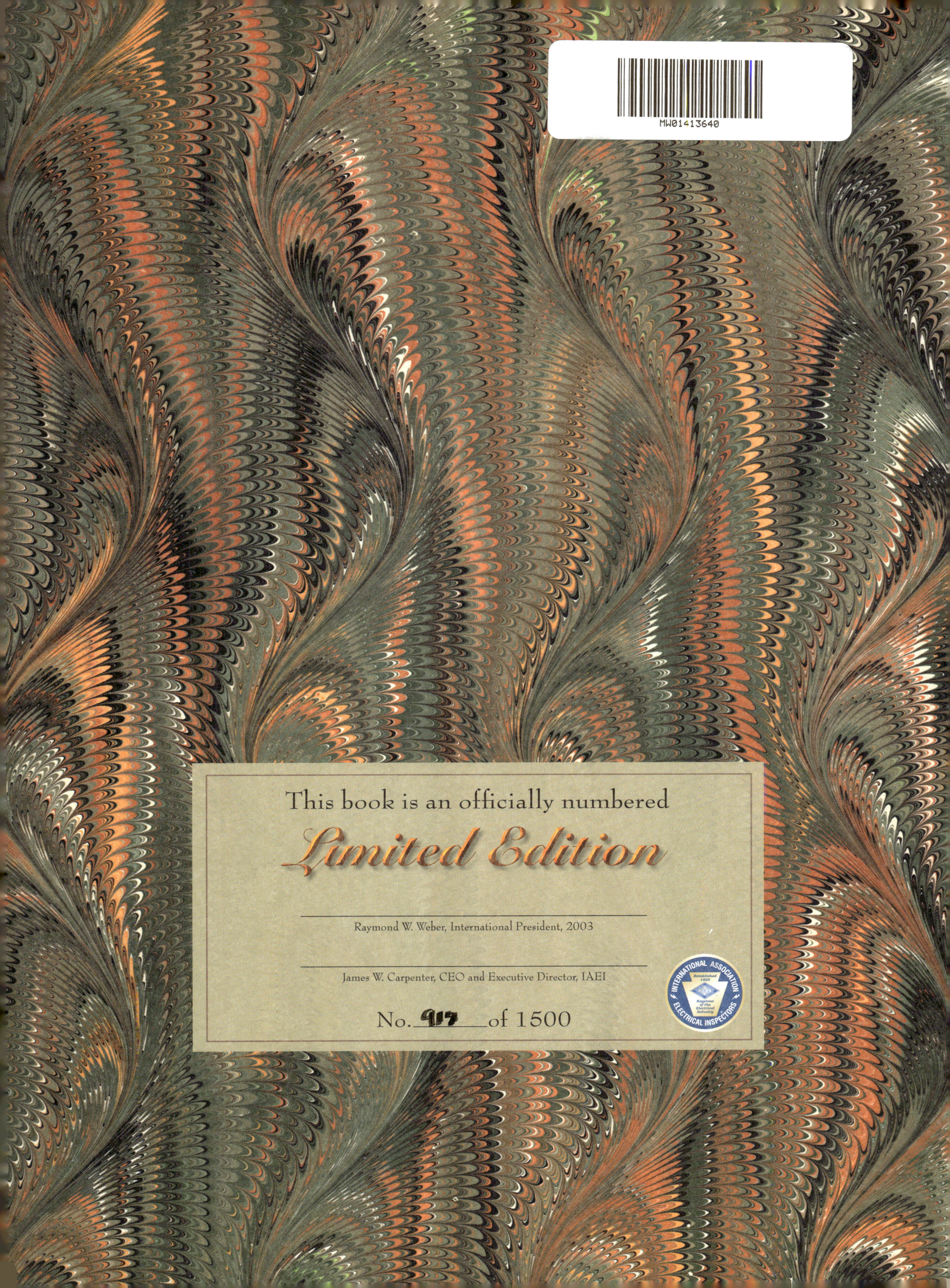
MW01413640
This book is an officially numbered
Limited Edition
Raymond W. Weber, International President, 2003
James W. Carpenter, CEO and Executive Director, IAEI
No. 917 of 1500
INTERNATIONAL ASSOCIATION ELECTRICAL INSPECTORS

A Passion for Safety

The IAEI Story

With a Foreword by
James W. Carpenter

International Association of Electrical Inspectors
Richardson, Texas

 NOTICE TO THE READER 

This book is a history of the 75 years of the International Association of Electrical Inspectors. It has been compiled from the bi-monthly magazines and many other books published by the association from 1928 through 2003. Although many of the articles are technical, it is not intended that these should represent current technology or approved methods of design or installation.

Publishers do not warrant or guarantee any of the products described herein are available or would meet today's standards. Publishers also do not warrant or guarantee any of the products described herein or perform any independent analysis in connection with any of the product information contained herein. Publisher does not assume, and expressly disclaims, any obligation to obtain and include information referenced in this work.

The reader is expressly warned that this is an historical volume and should not be used as a guide for electrical safety, design or installation considerations.

[1]*National Electrical Code* and *NEC* are registered trademarks of the National Fire Protection Association, Inc., Quincy, MA 02269

901 Waterfall Way, Suite 602
Richardson, TX 75080-7702

Printed in the United States of America
07 06 05 04 03 5 4 3 2 1

ISBN: 1-890659-30-4

Through the years, writers and publishers have generously given their permission to print or reprint the materials contained herein.

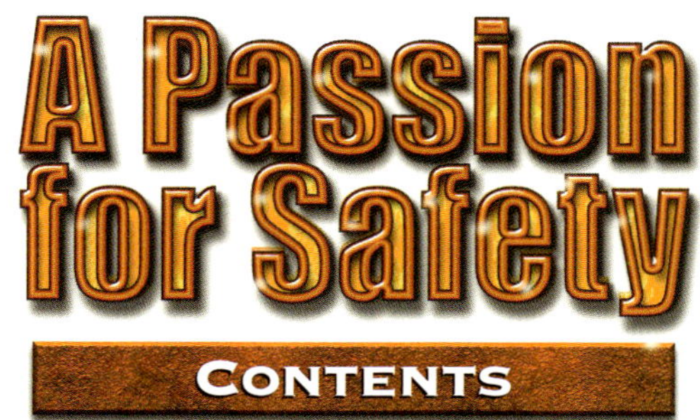

Foreword

Webster's dictionary defines *history* as "(1) an account of what has happened; (2) all recorded past events." I am sure most of us can remember as far back as our days in school and how we wondered why we had to study all that dry ole history. After all, the future was what we were interested in. But as time goes on and we look back to the "good ole days," history takes on a new meaning.

As we of the IAEI celebrate the 75th anniversary in 2003, we are reminded of the rich history of IAEI. That is what this book is all about. An account of what has happened—a record of past events! Contained in this book is the account of the actions of several people, working independently in different areas of the country, who got together and formed the International Association of Electrical Inspectors. This dedication and expertise exhibited by those early giants in the electrical industry is chronicled between the covers of this special souvenir limited edition, numbered and autographed book.

History not only tells about our founding—where we came from—but how we got to where we are today. In that journey, mistakes were made. We can learn from these past mistakes and not make them again. We can examine what was done right and redouble our efforts to continue the course set for us. Sometimes we stray from what our forefathers created this association for, so by studying our history we can reset the course. This by no means says that we can't do things differently, just as long as we maintain the principles set before us.

This book contains some amusing stories and incidents that happened during the 75-year journey. Look for the incident that prompted an author to remark, "Memory is a Funny Ghost." Learn about the cooperation and support of Underwriters' Laboratories and National Fire Protection Association during the early years. Look at the many other organizations that have been part of our history as well as the history of the electrical industry going about the business of harnessing and taming that powerful force—electricity. Examine the ways that IAEI got involved and participated in the code making process. Take note of the evolution of the educational process and the role that IAEI has taken in that process. Many things can be learned from this book—*A Passion for Safety, The IAEI Story.*

Many people have contributed to this endeavor and to try to list them all would surely leave someone out. A special thanks is extended to all the contributors, authors, and writers that have provided material to the IAEI, from the early *News-Bulletin* to the present *IAEI News*. Many names are identified in this book and if we have overlooked anyone, please be assured that it was unintentional. Many past and present members have contributed to the rich history and whether or not named you are much cherished and appreciated.

It would be obscene of me not to thank Kathryn Ingley and her staff of John Watson and Laura Hildreth for all the long hours and hard work they contributed to this project. All the rest of the staff was also pressed into some type of service and special thanks is issued to them. Phil Cox is also singled out for his diligence in obtaining historical photos from many different sources. He began that project during the early stages of planning for the Jubilee.

What does the future hold for IAEI? This book is not just a souvenir book that you would display on your coffee table or put in a special place for display. It is a textbook. All one needs to do is to study this work. A blueprint for tomorrow has already been laid for us. It is up to each of us to join together and continue on the path our founders laid out. After all, one gets out of any organization what one puts into it. As you read let your mind absorb what has gone on before. Wonder why. Get involved in the operation of your local division, chapter, and section. Be a contributing member, not just a member. Remember, we *are* tomorrow.

See you in 25 years at the 100th. We can reminisce about old times and talk about the history of these next 25.

James W. Carpenter
CEO and Executive Director, IAEI
Co-Chairman, Jubilee Planning Committee

Before there was electricity, there were gas luminaires.

The National Association of Electrical Inspectors 1913.

A Passion For Safety

Electricity came early to street cars and lights.

Electricity was early recognized as a dangerous friend. While it offered much good and many comforts, it could also turn as swiftly and as savagely as any wild beast. Those who worked with it knew this better than anyone, so they developed a passion for safety and made that their mission.

Prior To Edison

1660

In the course of his attempts to create a vacuum, 17th century German physicist Otto von Guericke made the first air pump (circa 1650), and the first machine to generate electricity. To demonstrate the pressure of air he devised the so-called Magdeburg hemispheres—two hollow copper hemispheres fitted together to form a globe about 14 in. (36 cm) in diameter from which the air could be pumped. A famous woodcut depicts the claim that it required two opposing eight-horse teams to pull the hemispheres apart. He invented (1660) a machine to generate electricity from the friction of the hand held against a rotating sulfur ball; he also predicted the periodicity of comets.

1862

Application of electricity to domestic illumination in 1862, before the invention of Edison's incandescent lamp: the Sawyerman electric light. The incandescent electric lamp was first devised in 1834 by James Bowman in Dundee, Scotland. In the absence of an electrical supply, he used voltaic cells and an evacuated glass tube. Warren de la Rue later produced a platinum filament incandescent lamp in an evacuated horizontal tube in 1840.

1752

Benjamin Franklin's experiment with kite and key. An undated painting from a wash drawing of Franklin and unidentified boy watching the glowing key after the kite was struck by lightening.

Thomas Alva Edison 1847-1931

Godfather of the Electrical Industry

His lifetime embraced four wars and as many depressions. More than any one man, his achievements have helped to lift America to the pinnacle of greatness. The world was his beneficiary.

Born in a brick cottage at Milan, Ohio, February 11, 1847, Thomas A. Edison, had little formal education, and to use his own words, "was usually at the foot of the class." However, even as a boy of pre-school age, he was extraordinarily inquisitive. His teacher, in fact, did not have the patience to cope with such an active and inquisitive mind, so his mother withdrew him from school and capably undertook the task of his education herself. Despite his lack of formal education, Edison recognized its great worth, and in his later years, sponsored the famous Edison scholarships for outstanding high school graduates. Most of Edison's vast knowledge was acquired through independent study and training. At the age of eleven, for example, he had his own chemical laboratory in the cellar of his Port Huron home. He had read such books as Gibbon's, *Decline and Fall of the Roman Empire*, Sear's, *History of the World*, Burton's *Anatomy of Melancholy*, and *Dictionary of Sciences*.

At the age of twelve, he maintained a chemical laboratory on a Grand Trunk train running between Port Huron and Detroit. His baggage car also reserved space to house a printing press on which young Edison ran off copies of *The Weekly Herald*, the first newspaper ever edited, published, and printed aboard a moving train. It was during this same period that a dramatic incident occurred which altered the entire course of Edison's career, and which may well have altered the course of the world's progress.

At Mt. Clemens, Michigan, the young Edison risked his own life to save the station agent's little boy from death under a moving freight car. The grateful father taught him telegraphy as a reward. Edison's association with telegraphy brought to a climax his interest in electricity—a word with which the name of Edison was to become inseparately associated—and led him to studies and experiments, which resulted in some of the world's greatest inventions.

As a telegrapher, Edison traveled throughout the Middle West, studying and experimenting to improve the crude telegraph apparatus of the era. At the age of twenty-one, he made his first patented invention—the Electrical Vote Recorder. Application for patent was signed October 11, 1868. This was the first of a total 1,097 United States patents granted to Edison during his lifetime, by far the greatest number ever granted to one individual. Three hundred fifty-six dealt with electric lighting and the generation and distribution of electricity. At twenty-three, he received his first money for an invention — $40,000 from the Gold and Stock Telegraph Company for his stock ticker. He opened a manufacturing shop in Newark where he made stock tickers and telegraph instruments. At twenty-four, young Edison assisted C. L. Sholes in inventing the first successful working typewriter model.

Through the years, he perfected many other inventions. On November of 1875 (Edison was 28) he discovered what was to be the foundation of wireless telegraph, radio, television and the electronic age. This was a previously unknown and unique electrical phenomenon which he called "etheric force." Twelve years later, this phenomenon was recognized as being due to electric-to-electric waves in free space. This was followed in 1876 by his patent on the electric pen, the beginning of the mimeograph. At thirty he completed the carbon

Inventor Thomas Alva Edison (1847-1931). While Edison did not invent the idea of the incandescent lamp, his invention, a one-piece carbon filament that glowed inside a vacuum, added hours of life to the light bulb and made it practical for everyday use. At the age of twenty-one, Edison had made his first patented invention, the electrical vote recorder. In 1883, Edison discovered another previously unknown phenomenon. He found that an independent wire or plate, placed between the legs of a filament of an incandescent lamp, acted as a valve to control the flow of current. This became known as the "Edison Effect." This discovery covers the fundamental principle on which rests the modern science of electronics. This photograph is circa the 1920s

Thomas Alva Edison

Godfather of the Electrical Industry, 1847–1931

telephone transmitter which made the telephone commercially practical. That same year came the phonograph, which he considered his favorite invention and doubtless it was one of the most original he ever created.

On October 21, 1879, at thirty-one, Edison invented the first practical incandescent electric lamp. Others before and in the same period with him, toiled long and hard to produce a practical incandescent lamp. The idea was not original with him, but it required the Edison genius to solve the difficult problems involved. Many tried to deprive Edison of the honor of having been the first to perfect a practical incandescent electric lamp, but they all met with failure. Edison's claim was too genuine to be set aside even by the courts which for one reason or another might have been inclined to challenge him.

An English jurist considering the claim of an English inventor, for example, might well be inclined to rule against Edison, if such a ruling were at all possible. But Lord Justice Fry, sitting in one of Great Britain's Royal Courts of Justice, made this commentary on the claims of Joseph W. Swan, an English inventor: "Swan could not do what Edison did—the difference between a carbon rod (as employed by Swan) and a carbon filament (Mr. Edison's method) was the difference between success and failure." Edison realized that the invention of a practical lamp alone was not enough to replace gas as the most-used means of lighting. Therefore, his work on the electric light is even more astonishing because in addition to performing a commercially practical lamp, he also invented a complete generation and distribution system, including dynamos, conductors, fuses, meters, sockets, and numerous other devices.

In 1883 Edison discovered another previously unknown phenomenon. He found that an independent wire or plate, placed between the legs of a filament of an incandescent lamp, acted as a valve to control the flow of current. This became known as the "Edison Effect." This discovery covers the fundamental principal on which rests the modern science of electronics. On October 21, 1929, commemorating the fiftieth anniversary of the incandescent lamp and in the presence of President Hoover, Henry Ford, and other world leaders, Edison reenacted the making of the first incandescent lamp. We have only mentioned a few of Edison's contributions to the world of today and tomorrow. However, in a volume of this size, we must limit ourselves to these few paragraphs and conclude with the following by Authur H. Palmer:

Edison Amberol Records were extremely fragile wax cylinders that originally gave two minutes of music. Later versions were introduced in 1911. Some titles were: "Red Wing Potter Chorus & NY Military Band" (1908); and Sousa's marches, "The Manhattan Beach" and "El Capitan Marches" (1912).

He led no armies into battle —
He has conquered no countries —
He has enslaved no people — yet he
Wields a power the magnitude of
Which no warrior has ever dreamed.
He commands a devotion more
Sweeping in scope, more world-wide
Than any other living man — a devotion
Rooted deep in human gratitude,
And untinged by bias or race, color,
Religion or politics.

—Excerpted from Welkin, A.H., *The Electrical Inspector,* IAEI, 1969.

Nikola Tesla 1856-1943

Invention of the Induction Motor — A Dream that Materialized

Electric power is the basis of modern mass production. Industries of all kinds use it. Everywhere that electricity is available, the electric motor operates mills, factories, farm equipment and home appliances. It is as universal as civilization. When it was first introduced, and for many years after, it was not widely used.

The early motor was not very powerful, and it was not very adaptable to different uses. Then too, it was difficult to care for. The commutator and brushes were apt to get out of order, and repair was difficult. The electrical experts claimed that the troublesome commutators and brushes were necessary, and that a motor could not be built without them. But a young man, a college student, did not believe it, and eventually he proved they were wrong.

One day in 1877, about the time Tom Edison's brain was active in his experiments leading to the electric lamp, a professor at the Polytechnic Institute of Gratz, in Austria-Hungary, was demonstrating to his class the action of a Gramme Dynamo. The machine had a wire-wound armature with a commutator attached to the end. Around the armature was a horseshoe form of field magnet. The class watched, fascinated. It was their first experience with an electric generator. One student, especially, young Nikola Tesla was completely absorbed in the performance. As the armature revolved, the copper brushes, through which the current reached the coil, sparked badly. "Those brushes shouldn't spark like that," said Tesla to himself, as the motor stopped. Again the professor started the machine, and again the brushes sparked. Nikola Tesla was suddenly excited. An idea had just occurred to him. Without stopping to think, he spoke loudly, above the sound of the dynamo. "A motor shouldn't need brushes and a commutator," he exclaimed. "I think it could be made to run without them."

The professor shut off the motor and looked scornfully at the bold young student. "A motor without a commutator! Ridiculous!" he said. "That's as impossible as a perpetual motion machine." One or two of the students snickered, and Tesla flushed. "Perhaps," went on the instructor sarcastically, "perhaps you are smarter than the electrical experts who design these dynamos. Maybe you can do what they can't — make an electric motor that doesn't need commutator and brushes." The class laughed, and Tesla, dreadfully embarrassed, said nothing more. But he did not forget it. Instead, he spent much of his spare time, in the years that followed, visualizing electric motors, trying to imagine one without the troublesome brushes and commutator. But even in his imagination he could not make one that would work. The professor might be right after all, but Tesla still did not believe it. There was a solution. Someday he would think of it.

Four busy years passed in which Tesla learned everything he could about electricity. But his "impossible" motor was far away as ever from reality. Then one day in 1881, while he was in Budapest studying the telephone system being installed there, he was walking through the park with a friend. He was not consciously thinking of his motor, but was reciting poetry as he walked. Suddenly he stopped, dumbfounded, for he could see in his mind, as clearly as if the real thing were before him, the motor he could build. "My motor!" he cried. "I see it now! No commutator…no brushes. Yet it will work. I'm sure of it. Look!" While his friend watched in amazement, Tesla snatched a stick from the ground, and began to draw diagrams in the sand. "See, here it is," he cried as he drew. "This is the armature in the center. It is made of iron bars instead of a coil of wire, and

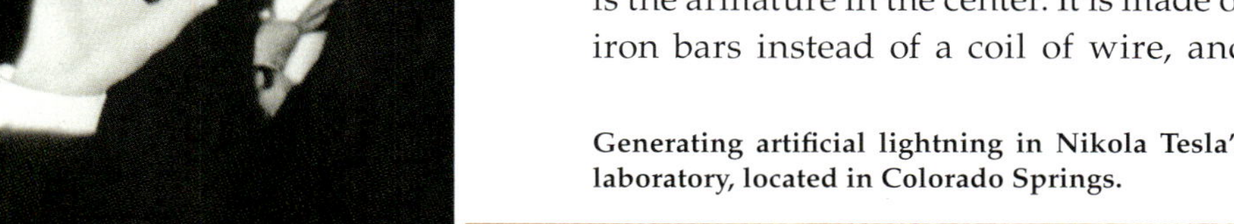

Generating artificial lightning in Nikola Tesla's laboratory, located in Colorado Springs.

Nikola Tesla 1856-1943

Nikola Tesla in His Laboratory. Inventor and discoverer of magnetic field rotations leading to the use of alternating-currents in electrical machinery and the induction coil known as the "Tesla coil."

has plates at the ends to short-circuit it. Thus it does not need a commutator or brushes. A rotating field is set up — a sort of magnetic cyclone. Current is induced in the armature, and the reaction between the revolving field and the induced current makes the rotatable part whirl. Do you understand?" His friend nodded. "Yes, I understand perfectly. I believe you have a great plan there, Nikola — one that will revolutionize electric power." And so it proved.

Tesla's induction motor, later designed just as he drew it there in the sand, has the simplicity, the adaptability, and the power necessary in electric motors for industrial use. Despite his professor's scorn, the young student proved his point. It is safe to say that our universal use of electricity for power dates from Tesla's invention of the induction motor, the motor the experts said was impossible.

Excerpted from Welkin, A.H., *The Electrical Inspector*, IAEI, 1969.

The debris of the downtown area of Chicago a few days after the devastating fire of October 8, 1871. A few survivors mill around the ruins. The Great Chicago Fire of 1871 signified the beginning of a new era. Chicago was quickly rebuilt and by 1875 little evidence of the disaster remained. It also signaled a new era in fire safety that culminated in the creation of safety codes such as the *National Electrical Code*.

Thomas Edison's electric lamp, patented January 27, 1880. Many tried to deprive Edison of the honor of having been the first to perfect a practical incandescent electric lamp, but they all met with failure. Lord Justice Fry, sitting in one of Great Britain's Royal Courts of Justice, made this commentary on the claims of Joseph W. Swan, an English inventor: "...the difference between a carbon rod (as employed by Swan) and a carbon filament (Mr. Edison's method) was the difference between success and failure."

RISING 1865-1943

FROM THE ASHES

RICHMOND, VIRGINIA

In the immediate decades following the close of the War Between the States in 1865, illumination of the city streets was again the source of considerable debate in Richmond, Virginia, especially in the legislative and executive branches of the municipal government.

As in other cities throughout the nation, the streets were lighted by gas from a municipally owned plant. This gas was also sold to its citizens for illumination of their homes and places of business. As a consequence of the war years and its aftermath, the plant and its distribution system suffered from maintenance and financial woes.

Threaten to Light the Streets By Electricity

During a meeting of the Common Council in 1877, in those days a bi-cameral council consisting of a Common Council and a Board of Aldermen were entrusted with legislative and some executive affairs of the city, while rates established for the municipal gas plants were under discussion "threats were made to light the streets by electricity" and in an earlier year, 1884, a local newspaper expressed the hope "that electric lights will soon be introduced and the gas works superceded for illuminating purposes."

In 1881, and the years immediately preceding, there were several technically minded citizens who were interested in the commercial possibilities of generation, distribution, and sales of electricity and had arranged private demonstrations of its use for street lighting. Among the first of these, if not the first, was a demonstration of electric lights as a part of the Yorktown Celebration held in Richmond in 1881. The demonstration was in charge of a Captain R. M. Poynter "one of the finest electricians in the state" as stated in newspapers of that date.

In 1883 a Mr. Roberts installed and demonstrated an arc light at the southwest corner of 11th and Main Streets, probably supplied from a "dynamo" in the immediate vicinity near 10th and Basin Bank, which was the basin for canal boats operating between Richmond and points in the western part of the state. This basin was used as a loading and turning waterway, known as the Kanawha Canal Basin. In 1886 another

View of the ruins of Richmond, Virginia, after the Civil War battles. To those civic minded-citizens of Richmond in the immediate post-war decades, illumination of the city streets was again a source of considerable debate. A Mr. Roberts, in 1883, installed and demonstrated an arc light at the southwest corner of 11th and Main Streets, which caused considerable discussion and heated debate. In 1884, a local newspaper expressed the hope "that electric lights will soon be introduced and the gas works superceded for illuminating purposes."

Joseph C. Forsyth was the chief electrical inspector and consultant of the New York Board of Fire Underwriters, and one of the early founders of the IAEI. Mr. Forsyth was employed by the Bureau of Surveys, later known as the Bureau of Electricity of the New York Board, on April 1, 1891, and he retired on September 15, 1942. His ability and efficient methods brought him early advancement.

In 1895, he was appointed chief electrical inspector, which position he held until 1925, when he was promoted to supervising engineer and given supervision of electrical installations throughout the entire area of the southern part of the state below the Dutchess County line. He served in this capacity until 1934, after which he acted as consultant to the bureau staff.

During this period, Mr. Forsyth compiled an enviable record in improving the rules, regulations, and standards of the electrical industry. His administration of the Bureau of Electricity commanded the voluntary respect of electrical contractors and manufacturers.

Mr. Forsyth, known through this country as the dean of electrical inspectors, was for years president of the Eastern Association of Electrical Inspectors, and became the first president of the IAEI when this association was organized in 1929. Honorary membership was conferred upon Mr. Forsyth in March 1934 when he retired from active service. He was a member of the Electrical Committee of the National Fire Protection Association, and had been instrumental in the promulgation of the *National Electrical Code* since its inception.

Mr. Forsyth has been honored on numerous occasions by the inspectors' association and by the electrical industry in the state of New York. In June 1941, a testimonial luncheon was tendered in New York City to commemorate his 50th year of service with the New York Board of Fire Underwriters.

A Westinghouse plant of about 1888. AC power plants grew rapidly. The early alternating current power plants used numerous small alternators that were driven by belts.

electrical lighting plant was constructed and operated under the name of the Old Dominion Electric Light Company, at 5th and Porter Streets in South Richmond, then known as Manchester, a separate city from Richmond. This plant consisted of a Thompson-Houston dynamo for supplying lights on Hull Street and in the shops of the Richmond and Danville Railroad (now the Southern Railroad) and J. B. Johnson's forging plant at the south end of the 9th Street Bridge. The charter for this Old Dominion Company was granted January 26, 1887 to M. B. Leonard, C. E. Wellford, H. T. Wickam, T. L. Chapman, B. B. Weiseger, with W. O. Randlett as operating engineer (still living in 1958).

In 1887 also, a charter was granted to the Progress Electric Company, with J. Thompson Brown as its director. Also the Excelsior Electric Light and Power Company was organizing to avail itself of rights granted Pizzini and Kates in 1884 for construction and operation of an electric plant.

Electric Street Cars

This year of 1887 also saw the application

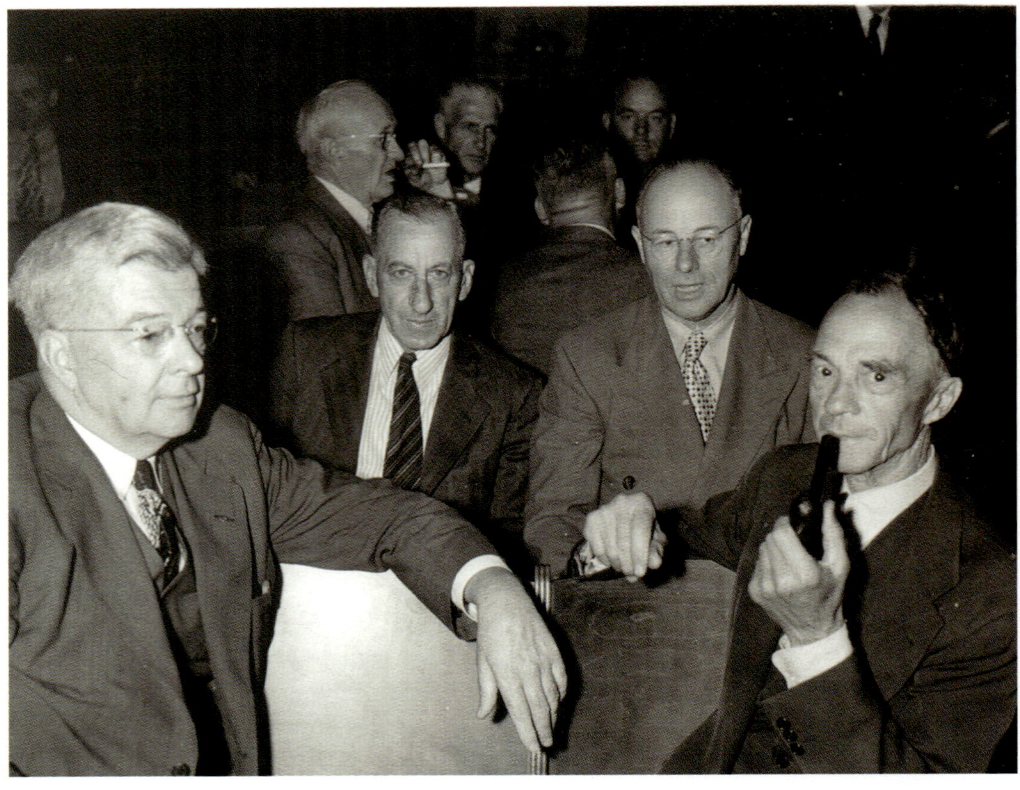

James "Jim" Mahan, H. V. Hannun, city of Anaheim, Leonard Hobbs, Smoot-Holman Manufacturing Company, and R. H. Manahan, retired chief electrical inspector, city of Los Angeles and city inspector for Laguna Beach at the Southern California Chapter meeting in Beverly Hills held on March 27, 1946.

The 17th annual meeting of the Wisconsin Chapter was held in Green Bay, November 19–20, 1942. The men in the photo are F. Lindner, president, Electricians Local 158 of Green Bay; J. E. Wise, Industrial Commission, Madison, Wisconsin; V. H. Tousley, NFPA and IAEI, Chicago, Illinois; A. A. Allen, electrical inspector, Watertown, Wisconsin; and J. C. Gerhard, president of the Green Bay Electrical Contractors Association. The chairman of the chapter, G. T. Fielder, was unable to attend the meeting but had sent a letter with reference to his new work with the National Youth Administration and the War Manpower Commission.

of electric power for street car propulsion to succeed horse drawn street car transportation. A bitter controversy raged over extending the lines of the Richmond City Railroad Company and the Richmond and Manchester Railway Company, because their plans for extension did not include any lines on Church Hill and a populous section north of Broad Street west of 9th Street. Mr. Leroy E. Brown, an associate with his brother J. Thompson Brown, while on a visit to Cincinnati, "made the acquaintance of several gentlemen looking for investment prospects," subsequently asking for a franchise for lines to connect Church Hill and the west end of the city, under the name of the Union Passenger Railway Company, the franchise was granted and they asked permission to use electricity as a motive power, permission being granted they contracted with the Sprague Electric Railway and Motor Company for entire equipment, to include also 40 cars, 12 miles of overhead power lines and a power plant, to be completed in 90 days. The time allowed was insufficient but cars were started in November 1887 and were in "more or less daily" operation in January 1888.

Power Plants Established

Water on the James River and Kanawha Canal, which provided power for some of these early electric plants, also supplied power for the operation, by water power and steam, of a number of plants on and adjacent of its route, prominent among them was the Tredegar Company whose plant extended south of the canal from 2nd Street to 7th Street; the Montague Manufacturing Company mill-working plant at 9th and Arc Streets for building materials; Gallego Mills and a number of other plants extending along its route to 14th Street. Many of these plants used water wheels as prime sources of power, with belted line and jack shafts to machinery used in the manufacture of a variety of products in vogue at the time, one of these water wheels was in use as late as 1957 at the Tredegar Plant.

In 1887 it was announced that the new power house at 7th and Canal Streets was being given its final touches and that no gas lights would be used for its illumination, light being obtained from "electric chandeliers."

Permits Required for Electric Wiring

It was also announced that the new tower and stone hoisting apparatus at the new city hall was used for the first time, the basement and first floor having been reached in its construction. This was the first building designed to be supplied by an underground service. In 1888 the first vestibuled train passed through Richmond on the Atlantic Coast Line R.R. In 1888 the Fire Underwriters notified all its insurance companies in Richmond that permits must be obtained from them for all buildings to be equipped with electric wiring.

The corner of 11th and Main Streets, selected for the demonstration of electric street lights in 1883, was very famous in these early years of 1900 and those pre-

Fred D. Weber, electrical engineer for the Oregon Insurance Rating Bureau of Portland, and secretary-treasurer of the Northwestern Section from 1929–1944, was one of the original founders of IAEI.

He graduated from the University of California in 1904 with a bachelor of science degree in electrical engineering. From 1904 to 1906, he was in the shops of the Westinghouse Electric and Manufacturing Company at East Pittsburgh, Pennsylvania, completed the electrical engineering apprenticeship course and obtained a diploma.

In 1917, he became a member of the Electrical Council of Underwriters' Laboratories, Incorporated, and of electrical examiners for the city of Portland, and during all that time he was the secretary of the board. In 1921, he was a member of the technical subcommittee on the protection of motors of the Electrical Committee of the National Fire Protection Association.

In 1926, he helped organize the Northwest Association of Electrical Inspectors, now the Northwestern Section of the IAEI, and became the secretary/treasurer of the section. He was later elected president of the association in 1932.

In 1927, he was made honorary member of the California Association of Electrical Inspectors. In July of that same year, he was appointed a member of the Electrical Committee of the National Fire Protection Association, representing the Northwestern Section, IAEI. In January 1929, he helped organize the Professional Engineers of Oregon. In 1933, he was appointed chairman of the Electrical Workers Sub-Commission of Oregon Building Congress, whose duties were to further the education of working apprentices in the trades.

Rising From The Ashes 1865-1943

Because of his hard work and patient, tactful manner in bringing together all interested parties to establish the IAEI in 1928, **Victor H. Tousley**, who had been chief inspector of Chicago, was made secretary-treasurer of the organization at its inception. The electrical industry, through the National Fire Protection Association, had engaged Tousley as field engineer and authorized and supported his work and office to enable him to serve as the secretary/treasurer of IAEI and to travel the nation on behalf of the organization. This continued for twenty years, until his death in 1948.

His contribution as secretary/treasurer of the IAEI guaranteed its growth to its present importance in safety accomplishment. The friendly patience and thoroughness displayed in his conduct of this office produced the confidence and respect essential to the success of the widely scattered and otherwise detached groups of the membership.

As secretary of the electrical committee and editor of several editions of the *National Electrical Code*, Tousley found other channels in which he contributed effectively to safety to persons and property and to orderly development within the industry. He labored steadily to "Let the *Code* decide."

Victor Tousley graduated from the Armour Institute (now Illinois Institute of Technology) in 1897, and went to work as an inspector for the city of Chicago from 1898 to 1912. He was promoted to the job of chief electrical inspector for the city of Chicago in 1912 and held this position until 1923. When he took over as electrical field engineer for NFPA in 1928, his conviction that electricity was to make further contributions to the national economy inspired continuing effort to keep himself abreast of the industry's new developments. Thus his advice on field conditions was in step with the times. He was also the co-author on eleven books on electrical subjects.

N.E. Cannady, electrical engineer and inspector for the state of North Carolina from 1914 to 1954, was one of the original founders of the IAEI, and served as its president in 1933. He also assisted in organizing the Southern Section IAEI in 1929 and was elected to the office of president that same year.

In 1930, he organized the North Carolina Chapter and held the position of chairman of that chapter for the first twenty-four years of its existence.

He attended Horner and Fishburne military academies and in 1903 entered the Navy. His electrical training came in

Young Roger Brown is the envy of all the children in Meriden, Warwickshire - he's Britain's most experienced racing car driver, for his age! Three-year-old Roger's father has made him a magnificent Grand Prix model car (1900), colored light blue, powered by electricity, and 5 feet six inches long. Mr. Brown (Senior) is chief engineer in the engine branch of Nuffield's (the famous car firm), and he made Roger's speedy model in his back garden workshop. Roger Brown is here taking his Grand Prix model out for a trip on the lawn. "I go very fast," he says, "and some day I shall go faster still."

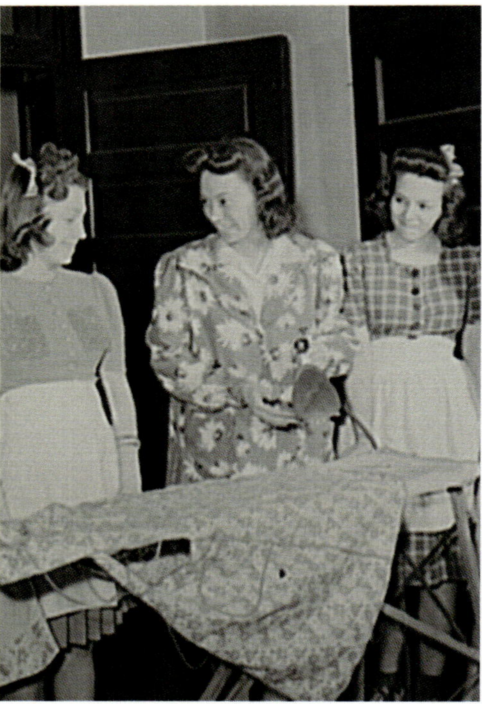

Ladies learning to use an electric iron at Farragut Agricultural School in Knox County, Tennessee (as part of the Tennessee Valley Authority), in 1942. The electric iron was invented in 1882 in France by Henry W. Seely using a carbon arc to create heat, a method that was found to be extremely dangerous. Irons using an electrical resistance were first shown by both Crompton and Co. and the General Electric Company, in 1892. This method was both safer and more efficient, setting the pattern for all further development. The earliest models looked like electrified flat irons with solid cast-iron sole-plates and cowls.

three years at the Naval Academy. In 1954, he was one of the eight North Carolinians who were fellows of the American Institute of Electrical Engineers. From 1915, with the exception of two years during World Wars I and II, he has conducted annually an electrical institute for electrical inspectors, contractors, electricians, utility representatives, jobber and manufacturers' representatives. During World War II, he was coordinator of electrical affairs for the North Carolina office of civil defense. In 1954, he was promoted to the position of chief engineer for the state of North Carolina, and took over both the electrical division and the fire marshals division.

Among his other activities and achievements are the following: chairman, State Board of Examiners of Electrical Contractors starting in 1937; member, Electrical Committee of NFPA beginning in 1937; member of the Electrical Council for Underwriters' Laboratories, Inc., from 1930; member of the AIEE from 1930-1947 and fellow, AIEE from 1947; and from 1941-1944, coordinator of electrical affairs, state of North Carolina, during emergencies.

These Victorian houses on Howard Street were damaged and collapsed from the 1906 San Francisco Earthquake. It struck with such force that buildings turned into heaps of rubble, power lines fell, roadways buckled, water and sewer mains were shattered. The San Francisco Gas and Electric Company suffered immense loss by earthquake and fire.

ceding. It was not only the financial center of the city, but also served somewhat as a trading center for those engaged in the building industry and its financial accompaniment through the banks and brokers in the immediate vicinity. Related businesses transacted much of their affairs on the northeast corner, and perhaps the term *curb-stone contractor* had its origin from this practice. Among its attractions, in addition to the financial facilities available, were several well known clothing establishments and numerous dispensaries of liquors and similar beverages with their free lunch counters under the watchful eye of barkeeps whose stern countenances discouraged mooching of the comestibles by empty hands; with a mug of nickel beer in hand the approach to the counter was sanctioned by a smile and one was permitted to satisfy both hunger and thirst in dignity, a far cry from the snack-bars of the 1950s with their raucous juke boxes. On December 6, 1881, The Brush Electric Light and Power Company obtained a charter to erect and operate an electric plant opposite the Academy of Music. This plant supplied street lights on a franchise from the city of Richmond, at 1st, 3rd, 5th, 7th and 9th Streets on Broad Street and on Main Street at 5th and 12th Streets and was known as Captain Pizzini's Plant. The street lights were of the carbon arc type without globes to enclose the carbons. A newspaper of that day stated before they were placed in service "these lights are expected to illumine streets to such an extent that a person can readily read a newspaper at a block from the source of light." Saks & Company at 1006 E. Main Street in 1883, had arc lamps installed in their store, also McAdams & Berry in the same vicinity. These were supplied from a plant at 10th and Basin Bank.

In January 1884 another franchise was granted by the city to Pizzini "and others that may associate with him" to erect poles and wires throughout the city for supplying electricity generally.

Types of Insulation

The writer endeavored to obtain more intimate details of methods and materials used in the earliest lighting installations mentioned in these sketches, in conversations with those engaged in the business in the early days, however, there was none that could provide descriptions desired. There were those with recollections of amazement at the demonstrations and the effect in those occupancies possessing them. None, however, observed much more than the effects. It should be borne in mind that considerable business in the electrical field, prior to its introduction for illuminating purposes, lay in the field of signal, communication and electric gas lighting supplied from batteries of wet

First recorded meeting of the Northern California Electrical Inspectors, at San Jose, California, on June 21, 1914. Claude Mitchell, with the little girl, at left, was the president and the founder of the association. Subsequent meetings were scheduled for July 11 in San Francisco and August 7 in Sacramento. For the next ten years, little was recorded anywhere of any activity of the cradle days of this association. Perhaps the unsettled times of World War I eclipsed the interest there might have been in the inspectors and the codes.

cells, either of the blue stone or carbon-zinc sal ammoniac type. Wire used for these purposes were either No. 16 or 18 containing a paraffin coated cotton insulation comparable to later days annunciator wire. The writer has seen lighting installations at 235/470 volts in which this wire was used. It is fair to assume that in the early days when insulated wire appeared desirable that this type was used, in connection with the arc lighting in buildings. After the general acceptance of arc lighting other insulations were developed, one of which was known as Underwriters or Ideal wire which was comparable to present day slow burning insulated wire consisting of impregnated asbestos with a cotton outer braid. Later still there was developed an insulation consisting of vulcanized India rubber (VIR) which is comparable to present day rubber insulated wire; soon thereafter the asbestos insulated wire was relegated to exposed wiring only, the rubber insulated wire being applicable to either exposed or concealed wiring.

Knob and Tube Wiring

With the invention of the incandescent lamp by Thomas A. Edison in 1879 and its commercial availability in 1888, the industry began to make great strides, methods and materials being developed rapidly. The early installations of this period consisted mostly of exposed wiring on insulators, using one piece tie knobs and tubes of unglazed clay. Experience soon revealed the highly hygroscopic qualities of the clay were to be avoided and this conditions led to the adoption of porcelain for such purposes.

UL and *National Electrical Code* Established

Losses incident to the growing number of electric lighting and power installations caused considerable concern to fire insurance companies and others in the infant industry and in 1897 a group of representatives from the insurance companies, power companies, architects and others interested adopted a set of rules and regulations for the installation of electric wires, to be known as the *National Electrical Code*, sponsored at that time by a National Electrical Conference, later and until the present day known as the National Board of Fire Underwriters.

Electricity from numerous overhead lamps provides lighting for this restaurant on board the steamship *Adirondack* in 1910. Experimental arc lighting was installed at Le Quai Conti and La Place de la Concourde, both in Paris, by L.J. Deleui and Dr. Henri Archerau in 1841.

Soon thereafter, the rules and regulations in this code were adopted as standard requirements by governmental agencies, insurance companies, power companies, and others concerned. With the general acceptance of these rules and regulations, there began a standardization of methods, materials, devices, and equipment. Previously, it had been recognized that in order to obtain desired results, some agency was necessary to investigate and test materials, etc., as they become commercially available and through the efforts of fire insurance companies the Underwriters' Laboratories had been established for the purpose in 1894 under the sponsorship of the National Board of Fire Underwriters. The establishment of Underwriters' Laboratories, with its findings, played a large part in bringing to the forefront the necessity for installation rules and regulations which resulted in the first *National Electrical Code* in 1897.

As stated before, in the earliest stages custom methods were used and much of the material was improvised to produce results without regard to other considerations. There were no formulae generally available, hence experience was the only guide and that had to be a matter of accumulation over the years.

Electrical Contracting Industry

With the adoption of rules and regulations the electrical contracting industry really had its inception; the phenomena and accompanying practice benefits to be derived in the use of electricity then appeared to the average individual to require special study and training for which he was not equipped and thus the electrician or contractor had to be called in to supply him with the necessary equipment.

In what may be termed the second stage of the contracting industry, installations were made with rubber or slow burning asbestos insulated wire, depending on whether for exposed or concealed methods were to be used. If exposed the wires were supported on solid tie knobs using short pieces of the same wire to secure it to the knob which was secured by screws to the supporting surface, or two-piece cleats which provided 2 ½ inch separation between the wires and secured by wood screws to the supporting surface. If such a surface wiring method offended the esthetic taste, the contractor would then resort to wood moulding. This method required more ingenuity in the making of a symmetrical appearance. Concealed wiring required considerable more labor, holes had to be bored through timbers for the insertion of porcelain tubes for each wire separately in order to provide the required code separation, terminated with knobs near the outlets and in intervening spaces exceeding 4 ½ feet.

Where the required separation could not be obtained flexible nonmetallic conduit, known as *circular loom,* was placed over each wire, such as outlets for lights, switches or receptacles. At lighting outlets no boxes were used and in many instances no boxes were used at switch outlets since they were of the surface type; flush type of switches were developed later.

All joints or splices in wires had to be soldered and taped with an insulation equal to that removed. For the connections, solder flux was in the form of a stick ¾″ x 6″. Screwdrivers of varying sizes and lengths were necessary for installing knobs or cleats. Each workman also carried a gasoline blow torch or an alcohol torch for fixture work.

Fixtures for many years were of the combination gas and electric type with mica insulating joints for connection to gas piping at outlets. Some of these were of very elaborate construction; all required much care in the assembly to prevent gas leaks and consequent explosions. Many pet birds and other pets were asphyxiated from lack of proper precautions, the gas was so odorous that persons would readily detect leaks and have corrections made.

With the introduction of two-piece knobs, with a groove for wires and its complement of a nail and leatherhead for securing to surfaces, many beers were consumed in discussions of its relative merits as compared to those requiring screws for supports as the old solid knobs with a tie wire to secure the conductor. Huge supplies of porcelain insulators were carried by some contractors, some purchased in car load lots.

With the advent of the dry cell contractors also carried large supplies of the item. Replacement of the old wet cells occupied them for many years, they were purchased in car load or barrel quantities. In the days of the wet cell, the writer spent many hours in packaging sal ammoniac of the correct quantity, from barrels; large quantities of circular carbon elements and pencil zincs were always stocked.

Bell and Fixtures

Bells in the early days consisted of the necessary coils, vibrating mechanisms and terminals mounted on wooden bases with a cover of the same material, known as wood box bells; with the advent of bells with metal bases and covers, many more beers were consumed in discussing the relative merits thereof. In the better class of dwellings solid brass push buttons were always used and it was not an unusual sight each morning to see servants polishing those at the front doors.

Among fixtures that were prized were those containing large numbers of crystal ornaments; also dome fixtures were the rage in home dining rooms. These were constructed of innumerable pieces of colored glass held in place with lead at intersections and the hold in frames of polished brass in varying sizes.

The earliest sockets (or lampholders as now called) for incandescent lamps were constructed in more than one form to permit insertion of the lamps of comparable base form, one was known as *Westinghouse base* which consisted of brass with a protruding ring around its perimeter and a center

A traffic officer stands on a platform under a Novalux Form 1 Mazda lamp fixture with an enclosed globe. This new lighting unit replaces the carbon arc lamp, circa 1910.

This particular telephone crew strung five copper wires from Omaha, Nebraska, to Denver, Colorado, in 1910. The woman pictured is the operator.

pin, the socket containing an opening in its center for insertion of the pin and its perimeter was provided with metal fingers which clasped the protruding ring of the lamp base, this and the center construction formed the circuit to the lamp.

Another type was known as the *Thompson-Houston base*; this was somewhat similar in construction except that the pin was threaded and its complement in the socket was also threaded. Then of course, there was the *Edison base* which is in use today and very soon superceded all the other types when lamp manufacturers began standardization of the industry.

The city hall was originally equipped with Westinghouse sockets and lamps, being replaced in 1912 when the building was rewired.

Underground Wiring Instituted

The city streets soon were covered with a maze of wires in the commercial district, all distribution using overhead construction; at one time in addition to two telegraph companies there were two telephone companies and several power companies operating, each with its own poles and overhead lines in the same general territory. To overcome this condition the city council adopted an ordinance requiring all distribution wires to be installed underground within what was defined as the Fire District. This change in distribution by the power companies required additional changes to services on customer premises, consequently electrical contractors were thus provided with additional business.

It was about this time that there was a tremendous surge in home buildings in the western section of the city, then known as Lee District from its contiguity to the Lee Monument, extending from Lombardy Street to what is now known as the Boulevard.

Branch Circuits, Panelboards and Fuses

In those days branch circuits were limited to 6 amperes, consisting of not more than 12 lamp sockets and permits were obtained from the city on that basis, also lamps from the power company were issued on the number mentioned on the permits, which were issued to the power company clerk daily in the city hall.

Panelboards were constructed of wood with asbestos lining and consisted of one or more plug or cartridge fuse blocks (or cutout bases) to which branch circuit wiring was connected where concealed wiring was involved, as in dwellings.

Installations of exposed fuse blocks and open knife switches were not uncommon. Knife switches were available from several manufacturers, notably Tower-Binford Electric and Manufacturing Company, with its plant in the rear of the southeast corner of 7th and Main Streets, adjoining its wholesale establishment at 711 E. Main Street in the form of an ell.

This company also manufactured electric fans, one of which was a ceiling fan under the trade name of Regina for direct current. Of a little later date, E. J. Willis established an electric motor manufacturing plant at 8th and McDonough Streets in what was then Manchester and known as the Richmond Electric Company, specializing in alternating current motors, any number were installed in Richmond and as late as 1958 some of their polyphase motors were still in service.

Before the adaption of electric motors for elevator service there were a number of elevators in the city using hydraulic power, notably in the Chamber of Commerce Building, and the city hall, the later being used until about 1914.

In the more pretentious buildings, slate panelboards were installed in wooden cabinets with asbestos lining, the earliest with terminal screws for open fuse wire, next followed those with terminals for enclosed fuses with a slot and hook to fit under the terminal screws, following this type were the more conventional type arranged for plug or enclosed cartridge type of the ferrule class of the present day.

Table or Desk Fans

The first table or desk fans for alternating current were of the induction type that had to be started by hand; later developments produced those with starting windings; these were, of course, for single phase operation and not of the oscillating type.

The first oscillating type did not contain any mechanical linkage between the revolving motor member and the oscillating mechanism but depended on air currents against stationary blades designed that they would turn at approximately 45 degrees thus using the air to force the revolving base against a spring which, in turn, then started it in the opposite direction, continuing the alternate sequence as long as the fan motor blades were in operation.

There were many other ingenious variations used for this purpose, none of which tended to lessen their weight and most were delivered by those using street cars for transportation.

It is worthy of note that at one time a person could ride from Seven Pines to Westhampton on the street cars for a nickel fare; some lines required only a three-cent fare.

Lighting the Streets

In June 1885 the Schuyler Electric Company and the Thompson-Houston Electric Light Company, of Boston, submitted proposals to the City Council for street lighting and subsequently the Schuyler Company was awarded a five year contract (at 29 cents per light, per night). Following this, the Richmond Schuyler Electric Light Company was organized and installed generating equipment.

This was a steam powered plant, obtaining water from the canal basin, with one engine on the first floor belted to shafting on the second floor, thence by belts to five 40-light Schuyler arc lighting dynamos for street lighting and two 40-light machines for commercial lighting, all for arc lighting purposes.

Image of the Electric Show at the Coliseum, taken from the floor of the exhibition room toward a columnar sculpture and showing display booths lit with various electric lights, circa 1911. The Coliseum was located at 1513 South Wabash Avenue in the Near South Side community area of Chicago, Illinois.

In 1886 work was started on another plant, in South Richmond, then known as Manchester, and in 1887, the Traylor Company also established a plant in Richmond for generation of electricity.

Energizer Bunny?

Many difficulties were encountered in these ventures, everything was new and untried, thus they contended with many failures. The Edison bi-polar machines however, "kept on going long after all else was scrapped," these were used for supply of current to the street car systems.

Finally, after much rebuilding of equipment the Sprague engineers succeeded in "making the cars stay in operation" and the Richmond Union Passenger Railway was a success, at a loss to Sprague of $75,000; the Richmond and Manchester was then electrified and extended.

Consolidation of Power Plants

With four or five electric plants in operation, consolidation became the order of the day; under the George E. Fisher interest all the railway and electric companies were merged into one and the power generation centralized in the Richmond Union Passenger Railway's plant, located at about 109 South 7th Street.

Most of the machinery was moved into this plant and continued in operation until 1894, subsequently the company was known as the Richmond Railway and Electric Company and built two new plants.

The plant was contained in two frame buildings with tin roofs and corrugated iron sides. The Boiler House was 120' x 60' with five boilers, known as porcupine builders, the arc-service was supplied by seven wood, 80-light dynamos, six Schuyler, 45-light dynamos and several Thompson-Houston dynamos.

The switchboards were built of wooden strips, strips with jack-plug and cable switching arrangements. A most unique feature of this plant was an enormous vertical boiler with feed water at the top, looking like an immense chimney, nearly 25 feet in diameter and over 100 feet high, around the base were seven hand fired furnaces.

This plant supplied all the street lights in Richmond until 1903 when developments in arc lights and transformers made the use of alternating current more economical, thus eliminating separate generators as required for the number of series lighting circuits then in use.

Series Arc Lamps

From 1878 efforts were made to construct an arc lamp with dependable self regulation of carbon movement necessary to form an arc and in this period Charles F. Brush developed the idea of using a shunt coil to lift and hold the upper carbon in a correct position, then the use of series arc lamps became possible.

At first the lamps used only one pair of carbons, these could not be made to last the long hours of night and later lamps were introduced with two pairs of carbons, burning one and then the other. All, however, were of the open type with consequent flicker from winds.

Towards the end of the 19th century an inner globe was developed to enclose the carbons, thus lamps had an inner and outer globe which was used universally to prevent flicker from winds and also contributed to carbon life of about 100 hours.

All this was the forerunner of constant current lighting systems for street lights. By 1916 practically all street lighting had been converted to the use of incandescent lights. In the old arc lamps it was necessary to "trim" or replace the carbons after each night of use.

They were varyingly capable of producing 1200 candlepower and originally cost the city 25 cents per night per lamp for operation on moon-lit nights and 40 cents for all night use.

In 1908 the City Council reconsidered a suggestion presented in 1882 that the water power available at the Old Pump House be utilized to generate electricity.

After all these years of discussion, work was started in 1909. In 1888 Mayor J. Taylor Ellison had urged the city to construct its own electric plant. The superintendent of the Gas Works in his report in 1890 had stated "this light (electric) has come to stay and all gas men had just as well reconcile themselves to the fact and act accordingly." However, financial stringency in 1891 eliminated all prospects of a plant construction for an indefinite period.

New Lighting at tire factory, circa 1910.

Alternating Current Distribution

With the advent of transformers and alternating current distribution systems a much more general use of electricity was envisioned. The first of such systems in Richmond used 1,100 volts at 133 cycles for distribution at 50 volts to users.

Among the earliest wiring of buildings was the City Hall, at this voltage, also the Dooley Mansion at Maymont, using impregnated paper conduits with a concentric wire (wire with a rubber insulated conductor having an uninsulated conductor concentrically around it and under a cloth envelope with a saturated compound).

There were a number of other buildings similarly wired, and in 1888 equipped with incandescent lamps.

The first church to be lighted electrically was St. Paul's. "On June 14, 1888, the Virginia Electric Light Company had hands at work placing electric light fixtures in the church; in the center was a large reflecting chandelier."

Raw Hide Gears

In December 1887 nineteen persons were in the electric car on its experimental run. It was noted that the cars developed considerable noise in the use of the gearing and in this connection an amusing incident is worth noting; on May 19, 1888, McFlinn's circus, while parading from Church Hill to the Chesapeake & Ohio Station at 17th and Broad Streets, when near the corner of 24th and Broad Streets, lost its performing elephant "Betsy" by death at the age of 93.

The body was moved to "horse heaven," a soap manufacturing plant on Bacon's Quarter Branch. The hide was removed and sold to I. Bluford (a well-known electrical man at that time and later an owner of an extensive business in electrical and mechanical supplies). The hide was placed in an abandoned well for curing but after many complaints of odors originating from the well, it was removed and converted into raw-hide gears for use by the street railway company to reduce noise; it was claimed that Mr. Bluford was the first to conceive the idea of such use and manufacture.

Rising 1865-1943
From The Ashes

Overcurrent Protection and Wiring Methods
The earliest interior electric wiring consisted of bare copper conductors with wooden cleats for support and separation of the conductors which was very soon succeeded by cotton covered conductors and clay or porcelain insulators for supporting and separation of the conductors.

Very soon thereafter the idea of drawing the wires in tubes was conceived and impregnated paper conduit was developed for use where necessary to be imbedded in masonry construction and also for concealed wiring in the better or more costly type of frame buildings.

This method was soon outmoded by the introduction of steel conduit which was more flexible for installation and consequently more economical as well as possessing safety not inherent in paper conduit.

Overcurrent protection was provided by the use of fuse wire (a fusible alloy of comparatively low melting point as compared to copper) mounted on wooden blocks with terminals for the connection of wires, and subsequently superceded by porcelain as experience from fires dictated.

These overcurrent devices were developed in different types, some rectangular shaped of porcelain with covers of the same material to enclose arcs by the interruption of fault currents and consequent melting of the fuse wire and were used for protection of service and feeder conductors.

Others were small rectangular or horseshoe shaped without covers and intended to be covered with tape in canopies of fixtures. Others still were used for open or concealed work for drop cords and were constructed as an integral part of rosettes of one- and two-piece construction.

Another wiring method consisted of wooden moulding, wooden strips about 2 inches wide with grooves for the retention and separation of wires and manufactured in 20 feet lengths. This method used porcelain devices for taps, drop cords, etc.; the devices containing porcelain covers for the contained connections.

Incandescent Lamps
Incandescent lamps were manufactured in 8, 16, 32 candlepower ratings of the Westinghouse or Thompson-Houston type of bases, superceded later in a standardized form by the Edison screw base. The lamps were given its customers free of charge by the power company on signing contracts for the number required; replacements were also free on return of burned out or bases of broken lamps.

Before the introduction of alternating current for general use in buildings, the power company supplied its customers from direct current systems at 235/470 volts, using the Edison system of distribution for lighting at 235 volts and power at 470 volts.

Due to transmission losses and consequent cost of distribution the direct current system other than for operation of street railway cars, was somewhat restricted geographically.

Among consumer requirements for light and power were electric fans for use on direct current; these were rated for use at 235 volts both in the suspended ceiling and table or desk types, the earliest fans containing brass brushes for commutating purposes and some were quite noisy in contact with the revolving commutator.

Contractor Shop Operation
It was the custom in those days that contractors were called in as autumn approached for removal, cleaning and storage of the fans until called in the ensuing spring, and a portion of the winter months were spent in the cleaning, repairing and wrapping during the storage period in contractor shops.

Signal work in the form of door bells for residences and, in the more pretentious homes annunciators and battery operated telephones constituted no small part of contractors' volume of business. Hotels, hospitals, etc., were equipped with elaborate annunciator systems that were battery operated; in the earliest days the batteries used were of the zinc-carbon, sal ammoniac type and were as unpredictable as modern day actresses and thus constituted a profitable maintenance item for contractors.

Circa 1930s wood tombstone table radio

The electrical business in the early days was not confronted with the do-it-yourself individual, practically all work being performed by workmen of contractors.

Some shop operations in those days, when viewed in the light of the present day practices, were very amusing, especially those in the hours of shop opening and preparation in getting materials to the jobs; few if any shops were equipped with means of transporting materials to jobs other than on the backs of their workmen, consequently it was not an unusual sight to see men loaded down with boxes of knobs and tubes, coils of wire and loom or bundles of moulding, tool bags and ladders, boarding street cars, some at fares of 3 cents.

Even bundles of steel conduit were so transported to the jobs at times, if not in very large quantities. The "wrong side of Broad Street" (north side) between 7th and 8th constituted a forum for discussion of current practices, by electrical workers on Saturday nights; more often than not they convened to nearby saloons where deeper studies of the problems would be in order, ending with the purchase of a boxed "half fry" for the little lady patiently awaiting his return to the domicile of peace and harmony.

Committee on Electricity Names City Electrician

The City Council of Richmond, impressed with reports of fires and fire hazards that might arise from unsafe methods and materials involved in the installation of wiring for the use of electricity in the streets and buildings in the city, adopted an ordinance on April 12, 1901, creating a Committee on Electricity consisting of four members of the Common Council and three members of the Board of Aldermen.

Pursuant thereto this committee held a meeting on April 15, 1901, and organized for the purpose outlined at its creation.

In the discussions it was recognized that some enforcement agency was necessary and a motion was adopted requesting the Board of Fire Commissioners to permit the superintendent of Fire and Police Telegraph to serve as electrician for the city. Subsequent to this action the Board of Fire Commissioners, on May 6, 1901, submitted its agreement to the arrangement and the superintendent was thereafter also referred to as the *city electrician*, W. H. Thompson being the incumbent at the time.

The chairman called a meeting for the preparation of a suitable ordinance to regulate installations of electric wiring and appliances on April 22, 1901; representatives of several electrical companies were present and were asked for their views. In the course of the discussions, Mr. A. M. Schoen, representing the Southeastern Underwriters Association, addressed the meeting, stating that the *National Electrical Code* of 1901, containing rules and requirements of the National Board of Fire Underwriters for the installation of electric wiring and apparatus had been adopted extensively by many cities throughout the country; that this code would be of great value in Richmond and probably as acceptable as any rules or requirements that may be drafted by this committee.

The electrical ordinance as drafted and amended, was authorized to be reported to the Common Council for adoption on May 13, 1901. Note: It does not appear that any definite installation rules were included.

While an unidentified woman rides in an electric automobile, Julia Rhoads and Hazel Ladora Gates ride in a gas powered automobile in Denver, Colorado, in 1910. Electric cars enjoyed great success in the early years of automobiles, but were later eclipsed by those powered by internal-combustion gasoline engines, which did not require frequent recharging.

In June 1901, the city electrician inquired of the Committee on Electricity if he should proceed to grant permits, under the ordinance, for "stringing of wires in the streets and houses," on a motion he was accordingly so instructed.

In July he submitted his first monthly report, giving the number of permits issued by him, stating that the Virginia Electric Railway & Development Company and the Richmond Passenger and Power Company were the only ones complying with the ordinance and that he was drafting a circular letter to be sent all electrical contractors calling their attention to the ordinance and its requirements with respect to permits.

Trouble in River City?

Then in August, the committee received a suggestion from the city electrician that a set of installation rules and regulations to embody similar rules of the *National Electrical Code* be prepared and submitted to the Common Council, the same sub-committee as before was appointed to prepare a code of rules accordingly and report at a future meeting.

The city electrician reported to the committee in November that electrical contractors were not giving their aid to the Electrical Department and suggested adoption of a rule that no electrical permits would be granted unless applied for before beginning an installation. Received and filed without any action.

The subcommittee chairman submitted a code of rules, marked (A), entitled 1901 *National Electrical Code* of the National Board of Fire Underwriters, which was adopted and forwarded to the Board of Aldermen. At this meeting the city electrician reported that Kingsbury, Samuel & Company were doing work at the Jefferson Hotel in violation of the city ordinance and asked for instructions on how to proceed with enforcement. On a motion, he was instructed to summon the offender to the police court.

In December, the city electrician reported to the committee that he had consulted with the city attorney regarding "dead" wires on the streets, and received an opinion that the conditions were serious and that council should be asked for an appropriation to remove them, in cases where owners could not be determined.

First Electrical Inspector in Richmond

This report also stated that work was being done without the knowledge of the department and that it was impossible to keep abreast of the volume of work being done and recommended that $74 a month be asked for the employment of a competent all-around electrical man to promptly inspect any and all wiring, also that $300 be asked for the purchase of electrical instruments for testing purposes.

A motion was adopted that a report be prepared and forwarded to the Finance Committee recommending the sum of $1200 be provided in the budget for 1902 to the credit of this committee for the following purposes: $900 for annual salary of an expert electrician and $300 for instruments and extra labor.

Adopted *NEC* 1901

Also received at this meeting was a copy of a resolution adopted December 5, 1901, the Common Council concurring that in the 1901 edition of the *National Electrical Code*, of Rules and Regulations of the National Board of Fire Underwriters as recommended by the Underwriters National Association, be and hereby are adopted in pursuance of an ordinance creating a Committee on Electricity, defining its powers and duties, as rules and requirements for the installation of electric wiring and apparatus to be used by all persons furnishing or receiving electricity for manufacturing, mechanical or other purposes within the city of Richmond. Note received and filed.

The city electrician submitted an extensive report in February 1902 on stringing overhead wires in the underground district and presented a number of complaints from property owners, insurance people and others, protesting such violations and asked for instructions on the enforcement of the ordinances related thereto. On motion he was instructed to reject any and all applications not in conformity with requirements of the ordinances. Complaints were also received regarding installation of a 200-light converter, designed to receive 2,000 volts intensity for conversion to a lower voltage, at 9th and Main Streets in front of the new Dispatch Building, to supply adjoining buildings. Note: The original ordinance requiring underground wiring in streets of certain districts was adopted in 1899.

Mr. Palmer, representing the Mutual Assurance of Virginia, appeared before the committee on March 3, 1902, with a request that police powers be delegated to their electrical inspector with the duties now invested in the city electrician. After a protest by a representative of the Richmond Passenger & Power Company, a motion was adopted requesting an opinion from the city attorney as to the legality of such an act. An opinion was rendered on March 10, 1902, to the effect that such an act would not be legal.

Licensing Proposed for Electrical Jobs

The city electrician presented a draft of an ordinance to license, control and regulate electrical contractors, interior electrical wiremen and operators of electrical machinery in March 1902. After some discussion, it was tabled.

The previous motion was taken from the table and a motion adopted recommending the former motion to Common Council for adoption on May 5, 1902. A representative of the electrical workers union, representing 150 electrical workers, appeared before the committee recommending that the appointment of an electrical inspector be made by the committee instead of the city electrician. This recommendation was later complied with, as authorized on May 17, 1902. Later that month, meeting of the committee was called for the purpose of "electing" an electrical inspector from a list of names, submitted by the city electrician. On the second ballot, W. H. Minor was elected and the city electrician instructed to notify the applicant that he was appointed at a salary of $75 per month.

A subcommittee was appointed in March 1903 to report an ordinance requiring electrical contractors and electrical wiremen to stand an examination and be licensed.

Permission Granted for Temporary Overhead Connections

On May 11, 1903, there appeared before the committee the secretary of the Home Electric Company, representing Virginia Electric Railway & Development Company and the Richmond Passenger & Power Company, with several electrical contractors, requesting permission to be granted for temporary overhead connections to furnish electricity for fans in buildings. It was stated that electrical contractors had large supplies of fans on hand and would suffer severe losses and citizens deprived of their use unless the power companies were permitted to make such connections, pending the time necessary for underground services were required by ordinance.

The city electrician was authorized to grant such permission.

NEC 1903 Adopted

The city electrician presented a copy of the 1903 edition of the *National Electrical Code*, with his recommendation that it be included in the committee report to Common Council for adoption. Accordingly, it was adopted on June 8, 1903.

Licenses and Fees

On January 14, 1904, the committee received a request for an increase in salary from the city electrical inspector as endorsed by the city electrician. Passed on to the Finance Committee for an appropriation.

The subcommittee presented an ordinance which would levy a license fee of $50 for electrical contractors and $1 for electrical wiremen. It was adopted and forwarded to the Board of Aldermen.

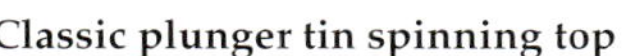
Classic plunger tin spinning top

Rising 1865-1943

From The Ashes

Circa 1920s household sewing machine

Licensing Required

On request of the committee, the city attorney rendered an opinion on January 27, 1907, that no electrician, except those in the employ of electrical contractors or those permanently employed by firms or corporations to do work on their own premises, may engage or be employed without a license and bond to do electrical work.

The next day, the city electrician began issuance of certificates on the "proficiency and capacity" to work as an electrician in the city of Richmond. The first certificate was issued to F. A. Fry, in the employ of E. B. Taylor Company (later a partner in the firm of Godsey & Fry). This firm specialized in electric fixtures in addition to its line of crockery, etc., for homes and commercial use.

First Electrical Examining Board

The first Electrical Examining Board was appointed by E. W. Trafford in 1913 and consisted of J. L. Speights as chairman; Morris Hunter, electrical contractor; A. W. Walton, electrical worker.

Names of electrical inspectors in the order of employment: W. H. Minor, 1902-1908; J. L. Speights, 1908-1924; T. W. Bowry, 1914-1948; R. B. Williams, 1922-1926; B. L. Mountcastle, 1924-1941; A. M. Miller, 1926-1958; R. C. Miller, 1922-1941; M. G. Folkes, 1941, present incumbent in 1959; P. A. Betlton, Jr., 1941, present incumbent; R. C. Owens, 1942-1943; F. F. Tuck, 1943-944; T. R. Conway, 1943-1945; B. J. Foster, 1945-1957; R. T. Sharp, Jr., 1949-1951; L. N. Wayne, 1956, present incumbent in 1959; H. A. Gray, 1956, present incumbent; J. W. Collier, 1951, present incumbent in 1958; W. B. Fox, 1957, present incumbent in 1958.

Excerpted from "Echoes from the Past," 1961-1963, by A.M. (Gus) Miller, associate editor, *News-Bulletin*, secretary-treasurer, Southern Section, IAEI and retired city electrical inspector, Richmond, Virginia.

Telephone and electrical wires were evident as early as 1911 near Byward Market on York Street, in Ottawa, Ontario. In its infancy, the electrical inspection service was largely confined to the Toronto, Ontario, area and usually only applicable to fire insurance company policy holders. That changed in 1912 and 1914 with significant amendments to The Power Commission Act. By order of the Legislative Assembly of Ontario, rules and regulations were made to cover the design, equipment, and workmanship of electrical installations. Municipal electrical inspectors were appointed, with jurisdiction limited to their own geographical boundaries

70 Electrical Years 1892-1943

The Taming of the Electrical Giant — Detroit, Michigan

Hendrick Antoon Lorentz

The Dutch physicist, Hendrick Antoon Lorentz, first advanced the electron theory in 1892. This theory, which is the basis of modern electrical progress, marked a dramatic change that in seventy short years has brought us the manifold marvels of electrical energy. That same year, 1892, as a boy eighteen years old, I started to work for the Electrical Construction Company of Port Huron, Michigan as an electrician's helper. Frankly, I knew nothing of the physicist's theory and cared less. Nor did I have any idea of where the electrical industry was going or what small part I would contribute to it. I had a job. I had a good boss. And I was earning a pay envelope worth seventy five cents a day.

My first construction job was with the White Building in Port Huron. Our energy power was 52 volts direct current. We used a wire trade-named "oknite." It was pretty crude stuff—just a rubber coating over the wire with no braid on the insulation.

Protection was afforded by homemade cutouts. These cutouts had open link fuses mounted on a wood base. We also used wood cleats for wire supports.

Building Construction

As crude as were our materials were our wiring methods. When we had to go through a joist, we bored a hole with a bell bit and strung the wire through. We mounted the cutouts on the back of wood baseboards and then screwed the baseboards in place concealing the cutouts. The net result was non-accessible fuses.

A few years later the White Building caught fire and burned to the ground. The newspaper reports claimed it was electrical wiring that caused the fire. It probably was.

Progress is sometimes painfully slow. When we wired the Opera House in Santa Claire, Michigan, we used our earlier materials and methods. But an insurance inspector singed by the experience of the White Building fire, insisted that we use non-flammable materials for wire supports. So we took out all of the wood cleats and replaced them with porcelain knobs. This was my first experience with an inspector insisting that a contractor rewire a job. I had not the vaguest premonition that some day the roles would be reversed, and that I might be the one insisting on safety regardless of first cost.

Electrical Manufacturing

It was about at this time that I had my first experience with electrical manufacturing. One of the early birds, Byron McCormick, started making electrical sign flashers. He hired me as an assembler. We nailed pieces of copper strips to a wood cylinder. The cylinder was rotated by a spring operated clock. The strips commutated against copper fingers causing the sign to flash on and off. Of course, the clock had to be wound daily. Very few of these flashers ever worked. They usually burned up after a few days of service. So I was in a business which took a financial loss.

Today, because of standardization, we can pick light bulbs of any make and replace burned out ones knowing they will fit. But consider the plight of the earlier uses of electricity. There were three manufacturers making sockets: Sawyer-Man, Thompson-Hudson, and Edison. Each used a different base requiring a different bulb.

Moreover, none of these sockets were lined with insulation. We had to carefully tin solder the lamp cord wire strands to keep them from fraying and causing a short circuit. But our labor was cheap and the manufacturer had not then designed materials to reduce labor time.

Ship Refitting

From building construction, to electrical manufacturers, to ship refitting. Across the river from Port Huron there were two excursion boats owned by a company in

Early light bulb

Sarnia, Ontario. These old wooden boats had formerly been lighted by hanging kerosene lamps.

The owners decided to modernize them and put in electric lighting. I remember how cold was the winter of 1894-95. It was magnified by the wintry blasts sweeping down the frozen St. Claire river. We worked ten hours a day, six days a week, with numb fingers trying to pull wire through wood moulding.

But it was well worth it when I opened my weekly pay envelope of four dollars and fifty cents. After all, seven and one half cents an hour and a sixty hour week was a good pay with good working conditions. I guess the toughening of my hide working in sub-zero weather served as a fringe benefit to assure me of a good appetite and good health.

Digging Pole Holes

In September 1895, I left home and came to Detroit, Michigan. I was now twenty-one years old, a well-trained electrician, and ready to go after bigger things. I had come to the Big City. However, the first job I got was digging pole holes. The horse drawn street car era was about to end.

The Citizens Street Railway Company was putting in the first electrified car line in Detroit. The line ran from the intersection of Harper and Woodward Avenues and out Woodward to the Highland Race Track. The decision to electrify this line was somewhat prophetic, as it was on the site of the Highland Park Race Track that Henry Ford erected his first modern automotive assembly plant, turning out Model T Fords on a mass production basis.

Lineman for Trolley Wire

So it was I started my career in Detroit digging holes — digging holes for the trolley wire poles for the Woodward Avenue line. It wasn't long until I was promoted to lineman, stringing trolley wire and installing feeder cables. But something new had been added to the electrical industry. Some insurance people had organized a rule book for wiring street car lines. They called this rule book, The *National Electrical Code.* The first issue covered only street car wiring.

Although the history books do not record the year of 1896 as a Panic year, it was, as I recall, a bad year. I worked for many electrical contractors. I was lucky to get work. Many men were out of work and electricians were lucky to get a job at $1.25 a day. But in 1897 I got steady work helping to usher in the world of instant communication.

The automobile was still not born, and most transportation was by old fashioned horse power. It was a noisy, glamorous, and spectacular sight to see the white horse teams come charging from the fire house pulling hook and ladder wagons. The steam boiler pumper was accompanied by the cacophony of galloping hoof beats, clanging bells, a steam whistle, and the roar of fire belching from its boiler.

Crowds would line the way to cheer the gallant men on their errand of daring and mercy. However, the fire was usually well under way and out of control before these knights in red helmets arrived.

Fire Reporting

Fires were reported in many ways: a citizen rushing into the fire house giving a breathless but somewhat belated report, a small boy furiously pedaling his bicycle to bring the news of an outbreak. But the main source of alarm was a high tower built on top of the fire house. There, firemen stood watch looking for a tell-tale plume of smoke. Once smoke was spotted the entire company would sally forth in the general direction at breakneck speed to hunt out the smoke's source.

As colorful and brave were these men the late and inaccurate warning system made fire protection quite inadequate. The AWX Fire Alarm Company was formed to provide instant and accurate communication that is even today the basis of our fire alarm systems. This company would rent and install fire alarm boxes in factories and stores with telegraphic connections to fire houses.

A new industry was born, a form of automation had arrived, and I worked as

Henry Ford and the ten million[th] Ford car.

The days of the horse drawn carriage were coming to an end.

Calling in the alarm in 1910

an electrician installing the equipment and wiring. From this communication system also came the night watchman report boxes. Installation and maintenance provided good steady jobs for electricians and I was well on my way.

By 1898 the impact of the servant, electricity, was being felt in even more dramatic ways. It was now possible to turn night into day. Detroit had installed in the downtown area several lighting towers. These were large cantilevered towers about 175 feet high.

They rested on a single pedestal and were supported by guy wires. At the top was a cluster of from four to six carbon arc lamps. The carbons needed daily replacement and cleaning. So I started my career as a civil servant working for the public light commission as a lamp trimmer.

I had eleven towers to maintain each day of a seven-day week. I would carry a six-foot ladder to the base of a tower and use it to get to the bottom cross trees. Then I would pull myself to the top on a small balance type elevator. On windy days stepping out from the elevator to the narrow servicing catwalk was a bit precarious. On these occasions I would strap a safety belt to the railing and cautiously edge my way around. For a while the dizzy height and the tower swaying in the wind frightened me. But I gradually grew accustomed to the potential hazard of the job, and it became a part of a day's work.

And I was doing well—steady, seven-days-a-week work trimming Brush and Adam-Bagley carbon lamps, and my pay was now up to sixty dollars a month.

Electrical Maintenance

The turn of the century brought me a nice promotion. From light trimmer to electrical maintenance man was quite a step forward. The city-operated utility furnished power and maintenance for schools and all city-owned buildings. Some budding leaders of the electrical industry were employed by the Public Light Commission. Austin Hatch was deputy commissioner. Bry Horton was the electrical engineer. In later years Bry Horton founded the Detroit Fuse Manufacturing Company which later became the Square D Company.

The expanding use of electricity soon outmoded direct current. As the lines of transmission lengthened it soon became apparent that higher transformable voltages were needed to minimize line voltage drop. In the years of 1901 to 1902 the city started changing from direct current to two-phase four-wire alternating current.

Two A. C. generators were installed to fill this growing need, and new switchgear was required. (However, in those days all switching central points were lumped into one word — switchboards.)

Switchboards nor their component parts were not available as manufactured items. Another electrician, Walter Jones, and I were assigned the task of building a switchboard from scratch. Our work was to be done under the watchful eyes of Al Saundersen, foreman of the lamp room.

We procured some Italian marble, tediously drilled it (without power tools), cut and shaped copper bus bars into switches, made wood switch bar handles, and installed switching jacks and meters on the face of the marble. I had no knowledge of the theory of alternating current. So I took a correspondence course.

Although, I did not complete the course, I found that it helped me quite a bit. It was during this period I got some more experience in the manufacturing business. Bry Horton got a patent on the first enclosed fuse. They were powder filled capsules with a pigtail at each end. I guess this is where the expression "blown fuse" originated. Because when those devices opened a circuit they literally blew open from the powder pack. Walter Jones and I worked night and weekends helping Bry assemble these fuses.

Distribution Substations

Alternating current transformation called for use of substations to distribute power around the city. In 1902 we built two of these substations. The first one was installed in the generating station under the supervision of a Westinghouse engineer. We started the second one in the basement of Southeastern High School; but before we could finish it, we had to run an underground feeder cable from the lighting plant. I helped pull this cable and gained a new skill in learning how to make cable splices.

City Electrical Inspector

While working on the third substation in a school on Horton Street near Brush Street I was appointed to a job that was to become my life's work. In 1905 J. B. McCarthy resigned as the city electrical inspector, and I was appointed to replace him. My salary was to be $1000 a year. Ben Clark, who came from the Detroit Edison Company, was to work with me. He had a depth of technical knowledge that was a great help to me.

I must digress at this point for a personal note. My sister introduced me to a pretty little eighteen-year-old girl who really caught my courting fancy. Maude Atkins and I were married in

Eastern Section Timeline

1903 First meeting of the **National Association of Electrical Inspectors**. Members of this organization went on to form the Eastern Section of the IAEI in 1928.

Western Section Timeline

1904 The **Western Electrical Inspectors Association**, precursor to the Western Section, is formed.

Southwestern Section Timeline

1914 First recorded meeting of the **Northern California Electrical Inspectors**, at San Jose, California, on June 21, 1914.

1904, and have raised two sons both of who are working in the electrical industry today. I doubt if Maude knows the difference between a volt and an ampere; but she has been constantly at my side, straightening my necktie, seeing that I keep my hair cut, accompanying me to all the conventions and meetings; encouraging me in disappointment and sharing those rare moments of success. Most of my friends in the electrical industry know her as well as they do me. Without her reassuring help I am sure the balance of this story would have been quite different.

Starting an electrical inspection department in a rapidly growing city brought many problems. First it was a new field to me. I was no longer working with the tools but was watching for the safety of the public; others spliced the wire, ran the cable, and installed the fuse cutouts. There was no code book, only a few Underwriters' special rules. We divided the city right down the middle. Ben Clark inspected east of Woodward Avenue and I inspected the west side. We covered our areas with bicycles and occasionally rode street cars. Buildings were going up so rapidly north of Grand Boulevard that we were hard pressed to keep up with them.

Our department had no clerical help. After pedaling a bike all day long chasing down wiring jobs we often came back to the office and worked far into the night filling out inspection reports, doing bookkeeping for inspection fees, and planning the next day's work.

I cannot say when, or how, but gradually we began to see our work as more than a job. We were beginning to be conscious of our efforts as being true civil servants. We knew that we were dealing with an energy giant that could turn machines, light homes, and take burdens off men's backs. Yet at the same time, if this giant got out of control, he could kill, maim, and destroy property. Yes, it was more than a job, it was a terrifying responsibility. We knew we could not enforce safety in the usual sense of law enforcement. We were only two against a large expanding city.

Some of the electrical contractors were resentful of inspection, and would go ahead and wire without a permit or any regard for safety. Frequently, we would furiously pedal our bicycles across open fields bumping over ruts and hillocks to catch a contractor wiring illegally. Later the city provided us with motorcycles, and eventually Model T Fords. Still these more convenient means of transportation would not allow us to catch all the evaders. It was during those busy and hectic days that we evolved a concept that I believe even today is the basis for success of any good inspections department. We must sell the idea of safety and the safeguards of inspection. Call it public relations if you wish. Or call it safety education. Today ours is a job of coordination. Coordination with utilities, with contractors, with insurance groups, with manufacturers of equipment, and with the public. There are not enough inspectors in the country to *enforce* safety. We learned that a major portion of an inspector's job was to convince contractors and the public that inspection and wiring safety were in their best interest.

During these early years of the rapid growth of the use of electrical energy the automobile was still the wealthy man's toy. Delivery trucks were still quite a way in the future. Consequently, electricians reported on the job carrying their tools and wiring materials with them. It was not uncommon to see these men with their tools in a newspaper bag and

Charter Members of the Western Association of Electrical Inspectors. This photograph was taken May 1905, in the yard of the first building occupied by Underwriters Laboratories, Inc., at 67 East 21st Street, Chicago. *First Row, left to right*: **Chas. Berry, L. A. Barley, C. N. VanCleef, C. B. Giles, H. C. Bettinghouse.** *Second Row, left to right*: **F. D. Varnum, R. L. Daniel, James K. Polk, Jr., Chas. E. Bean, Harvey Bloomer, H. G. Young.** *Third Row, left to right*: **Chas. Smith, Julius F. Jaeckel, Wm. S. Boyd, Waldemar Michaelsen, Frank R. Anderson, E. R. Townsend, A. J. Pruvot, Harry Deakins, Frank Sackett, George Cotton, A. L. Demond.** *Fourth Row, left to right*: **Fred Dustin, unidentified man, Frank R. Daniel, John Paul.**

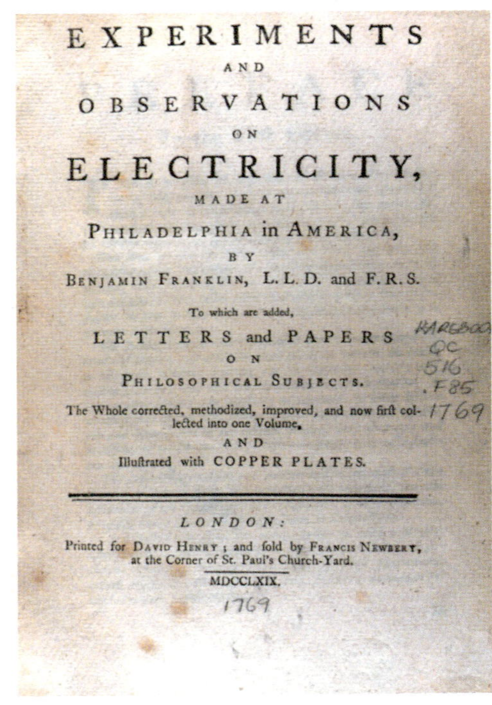

EXPERIMENTS
AND
OBSERVATIONS
ON
ELECTRICITY,
MADE AT
PHILADELPHIA in AMERICA,
BY
BENJAMIN FRANKLIN, L. L. D. and F. R. S.
To which are added,
LETTERS and PAPERS
ON
PHILOSOPHICAL SUBJECTS.
The Whole corrected, methodized, improved, and now first collected into one Volume,
AND
Illustrated with COPPER PLATES.

LONDON:
Printed for DAVID HENRY; and sold by FRANCIS NEWBERY, at the Corner of St. Paul's Church-Yard.
MDCCLXIX.

1769 paper on experiments and observations of electricity by Benjamin Franklin.

coils of wire slung over their shoulders. I remember seeing a short young man riding on the open back platform of a street car carrying lengths of wood moulding and armfuls of knobs and tubes. He was a delivery boy for one of the early electrical wholesalers, The Frank C. Teal Company. Today, that boy, Morris Bloomberg, is president of Madison Electric Company, one of the country's leading electrical wholesalers. *Memory is a funny ghost*. Whenever I see Morris my mind flashes back to that small boy with such a heavy load.

Like much of what we learned about safe or unsafe materials, good or poor wiring practices came from surmounting our problems. In 1907 we had so much trouble in getting electricians to correctly solder and tape joints in the tap wiring systems, we finally decided to abolish this wiring system. We required a loop system with boxes at each outlet and each point of connection. Manufacturing companies quickly formed to supply outlet boxes, switch boxes, and the hardware contingent to these new methods. In 1903 armored cable was approved for internal wiring which brought a great saving in labor over the earlier knob and tube system.

Our inspection department grew through these years and it became necessary to have a supervisory organization. In 1918 Ben Clark was appointed a chief electrical inspector and I as assistant chief To gain a better background for my new responsibilities I attended night school at Cass Technical High School, taking a course in alternating current. By 1919 we realized that inspection would be more effective if we could be sure that the electricians were qualified to do their work. So our city gave us a licensing ordinance. That year Ben and I gave an examination to the first journeymen electrician and journeyman fixture man. As yet we were not examining contractors. But contractors were required to have a journeyman electrician in their employ and to post a bond of $1000. Moreover, the contractor paid a license fee of $5 and electrician a fee of $1. Within a year the mayor appointed an examination board to prepare and supervise journeyman's examinations. The board was represented by a cross section of the electrical industry. The board met monthly to review license applications and examination papers. The chief electrical inspector was at that time the chairman of the examining board.

I find myself getting ahead of my story. Perhaps I have rambled on hastily because "inspection" is so close to my interest. But in 1912 the first electrical club was organized. There were only fifteen members; all were electrical inspectors. We met in the old Public Light Commission building and called it The Electric Inspection Club of Detroit. However, much earlier than this another inspection group was formed. William Boyd formed the Western Section of IAEI in Chicago in 1905. It was not until 1924 that I joined this now famous group. In the meantime the inspection club in Detroit dissolved in 1922.

Now the scope of the electrical inspection was growing national; *National Electrical Code* committees, chapter after chapter of the International Association of Electrical Inspectors were formed. A free and sometimes stormy exchange of ideas gave impetus to the development of standardization of safety practices. In 1927 the Michigan Electrical Inspectors Club was formed. Ben Clark was its first president. I presided in 1930–1931. This club did not join the IAEI as a chapter until 1950. Some of the inspectors held out for a few years before they would affiliate with the national organization. I had always felt the need for national unity so that some measure of uniformity in materials and methods could be achieved. Otherwise, fractured local rulings could run the cost of materials so high as to place too dear a price on modern convenient wiring. It is a source of pride to me to have been elected president of the Western Section in 1940 when the meeting was held in Kansas City, Missouri. I am still an honorary member of this section and have missed only three meetings in the past thirty-five years.

Ben Clark and I, early in our work together, became concerned because many new materials and methods were being developed by the electrical manufacturers. Yet because *Code* and UL standards had not been set for these newer methods it was difficult for the manufacturers to gain any field experience with which they could present their case to Underwriters' Laboratories or the Code Committee. We conceived the idea of allowing trial installations under controlled conditions.

In 1925 a representative from Rome Wire and Cable Company brought us a new type of non-metallic cable. He called it Romex. He wanted some field trials so he could present his case to UL. We told him we could not approve its use in just any building. We would need the approval of the building owner. Ernest Brown, superintendent of the McCleary Harmon Company an electrical contractor, was building a new home. He was a rather progressive fellow and asked if this new Romex could be installed in his home. We gladly cooperated. To my knowledge this was the first home ever to be wired with non-metallic sheathed cable. I often wonder how many million of feet of this cable have been installed since 1925. Still we had to be careful. We conducted many tests, insulation breakdown tests, short circuit tests, and many others before the wiring was covered. After the building was completed we went over and over these tests again. With these results we allowed fifty other homes to be wired this way. Within a year, and we like to think with our help, non-metallic cable was approved by Underwriters' Laboratories.

As the years passed other manufacturers came to us for help. We approved as a project for trial installation a new distribution method that was developed by the BullDog Electric Products Company, called Bus Duct. We also gave trial field experience for circuit breakers, for Electrostrips, and for dead front switchboards. All of these jobs were watched

"OH, FOR PETE'S SAKE, LADY! I'M OUT HERE GATHERING SOME INFORMATION REGARDING AN ELECTRICAL BID!"

carefully and installed under close supervision. It is no small source of pride to have played some part in the development of many of the products we use so commonly today.

After Ben Clark retired, I succeeded him as chief inspector. I stayed at this post until July 1, 1943. Under the city's retirement plan I found that I had to retire. Frankly, I felt I was too young a horse to be put out to pasture. Bill Frank, president of BullDog Electric Products, seemed to agree with me.

Electrical Manufacturing

The next day I reported to him for work as an electrical consultant. But what a change! After years of dealing with electrical manufacturers in what I thought was a liberal attitude, I really had my eyes opened. Now I saw the other side of the coin. I saw the painstaking research and development necessary to prepare a new product for first submittal. Test after test, redesign and redesign—styling to be considered, marketable price, lowered manufacturing costs— utilization of new materials, plastics, aluminum, paper thin tapes with dielectric strength better than wads of rubber. Finally the product is UL approved and then released to sell in a highly competitive market. Indeed this is a long way down the road from Byron McCormick's sign flasher.

I am in the autumn. The years gently float by as the dropping of the gaily-colored leaves. Now BullDog is a division of that industry giant the ITE Company. These have been a thrilling and exciting seventy electrical years. Sometimes they were tough years, but mostly they were rewarding. I have watched the electrical giant bring safe and massive help to man.

Excerpted from "Echoes from the Past," by James Galbraith, retired chief electrical inspector, Detroit, Michigan, *News-Bulletin*, March and May 1963.

James Steele Mahan, along with the other early leaders of IAEI, helped play an active role in the association's founding. His life had been devoted to the electrical industry, having served as an apprentice in the General Electric Shops at West Lynn, Massachusetts, starting in 1903. During his work in several divisions of GE, he did development work on mercury arc rectifiers, flaming arc lamps, Curtis steam turbines, and split phase motors.

Mr. Mahan became chief electrical inspector for the city of Memphis in 1910 and continued in that position until 1911 when he became affiliated with the Western Insurance Union in charge of inspection and rating of utility properties throughout the nineteen middle western states. In 1924, this position and Mr. Mahan transferred to the Western Actuarial Bureau where he continued to do supervisory work. He also had time to engage in additional activities in the Western Association of Electrical Inspectors. During this time, he was in close contact with the Underwriters' Laboratories, Incorporated, and the U.S. Bureau of Standards and his work took him into all sections of this country and Canada.

Mr. Mahan served on many committees of the Western Association of Electrical Inspectors, including a tenure of presidency. He also served on many committees of the NFPA including secretary of the committee on electric railway car houses and cars, committee on electric power houses and substations, and was alternate on the electrical committee and its article committee for several years.

In 1930, Mr. Mahan became field engineer for Steel and Tubes, Inc., at which time electric metallic tubing was first introduced into the electrical industry. In 1934, he elected to start his own business and opened an office in Chicago specializing in electrical inspection services, fire prevention surveys, and the introduction of new products.

Old (in experience but not in spirit Ed J. Stewart) called at Western Section headquarters for a little chat on association matters and incidentally let fall the information that he is now secretary of the Kansas Firemen's Association, and is quite busy preparing for a fire school next June. Ed has done some mighty good work in Kansas, especially since he has become chief engineer of the Kansas Inspection Bureau. Ed also informed us that Topeka has a new electrical inspector, Mr. O. C. Lake, whose application is before the executive eommittee, thanks to Ed's efficiency. Someone will wonder what has become of member Fichtner, and it is a pleasure to announce that he now has a fine position in the water department. Having been "faithful over a few things" he now has a fine promotion. Here's wishing Fichtner continued success in his new job as well as hearty congratulations. Things are certainly looking up in Kansas when honest, efficient service can bring prompt reward. It always pays to do one's best.

William S. Boyd

The approval of all electrical standards and the final approval of all appliances judged under these standards came under the supervision of the Electrical Council of Underwriters' Laboratories. This photograph was taken at the 1929 council meeting held in Chicago. ***Standing (left to right)*:** **Frank R. Donald, Walter J. Burke, C. K. Cregier, John S. Caldwell, J. Whitner, F. D. Weber, W. W. Vaughn, F. G. Waldenfels, F. H. Moore, R. L. Daniel, H. N. Beecher, W. S. Boyd** ***highlighted in photo*,** **F. A. Cambridge, George F. Sheridan, J. C. Forsyth, C. W. Mitchell, V. H. Tousley, and R. B. Shepard.** ***Seated (left to right)*:** **W. W. Wise, George L. Swan, L. C. Illsley, Ben W. Clark, M. B. Gleeson, A. G. Wilbur, F. O. Evertz, Dana Pierce, L. A. Barley, H. A. Patton, George Welman, K. W. Adkins, M. G. Lloyd, Warren Hadley, Oscar Frykman, and Robert M. Nesbitt.**

1931 Eastern Treasurer Hopkins, Eastern President Jim Mahan, and International President William S. Boyd at the 1930 Eastern Section meeting in Pittsburgh, Pennsylvania.

With the backing of the Stock Fire Insurance Underwriters and some of the electrical equipment manufacturers, William Merrill obtained necessary support for a testing laboratory in 1894. Two assistants were hired by the names of Edward Teall and William S. Boyd, and in a small test facility established over a fire station at 22nd and Wentworth in the city of Chicago, the Underwriters Electrical Bureau was established. Seven years later, the small laboratory would incorporate and change its name to Underwriters' Laboratories, and one of the original assistants, William Boyd, who later became the chief electrical inspector for the city of Chicago, was instrumental in the creation of the IAEI in 1928.

Boyd was the secretary of the Western Association of Electrical Inspectors at the time when C. W. Mitchell, secretary of the California Association of Electrical Inspectors, contacted him in 1925 about the possibility of the California association joining the Western. Boyd replied that a committee was working on such a plan to organize the electrical inspectors of the U.S. and Canada into a national or international organization. By 1927, the preliminaries to formation of the international association had progressed to a point at which an organizational meeting was held November 14, 1928, in New York. Records show that the IAEI was officially born on January 1, 1929, thanks to the hard work of Boyd and other individuals.

Mr. Boyd was the Western Section secretary from 1929–1936, and the international president in 1930.

Walter J. Burke, superintendent of the wire division, of the Boston Fire Department, worked for the city for over forty years. His first job after graduating from school was working on "zincs" for batteries used in portable electric gas lighting equipment, and then working at the George Williams' Company. With the experience from those jobs, he was employed as night inspector of street lighting by the Boston Electric Light Company, and then entered the employ of the city of Boston in 1891, in the Bureau of Inspection of Wires, where he was one of four interior wire inspectors. In 1919, with the enactment of a city ordinance making the wire department a division of the fire department, he was appointed superintendent of wires.

He was also one of the thirty-six members of the electrical council of UL, where he was constantly in touch with every development of the industry. He was a member of the IAEI, Massachusetts Municipal Inspectors Association, Metropolitan Electrical League, and the Boston Firemen's Relief Association.

Humanitarian instinct made him a prime mover in placing on the statute book a law requiring the insulation of all metal street lighting standards for the protection of workmen. For his efforts in saving horses from electrocution by fallen trolley wires on November 26, 1898, the fatal night of the "Portland" disaster, he was awarded life membership in the Society for the Prevention of Cruelty to Animals.

Excerpted from *News-Bulletin*, July 1931.

1915-1928

1925 Meeting of **Eastern Association of Electrical Inspectors** at Springfield, Massachusetts, November 17, 1925. This meeting was considered the first annual Eastern Section meeting.

1926 **New York Chapter** is formed.

Meeting of Eastern Association of Electrical Inspectors at Springfield, Massachusetts, November 17, 1925. Thomas Henry Day, retiring president, and J. C. Forsyth, who was elected president for the ensuing year, are shown in the center foreground. In the group are the following members of UL's staff: A. R. Small, vice-president; R. B. Shepard, electrical engineer and C. J. Peacock, service engineer. W. J. Canada, field secretary, Electrical Committee of the NFPA, is also in the group.

An old type gas lantern (*right*) is juxtaposed next to a new form 19 pendent lantern type General Electric Novalux lighting unit (left) on Alameda Avenue in Santiago, Chile, in 1925. The first practical installation in Europe of Edison's electric lighting was in London at Holborn Viaduct. Gas company rights prevented Edison from digging up the streets to install the wiring, but having discovered that the Viaduct had been equipped with channels and raceways, the wiring could be easily installed much to the dismay of the gas companies.

How They Grew

After 50 Years

A Look Back—A Look Ahead

It appears appropriate that as we gather to celebrate IAEI's 50th birthday, that we look back to see whence we have come, and that we look ahead to the challenges and opportunities that we are likely to encounter.

The IAEI is a relatively young organization in comparison with the early use of electricity in this country. Such uses date back to Morse's invention of the telegraph in 1837, Bell's invention of the telephone in 1875, and Edison's invention of the incandescent lamp in 1879. By 1881 fires associated with the use of electricity had increased to the point of attracting attention from the fire insurance industry, which published an electrical code which was the forerunner of the first *National Electrical Code.*

History buffs will no doubt smile to learn that this first *Code* contained some of the same safety concepts that we find in our modern day *Code*, namely,

1. Wires must have excess conductivity of load to be carried (50%).
2. Wires must be thoroughly insulated and doubly coated with some approved material.
3. Wires passing through floors and partitions must be secured against contact with metal and other conducting material in a manner approved by the inspector of the board.
4. A shut-off must be placed at the point of entrance of the supply wires for each building, and the supply turned off when the lights are not in use, and
5. Application for use of electricity must provide information as to the number and kinds of lights to be used, an electrician's estimate of the quantity of electricity required, and a sample of the wires to be used.

It is also interesting to observe that even though this first *Code* was primarily the product of the fire insurance industry and not government enforced, a number of manufacturers of lighting systems voluntarily agreed to produce their equipment so as to comply with the *Code's* provisions. This spirit of working together within the electrical industry in the interest of safe use of electricity has been a distinctive characteristic that still prevails and is best exemplified in the IAEI purposes and membership which I will touch on later.

First Electrical Inspectors

Probably the first electrical inspectors were those employed by fire insurance interests although the city of Chicago had an electrical inspection department

1928 Southern Section meeting in New Orleans, Louisiana, on October 28, 1928. The 1929 section meeting laid claim to being the first, so this may have been the organizational meeting of the Southern Section.

Southern Section meeting in New Orleans, Louisiana, on October 28, 1928

One by one these inspectors came together, in various states, and began to increase in number. In fact, they grew before they were organized into one. Many of the parts are much older than the whole, but no one cared. So the parts multiplied and reached across national borders to other lands, still pursuing safety.

Second annual Northwestern meeting in Portland, Oregon, January 17–18, 1927

1926 Fred Weber helps organize the **Northwestern Association of Electrical Inspectors**, now the Northwestern Section of the IAEI. First Annual Northwestern Section meeting.

as early as 1880. The concept of a main disconnect switch, protection of conductors, concept of permits, concept of approved materials and approval by the authority having jurisdiction were all contained in this first 1881 code which was issued by the New York Board of Fire Underwriters.

The forerunner of Underwriters Laboratories was an insurance bureau established in Chicago in 1893 to test and report on electrical materials and devices. This bureau published its first list of approvals in 1897. Underwriters Laboratories was chartered in the state of Illinois in 1901.

While the 1881 code produced under the auspices of the fire insurance industry achieved some national recognition, it was not until about 1897 when all segments of the electrical industry jointly participated with the insurance industry in producing a national code. This change recognized another aspect of the electrical industry that continues to permeate its operation, namely, that voluntary compliance with safety rules of the code can best be achieved by utilizing a code-developing procedure in which all segments of the industry can actively participate.

Regional organization of electrical inspectors preceded by several years the formal establishment of IAEI. The Western Association was formed in 1905. Inspectors from the southern states established a regional group in 1914, as did inspectors from the east coast in 1905-1906, and inspectors from the west coast in 1912.

Establishment of IAEI

The International Association of Electrical Inspectors came into being in 1928 largely through the efforts of William S. Boyd, an early chief electrical inspector of the city of Chicago. In addition to Mr. Boyd, Ellis Cannady of North Carolina, Jim Mahan of Los Angeles, Joseph Forsyth of New York, Victor Tousley of Chicago, and Fred Weber of Portland, Oregon, all played active roles in the association's founding.

But what is this organization of electrical inspectors, what does it seek to do, and who are its members?

Obviously, as its name clearly indicates, it is an association, but its membership is not restricted just to those persons actively engaged in electrical inspection work. Rather it is the one electrical association whose membership is open to all persons associated with the electrical safety system. I am sure you all know that the electrical safety system in the United States has been described by some Washington authorities as a nonsystem because it is not structured as a result of federal legislation or controlled by some single bureau in Washington.

The system comprises several loosely knit groups which recognize the *National Electrical Code* as their common core of interest. All these interests are represented through membership on code-making panels and by participation in other forums that provide input to the code-making process. Figure 1 lists the most widely recognized components of the system.

Persons who are a part of the electrical safety system are eligible for membership in IAEI and it is this common *code* forum provided by IAEI which qualifies it to properly refer to itself as the keystone of the electrical industry—that interlocking mechanism which ties the supporting pieces together. Figure 2 shows the broad distribution of membership in the association.

IAEI's Purpose for Existence

Every organization must have some identified purpose for existing and IAEI

COMPONENTS OF THE ELECTRICAL SAFETY SYSTEM

- ELECTRICAL INSPECTORS
- ELECTRICAL MANUFACTURERS
- UTILITIES
- INSTALLERS
- TESTING LABORATORIES
- ARCHITECTS AND ENGINEERS
- CODE DEVELOPERS

Figure 1. Interests comprising the electrical safety system in the United States.

MEMBERSHIP — IAEI

ACTIVE MEMBERS (INSPECTORS)	5,600
CONTRACTORS, FIELD ENGINEERS, SALES REPRESENTATIVES	3,500
ELECTRICAL JOURNEYMEN, WIREMEN	3,500
MANUFACTURERS	700
CITIES, TOWNS, MUNICIPALITIES	700
TOTAL	14,000

Figure 2. Broad distribution of membership statistics as of August 1978.

The objectives of the IAEI shall be:

(a) To cooperate in the formulation of standards for the safe installation of and use of electrical materials, devices and appliances.

(b) To promote the uniform understanding and application of the National Electrical Code and other electrical codes.

(c) To promote cooperation between inspectors, the electrical industry and the public.

(d) To collect and disseminate information relative to the safe use of electricity.

(e) To represent the Electrical Inspectors in all matters which are dealt with nationally and internationally by the electrical industry.

(f) To cooperate with other national and international organizations in furthering the development of the electrical industry.

Figure 3. Objectives of the IAEI.

is no exception. I think that attendees at IAEI chapter and section meetings and at NFPA electrical section meetings are likely to think that the IAEI is some kind of an informal debating society concerned solely with interpreting the *National Electrical Code*. While this activity is the most visible one, it is just one of six activities or objectives of the association. These objectives are listed in figure 3.

The first four objectives are clearly those aspects that relate to the mechanisms by which electrical safety is achieved. The two latter objectives relate to the welfare of the electrical inspector and the growth of the electrical industry.

In taking stock of the association on its 50th birthday, one might well ask how is the association doing in meeting its stated objectives?

Reference to the 1978 *Membership Directory* will show that the association is indeed quite active in the formulation of standards for the safe installation and use of electrical materials, devices, and appliances. The association has a representative on each of the 23 code-making panels, and underwrites the expense of each representative's attendance at meetings of the panels. Representatives are currently serving on 14 technical subcommittees of the *NEC*, on five subcommittees of the American National Standards Institute concerned with electrical equipment and procedures, five NFPA committees related to electrical matters not a part of the *National Electrical Code*, as well as on committees of Underwriters Laboratories and the National Safety Council.

The grass roots work of promoting uniform interpretation of the *National Electrical Code* and other electrical codes is carried on primarily through chapter meetings which are held on a regularly scheduled basis. Currently there are 86 chapters organized into six major sections. At both chapter and section meetings real field problems are presented to a panel of persons having first-hand knowledge of the *Code* requirements for discussion and resolution. While the opinions rendered at these meetings are strictly informal, nevertheless, they are most useful in bringing to light various aspects surrounding the basis of the *Code* requirements and hence contribute to a more uniform interpretation.

Another mechanism for promoting uniform understanding are the numerous discussion articles by recognized *Code* experts which appear in the *IAEI News*.

In almost all cases of official interpretations of the *NEC*, an electrical inspector serves on the interpretations committee, while the executive vice president of the association serves on the *NEC* correlating committee.

The fact that 60 percent of the association's members are drawn from other than electrical inspection interests supports the view that the association is indeed advancing cooperation between electrical inspectors and other segments of the industry and of the public. The continuing growth in membership further attests to the usefulness of the association in helping to achieve cooperation with the concerned safety interests of the industry.

Reporting Electrical Fires and Accidents

Over the years, the association has collected information related to electrical fires and accidents and has publicized these data in the *IAEI News*. It is my personal view that the association might well have been more active in collecting such information and might thereby have increased the credibility of the information that is given to the public concerning electrical fires and accidents. There is presently an NFPA

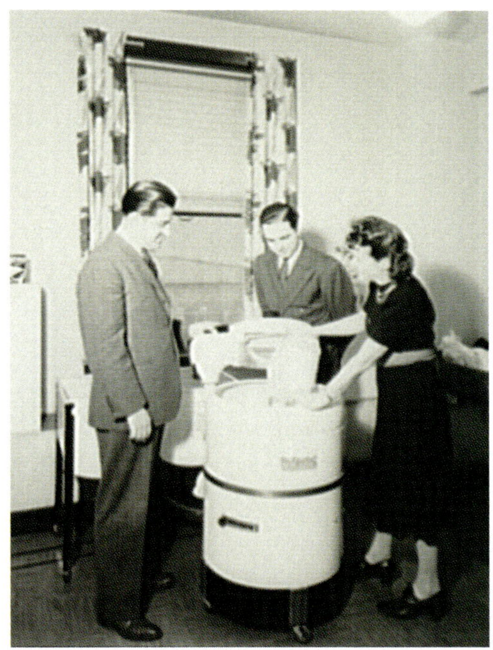

A washing machine demonstration given at the Electric Institute of Washington, Potomac Electric Power Company. The first electric-powered washing machine (the Thor) was introduced in 1908, by the Hurley Machine Company of Chicago, Illinois. Alva J. Fisher was the inventor. The machine was a drum type with a galvanized tub and an electric motor, for which a patent was issued on August 9, 1910. The machines worked reasonably well; but with the motor bolted to the side of the machine, they were not very safe as water often spilt over the side and into the motor or switch. It was not until after a few people got injured, that they enclosed the drum into a case in the 1930s.

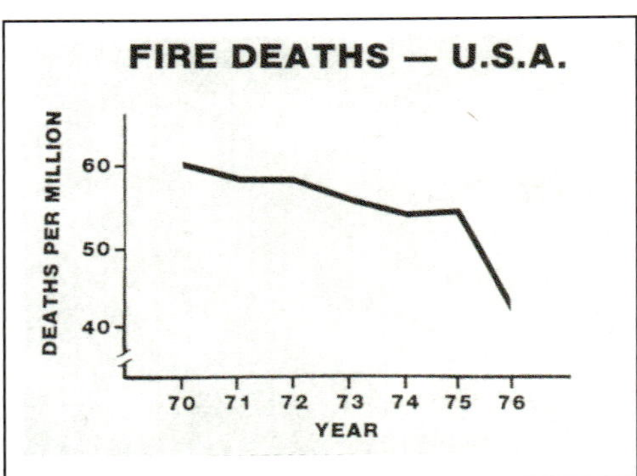

Figure 4. Fire deaths from building fires in the United States.

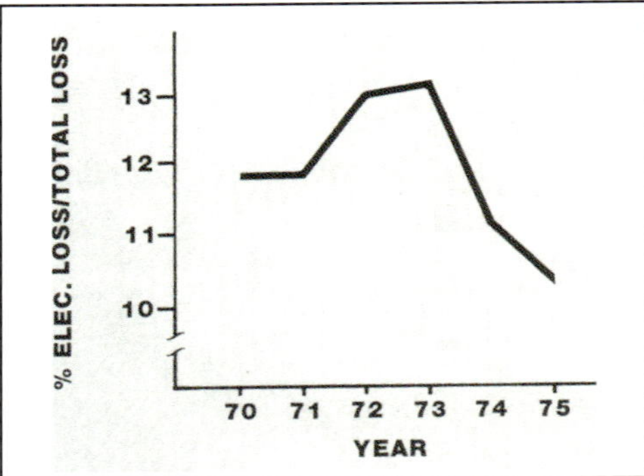

Figure 5. Percent electrical fires to all building fires.

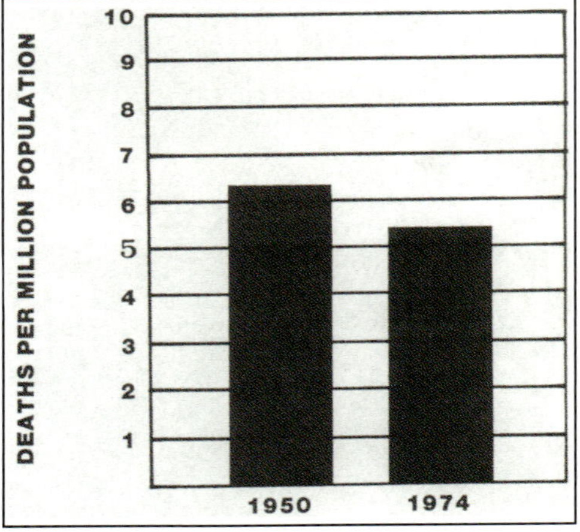

Figure 6. Deaths per million from electrical shock.

Twenty-first annual convention of the Western Association of Electrical Inspectors, Hotel Sherman, Chicago, January 26—28, 1926

1926 **Wisconsin Chapter** is formed.

1928 **The IAEI** came into being in October 1928 largely through the efforts of William S. Boyd, an early chief electrical inspector of the city of Chicago.

committee concerned with developing valid procedures for investigation of fires thought to be of electrical origin. Your association is represented on this committee and I would hope that this committee work would significantly increase the credibility of fire and accident data.

Taking stock should also encompass some evaluation of how well are the association and the electrical industry doing in promoting electrical safety. Finding suitable yardsticks to measure effectiveness in this area is not easy, for statistics which tabulate property that was not destroyed or injuries that did not occur as a result of the electrical inspector's efforts are most difficult to produce. I believe there are some rather indirect ways to evaluate the efforts of the electrical safety system—but I should point out that the data collection mechanism that has been used is not as reliable as we would like it to be.

As can be seen in figure 4, except for 1976, there is a gradual downward trend in the number of building fire deaths per million inhabitants in the U.S. There is a rather dramatic decline in 1976 for which no plausible explanation has yet been advanced. Since the 1977 data has not been released, it would be premature to assume that such a reduction represented some sensational breakthrough in lives saved.

Of greater interest to this group, however, are fires attributed to electrical causes. Figure 5 shows that while no definite trend can be concluded, the percent of electrical fire losses have varied within a very narrow range over the past few years with a downward slope for the last two years.

Electrical fatalities have varied somewhere between 800 to 1200 per year in the period 1950 to 1974. During this same period, the personal exposure to electricity has materially increased. The population has increased by a factor of 1.4, while the per capita residential consumption of electrical energy has increased a whopping 539 percent. Despite this significant increase in use and hence in exposure to electricity, the death rate per million from electrical shock has fallen from 6.3 to 5.4 as shown in figure 6.

While it would be wrong to rely too heavily upon these data, they do suggest that the safety system is making a substantial contribution toward increasing electrical safety. If this were not so these curves would parallel the increased exposure and instead of showing a downtrend they would show a decided upward slope.

Well, so much for the past—what are today's challenges and opportunities—for the way in which these are faced can well determine the course of the future.

Challenges Facing the Association

I would not attempt to rank the seriousness of challenges which I perceive to be facing the association today but I would certainly include the potential threat of the federal government to regulate the safety aspects of the electrical industry near the top. Currently the consumer product safety commission is trying to establish jurisdiction over electrical wiring used in buildings occupied by consumers or frequented by consumers. This effort ignores the fact that "electrical wiring" is a term used to describe a system by which products conforming to recognized standards are installed or assembled by qualified personnel in accordance with recognized safety rules and inspected by duly authorized electrical inspectors. The commission action appears to place the entire burden of electrical safety upon the individual electrical product manufacturer. If such regulation of the system is to occur, presumably it would commence gradually by requiring products to conform to federal standards which would require that installation instructions be furnished by the manufacturer. This would undoubtedly increase the do-it-yourself practice with increased disregard of permits and inspection procedures.

Another challenge soon to be faced comes from the Occupational Safety and Health Administration through its promotion of a separate walk-through electrical code covering electrical safety in America's work places. Even though OSHA has adopted the 1969 *NEC,* it is expected that OSHA will gradually withdraw its support of the *Code* and that the "work place" code will probably replace the *NEC* as the required level of electrical safety requirements to be met.

Probably a more subtle challenge which surfaces periodically is agitation and support for a federal building code—that is one developed and enforced by agencies of the federal government. The latest reason cited for supporting such a code is the need to conserve energy in all types of buildings. Control of the building industry has been a long time dream of some Washington bureaucrats and a popular issue such as energy conservation would undoubtedly engender considerable support in the political arena. All these challenges at the federal level deserve the watchful eye of the association and further the enlistment of its membership to become involved politically when it sees actions that move toward federal regulations in the electrical safety field.

But not all challenges to the electrical safety system come from Washington. Some are created when inspectors and other interests promote local codes which contain substantial deviations from the *National Electrical Code.* The existence of code differences is sometimes used to portray a picture of mass disarray within the electrical safety system and to support the concept that federal regulation is needed for the good of the industry as well as for the good of the public.

As our local governments have become more complex, there has also developed a need for more effective local administration. This has frequently resulted in combining a number of public safety functions into a single department with the result that the local electrical inspector finds that instead of reporting directly to the city council or the city manager, he now reports to the building inspector. This has become of grave concern to the inspector who sees a threat to his professional status as well as the need to acquire new skills just to maintain his present status. Fighting one's boss has never been considered to be real smart and as difficult as the change might be to accept, the smart money has got to be on the inspector who would seek to make his boss look good and thereby tend to promote himself as the chief assistant and subsequent successor to that position. The demands on tax payer's dollars are so tremendous that it is illogical to presume that consolidation moves in the interest of economy can be stayed on the basis that electrical inspection work is significantly more complicated than other types of inspection work related to building safety.

Because the *NEC* is one of the chief focal points of the association's activities, any action which threatens the integrity of the code-development process has got to be a matter of grave concern to the association. Within the last couple of years, a powerful group within the NFPA membership has pursued rather successfully the practice of packing the annual meeting with its members to achieve, by physical body count, those changes in safety requirements which could not be achieved within the technical committees. In fairness to this group, it should be mentioned that such

Electric range and oven, circa 1930s. Cooking became more advanced in 1910 when the first electric cooking unit was built using heating wires embedded in porcelain blocks. In 1915, in an attempt to solve his mother's problem of burning bread, a young man attached a gas water heater thermostat to a gas oven, developing the first oven temperature control. With technology expanding by the 1920s, cooks had a choice of ranges or separate ovens and cooktops. Consumers' kitchens were brightened-up in 1925, when ranges became available in a rainbow of colors -- black, white, red, green, buff, blue or gray. Previously, black was the only color option.

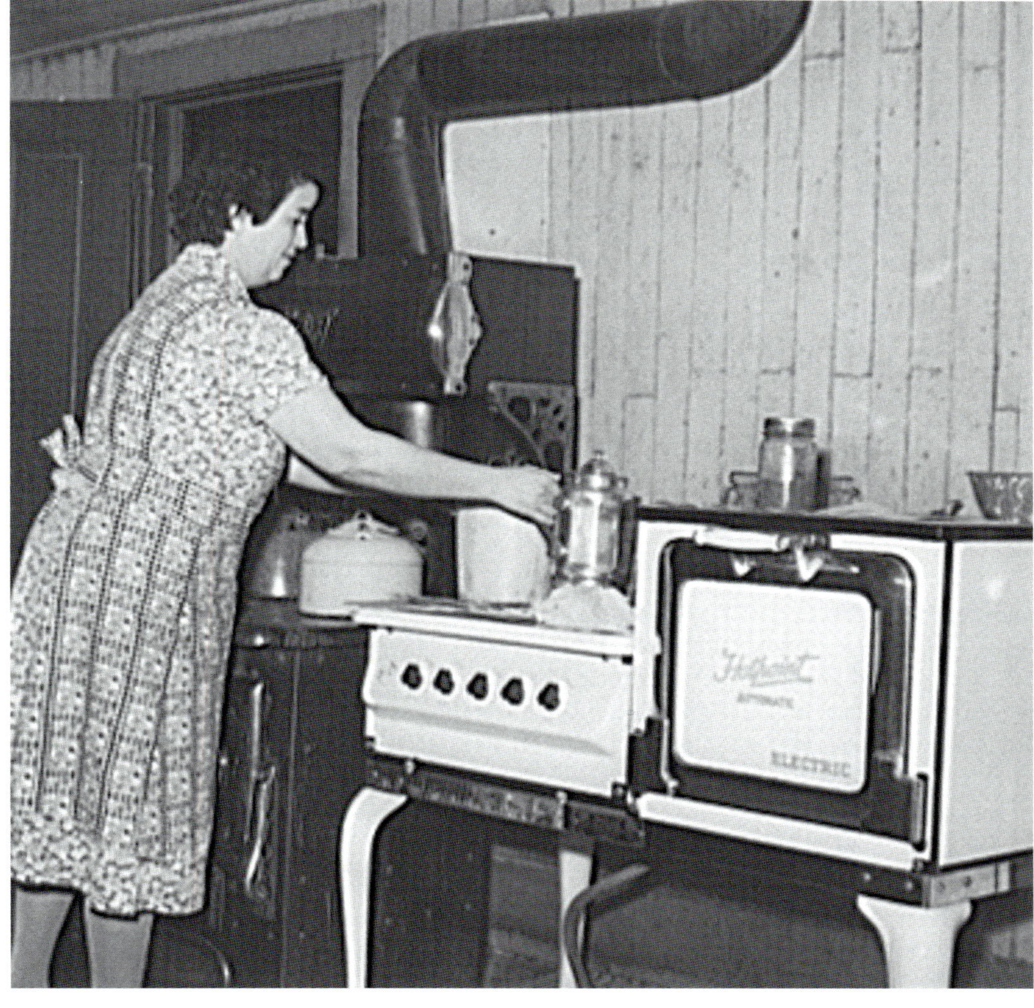

Workers pose proudly on and around a newly completed electric hydro-turbine generator, on June 27, 1924. The generator works like a water wheel, using the force of water to produce energy, and is entirely electrically driven. In 1915, Ontario Hydro was granted new powers, and electrical inspection became the responsibility of The Hydro-Electric Power Commission (HEPC) of Ontario with the power to make regulations, appoint inspectors, and set fees. Regulations kept pace with developments in the industry with appropriate amendments put forth by a committee comprised of representatives from manufacturers, contractors, the Toronto Hydro-Electric System and the HEPC. This system worked well until 1927, when due to an increasing lack of uniformity between the various provinces over the regulations and their interpretation, a National Code Committee was established under the auspices of the Canadian Standards Association.

practice has been used by others, but only sparingly, and not as a routine *modus operandi*. At stake is the large issue as to whether or not other interests will also adopt the "court-packing" concept as a means of combating the practice, or of using it to achieve their own objectives. The NFPA is deeply concerned about this situation and is actively studying the issue with a view to promoting remedial action.

Of most immediate concern to this association, and particularly to its active inspector members, is the so-called tax payer revolt. The hard results of such a movement is well illustrated by the very substantial loss of attendance at this convention from members residing in California caused by the adjustment to Proposition 13. It appears that the current mood of the country is to resist larger government, be it at local and state levels, as well as at the national level. Accordingly, government administrators must make hard choices as to the utilization of available resources. Activities which have minimum public appeal are the first ones to be cut. Electrical safety which is based primarily on prevention has never been promoted as a glamour type service as has fire fighting or crime suppression, hence it is not surprising that activities which do not produce immediately visible income by way of fees, will be early candidates for financial cut-backs.

But as serious and discouraging as these challenges appear to be, there is no reason to believe that opportunities do not also exist for advancement of the association as well as the welfare of its members.

The tax payer revolt suggests two immediate actions to be initiated. The first of these is to develop and launch, possibly through paid professionals, a broad public awareness program to educate the public, and particularly those involved with the management of government concerning the significance of the electrical inspector's work and his contribution to the safety and welfare of the community. Such a program has been needed for a long time and the combination of challenges to the electrical inspection fraternity make it even more imperative at this time.

The restrictions on funds as the result of the tax payer revolt make it necessary that each inspector carefully review his schedule of inspector fees and adjust such fees as to make his department as financially independent of tax dollars as can be accomplished. When compared with the total cost, or even the electrical cost, of a modern building the electrical inspection fees are only miniscule. If the inspector sincerely believes in the value added to the building as a result of his activities, then he should be able to convince his bosses that his department can be made financially self-sufficient.

Active Participation Essential

When presented as a mechanism for keeping the inspector's knowledge and skills current with rapidly moving technology, as to better discharge his public protection responsibilities, attendance at chapter, section, and NFPA meetings would appear to be ample justification for the inspector's active participation in the affairs of the association. Not only does such participation improve the inspector's skills, but it also adds to his professional status.

Much has been written and said about upgrading the inspector's capabilities through schooling and certification. It is only natural that the inspector with many years of actual inspection service is not likely to be enthusiastic about the real value of additional book learning. Despite the great job that the code-making panels do in writing the safety requirements of the *NEC*, understanding of the basic elements of electricity, and some of the peculiarities of specialized equipment greatly improve the soundness of the inspector's judgment exercised in interpretation of the rules. The electrical art advances each year and with each new technological breakthrough, the electrical inspector must keep up with these developments if he is to have his judgments based on sound engineering principals.

It seems to me that IAEI needs to continue its programs of education and certification, while recognizing the advantages of a certain amount of "grandfathering." Such recognition would permit the continued use of long-service inspectors, where background and experience are important job qualifications. New people entering the activity would be required to meet higher educational requirements so as to upgrade the inspection activity over a period of time. With such an arrangement, the contributions of the older inspectors can be equitably meshed with the higher education qualification of those just entering the activity. Many professional licensing groups have utilized such combination of qualification in launching new certification programs.

Need Greater Public Awareness

As part of its overall public awareness program, the association needs to place greater emphasis on its main function, that of assuring safety in the use of electricity. Too often the inspector and

California Association of Electrical Inspectors in convention at San Diego, California, March 22 – 24, 1926.

the *Code* are portrayed as unwarranted costs fostered upon the innocent builder or tax payer. It is in the best interest of the entire industry that the particular role that each segment plays be recognized and respected. It is only when each segment completely discharges its role that the maximum benefits of safe use of electricity are realized at the least costs. Public service announcements on TV and radio might well be utilized to help educate the public in safety matters at rather modest cost in time and dollars. One cannot achieve a position of respect as a recognized public safety-concerned organization by hiding his light under a bushel. In today's world it is not enough just to do a creditable job, one has to publicize his contributions if he wishes to be recognized.

I cannot stress too strongly the importance of having the association take a stronger role in collecting and dissemination information concerning electrical fires and accidents. The Consumer Product Safety Commission has a rather sophisticated operation known as NEISS for National Electronic Injury Surveillance System. Unless there are other data sources of equal or better reliability, the NEISS will constitute the entire database of accident information which can be used to regulate the entire electrical industry that is involved with electrical consumer products.

Where I live in the Chicago area, the local electrical utility has seized the current concern about energy to promote greater use of electricity by simply describing electrical energy as the "conservation fuel" and by publicizing that in its generating plants electricity is produced by using coal and nuclear energy which are available in rather generous quantities. Similarly, it seems to me that this association should join with other segments of the industry in promoting the continued *full* use of electrical energy—for the U.S. economy cannot begin to provide for full employment by following a policy of restricted activities that results from government dictated policies which rely solely on energy conservation.

I would not presume to be able to forecast the changes that may result from the current pricing of oil and natural gas that leads to the search for competitive fuels, nor can I forecast the impact of a political solution to the method of disposing of atomic wastes. I am confident, however, that the long-range solution to these and other energy related problems must be based on sound economics. Accordingly, I believe that the future of the electrical industry is bright even though challenges of an environmental and political nature will continue to be present. Electrical energy, the product of the industry, has too many advantages associated with its availability and use to assume any role other than that of continuing usefulness and growth.

Your association is a vital part of the electrical industry and its future and growth are also bright as long as it continues to play its essential role of public protection. Consistent with that posture is the dedication of each of you to do your job in the industry in a way that will reflect the pride which you share in being a part of a winning team.

I congratulate you upon reaching the 50-year milestone and I urge you to grasp, and vigorously pursue, the opportunities that the future holds for your organization.

Excerpted from *IAEI News*, January/February 1979, pages 30–37, "After 50 Years. A Look Back—A Look Ahead," by Baron Whitaker, consultant to the president of Underwriters Laboratories. This was the keynote address of the Golden Jubilee in 1978

1924 First annual of the newly formed **California Association of Electrical Inspectors** held in Long, Beach, California, on July 28–29, 1924. This section later became part of the Southwestern Section of the IAEI.

THE FIRST 50 YEARS

Southwestern Section

William Cyr *was an associate member of the Southwestern Section from 1926, after he first joined the staff of* Journal of Electricity, *which was later called* Electrical West. *He retired in 1962, but continued as consulting editor until the magazine suspended publication. He was elected a member of the Southwestern Section executive committee and served for several years—and was on the public relations committee from 1934.*

He assisted both Harold Gerber and Herb Ufer, secretaries of the Southwestern Section, during their tenures, in recording and preparing the proceedings of the annual meetings. He was appointed on Herb Ufer's history committee, which made its report in 1955 and from which he compiled this history.

In the beginning God created the heaven and the earth. And the earth was without form, and void, and darkness was upon the face of the deep. And the Spirit of God moved upon the face of the waters. And God said, Let there be Light, and there was light."

We descendants of Adam, the man that God created, have been centuries learning that the Light that God created was Electricity. In fact, only in the last 100 years of the millenniums of time since God issued that construction order has man learned how to generate, transmit, utilize—and protect that source of all energy—Electricity.

As our nation prepares to celebrate its 200th anniversary and the signing of the Declaration, remember they signed that Declaration by candlelight. Ben Franklin, who might be considered our first electrician apprentice, certainly tempted God by flying that kite. As we look back to that first centennial exposition held in Philadelphia in 1876, it is almost incredible to realize that the only electrical exhibits there 100 years ago were of the telegraph. Only two small dynamos were exhibited, one Belgian, the other American, which turned up enough energy to light a small carbon arc. The public was only mildly curious of this new toy.

Yet in a short 20 years after that, the complexities of generating and transmitting that electrical force had so increased (and so had the fires) that the underwriters of insurance on buildings brought together engineers, scientists, architects and the generating utilities of that time to write up rules for safe installation and utilization of this magic force of fluid or whatever it was. We hardly know yet what it is. Thus was brought about the first *National Electrical Code* in 1897. Every two or three years since has required a revised and updated edition to take care

William Cyr

James Howard Fenton was a pioneer whose career was full of good works and solid achievement. Charter members of the Western Section remembered that Jim Fenton helped organize the Western Association of Electrical Inspectors and was its president from 1921–22 as well as its memorable host in 1913 and in 1920.

Mr. Fenton's crowning achievement was the organization and management of the electrical inspection department operated under the control of the St. Louis Fire Prevention Bureau.

James Howard Fenton moved to St. Louis when he was about thirteen years old, and learned the carpenter's trade. He joined the Salvage Corps in 1885 and became electrical inspector for the St. Louis Board of Fire Underwriters in 1889, where he remained until the dissolution of the organization. A short time later the St. Louis Fire Prevention Organization was organized and Mr. Fenton took charge of the electrical department, remaining there until he resigned in 1925. A year or two later, he became associated with Frank Adam Electric Company where he remained until his death in 1929.

Mr. Fenton, for years, served on the electrical council of Underwriters' Laboratories.

of the new and more intricate ways in which electricity is employed.

The existence of this electrical inspectors association for only half of this last hundred years is what we celebrate this year. For once man caught on, he certainly has been fast to accelerate his knowledge of and utilization of this fabulous force.

Just think, in this 100 plus years, man has developed electric energy use from a dim filament glowing in a glass bottle and a primitive motor (the reverse of the dynamo), on up to lighting every home, all of our streets, powering every factory, moving people and equipment anywhere, sending beams to the moon and distant stars of the firmament, talking across the land and over the waters, sending pictures around the world—fantastically incredible miracles, they would have been thought a century ago.

So here we are, custodians for mankind of the duty to see that this terrific force is harnessed securely, is handed carefully, used in a safe manner, controlled by satisfactory means and methods, so that its benefits to man can be enjoyed and its dangers unfeared.

As an organization, we have been in existence for 50 years [*Editor's note*: California Electrical Inspectors Association, now part of the Southwestern Section IAEI.] We have endeavored to keep pace with the truly fantastic electrical complexity that has ensued.

There are a few reference points from the past with which to relate the progress of our association in its 50 years. The first *National Electrical Code* after a couple of years of work by committees of as many interested parties as could be brought together, was issued in 1897 by a National Conference on Standard Electrical Rules. Every two or three years thereafter revised editions have been issued.

The first mention of western cities adopting wiring rules and setting up inspection that I found in the back issues of *Journal of Electricity* was that San Francisco had done so in 1893; and that in 1899 the supervisors adopted order #267 regarding inside wiring and in 1901 #353, registration of electrical contractors and wiremen. You'll be interested, I'm sure, that the inspection fees were: 5 cents an outlet, 10 cents for four lights from one outlet, arc lamp 50 cents, additional arcs 25 cents, motors – 1 hp 50 cents, 3 hp $1, and 5 hp $1.50.

As another point of reference, even as late as 1916, only 8 percent of the homes of the country were wired. Possibly because development of electricity was faster in the west, the percentage was higher out there but not so much.

It was at the turn of this century that cities began to find electricians of some experience and appoint them as the electrical inspector for their jurisdiction. Some few were engineering graduates but many were electricians trained through apprenticeship and work with the tools of the trade.

Each, being an individual, had his own ideas of what should be done and many were the special rules they wrote. There was need for them to get together and exchange their ideas and experiences so that more reliance could be placed in the rules of the *National Electrical Code*. If there was a need felt that the national rules might be changed more realisti-

J. N. Mochon, chief electrical examiner, province of Quebec, Canada, was a charter member of the IAEI, and was active in the Western Association of Electrical Inspectors before the formation of the IAEI.

In 1919, the Quebec Provincial Government named a Board of Electrical Examiners to look into a report on the advisability of taking over the inspection of electrical installations and the licensing of electricians and contractors. Mr. Mochon was named as one of the three members on this board.

Those of the "Old Guard," who had been in this field of endeavor since or before the creation of this board could appreciate the reasons which prompted the Quebec government in the matter, when conditions existing at the time were taken into account and compared with those of 1946 as regards the development in the application of electricity in industry and the home, improvement in code requirements, the advancement made in the manufacture of electrical products and their acceptance by the laboratories as a recognized standard.

The report presented by Mochon and his associates on the board led to the enactment of a provincial statute called "The Protection of the Public Against Fire," limiting its application to the inspection of electrical work done in public buildings and industrial establishments. The results obtained were so conclusive that Mochon was promoted to the position of chief examiner in 1923 with instructions to study and report on the further possibilities of legislative action.

In consequence, the provincial government of Quebec took over the inspection of all electrical work in 1928 and entrusted the administration of this broadened field of action to Mr. Mochon as chief examiner and director of the service.

Mr. Mochon was a member of the Western Section, IAEI; AMAIEE; Canadian Standards Association; GE Test Alumni; Canadian Electrical Association and the Montreal Electrical Club.

cally, getting together offered a chance, perhaps, to send their ideas and requests for change to the national code-making committee. There was also a need to understand the national code; to be better informed should result in more uniformity of how the rules were interpreted and applied.

By 1912, although no record of them can be found, there had been some small meetings in California arranged by Claude W. Mitchell, electrical engineer and inspector for the Board of Fire Underwriters of the Pacific, to discuss and become informed of changes in the successive national code editions. On July 27, 1912, both he and Harry N. Beecher, chief inspector, city of Los Angeles, addressed the third annual meeting of California State Association of Electrical Contractors in San Jose, presenting statistics showing the number of fires from electrical wiring faults. Proposed new rules in the forthcoming 1913 *National Electrical Code* that would affect electricians were also discussed. The contractors association president appointed a committee to work with inspectors to organize a California Association of Electrical Inspectors. W. A. Spencer, San Jose city electrician, was named the president; Edward W. Jewell, San Diego city electrician, secretary; P. A. Anderson, Oakland city inspector, treasurer. Mitchell and Beecher were named to organize the inspectors of the state and report at the 1913 contractors association convention in Santa Barbara. However, no record has been found that such a meeting was held.

On March 21 of 1914, mention was found in *Journal of Electricity* of a meeting of California Section, National Association of Electrical Inspectors in San Francisco, at which Claude Mitchell presided. Then on July 10, the *San Jose Mercury-Herald* reported and published a picture of the Northern California City Electrical Inspectors, chaired by Mitchell, meeting in San Jose, with a picnic at Alum Rock Park. Subsequent meetings were scheduled for July 11 in San Francisco and August 7 in Sacramento. Little was recorded anywhere of any activity of those cradle days of this association

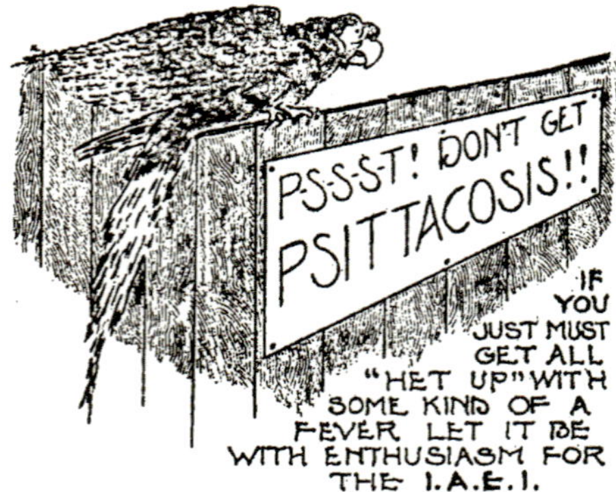

the next 10 years. Perhaps the unsettled times of World War I eclipsed the interest there might have been in the inspectors and the codes.

But another inspection body was launched in that period. When, in California, the Workman's Compensation Act was passed, a Division of Industrial Safety was created to cover hazards to everyone employed in business and industry. For electrical safety protection, Safety Orders were prepared by committees of interested people and organizations. These were to be enforced by state inspectors. In 1917, after the United States had entered the war, and industrial activity to support the troops was predominant in the national interest, the Electrical Safety Orders were adopted and George Kimball, who had been an engineer with Pacific Telephone & Telegraph Company, was appointed the chief inspector of the electrical division.

As a state code, the Safety Orders were designated to supercede the local codes and the national code in all places of employment. Emphasis was on safety to persons, not fire prevention. Residential wiring was not included.

The *National Code*, born of the insurance underwriters, had its first emphasis in fire prevention, but as the electrical inspectors of the cities increasingly demanded, it gradually was revised and improved to require personal protection as well as fire protection.

Addition of the Safety Orders to the *National Code* and the many local ordinances containing special rules and exceptions, brought about a need for an organization that could seek to coordinate and unify all of them into workable practical form. Feeling this particularly, two far-sighted pioneers, Claude Mitchell, inspector for the Pacific Board of Fire Underwriters, and George Kimball of the California Division of Industrial Safety, worked with Herbert Stitt, Fresno city electrician, to call together all the city inspectors of the state to a meeting in Fresno, January 24–24, 1924.

Ten cities were represented—H. W. Stitt, Fresno, who was made temporary chairman; Ralph W. Wiley, San Francisco; Carl Hardy and B. C. Hill, Oakland; R. H. Manahan, Los Angeles; R. W. Abright and R. B. Taplin, Long Beach; A.

Addition of the safety orders to the National Code and the many local ordinances containing special rules and exceptions bought about a need for an organization that could seek to coordinate and unify all of them into workable practical form. **George Kimball**, chief engineer, Industrial Accident Commission, and **Herb Stitt**, Fresno city electrician, helped Claude Mitchell organize the California Electrical Inspectors Association. This photo was taken at the official first meeting in July 1924 in Long Beach of the California Electrical Inspectors Association. That association later formed the Southwestern Section of the International Association of Electrical Inspectors in 1928.

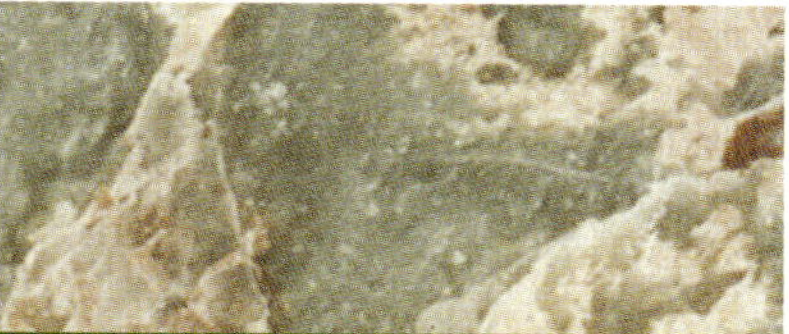

E. Johnstone, San Diego; J. M. Evans, Modesto; J. C. Hamilton, San Jose; J. I. Dixon, Santa Clara; F. A. Morrell, Stockton. The state was represented by George Kimball, San Francisco, and Frank Short, Los Angeles. Paul B. Wilson, district manager, San Joaquin Light & Power Company, was a utility representative. First steps were taken to form the organization and H. W. Stitt was named president pro tem; C. W. Mitchell, secretary. A committee to draft a constitution and bylaws consisted of Frank Short, chairman, R. H. Manahan and R. W. Abright.

At what was really called the "First Annual Meeting" of this newly formed California Association of Electrical Inspectors, held at Long Beach, July 28–29, 1924, the draft of a constitution and by-laws was read and discussed. Herbert Stitt was elected president, R. W. Abright, vice president and C. W. Mitchell, secretary-treasurer.

It was largely through the efforts of Claude W. Mitchell that the California Association of Electrical Inspectors was organized in January 1924, and he acted as secretary of this organization up to the time it was merged with the International Association of Electrical Inspectors. When this organization became the Southwestern Section of the IAEI, Mr. Mitchell continued to act as the secretary, a position he held until his death in 1936.

Mr. Mitchell was also active in the organization of the IAEI and became a member of the executive council at the organizational meeting in 1928. He was elected fourth vice president in 1932. He also became a member of the electrical committee of the National Fire Protection Association in 1918, and for many years was a member of the electrical council of Underwriters' Laboratories.

On the west coast, Mr. Mitchell was active in the San Francisco Electrical Development League. He was also affiliated with the Fire Underwriters' Association of the Pacific, and with the Blue Goose, International.

Some subsequent meetings were held in March 1925 at San Francisco and September in Fresno. In March 1926 at San Diego the articles of incorporation were adopted, with one change — one annual meeting instead of two.

With the assistance of electrical industry advertisers, a cooperation that has been accorded the inspectors since the beginning of its association and continues to this day, an annual *Proceedings* was published in 1924.

Secretary Mitchell had been in correspondence with the secretary of the older Western Association of Electrical Inspectors, William S. Boyd in Chicago, suggesting that the California association join the Western. Boyd replied that a committee was working on such a plan to organize the electrical inspectors of the U.S. and Canada into a national or international association. A chart and letter outlining the proposed organization was sent. This became the main topic of consideration at the meeting in Fresno, September 24–26, 1925. At the San Diego meeting, March 22–24, 1926, L. W. Going, Portland city inspector, one of the nation's most creative code makers, who had just been elected president of a newly-formed Northwestern Association of Electrical Inspectors on January 11–12, 1926, and F. D. Weber, the secretary of the Oregon Rating Bureau, came down to discuss the proposed international association. They were made honorary members of the California association and the following year's annual *Proceedings* contained the reports of both Southwestern and Northwestern associations.

By 1927 the preliminaries to for-mation of the international association had progressed to a point at which an organization meeting was held November 14, 1928, in New York. Records show that officially the IAEI was born January 1, 1929 and the first issue of the *News-Bulletin* was dated March 1929.

The first officers were: J. C. Forsyth (Eastern Section), president; William S. Boyd (Western Section, Chicago), first vice president; R. H. Manahan (Southwestern Section, Los Angeles), second vice president; F. D. Weber, (Northwestern Section, Portland), third vice president; N. E. Cannady (Southern Section, North Carolina), fourth vice president.

Because of his hard work and patient, tactful manner in bringing together all interested parties to establish the IAEI by 1928, Victor H. Tousley, who had been chief inspector of Chicago, was made secretary-treasurer. The electrical industry, through the National Fire Protection Association, had engaged Tous-

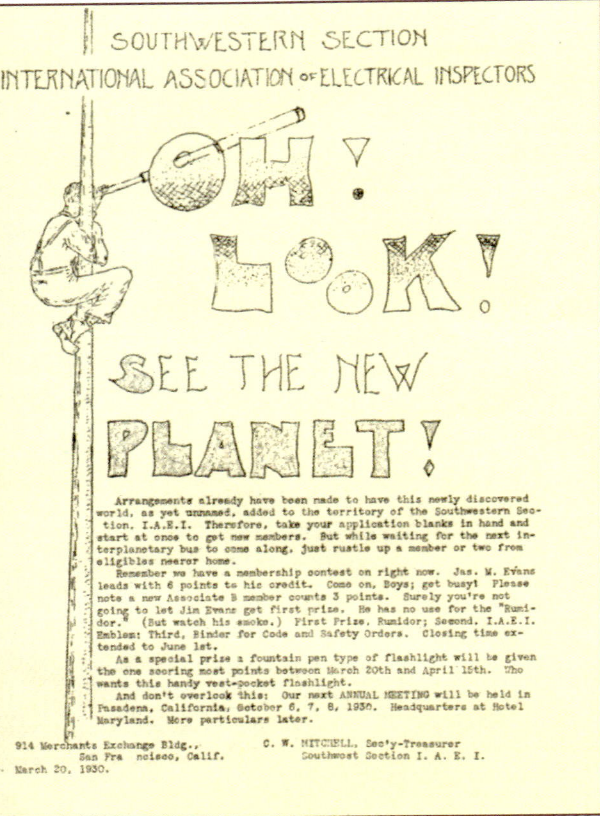

SOUTHWESTERN SECTION
INTERNATIONAL ASSOCIATION OF ELECTRICAL INSPECTORS

OH! LOOK! SEE THE NEW PLANET!

Arrangements already have been made to have this newly discovered world, as yet unnamed, added to the territory of the Southwestern Section, I.A.E.I. Therefore, take your application blanks in hand and start at once to get new members. But while waiting for the next interplanetary bus to come along, just rustle up a member or two from eligibles nearer home.

Remember we have a membership contest on right now. Jas. M. Evans leads with 6 points to his credit. Come on, Boys; get busy! Please note a new Associate B member counts 3 points. Surely you're not going to let Jim Evans get first prize. He has no use for the "Rumidor." (But watch his smoke.) First Prize, Rumidor; Second, I.A.E.I. Emblem; Third, Binder for Code and Safety Orders. Closing time extended to June 1st.

As a special prize a fountain pen type of flashlight will be given the one scoring most points between March 20th and April 15th. Who wants this handy vest-pocket flashlight.

And don't overlook this: Our next ANNUAL MEETING will be held in Pasadena, California, October 6, 7, 8, 1930. Headquarters at Hotel Maryland. More particulars later.

914 Merchants Exchange Bldg.,
San Francisco, Calif.
March 20, 1930.

C. W. MITCHELL, Sec'y-Treasurer
Southwest Section I. A. E. I.

ley as field engineer and authorized and supported his work and office to enable him to serve as the secretary-treasurer of IAEI and to travel the nation on behalf of the organization. This continued for 20 years, until his death in 1948.

In May of 1929, Tousley visited Los Angeles and San Francisco to discuss with members of the California association affiliation with IAEI and territory to be encompassed. Mitchell submitted a list of 166 members of the California association who became chapter members of the Southwestern Section. Territory was to include the states of Arizona, California, Nevada, Utah and the Philippine and Hawaiian Islands. Utah was later transferred to the Northwestern Section. By August 18, 1930, these official changes had all been made by the executive council of IAEI.

The first annual meeting (seventh of the California Association of Electrical Inspectors) of the Southwestern Section was held in San Francisco, September 18–21, 1929. First officers were: C. W. Beaton, Sacramento, president; A. E. Johnstone, San Diego, vice president; and C. W. Mitchell, secretary-treasurer. The first IAEI executive council members from the west were: Carl Hardy, Oakland; R. H. Manahan, Los Angeles; and C. W. Mitchell, San Francisco.

There were two joint meetings with the Northwestern Section — the first August 23–26, 1937, in Salt Lake City; the second during the Golden Gate International Exposition in San Francisco, August 14–16, 1939. A joint meeting of all IAEI sections was held in Chicago in September 1933, but only two members were able to attend. Another was held there in September 21–26, 1953, and plans were made for a 50th annual of the IAEI in New Orleans in 1978.

Chapters sprang up from the section organization as inspectors in several areas felt a need to work with fellow inspectors of neighboring towns or cities in relation to their own local ordinances and codes. Often they needed fellow support to resist some high pressured tactics from special interests who sought permission to deviate from the *Code* or use some untested materials or methods.

The first chapter in the Southwestern Section started from a Los Angeles meeting April 18, 1929, of city inspectors of Southern California. A formal request on October 28 of that year brought approval of the executive council and January 9, 1930, the first official meeting of the Southern California Chapter was held.

The inspectors from the cities around San Francisco Bay and Sacramento who had met with Mitchell to start the state association continued to meet and became the Northern California Chapter. Soon there was a Central California and then a Sacramento Valley Chapter. But the most active chapter organizer of all was Herb Ufer, Western Superintendent of Underwriters Laboratories, who traveled the western states, visited inspectors and inspired them to form chapters in Nevada, Arizona, Montana, Idaho, and Utah.

The first annual meeting to be held outside California was in 1954, at Elko, Nevada, when E. E. Carlton was president. The first in Arizona was in Phoenix in 1957, Frank Jones president. Another Arizona meeting was held in Tucson in 1963. New Mexico, now also in the Southwestern Section, having transferred in 1959 from the Western Section, had an annual meeting in 1967 in Albuquerque. And after many years of pleading from the delegations that came each year from the Hawaiian Islands, and after a trial run was made by a group from the section led by Carlton to a chapter meeting there in 1962, (64 attended from stateside) the section held a very well-attended annual meeting in Honolulu in 1972 with Hawaii's own Arthur K. C. Chong as president.

Each annual meeting has had at least one or more new and controversial problems to face up to and try to write changes in the national code to submit to the code-making panels or executive council for the next edition of the *Code*. At first there was no detailed procedure for processing such proposed changes. As field engineer for NFPA, Victor Tousley would go through the changes submitted by the various

William Brown Hubbell assisted in organizing the old Western Association of Electrical Inspectors in 1905, and was a loyal member up until his death in 1929. He was elected president of that association in 1924. Like so many prominent men in the electrical field, Mr. Hubbell began to take an interest in things electrical early in life and retained his interest to the very last. The life of Mr. Hubbell will always be a shining light to the electrical inspector searching for the true secret of success which might be summed up as follows:

Know your code.
Be loyal to its requirements.
Administer it intelligently.
Study to be helpful.
Listen courteously.
Explain patiently.
Always be fair.

Obedience to these rules in the spirit in which Hubbell followed them will bring to the electrical inspector a real satisfaction in the work performed, his friends will be without number, and his acclaim will reach to the uttermost parts of the earth.

Probably no one in the electrical industry had a wider circle of acquaintances than did Thomas Henry Day, and there were few in the electrical inspection business that did not know of him and his work.

Mr. Day started his electrical experience on October 10, 1876, when he began the installing of thermostats in the coal bunkers of the U.S. battleship *Tennessee*. From that time on he was actively engaged in electrical work, finally taking a position with the Hartford Board of Fire Underwriters and later with the New England Insurance Exchange.

Mr. Day was always active in inspectors' organizations and was one of the charter members of the International Association of Electrical Inspectors. He was secretary of the original National Association of Electrical Inspectors; and in 1930, he was elected life honorary member of the Eastern Section, and in the same year was elected to honorary membership in the international association in "recognition of his lifelong and successful endeavor in the application of the *National Electrical Code* and for his many contributions to the cause of electrical inspections."

panels and sections and these would be discussed. Then, wearing his other hat as secretary of the IAEI, he would take the recommendations and reactions of the members of this section along to the other section meetings and to the electrical committee, of which he also acted as secretary, a third hat. Inspectors felt that their proposals were not given adequate consideration and dissatisfaction with this loose and unprecise procedure—for inspectors are by nature sticklers for strict following of the written rules—finally brought about a change, a complete reorganization of the IAEI making for a stronger position in the writing of the *National Electrical Code*. Several of the Southwestern Section leaders had a dynamic part in this reorganization.

California is known for its share of activists or revolutionaries. Even city administrations in the state have had its rebels and there was a movement in Southern California among inspectors to set up an independent association and write a code for that area alone, which would have compounded the confusion that already existed.

After the death of Victor Tousley in 1948, the secretaryship of IAEI transferred to Charles L. Smith, former Detroit chief inspector. The pressure grew for such a change of national set up. In 1950 the then president, J. E. Wise, appointed two Southwestern Section members to committees whose efforts brought about important results.

Arthur Veit, a past president of both the section and later the IAEI, was named chairman of the IAEI articles of association and by-laws committee to revise and bring up to date the 20-year-old original.

Herb Ufer, who had been secretary-treasurer of the section since 1946 when

H. G. Ufer, an unidentified gentleman from Spokane, W. L. Gaffney, Northwestern secretary/treasurer, and Ed M. Tubbs, first vice president at a Northwestern Section meeting. (Date unknown)

New officers are sworn in at the 1951 Southwestern Section meeting in Long Beach. The new officers are (*left to right*): C. R. Meikel, first vice president; H. G. Ufer, secretary/treasurer; R. D. Johnson, president; A. C. Veit, international president; Ed Muller, retiring president; and E. E. Carlton, second vice president.

Harold Gerber of San Francisco had resigned, was named chairman of the dues structure committee. Both committees' reports were adopted at the Silver Jubilee meeting of all sections held in Chicago in September 1953. The amended articles were placed in effect January 1, 1954, and in 1958 IAEI became an independent body, no longer depending on NFPA for its managing secretary. The new dues structure made the IAEI self-supporting. The new articles provided a path through the jungle of procedures to get the recommended changes emanating from the section to the code-making committees of NFPA. That procedure, changed only as necessary in the interim, is what is used in the section meetings today.

Herb Ufer's novel idea that has aided the Southwestern Section so much financially, was the Type F membership for cities and counties themselves, supplementing the individual inspector memberships.

But hard-working, dedicated, articulate and dynamic Herb Ufer was caught in a backfire from the new ar-

After forty-three and one-half years with Underwriters' Laboratories, H. G. Ufer, western superintendent of that office in Los Angeles, California, retired on November 1, 1953. Mr. Ufer was long active in the IAEI, serving as secretary/treasurer of the Southern California Chapter for many years until he was elected second vice president of the Southwestern Section in 1945. In 1946, he became first vice president. Because he exhibited such intense interest in the affairs of the Southwestern Section, he was requested by the executive committee to take over the office of secretary/treasurer of the section. He handled his new position with efficiency and outstanding ability until resigning in 1953.

"Herb" as he is known to his many friends throughout the U.S. and Canada, was born in Chicago, Illinois. He completed his higher education at the Armour Institute of Technology, where he graduated in 1910 with a degree in electrical engineering.

Mr. Ufer began his career with UL in 1910 as assistant engineer in the protection department. When the label service department was created, he was transferred to it and remained there until he moved to the Pacific coast, which occurred five years later where he was made chief inspector. In 1927, he was sent to Los Angeles, California, and in 1929 was appointed western superintendent of UL, which position he held until his retirement.

Mr. Ufer was a registered electrical engineer in the state of California; a professional member of the Pacific Coast Building Officials Conference from 1927; honorary member of the Fire Chiefs Association; member of the Los Angeles Electrical Club from 1927, an honorary member of the Los Angeles Estimators Club and the Electragists and a member of the Los Angeles Elks Lodge #99 for more than twenty-five years.

ticles strict enforcement. After his long service as section secretary he had been elected an international vice president and in the normal procedure would have been president in 1956. But he had retired from Underwriters Laboratories and then become a consultant for Rome Cable Company, and thus no longer eligible for president of the association. The legal hassle over this strict interpretation of the new rules hurt Herb deeply but he continued to work as faithfully as ever for his "boys." He was later given the title of honorary president in 1956 and L. O. Trim took his place as IAEI president.

IAEI presidents from this section have included many of the section presidents, the latest of which was our Colin Watt who was section president in 1967 for our Albuquerque meeting. Lou LaFehr, who was our section president in 1953 and then became section secretary-treasurer in 1954, succeeding Herb Ufer, was chosen by the executive council to be the IAEI managing director in 1962 and is now executive vice president. Succeeding LaFehr as our section secretary in 1963 has been C. R. Pierce of Fresno, where our section began, and who was section president in 1962.

Our section secretaries, by the nature of their continuing position must truly be somewhat the manager of section affairs between presidents each year. Each contributes some special quality of his own to his leadership.

Claude Mitchell, a quiet, patient and reasoning man, with a sense of humor, was organizer and nurse to the organization as it crawled and learned to walk.

Harold Gerber, brash young chief inspector for Ralph Wiley's San Francisco Department of Electricity, pulled the association up by the seat of the pants to try to keep up with his dynamic brain and its self-taught but amazing knowledge of electricity and of the *Code* and the fantastic new developments in the field. Inspection was not creative enough for Harold; he quit and became a consulting engineer, with many achievements to his credit.

Norman Allan "Al" Cockburn, who was born, raised, and educated in Toronto, was a man who had many friends in the electrical industry throughout the North American continent, in Britain, and on the European continent. He became a member of the Association of Professional Engineers in 1938.

He joined the Approvals Laboratory on May 1, 1929, when it was a department of the Hydro Electric Power Commission (HEPC) of Ontario, as an assistant inspector. Working through the ranks, he was appointed supervising engineer of reinspection in 1945 and held this position until August 31, 1950, when he was appointed chief inspector and a member of management of the Canadian Standards Association Approvals Division (the approvals work was transferred from the Ontario Hydro in 1940, but not made official until 1950 when it was headed by Mr. "Gerry" Moes, former president of the Canadian Section). Ever active, Al assumed additional responsibilities of the Approvals Laboratories plant and project engineer, and in 1953 started working with the architects and engineers, etc., on the plans for the new 50,000 square foot modern testing laboratory now located in Rexdale, Ontario.

Al was an active member of the IAEI and was elected secretary-treasurer of the Ontario Chapter from 1949 to 1952. He is also past-president of the Model Railroad Club of Toronto, a member of the Engineering Institute of Canada, and a member of the Etobicoke Rate-Players Association.

Herb Ufer was the missionary, who taught the gospel of the code and the brotherhood of inspectors throughout the West and organized chapters; "missions," if you will.

Lou LaFehr pulled the now somewhat scattered section, seemingly at times to be going off in all directions, back together and did so good a job he was asked to do likewise with the International IAEI, which was then in a crisis itself.

Chuck Pierce has stressed education of the inspectors to earn a higher status in government. He still manages to keep all the balls in the air, juggling the many factors in the industry as he heads up the section affairs.

Each meeting of the section seems to have discovered some new and often strange device, method, hazard or problem. The first meeting in 1924 spent most of its time discussing the single fusing of branch circuits, proposed in the 1923 *Code*. Other meetings wrestled with outlawing black conduit, nonmetallic sheathed cable or "Romex," armored cable, knob-and-tube services, Type S fuses, circuit breakers—especially the interchangeable ones that the manufacturers thought were such a bright idea (and Bob Maxwell thought were inventions of the devil)—iron wire during war-housing days, plastic-coated wires, PVC conduit, aluminum wire, aluminum conduit, derating of wires and now ground fault interrupters—all of which issues somehow show either radioactive traces or are still explosive issues.

Grounding we have with us always—even after the special, high echelon conference session that was held during the 1961 meeting at Long Beach. But it would appear that electricity has sneaky ways to find some obscure new path to ground.

The California chapters have always had the special problems created by the differences between the State Safety Orders and the *National Electrical Code*. Special sessions of the section meetings are set aside to hear from the state's Division of Industrial Safety and to discuss these problems. The members from other states either take a recess or come in to learn about California's problems.

Harry A. Patton

Each year since 1960 joint meetings of chapters have been held. For instance, the Northern California, Sacramento Valley and Central California chapters met together on more or less state matters, with some national code discussion to get unanimity on code change proposals to be submitted to the section meeting. The Southern California Chapter, which has a Greater Los Angeles Division, met with the southern San Joaquin Valley group of the Central California Chapter. For the past several years quad-chapter meetings have been held to include both ends of the state. (Other divisions in the section now include a Shasta division in Northern California; a Maui division in Hawaii; and a Southern Nevada division.)

Pressure from the home building industry in California resulted in a housing law and a drive to write a code for housing that was intended to encompass all state codes that had anything to do with wiring, known as Title 24. On the wake of this, from the federal level has come OSHA, to override everything below it in the name of occupational safety. And now we hear the Federal Consumer Product Safety laws will bring more rules. So the IAEI and particularly the Southwestern Section and California are faced with the resolu-

Harry A. Patton was the third vice president of the IO in 1940 and electrical inspector for the Washington Surveying and Rating Bureau, Seattle. "Pat" came across the border from Ontario to New York State in 1882, going to work in a machine shop in Lockport.

In his early days he was interested in telegraphy and, while not employed by any of the telegraph companies, was known as a plug operator. His first real experience with electrical work was government line repairing, connecting up the various posts in the territory. At the expiration of his services in 1889, he received another diploma as an efficient lineman and rough rider. He then went east to Minneapolis, entering the employ of the Brush Electric Company as a wireman.

In 1891, he joined the Light and Power Company at Eau Claire, Wisconsin, as superintendent, remaining there until 1900. He then went west, entering the employ of the Light and Power Company in Seattle as a journeyman, remaining there until 1904, when he entered the employ of the Washington Surveying and Rating Bureau as electrical inspector.

Mr. Patton was a believer in organizing better working conditions for mankind and belonged to several fraternal orders and to a number of civic organizations. He was a member of the old Western Association of Electrical Inspectors. He was instrumental in organizing the Northwestern Electrical Inspectors Association, which later merged with the IAEI. Mr. Patton was president of the Northwestern Section in 1928–1929.

"Jimmy, go light a candle for the contractors."

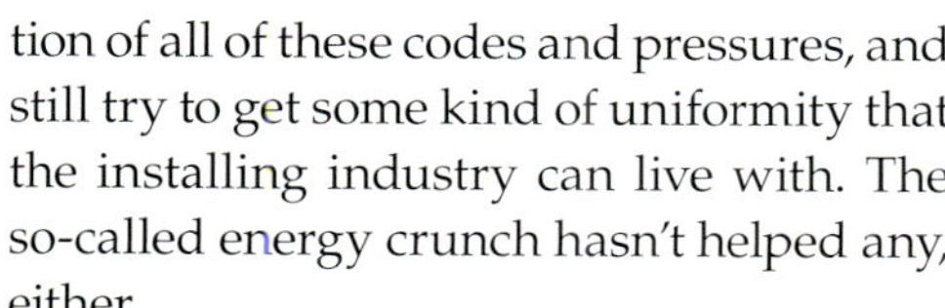

tion of all of these codes and pressures, and still try to get some kind of uniformity that the installing industry can live with. The so-called energy crunch hasn't helped any, either.

Such, in very brief, in the history of this Southwestern Section.

Codes deal with facts and figures, with materials, methods, standards. Associations are people, you and me, each with their own ideas, experiences, prejudices, theories. People change with the years and move on. New people come in to take their places. Very few of you here today knew or recall the founders of this association that have been mentioned. Many of you are new or only recently became inspectors and then members.

This history has been prepared so that you can be acquainted with what came before you, and appreciate your elders for all the work and heartache that went into this organization. All of this has been accomplished in a working lifetime—50 years.

It is yours to carry on for the next 50. The first 100 years are the hardest, they say.

Excerpted from *IAEI News*, January/February 1975.

Walter A. Dilzell was a charter member of the Southern Section and Louisiana Chapter at New Orleans, and was an original member of the executive council of the IAEI. He took an active part in the Southern Section's first convention held in Atlanta in October 1929. He was especially popular at these conventions because of his jolly and cheerful disposition and good fellowship.

In 1915, he founded the Dilzell Construction Company and later was connected with the Union Plumbing and Construction Company, which installed the plumbing and heating system in one of New Orleans finest buildings in 1930, the Masonic Temple on St. Charles Street. He was appointed city electrician in 1919 and served for two and a half years and was again appointed city electrician in 1925, where he remained until his death in 1930. Mr. Dilzell was also an active member of the International Association of Municipal Electricians and had served as treasurer of this association for many years.

Joseph P. Rohan joined the Electrical Inspectors Association in 1915, and was active until his retirement in 1946. He has held many offices in the association, including chairman of the Western New England Chapter.

In January 1895, Mr. Rohan went to work for Charles R. Reynolds Company, electrical contractors. In 1896, for Rice & Baldwin. Mr. Rohan had previously been a helper for Mr. Baldwin, while working for the Reynolds Company. The Rice & Baldwin Company later became the Baldwin-Stewart Company.

Except for two years, Mr. Rohan worked with the same contractor, and in 1915, he became inspector of wires for the city of Hartford. When he retired in 1946, he was the chief electrical inspector for the city.

On a sightseeing tour of the Windy City, looking south along Michigan Boulevard from the Chicago River in 1927. By 1927, the preliminaries to formation of an international organization were already being discussed in Chicago. William S. Boyd, chief electrical inspector for the city of Chicago at this time, was instrumental in the organization of IAEI.

A Backward Glance at Air Conditioning In America

Neon signs illuminate the facade of the Empire Theatre where crowds have gathered for a performance of *Lady Be Good*. The Empire Theatre opened in Atlantic City, New Jersey, in 1898, and claims to have introduced what we now call air conditioning that same year. What makes the story even more remarkable is that the cooling came from a refrigeration plant which was remote from the theatre site. The Atlantic City Cooling Company was organized in 1895 for the double purpose of operating an ice plant and to provide central refrigeration for business houses, hotels, and homes.

History will record that mankind achieved two important steps on its way to civilization: The first was its ability to generate heat and, thereby, to survive the ravages of extreme cold. The second was its ability to *remove* heat and, thereby, control the indoor environment in a way which had only been a dream for centuries.

The first step was taken when man was still crawling about in primeval caves, long before recorded history. The second step came not until hundreds of thousands of years later. If one were to transform centuries into minutes, it could be said that man learned to generate heat years ago but he did not learn to generate "cold" until a few heartbeats ago.

By the time of the American Civil War, engineers were building viable refrigeration systems. After the war, the primary application of this technology was the manufacture of ice.

The reality that food remains edible longer at low temperatures was well known. Ice was cut out of rivers and lakes during the winter and stored in sawdust to preserve it during the summer when it was most needed. The development of refrigeration machines relegated such primitive practices to the dim corridors of history.

It didn't take long for the inventive American mind to conclude that refrigeration could be used to conquer the second scourge of modern man, the debilitating effects of summer's heat.

The first application of refrigeration in space cooling is subject to debate. However, it is clear that within a few years after the turn of the century, there were refrigeration systems designed to cool the air within buildings.

One building claims to have introduced what we now call "air conditioning" as early as 1898. That was the year the Empire Theater opened in Atlantic City, New Jersey. What makes the story even more remarkable is that the cooling came from a refrigeration plant which was remote from the theater site. The following account is taken from the February 28, 1954, edition of the *Atlantic City Press*:

"The theatre's air cooling was accomplished by an underground system of refrigeration conveyed from a plant on Baltic Avenue, which served many other lines of business, as far back as 1895. The Atlantic City Cooling Company was organized in 1895 for the double purpose of operating an ice plant and to provide central refrigeration for business houses, hotels and homes. Pipe lines carrying a refrigerant similar to that used to make ice were laid underground in the streets and service was provided to all who wished, the same as city water and gas. It was ahead of its time, however, for not enough patronage could be obtained to pay a profit, and the service was disconnected after about eight years."

Some people, prior to the revelation of the Empire Theatre story, believed that the first air-conditioned theatre had been the Metropolitan of Los Angeles, equipped in 1921. The 1954 Atlantic City newspaper story quoted above tells of people then alive who had attended the opening of the Empire on July 1, 1898, and who described the indoor air "as cool as anyone could wish."

Forward-looking businessmen immediately saw the commercial advantages of air conditioning and the milestones began to come in quick succession.

Electric Institute of Washington, Potomac Electric Power Company, air conditioning display, circa 1920.

One of the first department stores to be equipped with air conditioning was Filene's Sons of Boston, Massachusetts. Installation was completed in June 1927. Twenty years later, the store owners were asked if the air conditioning had helped sales. With typical Yankee restraint, they replied: "There is no way of telling whether the air conditioning resulted in increased sales, but we have observed that when the air conditioning does not function as it should and the store becomes warm in certain areas, many customers go from the warm areas to the cool, air-conditioned areas."

At what year you peg the date for the first air-conditioned bank depends on how liberal you want to be with the term. A bank in St. Louis, built in 1916, employed a system called "washed air" wherein outside air was drawn through a spray of cool water taken from a cistern under the building. Such systems were widely tried but the excessive humidity they added to the air was considered unacceptable and eventually led to their demise. The St. Louis bank, however, continued to use the "washed air" system until they remodeled the building in 1946.

One of the first large apartment buildings in the East to be air-conditioned was equipped in 1936. Located at 400 Park Avenue in New York City, the 12-story building drew wide attention. An article in the May 1936 edition of *Buildings Magazine* carried the following story:

"The occasion marks a new step forward in the provision of modern conveniences and in the history of air-conditioning, for while one or two small apartment houses have recently installed this service, nowhere else in New York, certainly, has an apartment air-conditioning job of comparable size and thoroughness been undertaken. Although air conditioning is but one phase of the modernization, it is perhaps the most important one from the standpoint of the owner or manager. Installation of the service in a building of this size and character indicates not only that air conditioning for apartments has 'arrived' but also that the invention is adaptable to existing structures built long before the conditioning was in prospect. It will be interesting to see what this means as a renting feature."

The early years of the air-conditioning industry, between 1900 and 1940, must have been exciting times for those were involved in the birth of something so significant in the history of mankind.

One can only speculate about the technological, manufacturing and installation problems which were encountered by the industry pioneers of that period. But, we can safely assume one thing: The thrill of accomplishment for those people must have been tremendous.

Reprinted from the November 1981 issue of KOLDFAX published by the Air-Conditioning and Refrigerating Institute. — Excerpted from *IAEI News*, January 1982.

The Inspectors

1946 Northwestern Section

Calling themselves inspectors, they set out to ferret out unsafe installations and require more from the installers—more safety, and more safety. They would tame electricity if it were humanly possible. From these inspectors rose leaders, many of them fearless and determined, who challenged their followers to even more exacting margins

1929-1939

The Great Depression

The ***Golden Decade*** ended abruptly in 1929 when the Great Bull Market reached its crest in early September, and then plummeted into the depths on October's Black Thursday and Black Tuesday. The progress reaped in the earlier part of the century that had been marked in the industrialized portions of the world by increasing material prosperity for larger segments of the population suddenly shifted from the highest forward gear into reverse. By the time Franklin D. Roosevelt replaced Herbert Hoover in 1933, one-fourth of the American workforce was unemployed. It was not all negative, however, as the decade forced Americans to come together in a spirit of cooperation; to find a leader capable of shaping their undeveloped feelings into a political program; to agree to a few modest restraints being placed on the marketplace economy; to form a rudimentary welfare state; and to renew their faith in democracy—and this faith garnered from the decade helped America win the next world war. The decade began in the early stages of the worst economic collapse in modern history and ended in the early stages of the worst war in modern history.

1929 International President

Joseph C. Forsyth was the chief electrical inspector and consultant of the New York Board of Fire Underwriters, and one of the early founders of the IAEI. Mr. Forsyth was employed by the bureau of surveys, later known as the bureau of electricity of the New York Board, on April 1, 1891, and he retired on September 15, 1942.

Mr. Forsyth was the president of the Eastern Association of Electrical Inspectors, and became the first president of the IAEI when this association was organized in 1929. Honorary membership was conferred upon Mr. Forsyth in March 1934, when he retired from active service. He was a member of the electrical committee of the National Fire Protection Association, and had been instrumental in the promulgation of the *National Electrical Code* since its inception.

Quick Fact

First Lady

The IAEI is pleased to number among its members, Miss F. H. Pettee of the Simplex Wire and Cable Company of Jacksonville, Florida, the only lady member of which we have a record. — Reprinted from *News-Bulletin*, May 1930.

The International Association of Electrical Inspectors

Its Organization, Membership, How Governed and the Territorial Limits of Its Various Divisions

The International Association of Electrical Inspectors is made up of an executive council, five major divisions known as chapters, together with the individual members. A person taking membership in the association becomes a member of the International and at the same time becomes a member of the particular section in which he resides. A person may, if he so desires, hold membership in more than one section, but he can vote or hold office only in the section in which he resides. A member of the International Association is, however, privileged to attend the meetings of any section or chapter, no matter where held.

The states and territories of the United States and the provinces of Canada are assigned to geographical divisions knows as sections. The territory of these sections is as follows:

Eastern Section

States of Maine, New Hampshire, Vermont, Massachusetts, Rhode Island, Connecticut, New York, New Jersey, Pennsylvania, Maryland, Delaware and the District of Columbia, and the Provinces of New Brunswick, Nova Scotia, Quebec and Prince Edward Island.

Western Section

States of Ohio, West Virginia, Kentucky, Tennessee, Arkansas, Indiana, Michigan, Illinois, Wisconsin, Missouri, Oklahoma, Iowa, Minnesota, North Dakota, South Dakota, Nebraska, Kansas, Colorado, Wyoming, New Mexico and Montana, and the Provinces of Ontario, Manitoba and Saskatchewan.

Southwestern Section

States of California, Nevada, Utah, Arizona, and the Philippine and Hawaiian Islands.

Northwestern Section

States of Washington, Idaho, Oregon and Alaska, and the Provinces of British Columbia and Alberta.

Southern Section

States of Virginia, Georgia, Mississippi, North Carolina, Florida, Louisiana, South Carolina, Alabama, Texas and Puerto Rico, Cuba and South America.

The major work of the association is carried on by the sections. Each section is controlled by its own officers and directors. The sections each hold an annual meeting in some city within its territory, these meetings generally lasting through several days. The sections also appoint numerous committees from among its own membership to carry on the section work.

CHAPTERS

In order to broaden the work of the association and to permit more frequent local meetings, each section is authorized to form chapters. These chapters occupy only a limited territory, such as a state or metropolitan district. Chapters now in existence as a part of the International and the territory they occupy are as follows:

New York Chapter – Metropolitan New York district and New Jersey north of Trenton.

Western New England Chapter – States of Connecticut, Rhode Island, Vermont, New Hampshire, Maine, and that part of Massachusetts west of a straight line passing through a point just west of Baldwinville, Mass., and a point just west of Southbridge, Mass.

Wisconsin Chapter – State of Wisconsin.

Illinois Chapter – State of Illinois.

Philadelphia Chapter – Philadelphia County, Camden and New Jersey south of Trenton.

Other chapters are in the process of formation.

MEMBERSHIP

The association includes three classes of membership: **Active members**, or those who are engaged in electrical inspection work and including inspectors employed by the utility companies; **associate members**, or those interested in the purposes of the association but who are not eligible for active membership; and **cooperating members**, or those organizations and individuals having an interest in the association and desiring to encourage its activities. The dues vary somewhat throughout the several sections. The dues for active members is $2.00 per year in all sections except the Northwestern, where the dues for active members is $3.00 per year.

The dues for associate members in all sections is $3.00 per year for Class A members and $10.00 per year for Class B members. The dues for co-operating members is $100.00 per year.

Application for membership should be made to the section in which the applicant resides, or may be made direct to the International headquarters.

Membership in Chapters

The chapters are made up of members of the association residing in the particular territory of the chapter. A member of the International does not through his International membership automatically become a member of a chapter. He must make separate application and pay separate dues before becoming a chapter member. Application should be made direct to the chapter officers.

EXECUTIVE COUNCIL

The organization as a whole is supervised by a corps of officers and an executive council, the representatives to which are elected by the sections and on the basis of their total active membership. The executive council meets at least twice each year and considers and acts upon such matters as have a bearing on the association as a whole and particularly those matters having to do with the National and other electrical codes.

EXECUTIVE OFFICE

The International Association maintains an executive office at Room 705, 612 North Michigan Avenue, Chicago, in which office of the secretary-treasurer is located. The telephone number is Superior 0704. — Reprinted from *News-Bulletin*, March 1929.

1929 Ohio Inspectors Assistant Secretary

Miss Betty Kelly was the assistant secretary, Ohio Inspectors Association in 1929. At a meeting of the Ohio Association of Electrical Inspectors in 1929, the Ohio association took formal action towards becoming a chapter of the Western Section, IAEI. The charter for the Ohio Chapter was formally granted in 1938.

A Bendix Automatic Home Laundry washing machine, circa 1940. The first fully automatic machine was introduced at a state fair in Louisiana in 1937 by a company called Bendix Corporation. General Electric claims to be the maker of the first fully automatic machine in 1947 but this may be the first automatic machine with an agitator. In addition to being used as a washing machine, a number of Canadian machines in the early 1920s were offered with built-in gas or electric water heaters. The addition of a motor-driven drain pump at this time moved the machine one step closer to being completely automatic.

Two women work at an Ampule washing machine at the Hoffmann-LaRoche Incorporation, circa 1945.

Quick Fact

Kentucky Chapter was started on its way at a meeting held in the rooms of the Louisville Chamber of Commerce on the evening of August 12, 1929.

THE INTERNATIONAL ASSOCIATION

By J. C. Forsythe, president, IAEI

The idea of an International Association originated, I understand, in the Western Electrical Inspectors Association, and due to the hard work and tactful and patient manner in which it was handled, it came into being in October, 1928.

A bi-monthly bulletin is published and the issues thus far distributed have been of such high character, containing articles and items of so much general interest that it has caught the attention of the entire electrical industry.

I do not need to explain to you anything about the set-up of the International Association or the manner in which it is supposed to function for most of you are as familiar with that as I am; but I thought I would take up a little time in trying to elaborate on our aims and purposes.

On referring to the printed Articles of Association, you will notice that there are seven specific objects set forth. Seven, as you all know, is the number denoting completeness.

The first one states, "To co-operate in the formulation of standards for the safe installation and use of electrical materials, devices and appliances." The electrical inspectors, as a group, are the most unbiased and should be the best informed of all groups engaged in creating electrical standards for safety. This is true because no inspector is or should be interested in the manufacture, sale or installation of electrical materials, devices or appliances of any kind. They are in touch with more electrical equipment of all kinds and under more varying conditions than any other group of individuals in the electrical industry and are in a better position to know, first hand, the causes which produce electrical fires and accidents. For these and various other reasons, therefore, why shouldn't the inspectors, not only cooperate in the formulation of standards for electrical safety, but be the real leaders in securing the enactment of suitable rules, laws, and ordinances to this end. There should be created in the minds of inspectors a class consciousness and a realization that they are the guardians of the lives and properties of the public and that we must shoulder and carry that responsibility.

When a manufacturer sells his product to the jobber and gets paid for his merchandise, he may be indifferent as to where it goes or what happens to it. When a contractor completes his work and secures his certificate of approval, he has no further interest in the job assuming that his bill for the work and materials has been paid. But the inspector has to carry the responsibility for that equipment for an indefinite time. I was informed, just the other day in connection with a large building in which one of our reinspection men had criticized the electrical equipment, that we had no right to find any fault with the installation because the owner of the building held our certificate. On looking up the records I found that the certificate in question has

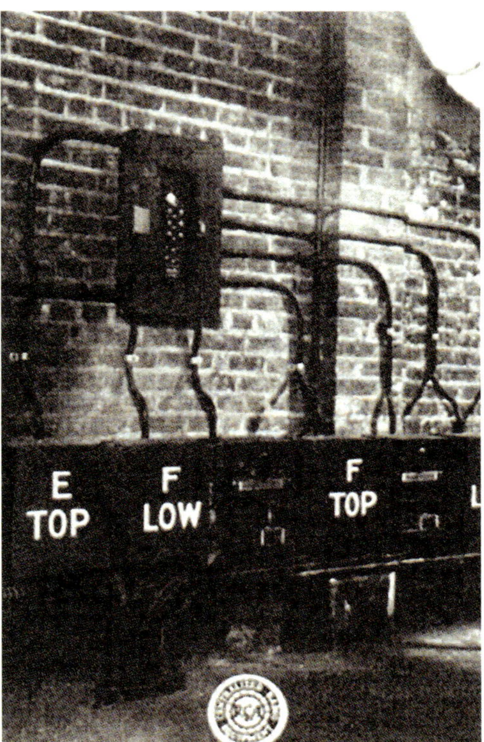

Central coupling units for antenna system in 1931. By the late 1920s, one central antenna was properly constructed at the most advantageous location and by means of a central coupler is connected to a number of transmission lines. These transmission lines ran down through the building and each apartment in a building is connected to one of these lines through an extension coupler. Tenants no longer find the radio connections cluttering up the courts and draped along the interior trim of the modern structure thanks to these new coupling units. The tangle of antenna wires no longer disfigured the roof of the modern dwelling or apartment house.

International Association of Electrical Inspectors

APPLICATION FOR MEMBERSHIP

Date, ... 1929.

To the I. A. E. I.

Gentlemen : I hereby make application for Active...., Associate...., Co-operating...., Membership in the International Association of Electrical Inspectors. I enclose $........, dues for 1929. I also subscribe for the I. A. E. I. News-Bulletin for the year 1929, fifty cents of the year's dues paid by me being for subscription to the News-Bulletin.

Name ....

Mail Address: St. and No. ....

City ....

Title ....

Associated with ....

Signed ....

Mail application and dues to Secretary of Section in which you reside.

1929 Original Application For Membership

been issued in 1901 or a little over 28 years ago. The obligation and responsibility of the inspector does not cease when he has issued his approval but has only begun. Under these conditions, do you believe that the inspector has a right to have a leading part in the formulation of the *Code*? I think so.

Second, "To promote the uniform understanding and application of the *National Electrical Code*." If there is one thing more greatly needed today than any other it is to not only have a standard, nationally accepted *Code*, but to interpret and apply that *Code* in a uniform manner. I have been told by a representative of a public utility that they are obliged to carry fifteen different types and styles of service equipment to meet the requirements of the different inspections departments. Such a statement does not need any explanation, as it is in itself a sufficient indictment of inspection methods and practices. I do not believe it to be possible to write any code in either such a broad or specific manner that interpretations of its means and methods of application in special cases would not be necessary. All men, and especially inspectors, do not think alike, do not reason alike, and hence their findings and rulings are often diametrically opposite to each other. We want individuality, we want expressions of opinion, but we also want a basis of understanding and common sense that will lead us to decisions which will be acceptable to all.

Have I overstated this situation, or given a wrong impression of the inspectors' attitude generally towards the *National Electrical Code*? If not, and I don't think I have, is there not a pressing need for some organization like the International, one of whose principal objects is to bring about a uniformity of interpretation of the *Code* and seek to secure a more general adoption of it by states and municipalities? The inspector who says that he does not care to join any association because he can't see how it is going to benefit him is, to say the least, very shortsighted. I have noticed that such a one is always willing to accept and use anything of value that may happen to come out of it. Don't be a parasite. Do we need a better understanding of the provisions of the *Code* among the rank and file of inspectors? From the reports of the manufacturers, the utilities, the jobbers and the contractors, I think we do. If you think so, join our ranks and help us push forward to this much desired result.

Third, "To secure and promote un-iform administrative ordinances and inspection methods." The results accomplished in promoting the adoption of uniform ordinances by cities throughout the country is due to the splendid and untiring efforts of Mr. Harry B. Kirkland as representing the Society for Electrical Development. Mr. Kirkland has done more to awaken the electrical industry to the great need for such action than any other person or organization of which I am aware. Let us place all of our influence back of Mr. Kirkland's efforts and assist him in every possible way. "How about uniform inspection methods?" What is meant by this statement? Simply this: We believe that where there are so many different ways of doing anything, there can be but one best way. How are your reports made up and how are they handled? To whom are they sent and why? If there is a better way than your way, wouldn't you like to know about it and, if possible, adopt it? The International is pledged by the publication of a statement in its constitution to investigate and recommend to its membership how reports can best be handled. Send to the secretary a complete outline of your daily routine and method, including application and certificate forms, and some day we may get to thinking pretty nearly alike on this problem also.

Fourth, "To collect and disseminate information relative to the safe use of electricity." We believe that every fire and accident of electrical origin should be investigated and the exact cause of the incident ascertained, and that these reports should be a part of the permanent records of every inspection department and copies filed with the secretary of the International Association for record and reference. No doubt, there are some who would feel that such action was unnecessary and unwarranted, that it would cause trouble and perhaps give too much publicity to such occurrences. If so, I must disagree with such conclusions. Electricity as employed today, if given even reasonable supervision and control, is the safest form of energy known; but for years it has been the scapegoat for fires and accidents of unknown or doubtful origin. There is not, in my opinion, any better way in which to remove these uncertainties from the public mind than by an honest, truthful and unbiased report as to the exact occurrence in each case. There is no better way to find out whether or not the rules under which we are working are adequate and complete. The facts developed by the investigation of fires from our office has done more to produce changes in the *Code* than all theories that have ever been advanced.

If you have an idea that a certain device or material or appliance is unsafe and you are inclined to prohibit its use, or if something comes along that you are not sure about, or that you would like to approve if you could find justification in the *Code*, would it not be a satisfaction to be able to learn from some reliable, unbiased source just how these things are being handled in other jurisdictions. If so, then you can or will be able shortly to obtain this information for the International. Would such a service be worth while? It would seem so.

March 1929 Membership Score Card

The president of the IAEI has requested the officers of each section to appoint a special membership committee for the section. There are throughout the territory of the association many inspectors and others eligible for membership who are only awaiting an opportunity to associate themselves with us, and in order to make our work more effective, an invitation should be extended to these individuals to join with us.

The International Association started off with 1,989 active and associate charter members on its books. The charter members by section are broken down in the following chart:

Section	No. of Charter Members
Eastern Section	1,041
Western Section	599
Southwestern Section	166
Northwestern Section	129
Southern Section	54

Reprinted from *News-Bulletin*, March 1929

On April 16-18, 1931, over sixty inspectors from all parts of the province of Quebec met at their regular annual meeting in the city of Montreal. Mr. J. N. Mochon, chief examiner for the province of Quebec, presided over the meeting devoted to a discussion of the Canadian Electrical Code.

This illustration was "unveiled" at the meeting, and it showed a caricature of familiar faces in probably what were quite unusual attitudes. The caption states, "With the Wire of Electricity." — Reprinted from *News-Bulletin*, July 1931.

Fifth, "To represent the electrical inspectors in all matters which are dealt with nationally and internationally by the electrical industry." Up until the present time the inspectors, as a group, have had no means of contact with the electrical industry. Groups of manufacturers, of public utilities, of electrical contractors get together and after making their decisions and agreements come to the individual inspectors and expect that their conclusions will be approved. It has often placed the inspector in a very embarrassing and sometimes a compromising position that is wholly unnecessary and avoidable. Let the other groups in the electrical industry call into conference with them representatives of the International Council and I can assure them that we will cooperate 100 percent, and if the past is any criterion such conferences will save many annoying and expensive mistakes. Would the knowledge that the plan or method, or device was acceptable in advance of its presentation to the public be of any value? It seems to me that is would be so.

Sixth, "To cooperate with other national and international organizations in furthering the development of the electrical industry." How can this be done? The electrical industry does not seem to need any assistance in its development. It is growing so rapidly now, and has been doing so for so many years, that the things which fitted last year are no longer adequate today; but there is more to bigness than growth. Any great structure that has not proper foundations is likely to crumble and fall. The inspector can and does perform a great service to the industry when he stands in the way of the installation and use of substandard materials and devices whether of domestic or foreign manufacture. This is a part, and a very necessary part, in the foundation for the support of the electrical industry.

A policeman in uniform properly performing his duties represents the Law in action. To him has been delegated certain authority and from him is expected certain performance in line with his prescribed duties. Any law will, at times, work hardships in particular cases because no law, if properly administered, can be sufficiently flexible to meet all conditions. Under the complex civilization in which we are living today, to attempt to live without law would result in chaos. Through the process of law, therefore, we have our liberty and while we may often chafe under it, yet it is our sole defense against destruction. An electrical inspector who is properly performing his duty represents the *Code* in action. To him has been delegated the policing of all electrical equipment. His power and authority is often regarded as autocratic and is frequently so employed. Let us assist the other groups in the electrical industry in providing for this power and control a safe, smooth and adequate channel in which to move.

Seventh, "To promote closer co-operation between inspectors, inspection departments, the electrical industry, and the public." How can you expect to have any real cooperation as indicated in this sentence without some channel of communication as provided by the International Association. The chief criticism of inspection departments today is that each one is a law unto itself. How can it be otherwise unless and until you provide a common ground on which inspectors and inspection departments can meet? This is one of the principal aims of the International and we will not have fulfilled our obligation to the industry and to the public until this has been accomplished.

1930 International President

William S. Boyd was one of the original two assistants who were hired by William Merrill to form the Underwriters Electrical Bureau, which became UL seven years later. Boyd, who later became the chief electrical inspector for the city of Chicago, was instrumental in the creation of the IAEI in 1928.

Boyd was the secretary of the Western Association of Electrical Inspectors at the time when C. W. Mitchell, secretary of the California Association of Electrical Inspectors, contacted him in 1925 about the possibility that the California association join the Western. Boyd replied that a committee was working on such a plan to organize the electrical inspectors of the U.S. and Canada into a national or international organization. Mr. Boyd was the Western Section secretary from 1929–1936, and the International president in 1930.

I hope that I have given you a little broader and a little clearer idea of the scope and purpose of the International Association. We mean every word of it, we are in earnest, and we believe that this organization is needed by the electrical industry, by the insurance interests, by the public and last but not least, by the inspectors themselves. If you are in sympathy with this movement then get back of it with all your energy and help us to put it over. If there are any two men in the International Association who deserve the sincere thanks of all the officers and members, those two are Mr. Jim Mahan and Mr. Vic Tousley. Give these men your assistance in anything and everything they may call on you to do.

None of the men who are active in the affairs of this organization, and who are giving of their time and energy for its up-building and for the promotion of its ideas, are receiving any personal benefit or compensation for their efforts. It is wholly an altruistic service, carried on for the improvement of the electrical industry in general and for the help and benefit of the electrical inspectors in particular.

We have been talking a great deal about co-operation. Perhaps it might not be out of place if we were to try to obtain a more definite idea of just what we mean by it from the standpoint of electrical inspections. Its dictionary definition is "To operate together or jointly for a common purpose or to a common end or result." And then this very significant sentence is added: "Men cannot co-operate successfully for any purpose if the sole bond between them is self interest." It is a rather difficult job for a man to co-operate with himself. There must be at least two persons with a common purpose before any real co-operation can exist. The greater the number of people having a common purpose, the greater need there is for some form of co-operation and if the end in view is the same, the easier it should be to secure a common basis for operation Have the electrical inspectors of this country and Canada a common end or purpose in view in all of their work? The answer cannot be controverted. That answer is "yes." What is this common purpose? It is, or should be, to secure the installation and use of electricity in the homes, the factories, the offices, or the public highways, or wherever it is employed or is present, in not only a manner that is reasonably safe to life and property but which will remain safe under proper care and supervision for years to come.

Why am I saying all this to you? I'll tell you why. It is because I have made the inspection of electrical equipment my life's work. Because my mind has been so continuously employed in the study of this problem that I can think of little else. Because I want to see, as my time of activity shortens, a real court of arbitration established that will provide for the proper and equitable settlement of all disputes arising among inspectors and in their work, and because I want that feeling of satisfaction which comes from having helped in the organization, in the development and in the operation of an organization which will be a benefit to all those who have made, or who are now making, or who may hereafter make, the business of electrical inspections their chief concern.

Reprinted from *IAEI News*, November 1929.

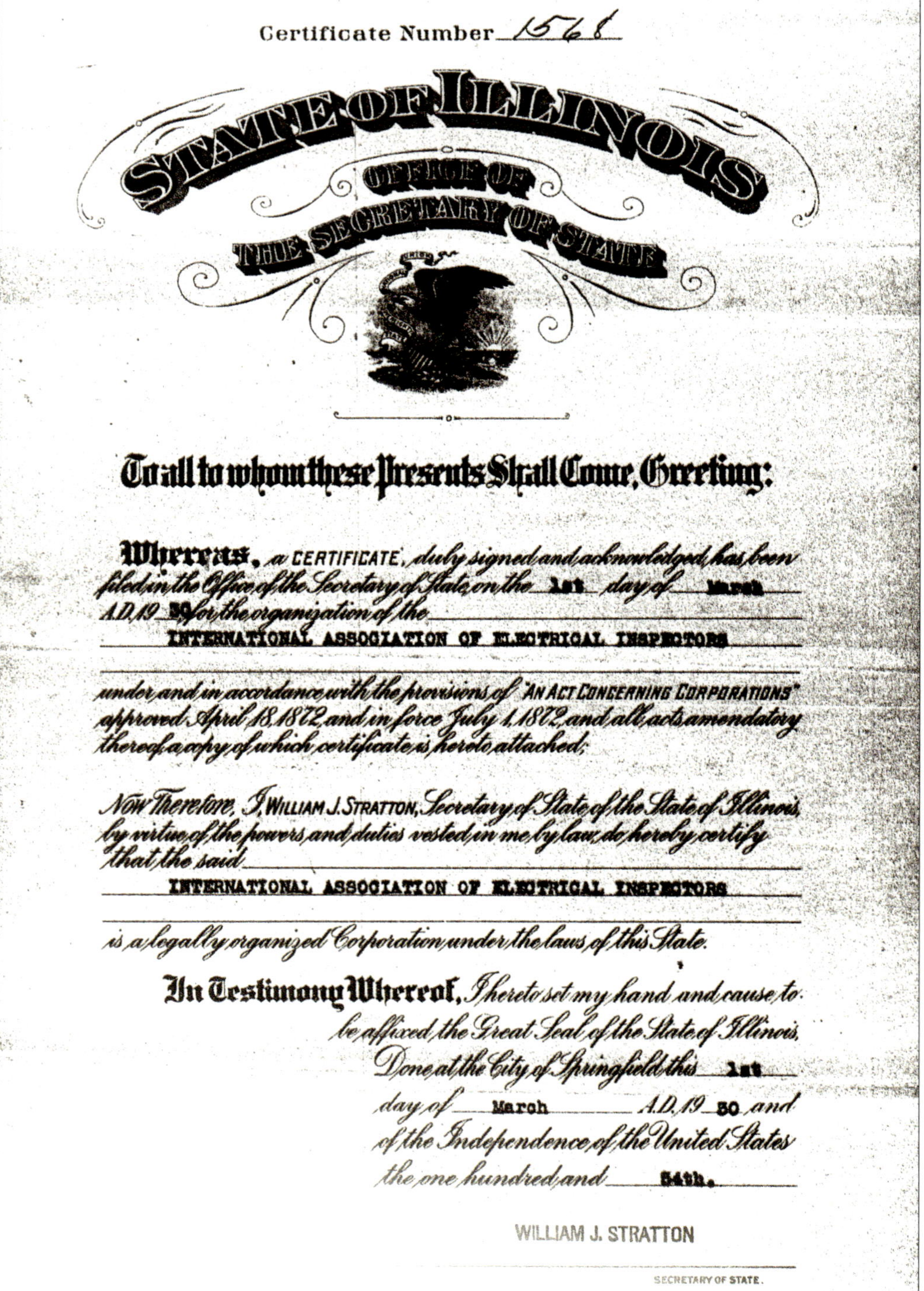
Certificate Number 1568

State of Illinois

Office of

The Secretary of State

To all to whom these Presents Shall Come, Greeting:

Whereas, a CERTIFICATE, duly signed and acknowledged, has been filed in the Office of the Secretary of State, on the 1st day of March A.D. 19 30 for the organization of the INTERNATIONAL ASSOCIATION OF ELECTRICAL INSPECTORS under and in accordance with the provisions of "AN ACT CONCERNING CORPORATIONS" approved April 18, 1872, and in force July 1, 1872, and all acts amendatory thereof, a copy of which certificate is hereto attached;

Now Therefore, I, WILLIAM J. STRATTON, Secretary of State of the State of Illinois, by virtue of the powers and duties vested in me by law, do hereby certify that the said INTERNATIONAL ASSOCIATION OF ELECTRICAL INSPECTORS is a legally organized Corporation under the laws of this State.

In Testimony Whereof, I hereto set my hand and cause to be affixed the Great Seal of the State of Illinois, Done at the City of Springfield this 1st day of March A.D. 19 30 and of the Independence of the United States the one hundred and 54th.

WILLIAM J. STRATTON

SECRETARY OF STATE.

In accordance with the action taken at the 1929 executive council meeting, the International Association of Electrical Inspectors was incorporated in 1930, under the laws of the state of Illinois as a corporation, not for profit. The current designation for this type of corporation is 501(c)(6).

The Inspectors 1929-1963

Growing into IAEI Leaders

Formative 35 Years

Southwestern Section members at the 1931 section meeting

1931 International President

R. H. Manahan, International president for 1931, was a chief electrical inspector, city of Los Angeles, and inspector at Laguna Beach.

Southwestern Section Timeline

1929 The first annual meeting (seventh of the California Association of Electrical Inspectors) of the Southwestern Section was held in San Francisco, September 18-21, 1929.

The first chapter of the Southwestern Section started from a Los Angeles meeting on April 18, 1929, of city inspectors of Southern California. On January 9, 1930, the first official meeting of the Southern California Chapter was held.

C.W. Mitchell is elected the Southwestern Section's first secretary.

1938 Imperial Valley Chapter organization meeting was held in the city hall in El Centro on December 15, 1938; formal organization meeting to be held January 10, 1939.

The inspectors from the cities around San Francisco Bay and Sacramento who had met to start the state association continued to meet and became the **Northern California Chapter**.

Central California Chapter charter granted on April 18, 1938.

Greater Central Valley Chapter granted charter.

1939 H. L. Gerber, of San Francisco, California, is elected Southwestern Section secretary.

1948 New Mexico Chapter granted charter.

H.G. Ufer, of Los Angeles, California, is elected Southwestern Section secretary.

1949 Arizona Chapter formed. The chapter was later divided into two chapters—the Central Arizona Chapter and the Southern Arizona Chapter—in 1986.

Hawaii Chapter formed.

1951 Nevada Chapter formed.

Sacramento Valley Chapter formed in California.

1953 L. E. LaFehr, from Alhambra, California, is elected Southwestern Section secretary.

RECD APR 1

SOUTHWESTERN SECTION
INTERNATIONAL ASSOCIATION OF ELECTRICAL INSPECTORS

JOIN THE I.A.E.I. DO IT NOW

IT IS SPRING!

And Harry Beecher says this is a Bum picture. But don't let the Spring Fever (or what have you) cause you to let your interest in the Association lag. Right now is the time to get that new member you promised to bring in. And, also, right now please note the following items:

1.- Our own Active Member, R. H. Manahan (our "Mannie") is President of the I.A.E.I. A Salute to President Manahan!
2.- I.A.E.I. Secretary Tousley advises that a new edition of our Year Book is going to press in a few days. To make sure that you are listed correctly in this pamphlet please write plainly (or print) on the enclosed post card the following:
(a) - Your Name.
(b) - Your Address.
(c) - Your Title.
(d) - Name of Firm, Individual or City Department with which you are associated.

Please do this promptly and mail the card at once; otherwise you may be left out.

C. W. MITCHELL
Secretary-Treasurer.

San Francisco, California,
March 27, 1931.

1931 membership recruitment ad for the Southwestern Section. C. W. Mitchell, the author of the ad, was the original founder of the California Association of Electrical Inspectors.

1956 Hawaii Chapter, Maui Division, was granted its charter by the executive board.

1962 Shasta Division of the Northern California Chapter is formed.

L. O. Trim, of Burbank, California, is elected Southwestern Section secretary.

Charles R. Pierce, of Fresno, California, is soon thereafter elected Southwestern Section secretary.

1951 Southwestern Section meeting.

EDITOR TOUSLEY COMPARES UNEMPLOYMENT TO AN OVERLOADED ELECTRICAL SYSTEM

The present condition of unemployment is such as to make all of us devote some thought to the possible solution to the problem and being electrical in our activities we are likely to be electrical minded in our solution.

The present condition might well be compared to a situation with which the writer was brought into contact a number of years ago. The lighting company in a large city supplied direct current to its underground network. These feeder circuits all originated in a large distribution switchboard built in the form of a horseshoe with each feeder fed through a large, lead strip fuse on the face of the board.

An unusually heavy load came on the system and one of these feeder fuses blew. This in turn threw a heavier load on those fuses remaining in service. Another feeder fuse soon went out and with the increased load on the fuses still in service, together with the heat and fumes of the blowing fuses, it was only a matter of seconds before the last fuse had blown and the whole system was out of commission.

Here then, was a problem of restoring service. To connect one generator to this network was to place it on a practical dead short circuit. The breaker of the generator would have operated or the generator would have burned up. Just how service was restored in this case the writer does not know, but undoubtedly, it became necessary to *segregate the load and connect generators across the isolated groups* until such time as regular service could be resumed.

It is not so far-fetched to liken this instance to the present economic situation. The load on the system increased to a point where it broke down and now we are in the position of the electrical system described above—where our generators are all ready to operate but we must devise some plan whereby we can successfully connect them to our waiting load.

Recently an advertisement contained this significant statement: "Do not think of unemployment in terms of millions of people out of work in this broad land of America. Think of unemployment as a few people out of work within a stone's throw of you—your neighbors." The advertisement, which then went on to list 100 items of possible employment, contained these two: "renovate electric light systems," and "install new electrical outlets."

Here apparently is a parallel with the electrical problem described. In order to restore service, it is necessary to segregate the load into many small groups until the whole system assumes a normal operating condition.

It is a duty of the electrical inspector to see that safe electrical installations are maintained. He can help the unemployment situation as well by making reinspections now.

The inspector may hesitate to place another burden upon the public in a time of unemployment, but by placing what at first glance may seem to be a burden, he is doing his part in bringing back a condition of employment which must in the final analysis result in the most good.

Make reinspections now and double the value of your work by getting safer installations through more outlets, and assisting to bring back the period of full employment.

Editorial by V. H. Tousley, Reprinted from *IAEI News Bulletin*, March 1931.

"IT WORKED, STEVE! THE WIRE'S THROUGH!"

1932 International President

Fred D. Weber, electrical engineer for the Oregon Insurance Rating Bureau of Portland, and secretary-treasurer of the Northwestern Section from 1929–1944, was one of the original founders of IAEI. In April 1917, he became a member of the electrical council of Underwriters' Laboratories, Incorporated. He was also a member of the board of electrical examiners for the city of Portland, and during all that time he was also the secretary of that board.

In 1926, he helped organize the Northwest Association of Electrical Inspectors, now the Northwestern Section of IAEI, and became the secretary/treasurer of the section. In July 1927, he was appointed a member of the electrical committee of the National Fire Protection Association, representing the Northwestern Section, IAEI.

PROBLEMS BEFORE THE IAEI WARRANT CAREFUL ATTENTION

There are a number of problems before the International Association which warrant the careful attention of the sections, the chapters, and the individual members for their proper solution. Some of these problems have had extended consideration by the association, but the efforts have not been sufficiently crystallized to justify recommendation by the executive council.

In those localities where chapters are functioning, these problems can and should be made the subject of special chapter study, consideration, and recommendation.

The sections should refer the subjects to appropriate section committees for their study and for the purpose of ascertaining and correlating the chapters' efforts.

The problems presented here do not, by any means, represent a complete list of the subjects before the association, but the solution of those mentioned will go a long way towards stamping the IAEI as an association of accomplishment.

The problems have been set down under three heads: General, or those having particularly to do with the association as a whole; Inspector-members, or those having to do with the individual; and *National Electrical Code* problems.

IAEI GENERAL

The association itself represents a problem of prime importance. The officers, members, and supporters of the association have ample reason to feel highly gratified with the results to date. The association has had a rapid growth in members. While the first years have been more or less formulative, there have been many notable constructive achievements. But the task is far from being completed. We need every inspector in our membership. We need to further develop the machinery of our organization and to make more efficient use of the means now at our command.

The International Association is unlike any other similar organization. It does not have a fully manned headquarters' staff. It does not have a corps of paid officials to carry on its work. The association must advance; it must build itself up; it must become more useful and valuable to its members; it must become more respected by the public and by the industry. The association has been built up by the individual members; the individual members can be relied upon to carry on this development.

Trial Installations

The problem of trial installations has been before the industry for some time but is not yet solved. The electrical inspector is particularly concerned in this subject and it has been squarely placed before the IAEI for solution. It is a big problem and its effects are far-reaching. Maybe trial installations are needed — maybe not. It is for the IAEI to express its opinion and, if this opinion is favorable, to make such detailed suggestions as will permit the problem to be worked out in a safe and satisfactory manner to all concerned.

Investigation of Fires and Accidents

No more important problem is before the IAEI. A committee has been at work on this subject since the organization of the association. The report of this committee was enthusiastically received and given hearty support at all the recent section meetings. In carrying on the work of prevention of electrical fires and accidents, it is essential to know the exact details of how these fires and accidents occur. A following out of the procedure recommended by this committee will provide the association members with authentic information covering the whole country.

The association will send to each member a copy of the manual and report form which has been adopted. Chapters should devote at least a part of their meetings to a study and discussion of these forms.

Flexible Cords

There is now effective a new method of labeling flexible cords, the details of which have been transmitted to all the members. This new method of marking consists of a band placed around the cord at five foot intervals showing it is Underwriters' Laboratories inspected. The figures on the amount of unapproved cord in use are astounding and undoubtedly much of this sub-standard cord has been the cause of fires and accidents. The success of the campaign to obtain standard cords will depend to a great extent on the

Western New England Chapter sponsored a banner inviting people to a chapter meeting held at the city hall in Torrington, Connecticut, on April 27, 1932. The air was filled with the beginning of snow, and there was a small attendance of thirty-seven present. The chapter had considerable discussion on refrigerator fires, and J.P. Rohan reported that an accident occurred in his city, which was due to a defective portable cord used in a garage. President W. J. Mahan of the Eastern Section gave a talk on Articles 8 and 10 of the *NEC*, and S. H. McClure of Colt's Patent Fire Arms Company gave an interesting talk on, "The New Meter Sequence." Mr. Haden of the Spring & Buckley Company held a drawing on an automatic electric toaster, a rarity in those times.

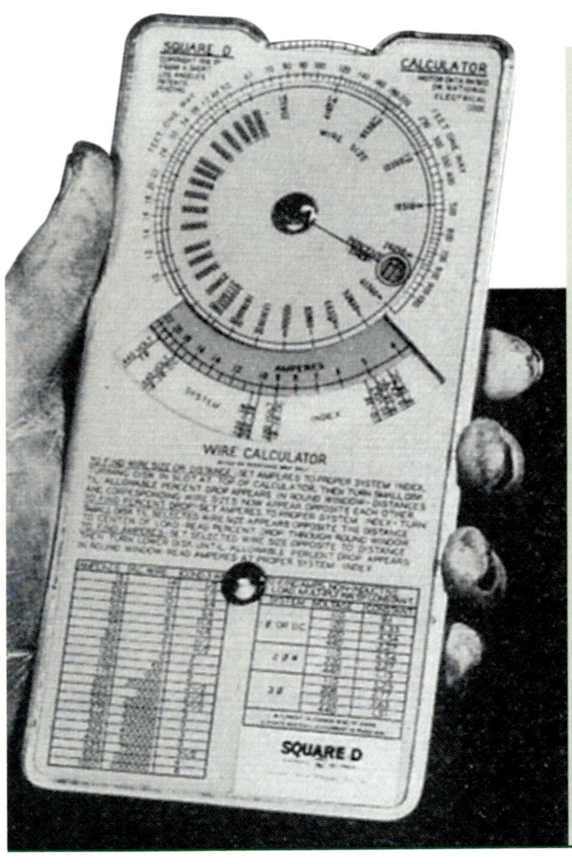

Frank A. Short, who was electrical engineer of the Industrial Accident Commission of California in 1932 and president of the Southwestern Section, introduced a new wiring and motor data calculator of unusual design and of particular interest to inspectors, electrical engineers, contractors, salesman, estimators, wiremen, etc. The compact device allowed the electrical man to attain all wiring and motor data, eliminating hours of figuring and providing him with accurate data at the turn of one of the three dials. There are two calculators really, one for computing wiring data and the other for computing motor data. The calculator could be purchased from the Square D Company of Detroit Michigan.

1933 officers of the Western New England Chapter elected at the annual meeting on December 7, 1932. From *left to right*: Leonard J. Wylie, third vice chairman; William E. Armstrong, secretary/treasurer; Henry E. Bolles, first vice chairman; Sherlon T. Baldwin, chairman; and Martin C. O'Rourke, second vice chairman. Mr. E. C. Alcott of the Anaconda Wire and Cable Company (Boston, MA) gave an interesting talk regarding the mining of copper and the manufacture of copper wire at this meeting. This was followed by a motion picture entitled, "From Mine to Consumer," which was given through the courtesy of the American Brass Company of Waterbury, Connecticut.

efforts of the members of the IAEI, and these members can as effectively eliminate the undesirable cord as they did the "old code" rubber-covered wire. This subject should be bulletined to section and chapter members.

Special Rules

There are in effect in many localities special rules which vary from those of the *National Electrical Code.* The IAEI executive council has recommended such a study of these special requirements as will make them uniform, to the end that they may be recommended for adoption in the *National Electrical Code.* Both sections and chapters should appoint committees to carry on this work. Reports of these committees should be made at both section and chapter meetings.

Inspection Forms

There is a constant demand for a set of standard inspection forms which can be used by inspection departments. While this demand comes from those localities which are creating new inspection departments, the compilation and study of such a set of forms will be of assistance to the older departments in presenting new ideas which may serve to make their own forms more effective or more efficient.

A committee is now working on this problem and its report should be presented to the association this year.

Adequacy

The matter of adequate electrical installations is of utmost importance to the industry as a whole. It is of particular importance to the inspector for adequacy is closely allied to safety. The industry has committees working on this problem and the International Association is represented on these committees.

Undoubtedly the results of this committee's work will be transmitted to the association, but both sections and chapters should continue their study of the problem so that the association's representatives will be intelligently informed as to the association's views in this matter.

Branch Circuits

The inspector is dealing continually with branch circuits and no one is better informed as to the difficulties of this problem nor as to the needs, than the electrical inspector. This is a problem which should receive the most careful and complete consideration by suitable committees of both the sections and the chapters, and these committees should be prepared to submit definite suggestions to the association's meetings.

Publicity

It has been called to the attention of the inspectors time and again that one of the things he lacked, both individually and collectively, was "publicity." He fails to "advertise" his activities, so that even those on whom he depends for support are unaware of his accomplishments.

The matter of publicity was deemed of sufficient importance by the executive council to appoint a special IAEI committee for this purpose. The field of this committee is broad. It involves not only the usual publicity of the association's affairs through the channels of the technical press, but includes the preparation of articles bearing on inspection matters that can be used by the member in his local papers. It also includes the preparation and transmittal to members of articles on standard subjects such as the newspaper releases sent out by the Western Section on the Christmas holiday hazards.

Each section or chapter should have its own publicity committee to work with the main IAEI committee as well as to carry on activities of its own.

Inspection Outside Municipalities

In many localities there is no inspection supervision of electrical work outside the corporate limits of municipalities. This includes the rural territories and, what is of importance to municipalities, that territory directly outside the municipal limits which will probably later on be annexed to the city. It is a matter of common knowledge that much cheap and defective work is installed in these territories. In self-defense, the utilities frequently make inspections of these installations, but the utility as a rule would welcome some official supervision.

Many efforts have been made to solve this difficulty, and a number of states have passed laws on the subject. It remains, however, for the IAEI to give careful study to this matter and, as the solution may involve state laws, this can well be handled by the chapters.

INSPECTOR-MEMBERS

Civil Service

The IAEI has pledged itself to use its best efforts to obtain civil service protection for all its municipal inspector members. Electrical inspection is a specialized and highly technical subject. It deals with the protection of life and property. It is not—or should not be—political. No position involving the safeguarding of human life and the prevention of the destruction or property should be political, nor subject to political influence. The inspector frequently gives the best years of his life to his chosen profession, and many times turns down offers of more lucrative positions. He should have all the protection civil service can afford him.

As the matter of civil service is under the jurisdiction of a municipality or a state, the subject is one in which the chapters can be effective.

Inspector's Salary

This problem is one that is close to the inspector's heart. It is not, of course, possible for the IAEI to carry on any activity that has for its direct purpose the raising of an inspector's salary. Indirectly though, the IAEI can be of real service in this problem. As a matter of business knowledge advancement in any position is brought about by the raising of the standard of the individual, and the IAEI can be made to supply the means by which the individual standard of the inspection in his profession can be raised. Then, too, the efforts of the publicity committee should be beneficial in the matter of salary.

BE YOUR OWN ELECTRICIAN!

Learn Something about Home Wiring in One Great Big Lesson!
"They laughed when I said I could do my own wiring. And they laughed harder when I showed them my work. But one big lesson taught me a lot of things I didn't know. P.S.—We had a fire one night and the wife and I barely escaped."

NATIONAL ELECTRICAL CODE

Grounding Outlet Boxes

There was presented the IAEI executive council a proposition to recommend such a revision of the *National Electrical Code* as would require the grounding of the outlet boxes when used on knob and tube work or on non-metallic sheathed cable installations, when the outlet box was in contact with wire lath or metal ceilings. There developed a considerable difference of opinion on the subject involved and the matter was referred back to the IAEI for further study. A considerable discussion took place at the recent section meetings and the association is probably now ready to make definite recommendations. section committees should investigate this problem and be ready to report at the 1932 meetings.

Crowding of Outlet Boxes

This is another problem which was referred back to the association for further study. It has been in the hands of suitable committees and tentative specifications have been submitted in some committee reports. Those committees should be ready to report at the 1932 meetings, but their tentative reports should first have chapter consideration.

Demand Factors on Air Heater

A specific proposal for demand factors on air heaters was before the IAEI executive council last year, but was ultimately withdrawn before final action was taken. This problem involves the demand factor on heaters used for heating the premises as distinguished from water heaters or ranges. The two problems are essentially different. The proper solution of a problem of this kind involves investigation and tests of actual installations. Inspectors having information bearing on this subject, or in a position to get such information, should transmit it to the proper section committees. It is also a proper subject for chapter study.

Demand Factors on Ranges

The present *Code* requires a 100 percent demand factor on range installations of one or two ranges. Recent tests have indicated that a demand factor allowance might safely be made on installations with one or two ranges. It is understood that extensive tests are now being made to obtain accurate data on this subject. The subject is one that could well be considered by section and chapter committees.

Carrying Capacity of Service Switches

The study of this subject was not sufficiently completed at the last section meetings to warrant definite recommendations. The problem involved here is the absence of *National Electrical Code* recognition on a limiting capacity of knife switches used as service switches.

Code reference to this matter is contained in the recommendation appearing in 1201-a, fine print note: "….that switches above 1000 amperes capacity be not used to break currents…." A specific *Code* rule on this subject will eliminate the necessity for local requirements. Section committees should be ready to make recommendations on this subject. It should also be studied by the chapters.

No. 12 Wire Minimum

A problem before the IAEI is, shall No. 12 wire be made the minimum allowed by the *Code* for general wiring purposes? Action on this subject was taken at several of the recent section meetings and the subject will undoubtedly come before the 1932 meetings for definite action. The problem is of importance from many standpoints, and the chapters should allot time to its consideration.

Multiple Services

The matter of multiple services to a building came up at all sections and it is evident from the discussions that the present *Code* provisions do not cover all conditions the inspector meets. Definite suggestions to clarify and make the provision more complete should be made by the IAEI. This matter should be considered by both sections and chapters.

Outside Wiring

The subject of outside wiring came before the executive council and was referred back to the association for further study. The problem here seems to be that Article 3 does not completely cover all conditions of outside wiring with which the inspector has to deal. Constructive suggestions for amplification for this *Code* article should be made by both sections and chapters.

Reprinted from *News-Bulletin*, March 1932.

Civil Service for the Inspector

The recent numerous political upsets throughout the country again call attention to the need for civil service for the electrical inspector. In one state alone word has come to the association headquarters of some nine or ten large cities where the electrical inspector has either been replaced or is expecting replacement.

For just how long will the citizens of this country allow those on whom their safety depends to be used for political capital?

Without doubt there will be some instances where the new incumbents will be better trained than those who are replaced, but these are apt to be the exception; for political appointees are not generally selected on the basis of their ability but for distinctly other reasons. Selection on ability is a product of civil service, not of political appointment.

An electrical inspector who receives his appointment as a political favor is not in the best position to impartially and strictly enforce those regulations designed to bring about safety. A proper enforcement of any safety regulation involves a freedom from political interference and a security in office.

No one would think, in a case of sickness, of consulting a doctor who had worked at his particular profession for a period of only one or two years. The knowledge which can only be gained from long and extended experience is valuable either in health or in safety.

And no one in charge of the business of a great corporation would think that just because the president or the chairman of the board of directors had been replaced that the trained heads of the various departments should all be discharged. The stockholders would not long stand for such a condition. Then why should the stockholders of a municipal corporation still countenance this relic of the spoils system?

The duties of the position of electrical inspector are exacting. They require study and years of careful preparation. They cannot be assumed by the ordinary individual, and even where the individual is otherwise well qualified several years will be consumed in properly fitting into the new position.

The IAEI has taken a definite stand on civil service for electrical inspectors. Some work has been done and something accomplished, but greater effort must be made to give this work more effect.

Reprinted from *News Bulletin*, January 1935

1933 International President

N. E. Cannady, electrical engineer and inspector for the state of North Carolina from 1914 to 1954, was one of the original founders of the IAEI, and served as its president in 1933. He also assisted in organizing the Southern Section, IAEI, in 1929 and was elected to the office of president that same year. In 1930, he organized the North Carolina Chapter.

Among his other activities and achievements are the following: chairman, State Board of Examiners of Electrical Contractors starting in 1937; member, electrical committee of NFPA beginning in 1937; member of the electrical council for Underwriters' Laboratories, Inc., since 1930; member of the AIEE from 1930-1947 and fellow, AIEE since 1947; and from 1941-1944, coordinator of electrical affairs, state of North Carolina, during emergencies.

MIDDLE DEPARTMENT RATING ASSOCIATION

MIDDLE DIVISION

414 WALNUT STREET, PHILADELPHIA

CARLYLE H. HILL, MANAGER

March 24, 1933.

TO ELECTRICAL INSPECTORS:

The present banking situation since the National Bank Holiday, has brought about conditions in connection with checks covering electrical inspection fees which has reached considerable amounts. To date we have checks amounting to $1300.00 returned which have been drawn on banks, some of which have not been given permission to reopen and others on which withdrawals have been restricted to a certain per cent of the deposits. Quite a number of our Inspectors' accounts are also under restrictions and these checks covering cash fees collected in the field cannot be deposited.

In accepting checks from contractors covering fees, we will expect that you use some discretion by making inquiries as to whether the amount will be paid by the bank on which it is drawn, and this under the present conditions should cause no offense since the check if not accepted by the bank has no more value at the time of deposit than a dishonored check. On banks in your district which you have knowledge, either personal or through the press, have not reopened, you will return any checks received to the contractor with request that cash fee or check drawn on an open bank without restrictions be furnished. This cooperation through the Inspector in the field will eliminate to some extent these worthless checks being accepted and also save the Inspector from making collections on a further number of checks returned through him to the contractor.

The collection of cash fees being retained by the Inspector and forwarded by check on a bank in which the deposit has been restricted will have to be discontinued. These fees to be forwarded with applications, either by money order or cash sent registered mail. If your bank is closed or your account restricted, please inform us at once and to what extent your funds are involved.

Very truly yours,

Carlyle H. Hill

Manager.

THE INSPECTORS 1929-1963

GROWING INTO IAEI LEADERS

FORMATIVE 35 YEARS

1949 Western Section, 45th Annual Meeting

1934 International President

William J. Mahan was a charter member of the Eastern Section, past president of the Eastern Section, and 1934 International president. Mr. Mahan was a former member of the electrical committee of UL and was considered as an efficient public official who had contributed a great deal to the electrical industry. He was a member of the building department of New Haven for twenty-seven years.

1935 International President

A.G. Hall, 1935 president of the IAEI, was from Toronto, Ontario; the first Canadian president.

1936 International President

Ralph W. Wiley, San Francisco, CA, Southwestern Section.

1937 International President

L.G. Going, Portland, OR, Northwest section.

Western Section Timeline

1929 **Michigan Association of Electrical Inspectors** holds meeting at the Detroit Edison Boat Club on June 20, 1929.

William S. Boyd, from Chicago, Illinois, is elected as the Western Section secretary.

James S. Mahan addresses a meeting of the Short Course for Firemen at the University of Illinois at Champaign on June 20, 1929. Mr. John Gamber, chairman of the Illinois Chapter has charge of the details of this school. The **Illinois Chapter** was formed earlier in the year.

Kentucky Chapter was started on its way at a meeting held in the rooms of the Louisville Chamber of Commerce on the evening of August 12, 1929.

Western Section holds its 25th Silver Jubilee on August 26-28, 1929.

The Electrical League of Cleveland, Ohio, organizes the Inspectors Association of Greater Cleveland. It is hoped the group of inspectors will ultimately become a part of the **Ohio Chapter**.

1931 **Rocky Mountain Chapter** holds its organizational meeting on April 23, 1931.

1932 **Missouri-Kansas Chapter** comes into play.

1933 **Indiana Chapter** is formed.

1936 **C. P. Holmes** is elected as Western Section secretary.

1938 The Ohio Association of Electrical Inspectors becomes the **Ohio Chapter**.

Charter for the **Iowa Chapter** is granted at a meeting on July 25, 1938.

St. Louis Chapter is granted a charter by the International office.

1940 **F. H. Moore**, of Indianapolis, Indiana, is elected Western Section secretary.

1945 Western Section forms the **West Virginia Chapter.**

1945 Although it was later moved to the Northwestern Section, the **Idaho Chapter** is formed as part of the Western Section.

Western Section Timeline

1948 Executive board approves the formation of the **South Dakota Chapter**.

1950 **Michigan Chapter** charter was presented on July 7, 1950.

Western Section's first division, the **Suburban Division** of the Illinois Chapter, is created on September 27, 1950.

Tri-county Division of the Idaho Chapter is mentioned as being created in 1950, in the 1951 executive board minutes.

1951 **Minnesota Chapter** lists its first chapter meeting in the *IAEI News* "Dates Ahead" section.

1953 Although it was later moved to the Southern Section, **Oklahoma Chapter** is formed in 1953, as part of the Western Section.

Nebraska Chapter is first mentioned in the November 1953 issue of *IAEI News*.

H. L. Parks, of Charleston, West Virginia, is elected Western Section secretary.

1956 Ohio Chapter creates its first division, the **Akron Division**.

1953 **David M. Lines,** of Topeka, Kansas, is elected Western Section secretary.

1953 **North Dakota Chapter** is formed in late 1961.

Western New England Chapter members on a visit to Anaconda Wire and Cable Company plant at Hastings on Hudson in 1938. Such visits to manufacturers were common for chapters in the early days of IAEI, and oftentimes the meetings were held at the plants themselves.

Florida Chapter meeting held in Fort Lauderdale in 1939.

1938 International President

H. N. Pye, from Atlanta, Georgia, was the 1938 International president.

1939 International President

Dr. M.G. Lloyd was awarded the Hector Tyndale Fellowship in Physics for three years, two of which were spent at Harvard and Berlin, after graduating from the University of Pennsylvania. This supplemented a course in electrical engineering with graduate studies in physics, chemistry, and mathematics. He was a member of the George Washington Chapter and of the Southern and Eastern Sections.

Dr. Lloyd gave a great deal of attention to traffic signs and signals and was a member of working committees of the National Conference on Street and Highway Safety. He represented the country upon an international committee, which had been organized by the International Commission on Illumination, dealing with this subject.

Dr. Lloyd was a member of 21 different committees, which developed standards under the procedure of the American Standards Association, as well as various sources. Prominent among these were the electrical committee of the NFPA, where he was a member for over twenty years.

Electrical fire-shock exhibit in Elgin, Illinois. The exhibit was created by Alvin R. Copeley, city electrician, during Fire Prevention Week.

1940-1949

The War Years

The struggle against Germany and Japan thoroughly permeated domestic life in the 1940s, dominating all other activities and inducting America into a grown-up world full of conflict and aggression.

BUY WAR BONDS

After the failure of U.S. intelligence at Pearl Harbor and the mass sinking of Allied ships by German U-boats, the feeling in the early part of the war was that Americans were close to being defeated, and Americans began to face the awful truth and began to resolutely put themselves into gear. The word *victory* took hold and instantly became the propaganda note of the war, and soon backyards were dug up and transformed into Victory Gardens, government bonds became Victory bonds, and the spread two-finger gesture enrolled the body itself in the Victory campaign. In order to win the war, the 1940s became a period of regulation and repression, and from 1942 to 1946, there was something like a socialist America. World War II reversed decades of official American isolationism, and the U.S. began playing a leading, stabilizing and permanent role in world affairs. This new outlook was hard won, however. We had shocked the world with the use of the atomic bomb, and soon it would become evident that trusting the Soviet Union was unwise, as they would soon become our enemy, and not our ally. The House Committee on Un-American Activities began investigating citizens from all walks of life, and began a new era of social repression. History began to be rewritten after the war, and the Age of Innocence was officially over.

NEWS-BULLETIN

OF THE

INTERNATIONAL ASSOCIATION OF ELECTRICAL INSPECTORS

National Defense

Since the last issue of the *News-Bulletin* the situation on National Defense has been materially altered by the declaration of war. The part which the electrical inspector must play from now on becomes a more important one in many respects. The attitude which the electrical inspector will be called upon to assume is a changing one, and one that must be determined by the seriousness of the present emergency.

While the executive council of the International Association of Electrical Inspectors has given careful study of the problem of the inspector's policy in connection with defense problems, as cited by the following resolution adopted by the council and published in the November *News-Bulletin*:

"That where some particular minimum standard be waived or reduced, the authority having jurisdiction make every effort to relax the mandatory compliance only to the least practicable extent; only as a permissive alternate; only during the duration of the present emergency; only when safety is assured; and that they discourage the acceptance of substitutes if standard materials are available."

There has been a vast change in the situation since the adoption of this resolution, and while the policy suggested is still applicable to a certain degree, the exigencies of the situation have materially altered.

As one of our section presidents so aptly said in his presidential address, the first and major objective of the electrical inspector is not only to assist the defense program, but to do nothing to interfere with it, except where the proposed action is fully justified by added safety from fire, added safety to life, or added assurance of the continuance of the production essential to the defense program.

It has already become necessary for the inspector to accept substitutes for much of the material entering into the electrical installation, and in some territories the inspectors' activities have been reduced because of the lack of material available for building construction or new electrical installations.

Scarcity of electrical material will undoubtedly become more pronounced as time goes on, and the inspector will be called upon to make many decisions in regard to substitute materials and methods. He should give careful consideration to each case; he should be guided by the suggestion of the executive council, but he should keep first in mind the situation of this country and his duty and interest as a citizen thereof.

The IAEI desires to be of the greatest help in this new situation, and the member should feel free to submit his problems to the association. If advisable, the problems will be submitted to the IAEI executive council for suggestion or recommendation in any particular case.

There follows a memorandum of some items affected by priorities or allocations in which the inspector will be interested.

Allocation

The priority system described in the last issue of the *News-Bulletin* is gradually giving way to what is known as "allocation." As described by one of the executive officers of the priorities division, fundamentally, priorities is a method of rating the comparative importance of orders, so that those orders which are most essential to the nation can be filled ahead of those which are less essential. Basically simple, this network of priorities ratings inevitably becomes highly complex when the number of competing demands becomes too great. Sooner or later, priorities ratings undergo a process not unlike the depreciation of currency which takes place in a time of inflation. To insure the filling of an order in reasonable time, it becomes necessary to make the rating higher and higher. You eventually get to a point where the priorities rating system in itself simply is not adequate to control the situation.

The allocations program rests on a foundation of knowledge about what our national requirements are going to be. As an illustration, investigation shows that we shall need 35 million tons of steel for military purposes during 1942. By subtracting this military demand from the amount available, it will be simple to discover how much steel there will be to meet all the requirements of the civilian economy. It will remain then to determine how much steel the different steel-using industries will require, and to adjust their production schedules so that the total of their requirements will not exceed the total supply. Material is apportioned or allocated, industry by industry, and in some cases factory by factory.

Copper

Copper has many uses that affect the work of the electrical inspector. First, of course, is the use of copper for conductors. Copper, or some alloy in which copper enters, however, is also used in building construction, and building construction with its accompanying installation of electrical equipment has a decided effect on inspection activities.

Conservation Order M-9-c is most far-reaching in that it sets up control over both domestic and imported metal and scrap. Use of copper in more than 100 civilian articles is restricted until January 1, 1942. Use of copper in the manufacture of articles listed is prohibited after January 1, 1942. Use of copper in non-defense building construction is prohibited after November 1, 1941.

The prohibited list includes seven categories, the inspector having a special interest in building supplies and hardware, and house furnishings and equipment. Under building supplies come such items as air-conditioning equipment; conduits and tubing; elevators and escalators; lightning rods except for electric power stations and industrial stacks; lighting fixtures; plumbing and heating supplies; switch and floor plates; and screws, bolts, and nuts. Beauty parlor equipment, chimes and bells, pole line hardware, radios, reflectors and signs, including street signs, are among the items included under the heading *Miscellaneous*.

In the modification of Order M-9-c, issued November 1, 1941, some revision was made of the original specifications. Under general exceptions is included: "For use to comply with Underwriters' Regulations, or Safety Regulations issued under governmental authority, provided the pertinent provisions of such regulations were, in either case, in effect both on October 1, 1941, and on the date of such use, and specifically and exclusively require the use of copper or copper base alloy to the extent employed; or primarily as conductors of electricity, but this exception shall be applicable only to the extent necessary to permit the conducting of electricity required.

Other metals which enter into the construction of electrical equipment is under priority such as zinc. Zinc dust, such as is used in Sherardizing, is not so restricted. Tungsten and nickel are also included in the critical list.

Appliances with which the work of the electrical inspector is indirectly involved have also been restricted. Under date of November 27, 1941, the manufacture of domestic vacuum cleaners was restricted. The manufacture of domestic washers and ironers and electric refrigerators has also been curtailed.

Rubber

Rubber, of course, is under very strict priority regulation. Among the important happenings affecting rubber is the recent fire of the Firestone Rubber and Latex Products Company at Fall River, Mass., in which it is reported that there was a $9,000,000 loss, and that some 18,000 tons of crude rubber was involved much of which was destroyed.

Among the lessons that this fire has brought out is the necessity on the part of those in charge of the electrical equipment of industrial plants, and inspectors engaged in the inspection of these plants, for the utmost care in taking all possible steps to prevent the start of fires from any electrical cause.

Chlorinated rubber is placed under

Annual meeting of The Little Brown Jug Luncheon Club held at the Kentucky Hotel, Louisville, on January 18, 1940. The Little Brown Jug Luncheon Club was founded in 1935 by the Kentucky Chapter IAEI, on the basis of good fellowship and closer cooperation with everyone connected with the electrical industry. It has been a good medium to cement the relationship of those individuals vitally interested in better understanding in the electrical business. It also has been a definite factor in increasing the attendance and attention at the Kentucky Chapter. The 1940 officers of the club were (left to right): F. H. Moore, R. J. Heffernan, Walter Diecks, E. M. (Butch) Nelson, G. S. Dunn, Robert Barry, R. C. Bennett, H. H. Hudson, and J. Warner Pyles.

priority control by General Preference Order M-46. Among its other uses chlorinated rubber is used for electrical insulation purposes.

Repairs, Maintenance, and Supplies

Preference Rating Order P-22 grants an A-10 rating to certain industries and groups for material and supplies necessary in the carrying on of their business. Among the groups affected are manufacturing, warehousing, charitable institutions, carriers, educational institutions, printers and publishers, radio, telephone, and hospitals.

Due to their importance in the defense program a special priority rating of A-3 has been granted for the repair of elevators, escalators, and conveyors.

Utilities

Under an amendment to Order P-46, issued December 11, 1941, utilities are forbidden to undertake any substantial expansion of property or equipment without express permission from the Office of Production Management. This order applies to publicly owned as well as private utility companies and will cover Rural Electrification Administration cooperatives.

However, projects already under way and at least 40 percent complete on December 5 may be finished if the utility has supplies on hand for the purpose, or if granted priority assistance to obtain them.

With one exception, utilities may not without permission withdraw materials even from their own stores or inventories for expansion projects costing more than $1,500 in the case of underground connections or more than $500 in other cases.

Electric Range Cords

Due to the need for conserving copper and rubber, the Belden Manufacturing Co. have requested Underwriters' Laboratories, Inc., to accept for portable connections attached to electric ranges short lengths of three-conductor, rubber-jacketed cable having two No. 9 and one No. 11 conductors, or two No. 7 and one No. 9 conductors. These conductor sizes will have the following carrying capacities: No. 11, Type R, 22.5 amps.; No. 11, Type RH, 32 amps.; No. 9, Type R, 30 amps.; No. 9, Type RH, 43 amps.; No. 7, Type R, 40 amps.; No 7, Type RH, 57 amps. The Laboratories will accept these cords.

Housing

On December 3, Charles F. Palmer, Coordinator of Defense Housing, stated that 2,785 new publicly financed homes for defense workers and enlisted personnel had been completed during the week ending November 29. There is now a total of 56,581 homes ready for occupancy. With 275 homes going into construction during the week, the total of publicly financed homes now being built or completed reached 105,802. Federal funds have already been allocated for 126,259 defense homes.

Privately financed homes that are FHA-inspected started during the week totaled 3,831. Since January, 1941, 200,540 homes have gone into construction.

Blackouts

"Blackouts," a comprehensive 60-page pamphlet, prepared by the War Department, was issued November 14 by the Office of Civilian Defense. It may be purchased for 25c from the Superintendent of Documents, Washington, D. C.

Vacuum Tube Contacts

Underwriters' Laboratories, Inc., has stated that in the interest of National Defense, and during the period of the emergency, contacts for vacuum tube sockets in radio sets will be excepted if made of steel suitably protected from corrosion by plating. The standard requires the use of phosphor bronze or brass.

Flexible Cords

The new requirements for the physical test and the aging properties of 30 percent rubber compound employed in Types S and SJ cords, and the 40 percent rubber compounds employed in Types S, SJ, AFS, AFSJ, and HSJ cords, which were to become effective on September 2, 1941, have been postponed until March 1, 1942, at the request of the manufacturers of flexible cords, because of the uncertainty of the rubber situation at the present time as brought about by the National Defense.

Pendent Weatherproof Lampholders

Heretofore the standards of Underwriters' Laboratories have required a six-inch length of conductor on pendent weatherproof lampholders. On account of the scarcity of rubber brought about by the National Defense, the requirement has been modified to accept a three-inch length of leads.

1940 International President

K. W. Adkins inspected the Central Station Watch Service rendered in St. Louis in 1929, and reported some interesting disclosures. He was impressed with the efforts put forth by the telephone and telegraph interests to safeguard their cables from fire damage within their own premises. The new methods would seem to reduce the possibility of such damage to the point where it practically disappears. The mounting and housing of storage batteries were accomplished in a manner calculated to conserve the life of the battery and improve its reliability of operation. Mr. Adkins was remembered as the man who developed the motor wiring tables that made the Western Association of Electrical Inspectors, the precursor to the Western Section, famous. — Reprinted from *IAEI News*, May 1929.

Canadian Specifications Revised

To assist the Steel Controller of Canada in his effort to conserve stocks of steel for war purposes, the Canadian Engineering Standards Association has agreed to accept sheet steel of lighter gauge than called for in the Canadian Electric Code. The Hydro Electric Power Commission of Ontario has agreed to accept the recommendations of the Canadian Engineering Standards Association during the continuance of the present war, or until the present restrictions on the use of steel for non-war purposes has been lifted. Reference is made to the following specifications:

1. Minimum Thickness of Sheet-Metal for Enclosures: Sheet steel sizes are reduced from 16, 14, 12, 10, to 18, 16, 14, and 12 U.S. gauge respectively.
2. Sheet Metal for Doors: Sheet metal sizes are reduced from 16, 14, 14, 12 to 18, 16, 14, 12 U.S. gauge respectively.

3. Outlet Boxes, Conduit Boxes, Flush-Device Boxes: Sheet metal sizes are reduced from 14 to 16 U.S. gauge.

4. Automatic Motor-Control Devices of Small Capacity: "Enclosures having provision for conduit connection and made of sheet metal" are reduced from 16 to 18 U.S. gauge.

5. Cabinets and Cutout Boxes: Sheet metal sizes are reduced from 16, 14, 12, 10 to 18, 16, 14, 12 U.S. gauge respectively.

6. Sheet Metal for Frames and Doors: sheet metal sizes are reduced from 16, 14, 12, to 18, 16, 14, 12, U.S. gauge respectively.

Rural Extensions

There has been a curtailment in the extension of rural lines by the Hydro Electric Power Commission. While the conservation of electric energy enters into the situation, the real reason lies in the inability to get transformers. A large percent of the material used in transformer construction, particularly silicon steel, comes from the United States and this supply has been curtailed. It is stated that during the fiscal year the commission has built 650 miles of extensions into rural communities servicing 8,600 new customers. These extensions have been encouraged by the desire to help the farmer increase products for home consumption and for export to Great Britain.

Reprinted from *News-Bulletin*, January 1942.

Southern Section meeting at the John Marshall Hotel in Richmond, Virginia, from October 19-21, 1942.

Southern Section Timeline

1929 Atlanta, Georgia, was the scene of the first annual meeting of the Southern Section, October 15-17, 1929.

Application for the creation of the **Louisiana Chapter** was filed with the IO. It was created in July 1929.

R. L. Gatewood, from Atlanta, Georgia, is elected the Southern Section's first secretary.

1930 Florida Chapter charter granted.

North Carolina Chapter/Ellis Cannady Chapter was formed in a meeting from December 2-3, 1930 in Durham, NC. Name changed to North Carolina Ellis Cannady Chapter in 1983

1931 Texas Chapter is formed.

1933 The organizational meeting of the **Georgia Chapter** was held on December 15, 1933; held first meeting on January 20, 1934.

1934 North Louisiana Division of the Louisiana Chapter is created.

1936 The International executive council approves the charter for the new **Virginia Chapter.**

1939 Mississippi Chapter is formed.

1940 Joseph Whitner, from Atlanta, Georgia, is elected Southern Section secretary.

1942 C. M. Jones, from Atlanta, Georgia, is elected Southern Section secretary.

1944 The IO grants a charter for the **North Louisiana-East Texas Chapter**.

A.M. "Gus" Miller, from Richmond, Virginia, is elected Southern Section secretary.

1949 Texas Gulf Coast Chapter held their first official meeting January 10, 1949, at the Texas State Hotel in Houston, Texas.

South Carolina Chapter, holds its charter meeting on April 14-15, 1949.

Tennessee Chapter is created.

1950 Board of directors approves the creation of the **Alabama Chapter**.

1951 George Welman Chapter is formed; changed its name to the Southeast Louisiana Chapter in 1999.

1956 Baton Rouge Chapter is created. In 1968, the board of directors considered a proposal to change the name of this chapter to the Felix Fluck Chapter, but it was declined.

Augustus M. "Gus" Miller

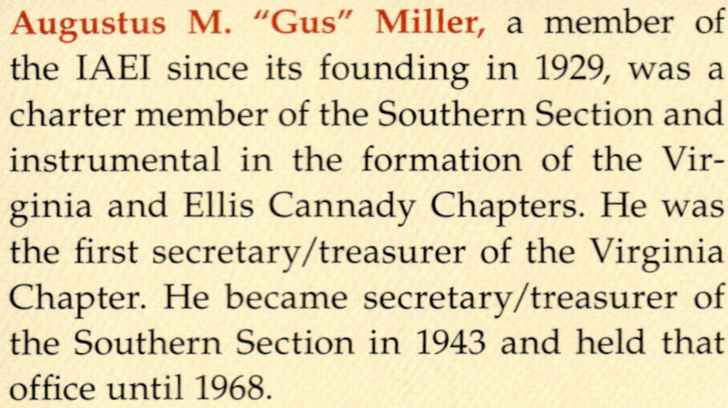

Augustus M. "Gus" Miller, a member of the IAEI since its founding in 1929, was a charter member of the Southern Section and instrumental in the formation of the Virginia and Ellis Cannady Chapters. He was the first secretary/treasurer of the Virginia Chapter. He became secretary/treasurer of the Southern Section in 1943 and held that office until 1968.

He was a member of several IAEI committees and a member of the board of directors for many years. He also wrote various articles for *News-Bulletin*. In 1954, while he was still actively employed, he made an honorary member of the Southern Section. Later he became an international honorary member, and retired from the city of Richmond in 1958.

1957 North Central Division of the Texas Chapter is born.

1959 Sabine Division of the Texas Gulf Coast Chapter is born. Eight years later, the division became the Sabine Chapter.

1963 West Texas Chapter is formed. Due to inactivity, the chapter was disbanded in 1977 by the board of directors and its territories were reassigned to the Texas Chapter.

1941 International President

G. E. Kimball from San Francisco, California.

Quick Fact

Mrs Anderson, secretary to the Board of Examiners of Electrical Contractors of North Carolina, was accepted as an associate member of the IAEI in 1940. This is the second female on record, the first being Miss F. H. Pettee of Jacksonville, Florida, who joined in 1930.

National Fire Protection Association
INTERNATIONAL

MEMBERSHIP CERTIFICATE

This is to Certify that

THE INTERNATIONAL ASSOCIATION OF ELECTRICAL INSPECTORS

IS A MEMBER OF THE NATIONAL FIRE PROTECTION ASSOCIATION

Percy Bugbee
General Manager

A NON-PROFIT TECHNICAL AND EDUCATIONAL ORGANIZATION. ORGANIZED 1896 — INCORPORATED 1930
COPYRIGHT 1940 NATIONAL FIRE PROTECTION ASSOCIATION, BOSTON, MASSACHUSETTS. PRINTED IN U.S.A.

IAEI's membership certificate from NFPA in 1940.

1942 International President

William L. Gaffney was the former chief electrical inspector for the city of Tacoma, Washington, and was elected as International president in 1942 and secretary/treasurer of the Northwestern Section in 1944. Mr. Gaffney joined the IAEI in 1926, and was chairman of the Puget Sound Chapter for three years. He has always been sold on what is now the IAEI slogan, "Let the *Code* Decide."

After graduation from high school in 1911, he drifted to Canada and went to work as a wireman's helper for the Hinton Electric Company. He returned to Tacoma during WWI and worked for Todd Dry Dock and Construction Company. In 1921 he went back to the contract shops until February 1925, when he entered the employ of the city of Tacoma as an electrical inspector. He was promoted to chief electrical inspector in 1939.

War Production Proclamation

Establishment of War Production Board

By virtue of the authority vested in me by the Constitution and statues of the United States, as President of the United States and Commander in Chief of the Army and Navy, and in order to define further the functions and duties of the Office for Emergency Management with respect to the state of war declared to exist by Joint Resolutions of the Congress, approved December 8, 1941, and December 11, 1941, respectively, and for the purpose of assuring the most effective prosecution of war procurement and production, it is hereby ordered as follows:

1. There is established within the Office for Emergency Management of the Executive Office of the President a War Production Board, hereinafter referred to as the Board. The Board shall consist of a Chairman, to be appointed by the President, the Secretary of War, the Secretary of the Navy, the Federal Loan Administrator, the Director General and the Associate Director General of the Office of Production Management, the Administrator of the Office of Price Administration, the Chairman of the Board of Economic Warfare, and the Special Assistant to the President supervising the defense aid program.

Charles "Carl" Schoninger, Eastern Section member from Yonkers, New York, shakes hands with President Franklin D. Roosevelt in December 1943. The electrical industry was vital in whatever progress the United States was to make in successfully carrying on production so necessary in supplying the war essentials.

2. The Chairman of the War Production Board with the advice and assistance to the members of the Board, shall:

a. Exercise general direction over the war procurement and production program.

b. Determine the policies, plans, procedures, and methods of the several Federal departments, establishments, and agencies in respect to war procurement and production, including purchasing, contracting, specifications, and construction; and including requisitioning, plant expansion, and the financing thereof; and issue such directives in respect thereto as he may deem necessary or appropriate.

c. Perform the functions and exercise the powers vested in the Supply Priorities and Allocations Board by Executive Order No. 8875 of August 28, 1941.

d. Supervise the Office of Production Management in the performance of its responsibilities and duties, and direct such changes in its organization as he may deem necessary.

e. Report from time to time to the President on the progress of war procurement and production; and perform such other duties as the President may direct.

3. Federal departments, establishments, and agencies shall comply with the policies, plans, methods, and procedures in respect to war procurement and production as determined by the Chairman; and shall furnish to the Chairman such information relating to war procurement and production as he may deem necessary for the performance of his duties.

4. The Army and Navy Munitions Board shall report to the President through the Chairman of the War Production Board.

5. The Chairman may exercise the powers, authority, and discretion conferred upon him by this Order through such officials or agencies and in such manner as he may determine; and his decisions shall be final.

6. The Chairman is further autho-

rized within the limits of such funds as may be allocated or appropriated to the Board to employ necessary personnel and make provision for necessary supplies, facilities, and services.

7. The Supply Priorities and Allocations Board, established by the Executive Order of August 28, 1941, is hereby abolished, and its personnel, records, and property transferred to the Board. The Executive Orders No. 8629 of January 7, 1941, No. 8875 of August 28, 1941, No. 8891 of September 4, 1941, No 8942 of November 9, 1941, No. 9001 of December 27, 1941, and No. 9023 of January 14, 1942, are hereby amended accordingly, and any provisions of these or other pertinent Executive Orders conflicting with this Order are hereby superseded.

Franklin D. Roosevelt

The White House
January 16, 1942

Reprinted from *News-Bulletin*, March 1942.

Convention During the War?

The question is occasionally raised as to section and chapter activities during the present emergency. Although neither the officers or the executive council of the IAEI have taken action on this matter, all expressions have indicated that there will be no change in the present practice. The need for meetings seems to be increased rather than lessened, as the problems with which the association members are confronted are more vital and important than ever.

This is not the first war that inspectors' associations have passed through, and during the first world war meetings were held as usual with the programs devoted to the problems brought on by the war situation. It has been noted that in the chapter meetings recently held the spirit of the emergency, and the problems arising from the emergency program, have dominated the meeting.

An editorial which appeared in an issue of *Electrical World* bears directly on this subject: "...Whatever the feeling may have been in the past, the problem today is not a local one for each to solve in his own way. War is something that is common to us all and we can accomplish more by working together. Conventions and meetings provide the time and place both for joint action and for getting a broader and more complete understanding of effective ways of meeting the common problem."

News-Bulletin, March 1942

1943 International President

T. W. Bowry from Richmond, VA., Southern Section.

1944 International President

James D. Lynett, supervising chief inspector, Department of Electricity for New York City, was elected IAEI president in 1944. He entered the electrical construction business in 1902 as an electrician's helper. He soon moved up and became the chief inspector of the Staten Island office in 1921.

For over eleven years, he taught in the evening technical high schools, and many of his pupils now hold responsible positions in the various branches of the electrical industry. He was also an examiner for the Board of Education of New York City, conducting examinations for licenses to teach electrical subjects and also promotion examinations for teachers.

Mr. Lynett was active in *Code* work for over twenty-six years and assisted Herbert S. Wynkoop in revising the present (1944) New York City Electrical Code. He was a member of the NFPA electrical committee, represented the United States Conference of Majors, was a member of the electrical council of UL, and a member of the American Institute of Electrical Engineers.

1945 International President

L. P. Dendel was from Lansing, Michigan, Western Section.

1946 International President

Ben C. Hill, formerly superintendent of the electrical department for the city of Oakland, California, was elected president of the IAEI in 1946. Previously, he was a member of the Oakland Electric Club and, at one time, was its president. He is also a past chairman of the Northern California Chapter, and an alternate on the electrical committee, NFPA.

He represented the inspectors' association in PCEA, and was active on the code and ordinance committee. His affiliations also included the Masons, Shriners, and Pan-American Association.

1946 R.W. Meullier

R. W. Meullier, of the Florida Chapter, and his pet dog. Mr. Meullier was born in Vermont, and his first electrical experience was with the New England Telephone Company, after which he worked at the electrical business in various locations throughout the country. He was an electrical contractor at Los Angeles and was foreman of construction and maintenance at Alaska-Yukon-Pacific (AYP) Exposition in Seattle. He went to Fort Lauderdale after World War I, and began working first for the Southern Utilities Company and later taking up an electrical contracting business. In 1935, he was appointed electrical inspector for Fort Lauderdale, a position he retained until he resigned in 1946.

Ladies at the 1944 Southern Section meeting in Atlanta, Georgia, on September 25, 1944. Southern President Dewey Johnson felt that this meeting was the most important since the beginning of WWII, and that the *Code* being revised would be a post-war code. War conditions brought lower standards and substitute materials, and it was quite a job for the electrical inspector to get a reasonably safe installation.

Post War Electrical Equipment

The post war period has developed into a series of electrical situations that is to have a very bad effect from the standpoint of the hazards from electrical equipment.

The post war period itself, the strikes, the lack of steel and other materials and particularly the lack of manpower, price regulation and other items, are making themselves evident.

Reports are received of electrical appliances being sold which are not marked with the manufacturer's name nor with any electrical ratings. Heaters are sold with the warning that they shall not be placed where heat would injure the surfaces unless an asbestos pad is used. The absence of manufacturer's names in noticeable.

Reports have been received of the absence from sales counters of the fuses used in the ordinary branch circuit, and the further discouraging statement that due to ceiling price limitation fuses are not likely to be available for some time. Incidentally, nothing has happened to indicate that the branch circuit fuse will discontinue its usual blowing.

It is probably safe to say that so far as appliances and other equipment that is purchased by the user is concerned the electrical inspector has before him one of the toughest jobs he has been called upon to solve.

Reprinted from *News-Bulletin*, March 1946.

Quick Fact

Leading Industry

Electricity in all its phases has become America's third largest industry, ranking next to agriculture and railroading, according to Charles M. Ripley, electrical engineer of the General Electric Company.

Reprinted from *News-Bulletin*, January 1931.

Fred D. Weber *(left)*, secretary/treasurer of the Northwestern Section, and J. Hyde Stayner *(right)*, first vice president of the Northwestern Section, at the second annual meeting of the Utah Chapter on April 23, 1943.

Don P. Caverly, commercial engineer, Sylvania Electric Products, Incorporated, and author of *Primer of Electronics*, spoke on "Electronics in the Lighting Industry," at the September 11, 1944, meeting of the New York Chapter. Mr. Caverly used a large board on which various types of lamps and tubes were set. This equipment was explained and demonstrated and included black light, cosmic ray, strobotrons, transmitting and power tubes, ultraviolet germicidal tubes, pirani tubes, fluorescent lamp equipment, and also an operating demonstration of cathode ray oscilloscopes.

1947 International President

W. R. Volheye, chief electrical inspector and safety inspector, Bureau of Labor, state of Oregon, began his apprenticeship in 1906, as an employee of the Claggett Electric Company in Portland, and has been continuously engaged in the field of electricity. He became a member of the Northwestern Section in 1935, and attended his first section meeting in 1936. He served as president of the Northwestern Section in 1942-1943.

Mr. Volheye entered the service of the state of Oregon as an electrical inspector in 1935, and was made chief inspector in 1936. In 1940, he was given additional duties as chief elevator inspector and chief safety inspector. He also served as director of apprenticeship for the state of Oregon during 1944 and part of 1945.

Clifford Prudhourne, city of Sacramento, H. C. Moore, city of Modesto and the new second vice president of the Southwestern Section, and Howard Neighbors, city of Berkley, at the 1945 Southwestern Section meeting.

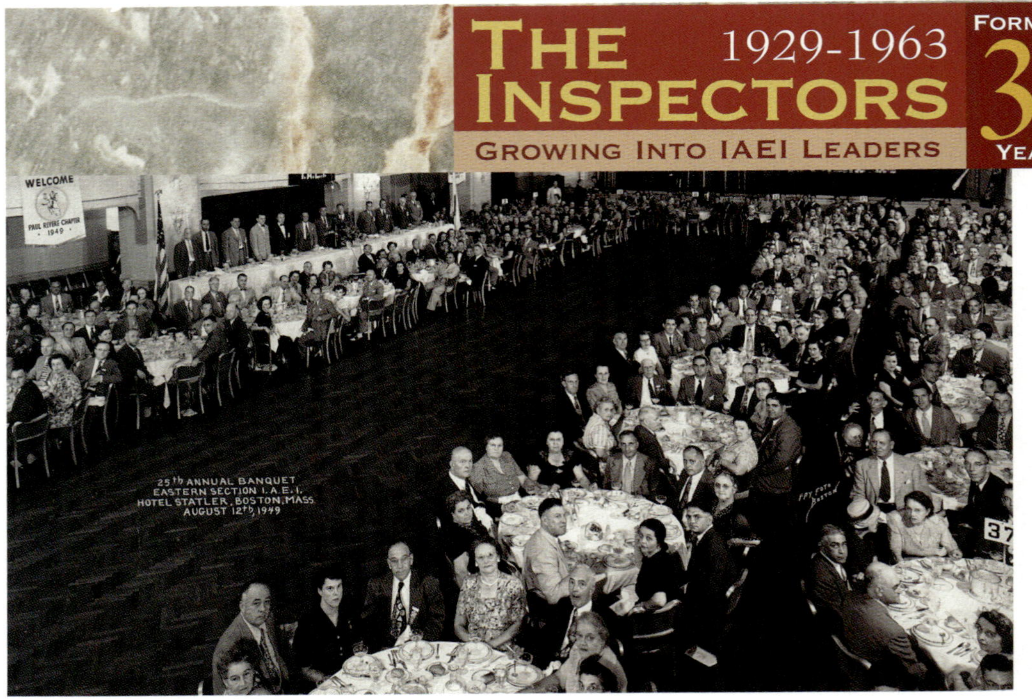

Annual Eastern Section meeting at the Hotel Statler in Boston, Massachusetts, August 12, 1949.

Eastern Section Timeline

1929 Western New England Chapter is granted its charter.

Board of directors approves the creation of the **Philadelphia Chapter**.

Westchester Chapter is formed.

Ray Walker, of Brooklyn, New York, is elected Eastern Section secretary.

1930 Eastern New England Chapter is created.

1931 Western Pennsylvania Chapter held its organizational meeting on April 7, 1931.

1932 George Washington Chapter is formed.

1936 Executive board of directors approves the creation of the **Long Island Chapter**.

1940 F. N. M. Squires, of New York, NY, is elected Eastern Section secretary.

1941 Empire Chapter's charter was granted November 24, 1941.

1943 A charter is granted to the **Roger Williams Chapter,** covering the territory of Rhode Island.

1950 Paul Revere Chapter is formed.

1952 Genesee Chapter held its organizational meeting on November 17, 1952.

Pine Tree Chapter is formed.

New Jersey Chapter is formed.

Western New York Chapter is formed.

John W. King, of Providence, Rhode Island, is elected Eastern Section secretary.

1953 Adirondack-Hudson Chapter is first mentioned in *IAEI News*.

1957 J. W. Hager, of New York, NY, is elected Eastern Section secretary.

1959 Robert A. Jutstrom, of Weymouth, Massachusetts, is elected Eastern Section secretary.

1962 R. A. Rockford, of New York, New York, is elected Eastern Section secretary.

1963 Eastern Pennsylvania Chapter is created.

Chesapeake Chapter is created.

James Clune, secretary, at left, and George Blend, chairman of the Montana Chapter, at a 1946 Montana Chapter meeting in Great Falls.

Women Indicate Electrical Preferences

In a recent Home of Tomorrow contest conducted by *McCall's* magazine to determine women's preferences and intentions in home building and remodeling, several facts were uncovered which will be of interest to electrical groups and which should help them substantially in planning their sales and promotional activities in the near future.

Of ten remodeling and replacement needs most frequently mentioned by the 18,850 contestants the addition of ventilating fans (kitchen and attic) ranked fourth in number of mentions and the installation of new lighting fixtures ranked ninth.

The Old Home

Participants in the contest were asked to list their general remodeling needs as well as specific room-by-room requirements. Of 13,210 readers, whose homes are in need of major repairs, 39.5% wish to install additional convenience outlets, 24.3% would like to rewire the entire house, and 45.9% want to replace present lighting fixtures. Of the 13,877 respondents interested in kitchen remodeling 44.4 % want to add a kitchen fan, 33.9% would like garbage disposers, 33.6% want dish washers, 24.8% expressed a desire for automatic washing machines, 19.3% want to add water heaters and 1.1% favor improving or changing their kitchen lighting fixtures. Of 6,745 contestants interested in attic remodeling, 41.8% want to install ventilating fans.

The New Home

Those women planning to build or buy new homes expressed considerable interest in certain major electrical appliances, but in general, will buy such equipment later rather than in the beginning. However, there were several exceptions to this: 51.6% of 11,101 respondents want to install water heaters right away; 46.5% of 11,501 would like fluorescent lighting immediately; while 35.3% of 9,814 want to put in circuit breakers now.

— Reprinted from *News-Bulletin*, March 1946.

MIDDLE DEPARTMENT ASSOCIATION OF FIRE UNDERWRITERS

401 WALNUT STREET, PHILADELPHIA 6, PA.

ELECTRICAL DEPARTMENT
C. M. HARMAN, SUPERINTENDENT
R. J. MORAN, CHIEF INSPECTOR

March 10, 1947

TO ELECTRICAL INSPECTORS &
CLERICAL STAFF:

In recent months, an increasing number of our field staff have been using the so-called ball point pen or pencil in the preparation of inspection reports and approval forms. We are advised that this type of pen uses a chemical compound in solid form as the writing medium and the compound, under some conditions, fades to such an extent that it is no longer legible.

We have been requested by some offices that receive our written reports or approval forms not to use the ball point pen in their preparation, and we request your cooperation in this respect.

Very truly yours,

C M Harman

C. M. Harman
Supt. Electrical Dept.

E-141

The so-called ball point pen is banned from inspection reports.

1948 International President

Jack G. Fisher, superintendent, electrical department, Mississippi State Rating Bureau (Fire Underwriters Bureau), was elected 1948 IAEI president.

Mr. Fisher first joined the Western Association of Electrical Inspectors in 1913 while with the Kentucky Bureau, and renewed his membership in 1924. He assisted in the organization of the Southern Section and served as president in 1935. He served on the electrical committee for twenty years and was on a number of article committees, and at the time the electrical committee was disbanded, was an alternate from two different groups; the IAEI and the Stock Fire Insurance Inspection Bureau group. He has been on the executive council of IAEI for a number of years.

1949 International President

Charles A. Ward started his career in the electrical industry as a stock boy with the late Philip H. Thorpe, a Paterson, New Jersey, electrical contractor, in 1908. From stock boy, he advanced to apprentice, helper and journeyman electrician. On August 4, 1910, he joined the International Brotherhood of Electrical Workers and still retains his membership in this organization.

Upon the formation of the electrical section of NFPA, Mr. Ward was appointed by Chairman Alvah Small to serve on Panel No. 5 of the newly organized electrical section. In 1934, he was elected president of the Eastern Section, IAEI, and in the following years represented the Eastern section on the executive council.

Paul Revere warns the attendees at the 1949 Eastern Section meeting that "the inspectors are coming! The inspectors are coming!" Mr. Revere is joined by his beloved horse [as played by John Furber (head) and R. E. Munroe (tail)].

Charles L. Smith

Charles L. Smith took over the reins as IAEI executive director and secretary to the board upon the death of Victor Tousley in 1948. At the time, he was chief electrical inspector for the city of Detroit, Michigan, and was selected by the NFPA board of directors to succeed Tousley as NFPA's electrical field engineer; IAEI had continued to depend upon NFPA's electrical field engineer to fill its office of secretary-treasurer. He was in this position until his untimely death in 1957.

It would take volumes to relate his contributions to the electrical industry in general, and the IAEI in particular. It might be said that his energy, while in office, was expended in devotion to the cause of the inspector. His efforts to have the *National Electrical Code* accepted as a standard by inspection authorities in municipalities, states, and by other governmental bodies were tireless. He aided greatly in assisting such authorities have a better and more uniform understanding of the *NEC*; and, in that capacity, was looked upon as a great authority on the *NEC* and other related codes and standards.

In his more than ten years as electrical field engineer, NFPA, and secretary-treasurer, IAEI, the association progressed by leaps and bounds. From a membership of approximately 3500 when he succeeded Vic Tousley, it steadily increased until it approached the near 10,000 mark in 1957. Many modern methods and business applications were introduced by him that increased the effectiveness of the services offered to the membership.

Among his affiliations were: American Institute of Electrical Engineers; International Municipal Signal Association; International Brotherhood of Electrical Workers; Society of Fire Protection Engineers; IAEI; and the National Fire Protection Association. — Excerpted from *News-Bulletin*, November 1957.

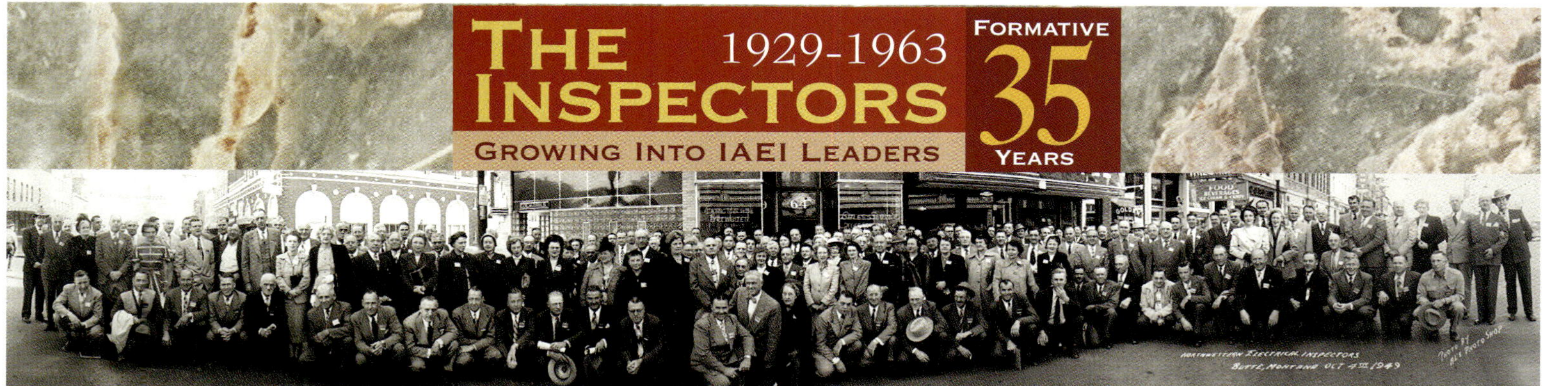

Northwestern Section Meeting in Butte, Montana, October 4, 1949

Northwestern Section Timeline

1929 **F. D. Weber**, of Portland, Oregon, is elected as the first Northwestern Section secretary

1936 **Utah Chapter** established.

1937 The first meeting of the **Puget Sound Chapter** is held on October 14, 1937.

1941 **Montana Chapter** is formed.

1944 **E. B. Morrison** is elected as the Northwestern Section secretary.

1945 Although it was initially formed in the Western Section, the **Idaho Chapter** is transferred to the Northwestern Section.

1946 **Tacoma Division** of the Puget Sound Chapter holds its first meetings.

1948 **W. L. Gaffney**, of Tacoma, Washington, is elected Northwestern Section secretary.

1949 **Oregon Chapter** holds its first organizational meeting March 11, 1949.

The first meeting of the **Tri-County Division** of the Idaho Chapter is held on November 9, 1949.

1950 **Eastern Washington Chapter** is created.

Boise Division of the Idaho Chapter is formed.

In 1945, Winston Churchill, Franklin D. Roosevelt, and host Joseph Stalin traveled to Yalta, a Crimean resort. With no other Allied leaders present, they devised a strategy to checkmate the Axis and drew up a postwar map. Stalin came away with rights to Eastern Europe, and the seeds of the Cold War were sewn. The fifties are sometimes remembered as an era of tranquility and order, but, in fact, dissent from Cold War norms was pervasive, turbulent, much publicized and even feted. From bomb shelters to the McCarthy hearings, the Cold War was a powerful entity.

This product exhibit shows examples of typical starter devices that were UL listed in 1950. This product exhibit is made up of three separate panels hinged together. The left and right wings mount enclosed NEMA Size 1, general-purpose, across-the-line magnetic starters. The center panel consists of an assembly of open type across-the-line magnetic starters arranged and wired to perform some special function as might be found in a typical multimeter, machine tool controller. The important point to note here is that these open-type magnetic starters, which are the building blocks of the assembled controller, are identical with the contents of the associated enclosed starter designated by the streamer running from the enclosed device to the open starter.

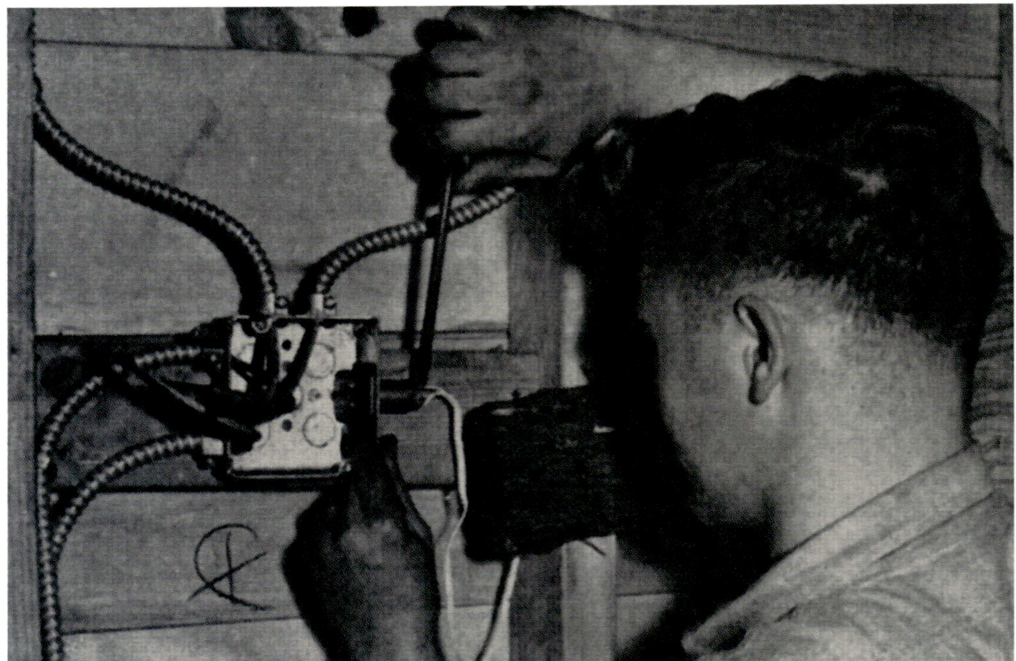

In the early 1950s, house wiring was considered ponderously conservative. Changes were absorbed slowly, even reluctantly. Bitter competition made the field aggressively cost-conscious. By and large, house wiring contractors were rarely organized to provide for the experimental jobs and field tests necessary to furnish cost data and know-how on new systems. Commercial work in stores, offices, and institutions were considered to offer a better opportunity than housing for initial experience.

Leaders of IAEI circa 1950. *Clockwise*: Charles L. Smith, IAEI managing director; Art Viet, 1951 international president; Bob Maxwell, San Jose, California; Ben Wheater, Long Beach, California (*rear*); an unidentified man; Everett Carlton, 1962 international president; Lou LaFehr, future IAEI managing director; Herb Ufer, Southwestern Section secretary; Mel Lundberg, Elko, Nevada; J. Hyde Stayner, Salt Lake City, Utah; and Larry O. Trim, 1956 international president.

1950 International President

John E. Wise, 1950 international president, entered the University of Wisconsin, electrical engineering department in 1912 and graduated in 1916 with the degree of bachelor of science in electrical engineering.

During the years 1930 and 1931, Mr. Wise served as chairman of the Wisconsin Chapter, and also as secretary/treasurer. In 1934-35, he was the president of the Western Section, and has served as a member of the executive council since 1930 and of the electrical committee of the NFPA from 1932 until it was disbanded in 1948. When the new electrical section was formed, Mr. Wise was appointed to serve on Panels No. 1 and No. 3.

He was a member of the electrical council of the Underwriters' Laboratories and is registered as a professional engineer by the Wisconsin Registration Board of Architects and Professional Engineers.

Quick Fact

Employee Annuity Program

After authorization, a plan for insurance and annuity for employees of IAEI was established in 1950 as described at the fall section meetings of 1949.

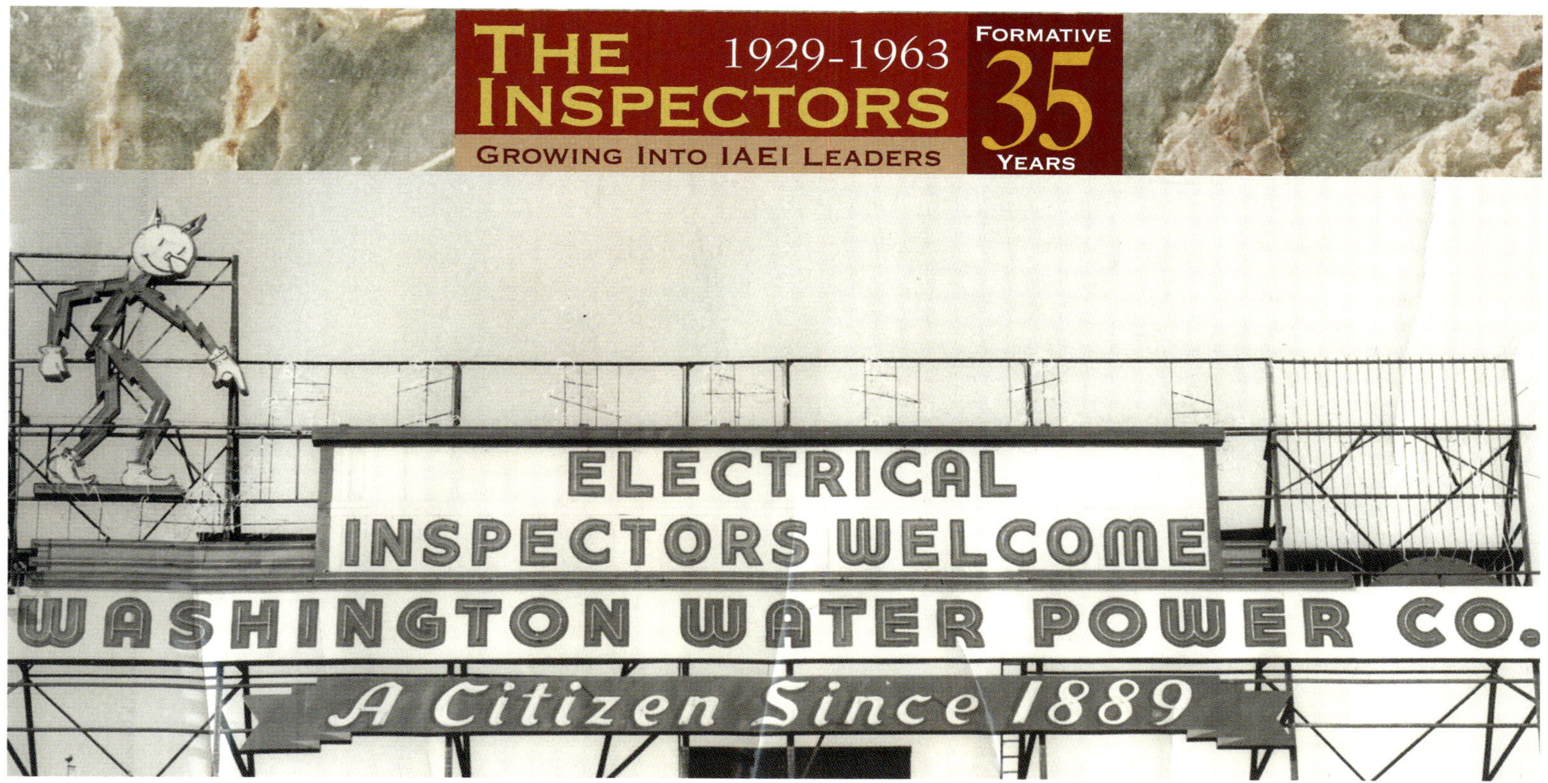

A sign atop the Power Company Building welcoming attendees to the 25th annual Northwestern Section meeting in Spokane, Washington. The meeting was held on September 19-21, 1951.

THE IAEI

By Fred H. Hintzman,
Indiana Chapter membership chairman, inspector for White County Rural Electric Membership Cooperative.

The International Association of Electrical Inspectors was organized in the year of 1928. It came about by combining several inspection groups with the old Western Association of Electrical Inspectors, which was one of the original participating bodies. The electrical inspectors were interested in forming an organization which would make it possible for them to meet, discuss and solve some of their electrical inspection problems.

This International association, which operates in the United States, Canada and Hawaiian Islands is divided into five geographical territories called sections. They are the Eastern, Southern, Southwestern, Northwestern and Western Sections. The state of Indiana is included in the Western Section. As the association grew each section was authorized to form other organizations called chapters in order to broaden the work of the association and to make it possible for more frequent local meetings such as the one you are attending here today. This our state of Indiana did on April 27, 1934. At this first meeting, Mr. Martin Braun was elected chairman. Mr. F. H. Moore, who was honored this morning by receiving an honorary certificate of membership was elected the secretary, has been serving in that capacity since that date. Mr. Moore has always been a constant builder and booster of our Indiana Chapter and the IAEI.

The International Association of Electrical Inspectors is now recognized by all groups in the field as a definite segment of the electrical industry.

The objectives of this association are best expressed in the objects of the IAEI as set down in Section I in the Articles of the Association as originally adopted. They are as follows:

1. To cooperate in the formulation of standards for the safe installation and use of electrical materials, devices and appliances.

2. To promote the uniform understanding and application of the *National Electrical Code* and other electrical codes.

3. To secure and promote uniform administrative ordinances and inspection methods.

4. To collect and disseminate information relative to the safe use of electricity.

5. To represent the electrical inspections in all matters which are dealt with nationally and internationally by the electrical industry.

6. To promote closer cooperation between inspectors, inspection departments, the electrical industry and the public.

The association is an inspectors organization, but it does not confine its membership to just electrical inspectors or electrical inspection departments. Any person or organization such as electrical journeyman, helpers, employees of electrical wholesalers, electrical contractors, manufacturer's representatives, salesmen, employees of municipal utilities or manufacturing organizations of electrical equipment and so forth, who are interested in the development of safety in the electrical field may make application for membership in the IAEI. The association now has a large number of these individuals and firms who are members, whom they appreciate very much. Since their electrical problems are of the same nature as the inspectors' they have been of great assistance in solving the mutual problems and have brought about a better understanding, standardization and uniformity of the *National Electric Code* in the entire country.

There are various classifications of membership in the association. They are classified as active, associate class A, associate class B and other classification. Other electrical organizations may obtain the services of the IAEI by writing to the Chicago office for additional information.

The amount of dues per year for Western Section active members is only $4.00 which includes those persons regularly engaged in the inspection of, or supervision of inspectors of, electrical materials, devices, appliances, or installations for the purposes of preventing loss or damage to persons or property on behalf of federal, state, provincial, county, municipal or insurance organizations, or on behalf of electric light and power companies.

The amount of dues per year for the associate members, class A is $5.00 which includes those individuals not qualified for active membership, but who are interested in promoting the objects of the association. These persons are the electrical journeyman, helpers, employees of wholesalers and other employees, other than the inspectors, in the electric light and power companies.

The amount of dues per year for the associate member, class B is $10.00 which includes those individuals—representatives of organizations, or firms who are interested in promoting the objects of the association. This group is for the electrical manufacturers' representatives, salesmen and the electrical contractors.

In each case the applicant not only becomes a member of the IAEI, but he also becomes a member of the section and a member of the chapter. This membership entitles him or the organization to all the benefits of the association, various publications that are published from time to time, especially the *News-Bulletin*, which keeps all informed on the subjects closely involved in the inspection work. The material found in this bulletin alone is worth the cost of the yearly dues to any member. — Reprinted from *News-Bulletin*, March 1951.

The first regular meeting of the New Jersey Chapter was held at Buchanan Electrical Products Corporation in Hillside, New Jersey, on September 11, 1951. The permanent officers that were elected at this meeting were: (*front row*) Elmer T. Quinn, first vice chairman; Charles A. Ward, chairman; George H. Schardien, second vice chairman; (*top row*) Rudolph H. Fries, secretary; Richard B. Swallow, treasurer; Herman W. Burkhardt, utilities member; S. N. Buchanan, manufacturer member; Frank A. Higgins, municipal inspectors member.

Chairman H. A. Whisenant received the Alabama Charter from Robert A. Peterson, assistant technical secretary to IAEI at the organizational meeting on April 9-10, 1951. *From left to right*: G. M. Ross, C. M. Baker, H. A. Whisenant, and R. A. Peterson. Robert Ward, second vice chairman of the Southern Section, outlined what is necessary to insure a good state chapter. The program at this meeting was a talk entitled "Insulated Wiring," given by Fred P. Oliver, Union Insulating Company, Incorporated. Mr. Oliver pointed out the many advantages of insulated wiring, including twenty years of service.

1951 International President

Arthur C. Veit assumed office on January 1, 1951, as international president. He became a member of the California Electrical Inspectors Association in 1921, which later became the Southwestern Section. Mr. Veit served as chairman of the Southern California Chapter in 1931. He was elected president of the section in 1935.

Mr. Veit has served on many national committees of IAEI and was a member of code-making panel No. 15 of the National Electrical Code Committee, NFPA.

He became an electrical inspector for the city of Alhambra in 1921, and was promoted to chief of the electrical department in 1925. He later became chief electrical inspector for Los Angeles County in the Department of Buildings and Safety in 1933.

New Type "F" Membership Authorized for Governmental Bodies

A new type of membership was authorized by the executive council in 1950, which would allow for cities, towns, municipalities, counties, townships, states, and other governmental bodies to participate as members in the IAEI.

This membership was known as type "F" participating membership. There were four classifications, and the fees were based on the population of the community and prorated as follows: the section in which the membership was held retained 80 percent of the fee with 20 percent payable to the international office as per-capita tax.

The membership provided for one representative who would be the inspector in charge from the community. He would have all rights of an active member of the association.

The new type "F" membership was the result of a proposal by the Southwestern Section, who had underway an active campaign attempting to interest communities in their jurisdiction to participate.

Paterson, New Jersey, Becomes First Type "F" Member

Past President Charles Ward was successful in having his city of Paterson, New Jersey, apply for the first type F participating membership in the IAEI in 1950. This was most appropriate in view of his being president in 1949, the year when the new type of membership was first authorized by the board of directors. Mr. Ward, as chief electrical inspector for Paterson, was the representative.

1952 W.W. Fowler

Woodrow W. Fowler, city electrical inspector for the city of Columbia, South Carolina, was the 1951 Southern Section president. He was also secretary/treasurer of the South Carolina Chapter and chairman of the executive committee of the Southern Section. He worked as an electrician until 1942, when he was elected by the Columbia city council to fill a vacancy as assistant city electrician. He served in this capacity until 1949 when the city created a department of public works, at which time the inspection department was removed from the city electrician and installed under the division of buildings.

Members and guests at the UL Electrical Council Meeting in Chicago, Illinois, on September 18-19, 1953. Row 1 (*from left to right*): K.W. Adkins, L.W. Going, W.A. Stall, G. L. Swann, B.F. Greene, D.J. Talbot, F.G. Waldenfels, and G.J. Tansey. Row 2 (*left to right*): T.P. Branch, H.N. Pye, H.G. Ufer, J.D. Lynett, R.L. Lloyd, E.C. Waud, C.J. Shukes, N.E. Cannady, and S.M. Streed. Row 3 (*from left to right*): J. Whitner, C.L. Smith, J.E. Wise, M.M. Brandon, E.E. Carlton, Arthur Lagadinos, Glenn Rowell, R.L. Tilford, and T.A. Lloyd.

C. D. Cole and Val Bizley, from the Hydro Electric Power Company of Ontario, at the 1954 Ontario Chapter meeting held at Sudbury, Ontario, May 14-15, 1954.

The Canadian Section was granted its charter at the 1953 Silver Jubilee Meeting of the IAEI. The 1954-55 Canadian Section executive officers had a large responsibility in uniting the existing Canadian chapters from various sections into one cohesive unit. The officers were (*left to right*): Fred Eley, executive officer; Rene Pare; N.A. Cockburn, treasurer; K.L. Bellamy, secretary; William J. Brake, first vice president; A. Kembry; L. Robson, president; and G. S. Whelpton, executive officer.

Changes in Membership Dues Structure Approved

In accordance with the Articles of Association, and after open discussion at all of the 1951 fall section meetings, the executive council of the International Association of Electrical Inspectors has approved a change in the dues structure of the association as follows:

Dues for active members beginning in 1952 will be $6.00.

Dues for associate members beginning in 1952 will be $10.00.

The above dues are standard in all sections and chapters excepting those chapters which charge additional dues for the chapter's own use. There are a few chapters in the association which carry on extra activities that require additional funds over and above the per capita tax ordinarily distributed to the chapters for its members.

The International office will mail to each member an invoice stating the exact amount of dues payable for 1952 and this invoice will contain information instructing the members to forward such dues to the International office at 612 North Michigan Avenue, Chicago, Illinois.

Members are requested not to send dues to chapter or section secretaries as it will only create extra work which can be avoided if the dues are sent directly to the International office. When the member's dues are received in the International office the member will be mailed a membership card immediately which will serve as acknowledgment that the dues have been received. We request that members note on the returnable portion of the invoice corrections with respect to the spelling of names, address, zone number, or other information which will correct apparent errors.

The International office is vitally interested in having full correct information on all memberships in order to assure that members will receive material mailed from the International office promptly after such material is released.

For the benefit of those members who were not in attendance at the section meetings, the raise in dues was recommended by a special committee appointed by the president after the committee had thoroughly explored the financial structure of the organization. We are confident that the members understand, with the ever-rising costs of printing and other services normal to an association of this kind, that the raise in dues is fully justified.

It will be very much appreciated if members will remit promptly their dues to the International office at 612 North Michigan Avenue, Chicago 11, Illinois, after receiving the dues notice. — Reprinted from *News-Bulletin*, January 1952.

The program committee at the 1954 Ontario Chapter meeting at Sudbury, Ontario. ***Left to right*****: Chavelles Rose; Mrs. J.D. Cooper; Mr. J.D. Cooper, chairman of the programming committee; N.A. Cockburn; Mrs. I. Mellon; unidentified man; and Ian Mellon, co-chairman.**

1952 International President

Chester M. Kirsop, IAEI president for 1952 and city electrician for the city of Olympia, was with that city for twenty-four years in charge of all city electrical construction and maintenance as well as electrical and plumbing inspections.

He is a past president of the Northwestern Section of the IAEI and the Northwest Section of the International Municipal Signal Association, which he aided in establishing in the Northwest.

He is a past commander of Post 318 of the Veterans of Foreign Wars, and also participated in local Legion activities and was chairman of the Veterans Council for many years. He was assistant local director of civil defense in World War II and was for some time state of Washington liaison communications officer.

Quick Fact

Active Service

Members of the association who are in good standing, and who enter active service in the armed (uniform) forces of the Allied Nations, shall retain their membership status without payment of dues.

Reprinted from *News-Bulletin*, January 1951.

The **Silver Jubilee** Meeting, in 1953, celebrated twenty-five years of exceptional progress and service towards electrical safety. The general meeting committee, under the chairmanship of Samuel R. Todd, spared no effort in its attempt to make the meeting one to be long-remembered. Complete facilities, exceptional committee staffs, and the comprehensive program, shown here, were at members' disposal to ensure their comfort at the convention. A separate ladies program, listing entertainment and affairs for the ladies, was available at the registration booth.

Silver 1953 Jubilee

You Should Have Been There!

The Silver Jubilee Meeting commemorating 25 years of steady progress in the electrical industry is now history. Never before in the annals of the International Association of Electrical Inspectors have its members witnessed such a stupendous event. The occasion, the well planned program, the precise coordinator of the various committees, the close cooperation of all the sections produced an affair that will be long remembered by those who attended the Jubilee. As a result, this meeting has left an indelible mark on the minds of the electrical inspector which fully convinces him that the International Association of Electrical Inspectors is established as a permanent and vital segment of the electrical industry.

The meeting was truly international. Approximately fifteen hundred members and guests were recorded by the registration group at the Edgewater Beach Hotel where the Silver Jubilee meeting was held. The Jubileeans came from all sections of the United States, Canada and Hawaii.

Meeting Theme

The theme of the meeting "A Broad Discussion of National Electrical Standards" was strictly adhered to with a panel of experts comprised of the chairman of each code-making panel. Each individual who had a problem dealing with the 1953 *National Electrical Code* was able to present it before this group for discussion in line with the reasoning that caused it to be included in the *National Electrical Code.*

The informal code discussions and inspectors' problems periods held Tuesday, Wednesday, and Friday mornings prior to the session meetings were well attended and produced some intense and lively code discussions.

A very prominent and outstanding feature of the Silver Jubilee Meeting was the exhibits sponsored by the leading associations and manufacturers in the electrical industry. There is no doubt that this group played a very important part in making this Silver Jubilee such a remarkable success. The manner in which the products were displayed and the courtesy shown to the hundreds of visitors who frequented the booths, solicited considerable praise and comments. It is certain that this close contact with the very latest in modern wiring methods and modern electrical equipment as exhibited there will be of great help to inspectors and inspection authorities in keeping abreast with the latest improvements in the electrical industry.

Canadian Section Charter

Friday morning, September 25th, the Canadian Section came into its own when

Display appearing in Lake Shore National Bank window, Chicago, during the Silver Jubilee week through the joint efforts of the Public Relations Committee, IAEI, and Safe Electrical Cord Committee.

The display exhibits and meeting rooms at the Silver Jubilee meeting were often crowded with people interested in electrical safety. The 101 display spaces were sponsored by leading associations and manufacturers in the industry. These organizations went to considerable expense and effort to bring an extensive range of products of vital interest, including the latest developments in electrical and allied products.

The Canadian Section charter was presented to President-elect Rene LaBelle on September 21, 1953, at the 25th Silver Jubilee Meeting. The Ontario Chapter was the first Canadian chapter formed in 1948 as part of the Western Section, although some Canadians, such as N. A. Cockburn, were members before that chapter was officially formed. K. L. Bellamy, of Toronto, Ontario, was elected as the Canadian Section secretary.

Beyond a doubt the more than 400 ladies who were fortunate enough to attend this Silver Jubilee meeting will never forget the well-executed program that kept them in a continual state of surprise, anticipation and enjoyment practically every minute of the day. What with the style show, shopping tour and breakfast in the Narcissus room at Marshall Fields; a tour of the many interesting parts of Chicago; participation in the Don McNeil Breakfast Club Radio Show, Tom Bartlett Welcome Travelers Radio Show and Ladies Fair Television Program; the floor show and dance; and the infamous luncheon at the fabulous Tam O'Shanter Country Club, the ladies hardly missed their husbands busily engaged in convention problems.

1953 Group at the Silver Jubilee Convention

the gavel was turned over to President-elect Rene LaBelle, by Walter A. Stall, international president. The Canadian Section charter was actually presented Monday morning during the opening Canadian Section session, when N. A. Cockburn, former Ontario Chapter secretary, and Rene LaBelle, Canadian president accepted the document from IAEI Secretary-Treasurer C. L. Smith and International President W. A. Stall. The creation and organization of the Canadian Section is indicative of the rapid expansion and growth of the IAEI. The electrical association is now actually international from that standpoint. Among the distinguished visitors present at the presentation was the Honorable Mr. C. C. Williams, Minister of Labor for Saskatchewan, who spoke briefly to the group.

George Monroe, for many years chairman of the chapter organization committee for the Western Section, was presented the charter of the newly organized Oklahoma Chapter during the opening session. He, in turn, presented it to Mr. Holmes, a member of the executive committee of the Oklahoma Chapter.

Founders Awards

Approximately 800 members and guests present at the "Get Acquainted" luncheon held in the Marine Dining Room at the Edgewater Beach Hotel witnessed the presentation of Founders Award by Alvah Small, retired president of the Underwriters' Laboratories, Incorporated, to N. E. Cannady and Williams S. Boyd living members; to Victor Tousley, Jr., who accepted the award in the name of his late father; to H. G. Ufer in the name of R. H. Manahan; Jim Lynett for the late J. C. Forsyth; and to William Gaffney in the name of the late F. D. Weber.

The convention group was privileged to hear some very fine and excellent papers delivered by some of the most outstanding speakers in their particular field. These papers will be printed in their full text in the "Proceedings of the Meeting" in the January issue of the *News-Bulletin*.

The six hundred thirty or more guests who visited the Underwriters' Laboratories, Incorporated during their open house on "U/L Day" will never forget their highly interesting tests and demonstrations that were specifically planned on this occasion for those who were taken on the guided tour throughout the laboratories. Everyone who witnessed these tests came away with a convinced mind that manufacturers goods bearing the Underwriters' approval can be safely used considering the rigid requirements and tests to which the products are subjected.

Honorary Memberships

Four outstanding members of the International Association of Electrical Inspectors were voted honorary memberships in the International by their respective sections. These men were L. W. Going of the Northwestern Section, A. M. "Gus" Miller, Southern Section, S. R. Todd, Western Section and G. H. Ufer of the Southwestern Section. At a meeting of the executive council, IAEI the honors conferred on these gentlemen were officially approved.

Safety Flies a Flag

Another important feature of the Jubilee was the excellent display that appeared in the Grand Ball Room, the site of the daily

sessions, through the efforts of the public relations committee headed by Arthur H. Welklin. Appearing on the display boards were many newspaper accounts, photographs and visible examples of materials attesting the misuse of electrical wiring and equipment which produce hazards that, in many instances, ended in death to individuals and destructive fires in buildings. Also displayed were the many publications, a record and film entitled, "Safety Flies a Flag," as produced through the efforts of the safe electrical cord committee.

Ladies Entertainment Program

How well, the ladies entertainment program was handled through a superb job performed by its chairman, A. A. Somer, can be summed up in an all inclusive word "super." Beyond a doubt the more than 400 ladies who were fortunate enough to attend this Silver Jubilee Meeting will never forget the well executed program that kept them in a continual state of surprise, anticipation and enjoyment practically every minute of the day. What with the style show, shopping tour and breakfast in the Narcissus room at Marshall Fields; a tour of the many interesting parts of Chicago; participation in the Don McNeil Breakfast Club Radio Show, Tom Bartlett Welcome Travelers Radio Show and Ladies Fair Television Program; the floor show and dance and climaxed with luncheon at the fabulous Tam O'Shanter Country Club, the ladies hardly missed their husbands busily engaged in convention problems.

Dinner Dance

The big social highlight of the Jubilee, was the dinner dance given in the famous Marine Dining Room at the Edgewater Beach Hotel. Over one thousand members and guests crowded this dining room in every available place. Besides enjoying an excellent dinner, the participants were delighted with one of the best floor shows ever produced by the hotel management. Following the dinner, there was dancing to the rhythms of Carl Sands and his Orchestra.

"Pig Groomin'" Contest

The "Pig Groomin'" Contest was perhaps the main attraction for the many individuals who had entered a pig in this contest. The ingenuity of the women used in dressing these little piggies was something outstanding in the manner of novel achievements. There was no question that the judges were hard pressed to make some hairline decisions in determining the prize winners. Many beautiful and wonderful prizes were given away to the lucky participants. Every entry received an award.

Sections Business

During the course of the convention, each section was given a period of time to conduct its own business sessions without interfering with the regular program. One of the most important items completed at each section session was that of the election of officers. The respective sections elected the following men for the year of 1954:

Eastern Section, President, F. L. Mattfield, Long Island, N.Y.; 1st Vice President, A. O. Hyde, Buffalo, N. Y.; 2nd Vice President, William Carroll, Brockton, Mass.; Secretary – Treas., John W. King, Providence, R. I.

Canadian Section, President, Rene LaBelle, Montreal, Canada; 1st Vice President, J. A. B. Kembry, Edmonton, Canada; 2nd Vice President, L. Robson, Vancouver, British Col.; 3rd Vice President, W. J. Blake, Regina, Saskatchewan; 4th Vice President, W. D. Smith, Toronto, Canada; Secretary, K. Bellamy, Toronto, Canada; Treasurer, N. A. Cockburn, Toronto, Canada.

Northwestern Section, President, J. R. Crawfore, Butte, Montana; 1st Vice President, J. C. Hewitt, Olympia, Washington; 2nd Vice President, Cliff Atkins, Portland, Oregon; Secretary-Treasurer, W. L. Gaffney, Tacoma, Wash.

Southern Section, President, J. E. Snakenberg, New Orleans, LA; 1st Vice President, R. B. Boyd, Jr., Raleigh, N.C.; 2nd Vice President, J. C. Steele, St. Angelo, Texas; Secretary-Treasurer, A. M. Miller, Richmond, VA; Assistant Secretary, J. Clifton Young, New Orleans, La.

Southwestern Section, President, E. E. Carlton, Menlo Park, Calif.; 1st Vice President, Ben Wheater, Long Beach, Calif.; 2nd Vice President, James L. Ambrosi, Oakland, Calif.; Secretary-Treasurer, L. E. LaFehr, Alhambra, Calif.

Western Section, President, C. M. Parks, Chicago, Ill.; 1st Vice President, J. E. Fisher, Elkhart, Ind.; 2nd Vice President, Glenn Rowell, Minneapolis, Minn.; Secretary-Treasurer, H. L. Parks, Charleston, W. VA.

Executive Council IAEI

A meeting of the Executive Council, IAEI, followed the conclusion of the Silver Jubilee meeting. The group met in session under the chairmanship of Walter A. Stall, international president. Among the many duties taken up before the council was the election of officers for the year of 1954. B. A. McDonald of Rochester, New York was chosen by the council as the new International President of the IAEI. Other International officers are 1st Vice President, S. R. Todd, Chicago, Ill.; 2nd Vice President, H. G. Ufer, Los Angeles, Cal.; 3rd Vice President, E. B. Morrison, Portland, Ore.; 4th Vice President, Dewey L. Johnson, Atlanta, GA.; 5th Vice President, (to be appointed). Secretary-Treasurer, C. L. Smith, Chicago, Ill.

General chairman of the Silver Jubilee Meeting was Samuel R. Todd. To him must be given a great deal of the praise for the excellent manner in which he directed the many and various committees under his chairmanship. It was a vast undertaking, surmounted with many obstacles that required extensive planning and considerable foresight. The successful Jubilee is a tribute to his proficiency, in this line of endeavor. Vice chairmen were Hoyte P. Steele and Wm. S. Stacy, finance; William S. Boyd, founder; C. L. Smith, program and treasurer.

Other committee chairmen were: W. J. Alcock, local transportation; Fred Bernard, radio and television; G. A. Berthel, transportation; T. W. Briegel, souvenir; E. F. Cogan, hotel reservation; Cal Condon, badge; N. H. Davis, Jr., U/L Day; August Eckel and E. T. Rowland, publicity; C. M. Jones and Mrs. W. J. Alcock, photograph; H. C. Moses, Jr., and J. J. Smith, displays; Vicent J. Mulligan and K. R. Horner, section hosts; E. M. Nelson and V. J. Mulligan, booster; A. Pertle, registration; George W. Reinke, entertainment; A. A. Sommer and Mrs. D. J. Talbot, ladies entertainment.

Reprinted from *News-Bulletin*, November 1953.

1953 International President

From an oiler in the Stone and Webster Company at Jacksonville, Florida, to the chief electrical inspector of that city is another "Horatio Alger" story of hard won success achieved by **Walter A. Stall**, 1953 international president.

He began his electrical career as an oiler in 1901, and soon completed courses in steam and electrical engineering, and began working for an electrical contractor as a helper. Two years later, he became a journeyman. To gain experience on DC equipment, he accepted a job as foreman electrician for the Pullman Company in 1910, and moved on to become car lighting inspector for the southern district of the A.C.L. Railroad Company in 1914.

After certification as master electrician, he entered the electrical contracting field in 1917, where he was very successful. The position of chief electrical inspector for the city of Jacksonville was accepted by Mr. Stall in 1935.

Quick Fact

It has been estimated that about 95% of the accidental electrocutions kill males rather than females.

—Reprinted from *News-Bulletin*, September 1956.

Canadian Section Timeline

1931 Meeting of Quebec Electrical Inspectors

1948 Ontario Chapter was created originally as part of the Western Section.

1949 N.A. Cockburn, of Toronto, Ontario, is elected as the first Canadian Section secretary.

1950 was the inaugural year for the **Alberta Chapter**, but there were so few members, that no meetings were held until 1951. The chapter was originally part of the Northwestern Section.

1953 Canadian Section charter was handed to President-elect Rene LaBelle on September 21, 1953, at the 25th Silver Jubilee Meeting.

K. L. Bellamy, of Toronto, Ontario, is elected as the Canadian Section secretary.

1956 Quebec Chapter is officially created.

Gibson Bailey, of Toronto, Ontario, is elected as Canadian Section secretary.

1957 J. J. Donnelly, of Toronto, Ontario, is elected as Canadian Section secretary.

1959 David S. Martin, of Scarborough, Ontario, is elected as Canadian Section secretary.

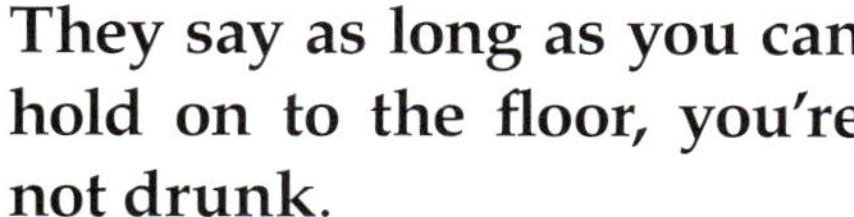

They say as long as you can hold on to the floor, you're not drunk.

The Western New York Chapter tried to make their meetings in the 1950s interesting both from the serious business side and a good fellowship angle. Roland D. Cranson, one of the executive committee members of the chapter, indicates that he had, according to the old saying, got happy.

Mrs. Ian Mellon and Miss Enid Olmstead run the registration booth at the 1954 Ontario Chapter meeting in Sudbury, Ontario. J. R. Duncan, a Perry Sound contractor, hands in his registration form.

Mississippi Organizes First IAEI Ladies Auxiliary Unit

The Mississippi Chapter added another colorful page to its history when a new women's club was organized during the chapter's two-day convention, held in Jackson, Mississippi, at the Heidelberg Hotel on March 28, 1955.

The group will be known officially as the Ladies Auxiliary of the Mississippi Chapter of the IAEI. The principal object of the auxiliary will be to promote better attendance and to assist in the planning of all social activities.

The 1955 officers of the ladies auxiliary, the first of its kind, are: Mrs. T. W. Sampson, president; Mrs. W. G. Bradley, vice president; and Mrs. C. B. Grauer, secretary/treasurer. Charter members also included: Mrs. W. R. Wood, Mrs. W. L. Strickland, Mrs. J. R. Hill, Mrs. L. D. Pepper, Mrs. A. T. Snider, Mrs. J. F. Barksdale, Mrs. Drad Porter, Mrs. Eva Grehany, Mrs. Dudley T. Smith, Mrs. Ben Segall, Mrs. H. F. Lowery, Mrs. J. N. McCammon, Mrs. Glenn Kelly, Mrs. James Graham, and Mrs. J. G. Fisher.

The group was heralded to be of great assistance to the members of the Mississippi Chapter in furthering the objectives of the association and in encouraging the membership to take a greater interest and a more active part in the affairs on the chapter level.

"We have the usual things, the refrigerator, the washing machine and dryer, the air conditioner, the broiler, my quarter-horse motor, and two heaters. Then, on the second circuit we have. . . ."

1954 International President

During World War I, **Bernard A. McDonald** was employed as an electrical inspector and expeditor with the Emergency Fleet Corporation of the United States Army.

Previous to his retirement in 1953, he was associated with the New York Fire Insurance Rating Organization and the New York Board of Fire Underwriters' for more than 33 years as an electrical inspector. He was also active in the development of the *NEC* for a number of years, especially through his membership on the electrical committee of the NFPA and through his membership on code making-panels 5, 7 and 8.

Mr. McDonald was extremely active in the affairs of the association, serving on countless committees.

Robert E. Rindell, chairman of the Western New York Chapter in 1955, appears to be washing dishes because of his being unable to pay his registration fee.

1955 International President

Samuel R. Todd, 1955 international president, received the degree of bachelor of science in electrical engineering in 1913.

Mr. Todd has served the IAEI as chairman of the Illinois Chapter in 1933, president of the Western Section in 1937, and for twenty years as the chairman of the meetings and program committee of the Illinois Chapter. At the fifth anniversary of the IAEI, at the all-section meeting in 1933 in Chicago, he produced and directed the two reel motion picture in sound, titled—"50 Years of Progress in Electrical Inspection," being a pictorial record of the highlights, speeches, and activities of the delegates at this first all-section meeting. He served as general chairman for the Silver Jubilee of the IAEI in 1953 in Chicago, at which time he was elected an IAEI honorary member.

He had been a member of the NFPA electrical committee for sixteen years. In 1933, upon request of the electrical committee, he prepared the first draft for the *National Electrical Code* standards covering installations of sound equipment and accessory apparatus in motion picture theaters.

In February 1949, he was the sole representative of the U.S. to a sixty nation conference held in Geneva, Switzerland, for the purpose of developing a new electrical safety code, for factories and industrial plants in Europe.

How Much From the Inspector...For How Little?

By Charles A. Stone, editor, *New England Electrical News*

HELP WANTED – MALE – HELP WANTED
Position of responsibility open for industrious, well-qualified man thoroughly familiar with all phases of electrical work from the wiring of the smallest home to the most intricate installation essential to the safe and efficient operation of the largest manufacturing plant, school or office building. Must be completely grounded in the laws governing such electrical installations and familiar with every detail of the extensive *National Electrical Code*. Must be capable of serving as educator, electrical consultant, business manager. He must be willing to work long hours, assume responsibility, make important decisions and stand by them, often in the face of unjustified but vigorous opposition. He must be prepared to sacrifice of his time, and home life, and prepared to study evenings and in all free hours in order to keep abreast of the never-ending developments in the world's greatest and fastest growing industry.

The above might well be an advertisement for an electrical inspector for any city or town in New England.

The average person reading it would assume, not unnaturally, that such a position automatically was one entailing a great responsibility, more than average personal integrity, a high degree of specialized knowledge, long experience, and the ability to find the right answers to intricate technical problems and to work with the public patiently, intelligently and diplomatically.

Qualifications High

And such is the case. The average electrical inspector has to have all those qualifications, and more. He is called upon to work long and uncertain hours, often under difficult and sometimes exasperating conditions, and to perform multitudinous functions with a smile, with pleasant good humor, with inflexibility when he's right, and with intelligent understanding at all times.

Naturally, with requirements for a position so extremely rigorous, it might likewise be assumed that the remuneration would be equally exceptional — that a well-qualified inspector, doing his job conscientiously, would be paid on a scale commensurate with his duties and obligations and special training.

But such an assumption would be entirely unwarranted!

National Schedule Low

The hard, unvarnished and obviously unjust truth is that the electrical inspector, almost without exception, not only here in New England but elsewhere in the nation, in big cities and small, is one of the lowest paid specialists in any industry anywhere. This deplorable situation is borne out conclusively in statistics and classifications of municipal inspectors throughout the country.

The electrical inspectors of New York City not long ago compiled the salary schedules and a resume of work assignments of inspectors in the United States. There are various methods of compensation, but all are uniformly low, compared with the remuneration for similarly highly-trained experts in other fields of endeavor.

The wages and incomes of those engaged in electrical work, from apprentice to engineer and contractor, have risen steadily over the years. But those of the electrical inspectors have lagged woefully behind, so much so that in some instances the lowliest electrical worker receives as much or more than the inspector responsible to the public for the entire electrical work performed in his area of jurisdiction.

1956 International President

Larry O. Trim, 1956 international president, served four years in the merchant marines in the engineering division. He then became interested in the electrical profession, entering this field as a helper of Ben Wheater, junior past president of the Southwestern Section.

Mr. Trim was the president of the Southwestern Section in 1947. He is also past president of the Burbank City Employees Association. He is a past master of Burbank Lodge No. 406 F. & A.M., serving in that office during 1954. He is a member of the American Legion and Veterans of Foreign Wars.

In 1934, he successfully passed a competitive examination with twelve applicants for the position of electrical inspector in the city of Burbank, California, and in May 1938, was appointed to that position. He was a registered electrical engineer in the state of California, and an accredited teacher for electrical subjects for the adult division.

While extracting the utmost in hours and effort from the electrical inspector, most communities have been negligent in rewarding this skilled, faithful and most important public servant, upon whose integrity rests the responsibility for making sure that all electrical work in the community meets fully the requirements of the law, and is safe and proper in every respect.

Who's To Blame

Just where the blame lies for this unfortunate condition is difficult to pinpoint. There is apparently no unified opposition to an improved salary schedule for qualified inspectors. But like the weather, "everybody discusses it, but nobody does anything about it." Certainly the electrical contractors, who come into direct contact with the inspectors, and constantly rely upon them for advice, would unanimously favor an income boost for them.

"I don't understand how it is possible to obtain the services of men of such ability for the money most communities pay," declared one leading electrical contractor. "They are responsible for the final decisions on every electrical installation, regardless of size and complexity, and yet their wages are less than those of most men on the job."

The inspectors, for the most part, are hard-working, competent men, who take pride in their work, and who could do much better financially in private business, and yet who stick to their jobs, conscientiously, at personal sacrifice to themselves and their families.

Deserve Better Treatment

"I think there should be some sort of concerted action to get them an increase. Most communities levy a fee for electrical permits and inspections, and since these departments are usually self-sustaining, there should be a division of income from permits in favor of the inspector much greater than at present."

"In my opinion, he should get a raise even if municipalities have to dip into the general fund to provide it — there is no public official who deserves it more, or who has been neglected for so long. The electrical industry itself should be a little ashamed that the salaries of its competent inspectors lag so far behind the wages paid everyone else concerned with the installation of electrical equipment."

In this Electronic Era, when almost everything depends upon electricity, the real life-blood of production, of jobs and comfortable living, the work of the electrical inspector has become increasingly complex. He must know what he's doing what's right, if disaster is to be prevented.

The electrical inspector has become something more than just a person who looks over a simple wiring system and gives it a cursory okay, as perhaps in the early days. The inspector today is usually a full-time official, with not enough hours in the working day to meet all of the mounting demands of his time. He has become more than an inspector, he is almost a "municipal adviser."

Helpful To Contractors

The busy electrical contractor doesn't always have time to keep himself posted on regulations of the various communities in which he may have jobs underway simultaneously. He relies upon the electrical inspector to advise him, in advance, of what he may or may not do. Furthermore, the inspector often comes up, gratuitously of course, with ideas

The 1958 Southern Section celebrates something.

1957 International President

Harold S. Morr, manager of the Utah Fire Rating Bureau, was employed as a valuation engineer with the Utah Power & Light Company after graduation from the University of Utah. He obtained a position as an engineer in the Salt Lake office of the Board of Fire Underwriters of the Pacific in 1936.

As a result of his interest in the electrical profession, Mr. Morr became a member of the Utah Chapter in 1943. He served as chairman of the Utah Chapter in 1945. In 1952 he was elected as one of the active members of the executive committee of the Northwestern Section and after serving for two years, was elected Northwestern Section president. Throughout his association with the Northwestern Section he had served on a number of code panel committees, acting as chairman of Panel 10 for three years. He also served on the Code Clearing House Committee.

He is a licensed professional engineer, Fire Protection Branch, under the Utah State law. He was a member of the NFPA Advisory Engineering Council, charter member of the Society for Fire Protection Engineers, member of the Pacific Coast-Intermountain Association of Fire Chiefs, and treasurer of the Salt Lake Safety Council.

that enable the contractor to do a better job at less cost.

"We have never encountered an inspector who wasn't willing to work with us and help us," asserted another prominent electrical contractor. "I will admit that sometimes we haven't always agreed, but I can honestly say that no inspector ever insisted on what wasn't right, and many times, with us at least, has come up with solutions to problems that were better than we had devised ourselves."

"I can recall any number of instances where the inspector has helped us do a better job for our customer, even though the customer was at first reluctant to spend the additional money. We as contractors naturally want to do the best possible installation but understandably one big obstacle often is the unwillingness of the customer to pay for more than the barest minimum."

"Time after time the inspector has helped us convince a customer that his own best interests would be served by doing the proper electrical job at the outset. The inspector's knowledge of regulations, his experience with other jobs, frequently proves the clincher where our own best arguments are of no avail."

The classification describing the duties of inspectors doesn't mention it, but the inspector soon discovers that his easy familiarity with the *National Electrical Code* and local restrictions often proves helpful to electrical contractors in avoiding costly mistakes, in getting a job underway properly so that changes aren't necessary later, in making sure that all requirements are met, and that nothing is overlooked that might subsequently prove embarrassing or expensive.

Rely On Inspector

Said one of Boston's top electrical contractors: "We rely on the inspector a lot, and get his advice constantly. One thing that we have learned and we are proud to pay tribute to the inspectors for it: they are always eager to help us and the other contractors, to avoid errors, rather than insisting on their correction after they are made. No one can know everything, and neither can any organization, however efficient."

"The electrical inspectors we have encountered know their jobs. We rely on them to perform them. It is of the utmost importance to us because our work involves large expenditures and a small error of fact or judgment could prove costly. The electrical inspector plays an important part in every electrical installation — without him all would be confusion, with each going his own way, to the detriment of all."

"I certainly believe, and I know that my colleagues feel likewise, that something should be done to make the inspector's job worthwhile financially so that it will continue to attract men of ability and integrity and sound judgment." — Reprinted from and by permission of *New England Electrical News*, August 1955. Published in *News-Bulletin*, November 1955.

Ladies auxiliaries began appearing throughout IAEI in the 1950s. Pictured are the elected officers of the auxiliary to the Eastern Section during this decade. *Left to right*: Secretary Mrs. Hyman Ferber, Brooklyn, New York; Committee Woman Mrs. John King, Providence, Rhode Island; Committee Woman Mrs. Elmer T. Quinn, South Mantoloking, New Jersey; Chairman Mr. George Bostley, Albany, New York; President of the newly formed ladies auxiliary Mrs. Frederick K. Sullivan, Belmont, Massachusetts; and Committee Woman Mrs. J. D. O'Connell, Yonkers, New York.

1958 International President

Dewey L. Johnson, superintendent of electrical affairs, Department of Electrical Affairs, Atlanta, Georgia, struck out on his own at 17, traveling to Jacksonville, Florida, to be employed with the Atlantic Coast Line Railroad in its shops. He eventually worked himself up to the position of locomotive fireman. Injuries from World War II prevented him from returning to his former position, so he was employed as an electrician's helper in the roundhouse shop. Attempting to further his education, he began a correspondence course in electricity.

Mr. Johnson is a charter member of the Southern Section and served as president of the Southern Section in 1944. He served as chairman of the Georgia Chapter consecutively from 1936 to 1939. In 1937, he was elected to the executive committee of the Southern Section and in 1940 because its chairman. He also was a member of the IAEI Standing Committee on Fire and Accident Prevention and Investigation of Fires and Accidents Caused by Electricity, and in 1937 was the chairman of the committee on Article 640, Southern Section.

He had served on the NFPA electrical committee as a representative to the United States Conference of Mayors, and was a member of code-making panels 1 and 3.

Important change: break from NFPA

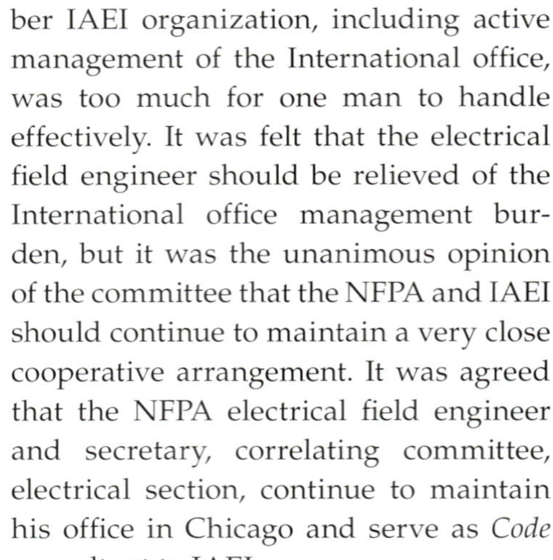

Careful attention should be given by the membership of the International Association of Electrical Inspectors to the recent change in administrative affairs as they relate to the responsibilities of the secretary/treasurer in the Chicago office. This change was brought about through the joint action of the National Fire Protection Association and the IAEI in separating the responsibilities of the electrical field service engineer, NFPA, from that of the secretary/treasurer. For more than thirty years, the joint office, together with all of its duties, had been under the jurisdiction of one individual. This is now completely changed.

The continual growth and expanding operations of the association required that the whole structural operations of the International office be reviewed for the purpose of alleviating a chronic condition caused by the increased work load and demands for the services of the staff officers, increased travel and long absences from the office. As a result, the executive council IAEI, at their annual meeting in Los Angeles, May 23, 1957, adopted a resolution to set up a joint committee of the NFPA and the IAEI to study the problems of the staff officials of the International office that were directly involved with the NFPA.

On December 16, 1957, at the NFPA's electrical field service committee meeting held in New York, it was the consensus that the dual responsibilities of the NFPA electrical field engineer and secretary/treasurer of the 9,000-member IAEI organization, including active management of the International office, was too much for one man to handle effectively. It was felt that the electrical field engineer should be relieved of the International office management burden, but it was the unanimous opinion of the committee that the NFPA and IAEI should continue to maintain a very close cooperative arrangement. It was agreed that the NFPA electrical field engineer and secretary, correlating committee, electrical section, continue to maintain his office in Chicago and serve as *Code* consultant to IAEI.

The executive council, IAEI, in session at their annual meeting at the Palmer House, Chicago, Illinois, May 18-20, 1958, after a full and deliberate review of the NFPA-IAEI Joint Committee Report, concluded that this arrangement was the most acceptable to them; and further, that the administration of the International office would come under the direct supervision and full responsibility of the newly elected secretary/treasurer, IAEI. The affairs of the association which covered membership, involving dues notices, dues payments, and so forth, the publication and editing of the *News-Bulletin*, the annual proceedings, bi-annual membership directory, and other strictly IAEI publications, the handling of correspondence concerning the functions of the association and advertising in the *News-Bulletin*, would all come under the jurisdiction of the secretary/treasurer IAEI.

Reprinted from *News-Bulletin*, July 1958.

Outgoing 1959 Southwestern President Chester Hefner congratulates newly-elected Southwestern President Ernest Nelson at the 1959 Southwestern Section meeting in Santa Rosa, California. Mr. Nelson was the chief electrical inspector of San Leandro, California, and also performed the engineering function pertaining to city faculties such as on street lighting and traffic signals. He was a member of NFPA, IMSA, IES, Pacific Coast Electrical Association (code committee) and the East Bay Uniform Electrical Code Committee.

1959 International President

Rene LaBelle, from Roxboro, Quebec, holds the distinct privilege of being the first member of the Canadian Section to become international president. He was elected in 1959. LaBelle is the second Canadian to hold this high office—the late A.G. Hall, who was a member of the Northwestern Section at the time, was international president in 1935. Mr. LaBelle was also the first president of the Canadian Section in 1954, after the section received its charter at the Silver Jubilee meeting in 1953.

Mr. LaBelle began his electrical career in 1927. In 1932 he went into the contracting business under the firm name of Rene LaBelle and Company Limited. In 1940, he was appointed by the Foundation Company of Canada to direct the electrical works of Shipshaw Power Development at Shipshaw, Quebec, which at the time was considered the largest hydro-electric power plant in the world. By early 1945 he was called by the Minister of Labor of Quebec to act as assistant chief inspector of the Board of Examiners of Electricians of the province. A few months later he was appointed by the provincial government as general director of service and chief electrical examiner for the same board. He was elected a member of the Provincial Parliament in 1936, and resigned in 1939 to return to private duty.

In July 1958, he was elected mayor of his home town of Roxboro, Quebec, a city part of greater Montreal.

1959 E.F. Cogan

Everett F. Cogan, acting secretary/treasurer of the IAEI since November 12, 1957, at the sudden death of Charles Smith, was elected to the office of secretary/treasurer by action of the executive council in 1958, a position he held until 1962.

After graduation from high school, Mr. Cogan spent two years working with the Southern Pacific Railroad as a carpenter and steel car repairman apprentice; he then entered the engineering college with the University of Detroit to study electrical engineering. He returned to the Southern Pacific Railroad and was employed as an electrician. In 1940, he was employed with the city of New Orleans as an electrical inspector. Following America's entry into World War II, he resigned from this position to work as an assistant electrical engineer with the United States Navy Bureau of Ships, 8th Naval District. In 1944, he was employed by the Consolidated Vultee Aircraft Corporation as an industrial and electrical engineer. In 1946, he resumed his work with the city of New Orleans as an electrical inspector.

In 1948, he became assistant electrical engineer to the late George Welman in the electrical department, Louisiana Fire Prevention Rating Bureau in New Orleans. In 1952, he resigned from this position and moved with his family to Chicago to accept the position of technical assistant secretary in the International office.

He was a registered professional electrical engineer, a member of NFPA, and the American Institute of Electrical Engineers. At the time of his death in 1972, he was employed by the U.S. Coast Guard.

1960 International President

Peter J. Hicks, Jr., served as public service engineer and chief electrical inspector for the city of Providence, RI, for forty-five years. He was appointed electrical inspector in 1928, and became chief electrical inspector in 1944, and was named public service engineer in 1949. He also served as deputy director of building inspection from 1957 until retiring in 1968. He was a past president of the Roger Williams Chapter, past regional and national officer of the International Municipal Signal Association, and was a member of the Rhode Island Board of Examiners of Electricians for twenty-eight years.

He was a member of the *NEC* board, which had the responsibility for writing the electrical code throughout the U.S. He was a member of the Underwriters' Laboratories Review Board, and organized and taught at the first school for electrical inspectors in the U.S. at the former Rhode Island Technical Vocational School.

Mr. Hicks was a member of the Rhode Island Society of Professional Engineers, the American Institute of Electrical Engineers, the National Fire Protection Association, and the National Association of Power Engineers. He was also an honorary member of Local 99, International Brotherhood of Electrical Workers.

1960-1963…
The Beginning of Change

The stakes were always high in the postwar years. Everything meant so much; everything counted—including a feeling that President John F. Kennedy's youthful confidence and jet-set glamour transmuted into a different, more cool and cosmopolitan style. Although our crusades during the sixties were not always well-advised, our idealism sometimes an obvious cloak for less worthy motives, whether we were rebels or conformists, we believed. Today, perhaps wisely, we live with multiple truths and narratives, a consumer's array of identities and attitudes with few final choices required, yet we continue to return, fascinated, to the voices and images of an earlier time—Elvis on the Ed Sullivan Show; Kennedy, grave-faced, elegant and masterful during the Cuban missile crisis; Martin Luther King transfigured by a dream before the Washington monument—those electrifying moments when the whole world seemed to stop, then change forever.

1960 Kennedy/Nixon presidential debate.

Financial and Membership Growth Reflected in IAEI Report

Members and guests attending the six annual section meetings, International Association of Electrical Inspectors, were visibly impressed with the glowing report made by the international secretary-treasurer on the progress of their association. It was with a great deal of satisfaction and pleasure, as well as sober reflection, that they listened to an account of the healthy financial status of the IAEI and the continued and steady growth of its membership. Evidence of complete approval was manifested by those present, expressing their acceptance of the effective work accomplished by the IAEI's executive council through its various committees.

1960 Curtis R. Kennedy

Curtis R. Kennedy, chief electrical inspector, Guilford County, Greensboro, North Carolina, was the Southern Section president for 1960. Mr. Kennedy is a member of the Ellis Cannady Chapter of North Carolina and has been active in the Southern Section, serving on the executive committee for a number of years, as a member of various *Code* committees, and on several of the section program committees. He was elected second vice president for 1958 and first vice president for 1959. — Reprinted from *News-Bulletin*, January 1960.

Perhaps the one major item of the secretary-treasurer's entire report that may be singled out for special attention was the financial picture covering the 1957-60 period. It may be recalled that in 1957 the association was faced with an impending financial crisis that required immediate attention and an immediate solution.

In that year, the financial report, as prepared by the auditing firm, showed a $4,000 deficit due to the fact that expenses in operating the association affairs exceeded the income derived from membership dues, advertising and other sources. It was quite evident that something had to be done, and quickly, if the association was to continue the services rendered to its membership, maintain office personnel and also provide additional revenues to meet increasing costs.

The executive council, after much study and deliberation, presented to the membership, a proposed dues increase which included the active, associate and type F memberships. It was the strong belief of the representatives of the various sections constituting the executive council that herein was the solution that would relieve this critical situation. The council was unanimous in its decision and confident that the membership would rise to the challenge and support the action of that body.

Drastic economies were effected in the International office to reduce expenditures and this resulted in an improved situation during 1958 as the auditor's report indicated. Operating expenses decreased and the report showed a slight gain of income over expenses.

The adoption by the executive council of recommendations made by the dues structure committee, followed by the ratification of the proposals by the active membership for a 1959 dues increase, resulted in a cash reserve balance by the end of 1959 in the amount of $30,000. By August 1960, the reserve funds showed a healthy balance of some $70,000 invested

1961 International President

George C. Monroe, 1961 president, was born in Chicksha, Oklahoma. He worked for Westinghouse Electric Manufacturing Company in Pittsburgh, Pennsylvania, in the switchboard department while attending night school until 1920. By 1952, he was recognized as a fire protection engineer and became a charter member of the Society of Fire Protection Engineers. In 1956, he was appointed district engineer for the Missouri Inspection Bureau in Western Missouri. He was appointed branch superintendent of the Spring district for the bureau in 1956.

In 1929, he became a member of the Missouri-Kansas Chapter. In 1938 he was elected to the Western Section executive committee and served as president of the section in 1946. The West Virginia Chapter was chartered during that year. He served as chairman of the chapters affairs committee of the section for 10 years, during which time the St. Louis, New Mexico, Michigan, Minnesota, and South Dakota chapters were organized and chartered. He served as chairman of Article 422 code committee under the old code. He has served on several IAEI code panels since that time, and was elected to the executive council in 1955.

in United States Bonds and United States Treasury Notes with slightly more that $20,000 available in the general and membership accounts.

Never in the past history of the IAEI has the association been in such a healthy and sound financial condition. It is no wonder that a spirit of optimism for the future growth and progress of the association permeated those members who were present to hear this report at the annual section meetings.

International President Peter J. Hicks, Jr. predicted that the next decade will witness astounding developments in the association, particularly in the advancement of the status of the electrical inspector. It is his candid opinion that the educational program, already greatly accelerated in the Southwestern Section, will provide the impetus that will assure the IAEI of reaching its long sought goal in elevating the electrical inspector to his professional status in the electrical industry.

Reprinted from *News-Bulletin*, January 1961.

1962 outgoing Canadian Section President R. Pare handing over the reins to the incoming president for 1963, Mr. J. E. Edwards at the 1962 Canadian Section meeting in Montreal, Quebec.

1962 International President

Everett E. Carlton received a bachelor of science degree in electrical engineering in 1933, and then completed one year of graduate study. He became a member of the Southern California Chapter in 1942, and in 1951 was elected to the executive committee of the Southwestern Section and served as president of the Southwestern Section in 1954. He was elected to the IAEI executive council in 1956.

He was a member of the American Institute of Electrical Engineers, registered professional engineer in California, member of the electrical council of Underwriters' Laboratories, Inc., and also a member of code-making panels 12 and 13 of the *NEC* committee of the NFPA association, serving as chairman of panel 12.

He represented IAEI on various committees, including the NFPA committee on machine tool electrical standards, technical sub-committees on three-phase motor protection, raceway fill and heating of conductors, and study of underwater swimming pool lighting.

1963 Hawaii Chapter. The chapter was granted its charter in 1956.

March 16, 1960, meeting of the Western New England Chapter at Bridgeport, Connecticut. *Left to right*: George J. Michel, chairman 1959; John M. Civitello, second vice chairman 1960; James F. Meehan, vice chairman 1960; Kenneth L. Babcock, chairman 1960; Charles J. Hosking, member executive committee; and Charles Berlepsch, Sr., member executive committee.

1962 L.E. LaFehr

L. E. LaFehr became the managing director of the IAEI in 1962, and was a member of the board of directors from 1954. In 1973, the title of managing director was changed to executive vice president as a result of action taken by the board of directors and as ratified by the membership to make his title commensurate with his duties.

His efforts to aid membership have been numerous. LaFehr was instrumental in establishing free membership to senior retired members. IAEI also prospered in other ways under his directions: from 9,000 to 14,500 members; from virtually no reserve funds to a comfortable reserve; a record of fifteen years with no deficits; efficient office procedures including IAEI's ownership of its own computer which manages the membership roster and provides addressing services to the chapters, sections, and to the electrical industry; the growth of the *IAEI News* from a small periodical to a well-known electrical trade magazine.

LaFehr's close alliance with other organizations such as the National Fire Protection Association (NFPA), National Electrical Manufacturers Association (NEMA), International Brotherhood of Electrical Workers (IBEW), Occupational Safety and Health Administration (OSHA), National Academy of Code Administrators (NACA), National Conference of States on Building Codes and Standards (NCSBCS), National Electrical Contractors Association (NECA), and Underwriters Laboratories' Inc., (UL), has contributed much to his status.

He was also a leader in IAEI's effort to cooperate with the three building official organizations in education/certification programs for electrical inspectors: International Conference of Building Officials (ICBO), Building Officials and Code Administrators (BOCA) and Southern Building Code Congress International (SBCCI).

1963 International President

Cliff Atkins began his early electrical career with a local contractor immediately following his high school graduation. After ten years of service with this firm, he resigned his position and became affiliated with a manufacturer's agent remaining in this capacity until 1935. In 1942, he became interested in the electrical inspection field and accepted a position as an electrical and safety engineer for the state of Oregon, Bureau of Labor.

He became a member of the Northwestern Section in 1942 and with the organization of the Oregon Chapter, became one of its charter members. His active interest in the affairs of the Oregon Chapter resulted in his appointment to a number of committees including chairmanships of the publicity and membership committees. His enthusiasm quickly resulted in his election to the executive committee of the chapter and eventually to the positions of vice chairman and chairman.

He was a member of NFPA code-making panel 10, and also a member of the technical subcommittee on swimming pool lighting. Besides maintaining a lively interest in the IAEI, he also contributed in his memberships to the Oregon Electric Club, the BPO Elks, the International Brotherhood of Electrical Workers, Local 48, and he served for four years as a member of the examining board and was chairman of commissioners for the local lighting district.

NEWS-BULLETIN
INTERNATIONAL ASSOCIATION
ELECTRICAL INSPECTORS

Their Voice

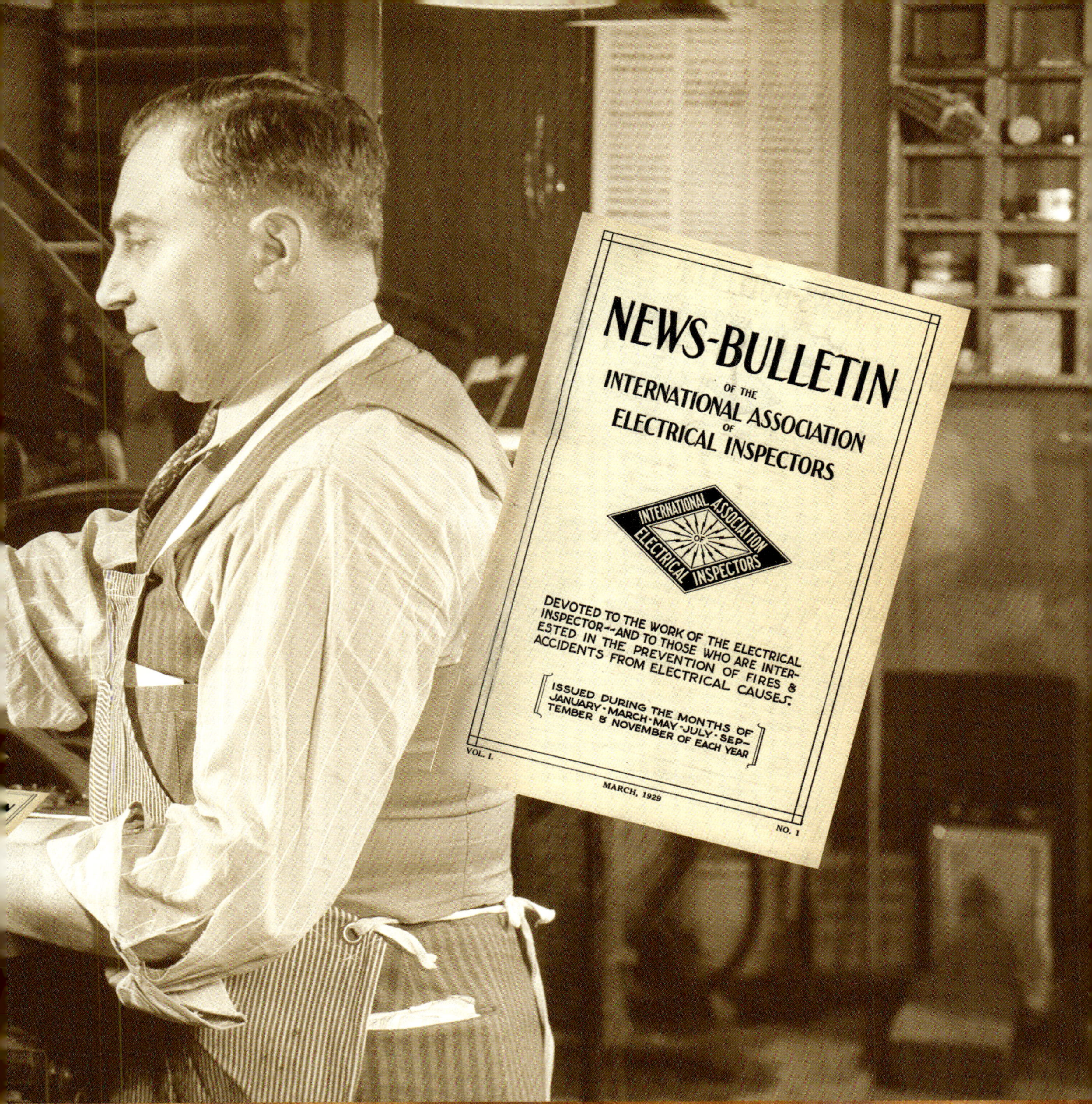

NEWS-BULLETIN
OF THE
INTERNATIONAL ASSOCIATION
OF
ELECTRICAL INSPECTORS

INTERNATIONAL ASSOCIATION OF ELECTRICAL INSPECTORS

DEVOTED TO THE WORK OF THE ELECTRICAL INSPECTOR--AND TO THOSE WHO ARE INTERESTED IN THE PREVENTION OF FIRES & ACCIDENTS FROM ELECTRICAL CAUSES.

ISSUED DURING THE MONTHS OF JANUARY·MARCH·MAY·JULY·SEPTEMBER & NOVEMBER OF EACH YEAR

VOL. I. MARCH, 1929 NO. 1

They found their voice in an unassuming publication called the *News-Bulletin*, and in it they shared information, facts, shortcuts, and safety—always safety requirements. As they shared, their voice grew louder and more persuasive and others joined the mission.

1941 January Issue

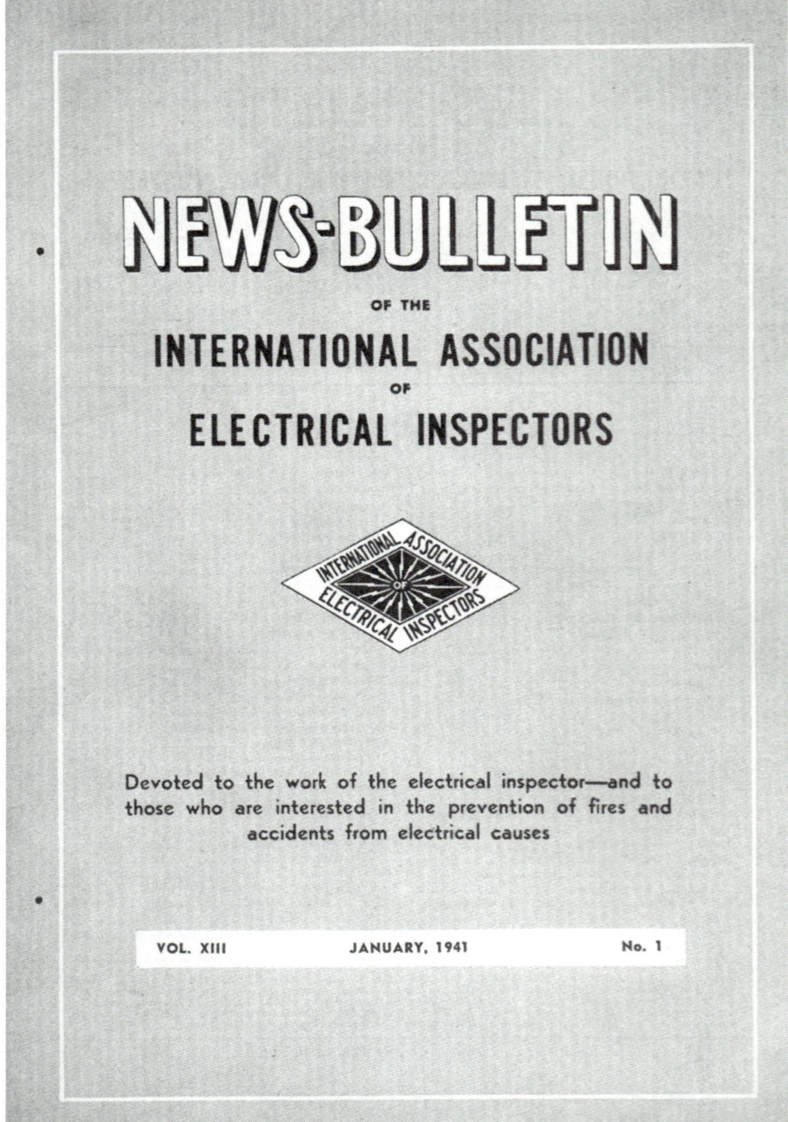

DATES AHEAD

Electrical Council of Underwriters' Laboratories, Inc., Chicago, Ill., Underwriters' Laboratories, 207 E. Ohio St., April 9, 1929.

National Fire Protection Association, Peabody Hotel, Memphis, Tenn., May 13, 14, 15, and 16, 1929. Mr. Franklin Wentworth, Managing Director, 60 Batterymarch St., Boston, Mass.

Western Section, I. A. E. I., Book-Cadillac Hotel, Detroit, Mich., August 26, 27, and 28, 1929. Mr. Wm. S. Boyd, Secretary, 175 W. Jackson Blvd., Chicago, Ill.

Northwestern Section, I. A. E. I., Hotel Vancouver, Vancouver, B. C., September 9, 10, and 11, 1929. Mr. F. D. Weber, Secretary, 414 Lumbermen's Bldg., Portland, Ore.

Southwestern Section, I. A. E. I., Sacramento, Cal., September 18, 19, and 20, 1929. Mr. C. W. Mitchell, Secretary, 914 Merchants Exchange Bank Bldg., San Francisco, Cal.

Southern Section, I. A. E. I., Atlanta, Ga., September 17 and 18, 1929. Mr. C. S. Crawford, Secretary, P. O. Box 36, Gretna, La.

Eastern Section, I. A. E. I., Atlantic City, N. J., October (Date not set). Mr. R. Walker, Secretary, 16 Court St., Brooklyn, N. Y.

The "Dates Ahead" column debuted in the March 1929 magazine with a small listing of the section meetings, along with a few dates regarding other organizations closely associated with IAEI. In the beginning, there were few chapters, so the column was relatively small, and included many events that were happening in the electrical industry. Today, this column encompasses two pages and lists happenings throughout IAEI — from annual section meetings to local division socials.

The *IAEI News* is the official organ of the International Association of Electrical Inspectors. First published in 1929, this periodical has reached the electrical inspector without interruption on a bi-monthly basis. Up until a few years ago, it was known as the *News-Bulletin*. With a new name came a brand-new format, lending itself better to the scheme of similar publications in the electrical industry.

Well-edited and with a wealth of current and pertinent information, this publication is a vital facet in the transmission of timely information not only to the electrical inspector but also to those associated with him in the electrical field.

Today the *News* ranks on the level of contemporary trade magazines such as *Electrical West*, *Lighting*, *Qualified Contractor*, and *Electrical Construction and Maintenance*.

Through its editorial content, the News aims at the dissemination of electrical safety by presenting technical articles that deal with problems encountered in the inspection field; with greater safety in using better wiring methods, etc.; with explanations of the more complicated sections and articles of the *National Electrical Code*; and other similar topics. The writers are prominent men in the electrical field. In addition, the *News* presents current listings of laboratory standards of electrical devices, materials, and appliances.

Important features to the membership are the dates of the chapter and section meetings, and the reviews of the activities of these meetings. True-and-false questions based on the *Code* are a regular item of interest. In addition, the *News* gives members an opportunity to state their opinions publicly, before the entire membership.

In short, for the electrical inspector of today, whose time is at a premium, this publication provides a ready reference for the latest data, an invaluable asset in every sense of the word. Membership in IAEI includes a subscription to the *News* at no further cost.

I appreciate this magazine to the extent of having copies of the year clothbound for my library.

I could expand on the content much further, however, I believe this brief reference will suffice for our present purposes.

Reprinted from *The Electrical Inspector*, by A. H. Welkin, 1969.

First article to appear in *News-Bulletin*, March 1929.

Talking Picture Equipment

Description of Circuits, Voltages Used and Methods of Installation

by Warren E. Bostwick

In this article no attempt is made to go into the details or give a technical description of the electrical apparatus used in connection with a talking picture installation and only those points which are thought interesting or instructive from the standpoint of the electrical inspector are taken up.

The equipment on the market will differ greatly. The method of running wires between units will vary from the use of flexible cords to lead covered wires in rigid conduits. The amplifier may be a portable type enclosed in a wood cabinet or consist of panels fastened to an angle iron frame work and securely anchored in place. This article will describe one of the better types; the safety provisions recommended, however, may be applied to all where connection is made to lighting supply circuits or storage batteries used.

To the ordinary motor driven motion picture projector, in order to run talking pictures, must be added the following apparatus:

(1) A device for converting sound from either mechanical cut records (ordinary photograph records) into an electric current; and where the sound record consists of photographic impressions on the edge of the motion picture film, the device causes current variations in a closed circuit, these variations representing the variations in the sound which is to be reproduced. This device is termed "the pick-up."

(2) An amplifier to amplify the variations in current reproduced from either type of sound record.

(3) Loud speakers which convert the electrical energy back into sound.

These are the three principal units required.

The motor driving the motion picture projector must be changed for one designed to run with minimum variations in speed. The motor is also equipped with one or two fly wheels which will tend to further eliminate variations in speed. The sound record must be run very smoothly; the same motor, of course, drives both the projector and the sound record.

American actor and director H.B. Warner behind a movie camera, circa 1929.

Phonograph Record Pick-Up

Where the pick-up current is generated by a transmitter and mechanical cut records operated on a turn table geared to the motion picture projector, the voltage in the pick-up current is very low. Wires from the transmitter to the amplifying panel are usually No. 18 or No. 20 lead covered wires in one-half inch conduit, the lead covered wire in conduit being used as a protection against mechanical injury and for operating reasons. The hazards of this circuit are negligible.

Photographic Record Pick-Up

In this type of sound record, with photographic impressions on the edge of motion picture film, variations of currents in a closed circuit are produced by means of a photoelectric cell. This photoelectric cell is a selenium wire enclosed in a tube from which the air has been exhausted.

A photographic sound record is made on the film when the picture is taken, a narrow strip on the edge of the film running its entire length provides space for recording sounds. The picture shown on the screen will, therefore, be slightly narrower where this method of reproduction is used. Briefly such records are produced as follows:

A ray of light from the mirror of a galvanometer is reflected on the photographic film. The field coil of the galvanometer is energized by a circuit in which a microphone is connected. Sound waves striking the diaphragm of the microphone are thereby reproduced by movements of the beam of light as photographic impressions on the film. The swing of the ray of light is confined to that part of the film used for the sound record and the impressions appear on the film as a series of waves of varying height and shape running crosswise of the sound record space on the film.

In order to reproduce these photographic impressions as sounds, the photoelectric cell is inserted in an amplifying circuit. A small incandescent light, called an exciting lamp, has its rays focused on an aperture over the photographic record on the film. These rays pass through the film to the photoelectric cell and as the film moves, the photographic impressions cause

variations in the amount of light striking the photoelectric cell. The resistance of the cell changes with the light variations and causes corresponding variations in current strength, thereby reproducing the variations of the sounds as recorded.

The exciting lamp circuit is supplied from a storage battery at 8 to 12 volts. This circuit should be fused and protected from mechanical injury.

Amplifier Panel

The amplifier panel must, for operating reasons, be located in the projection room. The first stage of an amplifier consists of very small radio tubes of which the filaments are lighted from storage batteries and the plate circuit supplied from 45 volt B battery. This stage is a separate panel but is usually mounted on the same framework as the main amplifier. In the case of the pick-up from photographic records using the photoelectric cell, current from the amplifier within the cell enclosures is taken directly to the main amplifier. For operating reasons and to protect from mechanical injury these wires are No. 18 or No. 20 lead covered and run in conduit. The voltage and current are so low that no particular inspection restrictions are usually required.

The main amplifier may consist of from one to three panels depending upon the size of the theatre and the volume of sound required. All panels are mounted on the same framework. On these panels are mounted tubes with amplifying transformers, filament lighting transformers, transformers and rectifying tubes for supplying up to 750 volts D. C. for the plate circuits of amplifying tubes. This apparatus is generally mounted on the back of the amplifying panel, although in some types, these tubes are on the face of the board. These tubes sometimes get very hot in operation and should be guarded.

The back of the amplifying panel is enclosed in a wire mesh or sheet metal cabinet. A door permitting access to the rear of this panel is equipped with a door switch which interrupts the 110-volt supply and thereby cutting off the entire panel when the door is opened. The door switch is a necessary requirement and it will also appear reasonable that the enclosures of the rear of the panel be made of sheet metal and fireproof.

The 110-volt A. C. supplied to the amplifier panel is No. 14 wire run in one-half inch conduit terminating in a junction box at the bottom of the amplifying panel and from this point runs

NEWS-BULLETIN 21

outside the transformer vault and wired in conduit under the floor to a circuit-breaker on switchboard, and with fuses in the transformer room in the leads to the two transformers and in each of the three leads to the motor, satisfies the requirements of the code. (Int. No. 12.)

N. E. C. OFFICIAL INTERPRETATIONS

The standard procedure of the Electrical Committee provides a means for obtaining an official interpretation of any Code rule. This privilege is open to anyone and requires simply the submitting of five copies of the matter upon which an interpretation is desired to the Chairman of the Electrical Committee, Mr. A. R. Small, 109 Leonard St., New York, N. Y.

Interpretation No. 28

Question: Over the top of a large switchboard a large pull box has been installed. This box is approximately 42 ft. long by 6 ft. wide by 29½ in. deep and contains 221 wires ranging in sizes from No. 14 to 1,000,000 CM. all rubber covered. The wires are neatly arranged, being racked on insulated iron bars with 9 in. vertical separation and practically no horizontal separation, the wires being carried horizontally through the box.

Does this box constitute a location "as in the rear of switchboards," as mentioned in section 1302-d, so that the Code would require covering the wires in the box with flame-proof outer covering?

Finding: No.

Interpretation No. 29

Question: Does paragraph (a) of section 404 of the 1928 edition of the National Electrical Code prohibit service conductors being run in attics?

Finding: The paragraph specifies that service entrance equipment shall be located "as near as practicable" to the point where the service wires enter the building. The paragraph may not be interpreted as prohibiting the running of service conductors, fused or unfused, through attic spaces when it is impracticable to locate the service equipment or the point of entrance of the service wires at points where the running of conductors through the attic space can be avoided. The authority enforcing the National Electrical Code for the territory in which a particular premises is located is presumably the judge of what is "impracticable" in this instance.

QUESTIONS AND ANSWERS

Question: I would like very much to obtain authoritative information as to the fire hazard caused by a drop in voltage on an ordinary 110-volt lighting circuit.

If we obtain 110 volts from the transformer, using No. 4 solid copper wire from the transformer to the main switch, and the total load throughout the various branch circuits in the building is 10 KW. At no time are all of the lights turned on. I assume that it would be proper to use 80% of the total load in arriving at the normal load.

If 80% of the total load should be used, would the drop in voltage at any point in the building cause the branch wires or mains to heat? In other words, does a drop in voltage cause wires to heat?

Answer: Voltage drop, in itself, does not cause heating of the wires. Of course, it is a fact that the more current you carry on a wire, the greater the I^2R loss and the greater the drop in voltage. The heating of wires, however, is caused by overloading the wires. I note in the case you cite that a No. 4 wire is connected to a 10 KW load. Assuming that only 80% of this load is in use at one time, you would then have approximately 73 amperes on a wire whose maximum carrying capacity is only 70 amperes, and if at any time the load should exceed 80% of the connected load, this overload in amperes would be still further increased.

I would be inclined to believe that the heating you refer to is due to an overload on wires.

Question: I have been told that it is contrary to the National Electrical Code to use Edison plug fuses on a 220-volt single phase motor. Some inspectors say you can, some say you can't. Will you please let me know.

Answer: This question is covered by paragraph 803-f of the 1928 Code which reads: "Approved plugs (or cartridge fuses in approved casings for Edison plug cutouts) not exceeding 125 volts, but including any feeder or circuit of a system having a

In the July 1929 issue of the *News-Bulletin*, leaders within the IAEI began responding to code questions to assist readers and members in understanding the requirements of the *National Electrical Code*. The standard procedure of the Electrical Committee of NFPA, which was later dissolved and formed into the code panels that we know of today, provided a means for obtaining an official interpretation of any *Code* rule. In 2003, IAEI's code consultants consist of representatives on the 19 code-making panels of the *NEC*, whose answers are published in the *Focus on the Code* column.

open as bus wires to the primaries of the filaments lighting and plate voltage transformers.

If the theatre is in a D. C. district a motor generator is installed to supply A. C. current for the amplifying panel. As this apparatus does not have to be in the booth for operating purposes it is better placed outside of same.

Speaker Circuit

The plate circuit of the last amplifying tube to the speakers located backstage is usually for operating reasons, run with No. 18 or No. 20 lead covered wire in conduit which terminates in a junction box at some convenient point from which the various speakers are connected by portable cords. This circuit is from 350 to 750 volts at a maximum of 50 watts, the capacity of the amplifying tube. The circuit is ground free due through connections to a 1-to-1 transformer, the impedance of which is very high, mounted on the amplifying panel and connected in the speaker circuit.

The exciting circuit of the dynamic type speakers may be supplied from either a 110-volt A. C. or a 12-volt battery. The maximum number of speakers may be 6, taking 1 ampere of current each. In the case of 110-volt excitations, the speaker frame should be grounded unless entirely out of reach and where the speakers are permanently located conduit should terminate at the speaker terminals.

Operation

Operators must regulate a device called a Fader, which is simply a variable high resistance connected across the pick-up circuit. The volume of each loud speaker is also controlled by a variable high resistance across each speaker circuit. These resistances are connected across the plate circuit of the last amplifying tube and therefore the mounting of these resistances should be a dead front type. The impedance of the 1-to-1 transformer connected in the speaker circuit is very high and although the voltage is that of the plate circuit of the last amplifying tube the probability that accidental contact, with this circuit on the secondary side, of the transformer, would result in serious injury is very small.

EDITORS' PAGE
The Aim of *News-Bulletin*

This official publication of the International Association of Electrical Inspectors is not intended to serve purely as a means of conveying the news of the association to its members. Neither is it intended as an instrument of diversion for the short time necessary to read its contents. Nor is it intended to be either a guide to better inspections or an instruction book on the *National Electrical Code* and its many problems.

Its aim is to awaken in the minds of the members of this organization a conception of those broad principles upon which the International is founded and to instill in them a desire to better understand the reasons for their existence as electrical inspectors and the purposes for which their positions as electrical inspectors were created. To bring them to a consciousness of their position as an essential part of that great industry which has to do with electricity and its many applications and to realize their obligations and responsibilities to this group and to the public which they serve. To develop a comprehension of the structure which they are erecting. To more completely overcome the individuality which has characterized their past and to realize that community of interest which exists between one inspector and all the rest. And to develop a pride in membership and a desire to study and search out those things which spell progress for themselves and their association and act to make these things effective.

This is a world of progress and he who stands still, in reality moves backward. No branch of any industry offers more interesting or more fascinating problems than does the electrical industry and no branch offers a more promising or satisfactory means of advancement and progress.

There is an old saying that in any task undertaken by a group, the individual who puts the most into the work receives the most benefit from it, and this is just as applicable to this work of ours.

The *News-Bulletin* will print the news of the inspection field and it will attempt to offer to the reader some diversion and much instruction and information, but underlying all of these will be this bigger, broader aim.

Reprinted from *News-Bulletin*, May 1929.

Safety Provisions

In addition to applying the present *Code* rules governing wiring in moving picture booths the following additional provisions will tend to eliminate hazards from the life and fire standpoint.

(a) There should be sufficient room in a booth so that the installation of the talking picture equipment will not obstruct working space around projectors or passage to the projection room doors.

(b) Storage batteries and all other equipment which operating conditions permit should be placed outside of booths.

(c) All storage batteries circuits should be properly fused and protected from mechanical injury.

(d) Transformers connected to lighting supply circuits, the rectifying apparatus and all wires in the plate circuits of large amplifying tubes should be enclosed in approved metal cabinets.

(e) Access to cabinet enclosing wires and apparatus connected to the plate circuits of large amplifying tubes should be arranged so that when the cabinet is opened the supply circuit will be disconnected.

(f) Panel framework, and loud speaker frames where the dynamic type is used with an exciting coil connected to regular lighting supply circuits, should be grounded if within reach.

(g) Tubes should be protected by substantial guards.

IAEI Managing Editors 1962-2003

Lou E. LaFehr — 1962
This was the first time they had a managing editor as well as an editor.

Marge V. Davis — 1964

Christine DiCarlo — 1967

L. D. Fisher — 1970

Lydia F. Johnson — 1970

Christine Spatara — 1972
Christine Spatara was formerly the Christine DiCarlo who was editor from1967-1970

Pamela Moroz — 1973

Emily Hildebrand — 1974

Shelly M. Burgan — 1992

Jerralyn Smith — 1992

Kathryn P. Ingley — 1998

IAEI Publicity Committee

John E. Wise, Chairman

This section of the *News-Bulletin* will hereafter be devoted to the activities of the IAEI Publicity Committee. This committee is engaged in preparing and circulating to members such means of publicity as will serve to inform the electrical industry and the public as to the aims, activities, and accomplishments of the association and its members.

From time to time articles headed "News Release" will be included. It is the desire of the committee that the members supply these releases to the local newspapers for publication. For the records of the committee, clippings showing the publication of releases should be forwarded to the association headquarters.

Experience of inspector members in any form of publicity such as newspaper articles, radio talks, lectures, addresses, exhibits, and the like should be sent in for including in this section of the *News-Bulletin*.

High Point of Interest in Electrical Safety Campaign Reached During Fire Prevention Week

Report of Public Relations Committee Activities

By John Wise, Chairman

For the next few years, the electrical safety campaign, being conducted by the International Association of Electrical Inspectors, has increasingly captured public interest. The high point thus far was reached this year during Fire Prevention Week, when more than 3,000 educational, governmental, municipal, civic and commercial organizations joined with the International Association of Electrical Inspectors throughout the country in an effort to influence the public to use electricity safely.

To secure widespread interest and cooperation in this campaign known as "Safeguarding Electrical Service in the Home," a promotional plan was developed. The next step in this program was to create advertising and promotional material designed to induce outside groups to actively participate in our electrical safety campaign. The following campaign was adopted:

Trade and Special Publications

Since a number of groups were extremely large, and were therefore too expensive to reach by direct mail, it was decided to select a number of magazines reaching these fields. As a result, *Safety Education* magazine was selected to reach school superintendents and teachers.

The *Journal of Home Economics* was chosen in order to reach those people who are affiliated in the American Home Economics Association and who are most instrumental in guiding public opinion in home economic and safety matters.

The *Parent Teachers Magazine* was selected in order to reach the officers and active members in the National Parent Teachers Council and some 22,000 affiliated groups.

Fire Protection magazine was selected for the purpose of reaching fire chiefs, marshals, and fire prevention organizations. All of the reputable electrical publications and trade papers reaching fields interested in the sale of electrical appliances carried an appeal to cooperate in this safety work.

Direct Mail

A series of fire prevention letters appealing to different groups to cooperate in Safeguarding Electrical Service in the Home were sent to numerous lists. Each letter was written on red paper, the lower edge of which was burned to make the appeal for cooperation more effective. These letters were sent to electrical inspectors, members of the National Fire Protection Association, special lists of the National Board of Fire Underwriters, the Public Utility Advertising Association, membership, home service

IAEI display at the 1936 American Home Economics Association meeting in Chicago. Commissioner W.A. Jackson and Chas. K. Cregier, chief electrical inspector for the city of Chicago, are sitting in the booth. The booth was part of the public relations committee's effort to raise awareness for Fire Prevention Week. To secure widespread interest and cooperation in this campaign known as "Safeguarding Electric Service in the Home," a promotional plan was developed by this committee that resulted in trade booths, direct mailing, and press releases.

This Advertisement Appeared in the September Issue of Electrical World, Lighting and Lamps, Lamp Buyers Journal, Electrical Dealer, and Electrical Merchandising.

employees, utility companies, Chambers of Commerce and numerous governmental agencies and their branches.

Publicity

Without planning a series of releases to tie into the national and local activities, a great deal of the effectiveness of this campaign would have been lost so a series of releases were developed featuring both the national scope of this electrical safety campaign and local participation. All national news releases were mailed from headquarters and releases relating to local activities were given out by participating organizations to city editors.

A series of feature articles were prepared for editors of home making page in national magazines and syndicate services.

Estimates indicate that 20,000,000 personal or printed messages on electrical safety were delivered to the public during Fire Prevention Week.

50,000 educational charts were distributed.

300,000 Home Inspection Blanks were requested.

78,000 booklets were sent to participants.

2,000 newspaper mats were required to fulfill demand.

2,000,000 reviewed electrical safety film.

Radio stations featured electrical safety talks.

National magazines, utilities, insurance companies and numerous governmental bureaus reprinted material, also trade publications.

3,065 educational, civic, governmental, municipal, and commercial organizations participated during Fire Prevention Week.

Exhibits and displays were prevalent throughout the country.

99,770 advertising messages were sent to members of the electrical industry, urging them to participate.

The International Association of Electrical Inspectors are going ahead with broader plans in the hope that interested electrical groups will participate more vigorously in the future.

Reprinted from *News-Bulletin*, January 1936.

1932 NEWS-BULLETIN 35

THE FORUM — A NEW DEPARTMENT

This new department of News-Bulletin, which is in response to a demand on the part of our readers, offers to members an opportunity to discuss before the entire membership any subject which is of general interest. It is, as its name indicates, a common meeting place for bringing out new thoughts, for commenting on existing subjects or practices, or for developing ideas through an exchange of views. It is possible also that a reader may wish to have discussed by the membership some subject on which he is not well enough informed to discuss himself. Opportunity is offered to those who do not find it possible to attend the annual Section meetings and lack an opportunity to present their views on a particular subject before the membership. It is hoped the membership will make free use of this department in developing constructive ideas. All communications must be signed but the writer's name will not be published if so requested.

Madison, Wisc., May 20, 1932.

Editor, News-Bulletin,

DEAR SIR:

The subject of Neon signs is presenting some difficulties to our inspectors. The so-called window signs, or skeleton signs, are being installed by persons who do not realize the danger, and who do not take any precautions to prevent contact with live parts nor to make sure that there will not be overheating of electrodes or connections. We find that in many cases agents who come in from other cities take orders for signs, and who later come back and hang them without making any contact with the inspection department. Some of these signs are connected with ordinary lamp cord and some with ordinary No. 14 wire with 600-volt insulation. In some cases, connections from one tube terminal to the next are made by means of single strands of bare wire, perhaps No. 18 or No. 20.

When installations of this class are discovered by the inspectors, the agents frequently state that they have no trouble with their signs in other cities. In other cases the inspector is not able to make contact with the agent since he is gone and has left no address.

I will be glad to know what has been the experience of other localities with these installations.

Yours very truly,
J. E. WISE, *Electrical Engineer,*
INDUSTRIAL COMMISSION.

Jacksonville, Fla., April 30, 1932.

Sears-Roebuck Company,
532 W. Forsyth Street,
Jacksonville, Florida.

Attention: E. J. Otto, Manager

GENTLEMEN:

I am just in receipt of a letter from Mr. C. S. Whitaker, City Electrical Inspector of Durham, N. C., a copy of which is enclosed herewith.

I am rather surprised to receive the information contained in this letter, as from past correspondence and information which has been furnished to me, I have been under the distinct impression that it was the established policy of Sears-Roebuck Company to handle and market only approved electrical materials, devices, and appliances, and to cooperate fully with administrative authorities in the enforcement of laws, rules, and regulations governing the installation of such materials, devices, and appliances.

Every city in the United States with which I am familiar has an ordinance requiring the installation of electrical wiring and apparatus to be performed under the supervision of duly qualified electricians and subject to approval by the proper administrative authorities acting under the Police Power of the Municipality.

The National Electrical Code as recommended by the National Fire Protection Association and the National Electrical Safety Code as promulgated by the United States Bureau of Standards, constitute the basis for all local rules, regulations, and ordinances governing electrical construction.

We must all recognize the fact that electrical energy, properly controlled, is the most useful servant which mankind has ever known, but improperly used and uncontrolled is a highly dangerous and destructive Natural Force, and possesses peculiar and inherent hazards which are well recognized by electrical experts, but which are not apparent to the average layman.

Having placed this dangerous and destructive agency at the beck and call of every man, woman, and child in the country, it is the duty of those of us who understand its inherent hazards to exert every effort toward the end that only com-

The Forum, or letters to the editor as it is known today, was introduced in July 1932. The original intent was to create a round-table similar to the Internet bulletin-boards of the 21st century. Members had an opportunity to discuss any subject of general interest, or to remark upon a published article. In the next few decades, members responded to each other in the "forum," and there are several listings from the 1950s in which members had a regular debate going on in each issue of the publication.

Quick Fact

A postal card from the Libreria Internazionale, Milano, Italy, asks for copies of the IAEI *News-Bulletin*, "as there is great scope for such extension of sales of your paper in Italy."

Reprinted from *News-Bulletin*, May 1947.

Victor H. Tousley, 1875-1948 first editor of the *News Bulletin*.
Looking backwards more than thirty years, I recognize a steadily increasing appreciation of Victor Tousley as a faithful public servant. Our first contacts were professional. He was chief electrical inspector in Chicago. Accordingly, he was properly concerned that the Laboratories' testing and listing of newly developed electrical products reflected appropriate consideration of practical field conditions. When expressing disagreement he was consistently firm, but was appreciative and sympathetic of a contrary view. Always alert to unsafe features, he could promptly modify his views and position when satisfied that safeguarding was not overlooked.

When he took over as electrical field engineer of the National Fire Protection Association, these fundamentals of his personality were more readily displayed. His conviction that electricity was to make further contributions to the national economy inspired continuing effort to keep himself abreast of the industry's new developments. Thus his advice on field conditions was in step with the times.

His contribution as secretary/treasurer of the International Association of Electrical Inspectors guaranteed its growth to its present importance in safety accomplishment. The friendly patience and thoroughness displayed in his conduct of this office produced the confidence and respect essential to the success of the widely scattered and otherwise detached groups of the membership.

As secretary of the electrical committee and editor of several editions of the *National Electrical Code*, he found other channels in which he contributed effectively to safety to persons and property and to orderly development within the industry. He labored steadily to have all concerned, "Let the *Code* Decide."

In recent years our contacts were on a close, personal base. If he was in town we often lunched together. Sometimes we discussed non-professional matters. He was a kindly, cheerful fellow, interested and happy in his home life, and had lively views on world, national and local affairs. I shall miss him always.

Alva Small. Reprinted from *News-Bulletin*, September 1948.

1948 September Issue

1973 January Issue

1984 May/June Issue

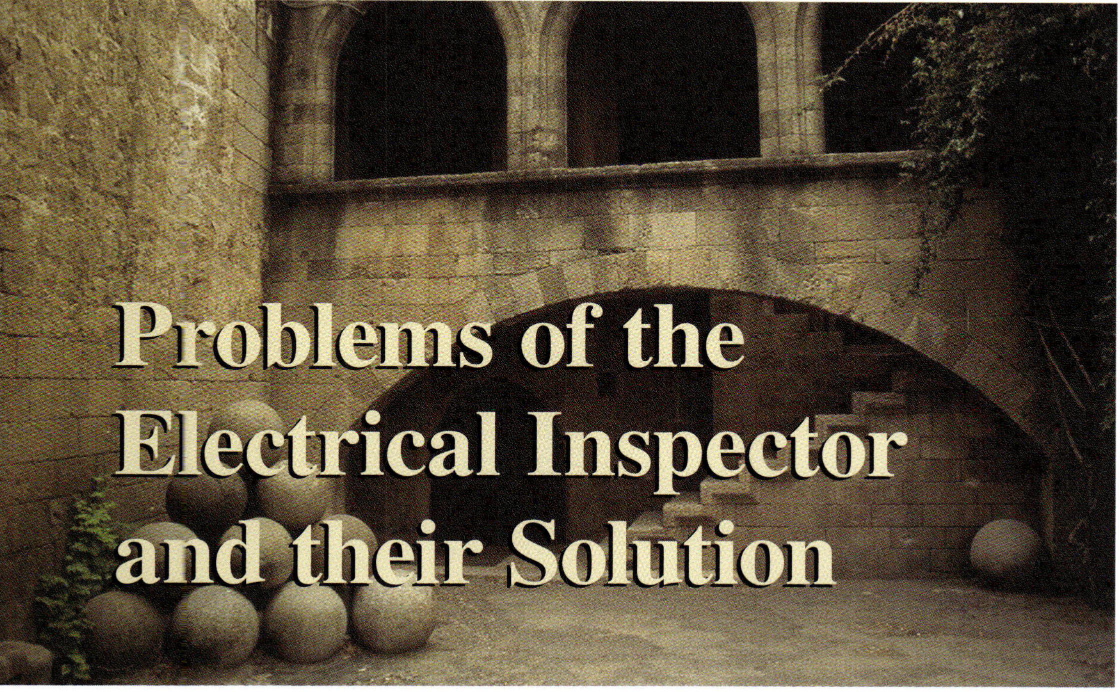

Orginal printing in March 1953 issue of the News-Bulletin. *Also used as a reprinted version in March 2003.*

Problems of the Electrical Inspector and their Solution

By Eustace C. Soares

Large capacity services on 208/120-volt AC network systems are increasing rapidly. Further they present an ever continuing challenge to the electrical inspector to see that the installation is safe and will not eventually become a fire hazard. Incidentally, that also means utilizing copper efficiently in the interest of our national economy.

A chief electrical inspector once remarked that he didn't propose to have his men go around with a thermometer hung around their necks, and he is right. The job of an electrical inspector is not that of a troubleshooter. However, a lot of later trouble can be nipped in the bud at the source through the application of fundamental principals in the approval of layout drawings.

It is the aim of this paper to set forth briefly the important fundamentals which affect the problem. Next the important factors covering the heating of large services are covered and finally the practical application of these to the job itself to provide a well designed service which will have all the elements of safety properly incorporated.

The important points to be discussed are: bus configuration and conductor assembly; magnetic induction heat losses; ventilation of equipment as well as room; arrangement of neutral; and grounding.

Fundamentals

Now let us consider a few fundamentals as applying to each of the above five major points under consideration.

1. Bus Configuration and Conductor Assembly

First, we will deal with cable and its ability to carry current for the same temperature rise under different conditions.

For direct current where the current is distributed equally throughout the cross section, the capacity of a conductor may be increased proportionately within fairly large limits merely by adding cables or bus bars allowing a reasonable air space for cooling.

If we consider cables, we also note that the *Code* restricts the carrying capacity based on the manner in which they are installed. Take any one type of cable, as Type

Canadian News and Notes

SERVICE CONDUIT AND CONDUCTOR SIZES

Owing to the critical shortage of rigid metal conduit that has again developed, one No. 8 bare and two No. 6 B & S Gauge insulated copper conductors in ¾" conduit will be accepted for 60 ampere 110/220 volt single phase services until further notice.

This does not authorize the use of a bare neutral in rural areas where the Rules and Regulations require an insulated neutral. (Reprint HEPC Quarterly.)

PLUG RECEPTACLES IN BATHROOMS

The Rule prohibiting the installation of plug receptacles in bathrooms has been withdrawn from the H.E.P.C. Rules and Regulations. The Electrical Inspectors have, therefore, been authorized to accept plug receptacles when installed in bathrooms in accordance with the minimum safe requirements for such outlets. It is necessary that the plug receptacle be so located in the bathroom that it is difficult of access for a person when in the bathtub or shower to plug in an attachment plug cap. If metal flush device boxes are used, they are required to be grounded. If an insulating-type flush device box is used, the cover plate shall be of the insulating type, but the screws used to attach the plate may be of metal.

Since the standard type of plug receptacle is now recognized for installation in a bathroom, a lighting fixture containing a plug receptacle will also be accepted when located in a bathroom, if its location in the bathroom meets the requirements indicated above the plug receptacles. The outlet box is required to be of metal and grounded. (Reprint HEPC Quarterly.)

SEALING OF CONDUIT IN STABLES

Non-metallic sheathed cable is frequently run from a stable to a room or loft above the stable and in doing so, Rule 47 of the Amendment to the Rural Regulations requires that it pass through a length of rigid metallic conduit sealed at both ends.

A report from the Laboratory advises that the upper seal alone is sufficient, and effectively curtails the passage of air through the conduit. The omission of the lower seal will prevent the accumulation of any moisture in the conduit. Consequently, installation with only the upper seal will be accepted. (Reprint HEPC Qurterly.)

WHAT DOES STANDARDIZATION MEAN TO YOU?

(Reprint from Canadian Standards Association Quarterly, April, '51)

Standardization no longer is the "bogey-man" that it was regarded by many organizations and individuals not so long ago. Prior to World War I, standardization was practiced only by organizations possessing far-seeing executives who believed in building for the future as well as for the present. To many, in those days, "standardization" meant "regimentation" and possibly exposing one's hand too readily to one's competition.

The Canadian Standards Association has an unofficial slogan proclaiming the benefits of standardization, stating to the effect that the term means Safety, Economy and Efficiency. A moment's reflection will establish the fact that, as far as industrial products are concerned, the three conditions are inseparable, — you cannot have either of the latter without depending upon the other two, — at least if you wish your organization to continue as a "going concern."

Industry, government and John Public alike are becoming more and more standards conscious. One can scarcely find an issue of a daily journal that has no reference, and even copious reference, to some standardization activity or proposal. Standardization of arms and defense equipment, standardization of fire prevention equipment, standardization of women's clothing, standardization of this and that and divers other things are referred to daily in our press.

17

Although the Canadian Section was not officially created until 1953, Canadian members have always had a role in the chronicle of IAEI. Many of these members were employed with the Canadian Standards Association. An earlier forerunner to the present *Ask CSA* section was the "Canadian News and Notes" section of the *News-Bulletin*, born in the July 1951 issue.

Underwriters Lab Announces

Television Receiver Without Isolating Power Transformer and Without Fire-Retaining Enclosure

In order to minimize fire hazard in radio and television receivers, the current edition of the Laboratories' Standard for Power-Operated Radio Receiving Appliances requires that circuit components be contained within a fire-retaining enclosure of noncombustible material, or be isolated from the power-supply by a transformer which is completely and individually housed in noncombustible material. A 285-watt television receiver which was recently submitted did not comply with these requirements in that there was no isolating transformer and the circuit components were not contained within an acceptable fire-retaining enclosure. The manufacturer claimed that the rectifier power supply of his television receiver provided a protection against fire hazard in circuit components of at least equal to the protection provided by the isolating transformer for the power supply of a comparable radio or television receiver. From tests, the Laboratories' engineers concluded that circuit components operating in the output of the rectifier power supply of this television receiver are provided with equivalent protection. The foregoing was reported to the Electrical Council and manufacturers of listed power-operated radio receiving appliances in a bulletin dated June 21, 1948 (Subject 492).

• LET THE CODE DECIDE •

Labels for Electric Signs

A bulletin dated June 28, 1948 (Subject 48) announced that the practice of determining the form denomination of labels for electric signs employing fluorescent lamps, is being modified to the extent that in the future, the factor representing the fluorescent-lamp ballasts in other than Form 1 signs, will depend upon the open-circuit secondary voltage rating of the ballast. In due course, paragraphs 161-165, inclusive, Of the Standard for Electric Signs will be revised. No change is being made in the method of determining the form denomination of incandescent-lamp, gas-tube, or combination incandescent-lamp and gas-tube sign labels.

• LET THE CODE DECIDE •

Change in the Requirements for Power-Operated Radio Receiving Appliances

Recent bulletins (Subject 492) to members of the Electrical Council and manufacturers announced two changes in the requirements for power-operated radio receiving appliances. One required that appliances employing record players be designed so that all moving parts of the record player mechanisms which involve accident hazard be inaccessible during normal operation of the appliance. The other, dealing with ac-dc type radio receiving appliances, required that a control shaft which involves shock hazard shall be rendered inaccessible by means of a suitable interlock or by means of a knob of suitable insulating material which is not removable from the shaft from the exterior of the enclosure.

• LET THE CODE DECIDE •

Recognition of Types RUF and RUFF Fixture Wires With Outer Covering of Nylon

A bulletin dated July 20, 1948 (Subject 66) announced that the Laboratories is prepared to recognize Types RUF and RUFF fixture wires with an outer covering of nylon having a nominal thickness of nine mils if the finished product is found to comply with all the applicable requirements of the Standard.

36 I.A.E.I. NEWS-BULLETIN

When IAEI was originally founded, the organization had no funds and no facilities, so they asked Victor Tousley to serve as their secretary-treasurer to get the organization started and for some months Mr. Tousley was given quarters at Underwriters Laboratories' chief testing station until the new organization could collect sufficient funds to rent a place of its own. This kinship with UL has lasted to this day, and in 1948, the *News-Bulletin* began publishing a new column called "Underwriters Lab Announces," a forerunner to today's *UL Question Corner*.

R, and examine its carrying capacity for various conditions (see table 1). For the best condition, a single conductor in free air, to the worst cited in the *Code*, seven to nine conductors in a raceway, we get a reduction in current-carrying capacity to only 43 ½ percent of the available without considering the other potentiality of a room temperature more than 30°C or 86°F, which would reduce the carrying capacity still further.

Then what about when we put 30 conductors in a raceway helter skelter. It becomes obvious that it should not be done yet we can find many such installations in service.

Further, when we are considering alternating current, the problem of increased capacity may become complicated. Adding copper bars or cables in parallel does not increase the current-carrying capacity proportionately and in fact can easily reach the point where an additional bar or cable may cause virtually no increase in capacity. This is owing to the so called *skin effect* which is a result of the reversing magnetic field around the conductor which crowds the current to the outer edge of the conductor.

The result of tests published by H. W. Papst of the Switchboard Engineering Department of the Westinghouse Electric Corporation in the September 21, 1929, issue of the *Electrical World* show that only too well.

Using 3″ x 1/8″ rectangular copper bars in parallel, the tests showed that current capacity is not increased proportionately to the number of bars in parallel. The comparative figures are shown in table 2. For the same temperature rise with a single bar, we get a current-carrying capacity of 600 amperes-per-bar, which unit capacity constantly decreases as we add bars until with twelve bars, the capacity per bar is only 242 amperes, less than 50 percent of the original. Note also that in going from ten to twelve bars the last two bars resulted in a capacity increase of only 75 amperes per bar or 12 ½ percent of the capacity of the same bar when used alone. This means that we had to add eight times as much copper as necessary.

It is plain that adding bars in parallel is not the economic way to get increased capacity for such increase may be ridiculously smaller than it appears it should be. Another point not shown in these tests is that the arithmetic sum of the current in each bar is greater than the total current.

Note that in going from ten to twelve bars, the last two bars resulted in an increase of only 150 amperes,

Allowable Current-carrying Capacity of 500 MCM, Type R Insulated Conductor	Amperes	Percent
1. Single conductor in free air	515	100
2. Three conductors in a raceway	320	62
3. Four to six conductors in a raceway	256	50
4. Seven to nine conductors in a raceway	224	43 1/2
5. Thirty conductors in a raceway	?	?

Table 1. Comparison of allowable current-carrying capacity of 500 MCM Type R insulated conductor in amperes.

We are very pleased to announce that Mr. Roy Burgess has joined our *News-Bulletin* staff as associate editor.

Mr. Burgess recently retired as acting chief electrical inspector for the city of Chicago. He was greatly instrumental in the formation and completion of the 1954 Chicago Electrical Code and received national recognition as a *Code* expert, giving freely of his time to bring clearer understanding of *Code* sections. Naturally, Roy has been a member of our association for years and was president of the Western Section in 1944.

Mr. Burgess received his technical education in electrical engineering at Armour Institute (now Illinois Institute of Technology). He entered the Civil Service in 1913 in the Chicago Bureau and his outstanding service over the years culminated in the esteemed position of acting chief electrical inspector for the city.

Again we want to welcome Roy; you'll be hearing from him in the coming issues of the *News-Bulletin*, we know he will be a great asset to our staff. — Reprinted from *News-Bulletin*, January 1957.

Current-carrying Capacity of Parallel Busbars for the Same Temperature Rise (Using 3" x 1/8" rectangular copper bars)

Number of bars	Square inches	Current-carrying capacity amperes	Average capacity per bar in amperes	Average current density amperes per square inch
1	3/8	600	600	1600
3	1 1/8	1500	500	1333
6	2 1/4	2350	392	1044
10	3 3/4	2750	275	733
12	4 1/2	2900	242	644

Table 2. Comparison of current-carrying capacity of parallel busbars for the same temperature rise using 3" x 1/8" rectangular copper bars.

or 75 amperes per bar, just 12 ½ percent of the capacity of one bar alone.

Note also that one 3″ x 1/8″ bar can operate at a current density of 1600 amperes per square inch and that the density constantly reduces till when twelve bars are used in parallel the average current density drops to 644 amperes, only 40 percent of a single bar. Note: the current density figures here shown cannot apply to other sizes of copper bar. For instance, they are too high for ¼″ x 4″ bar.

Then again when dealing with large capacities, we get a further distortion of current density owing to the interaction of the magnetic fields between phases. This is known as proximity effect and depends on the current as well as the spacing and arrangement of the conductors.

2. *Magnetic and Induction Heat Losses*

Next, consider the magnetic field surrounding a conductor. It varies as the square of the current. The magnetic effect of a current of 4000 amperes is thus 64 times as great as that of a current of 500 amperes although the current is only eight times larger.

Any conductor placed within an alternating magnetic field will have induced in it an electromotive force or voltage which will cause an induced current to flow within the conductor; while if the conductor is magnetic, a magnetomotive force also will develop. Both vary with the strength of the magnetic field or as the square of the current and both represent heat losses which may become appreciable.

If a magnetic conducting material such as steel is placed within an alternating magnetic field we thus have two losses: a magnetic or hysteresis loss, and an induced current loss.

If a non-magnetic conducting material such as aluminum alloy is placed within an alternating magnetic field we have one loss: an induced current loss.

The losses in either material will depend on the distance from the center of the conductor and will vary approximately as the square of the distance.

3. *Ventilation of Equipment as Well as Room*

In ventilation we must deal with and understand the properties of heat flow. Heat flows from a hotter body to a cooler body, never the reverse. The ratio of heat flow is a function of the temperature difference. The terms hot and cold are relative only. For instance, heat flows from a body having a temperature of 400°F to a body having a temperature of 300°F, although we will consider both bodies not only as hot but as very hot. The rate of heat transfer depends on the medium. Water is a good heat transfer medium. On the other hand, air is a very poor heat conductor, in fact, it is used as a heat insulator very effectively as evidenced by storm windows which depend for their insulating value on a relatively thin layer of air trapped between two glass surfaces.

Only a few watts are required to raise the temperature of a sealed metal enclosure or room materially if we depend on the heat being conducted away through air that cannot circulate outside the enclosure or room. Temperature rise of conductors within a sealed or nonventilated enclosure can be considered roughly as being double what it would be if means were provided for a natural free air circulation.

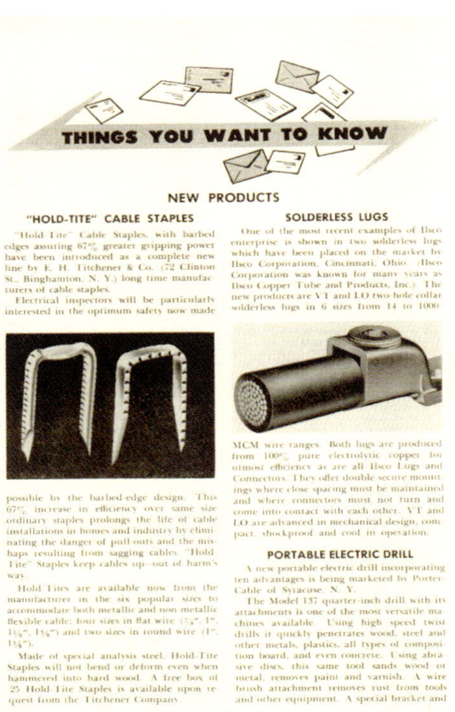
THINGS YOU WANT TO KNOW

NEW PRODUCTS

"HOLD-TITE" CABLE STAPLES

"Hold-Tite" Cable Staples, with barbed edges assuring 67% greater gripping power have been introduced as a complete new line by E. H. Titchener & Co. (72 Clinton St., Binghamton, N. Y.) long time manufacturers of cable staples.

Electrical inspectors will be particularly interested in the optimum safety now made possible by the barbed-edge design. This 67% increase in efficiency over same size ordinary staples prolongs the life of cable installations in homes and industry by eliminating the danger of pull-outs and the mishaps resulting from sagging cables. "Hold-Tite" Staples keep cables up—out of harm's way.

Hold-Tites are available now from the manufacturer in the six popular sizes to accommodate both metallic and non-metallic flexible cable: four sizes in flat wire (⅞", 1", 1⅛", 1⅜") and two sizes in round wire (1", 1¼").

Made of special analysis steel, Hold-Tite Staples will not bend or deform even when hammered into hard wood. A free box of 25 Hold-Tite Staples is available upon request from the Titchener Company.

SOLDERLESS LUGS

One of the most recent examples of Ilsco enterprise is shown in two solderless lugs which have been placed on the market by Ilsco Corporation, Cincinnati, Ohio. (Ilsco Corporation was known for many years as Ilsco Copper Tube and Products, Inc.) The new products are VT and LO two-hole collar solderless lugs in 6 sizes from 14 to 1000 MCM wire ranges. Both lugs are produced from 100% pure electrolytic copper for utmost efficiency as are all Ilsco Lugs and Connectors. They offer double secure mountings where close spacing must be maintained and where connectors must not turn and come into contact with each other. VT and LO are advanced in mechanical design, compact, shockproof and cool in operation.

PORTABLE ELECTRIC DRILL

A new portable electric drill incorporating ten advantages is being marketed by Porter-Cable of Syracuse, N. Y.

The Model 137 quarter-inch drill with its attachments is one of the most versatile machines available. Using high speed twist drills it quickly penetrates wood, steel and other metals, plastics, all types of composition board, and even concrete. Using abrasive discs, this same tool sands wood or metal, removes paint and varnish. A wire brush attachment removes rust from tools and other equipment. A special bracket and

40

Manufacturers and their products have always played an important role in electrical safety. In the January 1955 issue of the *News-Bulletin*, IAEI began listing approved products in their "Things You Want to Know" column, which is today known as *News Source*.

4. *Arrangement of Neutral*

It is well established and virtually everyone is thoroughly acquainted with the fact that the neutral must run in the same conduit as the phase wires or undue heating will develop. Every old timer has been up against that problem in his own experience and maybe learned the hard way. By the same token, although not as well recognized, when conductors are run in the open even a small piece of structural steel interposed between the neutral and the phase wires may cause undue heating.

5. *Grounding*

With a given voltage, the maximum current that will flow in a circuit is dependent on the resistance or impedance of the circuit. That fact is of great practical importance when we consider fault currents, and determines the method of grounding which must be employed. At this point, "It should be noted that even the best grades of rubber insulation will deteriorate in time, so eventually will need it to be replaced."

That statement is taken verbatim from Note 10 accompanying Tables 1 and 2, Chapter 10 of the *National Electrical Code.*

Since most faults occur to ground, we must never lose sight of that fact.

Application of the Fundamentals to Large Services

Now let us apply these fundamentals to a large capacity service and see how they affect:

1. *Bus Configuration and Conductor Assembly*

The service and load feeders may consist of cable or bus. Take a case where say ten 500 MCM cables are used per phase. There is nothing wrong about throwing these 30-phase cables plus the neutral cables in a steel duct or trough if we are willing to pay the very high price of reduced capacity. This method is not uncommon and because we do not figure usually on the high reduction of capacity to be expected, the cables are fully loaded when carrying perhaps even less than 50 percent of the allowable carrying capacity of three conductors in a raceway. This results in another source of undue heating and may cause hot spots that will create a fire eventually, owing to insulation breakdown.

If, however, unless the run were very short the cables were racked to give free access to air circulation and set up in groups of A, B, C, and N we will have an installation giving less voltage drop, better regulation, lower reactance and less temperature rise for the same current. Also, when multiple cables are used they should be protected with limiter lugs on each end.

If rectangular bus bar is used we find that multiple bars on ¼″ spacing is a very common practice much to be deplored. Reference is made here to 60 cycles AC circuits and not to DC circuits where such a practice would be perfectly correct within wide limits. By paying some attention to bus configuration we can get a marked reduction in heating. Let us examine facts as set forth in table 3.

An examination of that table shows that for the same temperature rise and with proper spacing only but using exactly the same number and size of copper bars we can carry: 15 percent more current for two bars; 28 percent more current for three bars; and 18 percent more current for four bars.

There is the greatest increase in capacity for three bars as compared with two or four. Why? Going back to our fundamentals we see that the skin effect of alternating current causes the current to crowd to the outside edge of the conductor so that the copper in the center of the conductor is working inefficiently. For two or four bars there is no copper exactly in the center of the conductor while for three bars, one bar is exactly in the center of the conductor. Spacing the three bars in special configuration removes one of the conductors from the center of the conductor and up goes the carrying capacity, in this case 28 percent.

Take a commonly used arrangement of four ¼ x 4 bars on ¼″ spacing and referred to as a 4000-ampere bus. We find that such a bus is capable of carrying only 2800 amperes for a 30°C rise over a 40°C ambient (four square inches of copper). Using only three ¼ x 4 bars and arranging them properly, we can get a capacity of 3120 amperes for only three square inches of copper. Although 25 percent less copper is used, we get an increase of 11½ percent in carrying capacity. Why then do we persist in putting copper bars on ¼″ spacing? It can be assumed that it is only the outgrowth of a habit pattern of the DC days that still persists in too many places. I venture to estimate that we have wasted millions of pounds of copper over the years, surely an economic waste.

If we use a single flat bar in a three-phase circuit and space the phases closely, we have the most efficient arrangement giving high current carrying capacity and very low reactance. Note the current-carrying capacity of a single bar from table 3. By using multiples of this arrangement, we get the interleaved bus in which the phase relation of the adjacent bars then become A, B, C—A, B, C, etc., depending on the number of circuits used. This is a simple construction and although it has rela-

Current-carrying Capacity — Rectangular Copper Bars 30°C Rise Based on a 40°C Ambient. All 1/4" Spacing

Capacity 1/4 x 4 bars	Square Inches	Current Density	Capacity 1/4 x 6 bars	Square Inches	Current Density
1220	1	1220	1660	1 1/2	1107
1925	2	962	2620	3	873
2440	3	813	3320	4 1/2	738
2800	4	700	3815	6	636

4" X 5/16" Ventilated square bus
3720 4.15 896 or equivilant to
3585 amperes for four square inches

Note: The above values do not take into account the loss in carrying capacity owing to proximity effect.

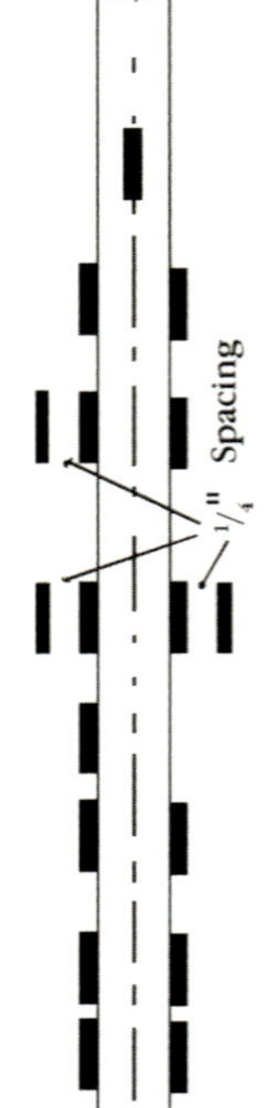

Current-carrying Capacity — Rectangular Copper Bars 30°C Rise Based on a 40°C Ambient. All 1/4" Spacing

Capacity 1/4 x 4 bars	Square Inches	Current Density Amps per Sq. In.	Capacity 1/4 x 6 bars	Current Density Amps per Sq. In.	Percent increase in capacity with improved configuration
—	—	—	—	—	—
2220	2	1100	3020	1007	15
3120	3	1040	4250	944	28
3315	4	830	4515	752	18

Note: The arrangements shown at left are the most effective for 3 or 4 bars but do not lend themselves readily for practical use especially if the bus is to be tapped.

Note: The above values do not take into account the loss in carrying-capacity owing to proximity effect.

Table 3. Current-carrying capacity — rectangular copper bars.

tively weak mechanical strength and the end connections may be complicated it has low reactance and low voltage drop and with proper supports is much used.

Aside from interleaved bus, ventilated square bus offers the only worthwhile way of designing any bus of more than four bars. The use of more than four bars in an AC bus is inadvisable from any angle, yet the practice persists.

2. Magnetic and Induction Heat Losses

These factors must be reckoned with in enclosure design. If not, undesirable and unnecessary heating will result. Since these losses vary as the square of the current they become increasingly more important as capacity increases.

Enclosures cannot be designed on the basis of voltage clearances only. If not given proper consideration in design work, not only do we get excess heating we can expect also annoying magnetic noise.

In the great majority of installations where noise is a factor, it is due nearly always to neglect of the problems of magnetic and induction effects.

If annoying noise exists in an installation, it is almost positive proof that the design did not properly allow for the magnetic and induction effects, always a very costly matter to correct after the job is installed yet relatively simple to avoid in the design stage. Also consideration must be given to proximity of building steel and to the distance from the center of the conductor to its enclosure side or any other magnetic material in the close vicinity.

3. Ventilation of Equipment as Well as Room

It is impossible to transmit current without using power. This power is expended as heat and is the I^2R loss. For a given conductor, this loss then varies as the square of the current. Twice the current means four times the loss in watts.

Two things are obvious. Whenever we transmit electricity we have heat loss and that heat must be removed if temperature rise is to be kept within bounds. The larger the capacity the greater the loss

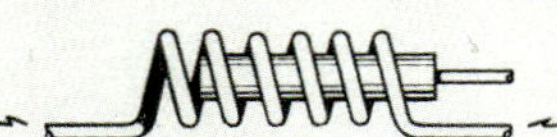

First ad to appear in the News-Bulletin, *March 1954*

Members of the IAEI will note that for the first time in 25 years of publication, the *News-Bulletin* is carrying advertising in this issue.

As many of you know, this advertising question has been under discussion for some time and the reasons, pro and con, as to whether it belongs in our pages have been very carefully weighed.

Many problems were involved in these discussions but the prime factors facing the association were: will the inclusion of advertising improve the quality and readership of the bulletin? Will the increased revenue afforded enable us to improve and enlarge the many other desirable services of our organization?

We feel the right answer to both of these questions to be a very emphatic Yes.

The right type of advertising, i.e., factual technical information on products which are in accord with national standards should be of great interest and value to all of our readership; and in turn, the revenue therefrom will definitely make it possible for us to improve the quality of the publication in every respect. Furthermore, since the IAEI is, and always will be, a strictly not-for-profit organization, we look forward with real pleasure to the chance which this additional revenue will give us to improve existing services and to create new means and methods whereby we may be of more service to the industry and the public.

We, the publishers of the *News-Bulletin*, are enthusiastic over these opportunities for improvements which this new policy affords.

Will you, the readers, send us your comments along with any suggestions which you believe will help both the association and our advertisers to bring you the type of information which you desire.

[*Editor's note*: The ad shown was the first ad published in the March 1954 issue, and the first advertisement published in any IAEI publication.] — Excerpted from "Editorial," *News-Bulletin*, March 1954.

1954 May Issue

1955 January Issue

and the greater the need for removing the heat generated. While it is possible to neglect ventilation in a small capacity circuit without undue temperature rise, ventilation becomes more and more essential as the circuit capacity increases.

Enclosed equipment then should be ventilated by providing proper means for air flow. Ample sized openings at top and bottom of an enclosure provide better air circulation than if the entire front of the enclosure were removed. From tests it has been determined that if equipment carrying 2000 amperes or more is enclosed and not ventilated, the temperature rise will be approximately double what it would be if it were properly ventilated. For instance, doubling the size of such an enclosure has no appreciable effect.

This matter of ventilation goes further than the enclosed equipment itself and must extend also to the room in which the equipment is installed. Inlet openings of the proper size at the floor level and exit openings at the ceiling level must be provided. Moreover such openings must be placed where they will have real value. To have openings which by their very nature and location will be blocked up in time will not be a solution. Illustrate: (1) carpenter shop; (2) in and out same interior basement room; and (3) outlet by steam pipes operating in summer.

Under certain conditions it is important if not essential that equipment must be totally enclosed but in such cases we must derate the equipment to allow for the lack of being able to properly remove the normal heat losses and thus keep the temperature rise within safe bounds.

4. Arrangement of Neutral

Because it permits a simple layout, switchboards for three-phase, four-wire systems have been built in which the service supply cables enter the top of the switchboard, the phase wires go through the service equipment to a bus usually on the bottom of the switchboard, and the neutral runs across the top. In nearly all cases some of the steel structure of the switchboard becomes interposed between the neutral and the phase wires. As the feeders leave the switchboard, a tap from the neutral completes each four-wire feeder circuit. For such arrangements where total currents did not exceed 1000 amperes with a correspondingly small neutral current, the excess heating was small and presented no problem. But let us not forget that there was some excess heating.

However, as the capacity of circuits increased, the heating caused by that arrangement became excessive and very noticeable. An unbalance of 200 amperes in a 3000-ampere circuit is not unusual. That unbalance is much more than enough to cause trouble if any of the steel structure is between the phase wires and the neutral.

5. Grounding

Both the service ground and the equipment ground introduce an element of safety to personnel, equipment, and property. Both must be installed in accordance with the accepted rules. Particular attention must be paid to insure operation of overcurrent devices on fault currents.

Recommendations

The proper time to insure the best installation is when drawings are submitted to the inspection department and not after the job is installed. The following represent specific recommendations for the five important points here discussed:

1. Bus Configuration and Conductor Assembly

For the approved carrying capacity of cables we can find data in the *Code* which can guide us, bearing in mind that we have various conditions all of which vary the carrying capacity. They are: (1) type of cable; (2) if in free air; (3) three cables in a single raceway; (4) more than three cables in a single raceway; (5) room temperature, if not over 30°C (86°F); and (6) putting multiple cables in a raceway or trough (see table 1).

For bus we must consider temperature rise as our guide. The old rule of 1000 amperes per square inch or, for that matter, any other rating per square inch is meaningless. For one square inch of copper bar the carrying capacity of 1000 amperes is conservative; but as square inches go up, density goes down for every square inch we add. Note the data in table 2.

We must give up the habit pattern of accepting bus bars in multiple on ¼" spacing unless the rating is accepted at its true value and not 1000 amperes per square inch.

AC busses, other than interleaved, should consist of not more than four bars with the configuration giving the least temperature rise. Where higher capacities are necessary, square ventilated bus had best be used. This does not mean that nothing else can be used but the arrangements cited will cover most cases, is practical and convenient.

2. *Magnetic and Induction Heat Losses*

Paragraph 3018 of the *Code* states that "...where a current of more than 50 amperes enters a metal enclosure the conductors...shall be so arranged as to avoid overheating of the metal by induction." The following distances from steel to center line of conductor are based on a 10°C rise of the steel enclosure when carrying currents as listed. They may be used as an approximate guide. An interleaved bus duct may be considered as carrying only that current carried by one of its component circuits, not the total rating of the bus.

Amperes	Distance from Center Line of 4" Wide Conductor to Side of Steel Enclosure
1000	6
2000	10
3000	12
4000	14

The above figures are approximately correct and are intended as a guide only. More test data are needed to offer accurate figures here. If the busway makes a right angle turn, all distances should be increased to the next higher rating.

If the enclosure and its structural members are made of aluminum alloy of the same cross section as the required steel, all of the above distances may be reduced materially but in any event should be somewhat more than necessary for voltage clearance only and preferably should be decreased little where actual load is 3000 amperes or more. It is recommended that where actual currents exceed 3000 amperes that enclosures be made of aluminum alloy. Tests have shown that with a load of 3500 amperes, there is a saving of 1000 watts loss if an aluminum alloy enclosure is used instead of a steel enclosure both having the same dimension as referred to. However, the difference in temperature rise is not much in both cases being only a maximum of about 5°C in favor of the aluminum alloy enclosure. The economic loss is a factor although by no means a very important one unless we are dealing with a load that operates continuously.

3. *Ventilation of Equipment as Well as Room*

Enclosed equipment, as well as the room in which it is installed, should be properly ventilated.

Enclosures should have an opening at extreme top and bottom the full width of the enclosure and not less than four inches, but preferably six inches, high protected with the proper screening. The rest of the enclosure should be covered to get the full chimney effect of air circulation.

The room in which equipment is housed should have an effective inlet opening near the floor having an area of about five percent of the square feet of area of the room and arranged to bring in outside fresh air. A similar sized exit opening near the ceiling and at the opposite end of the room should be arranged to deliver the air to the outside or to some room where an abnormal high temperature does not prevail. It is assumed that a normal ceiling height will prevail, natural ventilation is to be preferred although

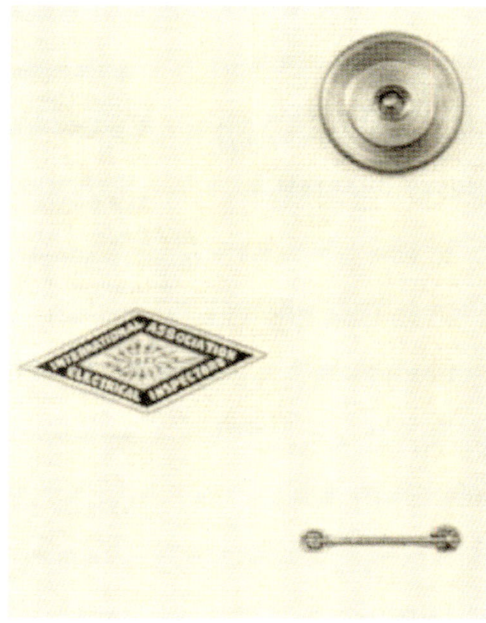

Here Is Your Official Lapel

The International office has a supply of the association's official lapel emblem, attractively designed in blue, white and gold in two styles — the standard button type (*top right*) or the safety latch pin-on type (*lower right*). These emblems are available to members at cost ($1 each) and may be obtained from IAEI, 612 N. Michigan Avenue, Chicago, Illinois. — Reprinted from *News-Bulletin*, November 1957.

Selling the IAEI at the 1957 Northwestern Section meeting. H. Morr (*standing*) points out a funny line in a contract read by William Gaffney, secretary of Northwestern Section, and Roy Crosby, secretary of the Eastern Washington Chapter.

Do You Have an Emblem of Your Membership?

The International office has a supply of the association's official lapel emblems, the Keystone, attractively designed in blue, white, and gold, in the standard button type. The actual size of this emblem is 5/8 inch by 5/8 inch. These emblems are available to members at cost ($1 each) and may be obtained from IAEI, 612 N. Michigan Avenue, Chicago, Illinois, Room 508. — Reprinted from *News-Bulletin*, January 1962.

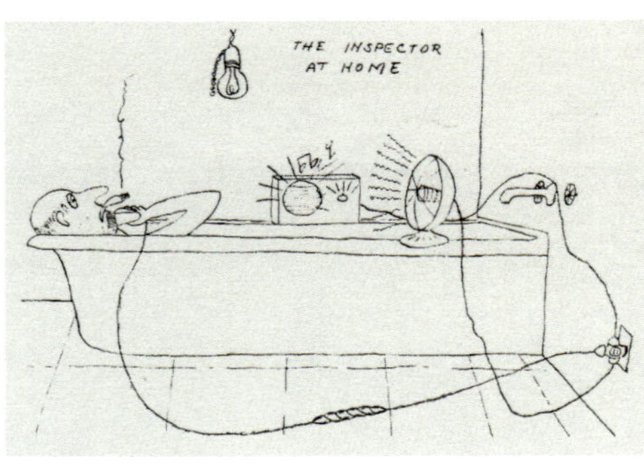

cases may arise where it may become necessary to use forced ventilation. In the latter case provision should be made to insure that the operation of the fan be as nearly automatic as is practical.

Air will not flow without a temperature difference any more than current will flow if there is not a voltage difference. An exit opening into a hot kitchen or near exposed steam pipes is little more effective than if there were no openings at all.

4. Arrangement of Neutral

The neutral should follow the phase wires through the distribution center. The neutral should not be carried across the top of the switchboard unless no steel whatever, not a single structural member, is interposed between the phase wires and the neutral.

There should be no exception to this.

5. Grounding

Particular attention should be paid to equipment ground impedance. All switchboards should have a ground strap extending the full length of the switchboard and bonded to each upright section. Also the service ground should be 25 percent of the capacity of the service. Bonding and the use of copper jumpers should be resorted to maintain a permanent low equipment ground impedance. On circuits with 4000 ampere overcurrent protection, the equipment ground impedance must be in the order of 1/100th of an ohm.

Summary

Of the five most important points to which we must pay particular attention we find that the first four— (1) bus configuration and conductor assembly; (2) magnetic and induction heat losses; (3) ventilation of equipment as well as room; and (4) arrangement of neutral — will show up reasonably early, although that means at least a year and long after the electrical inspector has forgotten about the job. They would show up immediately were it not for the fact that most new jobs require at least one year or more from the date of being put in service before they are operating at the load for which they were designed. The last point, grounding, seldom shows the effect of improper installation for many years, as much as ten or more, which is all the more reason why the layout should be inspected with a careful eye to what it will be after ten years of service. Several cases have come to my attention where equipment grounding and lack of attention being paid to bus and cable configuration was responsible for fires yet everything else was blamed except the true cause.

It might be said that all of these points are covered in the *National Electrical Code.* All that we need to get a safe installation is an insistence of a proper observance of the rules as they now exist.

Finally I would like to end up with a true story which aptly illustrates everything that has been said:

A commander of a garrison in Europe was transferred to another point. On arrival, he found a 24-hour guard duty posted in an area about one mile from the camp. He could see no reason for it. The former commander whom he was reliving could throw no light on it; he found the guard there and he continued it. But the new commander was a stubborn cuss. He was made of material that moves the world forward, not holds it static. He investigated and found that the area contained a powder magazine which was destroyed 230 years ago but no one thought to remove the guard.

Like this new commander I commend to electrical inspectors this same attitude as to why we do thus and so. It will improve safety and enhance the value of electrical inspection. That after all is our aim.

Eustace C. Soares, P. E., was employed by Industrial Engineering Services, New York 6, N.Y., when he wrote this article in 1953. Mr. Soares was one of the most renowned experts in the history of the *National Electrical Code* in the area of grounding electrical systems. His book, *Designing Electrical Distribution Systems for Safety* was originally published in 1966, and later grew into IAEI's *Soares Book on Grounding.*

Conducteur de Mise-a-la Terre Ou Isolation Double

By D. M. Manson, P. Eng.
CSA Testing Laboratories, Toronto, Canada..

Traduit Par: Paul Dubois and W. Kofman

L'Association de la prévention des accidents industriels a récemment mis en circulation une affiche murale pour souligner l'importance de pratiquer immédiatement la respiration artificielle quand il y a a eu choc électrique. Ce qu'il y a de plus frappant dans cette affiche c'est qu'elle contient des découpures de journaux relatant la mort de deux hommes par électrocution, accidents provoqués par des outils branchés sur le 115 volts. Ces accidents sont survenus l'été dernier dans le district de Toronto-Hamilton, et ce qu'il y a de plus troublant encore, une autre mortalité du même genre s'est produite depuis dans le même arrondissement.

Nous connaissons l'importance de l'application immédiate de la respiration artificielle. Cependant ne serait-il pas plus important que quelque chose soit fait pour réduire les accidents de ce genre? Les authorités en matière de sécurité affirment qu'il est possible d'améliorer cette situation avec la mise-à-la terre de la partie de métal extérieur de l'appareil ou en protégeant celui-ci par une isolation double.

Les idées exprimées par les termes mise-à-la terre et isolation double ne sont pas tout à fait nouvelles, mais dans plusieurs circonstances elles ne sont pas complètement comprises. Une étude plus appronondie de chaque sujet, particulièrement en ce qui concerne les appareils portatifs de 120 et 240 volts, met en relief des faits intéressants.

Mise-A-La Terre

La premìpartie du code canadien de l'électricité nous dit que le but de la mise-à-la terre est de prévenir un potentiel au dessus de terre d'apparaître sur la partie extérieure de métal d'un appareil électrique. En pratique, ceci s'accomplit quand on fait le raccordement de la partie extérieure de métal au conducteur neuter qui s'en va à la boîte de service d'entrée, c'est-à-dire au point où le dit conducteur est raccordé à l'électrode de mise-à-la terre. S'il y a court circuit entre les conducteurs sous tension et cette partie exposée de métal, un courant s'établira du fil sous tension au fil de mise-à-la terre et aux conducteurs neuters avec le résultat de l'éclatement de la fusible et le déchargement du circuit.

Il est évident maintenant que pour la mise-à-la terre effective d'un appareil, un circuit de mise-à-la terre continu à basse impédance est requis pour faire éclater la fusible et couper le circuit. Un tel circuit de mise-à-la terre s'étend cependant de la partie extérieur de métal de l'appareil jusqu'à l'électrode de mise-à-la terre à la boîte d'entrée et nécessairement comprend plusieurs raccordements. C'est comme une chaîne à plusieurs mailles dont n'importe laquelle peut malheureusement être une "mailee faible."

Retraçons un circuit de mise-à-la terre typique pour trouver ce que ces mailles faibles peuvent être.

Le conducteur de mise-à-la terre du fil d'ailmentation souple d'un appareil peut à force de manipulation répétée se couper et ceci à l'insu de celui-ci qui s'en sert, cependant l'autre conducteur du circuit reste intact et l'appareil continue à fonctionner.

La fiche de prise de courant au bout du fil électrique doit être raccordée correctement, et avec un fil électrique de trios conducteurs, il y a six manières différentes par lesquelles ces conducteurs peuvent être raccordés. Deux de celles-ci comportent un danger positif de choc, ainsi que deux autres si une corde d'extension est raccordée en transposant le fil sous tension avec le conducteur neutre.

Cependant la seule présence d'une prise de courant avec mise-à-la terre ne veut pas nécessairement dire que son attachement de mise-à-la terre est effectivement bon, particulièrement dans les vieilles bâtisses où les nouvelles installations des prises de courant peuvent être raccordées au tuyau à eau adjacent, sont maintenant permises par le code.

2002 July/August issue

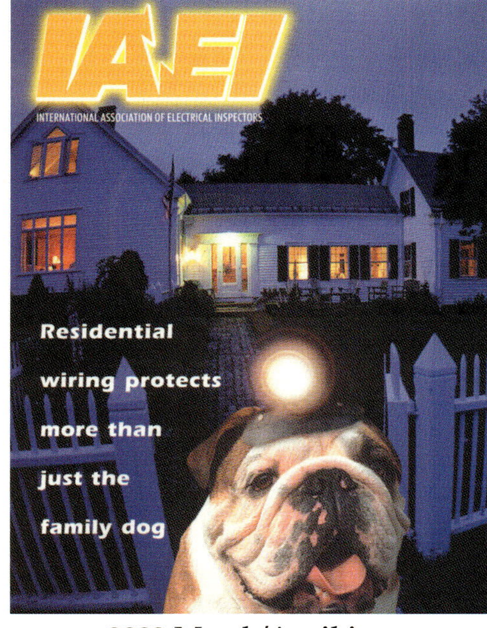

2003 March/April issue

Ces tuyaux sont la responsabilité du métier de plomberie, donc des joints ou tuyaux isolés peuvent être introduits n'importe quand sans qu'on le sache. A l'endroit où le système de fils électriques complete le circuit de mise-à-la terre de la prise de courant à la boîte d'entrée cela doit être conducteur du courant dans tout le parcours.

Les conduits doivent être pourvus de connexions conductrices sûres dans tout leur parcours et particulièrement entre la courroie de montage de la prise de courant et la boîte sur laquelle la prise de courant est installée. Les installations avec fil à gaine non-métallique comprennent plusieurs connexions dans le fil de mise-à-la terre pour aller d'une sortie à l'autre.

En considérant ce qui a été dit plus haut vous pouvez voir que l'installation et la maintenance de ces circuits avec mise-à-la terre comprennent un personnel de métiers différents dont n'importe qui peut sans mauvaise intention faire échouer l'intégrité de ce systéme.

Ainsi dans l'usage d'appareil avec mise-à-la terre il devrait y avoir quelques moyens possibles pour verifier le circuit de mise-à-la terre pour être assure qu'il est complet et capable de conduire le courant de "faute" nécessaire pour faire éclater la fusible.

Isolation Double

L'isolation double est un terme qui a été appliqué à cette sorte de construction où une isolation additionnelle est intentionnellement incorporée dans l'équipement, de telle manière que la probabilité d'électrisation du métal exposé soit réduite au stricte minimum. Pour des raisons pratiques une simple couche d'isolation améliorée est employée et referee comme "Isolation renforçée" mais son usage est généralement très limité.

L'isolation double n'est pas un nouveau principe. On en a fait un usage peut-être modéré dans la lessiveuse avec essoreuse depuis plus de 40 ans.

Ici le moteur (et plus récemment d'autres pieces électriques) a été isolé du métal exposé. Le rasoir électrique en est un autre exemple typique. Cependant c'est seulement récemment que le principe a été formé au point de vue technique en des standards de sécurité nationale à l'étranger. Une spécification de la CSA traitant du principe émis cidessus est en cours de préparation dans la partie II du code canadien de l'électricité.

Quelques unes des caractéristiques de construction et des principes qui entrent dans le dessin des appareils à double isolation sont d'un interêt particulier.

Premièrement: La construction doit être telle qu'il doit y avoir défectuosité de deux sections indépendantes d'isolation avant que la partie de métal exposée soit électrisée à moins que la dite construction soit telle que l'isolation renforcée soit acceptable.

Deuxièmement: Le fil électrique ne doit pas avoir de conducteur pour la mise-à-terre éliminant de ce fait la possibilité de mauvaises connexions quand la fiche de prise de courant est remplacée.

Troisièmement: La construction doit-être telle que l'usage normal de l'équipment (réparation incluse) ne résultera pas dans la perte de l'isolation supplémentaire. C'est-à-dire le métal ex-térieur ne doit en aucune circonstance être en contact avec l'isolation normale des parties sous tension.

C'est cette exigence que dans le passé beaucoup d' appareils, étant supposés avoir une double isolation, n'ont pas rencontrée. Peut-être la principale cause de ce manquement a été de se fier à l'espace d'air suppose donner l'isolation additionnelle sans s'assurer si ce même espace serait rigidement maintenu pour la durée de l'équipement, soit comme résultat de l'usage normal ou de la réparation. Finalement l'appareil doit être marqué indiquant qu'il a une double isolation. Au Canada on exige les mots suivants "isolation double—Ne requiert pas la mise-à-la terre." (Double insulated—Grounding not required) ou l'équivalent.

Estimant que le dessin d'un appareil avec double isolation demande un bon jugement avec expérience il doit de plus supporter des essais suffisants. D'un intérêt particulier est l'essai de haut voltage au moints 2500 volts aussi bien que l'essai de force mécanique tel que l'essai de dureté de rebondissement et l'essai de dureté de choc. L'essai de courant de fuite et de résistance de l'isolation sont aussi requis dans plusieurs standards.

L'isolation double donc, fourni en un même coup un apoareil avec un facteur de sécurité plus grand dans son système d'isolation et ceci étant incorporé par le manufacturier est par conséquent indépendant des autres métiers et circuits extérieurs.

L'Expérience Dans Les Pays Étrangers

Comme nous au Canada semblons commencer un programme pour augmenter la mise-à-la terre des appareils portatifs, il serait intéressant de connaître l'expérience de pays étrangers.

Plusieurs pays étrangers ont dans la passé essayé de mettre en vigueur les exigences de la mise-à-la terre des appareils portatifs. Leurs efforts n'ont pas été une réussite complète puisque la plupart de ces pays maintenant accepte l'isolation double de l'équipement comme alternative à la mise-à-la terre.

En Europe quelques pays l'exigent même à la place de la mise-à-la terre, dans certains appareils opérés par un moteur. Les Pays-Bas et l'Italie par exemple le demandent pour les outils à main dont on se sert dans les ateliers et les usines.

La Suéde et le Danemark le demandent pour les appareils à commande mécanique de service domestique tel que la balayeuse électrique, polisseuse à plancher, machine à coudre, phonographe, etc., appareils que l'on manipule ou que l'on touche normalement. En regardant les statistiques on peut trouver des faits intéressants.

Les statistiques les plus complètes que l'on peut confronter annuellement sont peut-être celles de la division de sécurité industrielle de la Californie département des relations industrielles. Leurs chiffres démontrent quelques 4594 accidents d'origine électrique à l'ouvrage durant la période 1955-60 sur les circuits à bas voltage 600 volts et moins.

De celles-ci 49 furent fatales. L'année dernière (1960) 951 accidents du même genre furent rapportes dont 11 furent fatales. Quatre de ces accidents mortels arrivèrent sur des circuits de 120 et 240 volts et tous furent dus à l'électrisation du chassis de l'équipement.

Les statistiques de la Californie pour 1960 démontrent aussi que 132 accidents ont été causes par des appareils portatifs dont deux furent fatales; supposant que ces outfils étaient branchés sur des circuits à basse tension i.e. 120 ou 240 volts ces 132 accidents représentent 13% du total de 951 sur de tel circuit. Encore 123 sur 132 i.e. 93% arrivèrent à des personnes au contact de pièces électrisées, pieces qui normalement ne devraient pas l'être. Une mise-à-la terre effective ou l'isolation double aurait donc éliminé la plupart de ces accidents avec des appareils portatifs.

Quand on lit les statistiques qu'on a au Canada on se rend compte que plusieurs accidents sont causés par des appareils portatifs. Même si nos statistiques ne sont pas aussi complètes que celles de la Californie une enquête de quelques 50 accidents causés par des appareils portatifs i.e. branches avec corde d'alimentation qui ont été rapportes aux laboratoires d'essai de CSA durant la période 1955-60 démontrèrent que sur 18 mortalités 4 furent causés par des appareils portatifs. Sur ces 50 accidents 165 furent causés par des outils.

Il y a peu de doute que la raison pour laquelle les outils portatifs démontrent si peu de sécurité dans ces statistiques soit leur usage ou peut-être pour dire mieux leur mauvais usage. Dans la plupart des cas on en abuse littéralement. Les statistiques démontrent aussi que les fils électriques souples sont la cause de plusieurs accidents.

Non seulements les fils électriques effilés exposent-ils les conducteurs sous tension mais de mauvais raccordements quand il y a mise-à-la terre conduisent à d'autres problèmes.

Une analyse d'information Australienne faite par J. B. Hays des Laboratoires du Bell Telephone Inc., démontre qu'un grand nombre de mortalitiés sont causées par des raccordements défectueux sur des fils électriques et des fiches de prise de courant avec mise-à-la terre, ou causé par des conducteurs coupés ou autres défectuosités qui permettent au fil de mise-à-la terre de venir en contact avec les fils à tension.

En fait 18% de tous les accidents mortels depuis une période de 5 ans ont été causés par des erreurs de raccordements. Un autre 9% ont été causés par des conducteurs de mise-à-la terre devenus électrisés à cause de raccords déconnectés au point de contact.

En d'autres mots 27% des fatalités ont été causées par un mauvais fonctionnement du système de 3 fils avec mise-à-la terre pas seulement un manque de fonctionnement suffisant de mise-a-la terre. Sans doute, la mise-à-la terre effective a sauvé plusieurs vies et il est impossible naturellement de donner des chiffres là-dessus.

Cependant la maise-à-la terre comme mesure de sécurité diffère de la plupart des autres moyens de sécurité en ce sens qu'il peut engendrer des accidents comme le prouvent les statistiques d'autres pays.

A cause de ceci de forts arguments peuvent être émis pour ne pas embarquer dans un programme général de mise-à-la terre parce qu'un tel programme pourrait résulter avec plus d'accidents que nous avons actuellement. C'est ce qu'actuellement pensent certains groupes aux Etats-Unis.

Conclusion

La politique que nous au Canada suivons n'est pas encore très définie mais il semble pour le moment, que nous allons reconnaîrte l'isolation double sur la même base que la mise-à-la terre.

Jusqu'à quell point cela s'étendrat-il, cela appartient à un souscomité spécial sur la mise-à-la terre des appareils sous la présidence de Monsieur K. L. Bellamy de 'Hydro-Ontario. L'industrie ainsi aura le choix de décider quelle sorte de construction elle désire suivre dans le dessin de tel équipment.

Plusieurs sortes de petits appareils incorporeront sans aucun doute l'isolation double. De cette façon celui qui se sert de certains appareils portatifs aura le choix et sa décision devrait cependant être prise seulement après de sérieuses considérations concernant l'usage de l'appareil.

Quand on se sert d'un appareil sur le même circuit et que l'on sait que la mise-à-la terre de ce circuit est en bonne condition alors l'usage d'un appareil avec mise-à-la terre devrait fournier assez de sécurité.

Cependant là où l'appareil doit fonctionner sur différents circuits dont la maintenance n'est pas sous le contrôle de celui qui se sert du même appareil alors l'isolation double est à recommander.

Sans considérer quell choix a été fait, la personne qui se sert de l'appareil est, cependant, en aucune circonstance dégagée de la responsabilité de maintenir cet appareil dans des conditions de sécurité complète. Elle doit aussi observer les règles de sécurité dans la manière de se servir de ce même appareil. Il est aussi a souhaiter que toutes ces précautions ne soient pas annulées par de fausses réclaimes.

Reprinted from *News-Bulletin*, January 1262.

News-Bulletin Format to be Revised

Plans are now in the initial stages to revise the format of the *News-Bulletin*, official publication of IAEI, beginning with the January 1963 issue. One of the most important revisions will be to change the size of the publication from its present form to 8 ½" x 11". The new format will incorporate the attractive features of present up-to-date trade magazines, journals, and periodicals. — Excerpted from *News-Bulletin*, November 1962.

For the first time, *IAEI News* was featured heavily on the cover, with the word "bulletin" blending into the background. This began the phasing out of the title *News-Bulletin* and the beginning of *IAEI News*.

Cord-Fault Circuit Interrupters

How cord technology reduces the risk of fire and shock

By Dr. Frank Brugner and Ned Schiff

Abstract

Residential electrical fires were responsible for 750 deaths, 6,000 injuries and nearly $1.3 billion dollars in property damage in 1994. Thanks to smoke detectors, education, reduction in smoking, and many other factors, the total number of residential fires attended by the fire service has decreased dramatically, from over 750,000 in 1980 to 451,000 in 1994. However, the number of fires involving electrical equipment has remained relatively constant, thus growing from 27 percent of the residential fires in 1980 to over 34 percent of the total in 1994.

One of the common causes of electrical fires is damage to cords. Extension cords caused half of the 6,600 cord-related fires attended by the fire service in 1993. These cord fires were responsible for 110 deaths and over $100,000 million in property damage. Even more frightening is a 1984 Consumer Product Safety Commission study that showed that unattended cord fires (incidents where the fire service did not have to be contacted) occur 10-20 times as frequently as attended fires.

Leakage-current protection devices (LCPD) have been developed over the past decade, which provide protection both from user shock and product damage. These products disconnect the power once the leakage current (to ground) exceeds a certain threshold. A new technology is available which combines an LCPD with a special cord to detect not only faults to ground, but also series faults and line-to-neutral faults in the cord, at levels well below those required for combustion. The cord-fault circuit interrupter (CFCI) eliminates a majority of cord-related fires and provides improved protection from shock and electrocution. In this article, we will review the cord fire problem, leakage current protective devices, CFCI technology, and the best applications for this technology.

Cord Fire Problem

Damage to electrical cords is a very common problem with potentially fatal outcomes. Flexible cords are frequently within harm's way and are thus subject to degradation during the course of normal usage. Cords, in violation of the *Code*, are frequently run under furniture or through doorways, which can result in pinching and crimping of the cord. This results in conductor breakage or damaged insulation. The standard duty extension cord is rated for 13 amps and is typically applied on branch circuits protected by a 15- or 20-amp device. These cords can easily be overloaded through misuse of cords while still within branch rating simply by plugging in a high current device such as a space heater or by combining multiple products. In addition, cords are often run under carpets or are coiled. This is an incorrect use of cords. It inhibits proper cooling,

1988 May/June Issue

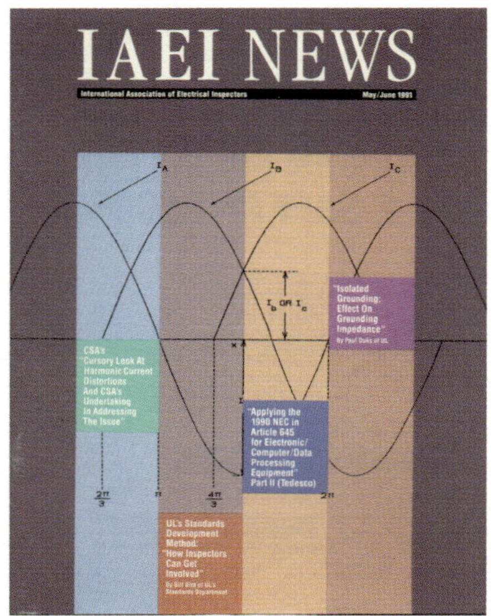

1991 May/June Issue

The *IAEI News* was displayed at INTERBIRO—15th International Exhibition of Information, Communication, Data Processing and Office Equipment, at the Zagreb (Yugoslavia) Fair on October 10–14, 1983.

thus overheating the cord and causing further cord degradation. In all these cases the damage is irreversible, often not visible, and can lead to a cord fault and a fire.

There are essentially two types of faults that are responsible for the majority of wiring-related electrical fires: series and parallel. A series fault is one in which a connection in series with the load is unintentionally broken, such as in the breakage of a conductor within its insulation casing. Heating will occur since breakage in the wire raises localized resistance to current flow. When the wire is severed, arcing may then occur across the gap. Both the increase in resistance and the arcing lead to localized heating.

A parallel fault is one in which there is a conduction path created between the phase and neutral conductors, between the phase conductor and ground (ground fault), or both. Parallel faults are generally considered to be the most common type of fault. There are three stages in the evolution of a parallel fault:

Leakage. Leakage currents will occur normally and safely in any cord set, related to the capacitance of the cable and the resistance of the insulation. As long as the insulation is in good condition, small, constant, leakage currents are considered harmless and safe.

Tracking (Treeing). As insulation degrades or becomes damaged over time, a conductive path may develop over internal insulating surfaces. Tracking is preceded by sporadic small current surges across the insulation called partial discharge. Partial discharge occurs at micro voids in the insulation. These voids contain the products of decomposed insulation in a gaseous state. Many times these gases are acidic and further accelerate insulation failure. These phenomena always lead to the destruction of the insulation system.

Arcing. Arcing is the final stage of this process when ionization of the gas across the insulation gap occurs, providing a conduction path between phase and neutral/ground. This arc generates intense heat leading to combustion.

Degradation can also occur internally to the insulation medium due to excessive heat. Fire may start from either combustion of surrounding materials or the insulation itself with localized heating or the later stages of insulation failure with arcing.

A ground fault is a type of parallel fault which is caused by current leakage from a current-carrying conductor to ground, such as a short from the phase conductor to the housing of an appliance. Even in the absence of arcing, if flammable material is present in or around the path to ground for leakage current, a fire hazard exists. In addition, it is possible for such a current to find its path to ground through the user of the appliance, giving rise to a risk for shock or electrocution. In fact, reduction of shock hazard has been the main impetus behind the development of a class of protective devices called leakage-current protective devices (LCPDs). It will be seen that risk of shock and fire arising from ground faults may be significantly reduced through the use of these devices.

Leakage-Current Protective Devices

The leakage-current protection device (LCPD) is a class of electrical or electromechanical devices that detect leakage of current in an electrical circuit. The basic schematic for an LCPD is shown in figure 1. Any current flowing in the phase conductor must return through the neutral conductor, unless there is leakage in the circuit.

Note that in the diagram both conductors pass through the toroid of the current transformer (CT), with the current flows having opposite sense. Thus, if the current on each conductor is of equal magnitude, there will be no net induction in the windings of the CT. However, when an imbalance occurs, current is induced in the secondary. This signal is typically fed to some type of trip mechanisms to shut off power to the circuit.

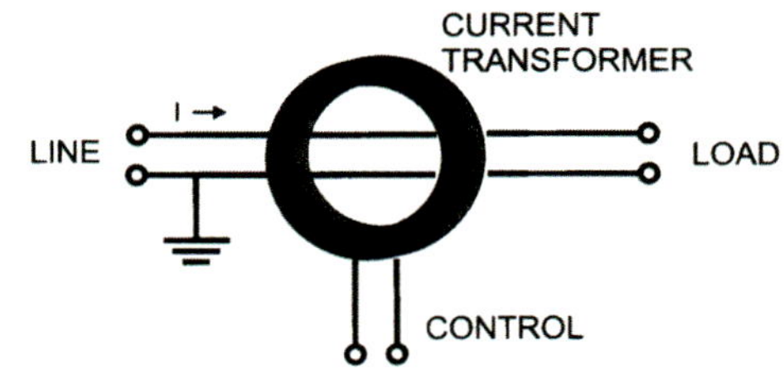

Figure 1.

UL has defined several classes of LCPD, related to the type and amount of shock protection they afford. Three of these will be discussed here, ground-fault circuit interrupters (GFCI), appliance-leakage current interrupters (ALCI) and equipment-leakage current interrupters (ELCI).

GFCI

A ground-fault circuit interrupter is an LCPD specifically intended to provide the most complete protection of people from shock hazard. Beyond the basic ground fault protection, GFCIs are required to provide both grounded neutral and broken neutral protection. A typical GFCI schematic is shown in figure 2.

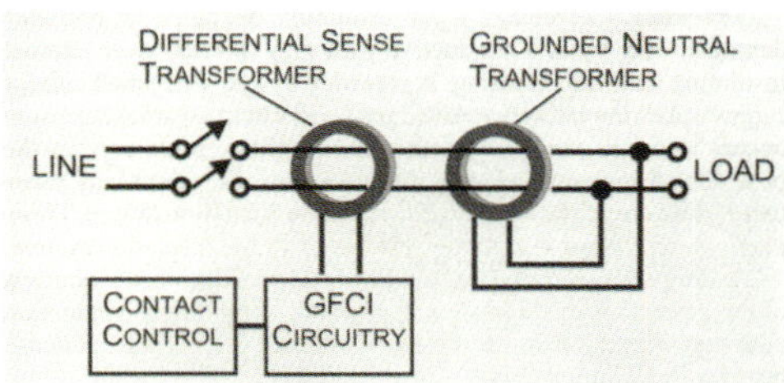

Figure 2.

When the differential transformer senses an imbalance in current between the leads, a signal is sent to the GFCI circuitry which commands a set of contacts to open, removing power from the load.

A notable difference between the GFCI of figure 2 and the generalized LCPD of figure 1 is the presence of an additional CT. The second CT is termed the grounded neutral transformer, which affords protection in the event the neutral becomes grounded on the load side of the protective device. This protection is a requirement of all GFCIs as defined in UL 943A.

Based upon medical research, UL has specified the leakage current trip levels for GFCIs to be in the range of 4-6 mA. The lower bound exists to limit nuisance tripping, since there is a level of leakage that would be considered both normal and acceptable.

In addition, there is a specified response time (the maximum allowable circuit disconnect time as a function of current) defined by the following equation

$$t = \left(\frac{20}{i}\right)^{1.43}$$

Where **t** is the response time in seconds and **i** is the current in mA.

ALCI

Appliance-leakage current interrupters are a class of LCPD closely related to GFCIs. In fact, they share the same limit for trip level and response time. The main difference is that ALCIs are intended for use only in circuits with a solidly grounded neutral conductor. Thus no requirement is specified for the double-grounded neutral protection or broken neutral protection, as in the case of GFCIs. Also, an ALCI-rated device must be an attended device, hence an extension cord with the identical protection level as an ALCI cannot carry the rating according to UL.

ELCI

Equipment-leakage current interrupters are a class of LCPD not considered to be "people protectors," and are generally only intended for equipment protection. ELCIs are virtually identically with ALCIs with the exception that the trip level is set higher than 6 mA. UL has defined no limits for the trip levels on ELCIs, though levels in the 10–30 mA range are common.

It is worth noting that though these devices are not considered adequate protection for all humans in all situations by UL, they still provide a level of protection for humans in many circumstances.

Cord-fault Circuit Interrupter

While GFCIs/ALCIs provide excellent shock protection and fire prevention in the case of ground faults, they provided no fire protection in the case of series arcing faults or other types of parallel arcing faults. CFCI power cords have been designed to detect leakage currents between and within conductors, and hence arrest the possibility of both parallel and series arcing faults before they can develop and ignite fires. Fire Shield accomplishes this by combining GFCI/ALCI technology with specially shielded conductors as shown in figure 3.

Because each conductor in the cable is completely surrounded by a metallic shield, any degradation in insulation or internal leakage (series or parallel) will pass current to the shield. When leakage currents reach a threshold value of 2.6 mA, the signal is carried along the shield to the GFCI circuitry, which will then shut off power to the load. Power is disconnected within 25 mS, well within the range defined by the formula referenced above. Faults are thus detected in the initial stages of cable degradation, well before arcing and combustion can occur.

Application Focus

This technology is well suited for a variety of applications. There are some common traits that make this premium technology desirable.

1. *Energized when attended.* Although all cord fires are undesirable, the most dangerous ones are those associated with unattended appliances, particularly those operating while people are sleeping. This includes window air conditioners, space heaters, counter top appliances such as bread makers, crock pots, and coffee pots, vaporizers, air quality products, electric beds, lift chairs, and extension cords.

2. *Portable.* Cords of portable products take a lot more abuse because of the frequent handling and storage in less than desirable locations. They are often located in high traffic areas as well. Window air conditioners, space heaters, and extension cords are good candidates.

3. *High Current.* High current applications operate closer to the maximum rating of the cord, placing them at a higher risk of overload. Additionally, if the cord is not provided with proper cooling, degradation can result in combustion. Exercise equipment, dehumidifiers, room air conditioners, heaters, major appliances, and extension cords are all desirable applications.

4. *Used with or near water.* These applications benefit from the ground fault protection built into the trip unit. Humidifiers, vaporizers, washing machines, and kitchen and bathroom appliances are potential applications for this technology. This not only protects against serious shock or electrocution, but also ground-fault related fires.

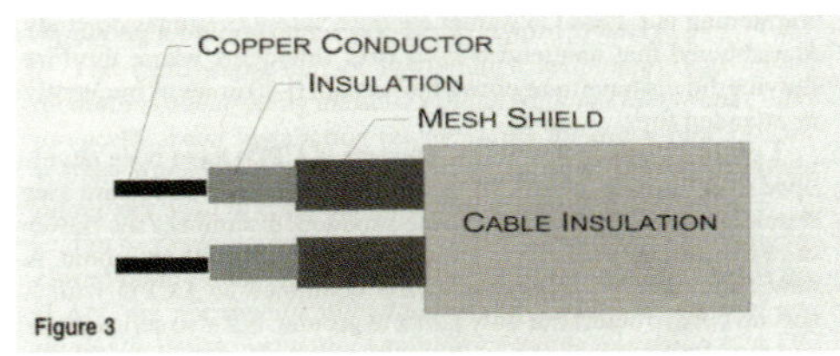

Figure 3.

5. *Products used around the elderly and children.* A disproportionate number of the fatalities in fires are with the elderly and children. Products used by the elderly including electric beds, lift chairs, and air purifiers. Products used in nursing homes and extended care facilities are excellent candidates as well. With children, an additional application concern is the frequent occurrence of mouth burns associated with infants' chewing on power cords.

Summary

Reducing residential electrical fires is an important and major challenge for the electrical industry. According to the U.S. Consumer Product Safety Commission's 1994 Residential Loss Estimates, the total fires attended by the fire service has decreased dramatically from over 750,000 in 1980 to 451,000 in 1994. However, fires involving electrical equipment have remained relatively constant in number thus growing from 27 percent of the residential fires in 1980 to over 34 percent of these fires in 1994.

The lack of progress in reducing residential fires involving electrical equipment can be attributed to many factors including:

1. We are using far more electrical products in our homes today.

2. Older residential distribution systems were not designed for the number or type of loads that are now in use.

3. Circuit breakers and fuses, by design, are not sensitive enough to detect faults before combustion occurs. Even the new AFCI breakers require a substantial arc to occur and do not detect all of the cord faults that cause fires.

4. Consumers do not understand electricity and, therefore, abuse and misuse electrical products.

Although these are valid issues, they should not deter us from applying new technologies to reduce the number of residential electrical fires. New products are now being marketed at a premium price based on safety (particularly where children are accessible to the product). CFCI technology provides premium protection that will reduce the risk of electrical cord fires and the risk of serious shock or electrocution. This protection is available at a very modest cost premium to manufacturers, even before the reduction in shock and fire liability is considered. When all costs are properly evaluated, CFCI protection provides very cost effective prevention for potential liability problems that all manufacturers encounter. As highlighted in this article, there are certain applications that benefit tremendously from this technology eliminating needless deaths and property damage caused by cord fires.

1. 1994 Residential Fire Loss Estimates, U.S. Consumer Product Safety Commission.

2. UL 943 Ground-Fault Circuit Interrupters

3. UL 943A Leakage-Current Protective Devices

4. Engineering Dielectrics, ASTM STP 66, Bartnikas/McMahon.

Dr. Frank Brugner has a masters in mechanical engineering and Ph.D. in material science and is the vice president of engineering for Technology Research Corporation. Ned Schiff has a bachelors of science in electrical engineering and economics and is the vice president of New Market Development for Technology Research Company.

Reprinted from *IAEI News*, March 1998.

Quick Fact 1994

At the International board of directors meeting on November 5, 1993, the board approved for new members' names to be printed in the *IAEI News.*

A CLOSER LOOK

Phil Simmons
IAEI Representative CMP-1

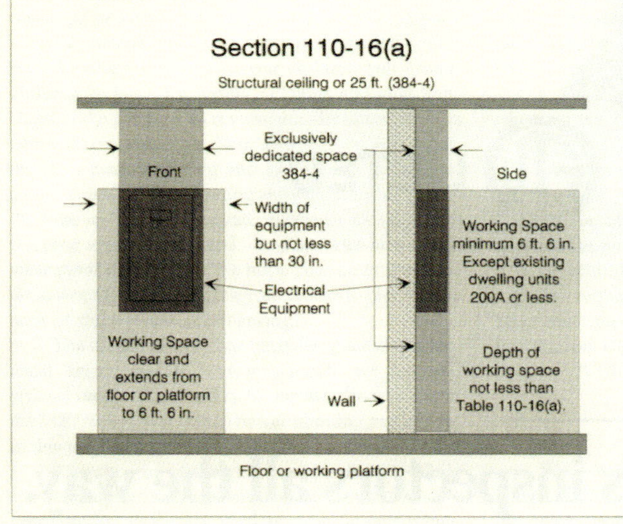

Section 110-16(a) has been revised in the 1993 National Electrical Code® to once again emphasize the importance of providing adequate working space about electrical equipment. The high cost of interior spaces in buildings and other structures make getting and maintaining adequate working and exclusively dedicated spaces more difficult.

The change occurred in the second paragraph of Section 110-16(a). A new second sentence reads, "The work space shall be clear and extend from the floor or platform to the height required by this section."

Someone once said that Ground Fault Circuit-Interrupters were the only "people protectors" in the Code. I think several Sections in Article 100 provide for "people protection." Adequate working clearances, headroom, exiting from electrical rooms and adequate illumination are examples of requirements critical to "people protection."

Working clearances in the direction of access to live parts operating at 600 volts, nominal, or less to ground and likely to require examination, adjustment, servicing, or maintenance while energized, must be in compliance with Table 110-16(a). First of all, a judgement must be made on whether the electrical equipment under consideration is likely to be worked on while energized. Usually, service equipment enclosures and sub-panels as well as industrial control panels, motor controllers and motor control centers are considered to require the working clearances. In many inspection jurisdictions, working clearance is also required about mechanical equipment such as heating, air-conditioning and refrigeration equipment. Since this section requires a judgement call in some cases, the installer is cautioned to verify the view of the local Authority Having Jurisdiction before installing electrical equipment in an unfamiliar area .

Once it is determined that working clearance is required, the minimum working clearance required is determined by reference to Table 110-16(a). Simply review the "Conditions" below the table to determine whether condition 1, 2 or 3 is applicable. Then, using the nominal voltage to ground, determine the minimum clear distance in feet required.

Distances must be measured from the live parts if such are exposed or from the enclosure front or opening if such are enclosed. This requirement is shown in the illustration by the words "Width of equipment but not less than 30 inches".

This space must be clear from the floor or working platform to a height not less than 6½ feet. [See Section 110-16(f)] Equipment such as transformers are not permitted to be located so they impinge on the working space.

It is not required that electrical equipment less that 30 inches wide be centered in the working space. It can be located anywhere in the working space. However, note that in all cases, the equipment must be located so equipment doors or hinged panels can be opened at least 90 degrees.

Shown in the illustration as well is the requirement in Section 384-4 for exclusively dedicated space above and below the electrical equipment within the scope of Article 384. No piping, ducts, or equipment foreign to the electrical equipment or architectural appurtenances is permitted to be installed in, enter, or pass through this space. This space is reserved for installing raceways, cables and electrical equipment related to the switchboard, panelboard or motor control center.

Providing adequate working space in compliance with Section 110-16 and the exclusively dedicated space required by Section 384-4 is critical to safety. Installers and inspectors must insist on compliance.

Illustration from IAEI Analysis of the 1993 National Electrical Code®.

This is the inaugural article of a new regular feature in the IAEI News. "A Closer Look" will be an in-depth analysis of a significant requirement in the NEC®. IAEI members of the 20 Code Making Panels will write on topics in their areas of expertise. Stay tuned!

6 IAEI NEWS

Our new column "A Closer Look" will be written by one of our code panel representatives and will be a regular feature in the *IAEI News*. Articles will explain the new requirements in the codes and the reasons behind the changes. Some articles will bring together requirements from several sections of the *Code* that impact a particular part of an electrical installation. If you have a subject or question that is in need of "A Closer Look" get in contact with us. — Excerpted from *IAEI News*, November 1992.

" PUTTING A JUMPER FROM TERMINAL 'D' OVER TO POINT 'X' DIDN'T WORK... ANY OTHER SUGGESTIONS? "

"It really isn't. I just want the cows to think it is."

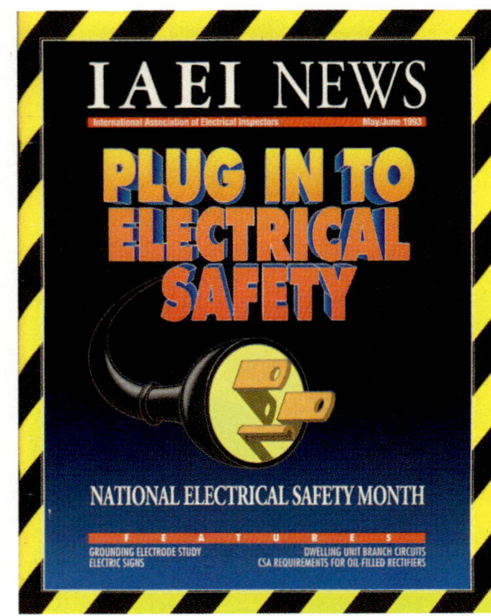

1993 May/June Issue

1996 November/December Issue

2002 March/April Award-winning issue

IAEI News recently placed silver in the scientific and technical journals (web) category of the prestigious Gold Ink Awards Competition. The March/April 2002 issue was submitted by IPC Communication Services, who print the magazine. This rigorous competition about quality was judged by accomplished professionals in the printing industry. Criteria for award-winning pieces included quality of printing, technical difficulty and overall visual effectiveness. Nearly 1800 entries competed in 40 categories; each category awarded only one gold, one silver, and one bronze. Winning entries will receive recognition in the special Gold Ink issue of *PrintMedia* magazine to be published in October. The Annual Gold Ink Awards Reception and Banquet will be held at McCormick Place in Chicago on the evening of October 7, 2002. — Excerpted from *IAEI News*, September 2002.

2000 May/June issue

1998 September/October Issue

IAEI NEWS 1915-2003
INTERNATIONAL ASSOCIATION OF ELECTRICAL INSPECTORS
OFFICAL PUBLICATION

A brief look at IAEI's logo history and development

1929 Association Emblem

The executive council in its February meeting adopted the official association emblem.

This emblem will be used on the official publications.

The emblem is also being made up in gold and enamel buttons and pins for members' use. The lettering and design is in gold with a center of white enamel and on the outer portion a deep blue enamel forming altogether a very attractive association pin which any member can be proud to wear. The cost with either a screw button or a clasp pin is $1 which should be forwarded to association headquarters, 612 N. Michigan Avenue, Chicago. — Excerpted from *News-Bulletin*, March 1929.

1929 Prize Offered for a Slogan

The officers of the International Association are of the opinion that a slogan descriptive or emblematical of the association or of its aim or activities will be of benefit to the association's work.

To this end President Forsyth has asked the executive council to act as a committee on this matter, and to excite interest in the undertaking, a prize of fifteen dollars has been offered by one of the members to be awarded to the person whose slogan is accepted.

All members of the association are eligible to this contest and a member may suggest as many different slogans as he desires, to send to International Association of Electrical Inspectors, Room 705, 612 N. Michigan Avenue, Chicago.

The slogan will be selected and the winner of the prize announced at the February 1930 meeting of the executive council.

The slogan "Let the Code Decide" as used by the Southwestern Section for some time, is shown. — Excerpted from *News-Bulletin*, November 1929.

[Editor's note: The slogan adopted by the Southwestern Section was eventually adopted by the IAEI as the official slogan.]

1960 A keystone was added to the association emblem (logo) in 1960, and it appeared in the September 1960 issue of the *News-Bulletin*. Similar keystones first started appearing in raw form on the cover of the magazine in the 1950s, but it did not officially take form until the aforementioned issue.

1965 While the keystone itself was introduced in 1960, the words "Incorporated 1928" did not appear until the September 1965 issue of the *IAEI News*. This version of the logo was registered in 1965, and would become the building block for the official logo that would later come in the 1970s.

1976 The circle logo officially premiered in 1976, with a debut on the cover of the May issue of *IAEI News*. When it first premiered, however, the color was on the keystone and the words, instead of the background.

1979 The colorless background changed in 1979, however, as the background color adopted the traditional blue favored by the organization. In 1929, the organization adopted the blue as a favored color of the emblem and this blue was used frequently until the modern adaptation of it, Pantone 300 blue, was chosen.

1995 The board of directors approved the creation of a member logo at its meeting in 1994. This *member logo* consists of the corporate logo with a wreath border and the word "member" at the top. It was produced in the same PMS 300 blue as the corporate logo. The logo was officially launched on January 1, 1995. — Excerpted from *IAEI News*, January 1995.

1998 The current official IAEI logo was trademarked in 1998. It was discovered at that time that the IAEI had not officially incorporated until 1930, and so the wording in the keystone was changed to reflect that fact. The logo's colors are blue and white, and, by law, cannot be changed in any way except for proportional resizing.

1998 The *IAEI News* lightning-bolt logo had its official launch on the cover of the November 1998 issue, and was trademarked in 2002. Since that time, the logo has come to represent IAEI as a marketing tool, used on books, pamphlets, and other corporate collateral.

Their Mission and Its Impact

C. W. Valentine, manager, switch department, Automatic Switch Company, spoke on automatic transfer equipment for emergency lighting and power at the Eastern New England Chapter meeting on November 15, 1944, in Boston.

Theirs was a single mission, one goal — to keep family and friends safe from the swift savage bite of electricity. The mission was broken down into small units and each pushed until the impact was felt around the globe. From this mission arose the need to train the second generation and from that need arose publications and seminars and close observance of the code.

April 1929. Talk of Organizing IAEI Chapter

About 50 inspectors from southern California met in the assembly room of the Los Angeles electrical department to consider the provisions of the 1928 *Code*. Mr. R. H. Manahan presided and the entire day was devoted to many interesting and valuable discussions of the new *Code* requirements. This enthusiastic group of inspectors have been holding regular meetings and are considering organizing an IAEI chapter. — Reprinted from *News-Bulletin*, May 1929.

May 1929. Proposed Committee on Talking Pictures

Chairman Alva Small of the electrical committee has issued a bulletin on a proposal to appoint a technical subcommittee on *National Electrical Code* regulations on wiring for sound reproduction in motion picture theaters and has asked for suggestions as to the interests and personnel to be represented thereon.

This is a very live subject with inspectors' organizations as the talking picture is being installed at a very rapid rate throughout the country in the smaller cities and theaters as well as in the more pretentious theaters.

Inspections will welcome prompt acting on the part of the proposed committee as standard regulations for the installation of this equipment is particularly desirable at the time of original installation. The *News-Bulletin* will try to keep inspectors informed with the development in this committee work. — Excerpted from *News-Bulletin*, May 1929.

January 1930. Campaign to Eliminate Fire Hazard

Mr. Charles A. Waller, electrical inspector of Saint Joseph, Missouri, instituted an active campaign over the holiday season looking toward the elimination of the fire hazard from defective wiring. In carrying out this effort, letters were sent to all merchants calling attention to the desirability of a strict compliance with *Code* rules and a use of only approved apparatus. The cooperation of the newspapers was also obtained and undoubtedly was very effective in lessening the hazard of holiday electrical decorations. — Excerpted from *News-Bulletin*, January 1930.

Students of the Industry

Students of the Code

From the very beginning the use and distribution of electricity was an adventure. Many were involved in the creative methods developed to handle this new and powerful force yet few realized the unseen dangers associated with electricity. It was a dynamic industry then and that feature is still apparent today. As the world evolved from candlelight to electric lamps, the dangers started to become apparent. The founding fathers and many of the association's first diligent ancestors of the IAEI recognized early on that education and training were going to be essential and inherent parts of the electrical industry. Electrical safety was and still is a primary objective and necessity. Not only were there going to have to be regulations to govern its use, but there would be a continuous need for training of industry professionals and installers, as well as electrical inspectors.

Electrical inspectors in the early years were primarily spawned from the industry and brought to the position a sense of competence through their knowledge of the electrical trade. Those involved in installation and enforcement realized and understood the need for staying current in their field. Today we call this "continuing education and training." It was a common fact that to be effective as an electrical inspector and apply the few rules available to electrical installations was a chore, but for safety it was evident of the worth in these services. Becoming a trained craftsman meant an investment in time and effort mostly on the job, learning by the school of hard knocks in many cases. As time passed classroom learning was the essential compliment to training of electrical trade workers.

Code Obsession

The term "*Code* Obsession" as mentioned in this publication relates to the interest and dedication to its presence in the electrical industry. The term is directly related to some primary important elements. These elements are all directed at a desire and need to develop and maintain the *NEC*. IAEI has demonstrated its commitment to this process by its active involvement from the early years. The following provides a gathering of thoughts relative to the meaning of the electrical industry's as well as IAEI's obsession with the *NEC*.

Develop and Maintain the *Code*

Since its birth, the *Code* has been molded and shaped by many pioneers in the industry. The process as well as the document has evolved into one of the most extensive accumulation of requirements in the electrical industry. IAEI has had and continues to have a strong voice in the production process of the *NEC*. IAEI is dedicated to the development of *Code* that is reasonable to comply with, and also one that is reasonable to enforce. This is often referred to in the industry as working for the development of "Good Code." If the *Code* is easily understood and also easily enforced, it has the benefits of consistency in understanding, and results in increased overall electrical safety. IAEI has been an active participant in the promotion and development of the *NEC* and continues to be committed to that cause as evidenced by participation on all NFPA-70 technical committees (code-making panels).

Learning the *Code*

For electricians, designers, engineers, electrical inspectors and others, the process of learning the *Code* starts early in one's career. One of the unique things about this business is that it is constantly changing and new technology is entering the field on a routine basis. Learning the *Code* is an essential process for success. It should be understood that the process does not end, but is ongoing. The *Code* gets more

Eastern New England Chapter meeting on November 15, 1944, in Boston. The main discussion of the meeting was a program by C. W. Valentine, manager of the switch department at the Automatic Switch Company, who spoke on "Automatic Transfer Equipment for Emergency Lighting and Power." He pointed out the need of emergency lighting in buildings such as theaters, auditoriums, and the like. At the end of the meeting, a moving picture showing the invasion of Italy was shown to the members.

extensive and complete from cycle to cycle and added emphasis on staying current with the requirements is essential. IAEI understands the value of staying current with the rules in the *NEC*, because they relate to electrical safety for persons and property. We are all students of the *Code* to one degree or another.

Teaching the *Code*

Inspectors are generally good teachers of the *Code*. As A.H. Welkin once wrote, "Inspectors that teach the *Code* not only provide an invaluable service to those in need of *Code* training, but also keep themselves current with the rules." The old saying, "Nobody learns more than the instructor" is still so true. Basically as inspectors move on to teach the *Code*, they find out that they benefit tremendously as they prepare to instruct students. One can easily conclude that those involved in the electrical industry are "students of the *Code*" and must remain current. The need for training and continuing education grows ever larger as the *Code* grows. IAEI has dedicated resources and efforts to be among the few authoritative electrical training arms that can provide insight as to the meaning and purpose of the *NEC*, and also provide valuable insight relative to the perspective of the inspector in their teachings. As inspectors perform their daily responsibilities, it often results in a learning process for both the inspector and the customer.

Code Application and Enforcement

One of the primary concerns and objectives of IAEI is to work for the uniform and consistent application and enforcement of the *Code*. It is vital that the inspector's voice be consistent and uniform in his or her day-to-day performance on the job. The consistency and uniformity is directly related to the credibility of the inspector and jurisdiction. This objective can only be met with a strong emphasis placed on education and training in the *Code*. It is vital that electrical inspectors not only understand how to find the information within the *NEC*, but that they effectively apply those rules to installations and systems. The *NEC* rules provide for installations that are essentially safe and free from hazards, but are only effective where they are properly applied.

IAEI Directors Emphasize Electrical Code Training

In the early years of the association, a great deal of emphasis was placed on organizing the IAEI and establishing primary objectives and goals. It is clear in the current objectives and mission of the organization that those remain as an important feature the IAEI continues to foster.

From the beginning, each IAEI executive director including Secretary Tousley, along with input and guidance from the IAEI board of directors had a hand in paving the road that IAEI is traveling on today. Teaching and education were apparent at the IAEI meetings through interactive *Code* training programs and *Code* question discussion forums and panels. In the 1970s and early 1980s it became apparent that IAEI needed to expand the training arm of the organization. While L. E. LaFehr was executive director, IAEI started placing increased emphasis on educational information in the *IAEI News*. The association had been growing in membership for decades now, and was experiencing some growing pains in some key areas. One of these was the education and training segment of IAEI. The need for growth in this area was becoming more evident.

During the period where Wilford Summers was executive director, the IAEI starting expanding and taking on new challenges that focused on providing training material and programs. Under Wilford's tenure, the IAEI started developing training publications in the interest of supporting the education and training needs of electrical industry workers and the inspectors. The first IAEI training publications were the *Analysis of Changes of the NEC* and *Soares' Grounding Electrical Distribution System for Safety*. IAEI purchased the copyright to Eustace C. Soares' original publication, and continues to update and produce it today in his memory. *Soares Book on Grounding* evolved into one of the most authoritative publications on the topic in the industry. With the publication of this material, the IAEI was also pressed into growth and expansion in the local and national seminar arena. IAEI started to provide numerous training seminars throughout the United States and beyond in some cases. IAEI also teamed up with major organizations like NEMA, NFPA, and UL to provide training seminars geared toward continuing education in the proper understanding of the *NEC*.

Group of early IAEI leaders, who were instrumental in teaching early seminars at local chapter and division meetings, examining a standard dead-front switchboard section (labeled), donated by Mullenbach Electric Manufacturing and Zinmeyer Company, exhibited at the Southern California Chapter meeting on March 27, 1946. *From left to right*: J. H. Crannell, retired chief electrical inspector for the city of Glendale; H. G. Ufer; R. H. Manahan, retired chief electrical inspector, city of Los Angeles, later the inspector for Laguna Beach; and Paul M. Rodet, chief electrical division for the city of Los Angeles.

In the early 1990s IAEI placed a new executive director, J. Philip Simmons, who took the IAEI educational training ball and ran with it. Under Phil's tenure, the job responsibilities of the executive director were expanding to include regular training material development as well as providing leadership for the association. It had become a monumental task to continue to produce IAEI training publications, training seminars, and tend to the mounting business needs of the association. During Phil's time as IAEI executive director, the association was able to continue to revise these first two publications and also add the first IAEI published material on *One- and Two-Family Dwelling Electrical Systems*, *Ferm's Fast Finder Index*, and the *Neon Installation Manual*. During this time frame the IAEI was also involved in the development and support of a national certification program for construction code inspectors (see chapter 7 for additional information on IAEI's role in the electrical inspection certification process). This spawned the need for the three IAEI certification exam study guides. The IAEI publications library had expanded to eight, each requiring revisions as new *Code* cycles arrived. The amount of work to keep the training material and seminar program of IAEI was growing, as was the association membership.

IAEI Seminar Instructors

Executive Director Simmons also recognized the value of training IAEI seminar instructors from the electrical inspector ranks. IAEI instructors many times were also directly involved with the code-making process by serving on the NFPA-70 technical committees. This quality is still apparent today as the IAEI instructors either have served on a code-making panel for the *NEC* or are currently serving in that capacity. Instructors like Summers, Simmons, Lawry, Helmick, and others recognized for their knowledge and professionalism were complimenting the electrical training circuit with their presence and efforts. The IAEI training provided by these instructors offers valuable and authoritative insight, as well as an unbiased approach to the meaning of *Code* rules as well as valuable background information on how they were developed. Probably the most important element of the IAEI instructors is that they teach the *Code* from the perspective of the electrical inspector. IAEI training seminars and publications were gaining in popularity and demand as the association continued to grow. Many new members were being recruited through the IAEI seminar programs.

In the mid 1990s the IAEI saw increased growth and Philip H. Cox took the reigns as executive director and CEO. Under Phil's tenure the growing pains and demands of IAEI in the education and training segment continued. Phil was involved not only in the needs to expand the IAEI internationally, but also continued the work started by Simmons. Phil recognized and identified a true and meaningful need for the development of a full Education Department.

Along with the guidance of the board of directors, IAEI affirmed its commitment to electrical education and training by expanding to include a department dedicated to handle development and revisions of training publications and programs, and manage the seminar and certification programs. (See chapter 10 for additional details about the IAEI Education Department.) IAEI saw increased expansion in the development of additional training materials, seminar offerings and implemented an additional on-site seminar program. IAEI also received accreditation from the International Association of Continuing Education and Training (IACET) as an authorized provider of continuing education units for its training programs. IAEI also added two additional publications to the library during Phil's time as executive director. *Neon Lighting* and the *Comprehensive Study Guide* were in the process of development under Phil's direction and saw completion and publishing under the leadership of the current executive director and CEO, James W. Carpenter. Expansion that includes additional training materials and publications are in the plans for the 2005 *NEC* cycle under Jim's leadership. Once again, IAEI continued to address the training needs of installers and inspectors.

Today the Education Department continues to work at an aggressive pace to maintain its standing among the best quality and informative sources for electrical *Code* training materials and seminars in the industry. This chapter takes a look back at some of the significant events and emphasis placed on the inspector and electrical training and how IAEI grew in these areas and maintains the flexibility and versatility to continue to move with the industry as an active participant in providing electrical training and continuing education programs. IAEI continues into the new century with a clear focus and vision of the industry electrical training needs and meeting important missions and objectives of the association.

by Michael J. Johnston, IAEI director of education, 2003.

Letter from President Forsyth to Presidents of Sections

It is my belief that the International Association should start a campaign looking to some improvement of electrical conditions from the standpoint of safety to life and property. The electrical industry is awaiting some action on our part along several lines and we must meet the situation as completely as possible in order that we may justify the existence of our organization and also that we may continue to have the financial and moral support of all branches of the industry. We should be a constructive force as well as a regulatory one.

There are two matters that appear to be of pressing importance and I would request that you consider them, if necessary, with your executive committee and, if agreeable, authorize in the name of your section, the necessary procedure to place in effect concerted action in these respects.

It is my suggestion that a communication be sent from the secretary of each section to every inspector who has authority to proceed along the lines indicated; this communication to urge that these inspectors appoint some member of his staff to visit all stores and supply houses selling or offering for sale electrical devices and materials and to take up with them from the question of discontinuing the handling of any device or material that is not in compliance with the *National Electrical Code* or local ordinances. It has been my experience from work of this nature carried on from this office that merchants, particularly in department stores, once they are acquainted with the situation will willingly follow the recommendations of the inspection bureau. A concerted action along this line would most certainly discourage all manufacturers of substandard cords and make it difficult to market this product on the basis of costs alone. Condemnation reports from various sections of the country would lead the manufacturer of the material to believe that there would be very little profit to be made from it.

The other matter which should be handled through the same channels and by the same group of inspectors is the question of adequate wiring particularly in residences and apartment houses. Each inspector should get into communication with the architects, builders, and electrical contractors in his territory and point out to them the advantages of adequate wiring being provided at the time the buildings are erected and to secure, if possible, newspaper items bearing on this subject. In this communication there should be an explanation as to what is meant by adequate wiring. This can be covered by specifying the number of additional outlets other than lighting outlets that should be installed in rooms devoted to particular purposes such as bedrooms, bathrooms, kitchens, etc.

It is my belief that concerted action by all inspection departments throughout the country would be not only of great value to the electrical industry and would secure their hearty assistance and cooperation but particularly would result in reducing the number of electrical fires from present unsafe methods of wiring. While these efforts would undoubtedly be of vale to the electrical industry, yet they would be of much more value to the public by providing them with easy, safe, and ready points for attachment of electrical devices and appliances and in doing away with the necessity for unsightly installation of flexible cords on walls and ceilings.

Very truly yours,
J. C. Forsyth, President.

—Reprinted from *News-Bulletin*, March 1930.

Sign in and registration for one of the IAEI section meetings, circa 1958. Educational speeches figured heavily in these meetings.

Spreading Knowledge of the *Code*

In a recent paper by the representative of a Wisconsin utility, there appeared the following:

"In discussing the matter of electrical installations with reference to fire protection, the first thing that comes to our minds is the *National Electrical Code*. I think we all have a rather hazy idea about the details of this *Code*. It is much like our life insurance policy—we know the amount and the company with which we have insurance but we are not very familiar with the details. If anybody should be thoroughly acquainted with the *National Electrical Code*, it should be those who are engaged in the business of furnishing electricity and making electrical installations."

It may appear to electrical inspectors and to those who deal directly and continually with the *Code*, that everyone who should be is thoroughly familiar with *Code* provisions, but such, evidently, is not the case.

The *Code* is designed to prevent electrical fires and accidents and everyone, therefore, has a direct interest in compliance with it. The general application of the *Code* involves two essentials — a "knowledge" of the *Code*, and its "enforcement;" and this latter cannot be successfully carried out without the former.

There is a characteristic of the *National Electrical Code* that makes a "knowledge" of it of unusual value. The *Code* is not "enforced" as we usually use this term in its application to laws. It is more a statement of fact to say that the *Code* is "conformed" to. And it is conformed to because it is reasonable and just and because it is to the best interest of all concerned to conform to it.

The first duty of an inspector in charge of an inspection department is to obtain a compliance with the electrical code provisions and any action which tends to spread a knowledge of the *Code* makes this effort easier to accomplish and more effective.

It would seem then that every inspector in charge of an inspection department should so arrange his affairs that he can devote some time at least to spreading the knowledge of the *Code*.

That there is presented an opportunity among some of the utility groups is evident from the paragraph quoted above. But there are many more. There has recently been organized a group of electrical maintenance engineers. These men are vitally interested in a knowledge of the *Code* and would undoubtedly welcome an opportunity to learn more about it.

Manufacturers, business men's associations, chambers of commerce, and neighborhood groups, all present fields for disseminating the message of the *Code*. A very fertile field is that of engineering college classes. These men become the engineers of tomorrow and the fundamentals of the *Code*, once established in their minds, pay big returns.

Last, but not least, is the public itself. It is the public that the *Code* is designed to protect. It is the public whose life and property are safeguarded. It is the public who gains or suffers with conformity to the *Code* or in noncompliance with it. The public is interested in the *Code* and that interest has been proven wherever an individual in charge of an inspection department has seen fit to take advantage of its opportunities.

Inspectors and chief inspectors should make this spreading of the *Code* knowledge a definite part of their activities.

Reprinted from *News-Bulletin*, July 1931.

Quick Fact

Everyone's Off At War

A. J. Diebold, instructor of electricity, resigned from the IAEI due to the fact that no students are taking instructions in electrical work at the present time. — Reprinted from *News-Bulletin*, March 1942.

The Electrical Inspector

The electrical inspector belongs to and is an integral part of a great industry—an industry that today plays a most important role in the life of our nation.

An industry that has given us the telegraph that decreased the size of our country and brought together the people of its extremes and then has followed with those greater developments: the telephone, the radio, and soon with television.

An industry that has lighted the streets of our cities and controlled their traffic, and has lighted the highways of the air and controlled its traffic too. That has lighted our homes and our factories and our churches, our theaters, and our parks, and gives us many more hours in which to live.

An industry that has transported us overhead and underground, through city streets and through mountain passes.

An industry without which neither the airplane nor the automobile could be operated, nor could they be made as they are today.

An industry that in its power application is ever expanding and limitless. This factory depends on it and the home life without it would be toilsome and drab.

Take away from the home the electrical light with its utility and its decoration, the range, the water heater, the oil burner, the refrigerator, the fan, the vacuum cleaner, the toaster, the humble electric bell, and the thousand and one devices and appliances that serve us in health or in sickness and ease our work and make life more worth living.

An industry that is so essential to our existence and our welfare that it ceases to belong to the group, but to the nation as a whole.

Note our Blue Eagle, the symbol of our national recovery. An eagle—the years old emblem of our nation—holding in one claw a cog-wheel almost the elementary in mechanics and in the other a symbol of electricity, that comparatively new but tremendously important factor in our lives and the life of our nation.

The electrical inspector should feel proud and should consider it a privilege to be part of this great industry. He should accept the honor and assume the obligation it imposes. He should completely understand the elements of the industry to which he belongs and should make himself a component part of its development and its advancement.

Reprinted from *News-Bulletin*, January 1934.

The Blue Eagle, circa 1934.

A Moving Picture on Electrical Safety

The IAEI public relations committee has produced a moving picture on "Preventing Fires Through Electrical Safety." The film is available to inspectors or to volunteer fire departments for showings to public groups.

This film was produced as a part of the association's program to instruct the public in safe handling of electrical wires and appliances which are being used in ever increasing numbers of homes. Electrical inspectors know that installations which are adequately safe when first installed, frequently become unsafe when occupants bring in substandard equipment and attach handyman wiring to the electrical system. They also know that most electrical inspection departments and most fire departments do not have the facilities to make re-examination in homes.

The association feels the most effective way of avoiding unnecessary hazards is through public education.

The New York Fire Department cooperated with the association in making the picture by providing firemen and equipment to appear in several of the scenes. A short version of the film was shown in the booth of the fire department in the New York World's Fair. The presentation takes the form of a talk given to a public audience by a uniformed fireman. After the lecture has discussed some particular hazard, the scene shifts to a home, where it shows how the hazard is actually created, and the fire started. In each case, the fireman explains how such fires can be avoided.

Prints are on 16 mm safety film and are silent. The pictures, with a few titles, tell the story completely. The film is 730 feet long and requires about twenty-three minutes to show.

The public relations committee has provided a number of copies of the film which have been placed in various sections of the country. All that is necessary to secure the film is to write to the nearest of the committee's representatives and ask to borrow the film for a particular date or a specified time. The user must pay the small shipping charge one way; the return shipment will be paid for by the committee.

Representatives handling the film are:

Paul Ferneding, 85 John St., New York, New York.

J. W. Dunning, City Hall, Columbia, South Carolina.

Frank G. Camus, City Hall, Shreveport, Louisiana.

John E. Wise, State Office Building, Madison, Wisconsin.

E. J. Stewart, 701 Jackson Street, Topeka, Kansas.

Marion M. Wilson, 804 Farlow Avenue, Rapid City, South Dakota.

E. G. S. Pryor, P.O. Box 1818, Seattle, Washington.

F. D. Weber, P.O. Box 70, Portland, Oregon.

K. W. Keene, 500 Sansome Street, San Francisco, California.

Herbert G. Ufer, P.O. Box 6360, Metropolitan Station, Los Angeles, California.

Electrical safety is a subject which has been given very little attention, and for that reason the film will hold considerable interest for public groups. The committee invites you to borrow the film and show it.

— Reprinted from *News-Bulletin*, March 1940.

IAEI Film Shown at Safety Council Meeting

The Massachusetts Safety Council Fire Prevention meeting was held at the Statler Hotel, Boston, on March 11, 1940. Among the interesting items on the program was a showing of the IAEI publicity committee's film "Preventing Fires Through Electrical Safety."

New York Chapter Exhibit

In a letter from F. E. Swane of the New York Chapter, he states the chapter's safety exhibit has had a very busy time. After a showing of the exhibit at the Hotel New Yorker, it was moved to a display window in the office of the Nassau County Fire Marshal at Mineola, Long Island, where it received considerable publicity.

The exhibit was then moved to Plainfield, New Jersey, where it was displayed at the Ben Eiseman Company, under the direction of Vernon Cowart of Plainfield. Here again the exhibit received considerable publicity.

Excerpted from *News-Bulletin*, May 1940.

Public Relations Through Electrical Safety Education

It goes without saying, that selling electrical safety is destined to become your biggest job. And while you are selling electrical safety you are selling the *National Electrical Code* and the IAEI. Incidentally, the people of your community will know there is such a fellow as the electrical inspector. There are plenty of avenues wide open awaiting your beckoning call to do a real public relations job. One of the most successful methods at your disposal, we believe, is through the medium of displays. The home show, the state and county fairs, and similar events present a challenge to every electrical inspector in the country. Up to now, we never heard of it costing a thin dime—merely your effort and you will be rewarded in a thousand ways. Try it. It is here that people seem to be in the mood to watch and listen. Attractive displays will captivate people. You will have large numbers of people willing to accept and digest the intelligence you provide them with.

You should have very little difficulty in arranging features with drawing power. Displays with action are bound to catch the eye. Contrasting "Model T" type service entrance equipment with the latest models always command a lot of attention. In fact, the showing of any wiring or appliance of early vintage along side the latest designs invariably prove interesting. If nothing more, you can illustrate your point with large photographs showing installations of a hazardous nature along with those of an approved type. You might also arrange an attractive and effective display depicting how overloading of circuits gradually develop and the result. Booklets appropriate for this type of publicity are available through Donald Benson, secretary/treasurer, Safe Electric Cord Committee, 155 E. 44th Street, New York City.

There are only a few suggestions on items which have met with success.

The sky is the limit on what can be done. Won't you do some exploring in your respective community and let us know the outcome? We hope the time will come when the public relations committee, through the IAEI office, will be in a position to offer appropriate items for use by our members.

—Reprinted from *News-Bulletin,* By Art Welklin, chairman of public relations committee, IAEI, November 1955.

Inspectors in School

First course on human relations for electrical inspectors conducted by the Northern California Chapter, International Association of Electrical Inspectors, was reported by E. E. Carlton, educational committee chairman, as a complete success. The course held alternately in Oakland and San Mateo on six successive Wednesday nights in April and May was conducted by Harry Swift, consultant.

Its purpose was to improve inspectors' relations in their work with contractors, building owners, people in the field and to adjust differences in viewpoints and enforce compliance and handle complaints. A total of 31 enrolled and of these 20 attended all six. The remainder attended practically all of the course also. Two even came each Wednesday from Monterey.

The report was made by Carlton at the Northern California Chapter meeting in Oakland July 16, 1958. He said that it was the first of a group of educational courses to be developed for inspector members. Charles Viss, Modesto Chapter chairman, presided. The afternoon was spent touring General Electric Company industrial control equipment plant in East Oakland.

—Reprinted from *IAEI News,* November 1958; Courtesy of *Electrical West.*

Quick Fact

Insurance Coverage

1950 was the first year that all section meetings of the association were covered by an injury liability and property damage insurance which was provided for by the International office, in a single policy, the cost of which was borne by the several sections.

Reprinted from *News-Bulletin,* September 1951.

IMPORTANCE OF TRAINING FOR INSPECTORS

This matter of training of inspectors is daily becoming a bigger program. I needn't tell you that you are engaged in probably one of the most important works that any human can engage in, the job of inspecting wiring and the job of preserving the lives and property of people. I don't know how you can engage in a more important work than this.

For five years I was chief inspector for the city of Topeka and my responsibilities were daily thrown in my face. I don't know how many of you have ever had the occasion of being called upon to go out to some home where a child had been electrocuted. Unfortunately, I had that too often in Topeka.

In case you haven't, let's hope that you never do. I want to kind of go over this with you, as to what happens to you in a case like this. You go to the door, you are met by some relative of the deceased child and, of course, he is in a very distraught condition and he proceeds to usher you into the locality where the accident happened. Meanwhile, you can hear the almost hysterical sobs of the mother of this child and the father in there trying to comfort her, and these people look at you like, "Why didn't someone tell us? Why didn't someone warn us of the terrible hazard that can exist right in the home?"

And then you start a little self-recrimination and you wonder, "Well, what could I have done? Is there anything I could have done to prevent this terrible calamity?" And if you stop and think long enough, you will find out that there is, and it is this facet of inspector training that I want to discuss.

Probably the greatest need that you have for training is in public relations and public information work. Your technical training largely can be gathered from such meetings as this. This great association, the International Association of Electrical Inspectors, has done a fabulous job in keeping all inspectors abreast of new developments in the electrical industry and of all the technical changes, changes in the *Code*.

An IAEI display for safety week, courtesy of Art Welkin and the Indiana Chapter, circa 1955.

In fact, you discuss them right here in your meetings before they enter the *Code*. You are largely responsible for the items that appear in this *Code*. But the public information and your public relations work is something that you have to develop on your own.

How can you best go about this? Well, my suggestion is to use the media that is available to you, of course, and then I think you will find the newspapers, radio stations, television stations, are really eager to get hold of information that is of general interest and general use to the public. And what could be more important than telling the public how they can save lives, their own lives, their own property and the lives of their children?

We are coming into the Christmas season and, of course, I know most of you municipal inspectors are now shuddering at the thought of some of these worn, ten-year-old, twenty-year-old Christmas tree lights that are going to be strung around the home at this joyous and festive season and they are going to be draped around a piece of highly combustible material. One little short-circuit and this joyous season of Christmas is turned into a holocaust where children are burned, maimed, houses are destroyed, and the season of joy becomes a season of sorrow.

Take this opportunity to contact these media that I mentioned to you, your newspapers, television stations, radio stations, get on and explain to them that worn and used cords of any kind should never be used. Use non-combustible trees if it is at all possible in the home.

Explain these things. You can do it better than I, because you are more in contact with it than I am. It has been five years since I have been with the inspection department of the city of Topeka and I have lost contact with a lot of your developments and actually this came home to me as I wandered through the fourth floor here and I saw all of these new developments.

Kansas Conducts Code Forum

Sanctioned by the officials of the city of Wichita, Kansas, and supported by the officials of the Kansas Gas and Electric Company, with their full cooperation and enthusiasm, a code forum was held under the general supervision of George M. Lancett, chief building inspector, city of Wichita, Kansas. The code forum lasting approximately three hours, was held in mid-January 1959.

Permission was given by the Gas & Electric Company officials to conduct the code forum in their comfortable auditorium. In spite of the unfavorable weather conditions, some three hundred interested people, including architects, engineers, electrical contractors, electricians, electrical inspectors, and high school electrical groups, attended the forum.

Some participants drove as much as 150 miles to attend. Besides furnishing the auditorium, the utility personnel spent many hours in planning the meeting with Mr. Lancett and also provided a dutch lunch for everyone attending, free of charge.

Mr. Lancett acted as master of ceremonies and together with a panel consisting of his board of electrical examiners, guided the forum. The first half of the forum was devoted entirely to the explanations of the various sections of the *Code*.

The second session comprised a question and answer period in which questions were asked directly from the floor, made convenient through the use of an aisle mike. Written questions taken from a question box set up in the auditorium were also answered.

The success of the code forum may also be contributed to the fact that Mr. Lancett and his committee met over a period of two months preceding the scheduled date of the forum and discussed thoroughly the various articles in the *National Electrical Code* to be discussed.

Mr. Lancett agreed that this planning required a great deal of work beforehand. Invitations were extended to various interested groups. However, all agreed that they received wonderful cooperation and were therefore well repaid by the interest and enthusiasm and the deep feeling that something really worth while had been accomplished.

Reprinted from *News-Bulletin*, September 1959.

You are a rapidly developing industry and you have got to keep in touch. But I want to dwell on that one point. Get your message across to the public, and this is one of the greatest things you can do.

As far as inspector training is concerned, I want to explain a little bit to you the functions of our department. Throughout the states of Kansas and Missouri we have had a lot of new inspectors.

We have had inspectors who were combination inspectors; they were electrical, plumbing and building inspectors. Some of them were fire chiefs; some of them were city clerks; but all of them needed the vital information that could be brought to them by the inspectors in the larger areas.

I worked with George Lancett, and we set up as school where each of these inspectors, the building, plumbing and electrical, would conduct schools for the inspectors in the smaller areas, these inspectors that have to inspect all of the facets in the building industry. This is one of the services my bureau can be of use to you on, no matter where you are.

Contact your apprenticeship representatives or your state supervisor and get the information from him about how these classes can be started. There is money available, federal funds, known as the George Barton Act, to provide teachers to teach these classes and wherever you live in smaller communities surrounding a large community, this would be an ideal situation, to have the inspectors in the larger community instructing the classes in these smaller communities.

We intend setting up one of those in the near future in Topeka. I am going back to Wichita and complete my arrangements for setting up a school there. This way, those of you who do not have the opportunity to come to these meetings of your IAEI, the inspectors in your smaller communities can have the benefit of the very fine training that they can get here at your sectional and even your chapter meetings.

When we talk of inspector training, this is where you get your technical training, right here, right at your International Association of Electrical Inspectors, from great guys like Sam Rosch, Josh Fisher, Bill Hogan, and all of the rest of them here who are capable and can give you their life's work in a few words.

By Thomas McGinnis, state supervisor, United States Department of Labor, Bureau of Apprenticeship and Training. This paper was delivered before the annual meeting to the Western Section, on October 5, 1960, in Kansas City, Missouri. Reprinted from *News-Bulletin*, March 1961.

The Need for Professional Status for the Electrical Inspector

To properly evaluate the need for technical personnel, let us first consider the engineering manpower team. There are several types of technical personnel. There is the professional engineer, the semi-professional engineering technician, and there is the craftsman, into which class the electrical inspector falls.

The engineer usually has four years as a minimum of academic training beyond high school, with at least a bachelors of science degree.

On the other end of the spectrum is the craftsman who in most instances, has arrived at his status through practical training on the job, as an apprentice or through vocational training.

What are the qualifications of an electrical inspector? It can be said, an electrical inspector is one who can carry out, in a responsible manner, either proven techniques which are common knowledge among those who are technically expert in this branch of engineering or those specially prescribed by professional engineers.

Under general professional direction, he is capable of carrying out duties which may comprise working on design, drafting, estimating, inspecting, locating faults, and activities connected with sales engineering and representation, advising consumers and training and education of those of the allied field.

In carrying out many of these duties, the competent supervision of the electrical inspector is necessary. The techniques employed, demand acquired experience and knowledge of all phases of the job, combined with the ability to work out the details in the light of a well-established practice.

The electrical inspector therefore has a background sufficient to enable him to understand the reasons and purpose of an operation for which he is responsible. This covers a span from a small residence to factory, a chemical plant, a hospital, a grain processing plant and so on.

The scope is tremendous, but the fact remains that the electrical inspector who is delegated by law or otherwise to enforce the electrical code, must, by education, training and experience, be in a position to see that the code rules are properly interpreted and applied.

He is the authority who has the responsibility for checking wiring designs by accredited professional engineers, regardless of the fact, that generally speaking, he has no professional status.

The electrical inspector is the liaison between the professional man and his client.

Such a paradox has been recognized and standards should be assembled whereby those inspectors who qualify could be recognized on a professional basis.

In addition to the technical qualifications of an electrical inspector, there is another consideration which is quite important. The ability to do a good job, under trying circumstances and maintain the respect and confidence of the public and the wiring industry, has developed a code of ethics whereby the relationship between the inspector, the contractor, the utility, the manufacturer, the dealer and the public has been harmonious.

While the engineer "plans," the inspector "makes and does." The electrical inspector is often the liaison between the professional man and his client. He has the same basic characteristics and fundamental educational requirements as the engineer, except that this interest and education are more in the direction of application with less mathematical and theoretical depth, combined with ability to understand the instructions of the professional engineer and translate those to action either by applying his own abilities or in the direction of others.

Full realization of the importance of the electrical inspector to his community and to his employer should be made, so that the stature of the inspector would be recognized to a degree compatible with the responsibilities assumed and services rendered.

K. R. Gallagher, area inspector, Timmins, Ontario.
— Reprinted from *IAEI News*, July 1963.

Resolution Adopted to Upgrade Electrical Inspectors

Acting favorably on a report presented by Mr. Barney Alverson, chairman, education committee IAEI the executive council unanimously adopted a set of resolutions as prepared by its chairman to establish a standard for the International Association of Electrical Inspectors' educational program. These resolutions were adopted by the council in session last May in Detroit, Michigan. They are as follows:

Whereas, it is the purpose of the IAEI to promote the best interest of the electrical inspector in any way possible; and

Whereas, the standards of electrical codes have continually been raised; and

Whereas, the majority of electrical inspectors are constantly acting in a capacity above that for which they are given recognition; and

Whereas, proper recognition and consideration have never been accorded the electrical inspector;

Therefore, Be It Resolved, that the IAEI executive council approve the establishment of an educational standards committee; and

Be It Further Resolved, that this committee formulate plans for the establishment of suitable standards to qualify electrical inspectors; and

Be It Further Resolved, that the IAEI arrange to grant certificates of competency to those electrical inspectors qualifying under the standards to be formulated; and

Be It Further Resolved, that the IAEI do all in its power to provide the means to raise the electrical inspector to this new level.

—Reprinted from *News-Bulletin*, September 1961.

ELECTRICAL SAFETY

Professor Charles F. Dalziel's career spans a wide and varied range of activities within the field of electrical engineering. Since 1932 he has been associated with the University of California in Berkeley where he serves as professor of electrical engineering. He is a registered professional engineer in the state of California.

In this paper on electrical safety, Professor Dalziel discusses the precautions to be taken when working around electrical circuits to avoid serious accident situations involving personnel and equipment. He discusses the steps to be taken in event of an electrical accident, and the effect of electrical shock on the human body. Statistical data is presented which gives the scope of the electrical accident problem. Evaluation of the techniques of isolation, insulation, grounding, and current limitation are discussed with relationship to electrical safety.

Electric Shock

Because of the havoc of lightning and on the other hand, the harmlessness of static sparks experienced with modern synthetic clothing materials, all persons are to some degree familiar with electric shock and its tremendous potential for damage to life and property. Normally, we achieve safety from electric shock by isolation, insulation, grounding, and current limitation. It is only when one or more of these safety measures become defective or are circumvented that there is an electric shock hazard. Even when home appliances or other low voltage machines become defective, the electric shock hazard can be mitigated by keeping one's body from becoming part of the circuit. Persons should never hold an energized electric appliance with wet hand or bleeding or when wearing wet shoes or when standing barefoot on the ground or on a wet floor. Water provides a most dangerous condition for receiving electric shocks and no person should use electrical apparatus with his feet dangling in water, as from a pleasure boat or wharf. In contrast, dry shoes, rubber overshoes, old sacks or newspapers, and ordinary floor coverings, when dry, provide a high degree of protection from defective appliances.

It is important that the slightest shock is an ominous warning of potentially hazardous conditions. The slightest shock when operating an electrical appliance in one location might, in another situation, result in instant death if part of the body made only slightly better contact with the ground or a grounded metallic object.

In case of an electric shock accident, free the victim promptly from contact with the circuit. Immediately break the circuit by removing the extension cord from its receptacle, or open the switch. If you do not know which switch to open, open all of them. If the victim is still receiving a shock, use a dry stick, dry rope, dry clothing, or any non-conductor to separate the victim from the energized conductor. Move either the conductor or the victim. This must be done promptly and safely. Do not touch any part of the victim's body as long as he is electrified. If the victim appears not breathing, immediately apply artificial resuscitation. Do not lose time arguing or pondering as to the best method, but use the method that you know how to apply. Continue resuscitation until the victim revives, until he becomes stiff, or until a physician takes over.

While dry shoes, or dry newspapers provide some protection against 120 or 240-volt residence or industrial utilization circuits, such insulations are inadequate for higher voltage distribution circuits and high voltage power lines. Unfortunately, traffic accidents in which energized high voltage wires are knocked down are so frequent that the public must know how to minimize the hazard. If a high voltage wire comes to rest on an automobile, warn the occupants to remain inside. Reassure them that they are safe from electric shock as long as they do not make contact with the pavement. Warn would-be rescuers and onlookers not to come close to either the energized automobile or to any of the high voltage wires on the ground. Unless you know that the wire is from a low voltage circuit, do not approach it closer than from the place where you first notice it, certainly not closer than 25 feet. Many circuits are tested by being re-energized several times by an automatic recloser, and therefore all high voltage wires must be regarded as alive.

In such accidents, the rescuer should limit his efforts to obtaining a policeman, notifying the electric utility of the location and nature of the accident, and in keeping the public at a safe distance until the utility service man arrives and

Deaths Caused by Electric Current in the United States*

Year	Home	Farm	Industry	Street And Highways	Electrocutions** From all Causes
1963	254	64	189	89	878
1962	241	56	198	79	849
1961	259	102	214	99	980
1960	277	97	186	93	999
1959	316	84	215	106	1001
Average	270	81	200	93	941

*Vital Statistics of the United States. U.S. Department of Health, Education, and Welfare, Washington, D. C.

** Excludes deaths from electric current classified as transportation or machinery accidents, or accidents in mines and quarries, in agriculture, and in forestry.

Table 1. Deaths caused by electric current in the United States.

states that it is safe to proceed with rescue efforts.

Except for possibly causing a painful fall or for its nuisance value, the smallest electric shock of importance is that current which causes loss of voluntary control of the hand when grasping an electrified object. The muscular contractions increase with increasing current. Sensations of pain develop and contractions of the muscles that lie in the current pathway become increasingly severe. Finally, a value of current is reached at which the victim cannot release his grasp of the conductor. The maximum current a person can tolerate and still let go of the energized conductor by using muscles directly stimulated by that current is called his "let-go current." Currents in excess of one's let-go current are said to "freeze" him to the circuit. Such currents are very painful, frightening, and hard to endure for even a short time.

The most dangerous effect of electric shock is a derangement of heart action known as ventribular fibrillation. In the fibrillating condition, the pumping action of the heart stops, and death is likely in about five minutes. Treatment consists of prompt and continuous application of artificial respiration, preferably the mouth-to-mouth resuscitation method. If the rescuer has been trained, artificial respiration should be alternated with closed chest cardiac massage and the resuscitation process continued as the victim is taken to a hospital and given a defibrillating treatment. It is believed that currents of only 100 milliamperes are sufficient to cause the heart to fibrillate.

Quantitative information regarding electric shock intensities necessary to cause other serious effects remain largely unknown. For example, the minimum current required to produce unconsciousness is somewhere between let-go and fibrillating currents. Somewhat larger currents passing through the chest, head, or vital nerve centers may produce paralysis of the breathing mechanism, an effect called respiratory inhibition. Much higher currents, such as those used in electrocution of criminals, may raise the body temperature sufficiently to cause immediate death. Currents sufficient to blow fuses and trip circuit breakers often create awesome destruction of tissue and may produce very severe shock and irreparable damage to the nervous system.

Fatalities Due to Electric Current and Lightning In the United States*

Year	Electrocutions**	Natural Lightning	Total
1963	878	165	1043
1962	849	153	1002
1961	980	149	1129
1960	999	129	1128
1959	1001	183	1184
Average	941	156	1097

*Vital Statistics of the United States. U.S. Department of Health, Education, and Welfare, Washington, D. C.
** Excludes deaths from electric current classified as transportation or machinery accidents, or accidents in mines and quarries, in agriculture, and in forestry.

Table 2. Fatalities due to electric current and lightning.

Fires Resulting from Known Causes of Ignition 1954–1963*

	Rank	Number	Percentage of Total
Matches and Smoking	1	441,628	20.6
Electricity and Electrical Equipment except Lightning and Static	2	437,955	20.5
Lightning	4	259,696	12.2
Static Electricity and Static Sparks	17	2,094	0.1

*Insurance Facts, 1965. Insurance Information Institute, 110 William Street, New York, New York.

Table 3. Fires resulting from known causes of ignition.

Burns suffered in electrical accidents are of two types, electrical burns and thermal burns. Electric burns are the result of electric currents flowing through the tissues. Typically, electric burns are slow to heal, but they seldom become infected. Thermal burns, on the other hand, may be the result of the high temperatures in close proximity to the body, such as those produced by an electric arc or hot gases released by the arc, or by overheated conductors or vaporized metals caused by short circuits. These burns are similar to burns and blisters produced by any high temperature source. Currents of only the let-go level, if they flow for an appreciable time, are more than sufficient to produce deep electric burns. Both types of burns may be produced simultaneously. Any serious burn should receive prompt medical attention. Many victims of serious electric shock accidents recover, perhaps after a considerable period of convalescence, but with no serious permanent after-effects.

Safe Starting Procedures for Electric Portables

Many electric shock and burn accidents would not happen if the operator of an electrically driven tool or appliance followed a few simple rules.

(a) Examine the equipment for possible physical defects. Many potentially dangerous defects are obvious even to an untrained observer.

(b) Operate the device on a dry floor away from grounded objects. Get the feel of the on-off switch, and be sure that it operates properly.

(c) Move the portable near a grounded object. With the switch off, and then with the switch on, watch for sparks as the frame is moved into contact with the grounded object.

(d) Hold the operating portable and gently touch the back of the same hand or the back of the middle finger to the grounded object.

(e) If the device is equipped with two-prong attachment plug, reverse the plug and repeat (c) and (d) above.

(f) If you have doubt regarding the safe condition or proper operation of any electric machine, discuss the matter with your supervisor, your neighborhood electrician, or power utility service man.

Practical Thresholds of Electric Shock

Many persons have a fear of electric shock from instinct, hearsay past experience, or education. Moreover, this fear is often surrounded by mystery and lack of knowledge. For those familiar with the technical aspects of electricity, perhaps part of this confusion might be dispelled by defining the limiting quantitative values controlling the hazards of electric shock.

(a) *Lethal Shock Hazard*: Those a-c and d-c circuits capable of passing through a 500 ohm resistor, an uninterrupted a-c current in excess of 100 milliamperes, an uninterrupted d-c current in excess of 500 milliamperes, or an impulse discharge having an energy in excess of 50 joules.

(b) *Shock Hazard*: Those a-c and d-c circuits capable of passing through a 500 ohm resistor, an uninterrupted a-c current in excess of 10 milliamperes, an uninterrupted d-c current in excess of 60 milliamperes or an impulse discharge in excess of ¼ joule.

(c) *Negligible Shock Hazard*: Shocks of an intensity less than those producing "shock hazard" defined above, or equipment and circuits operating at 25 volts or less.

The electric accident situation is partially evident from inspection of table 1, which presents the latest data available covering electrocutions caused by electric currents in the U.S.A. The data were compiled by the National Office of Vital Statistics, U.S. Department of Health, Education, and Welfare, Washington, D.C.

It is noted that the average number of electrocutions per year during the five-year period is slightly less than 950. Of these, 270 occurred in the home, and 81 on the farm. Thus, about 350 electrocutions occur annually on 120, 208 or 240 volt utilization circuits. Industrial deaths due to electric current account for an additional 200, and since most of these occur on circuits having a voltage of 480 volts or less, it is apparent that approximately one-half the electrocutions in America are due to contact with low voltage circuits.

The data of table 2 were taken from the same source and are presented to round out the picture. Electrocutions due to commercial electricity and deaths due to natural lightning average some 1100 per year. Over the years the writer has been unable to find any authenticated deaths ascribed to static electricity or static sparks. It must be realized that these data reflect only the recorded fatal accidents, not the much larger number of serious shock accidents in which the victim survives.

Fires in the United States for which the cause of ignition has been ascertained and which resulted in claims against the insurance companies, are reported by the Insurance Information Institute. These data do not represent the total number of fires in the United States, and excluded are all unreported losses, as well as all fires for which the cause of ignition was not ascertained. Data for the last ten-year period, namely 1954–1963, are given in table 3. Note that fires due to electric origin almost claim first place!

As stated earlier, electrical safety is achieved by isolation, insulation, grounding, and current or shock limitations. Isolation means placing high voltage wires high overhead and far out of reach, or by designing structures with ample clearances so that workmen can work or climb with safety. Unfortunately safety by isolation is often circumvented by kites with metalized strings, booms of cranes and derricks, climbers, those rescuing pets, workers knocking nuts off trees with metal pipes, and by storing objects in the work spaces in front of or behind switchboards, etc.

Electricity is kept in its proper place by electric insulation. Adequate insulation assures that our electrical machines, appliances, hand tools, and portable extension cords, etc., will permit safe operation with long and essentially trouble free life. However, all mechanical contrivances fail eventually and the public must be ever alert to spot potentially dangerous conditions. Many insulations become brittle and develop small cracks when they become old or worn; on the other hand, abuse can damage any insulation. Fortunately many pending failures are

Northern California Chapter goes to school at the John O'Connell Trade and Vocational School in San Francisco, California, on October 18, 1955. ***At the left*****, Charles Foehn, business manager, IBEW, Local No. 6, and a member of the San Francisco Board of Education, shows the switchboard equipment.** ***Left to right are:*** **Karl Tobber, Marin County inspector; Joseph E. Clisham, coordinator, trade and industrial education, San Francisco; one unidentified man, a member of the IBEW; Chester Hefner, San Mateo County inspector; Leo Kirkoff, the tall gray-haired man, Trumbull Division, General Electric Company; Alfred Cooper, contractor for Costa County; Mr. Allen, Division of Industrial Safety; and Seth Cohn, electrical contractor.**

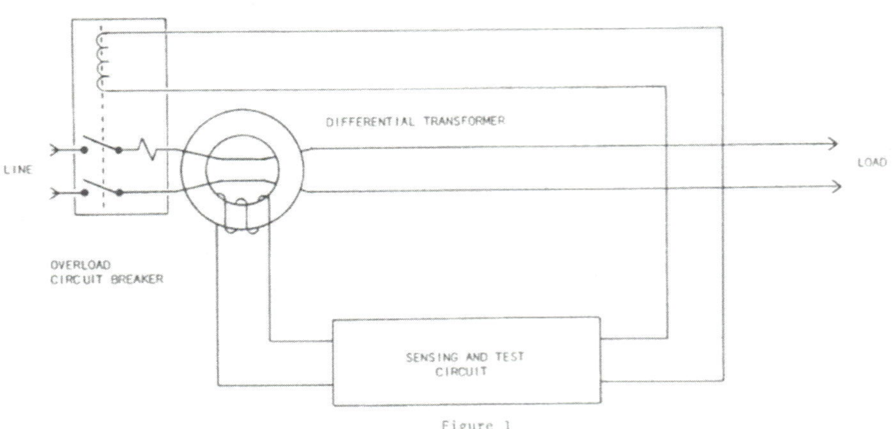

Figure 1. Rucker Electrical Safety Sentry; shown for typical 120 VAC branch-circuit protection.

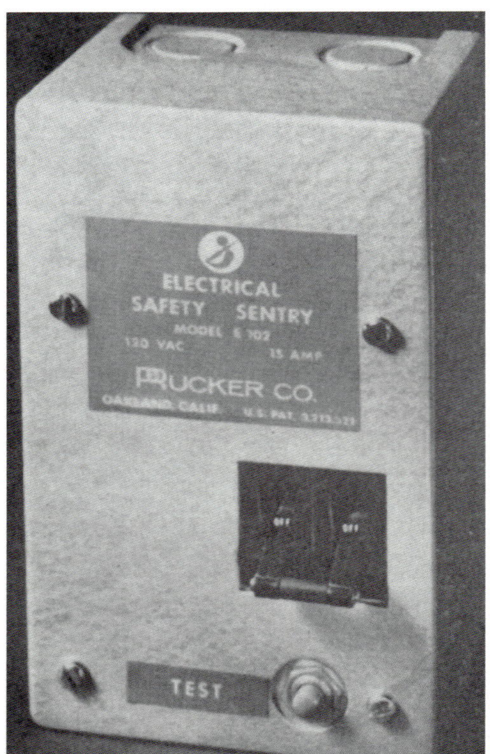

Figure 2. A 120-volt, 20-ampere, two-wire prototype for the home or swimming pool.

obvious, such as frayed insulation of extension cords, broken receptacles, or broken attachment plugs. Water and moisture often bridge small defects in the insulation of nearly worn out devices and cause the metal frame of the device to become electrified. Never use an appliance or electrically driven hand tool in the rain, or when it is obviously wet. The best assurance that the device was manufactured properly is to be sure that it carries the seal of approval of the Underwriters' Laboratories Incorporated. [*Editor's note*: UL Labels (seals) signify product listing rather than approval.]

The third means of achieving electrical safety is grounding. The purpose of grounding is to prevent the metal frame of an electrical device from becoming electrified and to maintain a low resistance circuit between the device and ground. In spite of all precautionary measures, should a device develop a defect and the metal frame become energized, it is anticipated that a current will flow of a magnitude sufficient to blow the protective fuse or to operate the branch circuit breaker. This is accomplished by connecting the neutral wire (color white) at the service entrance equipment, located at or near the utility watt-hour meter, to an effective ground. When available, this must be the cold water pipe of a continuous metallic underground water piping system. This ground will provide protection against extraneous high voltages such as a failure in the utility transformer and lightning.

However, to provide protection against defective equipment, the frame of each appliance or device must also be connected to an effective ground.

Some years ago the profession adopted the requirement that extension cords supplying hand tools contain a separate ground wire (color green). It is presently required that all receptacles (i.e., convenience outlets) in the home be of the approved grounding type. However, most 120-volt appliances such as electric toasters, irons, frying pans, mixers, coffee makers, portable heaters, radios, TV's, floor and desk lamps, etc., are factory equipped with two wire extension cords and two wire attachment plugs.

Although the *National Electrical Code* and the California Electrical Safety Orders require that all portable tools which are held in hand while being operated must be grounded, the writer has personally investigated many serious low voltage electric shock accidents in Northern California and by far the most common cause of injury was a defect in the grounding system. Since such a defect in the grounding system does not affect the physical operation of an otherwise operable electrical device, the writer is of the opinion that some other means of increasing electric safety is long overdue.

Moreover, unless the metal frame of each machine or device is connected to a truly "effective ground," the grounding system may have such a high resistance that an energized frame may not produce sufficient current to blow its fuse or actuate the branch circuit breaker. Even if the various device frames are connected to the nearest pipe, the ever increasing use of plastic pipe poses an interesting threat to the integrity of the grounding system.

Driven ground rods, such as lengths of pipe driven into the soil, are notorious for their high grounding resistance, especially toward the end of a long dry summer. Almost without exception, a driven ground will not permit a current flow sufficient to operate the circuit protective device. To be effective, the grounding system must comprise a continuous metallic system, such as the structural steel of a building, a metallic water system, or a separate copper ground wire.

Another consideration is that the resistance of the human body between major extremities, such as from hand to foot, is of such high resistance (currently believed to be about 500 ohms minimum) that accidental contact between an energized frame and a grounded object will permit a current much too small to actuate any commercial protective device presently available in this country. For example, the maximum current that can pass from a defective electric hedge clipper through the body between one or both hands and one or both feet is: I = E/R = 120/500 = 0.24 ampere or 240 milliamperes. Assume that the circuit is protected by a 20-ampere fuse. Should the frame of the defective device be not grounded, and should a person grasp the uninsulated metal frame energized at 120 volts when he is well grounded, such as when trimming the hedge barefoot, the maximum current that could flow would be 240 milliamperes, which is 0.24/20 = 1/83 of the current necessary to blow the fuse. There is simply no question that a current of 0.24 amperes or 240 milliamperes is much more than sufficient to freeze the victim to the circuit, to produce ventricular fibrillation, and to stop respiration.

The fourth means of achieving electrical safety, namely, current or shock limitations, is provided by the differential circuit breaker which limits the shock to a value less than that likely to produce dangerous injury.

The writer recently developed a simple semi-conductor actuated differential circuit breaker of sufficient capacity to operate commercial two and three-wire circuit breakers in common use in this country. One such circuit is given in figure 1. Before going into further detail, it must be stressed that such a highly sensitive fast acting protective device detects only line-to-ground currents, such as insulation leakage currents, or currents likely to flow during accidental contact with the "hot" wire of the 120-volt circuit and ground. This feature is in addition to the usual protection afforded by ordinary circuit breakers in protecting against high current short circuits.

Unfortunately, government statistics do not classify electrical fatalities as to the type of contact, such as whether the victim grasped both wires, or whether the circuit was completed by a line-to-ground current pathway; however, the writer believes that many fatal accidents are due to a person making contact with a "hot" wire while he is connected to a well grounded object, such as grasping a faucet or standing on a wet floor. Such possibilities include dislodging stuck toast from a toaster, basting fowl in an oven, or when turning meat in a grill with a metal utensil and accidentally making contact with the radiant heating element. The differential circuit breaker offers a tremendous increase in protection in comparison to presently available protective devices.

The Rucker Company of Oakland, California, has accepted the challenge and is preparing to offer a complete line of transistorized differential circuit breakers to protect both the home and industry with devices of capacities of 20 to 100 amperes and with voltage ratings of 120 and 240 volts. Figure 2 shows a photograph of a 120-volt, 20-ampere, two-wire prototype for the home or swimming pool. Such a device has sufficient sensitivity to interrupt the circuit for currents flowing to ground of 1 to 5 milliamperes. Because of the probability of somewhat excessive current leakage to ground during conditions of high humidity or excessive moisture, such as roof leaks wetting the wiring in the attic, or accidental spilling of water on the floor wetting the concealed wiring in the basement, such a high sensitivity might prove to be objectionable because of unwarranted nuisance tripping.

To be of practical value, the device is desensitized when the trip level is set in the factory. The exact value will depend upon extensive field experience and upon the decision of safety authorities. The Rucker differential circuit breaker is currently being evaluated by the Underwriters' Laboratories, Incorporated, and will be marketed under the trade name of Rucker Electrical Safety Sentry. [*Editor's note*: This device not yet listed by Underwriters' Laboratories, Incorporated.]

Although many fires are caused by short circuits, electric arcing, or overheated conductors, little is known regarding the minimum current necessary to start a fire. Limited laboratory tests indicate that when the current is limited to a few milliamperes, the sparks produced by 120 or 240-volt circuits are feeble, and they appear very unlikely to start a fire.

While the differential circuit breaker is no panacea for all low voltage electrical hazards, and certainly no license for unsafe practices in the use of electrical equipment, it does offer a tremendous increase in protection against fires of electrical origin, and serious electrical accidents due to line-to-line ground contacts.

Charles F. Dalziel

Charles F. Dalziel, P. E., professor emeritus, electrical engineer, at the University of California at Berkeley, was issued two patents adopted by the *National Electrical Code*, and provisions made mandatory by the U.S. Department of Labor in 1977: his patent for the ground-fault circuit interrupter, and electrical fencing. His was the first version of today's GFCI unit.

Dalziel became interested in developing the GFCI as a result of the many fatalities resulting from defective and unsafe underwater lighting fixtures before there was an Article 680 in the *NEC*.

Dalziel was frequently called as an expert witness in cases involving electrical accidents and was the author of over 150 technical papers. He had given technical lectures in France, England, Japan, Italy, Austria and Switzerland. His research covered electrical shock, electrical safety, electrical hazards, power system stability and special investigations into the causes of industrial short circuits, electrical fires and electrocutions.

His interest in safety led to his appointment as director of the Berkeley campus Disaster Committee. He also got his first certificate of commendation from the California State Disaster office.

Dalzeil was the recipient of the 1984 Distinguished Engineering Alumnus Award UC, Berkeley. He was a past member of the Henry Morse Stephens Lodge #541 F & A.M. honorary member American Society of Safety Engineers, life fellow of the Institute of Electrical & Electronic Engineers, and former chairman of the San Francisco section.

Article reprinted from *IAEI News*, September 1966.

Biography reprinted from *IAEI News*, March 1987.

Quick Fact

Nationwide Seminars

The IAEI board of directors approved recommendations that IAEI explore possibility of conducting *National Electrical Code* seminars around the country.

Reprinted from *IAEI News*, January 1978.

First Official IAEI Seminars on Changes to the NEC

The July/August issue of the *IAEI News* contained a two-page ad for the International Association of Electrical Inspectors sponsored seminars on highlights of the 1981 *National Electrical Code.* Your board of directors made a bold decision to move ahead aggressively in the field of education and these seminars are a result of that decision.

The four seminars presently scheduled are Houston, Texas, at the Astro Village Hotel on September 19–20, 1980: Denver, Colorado, at the Executive Tower Inn on October 17–18; Los Angeles, California, at the Biltmore Hotel on November 6–7; and Rochester, New York, at the Americana Hotel on November 14–15. Advertisements will appear in *Electrical Construction and Maintenance Magazine, Plant Engineering Magazine, Electrical Contractor, and the IAEI News*. Press releases will be appearing in *Electrical Consultant*, *IEEE Application Society Newsletter* and most of the other electrical industry media.

The seminars will consist of over 400 slides and audio-visuals describing the most significant changes in the 1981 *National Electrical Code*. The seminars will be moderated by your executive director, Bill Summers, and ably assisted by a host of nationally prominent *Code* experts including: Ben Segall, member of CMP-3 and CMP-6 and the author of the renowned book, *Electrical Code Diagrams*; D. J. Clements, electrical field representative for the National Electrical Manufacturers Association; George Flach, chairman of CMP-22, past member of CMP-10 and chief electrical inspector for the city of New Orleans; Ray Eckardt, member of CMP-9, engineer for Underwriters Laboratories; Bill Drake, member of CMP-17, Daniel Woodhead Company; George Waterhouse, director of the Colorado State Electrical Board; Norm Davis, member of CMP-5 and engineer for UL; Bob Pullen, field representative for NEMA; Chuck Pierce, chairman of CMP-20 and chief electrical inspector, Fresno, California; Bill Worthing, electrical field representative, NEMA; Daniel Boone, field representative, Federal Pacific Electric; Al Reed, member of the NFPA 70B Electrical Equipment Maintenance Committee and general manager of the New York Board of Fire Underwriters; Joe Ross, electrical field representative, NEMA; Jack Wells, chairman of the National Fire Protection Association 70B Committee and member of CMP-21, Pass and Seymour; and Jack Hogg, CMP-23, engineer for UL. The afternoon of the second day will be devoted to a question and answer session and the above named experts will respond to questions from the participants.

IAEI became involved in seminars for a variety of reasons.

• No one had really attempted to give the significant changes with the intent of assuring a high comprehension level of the participants.

The first official IAEI seminars were held in 1980. This was one of the first seminars.

• IAEI was the only group that could assure that the material was generated by the people who write, enforce, and interpret the *Code*. Generous assistance has been provided by our 23 code panel

Eastern Pennsylvania Chapter Begins Seminar Series

The Eastern Pennsylvania Chapter, IAEI, has just gotten off of the ground with the first of what they hope to be a series of *National Electrical Code* seminars.

On June 4, 1980, 130 eager participants showed up at Pagano's Restaurant in Philadelphia for a full and comprehensive program on Article 250, Grounding.

The participants were exposed to a diverse and extremely knowledgeable and experienced panel of speakers including: Arthur Parker, consulting engineer, who spoke on the "Story of Grounding — Why and Why not" and "Ground Fault Protection for Equipment." John H. Lewis and James W. Patterson of the Philadelphia Electric Company discussed "Utility Grounding Requirements." Duncan Graham, NECA, presented information on "Bonding," "Equipment Grounding Conductor," and "NEC Definitions." William Wusinich, IBEW, spoke on "Electrodes" and the "Electrode Grounding Conductor." Jack Saddler and Peter Gabrey of T. & B. Company, discussed "Manufacturer Grounding Hardware." William Thomas, OSHA, presented information on "OSHA Grounding Requirements" and "Ground-Fault Circuit Interrupters."

Chapter Chairman Salvatore Nazionale, extreme left, thanks the speakers who took part in the 1980 Eastern Pennsylvania Chapter seminar (*left to right*): William Thomas, OSHA; John Lewis, Philadelphia Electric Company; James Patterson, Philadelphia Electric Company; Jack Saddler, T & B Company; William Wusinich, IBEW; and Duncan Graham, NECA.

Chapter chairman Salvatore Nazionale moderated the seminar. The overall response of the participants was extremely positive and the requests for similar programs were numerous.

Officials of the Eastern Pennsylvania Chapter certainly feel that as far as education goes, they have definitely "Gotten Off the Ground!"

—Reprinted from IAEI News, September 1980.

James W. Patterson, Philadelphia Electric Company, illustrates a point during discussion of utility grounding requirements at the 1980 Eastern Pennsylvania Chapter seminar.

representatives. Underwriters Laboratories code panel representatives and other code panel representatives of various manufacturers.

- IAEI had the most widely recognized *Code* experts to write and explain the subtleties of the complex *Code* requirements.
- This was a method of publicizing the association before the public. An organized membership drive has not been undertaken for many years and there is a need to show the various segments of the electrical industry what we are capable of doing. In order to accomplish this goal, we will be supplying each participant with a copy of the May/June issue of the *IAEI News* and the 15-minute audio-visual "What Is IAEI" will be shown to explain the goals, accomplishments and membership services that are available to our members.

Even though these have been the primary goals of the board of directors, the program will reap additional side benefits for the association for many years to come. Initially it was planned that most of the artwork, audio and slides would be contracted out to private firms. However, investigation revealed that costs were so prohibitive that alternative methods would have to be found. This led to the conclusion that the art and technology to produce slides would have to be developed in-house. At the present time all artwork, photography and slide production is being done in-house. The side benefits include an 11-minute audio visual entitled "What Is IAEI" that was developed for our membership committee. This audio-visual was intended for showing to groups outside of IAEI and may be obtained from: D. J. Clements, Jr., Southern Section; O. J. Christiansen, Northwestern Section; L. S. Hickman, Canadian Section; B. L. Auger, Western Section; and L. E.

Those attending the IAEI 1984 Code Seminar held at the Queen Kapiolani Hotel in Honolulu, Hawaii, on March 9, included the following (*left to right*): *standing* — Ted Ralston, Hawaii Chapter secretary; Tamio Yatsushiro, supervising electrical inspector, county of Maui; Eugene Y. Fujihara, chief electrical inspector, city and county of Honolulu; Iemasa Kubo, supervising electrical inspector, county of Hawaii; *sitting* — Joyce Hatorri, estimator, Tri Electric; Kiyoshi Inouye, supervising electrical inspector, county of Kauai; Henry Sato, electrical engineer, city and county of Honolulu.

On February 7, 21, and 28, 1987, the Pine Tree Chapter co-sponsored 1987 *National Electrical Code* changes seminars. A total of 367 electricians enjoyed listening to commentator Ray Pelletier lead them through six hours of code changes. Ray used the IAEI *Code Analysis* as an outline, which made following the presentation easier for the participants using their own copies. To emphasize the changes, 75 IAEI slides were supplemented by another 210 real situation slides depicting the *Code* changes.

Waggoner, Southwestern Section.

A fee of $50 for the slides and cassettes is being charged to assure prompt return and the fee will be refunded on return. This program may also be obtained from the International office.

An audio-visual *How To Use the National Electrical Code* will be shown at all the section meetings and will be available for use at the chapter meetings shortly thereafter. An audio-visual "This is Your IAEI" will be shown at all the section meetings and will also be available to the chapters shortly thereafter.

What this all means, of course, is that the role of the International office is changing and will continue to change. We have now developed the capability to develop our own educational material and in all probability we will continue to grow in that area. We are also investigating the possibilities of publishing several books to supplement our income and to provide further services for our individual members. It is not inconceivable that we would develop an educational film library for use at our chapter meetings.

In order to have all these things at the present time we must also be prepared to sacrifice other things. The attendance by an IO representative to the chapter meeting has not been up to past standards. This is a necessity, of course, to carry out the wishes of your board and the energies of this office have been directed toward that end. Many chapters have come to expect participation of an IO representative yearly, and some even oftener. Many others have not had a visit in the last 20 years. This disparity of providing equal benefits to all can be overcome to a large degree by providing services that are available to all the membership.

Reprinted from *IAEI News*, September 1980.

First Woman Certified in Ohio As ESI

Phyllis Ann Sepeta-Wissman, University Heights, Ohio building inspector, is the first woman to be certified as an electrical safety inspector in the state. Ten years ago she earned concurrent degrees in physics from the Cass Institute of Technology and history from Western Reserve College and has completed three years' work toward a doctoral degree in high energy astrophysics.

She has worked in the aerospace industry in California and began doing field and design electrical work for her father's firm, the L. N. Sepeta Electrical Maintenance Company in 1971. In April 1976, she began her work as a University Heights housing inspector.

To her strong academic and theoretical background, Miss Sepeta-Wissman will add solid, practical experience. She states that she wants to be a community consultant, helping people make their homes safer places to live by making them aware of home maintenance problems that can be corrected while they are small. She also hopes to be able to add some worthwhile clarifications to the *National Electrical Code*.

Miss Sepeta-Wissman is a member of the Western Reserve Division, Ohio Chapter.

—Reprinted from *IAEI News*, July 1976.

Nebraska Members Receive Service Awards

Four members of IAEI's Nebraska Chapter have been honored with special service awards presented by the Nebraska State Electrical Board for their help in making electrical irrigation systems safer. Nebraska Lieutenant Governor Roland Leudtke (*third from left*), presented the special irrigation safety awards to (*left to right*): LaVerne Stetson, John Anderson, Larry Smith, Wayne Sides, and Bob Callies. These men were members of an ad hoc committee sponsored by the State Electrical Board and the Nebraska Rural Electric Association in 1976. Smith, executive director of the state board, stated that there were many difficulties with irrigation wiring at the time. He said rural electricians are not required to be licensed, and electricians without special training in irrigation wiring were installing the systems.

The *ad hoc* committee presented ten one-day meetings around the state for electricians, rural power district representatives and others with an interest in irrigation wiring. More than 480 persons participated in the programs which included the opportunity to become licensed for irrigation wiring. The program was also a training sessions for instructors, held in conjunction with the University of Nebraska's Cooperative Extension Service, and equipped participants to teach others principles of irrigation wiring. Smith said that since the safety program had begun, no fatalities have occurred.

Reprinted from *IAEI News*, March 1980.

The 35 graduates of the fourth electrical inspectors training program developed by the Michigan Chapter in 1982.

The Michigan Chapter of the International Association of Electrical Inspectors, in cooperation with the state fire marshal and the electrical industry, has developed an intensive two-week training program for Michigan's active electrical inspectors. Thirty-five graduates have come from the most recent fourth training program.

This program is acknowledged to be the first of its kind in the nation. The curriculum is designed to provide electrical inspectors with an opportunity to upgrade their skills and promote professionalism in the specialty of electrical code enforcement.

This opportunity for training has been received enthusiastically by electrical inspectors in Michigan. The training program is completely voluntary and is sustained solely by the interest and participation of Michigan's active electrical inspectors. So far, four training programs have produced 128 graduates. Plans have already been made for the fifth and sixth schools which are tentatively scheduled for the fall of 1982 and spring of 1983. Continuing education units (CEUs) are awarded by IAEI for completion of this program.

—Reprinted from *IAEI News*, September 1982.

Shown is the electrical class of the J. M. Perry Institute, Yakima, Washington. The class of fifty-nine students and three instructors attended the IAEI grounding seminar in Seattle, Washington, on February 5, 1982. All fifty-nine have become student members of IAEI.

FIRST ROUND OF IAEI SEMINARS SUCCESSFULLY COMPLETED!

The first four seminars on the 1981 *National Electrical Code*, sponsored by IAEI have now been completed. The attendance was extremely good with 250 in Houston, 375 in Denver, 134 in Los Angeles, and 246 in Rochester, New York. Many of your IAEI board of directors attended the seminars and at the November board meeting it was decided to continue with the seminars this spring. At the present time, we have selected Seattle, San Jose, Chattanooga, and Honolulu as the next sites. These seminars will be a one-day affair and you will find a two-page advertisement in this edition of *IAEI News*. Much experience has been gained at the first four cities and a number of changes will be made to improve our programs.

In order to more fully utilize the material that was developed for the seminars your board has decided to develop a complete training package to study the 1981 *NEC*. The training package consists of a book titled *Analysis of the 1981 NEC*, three cassettes with commentary on the changes in the current edition of the *Code*, and 100 slides of illustrations describing changes in the *Code*.

The 100 slides can also be obtained in 35mm filmstrip for those who have machines that will utilize the filmstrip. The book is a handy pocket size 4 1/2 –inch by 7-inch consisting of 148 pages of illustrations, photographs and commentary. Approximately 140 illustrations and photographs are used, as the old cliché that one picture is worth a thousand words is still true. The three cassettes feature 4 ½ hours of commentary contained within a attractive green vinyl album. We have obtained the services of a prominent radio and television announcer to serve as the voice of our cassette album. The cassettes are handy for those who wish to listen at odd times and perhaps do something else at the same time. The complete package (book, cassettes, slides) can be utilized by small and large groups to assure an accurate and efficient coverage of the changes in the *Code* without the necessity of committing a great deal of time in the preparation.

The slides and cassettes have been offered to each chapter and division to assist in the preparation of a chapter program on changes in the *Code*. You may wish to contact your chapter secretary or president to determine whether plans have been made to utilize these teaching aids.

Also contained elsewhere in this publication you will find application forms for the certification program for construction code inspectors. You will note that the various test sites are listed and you are required to select the test site that you wish to utilize. There are three electrical test modules offered: 2A electrical inspector—one- and two-family, 2B electrical inspector-general, and 2C electrical plan review. Your International office has a *Candidate Bulletin of Information* available that gives a full description of the tests including sample test questions. You may obtain a copy by writing the International office requesting a copy. At the present time IAEI is co-certifying the electrical modules with the Building Officials and Code Administrators (BOCA) and the Southern Building Code Congress

North Carolina Institute Meeting Draws Over 600

Attendance at the annual North Carolina Electrical Institute Meeting in Raleigh, North Carolina, numbered 616. This two-day meeting was jointly sponsored by the North Carolina Ellis Cannady Chapter, North Carolina Department of Insurance, and the State Board of Examiners of Electrical Contractors. It is the only meeting where all branches of the electrical industry meet to discuss public needs and mutual problems. The main purpose of this annual meeting is to promote uniform understanding and application of the *NEC* throughout the state and to collect and distribute information relative to the safe use of electricity.

The meeting was highlighted by a visit from Southern Section President William G. McClure of Columbus, Mississippi, and Southern Section Executive Chairman R. J. Edenfield of Augusta, Georgia.

During the session, Dick Edenfield asked IAEI members in the 600-plus audience to raise their hands. He challenged every member in the group to enlist one member in 1985. After asking for a show of hands of who would like to join IAEI, he asked for one

Over 600 attended the North Carolina Institute meeting in April 1985.

of them to volunteer to come forward and offered to pay his first year's dues if he would agree to sign up one of his friends during 1985. He then announced "I've got mine — now all of you members get yours."

Curtis R. Kennedy, executive director of the State Board of Examiners of Electrical Contractors, was awarded a plaque by chief electrical inspector Dick Boyd for over thirty years of outstanding service to the electrical industry in North Carolina. Chapter President J. R. "Sam" Thompson announced the upcoming retirement of Curtis Kennedy and awarded him an honorary membership to IAEI.

—Excerpted from *IAEI News*, September 1985.

The code panel at the North Carolina Institute meeting in April 1985 was composed of *(left to right)*: D. J. Clements, William R. Drake, George W. Flach, Richard L. Lloyd, Earl W. Roberts, Len H. Sessler, Peter J. Schram, and Robert W. Seelbach.

International (SBCCI). IAEI is automatically offering attractive wall certificates to all individuals that apply for the exams through IAEI, and successfully pass the test. Some concern has been experienced because we are also co-certifying electrical examinations with the International Conference of Building Officials (ICBO) that utilize a different set of test questions than those utilized by Educational Testing Services (ETS). In a recent meeting with Jim Bihr, executive director, ICBO, it was revealed that ICBO intends to utilize the ETS electrical examinations. This is good news to those that feel IAEI should not be involved in several certification programs.

In a report to the IAEI board of directors, the education committee reported that they are prepared to develop a refresher course to prepare IAEI members for the certification exams. Many individuals have been removed from formal study courses for long periods of time and the refresher courses will serve as a confidence builder to enhance the opportunities of the candidate to obtain a passing score.

Your International president for 1981, Roger Niedermeyer, has requested that the IAEI membership committee meet to formulate an effective program to assist the local chapters in obtaining new members and a uniform program of contacting drop-outs to build up our membership. The IAEI seminars have done much to advertise IAEI and the 15-minute audio-visual "What Is IAEI?" has been designated so that other audiences can be made aware of our goals and accomplishments. This slide program with sound can be shown to apprenticeship training classes (a new student membership category has been proposed by your IAEI board), NECA, IEEE, IBEW, college engineers classes, and independent electrical contractor groups. Regardless of the approach that is used to promote membership only a small percentage of contacts results in members. For this reason many contacts must be made to effect a substantial increase in membership. You may obtain a copy of the audio-visual "What Is IAEI?" from your section representative on the IAEI membership committee or by contacting the IO directly. Please let us know when the presentation will be used so that it will be delivered in time.

Reprinted from *IAEI News*, January 1981.

Mark E. Regan

Mark E. Regan joined IAEI in August 1996 as codes and standards and seminar coordinator for the International office. He brought with him to the position experience as both an electrician and a code enforcement officer for the state of New York.

Mark was involved in some of the editorial and development activity of the educational materials and the *IAEI News*, but he worked primarily as international seminar instructor. He was instrumental in implementing an initiative that focused on expanding the training and seminar services IAEI offered. The fairly new on-site seminar program saw growth under Mark's tenure. He was also instrumental in identifying other areas of growth needed in training and educational material offered by the IAEI.

Mark clearly understood the value of IAEI training to the electrical industry and that was apparent in his approach to his position and responsibilities. His energetic style and approach in the seminar setting brought him and the association recognition.

Employed by the IAEI from August 1996 to August 1998, Mark then accepted a position at Los Alamos National Laboratories where he worked primarily in an electrical instructor training role.

Mark is an inspector member and continues to work as an IAEI instructor. He is an active member of the Saudi Arabia Chapter IAEI and is working and promoting the association internationally. He and his wife Julie currently reside in Saudi Arabia under his current employment responsibilities. His current duties in Saudi Arabia include electrical inspections and quality control of major electrical installations in oil refineries in that region.

Mark provides IAEI seminar instruction occasionally while in the United States on leave from his responsibilities in that region of the world.

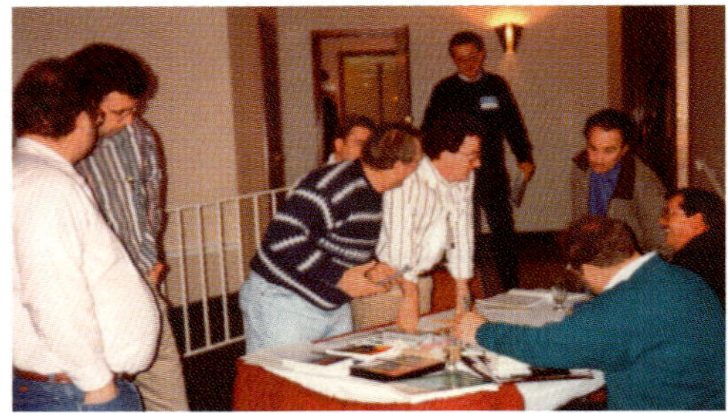

Michael Callanan (*seated left*), secretary/treasurer of the Eastern Pennsylvania Chapter, and John Whitney (*seated right*), vice chairman, register participants at the February 10, 1994, seminar in Philadelphia, Pennsylvania.

Quick Fact

Education Committee Gets New Secretary

At the 1999 board of directors meeting, the board decided to support the recommendation of the executive committee to designate the education department manager to serve as secretary to the education committee.

Reprinted from *IAEI News*, January 2000.

Permanent Training Facilities Planned for International Office

Through approximately 375 seminars and 100 publications, IAEI has trained thousands of people involved in various capacities in the electrical industry during the past seven years. Most of the training was done at various seminars throughout the country, involving considerable travel time and expense for the various instructors.

Ranging from simple brochures to bimonthly magazines to 400-page books, IAEI publications have been produced with a minimal staff and basic equipment. Despite this severe economy, these publications are recognized as authoritative standards of the industries.

Since education has always been a foundational principle of the association, establishing on-site training and publishing facilities became part of the goal for advancement when the International Office was moved to Richardson, Texas, in November 1991.

The Richardson office is a 12,000 square foot, two-story brick building built in 1985 for speculation and was unfinished inside when we bought it. The property was purchased for $150,000 or about $12.50 per square foot, an unheard of value. At the time, using contributions and funds from the sale of the Park Ridge office, we furnished the corridors on both floors and one-half of the office space.

The plan was to finish half of the upper floor into a conference and production center, where continuous classes could be held and production of educational materials escalated. Because of financial constraints, however, these plans have been slow in coming to fruition.

A recent renewed interest in this project has sparked three groups to make contributions toward its completion. Wisconsin Chapter, $20,000; North Carolina Electrical Institute, $2,500; North Carolina Ellis Cannady Chapter, $2,500. IAEI is encouraged by this new interest and hopes that other contributions will follow.

Total cost for elevator installation, HVAC equipment, finishing the space, and furnishings is estimated to be $125,000 or less.

Reprinted from *IAEI News*, September 1998.

Phil Simmons, Richard Loyd and John Taecker served as seminar instructors during the Trinational meeting of electrical engineers held in Cuernavaca, Mexico, in early February 1995. This meeting was also the site of the signing of an agreement of cooperation between IAEI and the Asociación de Ingenieros Universitarios Mećanicos Electricistos (AIUME). Front row (*left to right*): John K. Taecker, Richard Loyd, Phil Simmons, Francisco Lira, Eloy Munoz. Back row (*left to right*): Jorge Delgado, Gerardo Rubi, Pedro Sanhua, Guillermo Rivera, Efrain Ramirez, Adalberto Sanhua, Agustin Garcia, Ramon Garcia, Federico Trejo, Sergio Gonzalez, Luis Valdez, Manuel Vila, Ricardo Torres, Jesus Diaz (not pictured Jorge Ugalde).

L. Keith Lofland

L. Keith Lofland, who joined IAEI as education, codes and standards coordinator and seminar specialist in March, will assist the department by answering *Code* questions from members and customers, scheduling, coordinating, and conducting seminars, and will serve as a resource contact for the chapter, section, and division secretaries and treasurers.

Prior to joining IAEI, Lofland served as chief mechanical, electrical, and plumbing (MEP) inspector of the city of Garland, Texas, for 16 years. For thirteen years, he worked for various electrical contractors in the Dallas Metroplex as a journeyman electrician before accepting a position with the city of Rockwall to begin his 21-year career as an electrical inspector.

Holding many certifications, Lofland is well-qualified for his new position at IAEI. He holds a master electrician license for the Dallas County area, and has electrical inspector certification from both IAEI and ICBO. He is licensed as a plumbing inspector in the state of Texas and is a certified code enforcement officer with the Texas Department of Health.

Through the years he has been active in industry organizations. He served for four years as chairman of the Dallas County Regional Electrical Advisory Board, which administered electrical exams for over 40 cities in the Dallas Metroplex. He served as chairman of the Texas Chapter of IAEI in 1989. For the past six years, he has served Texas Chapter as secretary-treasurer.

The "Building Official/Building Inspector of the Year" award was presented to him in 1999 from the Construction Research Center, University of Texas at Arlington.

Reprinted from *IAEI News*, July 2000.

IAEI Training Seminars Reach the Cayman Islands

Approximately sixty persons attended the first IAEI electrical code training seminar on Grand Cayman Island. Cayman Islands is governed by the British and utilize the *National Electrical Code* for conformity assessment. They first adopted and enforced the codes and standards in the early 1980s. The Cayman Islands, like many other countries who have adopted the *National Electrical Code*, is challenged with ensuring uniform and consistent enforcement and application of the *NEC* and other codes and standards as well.

The building safety department in Grand Cayman provides continuing education for not only the inspectors, but for all involved in the industry. This commitment to electrical safety and education is under the direction of McCleary Fredrick, the building official in Grand Cayman, who recognizes the need for training not only for inspectors but installers, engineers, utilities, and others.

More and more IAEI is faced with challenges that will pull it into the international training arena. As the *National Electrical Code* is adopted and applied by countries outside of North America, their needs and challenges spawn opportunities to provide electrical safety training. IAEI is committed to representing the electrical inspector nationally and internationally and to providing high quality training. As interest in IAEI chapters abroad increases, the IAEI is poised to assist in proper application of code rules and to work toward electrical safety.

Communication and education are key elements in the electrical trade. Education involves helping those in the trade stay current with the requirements of the *NEC*; while communications covers all those activities that spread the information—from publications to code breakfasts to seminars. IAEI salutes Grand Cayman, McCleary Frederick, and the other individuals and organizations that are actively providing continuing electrical education at all levels.

Reprinted from *IAEI News*, July 2002.

Bill Clark talks about wiring and protection at the Train the Trainer seminar held at the International Office on February 2, 2002.

IAEI instructor Jim Rogers talks about the 2002 changes to the *NEC* at a seminar held in Iowa in April 2002.

Hazardous road conditions caused by snow could not keep these attendees away from the February 2002 seminar held in St. Louis, Missouri.

Keystone Chapter members listen intently at the 2002 Code workshop on April 6, 2002.

Director of Education Mike Johnston discusses the *Neon Lighting* book produced by the IAEI at the 2003 Neon Lighting seminar held at the Richardson office in February 2003.

Mississippi Chapter Vice Chairman Martin Jack addresses attendees at the code seminar sponsored by the chapter on July 27–30, 2002. About sixty-five people attended the seminar.

Components of neon lighting on display at the IAEI Neon Lighting seminar held at the International office on February 21, 2003.

THEIR MISSION 1928-2003
AND ITS IMPACT

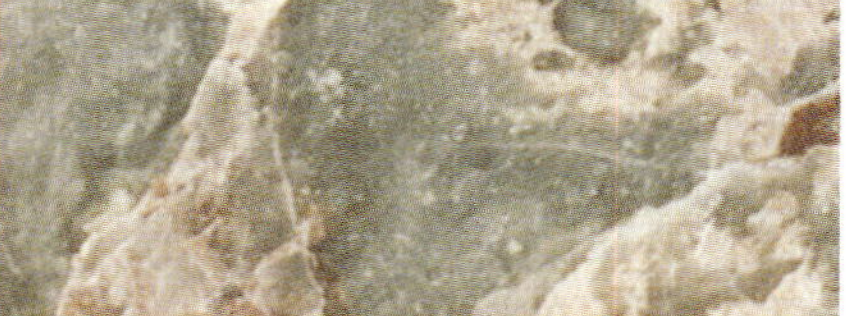

Learn electrical safety from this teacher...you bet!

Jim Rogers
Electrical Inspector
Alternate, CMP-12

Robert A. McCullough
Director of Inspections
Chairman, CMP-19

Electrical Training from IAEI
Everything you need to know.

Richard Owen
Senior Electrical Inspector
Chairman, CMP-3 [2005]

Tim Owens
Senior Electrical Inspector

Donny Cook
Chief Electrical Inspector
Chairman, CMP-14

Keith Lofland
Education, Codes and Standards
Coordinator, IAEI

Russell J. Helmick, Jr.
Supervising and
Chief Electrical Inspector
Alternate, CMP-1

Michael J. Johnston
Director of Education, IAEI
Principal, CMP-5

Lanny McMahill
Electrical Inspections Supervisor
Member, CMP-1

Philip H. Cox
Past CEO/Executive Director, IAEI
Past Chairman, CMP-1

Robert R. Sallaz
Retired Electrical Inspector
Past Member CMP-6

J. Philip Simmons
Author and Lecturer
Past Member CMP-1 & CMP-17

Mark E. Regan
Supervisor
Saudi Aramco Engineering
Project Inspection Department

Willam Clark
Retired Chief Electrical Inspector
Past Member CMP-1

STATE	CITY	SEMINAR TYPE	DATE	LOCATION	ADDRESS	ZIP	PHONE
California	Sacramento	Analysis of the 2002 *NEC*	6/6/03	The Heritage Hotel and Conference Cntr.	1780 Tribute Rd.	95815	916.929.7900
	Anaheim	1 & 2 Family, 2002 *NEC*	6/28/03	Holiday Inn Anaheim at the Park	1221 S. Harbor Blvd.	92805	714.758.0900
	San Francisco	Soares Grounding, 2002 *NEC*	7/12/03	Best Western Grosvenor Hotel	380 S. Airport Blvd.	94080	650.873.3200
Michigan	Grand Rapids	Soares Grounding, 2002 *NEC*	7/19/03	Crowne Plaza Grand Rapids	5700 28th St. SE	49546	616.957.1770
	Lansing	Analysis of the 2002 *NEC*	6/26-27/03	Best Western Midway	7711 Saginaw Hwy.	48917	517.627.8471
N.Carolina	Charlotte	Soares Grounding, 2002 *NEC*	6/7/03	Holiday Inn Airport	2707 Little Rock Rd.	28214	704.972.3254
Texas	Richardson	Neon Lighting	5/29/03	IAEI International Office Barbara Eastwood, x27	901 Waterfall Way, Suite 602	75080	972.235.1455 800.786.4234
		Health Care Facilities	5/30/03				
		1 & 2 Family, 1999 *NEC*	7/11/03				

For more information contact IAEI Education Department at 972-235-1455 • Michael Johnston, Director of Education (ext. 37) mjohnston@iaei.org • Keith Lofland, Seminar Specialist (ext. 36) klofland@iaei.org • Barbara Eastwood, Administrative Assistant (ext. 27) beastwood@iaei.org

2003 IAEI Seminar Ad.

National Weeks

Out of over a hundred national weeks in connection with which proclamations are issued, three stand out as an opportunity for the electrical inspector to place emphasis on the subject of electrical safety and the electrical codes. These features all stand high on the agenda of public relations, however, we have devoted a separate chapter to them in the interest of emphasis.

I suppose electrical inspectors are more completely involved in electrical week than in any other national week for the simple reason that they initiated it. It was during the Silver Jubilee meeting of the International Association of Electrical Inspectors, held at the Edgewater Beach Hotel in Chicago, that action was taken to recommend establishing an annual Electrical Safety Week. Later the industry decided it should be called Electrical Week, which naturally includes electrical safety while comprising the entire electrical field. The celebration takes place the week of Thomas A. Edison's birthday each year. It seems the electrical industry and the electrical inspector, in particular, short change themselves and the community by not becoming actively engaged through this week in alerting those willing to listen on the subject of electrical safety.

Through the years since the inception of Electrical Week, the national committee established by the industry to provide usable data, have done a top job in this respect and certainly need to be commended. This is where the press, radio, and TV are always glad to participate. Some communities have gone so far as to stage parades with floats depicting the "Electrical Safety Message." This is your week, Mr. Electrical Inspector—make the most of it.

Next in importance as far as the electrical inspector is concerned is Fire Prevention Week. I have been a member of the fire prevention committee of the Chamber of Commerce for many years. The chairman of this committee is invariably the fire chief. By virtue of his office, he is the logical man for the job. The committee meets at a luncheon once a month except during the summer months. Though various fire prevention methods are discussed other than electrical, the electrical inspector is a vital link on this committee and is at liberty to emphasize the electrical phase of fire prevention. I have found it a great help in associating with members of this committee, who generally consist of the fire chief; his assistant; safety committee secretary of the Chamber of Commerce; representatives of insurance companies; public and parochial school representatives; an electrical contractor representative; an insurance rating bureau representative; downtown merchants representative; industry fire prevention officials and a few others. We know of no better authoritative group than this where an electrical inspector has the opportunity to share his enforcement problems. Likewise, the opportunity for the dissemination of the electrical safety message is exceptional. Of course the life-blood of this committee is the fire prevention bureau of the fire department. In many cities the fire prevention bureau has been instrumental in bring-

IAEI display booth promoting the 1954 National Electrical Week in Tampa, Florida.

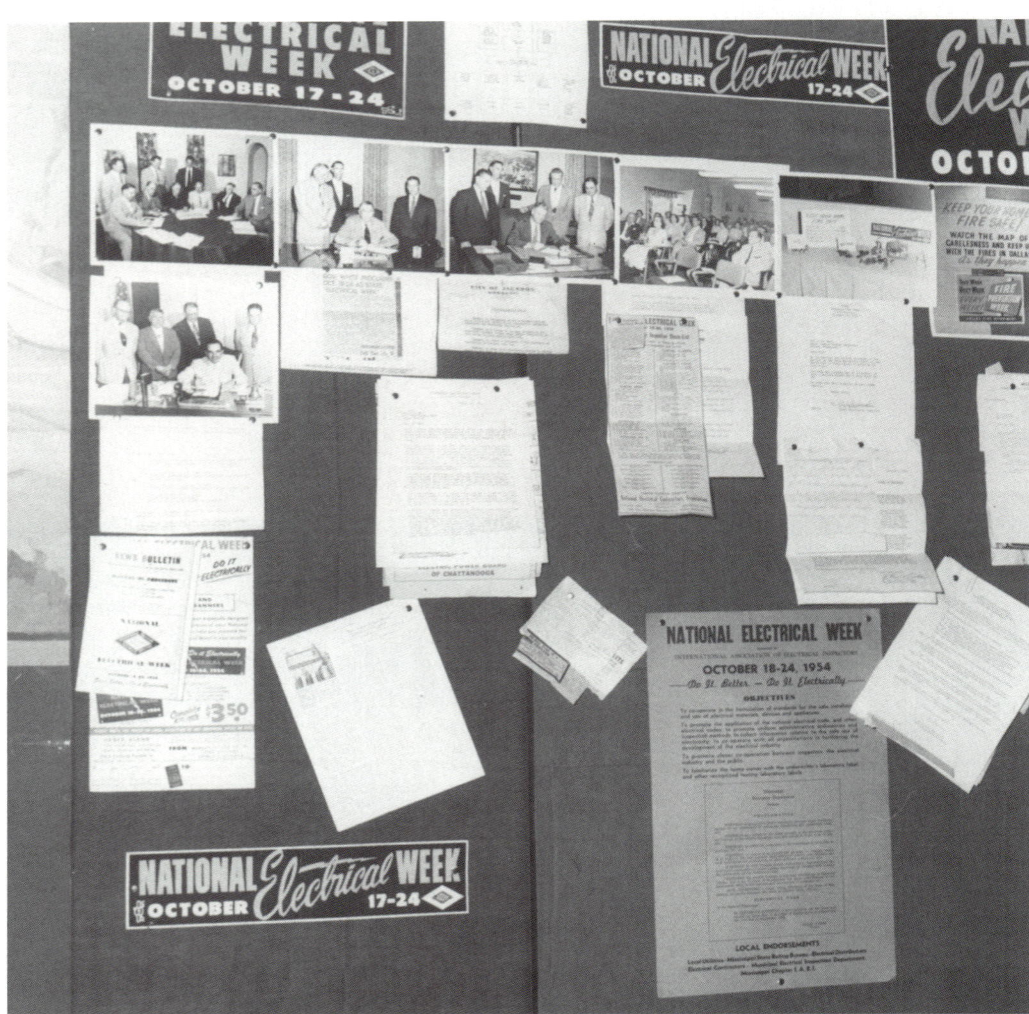

IAEI's Influence on National Safety Weeks

ing to the electrical inspector's attention information of the location of substandard wiring within old buildings. Membership on this committee often breaks down prejudice and effectively builds up good public relations.

Finally we call attention to Clean-up-Fix-up week. This is another opportunity to tell your story through the mass media of communication available to most every electrical inspector across the land. It goes without saying, surely electrical wiring can be included in the category of Clean-up-Fix-up. If it were possible to clean-up the substandard wiring of the country, we could expect fire losses to be reduced substantially, not to mention other improvements such as appearance and efficiency.

Reprinted from *The Electrical Inspector* by A. H. Welklin, 1961.

Fire Prevention Week October 3–9

Announcing that Fire Prevention Week will be observed from October 3 to 9 by proclamation of President Truman and the governor, the local fire department today called upon every citizen to join in the annual crusade against fire. Local leaders, fire prevention associations, manufacturers, insurance organizations, civic clubs, women's clubs, parent-teacher associations, schools, farm extension organizations, the Chamber of Commerce, and the National Grange have all pledged their support in making this community the most fire-safe in the country.

Quoting statistics recently released by the National Fire Protection Association showing a sharp increase in fire losses, the local fire department reports that every day there are fires which take a toll of 22 lives across the nation on the average.

"Most of these fires are unnecessary," the local fire department said in a statement today. "The twin objectives of Fire Prevention Week are to rid our homes and community of the hazards which account for the majority of fires, and to focus attention on the careless habits which take such a high toll of life and property."

"Fire prevention is a team job. If we all 'pull together,' inspect our premises for fire hazards and correct them, we make this town of ours one of the most firesafe communities in the nation. Take the slogan for the 1948 campaign to heart—and 'help yourself to fire prevention.'

Reprinted from *News-Bulletin*, September 1948.

The Baton Rouge Chapter helped create brochures and other literature for National Electrical Week, February 8-14, 1959.

Chris Grauer, congenial secretary-treasurer, Mississippi Chapter, is shown in the above photo with a number of prominent leaders in the electrical industry as the local National Electrical Week Planning Committee met in the office of Governor Ross R. Barnett, state of Mississippi to officially proclaim National Electrical Week.

The members of the NEW Planning Committee in the photo are as follows (*left to right*): Seated—B. V. Jones, Mississippi Rural Electrification Association, Jackson, Mississippi; and Ross R. Barnett, Governor, state of Mississippi. Standing — Bufkin White, Mississippi Power Company, Gulfport, Mississippi; C. S. Shaffer, Local #605, IBEW, Jackson, Mississipi; M. D. Woodward, Local #480, IBEW, Jackson, Mississippi; W. H. Maddox, Capital E.P.A., Clinton, Mississippi; C. E. Strahan, chairman., Local Chapter, IES, Jackson, Mississippi; S. C. Irby, Sr., NAED, Jackson, Mississippi; B. M. Davis, Mississippi Power & Light Company, Jackson, Mississippi; and Wayne Hegwood, NECA, Jackson, Mississippi. Standing (*right of Governor*): C.B. (Chris) Grauer, secretary-treasurer, Mississippi Chapter. — Reprinted from *News-Bulletin*, March 1960.

IAEI's Influence on National Safety Weeks

Electrical committee meeting at the Stevens Hotel in Chicago, Illinois, on October 8–12, 1945.

Code Obsession

New York Board Fire Underwriters
{Boreel Building}

Room Nos. 32 to 38 115 Broadway , New York Oct. 19th, 1881

The New York Board of Fire Underwriters, at a meeting held this day, adopted the following standard for Electric Light Wires, Lamps, etc., subject to future additions.

1. Wires to have 50 percent conductivity above the amount calculated as necessary for the number of lights to be supplied by the wire.

2. Wires to be thoroughly insulated and doubly coated with some approved material.

3. All wires to be securely fastened by some approved non-conducting fastening and to be placed at least 2 1/2 inches for Incandescent lights, and 8 inches for Arc lights from each other, and 8 inches from all other wires, and from all metal or other conducting substance, and to be placed in a manner to be thoroughly and easily inspected by surveyors. When it becomes necessary to carry wires through partitions and floors, they must be secured against contact with metal, or other conducting substance, in a manner approved by the Inspector of the Board.

4. All Arc lights must be protected by glass globes, enclosed at the bottom, to effectually prevent sparks or particles of the carbons from falling from the lamps, and in show windows, mills and other places, where there are materials of an inflammable nature. Chimneys with spark arresters shall be placed at the top of the globe. Open lights positively prohibited. The conducting frame work of chandeliers must be insulated and covered the same as wires.

5. Where electricity is conducted into a building, from sources other than the building in which it is used, a shut off must be placed at the point of entrance to each building, and the supply turned off when the lights are not in use.

Application for permission to use electric lights must be accompanied with a statement of the number and kind of lamps to be used, the estimate of some known electrician of the quantity of electricity required, and a sample of the wire at least three feet in length to be used, with a certificate of said electrician of the carrying capacity of the wire. The applications should also state where the electricity is to be generated, whether the connection will have metallic or ground circuit, and as far as possible give, the full details of manner in which it is proposed to equip the building.

Applications should be sent to Wm. M. Randell, Secretary of the Committee on Police and Origin of Fires.

Wm. W. HENSHAW, Secretary

Late into the evenings, on weekends, and on holidays, these passionate inspectors helped write down what they had learned and helped develop code, the all-important requirements for safety. As they memorized the code, they passed it along to others, through seven decades. This education, too, grew and grew and embraced technology and exulted in its strength and its fulfillment of the mission.

ELECTRICAL EXAMINATION PROCEDURES

Invariably cities, counties and states have examining boards whose responsibility it is to conduct examinations to determine qualifications of applicants for the various licenses as set forth in their respective codes. It goes without saying, such boards should be chosen with great diligence. Various segments of the directly interested industry should be represented on such boards. For example, many of these boards are comprised of an electrical contractor, an IBEW member, a utility inspector and perhaps an insurance inspector (Underwriters' representative), plus the electrical inspector, who usually is the ex-officio member. This is just an example of a good cross-section of representation. This division of representation usually has a tendency to keep things on an even keel. In some communities, it may be more feasible to provide a different format, yet, we must always remember the most democratic plan will always be the least questionable.

Fairness is always a vital factor in giving examinations. Failure in this regard is equivalent to failure of an Electrical Inspection Department to survive. Certainly few court decisions would be won. In fact, the ultimate abolishment of an electrical ordinance might very well be forthcoming.

Examinations should cover areas that will provide the board with sufficient information so that the qualifications of the one seeking a license might very well be determined. We believe, the broader the scope of the test, the better it is, not only for the applicant but the board as well. The examination should be broad enough to cover the basic principles involved plus provide sufficient time to the individual to think the problems through so that he does not have to resort to cramming. We all know that some people have the ability to arrive at the right answer very quickly while others must take more time. We have noted the latter are sometimes more qualified in the field than the former. However, this is a matter better left to individual boards to determine. Some allow use of the *Code* for certain types of tests. Some do not. In our opinion the *Code* should be allowed in all examinations. Just becoming familiar with the *Code* is a matter of great importance. It is interesting to note that those who failed to pass their examination the first time did so later and went on to become topflight supervisors. These men believe their failure contributed to the acquisition of greater *Code* knowledge.

We believe an examination should include a "where to find the code rule." For example: Give Article, Section and Paragraph which prohibit the use of wooden plugs. Fifty or hundred such items would seem about right. However, we must allow but a fraction of the entire examination time to this segment of a test. True and False questions have always been a favorite with most examining boards, but again, it should only comprise a small portion of the total examination. A statement that is true should be marked with the letter "T", and a false one, with the letter "F." In grading a true or false test, the final mark is obtained by subtracting the ones incorrectly marked from those correctly marked. In other words, if out of 100 statements, 95 were correctly marked, the final grade would be 90. The 5 wrong ones would be subtracted from the 95, which were right.

The major portion of the examination is composed of problems which the examinee must solve such as sample problem A.

Some examiners like to have as part of an examination a sketch showing a good number requiring the examinee to list for example, WHAT'S WRONG HERE. There isn't much chance for guesswork in this kind of test. If the examinee can arrive at the right answers, chances are he is very familiar with the *Code*.

J. Hyde Stayner leads a code breakfast discussion of the Nevada Chapter. This picture is circa 1940s.

Ben C. Hill, support electrical department of Oakland, California, and first vice president of the IAEI, and Martin C. Sandler, supervising inspector for the city of Oakland and president of the Southwestern Section at a section meeting in 1946.

NEW CODE PROCEDURE AS OF 1948

The following indicates the progress made by the correlating committee of the National Electrical Code Committee of the newly organized Electrical Section, National Fire Protection Association, in preparing a procedure for the code-making panels which are to process future revisions of the *NEC*, they are:

1. The procedure of the *NEC* Code Committee.
2. The list of code-making panels of those thus far invited to serve on the panels. Additions to the procedure as well as to the list will prepare subjects as handled by the correlating committee.

The provisions for supplements to the *Code* to appear annually, except when a general revision is scheduled permits resuming a publication method followed in the earlier years of the *Code*'s development.

Proposals for changes include additions to the 1947 edition of the *NEC* are invited from individuals and others concerned. These should be forwarded to the secretary. They will be referred to the appropriate code-making panel and be the subject of a report in due course. When a supplement to the *NEC* will be available for publication in 1949 remains to be determined.

The steps to be taken in handling interpretations of the *NEC* and proposals for tentative interim amendments of the *Code* are not announced at this time. The correlating committee plans only editorial and minor changes of the methods followed by the former electrical committee.

It will be noted that the procedural plans is generally consistent with the proposals made by the IAEI. It is assumed that procedural time tables for the filing of reports, etc., will be forthcoming in the near future.

THE CORRELATING COMMITTEE

Personnel

The personnel of the correlating committee shall be appointed by the board of directors of the National Fire Protection Association. The board also appoints the chairman of the National Electrical Code Committee and of the correlating committee and a non-voting secretary of both committees.

Functions

The correlating committee, acting for the Electrical Section, has the following functions:

1. Determines the policies and steps incident to revising the *National Electrical Code.*
2. Organizes the code-making panels.
3. Reviews all reports by code-making panels that recommend changes or additions to the *National Electrical Code* and supplements; approves them, or directs they be referred back for further study.
4. Determines upon the approved procedure for interpreting the *National Electrical Code*, or supplements.
5. Determines the general procedure with regard to proposals for tentative interim amendments of the *Code* or supplements; and reviews

Peter J. Hicks, Jr. chairman of the Standing Committee on Professional Status of Electrical Inspectors, established by executive council action in Boston, MA., June, 1956.

Part of the code panel report presenters at the 1994 Eastern Section meeting (*front row, left to right*): Bill Wusinich, John Caloggero, and Ernie Davis. Back row (*left to right*): Fred Hartwell, John Brezan, Phil Simmons, and Earl Roberts.

recommendations of code-making panels with respect to tentative interim amendments, and, if acceptable, approves them in the name of the National Electrical Code Committee.

6. Reports to the Electrical Section and to a general meeting of the NFPA, the sponsor, its approval of a proposed new edition, or of a supplement, of the *National Electrical Code*, recommending final approval as a standard.

Iowa Chapter code panel at the annual meeting in July 1996. *From left to right*: **Charlie Forsberg, John Steinke, Mike Forister, and Richard Loyd.**

Meetings

Meetings of the correlating committee shall be held at the call of the chairman. Seven members shall constitute a quorum. Action by the committee approving changes in the *National Electrical Code* shall be on the basis of at least seven affirmative votes; provided that if any absent member registers disapproval the action must be reaffirmed by letter ballot or at a later meeting of the committee.

Revisions of the *National Electrical Code.*

To be approved and recommended by the correlating committee a revision of the *National Electrical Code* shall be:

1. A tentative interim amendment,
2. A supplementary revision, or
3. A general revision.

A. Tentative Interim Amendments — A tentative interim amendment is a revision applied for and processed in accordance with the approved procedure for tentative interim amendments.

Note: This procedure as now approved by the correlating committee is, in principle, that previously in effect, in accordance with which several tentative amendments were announced by the former electrical committee.

B. Supplementary Revision — A supplementary revision of the *National Electrical Code* will ordinarily appear at yearly intervals as the result of reports from one or more code-making panels that recommend amendments of articles of the *Code* or propose new articles. Supplementary revisions will be identified according to the year of their publication. Their respective contents may have further consideration when a general revision is undertaken.

C. General Revisions — A general revision of the *National Electrical Code*, will be planned according to conditions, as follows:

1. Upon the initiative of the correlating committee after a four or five-year interval since a previous general revision.
2. After a shorter interval upon the request of the publishers of the *Code*.

Code-making Panels

The number of code-making panels and the code articles assigned to each shall be determined by the correlating committee which shall also appoint the chairman of each panel and the individuals formerly designated to serve with him. It shall also designate alternates for such individuals when conditions seem to warrant.

It will be the responsibility of the correlating committee to provide for proper representation on the various panels of those concerned with their respective article assignments.

Additional personnel (and alternates) may be added by the correlating committee following its consideration of nominations from groups that are concerned. The correlating committee does not expect that every group will require representation on every code-making panel.

Each code-making panel may be organized by its chairman as seems most appropriate for efficient disposal of contemplated revisions of the one or more articles that are assigned to it.

Each panel may develop its own working methods, subject to the requirement that its recommended revisions of the *National Electrical Code* must represent, in a major degree, the consensus of those substantially concerned with the *Code* article by which the recommendations are recorded.

Technical subcommittees to consider any designated topic shall be appointed by the chairman of the National Electrical Code Committee, if directed by the correlating committee or upon his own initiative. The personnel invited to serve on a technical subcommittee shall be chosen on the basis of familiarity with the problem or topic and need not be members of the National Electrical Code Committee. Its report, if containing proposals for changes or additions to the *National Electrical Code*, shall be referred to that code-making panel to which the affected article of the *Code* has been assigned and, if approved, shall be submitted to the correlating committee for further processing.

It is expected that the various panels will each solicit from individuals or groups concerned with the scope of an article the technical assistance and co-operation that will contribute to having its recommendations represent a consensus. Those cooperating in this manner shall have mention in the report of the panel.

When reporting recommended revisions, the outcome of voting by the designated members of a panel shall be recorded with the correlating committee by the chairman of the panel. This report shall advise respectively as to the number (of designated members) voting in favor or against and also those formally refraining from voting; if requested by a member, his reasons for a negative vote or for refraining from voting shall be included in the report. The required voting record shall not include such individuals serving without having been formally appointed to membership in the panel.

Each panel shall report also its having given consideration to any proposals for *Code* changes that have been referred to it and which are not recommended.

A panel may report at any time its recommendations for revision of one or more of the articles which are assigned to it. These recommendations will be processed with similar reports from other code-making panels by the correlating committee and the electrical section for release as an annual supplement to the current edition of the *National Electrical Code* or will be included in the program for a general revision of the *Code*, if one is scheduled.

Reprinted from *News-Bulletin*, September 1948.

"OH, NO! NOT THROUGH **MY** PLANT, YOU DON'T!"

" THAT'S JUST THE TYPE OF THING THAT MAKES MY JOB DIFFICULT, MISS SMITH! "

The Contribution of the IAEI to the National Electrical Code

By Merwin Brandon, vice president, Underwriters' Laboratories, Inc.

The *National Electrical Code* has been so long established and electrical people are presumably so familiar with its operations that I have a certain amount of hesitancy in discussing its formation before a group as familiar with it as those that are attending an IAEI section meeting. At the same time, I realize that many new people are coming into our industry as it expands and that some of the things the older ones take for granted have never been presented to the younger ones. Also from time to time I, myself, run into new information on the background of the *Code* that has not previously been familiar to me

As an illustration of the latter statement, I recently read some old records relating to the *Code* between 1905 and 1911 that showed the surprising amount of activity taken by the city of New York in support of the *National Electric Code* and its more universal recognition.

The Old Pearl Street Generating Station in New York is generally accepted as the first source of public power in this country, although there are claims that the midwest had some plants at about the same time. It is a fact, that New York City did have electric power at an early stage and went through some of the pains of the pioneer. One of these troubles was inadequate building wire and I found that Mr. Wynkoop of the New York City Electrical Division was most active in working with Mr. Pierce and Mr. Merrill of Underwriters' Laboratories, with Mr. Cabot, Mr. Forsyth, and Mr. Sweetland and others in the insurance field and with wire manufacturers to improve the insulation of building wire and thereby reduce the breakdowns and fires that were so prevalent in the early days.

One of the first of these activities was the formation of a Wire Inspection Bureau operated by the wire manufacturers with some testing done by Underwriters' Laboratories. It did not work out as hoped and as building wire continued to cause trouble, the Wire Inspection Bureau went out of business and Underwriters' Laboratories took on the assignment of investigating building wires and assuring their safe performance. One of the first steps in this process was the incorporation in the *National Electrical Code*, the 1911 edition, of comprehensive and, for those days, very severe test requirements on rubber-covered building wires and here again Mr. Wynkoop threw the whole weight of the city of New York into the fray in support of the *National Electrical Code*. Other municipalities joined in the effort, the wire manufacturers cooperated, and from that day to this, building wire has given an increasingly good performance as the use of electricity has become universal.

At the time all of this took place, there was no International Association of Electrical Inspectors. There were some local groups, competent and anxious to help, but there is little evidence in the files I read to show that they were able to do very much, except as outstanding individuals, like Joe Forsyth and Mr. Wynkoop, made their talents available.

The picture today is far different and one of the decisive factors is the contribution of the International Association of Electrical Inspectors. These men bring not only a wealth of experience in the installation of equipment; they also bring a devotion to the public welfare and a practical knowledge of working as a group to achieve a desired end.

Now there are many groups in the electrical industry aiding in the formation of safe installation requirements for electrical wiring and equipment, the contractors, the manufacturers, the utilities, the insurance groups, as well as the inspectors. Each brings a point of view and an experience that results in broad consideration of every problem relating to the safety of the public, but certainly the electrical inspectors are one of the major contributors to this effort. Individually these inspectors could, of course, do a great deal in the way of giving opinions and citing experience and throwing the weight of their individual organizations back of good safety practices, just as Mr. Wynkoop and Mr. Forsyth did in the early days, but this would not be nearly as effective as the present arrangement whereby virtually all of the active inspectors in the United States participate through delegates of their choosing, competent men who can convey not only their own experience, but through discussions with their associates in other parts of the country, the experience of all the electrical inspectors.

Presumably most of you realize that when a proposal for a change in the *Code* reaches the floor of a meeting such as this that is only the beginning. That proposal must run the gauntlet of the group in attendance at the meeting and subsequently be subject to the scrutiny of various committees in the association itself, until it is finally adopted as the considered recommendation of the IAEI. As such it carries a tremendous weight with a code-making panel.

All of this is not to say that the proposal will necessarily be adopted as submitted. Our democratic process provides a forum for all interested groups to express their views and all these divergent views must be reconciled before a firm proposal is made by the panel for public review.

This procedure is at times annoying and is always time consuming, but no better method has ever been found for the regulation of free people other than their full participation during the process of formation, so that the requirements finally adopted would be representative of informed thought and, therefore, acceptable with a minimum of conflict and friction.

If you will look at the composition of the code-making panels, you will see that there are one or more electrical inspectors on every panel. There is, however, one flaw in this arrangement that is not apparent by a review of the code panel membership and that flaw is that many of the municipalities do not provide funds to enable their representative to attend code panel meetings. To that extent the *National Electrical Code* suffers. These inspector representatives do have the opportunity to review all proposals and comment on them through correspondence, but that is not a suitable substitute for participation in discussion of the proposals by the full committee. The other groups provide sufficient funds to pay the expenses of their delegates and a program in now under way to provide funds for the expenses of electrical inspectors attending code-making panel meetings. If that effort is as successful as it should be, *Code* work will then receive the full benefit of IAEI representation and that would be a relief to the other segments of the electrical industry as well as to the inspector representatives, because all of these groups are aware of the inspector contribution and are most anxious that it be continued to the fullest extent so that the public will receive the safeguarding that it deserves in the use of electricity.

Reprinted from *News-Bulletin*, March 1956.

No, 3 Miles In 3 Minutes Isn't Fast—I'll Admit I'm No Barney Oldfield If You'll Admit You're No Electrician!

New Hampshire Says No to Licensing Electricians!

By Charles A. Stone, editor, *New England Electrical News*.

Once again, the legislature in New Hampshire has turned down a proposal to license electricians in that state. Just why in this enlightened age, when there is virtually complete dependency on electricity in everyday life, anyone would seriously oppose such protective legislation is difficult to imagine. No one doubts the wisdom of requiring doctors to show proof of their qualifications before practicing the healing art. Ignorance in electrical work can prove just as deadly.

Today, the life-blood of industry is electrical current. It is the principal servant in every home. It provides the necessities and comforts of life at every level. Electrical work is highly specialized. It calls for training and knowledge. Electricity is a deadly weapon in the hands of the incompetent. Allowing the unqualified to make electrical installations is like granting a permit to commit arson or worse.

Is It Bad?

One of the proponents of the law in New Hampshire declared with bitter truth that the state will continue to operate without a licensing law until tragedy forces its adoption. But why wait? Licensing laws where they are in effect have not proved onerous, or burdensome, or detrimental to anyone's welfare. Their benefits are such that no one would ever think of asking their repeal.

It does not seem unreasonable to ask an electrician to know what he's doing, and to show proof of it. In fact, not to require such proof seems much more unreasonable. Is it more unreasonable to license the driver of a car than the agent of death-dealing electric current?

We don't advocate that those in New Hampshire be forced to enact legislation in which they are opposed, even if such enactment is for their own best interests. As long as there is strong opposition, why wouldn't an investigation be advisable? The same might be equally desirable in Connecticut, where a licensing law is also pending, and likewise meeting with obstacles.

Study the Advantages

There would be much to gain in sending committees from both states to study the electrician licensing laws in Massachusetts and Rhode Island and Maine. A thorough study would definitely show many advantages for adoption of such a law. It might also serve to uncover ways in which the laws in those states could be improved.

We at this editorial post have for many years been in favor of licensing laws, and their strict enforcement. When we hear the arguments offered against such legislation they have a familiar ring to them. It is something we've heard many times before whenever, in fact, an enlightened community has considered licensing its electricians.

And we can say with truth and candor, unequivocally, that all the dire things predicted as the consequence of enactment of such protective legislation just never happen. No community can ask for a greater boon than a good licensing law honestly administered.

— Reprinted from and by permission of the *New England Electrical News*. Reprinted from *News-Bulletin*, July 1957.

Code discussion period at the Western New England Chapter meeting on March 16, 1960, in Bridgeport, Connecticut.

PROFESSIONAL STATUS FOR ELECTRICAL INSPECTORS

Peter J. Hicks, Jr., chairman of the Standing Committee on Professional Status of Electrical Inspectors, established by executive council action in Boston, Massachusetts, June 1956, presented a report approved by this committee to an industry advisory committee in New York, December 6, 1956, calling for specialized training for electrical inspectors throughout the country leading to the establishment of professional status.

The standing committee is of the opinion that only through competent electrical inspectors could the public be assured against inferior equipment and workmanship. Properly trained inspectors, who maintain high standards of inspection, contribute much to the electrical industry in all of its phases. Competent inspection protects the reputation that years of effort and millions of dollars have built into the products of the electrical manufacturers. It plays a large part in keeping inferior products off the market and protects the good name of the entire industry, from the journeyman to the public utility and the producer of electrical equipment. Competent inspectors provide the only safeguard against attempts to ignore the testing services and to install equipment and material that contravenes the law, victimizes the purchaser and belittles the reputation of the industry.

In addition, electrical inspectors need security and adequate compensation for the service rendered.

Three major recommendations are proposed:

1. A program to familiarize inspectors with the requirements of various codes and standards.

2. A refresher course in the fundamentals of electricity.

3. Seminars throughout the nation on modern electrical development.

The committee proposed that a program be set up to acquaint the inspectors with the requirements of the *National Electrical Code*, Underwriters' Laboratories, Inc., the National Fire Protection Association, National Electrical Manufacturers Association (NEMA), the National Board of Fire Underwriters standards and the standards of other nationally recognized testing laboratories and associations.

Point 2 is for the purpose of establishing a refresher course for inspectors. A course in fundamentals of electricity could be conducted by correspondence or by direct personal instructions. The course could be supplemented by lectures by representatives of the industry or other qualified persons. These in addition to proper literature and materials would serve to keep inspectors up-to-date with the advances in the industry.

The seminars as outlined in point 3 would be held at state colleges and universities during vacation periods. This part of the program would be limited to key inspection personnel and inspections recommended by them. Later, all inspection personnel could be invited to attend these seminars.

Mr. Hicks speaking for the committee was of the opinion that it would be possible for the present inspection personnel to improve their skill and that it would be possible to seek recruits among graduates of technical high schools and junior colleges to meet the problems of the field. Their academic and technical education would provide a good foundation on which to build towards a professional career.

Mr. Hicks' standing committee, including Delbert H. Hanson, Southwestern Section, William Hogan, Western Section, L. W. Cosens, Southern Section, and Chester M. Kirsop, Northwestern Section, also urge the establishment of sectional committees in the IAEI to maintain liaison between the membership and the standing committee.

On the advisory committee are:

C. W. Higbee, United States Rubber Company, representing the National Electrical Manufacturers Association.

E. A. Brand, Niagara Mohawk Power Corporation, representing the Edison Electric Institute.

Hendley Blackman, Westinghouse Electric Corporation, representing the American Institute of Electrical Engineers.

Merwin Brandon, vice-president, representing Underwriters' Laboratories, Incorporated.

E. R. Cornish, research director, representing the National Electrical Contractors Association.

Percy Bugbee, general manager, National Fire Protection Association.

Reprinted from *News-Bulletin*, January 1957.

Industrial code panel on busways for service at the 1960 Nevada Chapter meeting. ***From left to right:*** **O. G. Wedekind, UL; L. O. Traine, inspector and moderator; E. E. Carlton; E. G. Brolin; H. K. Glenn; and Kent P. Steiner.**

REPORT OF IAEI EDUCATIONAL COMMITTEE

To IAEI Members: A great progressive step has been taken by the executive council in recognizing a need for the following program, a program that has long been the dream of many IAEI members. A program of this nature and magnitude must have the support of the entire industry as well as those directly involved. To determine the need and the direction, questionnaires were sent throughout the country. This program is based, largely, on the answers we received. I am happy for the opportunity, at this time, to thank the committee, Past Presidents George Monroe and Peter Hicks, Jr., for their help in making this report possible. This program is for every member of IAEI, especially the electrical inspector, so too is the responsibility for its success. If you participate actively and enthusiastically, the "up-grading" of the electrical inspector will no longer be a dream but an accomplished fact.

Sincerely,

Barney B. Alverson

When I appeared before you at the last executive council meeting in Detroit, I asked for a year to determine the best approach to accomplish the upgrading of the electrical inspector. Fortunately, the committee has been a conscientious, sincere group. The quality and amount of work has been outstanding.

In a program such as we outlined to you last year, it was apparent that we would need the cooperation and support of the entire industry. Therefore it was necessary for the committee to determine the industry's attitude toward such a program.

To that end we composed a questionnaire of six questions with spaces for answers and nothing else, so the person answering would not have to be identified and would feel free from restraint in his answers. Each member received twenty-five questionnaires along with a cover letter of transmittal. President Monroe also circulated some.

In sending these letters out we attempted to get a sampling of opinion from other than electrical inspectors, such as manufacturers, utilities, engineers, architects, distributors, contractors, and journeymen. The response was tremendous!

Some were answered very simply but most of them showed a great concern and a sincere effort to help the program with constructive criticism and suggestions.

This survey showed there was a definite need for an upgrading program and a partial solution would be certification by the IAEI. The committee realized that this is only a partial solution but it was an excellent starting place. For the overall solution we established a ten-point program which would carry us along the path we have chosen.

Ten Point Program

1. Establish standards for certification.
2. Establish certification procedure.
3. Coordination of education in the various sections of IAEI.

(A) Setting up uniform courses of study in each section.

(B) Securing new educational and technical materials for integration and supplementation of section materials.

(C) Extend and enlarge use of *News-Bulletin* as educational media.

4. Securing any available financing for furthering this program.
5. Organizing educational seminars relative to our needs.
6. Feeding and receiving pertinent material to and from the electrical industry.
7. Soliciting new membership through our program.
8. Soliciting moral, political and financial support from other organizations for our program.
9. Representing IAEI in other organizations.
10. Issuing news releases relative to the safe use of electricity.

Beginning with the first point we established standards for certification based on the information gleaned from the survey and knowing that the standards would determine the merit of the certification. The standards must also be in the realm of attainment by every member of the IAEI.

Qualification for Certification

1. Good moral character.
2. At least thirty years of age.
3. An electrical engineer (EE) or certification as an EE by a state with registration laws plus five years experience in the electrical inspection field, or
4. Four years apprenticeship plus five years experience as a journeyman wireman, plus five years experience in the electrical inspection field with at least two years of the ten years in a supervisory capacity, or
5. Ten years experience in the electrical inspection field of which two years shall be in a supervisory capacity plus specific educational courses (exception: specific training in supervision may be substituted for the two years of supervisory capacity above) or
6. Eminence. Thirty-five years of age with twelve years experience in the electrical inspection field of a nature which, in the opinion of the section executive committee, would qualify him for certification and should include those men who have served as officers in the section as well as the chapter for at least one term.

An IAEI member meeting those qualifications and being certified by the IAEI should certainly not be called an "electrical inspector." He is that already. We considered many designations and in keeping with the survey decide to use the term "electrical safety engineer" defined as follows:

An electrical safety engineer is a person who is especially qualified by education, training and skill to offer a professional service for the prevention of accidents and fire caused by electricity. The application of special knowledge to the service and creation in planning, design, investigation, evaluation, consultation and supervision of practices, methods and materials relative to the safe use of electricity.

The second point in our program is the establishment of a procedure whereby an IAEI member desiring the honor of being certified as an electrical safety engineer would have a uniform method to follow in all sections of the IAEI.

Code panel at the Westchester Chapter meeting held on February 9, 1960. ***Seated from left to right*****: Thomas Mackie, chairman; Carlton Schaad and Nicholas Adams, New York Board of Fire Underwriters; Robert Sonneville, Whiffen Electric Company; Herman Metz, Cuccinell Electric Company; and Leonard Turner, Consolidated Edison Corporation.**

Certification Procedure

An inspector desiring to be certified by the IAEI would secure an application for certification from the chapter secretary. If the applicant is known to be of good moral character, 30 years of age, and has the necessary experience, the secretary and the chairman of the chapter sign as recommending and submit application to the section secretary.

The section presents the application, containing experience and education background, to the section executive committee, for final approval or denial. The section executive committee shall determine if applicant meet the standards by a majority vote.

They may ask for personal interview or take any other steps they feel necessary in order to make their determination. The application is then forwarded to the IAEI executive council, if approved by the section executive committee, for final action at the executive council annual meeting.

If it is approved by the executive council, a certificate is then prepared, signed by the president and presented by the president to the applicant at the next section meeting. If the chapter secretary and/or chairman are in doubt as to the age or moral character of the applicant, they may require additional proofs or references or may send the application to the section with a note of their findings.

The section executive committee may take three different actions on an application: (1) Approval; (2) Denial; (3) Referral to the section education committee. The applicant shall be notified of the action by the section executive committee.

In case No. 3 the referral would be based on a lack of vocational training and the applicant could then avail himself of the educational courses offered by the section. When he had satisfactorily completed the necessary training, the executive committee would be informed by the educational committee and could reconsider his application.

The executive council could take two actions based on the information furnished by the executive committee: (1) Denial; or (2) Approval. In the latter case, the certificate would be prepared and presented by the president or someone designated by him at the annual section meeting in appropriate ceremony.

The application and certificate format and design would be a product of the IAEI educational committee as would the responsibility for the uniformity and coordination of educational programs of the sections.

The IAEI educational committee would be the final appeal in case of a dispute arising between the applicant and the section or IAEI regarding the intent and meaning of the standards of qualifications or ethics.

Emphasis should be placed on the fact that the entire certification program is voluntary. It in no respects impairs or affects membership in the IAEI.

Issuing the certificate by the IAEI is, purely and primarily, an incentive to the individual inspector for self improvement. The secondary benefits vary all the way from self improvement to classification change to recognition and registration.

I am sure that the certification program if properly exploited would stimulate competition within departments, within units, within chapters and sections. It would also stimulate active membership by virtue of involvement of more members on every level. It would also create a desire for membership among those seeking more knowledge in this field and only being able to secure it through membership in the IAEI.

The Southwestern Section executive committee at its meeting in Long Beach, California, granted permission to the IAEI to use the educational material developed by the section, in other sections. This material covers the basic theory of electricity, a study of the *National Electrical Code* with the aid of B. Z. Segall's *Electrical Diagram* and an opaque reflector, inspection procedure and public relations. With the addition of material relative to fire and accident investigation and prevention together with a course in supervision, we would have a fairly complete educational program.

It would be necessary to have an active educational committee in each section to work out the details of disseminating the necessary educational material and grading one's efforts.

The first two points of this program are with the exception of maintenance and changes as prescribed by the executive council fairly well set but the third point is where the IAEI educational standards committee plays its biggest role, that of coordinating education in the various sections so that uniform procedure and education will guarantee the integrity of the certification, securing new educational and technical material to aid the section educational committees and to find ways of using our *News-Bulletin* to further our program, to develop new courses of instruction as needed and to act in advisory capacity to the council and the section committee.

Summary of Cost

As you can see from this report, so far, the constant cost of this program will be that of supplying the application forms and the certificates. The cost of providing the educational programs will be borne by the sections or passed on to others.

The cost of using space in the *News-Bulletin* is indeterminate at this point. The cost of the applications are very nominal. The cost of the certificate would vary depending on the type, size and frame.

It is expected that after the first big issuance that the probable need would drop considerably and from there on be constant. With six sections made up of some sixty-five chapters and divisions the original order of applications should be at least 2000; as these were used, a rate of use could be determined. The cost of 200 applications would be approximately $60.

The cost of printing the certificates would be nominal after the original plate was made. The cost of the plate would be less than $100. Thereafter the type of paper and the labor would determine the cost. The original order should be based on the cost per block, but not less than 2000.

The future cost of installing uniform systems in each section can be carried on largely by mail and entails very little cost. This budget should be reviewed by the secretary/treasurer and detailed, but it should not be a great deal in comparison to the total budget.

The other seven points in the program must yet be explored and exploited but with a program under way, the educational committee can stimulate activity to accomplish the other points. As you can see, it is going to require more than just the committee to bring the entire program into operation. It is, however, evident that the whole electrical industry is concerned and willing to help.

The educational committee presents this report for your approval as an overall program to accomplish in part the upgrading of the electrical inspector and the recognition he so richly deserves.

Barney Alverson was from the Southwestern Section and was chairman of the IAEI committee. Committee members: Chris Klawa, Northwestern Section; H. B. Love, Western Section and George W. Flach, Southern Section.

Reprinted from *News-Bulletin*, January 1963.

International President P. J. Hicks addressing the Nevada Chapter at a 1960 chapter meeting in Reno, Nevada.

Educational Program Gets OK "Grandfather" Certification Re-opened

The long-awaited IAEI education program (correspondence course) appears to be ready for release to IAEI active members. The program was approved by the board of directors at their regular meeting last November.

Although some detail work remains to be finished by the educational committee, it is expected that they will have the job done by February 15, 1967.

Survey Questionnaire Important

There is a questionnaire intended for active members in this issue. This survey is designed to provide information needed so that the mechanics of administering the course can be determined.

The educational committee will study the results of this survey. The survey will enable the committee to determine the interest, size, cost, scope, time element and other factors related to the course. As soon as sufficient questionnaire returns are available, the committee will meet, probably, in April or May, to assess the result.

After the Spring 1967 meeting of the educational committee announcement regarding the educational course will be made, probably in the July 1967 issue of the *News*. It is expected the announcements will include an availability date, cost data and an application form.

Keen Interest

Many members have expressed an interest in this educational program. This questionnaire is your opportunity to show your interest, help the committee, and get IAEI's educational work underway. The more students we enroll in the course the less it will cost per student. So, let the committee know by returning the questionnaire. But only if you plan to take the course when available.

Aimed at Inspectors

This course was designed with the novice inspector as the principal benefactor since electrical inspectors with ten or more years of inspection experience are generally sophisticated. Even so, this is an educational opportunity for all inspectors.

The course will include such basics as elementary theory of electricity, code, office procedures, field work, public relations and other facets of what should be in the educational background of an electrical inspector. This course is intended to develop a professional electrical inspector and to help him attain a better status financially. In our opinion, the course is equivalent to an associate arts—college level course.

IAEI Certification

IAEI will administer and conduct this course. Its successful completion by active inspector members of the association will result in certification as an electrical safety inspector or engineer. (Engineer where permissible).

Grandfather Clause for Certification

For the old-timers, (sophisticated inspectors), the board of directors reopened the grandfather clause for "certification." Filing for certification by eligible active inspectors is now open until September 30, 1967. Application forms for filing for certification may be obtained by written request to the international office.

Reprinted from *News-Bulletin*, January 1967.

Commercial code workshop at the 1962 Southwestern Section meeting. Henry Chateau, Underwriters' Laboratories, secretary; and Glenn Eastman, chairman.

Time for Action

Within the past several years we have been hearing and reading about the need for more electrical inspectors. Many trade magazines carry articles emphasizing this need, with the belief that wide circulation and repetition will seek out the men suitable to fill these vacancies.

The authors of the articles are persons closely connected to the electrical industry. They are cognizant of the demands of the electrical industry. They are aware of the future increased use of electricity, and the need for an immediate increase in the number of available electrical inspectors, so that all installations will receive proper electrical inspections in the interest of safety.

The lack of qualified inspectors means more responsibility on the shoulders of fewer people, resulting in hurry-up inspections, less time to review various problems with the electrical contractor, delays in the progress of building construction, and a general deterioration of a program so vitally needed by the general public. These conditions must not and will not come to pass if all of us interested in the electrical industry use just a few minutes of our time to inform those desirous of becoming electrical inspectors there is a solution through an educational program available to them for study and completion in their own homes.

Fortunately, the International Association of Electrical Inspectors saw the need for this type of an electrical educational program comprised of courses directed to those seeking employment as electrical inspectors, and to the electrical inspector that is constantly trying to keep abreast of the ever-growing electrical industry. Never before has there been offered such diversified courses to the inspector through a "learn while you work" program. Never before have there been courses prepared solely for the inspector, or the would like to be inspector, in terms that are directed to them, rather than electrical or designing engineers.

To you who are interested in the electrical inspection field, or those wishing to increase their knowledge of electricity, take advantage of this oppor-

THE UNIVERSITY OF NEBRASKA

University Extension Division

REGISTRATION FOR

ELECTRICAL INSPECTION 1x FUNDAMENTALS OF ELECTRICITY I BY CORRESPONDENCE STUDY	ELECTRICAL INSPECTION 2x FUNDAMENTALS OF ELECTRICITY BY CORRESPONDENCE STUDY
• The first of a series of six courses, each with a certificate	• The second of a series of six courses, each with a certificate
• A review of the "why" in the inspector's work	• Theory of alternating current as related to practical problems
• To promote wise decisionmaking by electrical inspectors	• To promote wise decisionmaking by electrical inspectors
• Course content prepared by IAEI Education Committee	• Course content prepared by IAEI Education Committee
• Fee $45.00 (Fee includes syllabus, lesson evaluation, certificate)	• Fee $45.00 (Fee includes syllabus, lesson evaluation, certificate)

REGISTRATION—Order Form Date______

University Extension Division, University of Nebraska, Lincoln, Nebraska 68508

Check below

Please enroll me in Electrical Inspection 1x — Fundamentals of Electricity I, a noncredit correspondence course. ______

Please enroll me in Electrical Inspection 2x — Fundamentals of Electricity, a noncredit correspondence course. ______

Please check ✓

☐ Tuition $45.00

☐ Cost of materials .... ______

FOR LESSON IX ONLY

Static Electricity 1966. NFPA No. 77. Boston: National Fire Protection Association, 1966 .... 1.00

FOR BOTH LESSONS

Carr, Ed. **Croft's American Electricians Handbook.** Eighth Edition. Text Edition. Manchester, Missouri: McGraw-Hill Book Company, Inc., 1961 .... $18.50

McPartland and Novak. **Practical Electricity.** Manchester, Missouri: McGraw-Hill Book Company, Inc., 1964 .... 4.50

Nebraska residents add 2½ per cent tax to cost of supplies .... ______

Total amount enclosed .... ______

Name______ Social Security Number______

Address______

tunity. Study while carrying out your everyday duties. Take advantage of the courses given by the correspondence study program which has been prepared for the practical person. Take advantage of a program under the direction of the University of Nebraska. Take advantage of a program that is offered at a very low nominal charge. Take advantage of a program where the cost of textbooks, reference books, and other applicable materials needed have been considered and kept to an extremely low cost to the student. Don't wait—don't waste your talents—increase your knowledge of electricity. Act now—enroll—start and complete all six courses. If an inspector at present, increase your knowledge. If wanting to become an inspector, prepare for the position. If employed in the trade, become a first class electrician. Send in the registration order form now.

Reprinted from *IAEI News*, March 1971.

From The Field

The Legislature has finally enacted the perennial bill to require inspectors of electrical installations to prove their own competence before being authorized to approve electrical wiring system. Several major fires have been attributed to incompetent local inspection officials. Under the new act, all electrical inspectors must be examined in accordance with standards established by the Board of Building Standards in the Department of Industrial Relations.

Electrical Inspectors to be Licensed in Ohio

The Ohio State Legislature completed its work on a bill to license electrical inspectors.

The Ohio Senate, on May 26, 1970, passed by vote of 31 to 0 an amended House Bill 991. Favorable action by the Ohio House was taken some time ago.

The bill was presented by Clara E. Weisenborn, Senator from Dayton, Ohio, as follows:

Mr. President, members of the Senate:

Amended House Bill 991 is a very important bill to this general assembly and the citizens of Ohio. The bill is quite simple in form and the amendments made to it in the elections, commerce, and labor committees have improved it to the extent it is an agreed bill by those directly affected.

House Bill 991 provided for the licensing of electrical safety inspectors by the Board of Building Standards. This is highly important as it will upgrade the caliber of those inspecting electrical installations whether they represent the state, a municipality, an utility or a private organization. All of us recognize the fact that newly installed electrical systems have become increasingly complex and sophisticated. Consequently, it is imperative that those persons charged with the responsibility of inspect-

continued

ing such installations be thoroughly qualified to ascertain the installation is properly made in accordance with recommended building standards thereby protecting life and property.

There is a temporary "grandfather" clause in the bill. It authorizes the Board of Building Standards to issue a temporary certificate of competency for a period of twelve months to any person, who is already engaged in the practice of electrical inspection. Such person is then required to take an examination and upon satisfactory completion of same is to be issued a permanent certificate.

Amended House Bill 991 has been approved in its present form by the Department of Industrial Relations, by the Board of Building Standards and by the Electric Utility Companies of Ohio.

We have passed in this 108th General Assembly three bills which have some bearing on HB 991 and each of which I consider important. These are Amended House Bill 709 which established minimum building standards. This passed the Senate 26-0.

Amended Substitute Senate Bill 180 requiring safety equipment for gas plumbing in certain public buildings. This passed the Senate 31-0.

Amended Senate Bill 190 relative to the installation and inspection of plumbing. This passed the Senate 29-0.

Amended HB 991 in my mind is even more important than the three bills I have just enumerated. I hope the Senate will give HB 991 the same support.

Clara E. Weisenborn

This is an important event in the history of electrical inspection and should lend encouragement to inspectors in other states for similar legislation.

Electrical inspectors in other states, in working toward such legislation, should be aware that the task is not so easy. Hard and serious work, plus a lot of personal time, is involved.

The Ohio Chapter, IAEI, dedicated itself to the job of obtaining state licensing for electrical inspectors several years ago. Their effort has resulted in this new law. Although the new law may not please all of the Ohio Chapter members, it is acceptable to the majority of the members according to an action taken at the chapter meeting on May 22, 1970.

Reprinted from *IAEI News*, July 1970.

IAEI Expands Its Certification Program

The IAEI board of directors, on the recommendation of the IAEI educational committee, approved an expansion of the certification program. One of the main new features of this expansion is the following:

If an inspector has fourteen years of experience in inspection, as of September 30, 1967, and in addition to this, holds a journeyman-electrician's certification of competency, he may apply for certification as an electrical safety inspector or an electrical safety engineer, whichever is appropriate, without having to enroll in the IAEI-University of Nebraska educational courses.

Anyone having this experience and the journeyman-electrician's certificate may now apply for certification. The journeyman-electrician certification of competency must be verified by either the local chapter of which the applicant is a member or through the educational committee of the chapter or section. This must have been a written examination of competency at the time the license was issued.

The chapter or section educational committee will have the responsibility of verifying the certificate of competency. Anyone submitting an application for certification under this clause must submit a letter with his application stating the journeyman-electrician's certificate he holds and from what city, county, or state. A brief resume of the type of examination must also accompany the application.

Upon receiving this application, the chapter will investigate and verify the type of license held by the applicant and, if approved, will forward the application to the International office for the issuance of the certification credentials.

It will be the responsibility of the chapter to see that the license issued was through a written examination on electrical work which would be in conjunction with a journeyman-electrician's certificate. Licenses held that were obtained for revenue purposes only will not be accepted for this new phase of certification.

The requirements set forth by the educational committee are that before filing for his journeyman-electrician's examination, the applicant had four years or more experience in the electrical industry prior to taking this examination.

Equivalency Tests

IAEI certification through equivalency testing, in lieu of the educational syllabus offered through the University of Nebraska, will be available soon through the University of Nebraska on Lessons 1X and 2X. Due to the fact that Lesson 3X deals with inspection procedures, there will be no equivalency test on 3X and everyone filing for certification will have to complete this portion. Equivalency tests will also be available for 4X, 5X, and 6X, so that those who wish to obtain certification without taking all of the educational program may do so.

Your educational committee is working diligently to complete 6X. Lessons 4X and 5X are in the final states at the present time. With this, we will have the first phase of our educational program completed. Later we hope to offer a more in-depth program for upgrading the experienced inspector.

The educational committee hopes that in the future various specialized programs can be offered through the IAEI on specific portions of the *Code*, theory, and public relations. If you have any suggestions as to material that you would like to have covered in future programs, please contact our International office or the chairman of the educational committee.

Submit Certification Applications to Your Chapter for Approval

Editor's note

The committee recognizes that not all jurisdictions have provisions or requirements for competency examinations and licensing of journeyman electricians. The committee did not provide any alternate or substitute for this requirement. So if you do not have this qualification or it is not available to you, you should not apply for certification.

The committee will, however, evaluate a completed educational course (other than the University of Nebraska) which may be considered equivalent and, thereby, approve certification.

—C. R. Pierce, chairman, IAEI Educational Committee. Reprinted from *IAEI News*, July 1972.

Certification By Education Or Testing

The educational committee of IAEI is happy to report that a complete educational program for the inspector is now available. The program will be in association with Block and Associates, Gainesville, Florida, who will be administering the *Code* sections of our program. These *Code* lessons are 4x and 5x of our original program.

The committee met with J. Morris Trimmer of Block and Associates and final arrangements are now complete. Four x (4x) of the *National Electrical Code*, Chapters 1-4, is now available. Five x (5x), covering Chapters 5, 6, 7 and 8, is in final preparation and will be available shortly. This program will include a review and a study of the *National Electrical Code*. The basics text will be the *National Electrical Code*. A supplementary text, *Learning the Electrical Code* by J. H. McPartland, will also be used. Mr. McPartland is editor of *Electrical Construction and Maintenance*.

Block and Associates will handle equivalency tests on courses 1, 2, 4 and 5x. These tests are for those who wish to obtain certification through testing rather than completion of independent study program.

Those interested in enrolling in courses 1x, 2x, 3x or 6x, should apply directly to the University of Nebraska, University Extension Division, Lincoln, Nebraska 68508.

Those wishing to enroll for the *National Electrical Code* Lessons 4x and 5x, or who wish to take any of the equivalency tests, will make application directly to the International Office of the Association, 802 Busse Highway, Park Ridge, Illinois 60068.

The cost for lesson 4x will be $25.00 plus $7.50 for the supplementary textbook. The *National Electrical Code*, to be used as the basic text, is not included in this cost.

The fee for 5x will also be $25.00. No additional textbook will be required.

Fees for the equivalency tests will be $15.00 each for 1x and 2x and $10.00 each for 4x and 5x. These equivalency tests will be open book type tests to be proctored and timed. Anyone wishing to take the equivalency tests should contact their chapter educational program representative to make arrangements for the proctor. The cost of proctoring is an additional cost.

The International office will issue certificates of completion for any of the courses taken through Block and Associates as well as for those taking the equivalency tests.

With the completion of this program, it now makes certification a reality and we hope that all our active members will take the necessary courses or apply for certification through equivalency tests. The association hopes that through our certification program, we can elevate our active members of the association to a *professional level within our* community.

—A Report from Educational Committee Chairman C.R. Pierce. Reprinted from IAEI News, July 1974.

Charles Schram and Ed Lawry seem to enjoy being stranded in the flood waters when a record 9 ½ inch cloudburst hit the Chicago area on August 14, 1987. The gentlemen were part of an ETS/IAEI certification committee meeting that continued as usual, despite the flood.

Inspection Officials Close Rank

The IAEI board of directors, at their last regular meeting, declared a policy of cooperation with the several building officials organizations in the United States. These are the: International Conference of Building Officials (ICBO), Southern Building Code Congress International (SBCCI), Building Officials Conference of America (BOCA) and the National Academy of Code Administrators (NACA).

IAEI's major endeavor in these cooperative efforts is to obtain a better understanding of the *National Electrical Code* among building officials; to relate the *NEC* to the model building codes and to provide an avenue of input from building officials into the *NEC*.

IAEI will also become a partner in jointly sponsored programs to certify electrical inspectors, a worthy project to upgrade the knowledge and prestige of electrical inspectors.

As a starting point in this endeavor IAEI and ICBO recently held a joint meeting of the Arizona Chapters of the two organizations and a resolution therefrom follows.

IAEI has held staff meetings with ICBO and SBCCI wherein plans have been made for continuing cooperation in the related fields of *Code* administration. This will lead to additional advantages in the future for both electrical and building officials.

by L. E. LaFehr, Editor, reprinted from *IAEI News*, May 1976.

Quick Fact

At the 1981 board of directors meeting, the executive committee reviewed and approved format for study manual, *Guide for Electrical Inspectors Certification Program*.

Reprinted from *News-Bulletin*, January 1982.

ANNOUNCING

A Study and Certification Program

Jointly Sponsored By
The Southern Building Code Conference International
and
The International Association of Electrical Inspectors
for
Certification of Combination Inspectors

Of 1 and 2-family dwelling with the electrical portion based on
The 1975 NEC 1 and 2-family Electrical Code
An application form and details of the program will be
Published in the September/October **IAEI News**

Or you may request an application form by writing to :

Southern Building Code Congress International
c/o Director of Education
3617 Eighth Avenue, South
Birmingham, Alabama 35222

IAEI News, July/August, 1976

Michigan Chapter Establishes Electrical Inspector Training Program

The Michigan Chapter of IAEI has established an electrical inspector training program in cooperation with the fire marshall division of the Michigan State Police and other segments of the electrical industry.

The curriculum which has been developed comprises a two-week course in the *National Electrical Code*, related to NFPA standards for hospitals, schools, hazardous occupancies, and places of public assembly. In addition, such topics as liability, court procedures, testing laboratories, plan review, report writing, communications, public relations, interrelationship of fire and building codes will be addressed.

The course will be offered at the Michigan State Police Academy in Lansing, Michigan, the weeks of February 11 and February 25, 1980. Active Michigan electrical inspectors may contact: Frank Nesbitt, Sam Curry, John DeMarais or Peter Van Putten for further details.

Certification of Electrical Inspectors

Certification of electrical inspectors was called for by Michigan State Fire Marshall William Rucinski as he spoke recently at Michigan State University in East Lansing, Michigan.

He also called for a training program to prepare additional electrical inspectors. The state has about half enough, he said.

"Michigan has the potential for a Beverly Hill Supper Club-type fire," Rucinski warned 200 Michigan state and municipal electrical inspectors, noting that electrical violations abounded at the site of the Kentucky fire which killed close to 200.

"The electrical enforcement authority in Michigan has been given to nearly 500 counties and municipalities, who procedure and enforcement varies from excellent to poor," he counseled.

"We are lacking in minimum qualifications for an electrical inspector; we lack training and certification capabilities, and we need uniformity in *Code* application and interpretation, variance and appeals," he said.

National associations and federal agencies have been slow in the development of a certification program, Rucinski added, as he called for Michigan leadership and teamwork to "re-establish professionalism" in the field.

"Our goal should be to establish the electrical inspector's minimum qualifications, a training school, a certification procedure and a continual certification program," he declared.

Industry, utilities and the state police fire marshal's division will cooperate, he proposed.

Reprinted from *IAEI News*, September 1979.

Register early for the IAEI sponsored seminars on changes in the 1981 *National Electrical Code.* On the final day, you will have an opportunity to ask questions of nationally prominent electrical code experts. The seminars were moderated by Wilford "Bill" Summers, executive director of IAEI, former secretary of the NEC Committee, editor of the *NEC Handbook*, and editor of McGraw Hill's *American Electricians' Handbook*.

Reprinted from *IAEI News*, July 1980.

Shown discussing the legal ramifications and liabilities of certification is Assistant General Counsel Stanford von Mayrhauser, New Jersey. Members of the National Board of Governors *from left to right are:* **William Connolly, acting chairman, New Jersey; Stanford von Mayrhauser, New Jersey; and William Hogan, program director, Educational Testing Service, Princeton, New Jersey.** *Not shown:* **Robert Wible, States Building Codes and Standards, acting secretary; and Trevor Jacobsen, representing Oregon.**

Meeting of the "National Board of Governors" of the Multi-State Testing Program for Construction Code Inspectors

On January 10-12, 1980, the National Board of Governors for the certification of Construction Code Inspectors met in Princeton, New Jersey, at the Henry Chauncey Conference Center on the campus of Educational Testing Service. The purpose of this meeting was to: review 128 electrical pretest examinations; examine setting minimum competency test scores; examine the national board's legal ramifications and liabilities; consider formulation of a permanent body; and discuss the need for an umbrella organization.

History

The state of New Jersey passed a law requiring the certification of construction inspectors. In reviewing the competency of existing programs, it was found that none was adequate. At this time, ETS was approached with $300,000 seed money to develop competency examinations. Educational Testing Service is a large non-profit organization that was established to conduct educational research, and to advise and instruct individuals and groups about educational measurement. ETS is one of the two most highly respected organizations of its kind. In order to assure a broader base of support, the National Conference of States on Building Codes and Standards (NCSBCS) agreed to provide a secretariat by setting up a multi-state testing program subcommittee that was later to be known as the "National Board of Governors." IAEI individual members have participated in this effort from its inception to provide an overall job description, to enumerate the dimension of electrical inspection activities, and writing examination questions. Fairfax, Virginia; Frankfort, Kentucky; South Bend, Indiana; and Trenton, New Jersey, were set up as pretest sites.

Setting the Minimum Competency Passing Points

An examination to establish minimum job performance standards to determine which candidates meet minimum competency standards, in order to be legally defensible, must be established by examining the "content validity" through a systematic judgmental/statistical analysis.

A certification examination must respond to two basic interests:

(1) Provide the certifying authority and the affected public with the reasonable assurance that the passing point represents a meaningful and useful level of competence.

(2) That the examinee is assured of a reasonable level of accuracy to assure that the passing point is not unnecessarily or unreasonably high.

The validity of these exams have been verified by the following:

(1) Review of job analysis data, development of test specifications; development of test questions by panels of job subject matter experts to provide assurance that minimum competency established by the test is critical; and

(2) That statistical analytic approaches have been used to establish the basic pass/fail level.

The question-of-being in a sound legal position regarding sponsorship or co-sponsorship of a certification affecting a man's livelihood is critical to our association.

The adoption of a 60 percent passing level for the multi-state testing program legally is sound, substantiated by a tape recording of the entire proceedings and, based on a completely defensible statistical/analytical approach.

How Will This Certification Program Work?

Examinations will be given in four categories: building, electrical, fire, and plumbing. The building, electrical and plumbing will consist of three types of certifications: 1- and 2-family, general, and plan review. The fire will consist of general and plan review. The examinees will be allowed two hours to answer 50 questions from an open *Code* book with a passing grade of 60 percent. The questions were written by a team of experts based on a job description that points out the critical elements that an electrical inspector must perform in his daily work.

The examinations will be given in all fifty states, on a voluntary basis, on the same two Saturdays in September 1980 provided there are sixteen or more candidates. If there are more than forty-five candidates, there will be two or more sites set up. ETS will administer the tests through a network that already exists at colleges and high schools in every state. Proctors will be professors and teachers who presently give exams for ETS on every conceivable subject and job category. Security of the test questions is extremely thorough. After all, $500,000 is too high a price to pay to develop a new set of questions. Multiple identification is necessary and signatures on applications are checked by handwriting experts against the signature on the exam. An attorney for ETS is on a committee that meets weekly to review suspected cases of cheating. Any suspect will be required to take another exam, free of charge. All exam material is numbered, so that missing material can be tracked down. The exams are reviewed regularly to weed out weak or misleading questions.

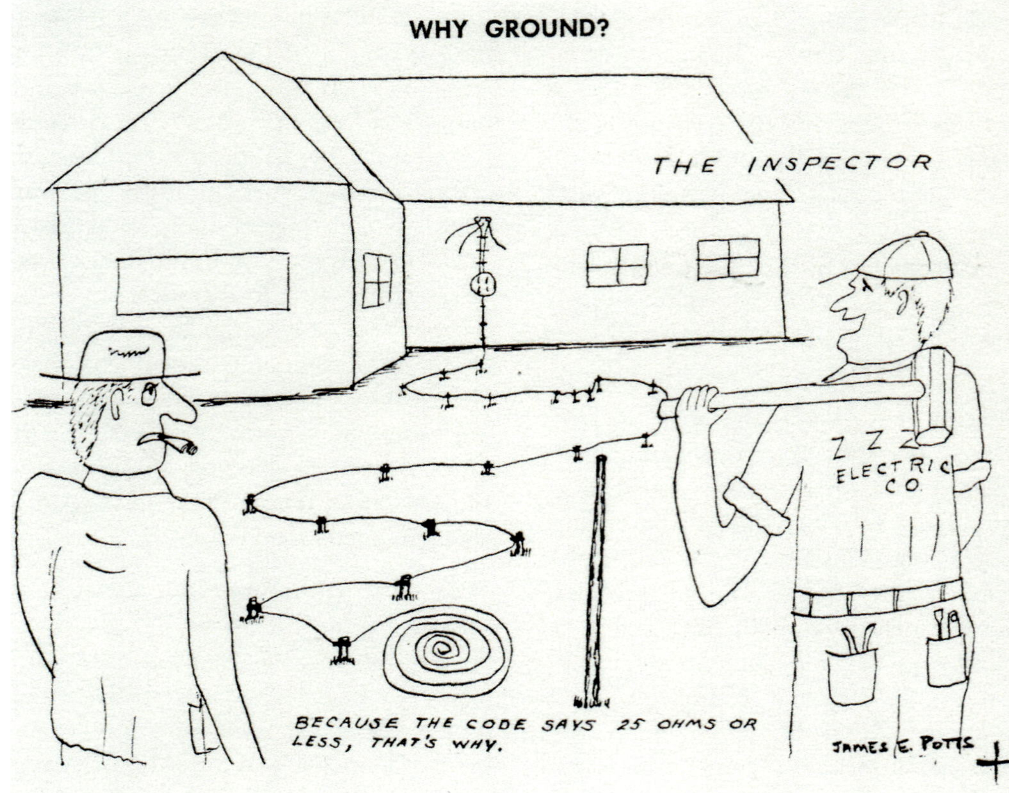

Who Will Be the Certifying Organization?

The National Board of Governors for Certification of Construction Code Inspectors has been limited to *users* of the certification. Invitations will be extended to one member from each state, BOCA, SBCCI, and IAEI. These users must be willing to certify examinees that attain passing grades.

The National Board of Governors recommends that the National Certification Program for Construction Code Inspectors be recognized by the several certifying states as a nationally acceptable examination suitable for reciprocity.

Should IAEI elect to be a certifying organization, they could issue certificates under their own name or co-sponsor with any of the other users.

Editors Note: As this magazine is going to press the IAEI board of directors is voting on the desirability of joining the National Board of Governors as a certifying organization for the testing program.

W. I. Summers, IAEI executive director. Reprinted from *IAEI News*, March 1980.

Arkansas Establishes State Board of Electrical Examiners

The highlight of IAEI's Arkansas Chapter in 1979 was the development and passage of Act 870 of 1979 by the Arkansas Legislature.

On hand for the signing of Act 870 by Governor Bill Clinton, which establishes the State Board of Electrical Examiners, and licensing for contractors and electricians, are (*left to right*): Philip H. Cox, Jr., chief electrical inspector, city of Little Rock; Charles McKenney, chief electrical inspector, city of Pine Bluff; Representative Robert Johnson, who introduced the legislation; W. M. Alberson, Jr., manager, Arkansas Chapter, NECA; Doyne Moore, president of the Arkansas Chapter, NECA, (now deceased); and Clark Daviss, secretary-treasurer, Arkansas Chapter, IAEI.

The act is considered permissive legislation as no one is required to take the state license. The measure allows contractors and electricians who hold state licenses to work any municipality in the state without being subject to licensing and examination requirements as specified by each individual city.

The bill was seen as a consumer measure in that the legislature felt that the quality of electrical construction would be upgraded as soon as an overall system of examination was implemented. Cox, an active member of the Arkansas Chapter, is currently serving as the chairman of the State Board. Over 3,000 electricians and contractors were licensed under the grandfather provision.

— Reprinted from *IAEI News*, January 1980.

Quick Fact

William Jefferson Clinton

William Jefferson Clinton became the 42nd U.S. president in 1993. Prior to his election, he had taught at the University of Arkansas from 1974–1976, was elected state attorney general in 1976, and in 1979 became the nation's youngest governor. After being defeated for reelection in 1980, he was elected again in 1983 and served until he ran for president in 1992.

Excerpted from Whitehouse.gov.

IAEI Joins NCPCCI as a Certifying Organization

The March-April edition of the *IAEI News* contained an article on the National Board of Governors for the National Certification Program for Construction Code Inspectors. Since this article was written the IAEI board of directors has voted unanimously to become a certifying organization for the testing program. This represents a giant step forward for our association as we have been thrashing around for some time with no apparent sense of direction. As far as IAEI is concerned this program is strictly voluntary; however, such a certification program is suitable for adoption at the city, county, state or federal level. IAEI will be issuing certificates to applicants that attain a 75 percent passing grade in the categories of electrical inspector one-and-two family, electrical inspector general, and electrical plan review.

Examinations will also be given in the categories of building, fire and plumbing. Building and plumbing tests will have examinations on the same three types of inspectors as the electrical; however, fire inspector examinations will be limited to fire general and fire plan review. At the present time two model code groups are prepared to participate in the National Certification of Construction Code Inspectors. They are the Building Officials and Code Administrators and the Southern Building Code Congress International. The examinations will be given in every state that has sixteen applicants on two successive Saturdays in September. Anyone who wishes to take all three examinations may then split up the tests on two weekends. Even on a voluntary basis such a certification enhances an inspector's job security and is an excellent bargaining position for merit increases. Further information on fees and examination sites will be forthcoming in the July/August issue of *IAEI News*.

In this issue of the *IAEI News*, you will find information on IAEI's use of the continuing education unit. Your board of directors has decided to issue CEUs to enhance the educational quality of our chapter and section meetings and to reward participants who desire to improve their professional development. The rapid expansion of knowledge in the electrical field and the demand for continuing education dictates the necessity for updating and upgrading one's knowledge. It is not merely good enough in today's rapidly changing technology to complete one's formal education without expecting to continue individual development.

The IAEI educational certification committee recently completed work to update the refresher courses to the 1984 *NEC*. Shown *left to right* are Peter Van Putten, Andre Cartal, David Maddrey, and Chairman Ray Olsen.

Participation in a CEU program will permit our members to continue their professional education with the ability to accumulate, update, and transfer the records of their educational experiences. In at least one state, mandatory participation in continuing education is required as a basis for continuing to be certified as an electrical inspector. The use of CEU units to promote merit increases for employees is also practiced by some localities.

One CEU unit is defined as ten contact hours of participation in a typical 50-minute classroom instructional session, or its equivalent. The minimum level that IAEI will recognize is four hours or .4 of a unit. Application forms will be made available to chapter and section secretaries on request.

Your international membership committee will be making an all-out effort in the coming year to acquaint the electrical industry with the International Association of Electrical Inspectors. Your international staff has prepared a 15-minute audio-visual to assist the membership committee in this endeavor. This presentation is titled "What is IAEI?" It consists of a cassette sound track and 55 slides and can be used with any recorder-player that is designed to transmit impulses to a Kodak carousel for changing the slides. Where recorder-players are not available, text will be provided so that a moderator can give the presentation using a Kodak carousel. In addition an attractive hand-out will be made available. This educational material is designed to tell the listener what kind of organization we are; our goals; our achievements and what we have to offer new members.

An all-out effort should be made at the local level to show this audio-visual to all NECA chapters, IBEW locals, apprenticeship training classes, independent electrical contractors, college engineering classes, high school and vocational training classes, and any other group associated with the electrical industry. The following international membership committee members have copies of the audio-visual for your use:

D. J. Clements, Jr., chairman, Southern Section

O. J. Christiansen, Northwestern Section

S. Leiman, Eastern Section

L. S. Hickman, Canadian Section

B. L. Auger, Western Section

L. E. Waggoner, Southwestern Section

A fee of $50 for the slides and cassette will be charged and will be refunded upon return.

—Reprinted from *IAEI News*, May 1980.

CERTIFICATION EXAMINATIONS FOR CONSTRUCTION CODE INSPECTORS

The Construction Code Inspector Certification Examinations have been developed by several model code groups, national inspection organizations and twelve states in collaboration with Educational Testing Service. These organizations have joined together to establish a testing program that will provide nationally recognized evidence of competence and professionalism in construction code enforcement. The examinations are based on the model codes for each discipline.

The purpose of the examination program is to provide a basis for determining competency of a person as a construction inspector or plan reviewer. In order to take an examination you must register with one of the states, organizations or authorized agents listed in the *Candidate Bulletin of Information*. The states, organizations or authorized agents have agreed to recognize the scores obtained on an examination.

The examinations are scheduled semi-annually and are given at approximately 100 locations throughout the United States in April and September. The examinations are scheduled on two consecutive Saturdays and are given at the same time and date at each location.

Description of Certification Tests

There are twelve separate examinations designed to measure competence in the areas of building, electrical, fire protection, mechanical and plumbing. All examinations are open-book examinations. A list of specific code books (by examination area) that may be used and recommendation regarding other reference materials are given in the Practice Test section of the *Bulletin of Information*. However, the use of published copyrighted materials other than those listed in the *Bulletin* is permitted.

The 12 examinations are as follows:

Building 1 & 2 Family Dwelling
Electrical 1 & 2 Family Dwelling
Mechanical 1 & 2 Family Dwelling
Plumbing 1 & 2 Family Dwelling

Building General
Electrical General
Fire Protection General
Plumbing General

Building Plan Review
Electrical Plan Review
Fire Protection Plan Review
Plumbing Plan Review

The emphasis in the one and two-family dwelling test is on inspection and basic plan review functions.

The general inspection tests cover structures/installations other than one- and two-family. The emphasis is on the major occupancy/use/installation problems in one to four-story structures. (Some basic high-rise-specific problems are covered).

The plan review tests are mainly concerned with the identification of design errors, the ability to perform required calculations accurately, and verification that proposed installations, systems, devices, or materials meet code requirements. Emphasis is on the occupancy/use/hazard classifications and problems that are most frequently encountered.

In several of the examinations, building plan review, plumbing general, and plumbing plan review, you are presented with a set of plans (or layout of an installation) and you are asked to record on a report sheet the design (or the installation) errors. Once you have recorded the errors on the report sheets, the plans (or layout) are taken away and you then must answer questions about the errors that you found on the basis of what you recorded on the report sheet.

It is recognized that on-the-job you should always have access to a set of plans (and until or unless a particular installation is covered, you can always review the layout). The point is that once you have made a determination as to what is wrong (errors of omission and commission), a report is made. What needs to be evaluated is the completeness and accuracy of the reported list of errors. The only way to test this in an objective manner is to have you list all the errors that you would include in a report and then have you use this list to answer questions about possible design or installation errors.

The first two national test administrations are scheduled on consecutive Saturdays in September 1980 and April 1981.

The dates are:

Saturday 9/20/80 Saturday 4/11/81
Saturday 9/27/80 Saturday 4/18/81

How To Register

Before you fill in any part of the form, read the instructions carefully, and then fill in the form using a typewriter or pen. Please print everything except your signature, which should be written just as you would sign a check or other document.

Item 1. Name. Print your last name, first name, and middle initial. Do not use nicknames or initials only. Use exactly the same name each time you register.

Item 2. Home Address. This address should be your home address or an address at which you will get mail for at least two months after you take the tests. Enter your address, printing only one number or letter in each box. Skip a box where a space would normally appear, but do not use any punctuation such as a coma, hyphen, or apostrophe. Be sure to enter your ZIP code in the boxes provided so your mail will not be delayed.

Item 3. Date of Birth. Enter month, day and year, using numerals only. This information is important for research purposes.

Item 4. Telephone Number. Print your area code and your telephone number in the boxes provided.

Item 5. Test Center. Choose a test center city that is nearest you. Enter the name of the city and state and four-digit code number on the line provided. A list of the cities and code numbers for potential test centers is given on the back of this page.

Item 6. Test Date. Check the appropriate date for which you are registering.

Item 7. Education. Instructions for filling out Item 7 are on the registration form.

Item 8. Experience. Check the box that best fits the time you have as an 8a. –Inspector/Plan Reviewer or 8b.–in a related field.

Item 9. Test you plan to take. Mark the boxes next to the test(s) you wish to take. (you may take up to two tests per session.)

Item 10. State, Organization or Authorized Agent. Refer to the list of state codes on the back of this page. Fill in your two digit state code in the boxes provided.

Signature: Sign your name as you would sign a check or other document.

Test Fees: $20 registration fee plus $20 for any one of the one- and two-family examinations; $25 for any one of the general or plan review examinations.

Return your registration form and test fees to the address listed in Item 10.

— Reprinted from *IAEI News*, July 1980.

Quick Fact

At the 1983 IAEI board of directors meeting, the executive board approved discontinuance of ICBO-IAEI co-certification of ICBO certification examinations. The IO will continue to encourage ICBO participation in the National Certification Program for Construction Code Inspectors. — Reprinted from *IAEI News*, January 1984.

Signing the Agreement. *Front Row (l to r)*: **John Stricklin, IAEI president and Phil Herrington, ICBO board of directors chairman.** *Back (l to r)*: **Phil Simmons, IAEI; Norm Scott, IAEI; Don Germain, IAEI; Paul Bowers, IAEI; Tom Trainor, IAEI; Paul Edgerton, ICBO; and Andre Cartal, IAEI.**

History in the Making

The International Association of Electrical Inspectors and the International Conference of Building Officials recently completed an agreement covering several major facets of the programs of both organizations. This historic agreement opens significant opportunities for cooperation between the two organizations.

Signing the agreement are (front row, left to right): John Stricklin, IAEI president and Phil Herrington, ICBO board of directors chairman. Back row (left to right): Phil Simmons, IAEI; Norm Scott, IAEI; Don Germain, IAEI; Paul Bowers, IAEI; Tom Trainor, IAEI; Paul Edgerton, ICBO and Andre Cartal, IAEI.

The major features of the agreement include the following:

a) Training programs. ICBO agrees to jointly sponsor electrical inspector training programs with IAEI. These training programs will be held at various times and locations that are mutually agreed upon. For these joint-sponsored programs, both the IAEI and ICBO logo will appear on various materials.

(b) IAEI publications. ICBO will be stocking, and making available to ICBO members, various IAEI publications.

(c) Inspector certification programs. IAEI and ICBO will be jointly sponsoring electrical inspector certification programs. Both IAEI and ICBO logos will appear on certificates issued to successful candidates of the program as well as on promotional materials. ICBO will appoint three representatives from IAEI to serve on the examination advisory committee. These members will actively participate in the certification program development and maintenance and will monitor the overall quality of the program.

Notices of the electrical inspector examinations and details of the program will appear in both organizations' publications on a periodic basis.

Electrical inspector certification examinations to be held in conjunction with the IAEI section meetings this fall are already planned. Additional information on these examinations is found elsewhere in this issue. The availability of these certification examinations at IAEI section meetings should add a new dimension of convenience for certification examination applicants as well as increase section meeting attendance.

ICBO electrical inspector certification is commonly accepted or required throughout the area where ICBO model codes are adopted. This agreement will allow ICBO to recognize and issue a reciprocal certification to those who have passed an IAEI electrical inspector certification examination. In addition, those who have passed an ICBO certification examination will be eligible for an IAEI certification and recognition. These holders of a certificate will be eligible to participate in inspector recertification programs. (ICBO has had a recertification program for some time; IAEI is presently developing one.) Where local regulations require electrical inspector certification, often, recertification in some form is also required.

As shown in the symbolic signing ceremony photograph, representatives of IAEI and ICBO met in Boise, Idaho, the first week of June to complete the agreement. The IAEI board of directors approved the concepts contained in the agreement at their November 1992 meeting.

We believe this agreement will open the door of opportunity for other significant areas where IAEI and ICBO can cooperate to achieve improved membership services for both organizations.

IAEI is already at work exploring similar agreements with other model building code agencies. — Excerpted from *IAEI News*, July 1993.

The general meeting at the 2001 Northwestern Section meeting drew questions regarding changes in the *NEC*; attendees focused on every answer.

Introducing the NCPCCI Computer-Based Testing Program

In December 1998, The National Certification Program for Construction Code Inspectors (NCPCCI) examinations will be administered on the computer in testing locations throughout the United States, Canada and U.S. territories. Computer-based testing (CBT) allows NCPCCI to offer greater testing flexibility, security, and immediate score reporting. The computer-based NCPCCI examinations will be given on an IBM or compatible pc with a mouse.

- You will be able to conveniently test by appointment in February, April, June, August, October, and December at more than 220 test centers throughout the United States, Canada and U. S. territories. The list of current test sites is subject to change.
- During the months in which the examinations will be offered, you will have a seven-day testing window to schedule your appointment to test (Saturday through Saturday, excluding Sunday).
- All NCPCCI certification examinations will be delivered on the computer only, including: electrical one- and two-family dwelling (2A), electrical general (2B), and electrical plan review (2C).
- You are encouraged to spend as much time as needed to become comfortable with the tutorial, which may take up to 15 minutes. Candidates who have taken other examinations on the computer have reported that the tutorials provided adequate preparation even to examinees who were novice computer users.
- The NCPCCI examination delivered by computer will contain 50 questions each, the same number of questions as the paper and pencil examinations.
- Just as you are permitted with the paper and pencil examination, you will be able to bring appropriate references into the computer testing site.
- Registration is similar to the paper and pencil process. See the previous page for registration and fee information.
- You will be able to schedule your testing appointment around a time and date most convenient to you.
- Immediately following the test, you will receive your score report on screen and a paper copy.

Reprinted from *IAEI News*, September 1998.

Electrical Inspector Certification Program in the United States

Certification is an important step in the progression of becoming a truly professional, highly trained and skilled electrical inspector. The Canadian Section of the IAEI promotes an inspector certification program in Canada and operates separately from its counterpart in the United States. An article on the Canadian Electrical Inspector Certification Program is scheduled for a later date.

The IAEI participates in an electrical inspector certification program along with the Building Officials & Code Administrators International (BOCA). Several states also participate in the program. BOCA and the state of New Jersey had major roles in the development and implementation of the program. The Educational Testing Service of New Jersey worked with the sponsoring organizations in providing professional services in both development and administration. The Chauncey Group International presently serves as the administrator for the

Code Panel at the fall meeting of the Tennessee Chapter on November 3–4, 2000. The panel consisted of *(from left to right):* John Minick, Mark C. Ode, Ernie Broome, and Harvey Johnson.

program. Other inspector certification programs also exist. The International Conference of Building Officials (ICBO) and the Southern Building Code Congress International (SBCCI) each have an inspector certification program. The IAEI and ICBO have a memorandum of understanding to recognize one another's certification.

IAEI bylaws include provisions that contain the basic framework for establishing and maintaining an inspector certification program. They are: "The IAEI is to establish an electrical inspector certification program designed to meet all IAEI program objectives and, if deemed necessary, to participate with other national, regional, state or provincial authorities, agencies or groups in established and recognized certification programs. The IAEI program is to have inspector certification modules consisting of not less than: (1) electrical inspector, general; (2) electrical inspector, one- and two-family; and (3) electrical inspector, plan review." In following this provision of the IAEI bylaws, the IAEI actively works within the established program to assist in providing the necessary administrative and technical support to help make the existing program meet its objectives.

One objective that the IAEI has not achieved is the implementation of a recertification program to help those who hold inspector certificates maintain an acceptable level of continued training. The provisions authorizing a recertification program are already in the IAEI bylaws and plans are to take steps necessary to have the program operational by the end of the year. It is important for this service to be offered to members and others who hold certification issued by the IAEI. The IAEI education committee is scheduled to meet within a few months and one major item on the agenda is to provide recommendations on how to best implement the program. Additional provisions or guidelines need to be developed before the recertification program can be fully functional. In addition to meeting the need of IAEI certificate holders, it is important that the program implemented will also be recognized by other organizations which have recertification programs.

While the existing program used by the IAEI effectively tests a person's knowledge of the *Code*, recommendations are coming from within the electrical industry to develop a more comprehensive inspector certification program. Concern expressed by industry is that one who has no experience in electrical construction can become certified through existing programs simply by learning *Code* rules well enough to pass the examination. The complaint is that knowing what the *Code* rules are does not necessarily mean that the individual either understands the significance of the rules or knows how to apply them. It is stressed that an electrical inspector must not only know electrical code rules, but he or she must also understand electricity and electrical systems in order to know how to evaluate what they see in an actual installation in the field and know how and when to properly apply *Code* rules. The issues raised by members of the electrical industry will need to be addressed in the near future.

Reprinted from *IAEI News*, March 1999.

A gentleman asks a code question at the 2000 Eastern Section meeting code breakfast. These breakfasts are an important, and popular, part of the meetings where members are allowed to take an active role in the code analyzing process.

New IAEI Eastern Section members proudly display their IAEI electrical inspection certifications as presented to them by Joe Tedesco in 1993 at an informal meeting of their electrician's society. *From left to right:* Ed Schick, Jr., Harold Endean III, Joe Tedesco, Richard Lintz and Wally Harris. These members are part of a 20-member group who talk electrical shop on the careers bulletin board through Prodigy Services Company. These individuals are interested in helping people do safe, effective electrical wiring and repairs. At least six of the members have become electrical inspectors and members of IAEI through both the encouragement and study assistance of Joe Tedesco, IAEI's codes, standards and seminar specialist, and the support from other cyberspace study partners. They continue to study hard for remaining electrical inspection certification exams.

IAEI Re-certification of Electrical Inspectors

The IAEI has participated in inspector certification programs for several years and is pleased to see a growing interest in certification by code-enforcing organizations and electrical inspectors. Many inspection jurisdictions have progressed to the point of requiring proof of certification as an inspector before one is permitted to perform the duties of an inspector. Certification through a professionally developed examination process is an important tool in demonstrating an individual's knowledge in those areas covered in the testing. Credit should be given to those individuals who have taken the required examinations because of their desire to better themselves. Those who have taken the certification exams because their employers recommend or require it should also be commended for successfully achieving certification. The general public certainly benefits from electrical inspector certification programs that effectively determine an applicant's level of knowledge and ability.

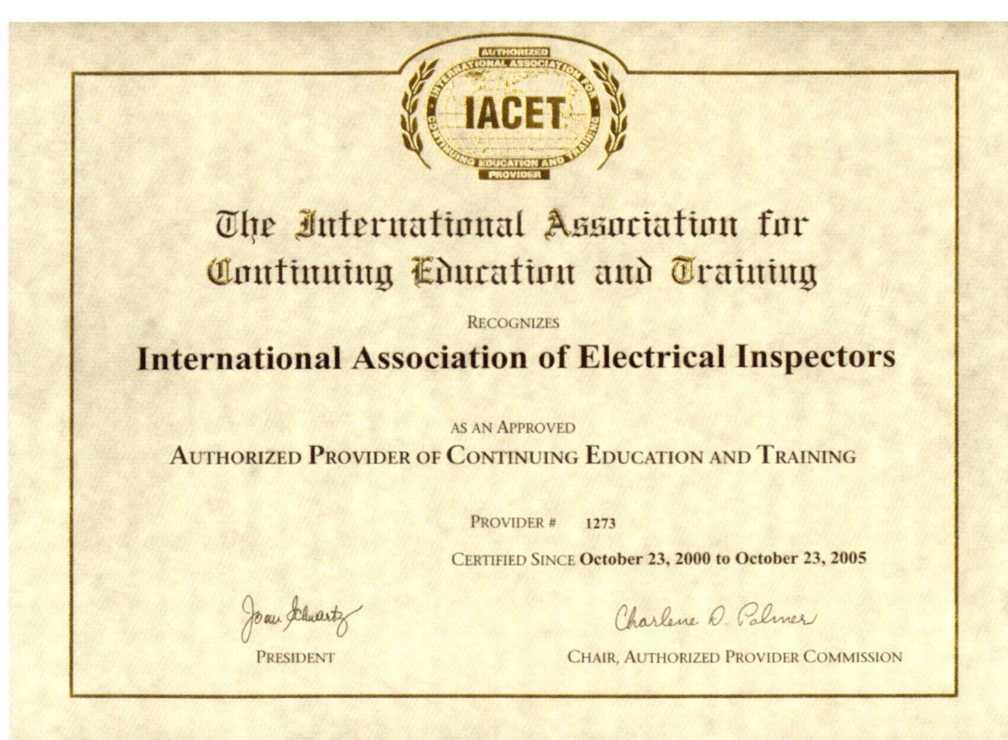
IACET

The International Association for Continuing Education and Training

Recognizes

International Association of Electrical Inspectors

as an Approved

Authorized Provider of Continuing Education and Training

Provider # 1273

Certified Since October 23, 2000 to October 23, 2005

President

Chair, Authorized Provider Commission

Achieving an electrical inspector certification is certainly an accomplishment in which one can take pride. However, becoming certified is only one of many steps needed to adequately fill the role of a professional electrical inspector. Inspectors who become certified can't afford to be satisfied with just that achievement. The demand to continue learning in order to keep up with the industry is too great for one to neglect opportunities to gain that knowledge. The IAEI provides many opportunities for certified electrical inspectors to continue their education. While electrical inspector certification has been promoted by the IAEI, training programs made available, and continuing education units (CEUs) awarded for training, those holding inspector certifications have not been required by the IAEI to be re-certified. The IAEI does recognize that re-certification of inspectors is an important part of an effective certification program and is taking steps to fully develop and administer a re-certification program as authorized by the bylaws.

Nancy Thomas of Educational Testing Service and the IAEI "boys" on the occasion of establishing the cut-score ratios of the electrical certification examinations at the meeting held in the Chicago area on August 15, 1987.

The IAEI education committee recommended that changes be made in the IAEI bylaws covering the inspector re-certification program and that the necessary steps be taken to properly implement the program. The proposed changes and recommendations were approved by the board of directors during its November 1999 meeting. Section 820(A) of the IAEI bylaws states "The IAEI shall establish and maintain an inspector re-certification program to effectively measure the level of competency being maintained by those holding IAEI inspector certification(s)." That provision is expected to be implemented this year.

Those who hold one or more IAEI certifications in the classifications of electrical general, electrical 1- & 2-family dwelling, or electrical plan review will need to re-certify within a three-year period. The methods of obtaining the necessary re-certification include passing an approved written examination, obtaining not less than 2.4 CEUs of approved training, or a combination of those two methods. Of the total training, 0.8 CEU is to be in electrical code changes. Continuing education units are awarded on the basis of 0.1 CEU for each hour of approved training. As an example, 0.8 CEU is issued for participation in an 8-hour seminar on the *Analysis of the NEC*. Individuals who let their certification lapse for more than one year beyond the renewal date will be required to retest to regain their certification. Individuals holding inspector certification according to IAEI records will be notified as to the re-certification program and will be provided with details on what is needed to maintain their certification.

The IAEI is a strong supporter of electrical inspector certification and encourages all inspectors who have not already achieved that status to do so. Being an electrical inspector carries serious responsibility with it. The better trained an inspector is, the better that person can do his or her job. Certification not only gives the electrical inspector a feeling of accomplishment, it also proves to others that a certain level of knowledge has been demonstrated. The educational program offered by the IAEI is intended to provide a source of training that inspectors, potential inspectors, electricians, and others can rely on to help expand their knowledge. The IAEI is working as fast and effectively as it can to develop new educational material and to improve on existing products to aid people within the industry. It is believed that the educational program will be an asset to those needing to prepare for certification and to those who wish to maintain that certification. It is difficult for others to legitimately criticize an electrical inspector who has a well-rounded knowledge of electrical codes, standards, wiring methods, electrical products, and the electrical system in general and who performs his or her job in a professional manner.

Excerpted from *IAEI News*, March 2000.

Texas Chapter Chairman Bob Younger (*center*) led the code panel at the July 2001 Texas Chapter meeting. Pictured with Bob are, *from left to right:* Wayne Loyd, Brad Scates, Bill McGovern, and James Hathorn.

Tennessee Chapter 2001 code panel at the Spring Meeting held on April 30–May 1, 2001. *From left to right:* Mark Ode, UL; Alan Manche, Square D; John Minick, NEMA. Ernie Broome was moderator for the panel.

Don Nissen, NFPA, moderating a code panel discussion at the 2002 Western Section meeting in Kearney, Nebraska.

IAEI/NFPA Certification Program

The need for an IAEI/NFPA Certification Program was identified by local entities, state agencies, and national organizations. Their recommendation was that IAEI and NFPA jointly develop state of the art certification programs based on knowledge and the practical application of the *National Electrical Code*.

In response to these industry needs, IAEI and NFPA have undertaken the responsibility for designing valid and reliable Residential and Master Electrical Inspector Certification Programs and ensuring these programs are accessible to all electrical inspectors.

Our Goals

- Professionalism
- Fair and accessible process
- Proficiency in Code usage
- Continuous learning
- Evidence of competence

Your Benefits

- Certification by IAEI and NFPA, the most recognized international organizations in the electrical inspection industry.
- Professional recognition through listing in the International Registry of Certified Electrical Inspectors.
- Demonstrated competence and knowledge in electrical inspections
- Advancement in your career.

Apply and Take the Exam

- Contact either NFPA or IAEI
- Entry requirements are detailed in application
- Cost: US $250 per testing
- Timeliness: Once accepted, you have 180 days to complete both the test and the practicum. The written test must be successfully completed within 90 days.

Your Preparation

You will also need the following in the 2002 editions to help in your preparation:

- *IAEI Comprehensive Study Guide*
- *NFPA Electrical Inspection Manual with Checklists*
- *NEC*
- UL White Book

Your Written Examination

The exams are designed to evaluate your knowledge of electrical inspection principles and code application skills. The CEI-R and CEI-M examinations are open-book, 3 and 4 hours, 90 and 120 multiple-choice questions, respectively.

Do the Practicum

- For CEI Residential, you will inspect 20 residential dwellings, including two swimming pools. Five of these will be under supervision.
- For CEI Master, you will inspect 30 properties, eight of which will be under supervision. These properties include: one and two-family dwellings, multifamily dwelling, commercial occupancies, health care facility and supervised inspections of agricultural, marina, industrial, and manufactured home.

Verification forms and supervisor evaluations must be sent to: NFPA Certification Department, 1 Batterymarch Park, Quincy, MA 02169.

Hang Your Certificate and Keep It There

When the audit is complete, the information is sent to IAEI/NFPA for final validation. If everything is in order, you will receive your official certification by mail. At that time, hire a band, call all your friends, and celebrate for you will have achieved title power.

Oh, one other thing, you will need to renew each year and re-certify every three years.

Excerpted from *IAEI/NFPA Certification Program*, 2003, and *The Power of 4*, 2003.

Quick Fact

At the 1999 meeting of the IAEI board of directors, the executive board authorized the International office to establish a "Train the Trainer' program to promote more uniformity in the interpretation and presentation of educational material.

Relationships

1941 Meeting of Underwriters' Laboratories, Inc., electrical council and guests at the meeting in Chicago, Illinois, on June 12–13, 1941. Front row, *left to right*: N. E. Cannady, F. G. Waldenfels, O. M. Frykman, R. B. Shepard, J. D. Lynett, C. S. Whitaker, L. A. Barley, and J. Galbraith. Second row, *left to right*: K. W. Adkins, J. G. Fisher, C. Goldsmith, J. S. Zebley, F. D. Weber, C. M. Harman, F. C. Camus, L. C. Ilsley, F. H. Moore and T. W. Bowry. Third row, *left to right*: J. F. Whitner, G. L. Swan, L. S. Bush, L. W. Going, H. N. Pye, W. E. Kern, R. W. Wiley, R. H. Manahan, G. Welman, and R. W. Wetherbee. Fourth row, *left to right*: G. E. Price, P. Ferneding, G. Rowell, W. L. Gaffney, G. E. Kimball, J. E. Wise, C. A. Ward, F. O. Evertz, R. J. Moran, J. B. Wilkinson, and F. N. M. Squires.

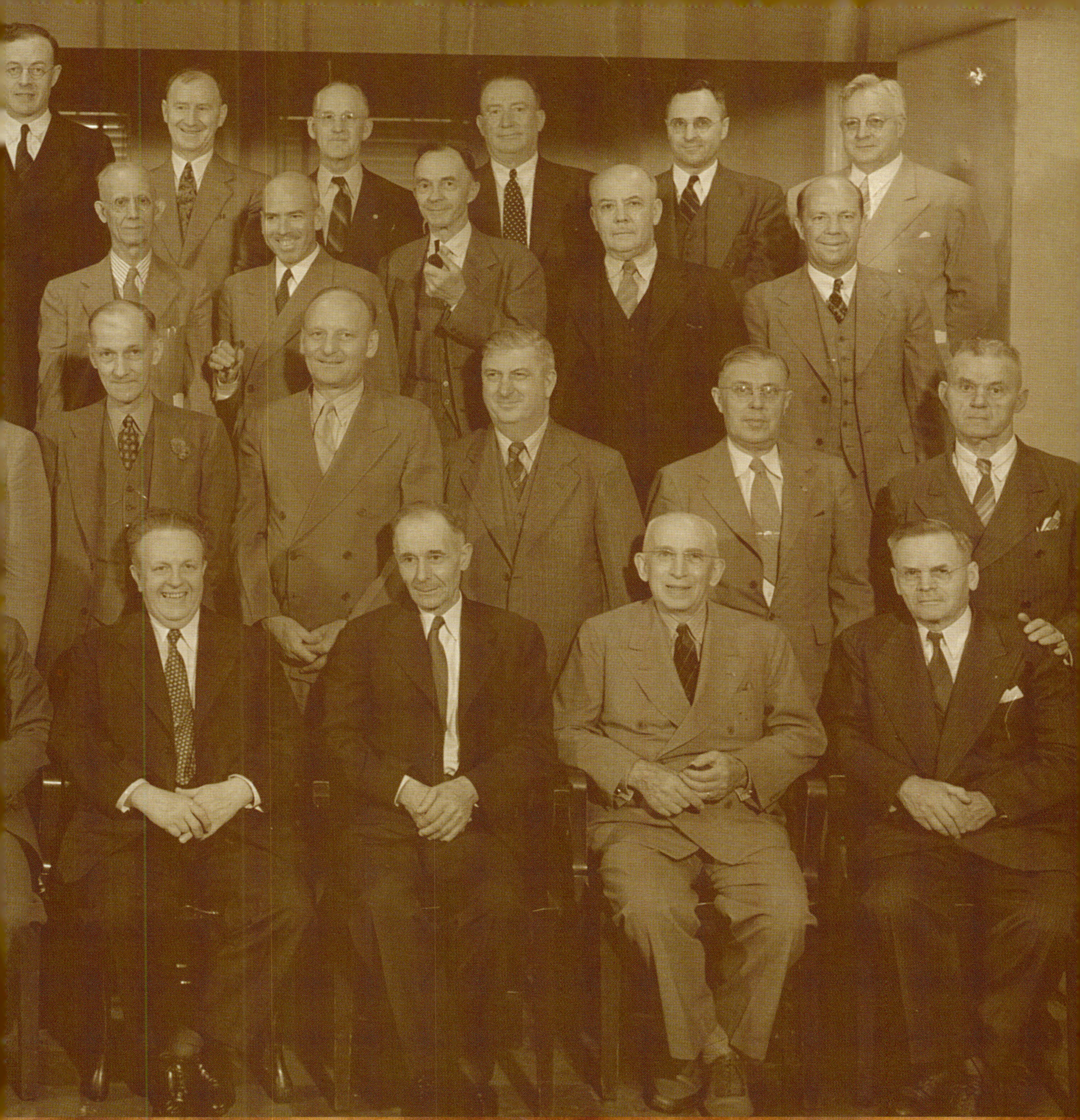

But none of this was done without solid, strong, abiding corporate relationships. From the beginning, other organizations and corporations nurtured the fledgling association, pouring in manpower, time, money, and exposure. They recognized that this association, like the plant which pushes through the cracks in the sidewalk, was determined to live, that it contained the seeds of perpetuity, that it was focused on its mission.

National Board of Fire Underwriters

The stock fire insurance companies established the National Board in 1866 as an educational, engineering, statistical, and public service organization. Originally the National Board had some jurisdiction over rates, premiums and commissions or compensation of agents but these functions have not been a part of the board's work for more than thirty years. While theoretically, the service it renders is to its membership, practically it has become almost entirely a public service institution. One of the outstanding activities in recent years has been fire prevention, which is in the interest of the public.

Committees of executives of stock fire insurance companies direct the different phases of the work. These are coordinated under the control of the general manager to whom the branch offices in Chicago and San Francisco also report. The electrical inspector would be most interested in the following committees: Actuarial Bureau, Construction of Buildings, Fire Prevention and Engineering Standards, Incendiarism and Arson, and Public Relations.

Actuarial Bureau

The actuarial bureau of the National Board provides one central organization for the compilation of fire loss statistics. Losses are classified and tabulated under a standard list of occupancy hazards, of which there are now twenty-eight, while the causes of fire are assigned under twenty-six headings.

Underwriting information required by insurance departments of several states is compiled by this bureau and it reports losses in behalf of its members to the fire marshals of nineteen states as required by law.

Part of the work of the actuarial bureau is the gathering and preparing of records of suspicious fires where there is indication of fraud or dishonest circumstances. The records of over twelve million fires are kept on file and the information afforded by the Actuarial Bureau is a direct contribution to the interests of fire prevention and fire insurance.

Construction of Buildings

One of the phases of the work of this committee is to act as a clearing house for technical information on fire resistive construction. A large percentage of the proposed building codes throughout the United States are sent to it for criticism and review. Helpful suggestions are offered and advice given as to the best forms in practice in other sections of the country.

An important contribution to the improvement of building construction in the United States is the recommended building code prepared by this committee. This code is a guide in making building laws and thereby tends to prevent construction that will be subject to conflagrations and increase fire losses.

Shown attending the April 23, 1985, meeting of the Westchester Chapter meeting at Con Edison's Westchester Division headquarters in White Plains, New York, are (*left to right*): Al Reed, vice president of the New York Board of Fire Underwriters; Frank Vitaliano, chairman of the Westchester Chapter; C. J. Papakrasas, assistant vice president of Con Edison's Westchester Division; Desmond W. Swayne, president of the Eastern Section, IAEI; and Thomas N. Murray, assistant senior inspector of Westchester for the New York Board of Fire Underwriters.

Fire Prevention and Engineering Standards

One of the earliest phases of the work of the National Board which has been continued to the present day with increasing service to the public is the activity of the committee on fire prevention and engineering standards. Realizing that the development of large cities makes conflagration almost inevitable, the National Board has endeavored to suggest recommendations, through this committee, which increase the fire prevention and fire protection facilities of cities, enabling them to avoid disaster. The study and work of this committee have been largely responsible for the improvement of American municipal conditions in the matter of fire hazards, and their engineers have personally inspected more than four hundred cities. This work is usually done by a force of three men in order to report on fire departments, water-works practices, fire alarm systems and fire department auxiliaries, as well as physical conditions in the mercantile and manufacturing districts. Every phase of fire protection and fire prevention is included in the report that is finally drafted. This is of great assistance not only to the municipality that it covers but also to fire prevention organizations and the underwriters of insurance companies.

In addition to the actual inspection of cities, many other important activities in connection with fire prevention are accomplished. Standardization of fire hose couplings has been developed and every community has been urged to make its hose couplings conform to the national standard in order that out-of-town departments may use its hydrants, should there be need of assistance in conflagrations.

Every innovation in industrial or commercial life has the attention of engineers representing the National Board. Suggestions and recommendations are made to decrease fire hazards in industry and to promote the proper use or storage of materials, processes and manufactures.

John A. Coffey, former secretary of the Adirondack-Hudson Chapter, IAEI, retired from the New York Board of Fire Underwriters in 1987 after 35 years with the Bureau of Electricity, Albany Division, New York. He was employed from 1950 until his retirement. He is shown with Albert J. Reed, (left), vice president, New York Board of Fire Underwriters, at a recent banquet where Coffey was honored for his long years of service.

Incendiarism and Arson

One of the most interesting and effective efforts of the National Board has been to aid in the apprehension, conviction and punishment of criminals engaged in starting fires for gain or revenge. Whenever a suspicious fire occurs, an investigator for the arson department studies the premises and considers the evidence, working in close cooperation with the state fire marshal, local sheriff, police officials, and the district attorney to bring the criminal to justice.

This work has a broader purpose than mere protection of the resources of the insurance companies. Its real purpose is to save innocent lives and protect property. It is the purpose of this committee to bring about the punishment or confinement of those responsible for starting incendiary fires.

Public Relations

In order to bring about a better understanding of the stock fire insurance business the committee on public relations employs modern advertising in newspapers, and prepares magazine articles, speeches, and pamphlets. Every effort is made to make the public realize the economic soundness of stock fire insurance as well as the need of fire prevention. It is the belief of this committee that when the public understands that it is false economy to build without thought of fire, that it is false economy to allow property to remain inadequately protected, that is false economy to take the chance of fire loss without adequate fire insurance, there will be a change in the habits of the American people. The cost of fire in this country represents more than the burning of property because it also means the destruction of natural resources and raw materials that can never be replaced. Every year 10,000 people who are burned to death and an annual property loss averaging over $450,000,000 bear witness to the fact that the people must understand and must cooperate in the fire prevention movement. It is the purpose of this committee to bring these facts to the attention of the people of America.

The National Board in all its activities throughout the United States is endeavoring to do everything it can to reduce the fire loss, promote better building construction, urge more efficient fire protection and safeguarding the public in every way.

by George W. Booth, chief engineer. Reprinted from *News-Bulletin*, July 1930.

Dennis L. Rowe

Eastern Section past president **Dennis L. Rowe** was elected president of the New York Board of Fire Underwriters at the board's annual directors meeting. He succeeds Alexander Pirnie who retired after serving 38 years with the New York Board of Fire Underwriters.

In 1986, Rowe began his career with the New York Board of Fire Underwriters, Bureau of Electricity, Albany Division, as an inspector. He was promoted to senior inspector in 1988, and to branch manager/chief inspector of the division in 1990. He was reassigned to the corporate office of the board and advanced to the position of general manager in 1995. Rowe was later elected vice president of the New York Board of Fire Underwriters in 1996.

Rowe is past chairman of the Adirondack Hudson Chapter and IAEI Eastern Section president. He is IAEI certified in 1&2 Family, general and plan review as well as holding certification as New York State code enforcement officer. He is a member of the *National Electrical* code-making panel as a voting member of CMP-8. He also serves on the electrical technical advisory committees for Underwriters Laboratories and Intertek Testing Services.

Excerpted from *IAEI News*, May 2001.

American Institute of Electrical Engineers

Fostering Electrical Developments

The American Institute of Electrical Engineers is the national organization representing the electrical engineering profession. It was founded in 1884, when the possibilities of an organization which would foster and encourage electrical developments were beginning to be realized. The objects of the institute are the advancement of the theory and practice of electrical engineering and of the allied arts and sciences, the maintenance of a high professional standing among its members and the development of the individual engineer.

Membership. All branches of electrical engineering are represented in the membership, which includes consulting engineers, professors of electrical engineering, chief engineers, managers, and other executives associated with electric lighting, railway, power, telephone, telegraph and manufacturing organizations constituting the electrical industry, and other persons interested in the advancement of the electrical profession. The value of institute membership in the estimation of electrical engineers is indicated by the continuous growth in membership from 1260 in 1901 to more than 18,000 in 1931.

Officers and Committee. The officers include a president, ten vice presidents, one elected from each of ten geographical districts, twelve additional directors, a national treasurer, and a national secretary. Much of the important work is accomplished through committees having jurisdiction over numerous administrative and technical activities; also through representatives on various bodies organized jointly with other scientific and engineering societies, such as the American Engineering Council, the Engineering Foundation, the American Standards Association, the International Electrotechnical Commission, the Intern-ational Committees on Illuminations.

Meetings and Other Professional Activities. Several national and regional conventions are held each year in various parts of the country for the presentation and discussion of professional papers and reports.

For the purpose of more effectively carrying out the aims of the institute and for the convenience of the members, fifty-nine local groups, called sections, have been organized in the principal electrical centers of the country.

Similarly, student branches have been formed in 109 of the leading educational institutions in which courses in electrical engineering are given.

Publications. A monthly journal called *Electrical Engineering* and a *Quarterly Transactions* are published. These are high-grade, electrical engineering periodicals containing in full or in abstract, engineering and scientific papers and discussions as presented before the meetings of the institute and its sections and branches; descriptions of new developments characterized by notable advances, and items regarding the activities of the institute and related organizations.

Headquarters. The institute has its headquarters in the Engineering Societies Building, 25 to 33 West 39th Street, between 5th and 6th Avenues, New York, New York. The building was made possible by the gift of $1,050,000 by Andrew Carnegie to the engineers of America as represented by the American National Societies of Civil, Mining, Mechanical and Electrical Engineers.

Standards. At an early date in the development of electrical engineering the institute recognized the importance of standardization of electrical apparatus; and at a meeting of its members in January 1898 there was an important discussion of the "Standardization of Generators, Motors, and Transformers." This resulted in the appointment of a committee, the personnel of which represented qualifications and experience from design, manufacturing, and operating standpoints. The report of this committee on standardization was represented and accepted at a meeting of the institute in June 1899; and the rules embodied became the authoritative basis of American practice.

International Relations. Reciprocal arrangements have been made by the institute with a number of foreign electrical engineering societies for the exchange of "Visiting Member Privileges," which entitle members of the institute while abroad, to membership privileges in those societies for a limited period; and similarly, members of foreign societies visiting the United States are extended the privilege of institute membership for a like period.

Summary. Briefly, the institute provides opportunity for and encourages comradeship, the interchange of ideas, the presentation, discussion, and publication of papers, the formulation of standards and codes, the development of international relations, particularly within the field of electrical engineering, the advance of ideals, the cultivating of the spirit of cooperation, and the inspiration which gives vision and incentive for new effort and greater achievement.

The institute has contributed largely toward the remarkable progress that has taken place in the electrical industry and has been an important factor not only in advancing the interests of its members and of the entire engineering profession, but also in its contributions to the solution of the great social and economic problems which underlie human progress.

by F. L. Hutchinson, national secretary of the Institute. Reprinted from *News-Bulletin,* July 1931.

Quick Fact

Edith Clarke was the first woman to be elected fellow of the American Institute of Electrical Engineers in 1948.

Reprinted from *Women's World: A Timeline of Women in History* by Irene M. Franck and David M. Brownstone, HarperCollins Publishers, 1995

International Brotherhood of Electrical Workers

Preventing Electrical Hazards

The International Brotherhood of Electrical Workers (IBEW), whose membership contains a substantial percentage of the workers who install and manufacture electrical equipment has a number of long standing and well developed activities in the field of accident prevention in the home as well as on the job. These stem from a basic policy of the Brotherhood that each member has the obligation to perform his work in such a manner that no job is left in a hazardous condition, either to fellow workers or the public. By way of implementing this policy, the Brotherhood engages in a number of programs and participations, including the following:

1. The IBEW has long sponsored the licensing of electricians as a means of upgrading the quality of electrical work in order to prevent accidents and fires.

2. The Brotherhood has promoted state electrical inspection codes throughout the nation, and many of its members serve on state code committees and are electrical inspectors.

3. The organization is a member of the National Fire Protection Association and its representatives service on many of the panels of the *National Electrical Code* committee.

4. The IBEW is an active member of the National Safety Council; its director of safety has been elected to the board of directors of the NSC and many of the IBEW members work on National Safety Council committees.

5. The Brotherhood has a close affiliation with the National Electrical Contractors Association, with which it has a joint apprenticeship training program into which is integrated compliance with safety codes and accident prevention in general.

6. Joint labor-management safety committees are promoted throughout the organization.

7. The Federal Departments of Health, Education and Welfare and of Labor utilize IBEW members on various committees dealing with codes and standards. As a current example, it has membership on the technical electronic product radiation safety standards committee (of HEW) and the labor-management advisory committee to the Bureau of Labor Standards.

8. The Brotherhood also holds membership in the American National Standards Institute and its members appear on many of the standards committees of the institute.

9. The Brotherhood continues to stress off-the-job, at-home safety through the media of the organization's *Journal*, which has a mailing list of over 1,000,000 copies per month. In addition, the organization publishes and distributes, as a public service, pamphlets on home safety.

Reprinted from *Electrical Safety Study*, NEMA, 1969.

IBEW Endorses National Electrical Week

The International Brotherhood of Electrical Workers has endorsed National Electrical Week as "an outstanding program for the industry" and has become a contributing sponsor to the 1957 observance, Merrill E. Skinner, chairman of the National Electrical Week Committee, announced today.

The IBEW, representing more than 650,000 members in all branches of electrical work, is the ninth major group in the electrical industry to give full support to the week which is scheduled for next February 10–16.

"We believe that this program shows excellent promise of generating considerable nationwide public impact for the benefit of the electrical industry," Gordon M. Freeman, international president of IBEW, said in announcing the action.

The primary objective of National Electrical Week, which will be held each year during the week of Thomas A. Edison's birthday, is to develop an information program on both national and community levels that will enhance public appreciation of electricity and the contributions of the electrical industry to the nation's progress and economy. It has the support of representatives of the entire industry-power suppliers, manufacturers, inspectors, distributors, dealers, contractors, and electrical leagues.

The N.E.W. Committee is developing a complete kit of materials for local committees that will be formed this fall to carry out community observances. Also, in addition to national newspaper and magazine stories and N.E.W. events that are planned, one of the features of the week will include N.E.W. messages on network radio and television programs sponsored by companies in the electrical industry.

Sponsors of the observance are: the Air-conditioning and Refrigeration Institute, Edison Electric Institute, International Association of Electrical Inspectors, International Association of Electric Leagues, International Brotherhood of Electrical Workers, National Appliance and Radio-TV Dealers Association, National Association of Electrical Distributors, National Electrical Contractors Association and National Electrical Manufacturers Association.

Excerpted from *News-Bulletin*, November 1956.

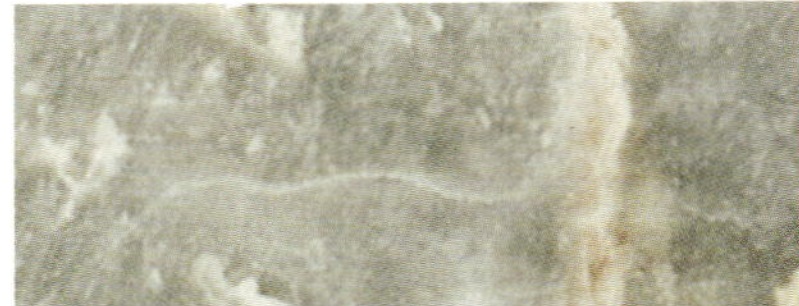

UL Founded 1894

UNDERWRITERS' LABORATORIES, INC.

AFTER 109 YEARS

UNDERWRITERS' LABORATORIES, INC.

UL and the Electrical Industry

Underwriters' Laboratories' close association with the electrical industry is as old as the industry itself. As a matter of fact, origin of UL in 1894 was the result of the first large-scale use of electricity for illuminating at the Columbian Exposition in Chicago. Edison had just recently perfected the incandescent lamp, and the exposition was to be the first real demonstration of lighting by use of electricity. There was such a rash of claims filed with the fire insurance companies who had underwritten the exposition that they decided to send a young engineer from Boston out to investigate the situation. His work led him to conclude that electricity had great potential as a servant of mankind that it must be used with care and understanding of its potential hazards or it would become a source of great fire loss. The man was named William Merrill, and is was he who conceived the idea of a laboratory that would be qualified to render expert opinions to the insurance industry relative to the fire hazards of materials, devices, and systems. Merrill's reports attracted widespread attention in the insurance field, and by 1901 the enterprise was incorporated in the state of Illinois, listing at that time a staff of three persons and $350.00 worth of laboratory test equipment.

Although Underwriters' Laboratories was organized to render service to the fire insurance companies, it very early took on the quasi-public aspects with which it is identified today. This development was a natural one because safety has always been a concern of our form of government, and police power has been used to insure an adequate level of safety for the public.

The identifying marks of UL are its publications — "called Lists," its Marker (the UL in a circle), and its Label, bearing the inspection manifest — "Und. Lab. Inc. Listed." I'm sure that all of you have seen these markers on products many times, but I'm not sure that you fully understood exactly the significance of the marker.

Essentially the marker serves to identify the product as being one, which conforms to the safety requirements of UL for the class. It means that the manufacturer has voluntarily submitted a prototype of this particular device to one of the testing stations of the Laboratories, that the engineers of the Laboratories have (1) conducted appropriate tests to insure that the product does not constitute a fire or accident hazard under conditions of normal use or under certain abnormal use conditions, (2) that the materials and forms of construction employed are such as will likely maintain the integrity of the assembly during the normal life of the product, (3) that the product can be installed in accordance with nationally-recognized installation code (*NEC*), (4) that the product can

William Henry Merrill, founder, Underwriters' Laboratories. The modest beginning of Underwriters' Laboratories was a bench, a table, some electrical measuring instruments and a few chairs located on the third floor of Fire Insurance Patrol Station No. 1, on Monroe Street, Chicago. The staff consisted of the writer, one helper, and a clerk. Previously to taking up work in Chicago I had been employed as electrical inspector by Osborne Howes, Jr., then secretary of the Boston Board of Fire Underwriters, and had suggested the laboratory idea, but the Boston Board at that time had preferred to have the small amount of test work which it required undertaken by a local engineering firm. On coming to Chicago in 1893, as electrician of the Chicago Underwriters' Association to solve some problems in connection with automatic fire alarm service in Chicago and inspect electrical installations at the World's Fair, I again advanced the laboratory idea and the little room over the horses of the Salvage Corps was the result. The work extended to embrace the territory of the Western Union as well as the Chicago Board, the organization being called Underwriters' Electrical Bureau and operated as a joint effort of the two organizations, Major C. E. Bliven being chairman of the Union Committee at the time and Edward M. Teall president of the Chicago Board. W. S. Boyd, my first helper, is now secretary of the Western Association of Electrical Inspectors and electrical inspector of the Union. Franklin H. Wentworth, my first field man, is now secretary of the National Fire Protection Association, and Bradshaw Squires, my first boy in the laboratory, is now a successful manufacturer's agent and jobber on the Pacific Coast.

—By W. H. Merrill, manager. Reprinted from *Reminiscences of Underwriters' Laboratories, Inc.*, by Merwin Brandon, April 1964.

be operated and maintained without undue hazards to the user or servicing personnel.

The primary tool used by the Laboratories' engineer in evaluating a product will generally be a published standard which the Laboratories has developed to prescribe the tests and constructions which it is deemed necessary to insure a minimum level of safe performance. For entirely new products, there will not be published standard available, because the standard reflects past experience and judgment of the Underwriters' engineers. In these situations, UL engineers develop requirements based on levels established for similar products, constructions, and situations which have proven to give satisfactory field performance.

Once the engineers have determined that a product complies with the requirements, they prepare a report — which generally contains photographs, prints, and other descriptive information — detailing those items of construction embodied in the product which were germane to the product's successful compliance with the requirements. A copy of this report is sent to the manufacturer, and he agrees in writing that all subsequent production bearing the label or having this particular catalog designation will be so constructed. A copy is also provided to the Laboratories' field inspector who initiates a program of periodic factory visits and inspections to assure that the product as it leaves the plant of the manufacturer does in fact comply with the Laboratories' listing requirements. An essential ingredient of each report is a section describing the marking to be provided by the manufacturer by which the product may be identified in the field as being listed.

In summary, the operation of Underwriters' Laboratories provides a form of safety evaluation, inspection, and certification service which has and does form a vital link in the chain of parties separating the manufacturer from the user.

After the manufacturer has assembled the product and shipped it from the factory, the product generally passes from distributor to installer, via the contractor, via approval of the inspection authority, with ultimate connection to the lines of the local electricity supply company for subsequent use by the consumer.

Through its testing, listing, and subsequent factory follow-up service the Laboratories has rendered a distinct service to each of these parties.

In most cases, the manufacturer benefits by producing a product, which causes less fires and accidents than, might otherwise be the case. Undoubtedly, the greatest service rendered to the manufacturer is the assurance of almost universal acceptance by inspection authorities. Without this broad acceptance, the manufacturer could not enjoy the benefits of mass production and distribution. Because of its unique position in the electrical industry, Underwriters' Laboratories' operation serves as a balance between the widely separated views of the inspection authority and the manufacturer. Minimum safety involves building a floor under quality so a fringe benefit to the manufacturer is an indirect establishment of such a level among competing manufacturers. Merchandising a product built to a nationally recognized safety standard also improves its position with respect to product liability insurance, and even before the courts, in event of legal action arising out of the use of the product.

Since the distributor is in the flow of commerce, the likelihood of his being involved in legal action arising out of use of the product is also reduced, because the product is less likely to cause fire or injury. The distributor can proceed with the marketing operations with the assurance that the product will not likely be returned because it is unacceptable to the local inspection authority.

It has been said that the contractor bets on each installation job that he can make the installation satisfy the requirements of the *National Electrical Code* as interpreted by the local inspector. The contractor, by use of listed products, has taken the best insurance that is available to him in this regard. The Laboratories' listing of wiring materials and other components of a wiring system also serves to classify the components so that they might be properly installed in accordance with the provisions of the *National Electrical Code*. Like the

Dana Pierce, president of Underwriters' Laboratories, Chicago, graduated from Amherst College in 1892. He then became an instructor at the Hotchkiss School in Lakeville, Conn., and while teaching took special work in physics at Harvard and Cornell. He resigned from Hotchkiss in 1899 and spent a year as graduate student in physics and mathematics at Johns Hopkins University, following which he joined the instructing staff at Pratt Institute, Brooklyn, N.Y. Here he remained until March, 1906, when Mr. Merrill, then president of Underwriters' Laboratories, selected him to take charge of the electrical department of the Laboratories.

For six years Mr. Pierce was located at the Chicago office, in charge of the electrical and signaling work, but in 1912 he established the testing station in New York and moved to New York to give it his personal attention, while maintaining direction of the electrical work in Chicago as well. In 1916 he was appointed vice-president of the Laboratories.

For many years Mr. Pierce has been prominent in the work of the National Fire Protection Association and was at one time president of this organization. For several years he acted as chairman of the electrical committee of the NFPA. This is a most important post, which has entire charge of the *National Electric Code.*

In 1923 Mr. Pierce was elected president of Underwriters' Laboratories and moved to Chicago in November of that year.

Mr. Pierce was elected an honorary member of the IAEI at the time of its organization meeting. He has always been an enthusiastic supporter of the association and has attended and taken part in many of our meetings.

Combined with those qualities that made him so valuable to the Laboratories and to the electrical world at large, Mr. Pierce possessed so much kindness, consideration, and all that is properly contained in that word "culture," as to endear him to us, in addition to commanding our admiration and respect.

Excerpted from *News-Bulletin*, January 1935.

With deep regret we record that **Alvah R. Small**, retired vice chairman of Underwriters Laboratories, died on October 8, 1954, at his home in Pompano, Florida, at the age of 71.

Mr. Small received his B. S. degree in civil engineering from the University of Maine in 1904. Because of a paper he prepared on Concrete Blocks he received an advanced degree of civil engineering from the University of Maine in 1929.

Upon graduating from the University of Maine, he joined the staff of the New York Fire Insurance Exchange until 1906.

On October 1, 1906, he joined the staff of Underwriters' Laboratories in Chicago as an assistant electrical engineer. In 1910 he formed the Label Service Department which was charged with the factory follow-up inspection of listed products. In 1916 he was promoted to vice president. In 1924 he was transferred to the Laboratories' office in New York. In January 1935 he was elected president of Underwriters' Laboratories and transferred to the main office and testing station in Chicago. In June of 1948 he relinquished active control of the Laboratories' work and was made vice chairman of the Board of Trustees.

Although a past president of the National Fire Protection Association and active in many committees of the NFPA, he was probably more widely known as chairman of the Electrical Committee of the NFPA. This committee compiles, amends, revises and publishes the *National Electrical Code*, the most widely adopted and observed safety code in the United States. He was also a member of the advisory engineering council of the National Board of Fire Underwriters, as well as holding committee memberships in many other groups of the NBFU. He was also on the board of directors and a member of many committees of the American Standards Association. The American Society for Testing Materials, Building Officials Conference, International Association of Electrical Inspectors and a fellow of the American Institute of Electrical Engineers. He was also a member of the Lake Shore Club, University Club, and Indian Hill Golf Club.

Reprinted from *News-Bulletin*, November 1954.

distributor, the contractor is provided with a floor under quality of products and materials as a safeguard against progressively inferior grades.

The electrical inspection is an exercise of the police power of the state to protect its citizens from hazards of fire and shock in the same way that the policeman protects against traffic hazards and crimes, or the public health official against contaminated drinking water or spread of infectious disease. This responsibility is given to the inspector by local ordinance, and includes the safety of the equipment as well as the installation. In most cases, the inspection authority does not have the time or facilities to make proper evaluation of the equipment; hence, he is generally glad to share a part of his responsibility with Underwriters' Laboratories, Inc. In some cities the inspection authorities have instituted sales control laws governing electrical products, which require that all products offered for sale or installation in their territories meet the product safety requirements of a nationally recognized testing laboratory.

The public utility is naturally interested in promoting the maximum use of electrical energy. Hence, any program, which tends to provide safe electrical appliances and materials so long as it does not increase the cost of the product as to discourage purchasers, serves the interest of the utilities. Also, to a degree, the utility company has a legal responsibility for equipment connected to its lines, and again, any reduction of fires or accidents also serves this interest.

Last, but by no means least in the chain, is the using public. The chief benefit to the user is that the electrical products listed by UL offer reasonable assurance against fire or electrical shock destroying his property or injuring his family. UL is in no sense a warranty or guarantee — but rather a declaration that

Alvah R. Small

the design of the product conforms to the requirements for the class. Underwriters' Laboratories does not purport that it tests or examines each and every unit that is produced, since to do so would simply make the cost of the service prohibitively expensive. The listing does contemplate that the manufacturer will conscientiously carry out his own inspection and quality control programs, and will thereby apply labels only to those units found to comply fully with the listing requirements. Inspection of the factory production by the UL's field force is primarily a spot check of the manufacturer's own inspection and control program.

The electrical equipment falling within UL's scope of operation does not include that generally used by a public utility in generating and distributing electricity. Neither does it include all the large ratings, which are generally installed and operated under competent supervision. In this regard, Underwriters' Laboratories seeks to make its services available to cover those products and materials used by the general public — thereby, fulfilling its primary obligation — "Testing for public safety."

By Baron Whitaker, president, Underwriters' Laboratories, Inc. Reprinted from *The Electrical Inspector*, by A. H. Welklin, 1969.

"Underwriters' Laboratories, Inc." Now Registered

The Laboratories has been issued Principal Register No. 636,273 by the United States Patent Office, under the Trade-Mark Act of 1946 covering the wording Underwriters' Laboratories, Inc.®

As evidence of this registration the letter R in a circle, somewhat as indicated will appear with this insignia. The labels, which are evidence of the listing and inspection of millions of products complying with the safety requirements of the Laboratories will thus bear a registered certification mark.

The effect of the registration is to increase the Laboratories control over the use of its name on products or otherwise.

Reprinted from *IAEI News*, January 1957.

UL and IAEI

Partners in Electrical Safety

As I became acquainted with more and more electrical inspectors both through my work with Underwriters' Laboratories and through the *National Electrical Code*, I began to read something of the relationship between our two organizations and I was fascinated by the manner in which the organizations had come to work together for public safety, one on the performance of the equipment and the other on its installation.

During the Chicago World's Fair or Columbian Exposition as it was called in 1892, Mr. Merrill worked as an electrical inspector for the insurance company organizations in Chicago and one of his associates was William S. Boyd. After the World's Fair was over and Mr. Merrill had obtained the backing of the stock fire insurance companies who comprised the National Board of Fire Underwriters, he began his work of testing electrical equipment to determine its safety just as he had done for manufacturers during the exposition. Mr. Boyd was so interested in this operation that on his own time he designed and built much of the equipment, which Mr. Merrill used in his early testing. As a matter of fact, Mr. Boyd kept up his interest throughout his entire life and worked closely with the Laboratories in every way until the time of his retirement in 1933.

Mr. Boyd also saw the desirability of having an organization, which would help the inspectors to understand their work better and to unify their requirements, and he worked hard toward this end until in 1904 or 1905 he was instrumental in forming the Western Association of Electrical Inspectors. By this time many of the municipalities had begun to recognize their responsibility for seeing to the safety of the public with respect to its use of electrical equipment and had taken over inspections which the insurance companies had conducted earlier because there was no one else available to see to proper installation from the standpoint of hazard. This process of relinquishing responsibility for electrical inspections and concentrating on their own problem of fire insurance protection continued until today only a few areas in the United States have electrical inspections conducted by representatives of insurance organizations. It may perhaps be worth noting that the only reason these inspections have been continued is because of the insistence of the

Lou LaFehr, managing director, IAEI, and R. L. Lloyd of Underwriters Laboratories, Inc., New York, seem pleased with the 1963 Northwestern Section meeting.

public and the local electrical contractors who have persuaded the city officials to formally designate the insurance inspectors as public representatives for the purpose of electrical inspections.

In the eastern part of the United States in the 1890's, Joseph Forsyth of the New York Board of Fire Underwriters was an outstanding electrical inspector and had much to do with writing the early requirements and checking installations for enforcement of the safety requirements. Joe worked closely with the municipal electrical inspectors throughout the East and they formed an Eastern Electrical Inspection group.

Electrical inspectors in other parts of the country, such as the Northwest, Southwest, and the South formed their own independent groups and all of these combined into the International Association of Electrical Inspectors on November 14, 1928, with Joe Forsyth as the first president.

One of the active workers in the formation of this International Association was Victor Tousley, chief electrical

inspector for the city of Chicago and recognized as an outstanding electrical engineer in safety work. He was subsequently employed by the National Fire Protection Association as their electrical field representative and continued in that position until his death, working tirelessly for greater safety and uniformity in the installation of electrical equipment.

When the International Association of Electrical Inspectors was formed they were an impoverished organization with no funds and no facilities, so they asked Victor Tousley to serve as their secretary-treasurer to get the organization started and for some months Mr. Tousley was given quarters at Underwriters' Laboratories Chief Testing Station at 207 East Ohio Street, until the organization could collect sufficient funds to rent an office of its own. Throughout his life, Mr. Tousley continued to hold the jobs, one with the NFPA and the other as secretary-treasurer of the IAEI. He was paid by the NFPA but given quarters by the IAEI which also made contributions to the NFPA Electrical Field Service Committee Fund to support the work which Mr. Tousley was doing in the promotion of safe electrical installations.

From the formation of the IAEI to the present time, the IAEI and Underwriters' Laboratories have continued to co-operate in the interest of public safety, and this has done much, not only to help the public use electricity safely, but also to unify requirements throughout the country so that mass distribution on which mass production depends could be obtained and the standard of living of our people improved accordingly.

—By W. H. Merrill, manager. Reprinted from *Reminiscences of Underwriters' Laboratories, Inc.*, by Merwin Brandon, April 1964.

Merwin "Money" Brandon, president of *Underwriters' Laboratories*, circa 1955.

Merwin Brandon, president of Underwriters' Laboratories, Inc., makes stirring farewell speech at the 1963 Northwestern Section meeting. He urged that the *National Electrical Code* be kept voluntary and free. At head table *(left to right)*: E. E. Carlton, L. E. LaFehr, Cliff Atkins, A. C. Veit, W. F. Reed, Paul Davison, C. D. Merger, and Del Hansen.

UL Founded 1894
UNDERWRITERS' LABORATORIES, INC.
AFTER 109 YEARS

UNDERWRITERS' LABORATORIES, INC.

and The Electrical Inspector

The work of the electrical inspector is extremely detailed and covers a wide field of devices and materials; it requires a large amount of specialized knowledge as to the suitability of many devices and materials. The requirements for original knowledge on the inspector's part of such devices is lessened by the work of the National Fire Protection Association, National Board of Fire Underwriters and other organizations in establishing standards for construction and installation. In addition to this, Underwriters' Laboratories furnishes him in simple and condensed form the specific knowledge that under the codes and standards established by these bodies, the devices and materials that he meets with in his work are acceptable as far as their designs and operations are concerned for use under the installation codes so established.

The American mind is progressive and not bound by precedent. We try anything and without these codes the work of the electrical inspector would be impossible. No one person can possibly accumulate in a lifetime sufficient knowledge of all the new devices and materials produced by our swift moving economic life to pass reasonable judgment on their probable performance under fire conditions.

A reasonable and fair judgment of these things can only be made by a group of men, supported by extensive testing facilities, devoting their lives to a study of how devices and materials act in regard to fire hazard or fire prevention.

Underwriters' Laboratories' staff consists of men whose life interest is a study of these features, a study always undertaken with a consideration of cost to the public, and their findings are available to you in the List of Inspected Electrical Appliances issued annually with frequent supplements and in their label.

Through these means it is relatively easy for anyone to find devices and materials for almost any application which have been carefully examined and tested and can be relied upon to do their work with a reasonable freedom from fire and accident hazard when properly installed. It is similarly easy for the inspector to judge devices and materials as to these points by reference to Underwriters' Laboratories' lists and the label.

The Electrical Council of Underwriters Laboratories, Incorporated, circa 1956. Back row *(left to right)*: J. E. Wise, R. L. Lloyd, L. M. Christensen, D. H. Hansen, E. Carlton, A. G. Clark, W. E. Stewart, A. Lagadinos, W. P. Hogan, C. J. Shukes, and M. M. Brandon. Middle row *(left to right)*: J. Whitner, M. G. Folkes, R. L. Tilford, R. E. Ward, J. F. Gray, L. S. Bush, B. A. Hartley, J. A. Graham, and S. M. Streed. Front row *(left to right)*: R. B. Boyd, S. Cowan, and D. L. Johnson.

Baron Whitaker, at age 50, was one of UL's youngest presidents. He started work with UL in 1936 and was elected president by the Board of Trustees in April 1964. His life has centered around the workings of Underwriters Laboratories. He has been totally involved in maintaining a suitable balance between government regulations and private sector involvement in safety; and in administering policy for more than 2000 UL employees.

It's been a busy fourteen years for Mr. Whitaker. He has traveled extensively both at home and abroad. He has spoken at meetings in almost every state; been on television and radio programs; worked with various departments and agencies of the federal government; and testified before various Congressional committees and subcommittees. He has worked on special committees, and accepted special appointments to work in all phases of the product safety picture—the worldwide safety picture. He has given generously of his time and energy; has always been available to spend time helping, solving, advising, doing whatever it took to keep UL operating in the public interest.

Underwriters has more than doubled in size during Whitaker's term of office. In 1964, the year he was elected president, UL's engineering departments handled 19,000 original investigations, in 1977 over 47,000 jobs were completed. In 1964 over 113,000 factory inspections were conducted to determine continued compliance with listing requirements. In 1977, over 255,000 factory inspections were executed. In 1964, UL's total office and lab space was 310,000 sq. ft. By 1977 this total was 760,000 sq. ft. and it is anticipated that this will increase to approximately 935,000 sq. ft. by 1979. In 1964 there were 406 engineers on UL's staff. By 1977 the number of engineers on the staff had increased to nearly 1,000 and the total number of employees was 2,331.

Through the years there have been happy times and sad; victories and defeats; good years and lean. Whitaker has always made public safety his main goal. He leaves UL in May of 1978, with the good wishes of all who have worked with him in the field of public safety. Whitaker, from North Carolina, is also a member of the International Association of Electrical Inspectors, and is very active in the Southern Section.

Reprinted from *IAEI News*, September 1978.

Baron Whitaker, president of UL in 1973, watches Paul W. Wyckoff, president of Chrysler Airtemp affix the first UL label ever applied to high capacity commercial and industrial air conditioning machinery. Observing are William Love, international president of IAEI (*standing left*), and John C. Hewitt, Department of Labor and Industries, state of Washington.

Jack Bono, president, Underwriters Laboratories, and Bill Summers, executive director of IAEI, are shown discussing cooperation between their respective organizations in 1980. On this occasion, it was announced that UL is releasing a 30-second public service TV message giving electrical safety tips from electrical inspectors.

The object of Underwriters' Laboratories is to bring to the user the best obtainable opinion on the merits of devices and materials with respect to life and fire hazard.

In order to insure the continued integrity of these opinions which are promulgated in their lists against change of the device by the manufacturer in a manner to increase the fire or accident hazard, Underwriters' Laboratories operates a large and carefully organized follow-up and inspection system by which the devices so examined and listed are kept under constant supervision by one of two forms of inspection service. These are the Label Service and the Reexamination Service.

Certain goods are manufactured by processes which inherently of themselves tend to produce a uniform product such as the stamping of devices by means of dies and molding of products. With such devices integrity of the product with the samples tested is properly maintained with a lesser frequency of inspection than is the case with devices which are assembled and which depend for their freedom from hazard on more human features concerned with the assembly of the device. For the device of this first character the Laboratories often operates the Reexamination Service which provides for periodic inspection of the product at the factory. The Electrical List shows clearly which devices are followed-up by this form of supervision. In such cases the identifying mark which distinguishes the listed device is specified in the list, thus making it easy for the electrical inspector to determine by reference to the list, whether or not the device has been examined by the Laboratories and is entitled to recognition.

Under the Label Service all the devices or materials are inspected at the factory and the evidence of this inspection is the Underwriters' Laboratories' label to be found on goods so listed. This label is your evidence that the device has been inspected at the factory and conforms to the requirements as to fire and safety hazards that have been established.

In both of these services Underwriters' Laboratories pick up samples on the open market from time to time for further check on the product.

As will be seen, the difference in listing under Reexamination and Label Service does not imply a different degree of freedom from hazard, but is largely dependent upon differences in method of manufacture. The listing of a device under Reexamination Service and the listing and labeling of a device under Label Service are each a dependable notification to you of the acceptability of the device when installed under the codes and regulations concerned.

The label is evidence that the device or material has been inspected and is up to the required standard. The reexamination listing tells the same story.

When you see a label or a listing you are, in effect, reading the conclusions of the final report of all the previous work by Underwriters' Laboratories of testing and inspecting the devices concerned. It is the aim of Underwriters' Laboratories to be as effective as possible in furnishing you with information as to the suitability of the various devices and materials met with in your work for installation under the governing codes and standards.

Reprinted from *News-Bulletin*, May 1930.

Underwriters Laboratories, Incorporated (UL) has announced the election of **Guy Thomas (Tom) Castino**, 52, as president. The announcement was made in April at UL's annual meeting in Itasca.

Castino first joined UL as an engineer in the Fire Protection division in 1960. He was appointed managing engineer of that division in 1974. In 1980, he was named chief engineer of the Fire Protection division. He was elected assistant vice president and chief engineer in 1982, and vice president and chief engineer in 1984. He served in that position until his election to executive vice president in 1988. For the past year, he has served as UL's chief operating officer.

Castino earned a bachelor's degree in mechanical engineering from the University of Illinois and is a registered professional engineer in Illinois. He is active in the National Fire Protection Association, the Society of Fire Protection Engineers, and the American National Standards Institute.

Underwriters' Laboratories Discontinues Canadian Listing

Following the adoption of the Canadian Electrical Code in 1927 and subsequent arrangements for the development of what is called Part II of that code in the form of standards applying to different classes of electrical devices and materials, the majority of Canadian electrical manufacturers, whose products have heretofore been listed or labeled by Underwriters' Laboratories, have expressed a preference to employ the services of the Hydro Electric Power Commission of Ontario for these products rather than those of Underwriters' Laboratories.

On January 1, 1933, therefore, Underwriters' Laboratories' listing, label, and reexamination services on electrical devices and materials manufactured in the Dominion of Canada is to be discontinued. All, or nearly all of these Canadian electrical products, will be listed by the Hydro Electric Power Commission of Ontario which will extend to them its listing and label service as already applied to other Canadian electrical products.

However, lightning rods and motors, controllers and fittings for use in hazardous locations will continue to be tested and listed by Underwriters' Laboratories.

Underwriters' Laboratories will continue its present listings and labels and reexamination services on products other than electrical as made in Canada by Canadian manufacturers. These include fire doors and windows, extinguishers, tanks, roof covering materials, refrigerators, hose, oil burners, and other non-electrical items.

The Hydro Electric Power Commission will continue as heretofore and under the same arrangements with United States' manufacturers to list a large number of electrical products manufactured in the United States on the basis of their being listed and labeled by Underwriters' Laboratories. It is expected that Underwriters' Laboratories will cooperate with the Hydro Electric Power Commission and with the Canadian Engineering Standards Committee of Ottawa for the maintenance so far as possible, of equivalent electrical standards.

Reprinted from *News-Bulletin*, January 1933.

Another successful meeting of the Florida Chapter IAEI, hosted by the Palm Beach County Division, took place at Palm Beach Shores, May 1998. Attendees received their meeting materials in bags donated by Underwriters Laboratories, Incorporated. Florida's casual demeanor is apparent from Paul Duks, assistant to the chief engineer, Global Engineering Division of UL. Paul served as a code panelist and a presenter at the technically excellent meeting.

Underwriters' Laboratories completed investigation and listing of a new line of mobile homes manufactured by Conner Homes Corporation of Newport, North Carolina. In 1970, mobile homes were the fastest growing market in U.S. housing, and mobile, prefabricated homes presented special problems of enforcement for regulatory agencies for public health and safety. As a result of discussions with members of the UL Electrical and Casualty Counsels on May 8–9, 1969, modifications were made in their method of investigating and inspection of mobile homes, modular or prefabricated homes. Inspecting newly listed mobile homes are (*left to right*): G. H. Wright, supervisory field engineer, Follow-up Services of UL; Floyd Green, vice president—Manufacturing, Conner Homes Corporation; Kern Church, North Carolina Department of Insurance, Raleigh; and Wallace J. Conner, president of Connor Homes Corporation.

R. D. "Derek" Barton, senior vice president, Underwriters Laboratories, Incorporated, Northbrook, Illinois, spoke on the Federal Trade Commission's proposed regulations pertaining to product safety and certification at the IAEI seminar held in Carmel, California, on April 19, 1979.

Underwriters Laboratories, Inc., announced the election of **Loring W. Knoblauch,** 59, as its ninth president and CEO at a special meeting of its board of trustees in 2001. He was also elected to the UL board.

Mr. Knoblauch served most recently as president and CEO of Talon Automated Equipment Company, a privately-held manufacturer of industrial processing equipment. Prior to that he served for three years as Hubbell Inc.'s president of international operations. He also spent twenty years with Honeywell International where he held a broad range of top management positions, including president of Honeywell Asia Pacific (Hong Kong) and vice president of international business development (Minneapolis).

Knoblauch's knowledge of industry is extensive and he brings a unique blend of international experience and business acumen.

Excerpted from *IAEI News*, July 2001.

Testing Laboratories

Through the years, testing laboratories have interacted with and supported IAEI. We wish to acknowledge them.

1878	SGS U.S. Testing Company, Inc. (SGSUS)
1885	Intertek Testing Services NA, Inc. (ITSNA)
1894	Underwriters Laboratories Inc. (UL)
1919	Canadian Standards Association (CSA)
1925	ETL Semko
1944	NSF International (NSF)
1947	Southwest Research Institute (SWRI)
1949	Applied Research Laboratories, Inc. (ARL)
1949	Wyle Laboratories, Inc. (WL)
1959	MET Laboratories, Inc. (MET)
1961	National Technical Systems, Inc. (NTS)
1971	Communication Certification Laboratory, Inc. (CCL)
1971	Electro-Test, Inc. (ETI)
1974	Entela, Inc. (ENT)
1980	TUV Rheinland of North America, Inc. (TUV)
1987	TUV America, Inc. (TUVAM)
1990	TUV Product Services GmbH (TUVPSG)
1995	Curtis-Straus LLC (CSL)
1999	FM Global Technologies LLC (FM)

National Fire Protection Association

Establishing Safeguards for Fire Safety

The National Fire Protection Association (NFPA) is a non-profit voluntary membership organization whose sole objective is the reduction of fire waste in lives and property. Organized in 1896, its stated functions are to promote the science and improve the methods of fire protection and prevention, to obtain and circulate information on these subjects, and to secure the cooperation of its members and the public in establishing proper safeguards against loss of life and property by fire.

The association has two classes of members, organization and associate. As organization members there are approximately 210 trade, professional, and public service associations. There are approximately 25,000 associate members, consisting of organizations or individuals from industry, commerce, government agencies at all levels, the military forces, insurance, architects, engineers, the professions, hospital and school administrators, and others who have vocational or avocational interests in fire control. The bulk of the members come from the United States, with sizeable representation from Canada, and a scattering of members in most of the countries of the Free World.

The basic function of NFPA is the preparation of standards and codes. The association has no power to legislate or enforce its standards and codes, but they are widely adopted as the basis of laws and regulations, and extensively used as the basis of good practice.

NFPA standards and codes are developed by more than 100 technical committees on which approximately 1500 persons serve without compensation. Committee make-up is widely representative of all parties, including users, who may be affected. Standards and codes are developed in a quasi-legislative process completely democratic in nature, and official adoption is by vote of members assembled at the association's annual meeting.

The educational and informational functions of the association are carried out by publication of a wide range of technical, informational and educational literature.

Public educational materials prepared by NFPA and distributed extensively by local organizations include a number of folders, booklets and check lists, plus films, dealing entirely or partly with electrical safety in the home. Among them are materials for children. The association annually services several thousand newspapers and house organs with clipsheets containing prepared materials on fire safety, frequently including one or more on home electrical safety, and likewise services all U.S. fire departments and county extension agents with prepared releases for use with local media which also frequently contain items on home electrical safety.

Fully realizing that "professional" electrical inspection generally stops at

"The Father of Uniform Electrical Wiring Rules"

Death has ended the career of Christopher M. Goddard, former secretary of the New England Insurance Exchange. As secretary of the Exchange from 1891 until 1925, Mr. Goddard was an outstanding factor in the fire insurance business in New England, taking a leading part in its development, while he is nationally known and remembered as the "father" of Fire Prevention Week and the *National Electrical Code.*

Mr. Goddard graduated from Dartmouth College in 1877. After teaching mathematics in a private school at Suffield, Connecticut, he engaged in electrical contracting in New Jersey. In May 1890, he joined the New England Insurance Exchange as electrical inspector and was appointed secretary in 1891.

In his official capacity Mr. Goddard was instrumental in securing the cooperation of electrical inspectors and launched the movement which resulted in the adoption of the Underwriters' National Electrical Association Rules, since 1897 known as *National Electrical Code.*

He also inspired the movement in the field of fire protection and prevention which took shape in the National Fire Protection Association. The NFPA was organized in the offices of the Exchange in 1896, and Mr. Goddard became its president in 1908. As president, he initiated the nationwide publicity campaign carrying the message of fire prevention, now the annual observe known as Fire Prevention Week.

In November, 1925, Mr. Goddard voluntarily asked to be relieved of his duties as secretary of the Exchange and was succeeded January 1, 1926, by Ralph Sweetland. Only a month before he sought retirement, Mr. Goddard was signally honored by the Western Association of Electrical Inspectors, who passed resolutions expressing their appreciation of his service and terming him "the father of uniform electrical wiring rules."

Mr. Goddard was made an honorary member of the International Association of Electrical Inspectors at its organization in 1928.

Mr. Goddard married Emilie G. Brandner in 1882, but Mrs. Goddard died several years ago. He is survived by several nieces and nephews, among them Dana Pierce, president of the Underwriters' Laboratories: Edward M. Goddard of the claim department of the Standard Surety & Casualty Company of New York, and Frederick W. Goddard of Johnson & Higgins, New York.

Reprinted from *News-Bulletin,* January 1935.

the plug outlet in the wall, the NFPA has developed literature and films for the homeowner and layman. One of NFPA's latest films "Hot Cords Can Burn" clearly illustrates the adverse effects which result from the improper use of extension cords. The film also shows how to select proper cords and how to use them safely.

Other brochures encourage homeowners to hire competent electricians to do permanent electrical wiring.

The *National Electrical Code* (Sections 210-22b and 220-3b) specifies that all residences must have receptacle outlets every 12 feet around habitable rooms and three 20-amp appliance branch circuits are required to handle the heavier current-rated appliances used in kitchens, dining rooms and laundry areas. This reduces the need for extension cords.

Section 250-45(c) of the *NEC* requires the grounding of metal parts of refrigerators, freezers, air conditioners, clothes washers, clothes dryers, and portable, hand-held motor-operated tools and appliances such as drills, hedge clippers, lawn mowers, wet scrubbers, sanders and saws. Since 1962, the *NEC* has required all 15- and 20-amp receptacles to be of the grounding-type to handle the grounding-type appliances and tools being developed. As an alternate safety feature, some of these home appliances or tools can be of the double-insulated types.

All NFPA literature suggests that wiring in the home conform to the requirements of the *NEC*. The NFPA (Sparky) Home Fire Inspection Form includes a check list for worn-out electrical cords and checking for the correct sizes of overcurrent devices.

Reprinted from *Electrical Safety Study*, NEMA, 1959.

Quick Fact

The first overseas members joined the NFPA in 1903. They were John Smith of the Sun Insurance office in London, and George Smith from an insurance office in Sydney, Australia.

Excerpted from NFPA.org.

IAEI Managing Director Everett Cogan and Frank Stetka, electrical field inspector for NFPA, at the 1969 Northwestern Section meeting.

Percy Bugbee, general manager of the National Fire Protection Association, spoke at the Western Section meeting on September 8, 1950. He spoke briefly on the close relationship that exists between the IAEI and NFPA. He mentioned that Charlie Smith, IAEI executive director and secretary/treasurer, had three jobs, not one. He is NFPA's electrical field engineer, secretary of NFPA's electrical section, and the general secretary of IAEI. Mr. Bugbee also talked about the new electrical committee procedure that went into effect in 1950.

NATIONAL FIRE PROTECTION ASSOCIATION

CODE MAKING PANELS

MEMBERSHIP: Appointed by the Correlating Committee. No specific number of members on each panel. Individual appointees considered as representing and speaking for the organizations with which they are affiliated. All organizations having a fundamental interest in activities of a particular panel are given representation. Appointments usually chosen on the basis of their interest, knowledge and available time to properly consider matters coming before the panel.

It is the responsibility of the Correlating Committee to provide for proper representation on the various panels of those concerned with their respective Article assignments.

The number of code-making panels and the *Code* articles assigned to each are determined by the Correlating Committee which also appoints the chairman of each panel and the individuals formally designated to serve with him.

FUNCTIONS: A code-making panel has referred to it, considers, and reports as to its recommendations proposed amendments or revisions of the *National Electrical Code*. Each panel has sponsorship of one or more related articles of the *Code*.

HANDLING PROPOSED REVISION

1. Proposal is prepared by some person and is assigned to a panel.
2. Panel considers and forwards to the Correlating Committee.

2a. Panel may refer it to a subcommittee for recommendation.

3. Correlating Committee submits revisions to Electrical Section.
4. Electrical Section discusses and returns it to the Correlating Committee with its comments, or for further consideration by the appropriate panel if necessary.
5. Correlating Committee may make final check for correlation.
6. Revisions reported to NFPA annual meeting.
7. NFPA acts in annual meeting, and may refer to Board of Directors.
8. NFPA submits it to American Standards Association.

ELECTRICAL SECTION

MEMBERSHIP: All interested NFPA Associate Members and representatives of Organization Members.

FUNCTIONS: To provide an opportunity for presentation and discussion, in open meeting, of proposals for revisions of the *Code*. Proposals also may be filed by members of the section or the public with the secretary and Correlating Committee. It reports its recommendation to the NFPA concerning revisions of the *NEC* which have been proposed by the National Electrical Code Committee.

NATIONAL ELECTRICAL CODE COMMITTEE

CONSISTS OF 1. Correlating Committee 2. Code-making Panels 3. Interpretations Committee.

FUNCTIONS: To interpret provisions of the current edition of the *NEC*; handle proposals for tentative interim amendments; develop, periodically, revised editions of the *NEC*.

CORRELATING COMMITTEE

MEMBERSHIP: Appointed by the Board of Directors of NFPA. Individual appointees not considered as representing any specific industry or organization.

FUNCTIONS: 1. Determine the policies and steps incident to revising the *National Electrical Code*. 2. Organizes the code-making panels. 3. Reviews all reports by the code-making panels that recommend changes or additions to the *National Electrical Code*; approves them, or directs they be referred back for further study. 4. Determine upon the approved procedure for interpreting the *National Electrical Code*. 5. Determines the general procedure with regard to proposals for tentative interim amendments of the *Code*; and reviews recommendations of code-making panels with respect to tentative interim amendments, and, if acceptable, approves them in the name of the National Electrical Code Committee. 6. Reports to the Electrical Section and to a general meeting of the NFPA, the sponsor, its approval of a proposed new edition of the *National Electrical Code*, recommending final approval as a standard.

INTERPRETATION COMMITTEE

MEMBERSHIP: Chairman of the Correlating Committee; Electrical Field Engineer; Chairman of the code-making panel concerned; at least two other members of the National Electrical Code Committee.

INTERPRETATION PROCEDURE

1. Those desiring an interpretation shall supply the chairman with five identical copies of a statement in which shall appear specific references to a single problem, paragraph, or section. Such a statement shall be on the business stationary of the enquirer and shall be duly signed.
2. When applications involve actual field situations they shall so state and all parties involved shall be named.
3. Two general forms of findings will be recognized:
   (a) Those making an interpretation of the literal text.
   (b) Those making an interpretation of the intent of the National Electrical Code Committee when a particular rule was adapted.
4. The findings of the Interpretations Committee will be in its name and for the National Electrical Code Committee as a whole. The applicant will be informed of the finding promptly following its having been determined.
5. Each code-making panel will be expected to give appropriate consideration to the text of any section or paragraph which has produced an interpretation. Finding to the end that suitable revision of the text involved may be recommended.
6. Requests for interpretations should be addressed to the National Fire Protection Association, 60 Batterymarch Street, Boston 10, Massachusetts.
7. NFPA has no power of enforcement of interpretations at any local level of inspection jurisdiction.

Reprinted from *News-Bulletin*, March 1953

Purposes and Objectives of National Code Making Panels

If today is an average day, there will be approximately 7,000 fires. These fires will cause 32 deaths and property losses of about $5,000,000. Some 1,500 of these fires will be in dwellings.

Fires of electrical origin are the second most frequent cause of fires in buildings, being exceeded only by fires caused by careless smokers.

The National Fire Protection Association was organized 70 years ago as a non-profit engineering and educational society solely devoted to the reduction of loss of life and destruction of property by fires.

Lest you think that in view of the fire record I have just given you that we have miserably failed in our mission, I hasten to point out measured against the vast growth of population and the vast increase in the amount of physical property that there is to burn, that our fire losses are not increasing in proportion. We are burning substantially less than we did ten and twenty years ago.

The NFPA and the National Electrical Contractors Association have been working together in the public interest for a long period of years, and for you to understand why this is so, I think that I should give you a condensed description of the National Fire Protection Association. The membership of our association may be of interest to you. There are a wide variety of kinds of people interested in preventing, controlling, and extinguishing fires. Our membership set-up is uncomplicated. We have two classes of members. Organization membership, which is limited to national and regional associations, and associate membership, which is open to any company or individual. There are over 200 organization memberships. This class of membership includes 96 of the national trade associations like your own, seven federal government departments, all of the national and regional associations in the fire insurance field, and such well-known national groups as The American National Red Cross, The American Automobile Association, The American Hospital Association, The American Institute of Architects, National Association of Manufacturers, and The National Association of Home Builders, to name just a few. I can think of no other association that has the wide breadth of support as does the NFPA. The reason for this is fairly obvious when you come to think of it. Fire affects, in one way or the other, every person, every building, and every type of industry.

At a recent meeting in Boston, newly-elected president of the National Fire Protection Association, Robert Grant, and the new executive director of the IAEI, Bill Summers, discuss the agreement that NFPA will continue to supply free copies of the *National Electrical Code* to all IAEI active members in 1980.

Our associate membership of some 21,000 includes thousands of people in industry, thousands of federal, state, and fire officials. Our membership is international and is now drawn from 70 countries throughout the world.

Now let me tell you a little about what we do. A basic activity of NFPA since its inception has been the development and promotion of standards for fire control. This is a large and complicated operation. Each year, we publish all of our standards in what we call the National Fire Codes. Current edition, which is now coming off the press, includes over 190 different standards. They will appear in 10 sizeable volumes which total 6,600 pages. Well over 100 different technical committees work on these standards, and more than 1,500 people serve on these committees.

Another basic activity includes the keeping and analysis of fire experiences. Our Fire Record Department issues annual estimates of fires by cause and occupancy, reports on interesting and unusual fires, and makes special study of occupancy fire records.

Another very large task is that of public education. We prepare and distribute millions of pieces of educational material simply to get the message of the principles of fire safety across to both adults and children.

There are some 22,000 organized fire departments in the U.S. and Canada, and in this area, we develop standards for fire department equipment, training

Newly elected president of the NFPA, Robert Grant and other NFPA staff members met with the National Electrical Code Correlating Committee at the 1980 Correlating Committee meeting in Houston, Texas. Seated *from left to right* are: Len Sessler; Dick Biermann; Richard Osborn, chairman; Bob Grant, president, NFPA; Rita Good, recording secretary, NFPA; and Kim Parker. Standing (*left to right*): Bill Summers, executive director, IAEI; Dick Stevens, vice president, chief engineer, NFPA; Don Fleckenstein; Howard Reymers; Mel Borleis, Bill Milby; Len Corey; Fred Hedlund; Sil Patti; Joe Ross, electrical field specialist, NFPA; and Tony O'Neill, vice president, NFPA.

procedures, and a whole library of texts on fire fighting methods. NFPA operates the Fire Marshals Association of North America for the benefit of the men in the states and in the cities that are in the front line of the administering and enforcing of fire standards. We operate the Society of Fire Protection Engineers, which is the professional engineering society in this field. We also have a section for industrial fire protection people, and another section for those of our members who are particularly interested in electricity. We operate special field services in the fields of electricity, flammable liquids, gases, and marine fire protection.

Your direct interest in the work of NFPA lies in the simple fact that we sponsor and produce the *National Electrical Code*. Attempts to write an electrical code started way back in the 1890s. By 1895, there were five different electrical codes in use in the United States. This created confusion and no end of controversy, and for a number of years, attempts were made to produce one *National Electrical Code*. In 1911, NFPA was asked to assume sponsorship of the *Code* and for the past 55 years, we have had this responsibility and have issued approximately every three years since that date, a new edition of the *Code*.

I would hazard the opinion that there is no more widely known or widely accepted standard anywhere in the United States today than the *National Electrical Code*. One reason for this, is the remarkably fine support that your association has given and is giving to the *Code*. The *Code* schools that your association sponsors are a great contribution, and we are most grateful for this activity. I would like, at this point, to pay a personal tribute to your present president, Dick Osborn, for his dedicated leadership in the development and promotion of the *National Electrical Code*. As most of you know, he is a member of the Electrical Correlating Committee, chairman of Panel 11, and now a member of NFPA's Board of Directors.

No standard, no matter how well prepared, is of any value if it doesn't gain acceptance and use. For the past 40 years, NFPA has operated an electrical field service program solely designed to support, promote, and interpret the *National Electrical Code*. This activity has been financed by contributions from your association, from the National Electrical Manufacturers Association, from the Edison Electric Institute, from the International Association of Electrical Inspectors, from the International Brotherhood of Electrical Workers, from Underwriters' Laboratories, and from the American Insurance Association. Frank Stetka, who is well-known to many of you, is our present electrical field engineer.

This is the first public announcement of the fact that we have, this month, hired

Mark W. Earley of Cumberland, Rhode Island, has been appointed chief electrical engineer of the National Fire Protection Association (NFPA), announced association President Robert W. Grant. Formerly assistant chief electrical engineer, Earley will be responsible for supervision of NFPA's Electrical Department staff and its technical activities including the *National Electrical Code*, the *National Electrical Code Handbook*, related seminars and products, NFPA's Electrical Section and representation of NFPA in the activities of other electrical organizations. As chief electrical engineer, he also serves as secretary to the National Electrical Code Committee.

Earley holds a bachelor's degree in electrical engineering and is a registered professional engineer. He is co-author of *Electrical Installations in Hazardous Locations* and is the editor of the 1990 edition of the *National Electrical Code Handbook*.

Prior to joining NFPA in 1986, Earley was with Factory Mutual Research Corporation for eight years. He has published numerous technical articles on the fire protection of electrical equipment and is a member of the International Association of Electrical Inspectors, the Institute of Electrical and Electronics Engineers, and the Society of Fire Protection Engineers.

Reprinted from *IAEI News*, January 1990.

Walter Stone, who is nationally known as an expert on the electrical code, to undertake a complete editorial revision of the *Code*. We are sure that in time, this will be a most valuable contribution in making the *Code* more understandable and easier for you to work with.

I think it is important for you to know at least the names of other NFPA standards in your general field of operation. Many of them may have an important bearing on your own work. There are standards on air conditioning, on blower systems, on signaling systems, on electrical equipment in chemical atmospheres, on electrical metal-working machine tools, on electrical systems for hospitals, on lightning protection, on static electricity, and on electric computer systems. For those of you that may be interested in any of these areas, a postcard or letter addressed to National Fire Protection Association headquarters at 60 Batterymarch Street, Boston, Massachusetts, will bring you a free, complete list of all of our standards and other publications.

I'm grateful to you for giving me the opportunity to tell you a little about the work of the NFPA and to express to your great association, our appreciation for your strong support of the *National Electrical Code*.

Houston, Texas, October 21, 1966—Text of the address given by Percy Bugbee, general manager, National Fire Protection Association before the 65th Anniversary Convention of the National Electrical Contractors Association. (Reprinted by permission from October, 1966 issue of *Qualified Contractor*.) Reprinted from *IAEI News*, January 1967.

Ray Weber and Jim Carpenter listen as Mark Early, NFPA, presents the latest issue of the *nec digest*™ at the 2002 Northwestern Section meeting. *nec digest* is the official source for information about NFPA's *National Electrical Code*.

NECA Founded 1901

NATIONAL ELECTRICAL CONTRACTORS ASSOCIATION

AFTER 102 YEARS

NATIONAL ELECTRICAL CONTRACTORS ASSOCIATION

Representing Electrical Contractors

The National Electrical Contractors Association was organized in 1901 as a trade association to represent electrical contractors. Membership is limited to electrical contractors and in 1969 there are more than 5,000 members organized in 128 affiliated but autonomous chapters throughout the entire United States.

The purposes and objectives of the association are to represent, promote and advance the interests of the electrical contracting industry and of the consuming public including but not limited to:

— Promotion and encouragement of more efficient, safer and more economical electrical installations.

— More efficient and economic distribution of electrical supplies and equipment.

— The collection and dissemination of information and data of value to the industry.

— The encouragement of active competition and sound business practices.

— The promotion of cooperation and good will among members of the electrical contracting industry and between them and the employees of the industry, the members of allied industries, governmental bodies and the public.

— The fostering and conducting of educational courses and programs for the electrical contracting industry, its members, its employees and the public.

These purposes and objectives are stated in the association's articles of incorporation and to a more or less degree are concerned with safe electrical installations and the safe use of electricity. NECA pursues these objectives through the activities of its officers, members, committees and staff. The NECA national office and headquarters staff are located in Washington, D. C. and the association maintains four geographic regional offices each with a director and field representatives. Local activities are sponsored and conducted by the NECA chapters each of which employs a chapter manager who is a professional trade association executive.

NECA has many programs and participates in many activities concerned with electrical safety in the home.

National Electrical Code

From the very beginning electrical contractors have been interested and concerned with rules for safe electrical installations. Through NECA electrical contractors have actively participated in the development and promulgation of the *National Electrical Code*. Today, electrical contractors have representation on all seventeen code-making panels and the correlating committee of the National Electrical Code Committee and on many technical subcommittees and ad hoc committees established by the National Electrical Code Committee to study particular problems. Electrical contractors feel that they have a responsibility for this work because of their expert knowledge gained from day-to-day, everyday experience with electrical installations.

NECA has always believed that it is in the public interest and the interest of the electrical contracting industry that local codes that provide safety standards for electrical installations be adopted. It recognizes that the *National Electrical Code* together with proper enforcement provide the minimum requirements necessary in the interests of the public and the industry. This has been included in a formal policy statement adopted by NECA.

Since 1963 NECA chapters have been sponsoring and conducting Code Conferences. The Code Conference Program is intended to acquaint the participants with the use of the *National Electrical Code* and to explain how it is developed and the procedure for proposing changes. Since its inception the NECA chapters have conducted about 500 local Code Conferences with a total attendance of approximately 30,000 persons. In addition to those directly involve with performing electrical installations, participants have included public officials such as fire marshals, public safety directors and members of local legislative bodies. Because of this participation, the Code Conference has been directly responsible for the adoption of the *National Electrical Code* by many communities that previously had no electrical safety requirements.

NECA as an association and many of its members individually are members of the National Fire Protection Association and its electrical section. It is a contributor to the NFPA electrical field service which promotes the use and understanding of the *National Electrical Code*.

Electrical Wiring Materials & Equipment

Electrical contractors through NECA participate on several committees of the American National Standards Institute concerned with material standards. A NECA representative is a member of the electrical and electronic standards board of ANSI. A NECA representative has also been elected to membership in Underwriters' Laboratories, Incorporated.

Electrical Installations

Skill is the cornerstone of the business of electrical contracting and the safe application of electricity to use demands skill. To develop this skill and to preserve skill in a growing and rapidly changing technology, NECA together with the International Brotherhood of Electrical Workers sponsors the National Joint Apprenticeship and Training Committee for the Electrical Industry. This joint committee develops and promotes standards and training materials for use by local joint committees for the training of apprentices and the continuing training of journeymen.

Recently NECA has developed and published the *NECA Standard of Installation*. This standard is intended to define what is meant by the phrase "installed in a neat and workmanlike manner" as it applies to electrical construction. It is published as a guide to improved electrical construction.

NECA believes in and supports strict inspection and enforcement of local electrical codes and ordinances. It maintains a membership in the International Association of Electrical Inspectors and actively participates in their affairs. However, since it is not practical for an electrical inspector to examine

in detail all parts of an electrical installation, NECA believes that electrical installations should be made only by competent and responsible persons and organizations. NECA through its chapters promotes legislation to establish examination and licensing of electrical contractors and journeymen as an adjunct to electrical inspection. This is to assure that electrical installations are performed in a manner that provides protection to persons and property.

General

NECA promotes better wiring in the belief that adequate and efficient wiring systems provide a higher degree of safety than the minimum requirements of the *National Electrical Code*. Inadequate wiring has the tendency to result in unsafe situations and conditions.

This promotion is carried out by NECA nationally and locally. Local chapters engage in programs to educate the public regarding the safe use of electricity especially during National Electrical Week, Fire Prevention Week and at home and electrical shows.

NECA also participates with its industry allies in inter-industry promotions of greater and safer use of electricity.

Reprinted from *Electrical Safety Study*, NEMA, 1969.

Quick Fact

NECA is a co-sponsor of the National Joint Apprenticeship and Training Committee (NJATC).

Excerpted from necanet.org.

Full Membership in IAEI Endorsed by NECA

Two significant and noteworthy articles appeared in the February 1962 issue, *Qualified Contractor*, official publication of the National Electrical Contractors Association that should provide much food for thought for all concerned.

Most significant was the stress placed by NECA's editorial staff on the importance of its members affiliating with the IAEI, reiterating NECA's recommendations made over a period of years, encouraging all electrical contractors to endorse and support the IAEI.

Through the cooperation of the officials of NECA, the first of two articles written for this purpose appear in this issue. Prepared by Art Welklin, chairman, public relations committee, IAEI, Fort Wayne, Indiana, and titled, "IAEI: Keystone of the Electrical Industry," it gave the origin, history, purposes and objectives of the IAEI and the need of a closer relationship between the electrical contractor and the electrical inspector.

A second article to be prepared by an NECA official will tell of the benefits that can accrue to the electrical contractor through membership and participation in the activities of the electrical inspectors association. Cooperation between these two groups would result in benefits to the entire electrical industry and the public as well. This article is scheduled to appear in the March issue, *Qualified Contractor.*

The second significant factor and pertinent to the necessary and needed cooperation expressed by the editor, *Qualified Contractor*, appeared in an article on page 82 of the February, 1962, issue, describing a series of debates held during a recent meeting of the Inland Empire (Spokane) Chapter of NECA in which 38 electrical inspectors and contractors participated. The debate technique was selected as a means of getting the most constructive comments on each question debated in the least time. Several prominent and outstanding electrical inspectors from the Pacific coast engaged in this activity.

Indications of such cooperation between these two large segments of the electrical industry speaks well for the future in a better understanding of the complex problems that face the industry today as they relate to the installation of wiring and equipment in conformity with the *National Electrical Code* and other related electrical standards. The medium of communication must be improved through common discussion. A breakdown in intelligent communication brings only disagreements, misunderstandings and aggravations.

Membership in the IAEI by electrical contractors in particular will afford them greater opportunity to meet the electrical inspector on common grounds at chapter and/or section annual meetings to engage in open discussion on mutual problems that are of vital concern to both groups. Such discussions will reduce interpretations of rules and regulations to a common denominator applicable and understandable to both with a resultant benefit to the public in matters of electrical safety.

Reprinted from *News-Bulletin*, March 1962.

Six Illinois chapters of the National Electrical Contractors Association (NECA) hosted a cocktail party for participants of the 53rd annual spring meeting of the IAEI Illinois Chapter. Pictured are (*left to right*): Ken Clawson, Midwestern region field representative, NECA; Larry King, program chairman; Dennis Coffey, chairman, Illinois Chapter; James M. Henneberry, chapter manager, Illinois Chapter, NECA; and George Ronchetti, chairman of the executive committee, IAEI.

NATIONAL BUREAU OF STANDARDS

The Measurer of Standards

The National Bureau of Standards was created by an Act of Congress in 1901, by which it superceded the Office of Weights and Measurements in the Treasury Department. The functions of this bureau were stated to be not only the custody of the national standards and making comparisons with them of the standards used in manufacture and commerce, but also the determination of physical constants and properties of materials, the construction of standards, and the solution of problems which arise in connection with standards.

Upon the creation of the Department of Commerce, the Bureau of Standards was transferred to it. The bureau now occupies a tract of forty-three acres in northwest Washington. It has eleven main buildings and seven minor buildings. A new hydraulic laboratory is to be built, an appropriation for the purpose having been made at the last session of Congress. Its staff numbers about 1050, of which 950 are located in Washington, the remainder being distributed among eight field stations of the bureau. The director of the bureau is George K. Burgess, who has been connected with the bureau since 1903 and was formerly its chief metallurgist.

The bureau has issued approximately 2,000 publications, which formerly were variously designated as scientific and technologic papers, handbooks, circulars, etc. Recently the *Journal of Research* was established, which includes all scientific and technologic papers now issued, although many of these are still to be had as separate reprints. Other publications are known as circulars, simplified practice recommendations, commercial standards, building & housing, and miscellaneous publications.

The functions of the bureau in the field of standardization may be listed as follows:

1. Standards of Measurement—Custody of the fundamental standards for measurements of all kinds, and comparisons with these and with working standards of the instruments and standards used in commerce and industry.

2. Standard Constants—Such as the velocity of light, the ratio of the electrostatic and electromagnetic absolute units, specific heats and heat capacities of different chemical substances, electrochemical equivalents, atomic weights, the gravitation constant, conductivities of materials, etc.

3. Standards of Quality—Specifications for materials and apparatus such as cement, dry-cleaning solvent, and electric transformers.

4. Standards of Performance—Such as operating efficiencies of fans, motors, generators, lamps, and batteries; life of lamps; ratios and phase angle of instrument transformers, etc.

5. Standards of Practice—Such as electric and gas service standards for public utilities, safety codes, elimination of unnecessary sizes or models, etc.

The bureau's research and testing work is divided among nine divisions devoted respectively to fundamental weights and measures, electricity, heat and power, optics, chemistry, mechanics and sound, organic and fibrous materials, metallurgy, and ceramics. The Commercial Standards Group comprises four divisions dealing respectively with simplified practice, building and housing, specifications, and trade standards.

The Electrical Division, which developed at first under the direction of E. B. Rosa, has as its present chief E. C. Crittenden.

The more fundamental work of this division naturally has to do with the fundamental units and standards for electrical measurement, which are based, by Act of Congress, passed in 1894, upon the mercury ohm, the silver voltameter, and the Clark cell.

The international units are maintained by the use of resistance coils of manganin wire and by standard cells of the Weston type. Alternating-current standards are derived from these by the use of dynamo-meter types of instruments. In addition to maintenance of the fundamental standards and measurements based upon them, there are sections dealing with photometry, magnetic measurements, radios, batteries, electrolytic corrosion, public utility standards and safety standards.

The application of electrical measurements to the determination of the quality and performance of electrical materials and electrical apparatus introduces a large amount of work which is carried out mainly for other government departments. This work involves the testing of wires, cables, dry cells, storage batteries, rectifiers, radio apparatus, lamps, headlights, fuses, spark plugs, rubber gloves, condensers, inductances and other objects too numerous to mention. Investigations have been made along such lines as the resistance of the human body, the salinity of sea water (by resistance), the properties of submarine cable, the velocity of projectiles, the movement of turrets on battleships, the effects of electrolysis in underground structures and methods for its mitigation, sound ranging for the location of enemy batteries in war.

The sections dealing with public utility standards have established standards for electricity meters and for electric service, and are working on standards for quantity units in telephone service. A number of safety codes have been developed at the bureau, prominent among them which are the National Electrical Safety Code and the Code for Protection against lightning.

Other important researches which have been carried out at the bureau are the determination of the ratio of electrostatic and electromagnetic electrical units, measurement of the properties of insulating materials, the development of frequency standards in the form of piezo-electric crystals, the investigation of storage-battery electrolytes, development of an electrical method for determining strain and stress in the members of engineering structures (such as bridges and dams), and the investigation of soil corrosion of underground pipes as distinguished from electrolytic corrosion.

The bureau carries on a great deal of research work, some of which is for the aeronautics branch of the Department of Commerce and some for other departments of the government. Many of its researches are carried on in cooperation with technical societies or organized industries. Arrangements are frequently made for the appointment of research associates, whose salaries are paid by some association or committee and who devote their time to working on research problems which are of interest to such associations. At the present time there are nearly one hundred research associates working in the bureau laboratories on special problems.

The bureau also cooperates with technical societies in their committee work. Members of its staff are found on many committees of the National Fire Protection Association, the American Institute of Electrical Engineers, the American Society for Testing Materials, etc. The bureau is officially represented upon the American Standards Association and a great many of its sectional committees, such as the electrical committee of the National Fire Protection Association. It thus has a part of the periodic revisions of the *National Electrical Code*.

The bureau is also active in international standardization work. It helps support the International Bureau of Weights and Measures. It is represented upon the International Electro-technical Commission, the International Commission on Illumination, the International Scientific Radio Union, the International Advisory Committee on Electrical Units and Standards, and the International Committee on Standard Wave Lengths and Solar Spectrum Tables.

By Morton G. Lloyd. Reprinted from *News-Bulletin*, January 1931.

Mitchell Bursts Into Poetry On Electrical Council Meeting

Electrical the Council's called that just has held a meeting
In Underwriters' Labs, you know and 'tis no use repeating
The story of the wond'rous work the Labs are daily doing,
Though they deserve more praise by far than to them is accruing.

Our Dana Pierce, the well known sire of that great institution,
Presided o'er the gathering and guided to solution
The many problems that came up before the Council members
And quenched betimes the threat'ning fires while they were still but embers.

"Bob" Shepard, too, was up ahead and aided in the guiding
along the straight and mainline track when threatened with a siding;
And Dr. Lloyd of Washington with usual words of learning
Spoke always to the point in view quite clearly and discerning.

"Bill" Boyd was there and had his say—this thought his mind was gripping:
that things we did might not be right and that we might be slipping.
Fred Weber from the great Northwest seemed much concerned with sockets
That hang out where the raindrops fall and for these drops form pockets.

"Hootnannie" Patton finds a dearth of samples in Seattle.
And so for these and "lower cost" he put up quite a battle.
And Evertz from Ohio State was quite elucidating;
(Inspection work has been his task, connected up with rating).

While Joe Forsyth, the patriarch of all New York inspectors,
Spoke words that showed himself to be one of the great dissectors
Of knotty problems that arise, and so did Harry Beecher.
(Yes, he's the boy who will make friends with any living creature.)

George Welman from the Sunny South brought up some armored cable.
(That lad will surely "fight the fight" as long as he is able.)
And Cambridge from the Northern land that's just beyond our border
Told what he'd done in Canada to keep all things in order.

Vic Tousley with his usual mien, both dignified and stately,
Joined in and showed that for the job that's come to him quite lately
He's qualified to take the wheel and steer the way that's rational
To bring success and glory to Inspectors International.

And nearly all the members there took some part in the meeting—
The thought of each seemed but to be, "The time is all too fleeting."
For each had gained more knowledge of the many complications
The Lab'ratories' Staff meets with as part of daily rations.

And friendly bout of argument anent the points in question
Gave each some thoughts that will relieve his mental indigestion.
And so that we might have a chance to get some little notion
Of what the daily work is like with all the wheels in motion.

They took us 'round to see the sights and one was quite appalling—
A big steel safe got "all het up," was raised, then let go, falling,
And when it landed on the floor, as though in fire-swept ruins,
We realized how practical the Labs are in their "doin's."

And then they showed us how some arcs, the products of high tension,
Would dance around and seem to find the missing fourth dimension
They made a test upon a switch and showed how power factor
For any value can be set upon their new reactor.

The entertainment that they gave both in the Labs and elsewhere
Was wonderful as was the way, providing for our welfare,
They housed us at the Lake Shore Club where we were quite contented
To eat—but sleep, I must confess, was almost quite prevented.

By indoor sports which all enjoyed, including one of cunning
By Dana Pierce whose nickel rolled in compound curves most stunning.
While at the dinner Wednesday night we all were feeling happy
Good things to eat, good company, good talks, not long but snappy.

And at the close two of the staff (Welborn and Brandon) Charmers,
Gave proof the Labs can show the world the best relief for farmers.

—C. W. Mitchell, San Francisco. Reprinted from *News-Bulletin*, July 1929.

ESA Founded 1915

ELECTRICAL SAFETY AUTHORITY

Electrical Safety Authority

Building on Our Heritage

Kingston, our host city, has a great heritage. Founded in 1673, it was the first capital of the united Upper and Lower Canadas before the national seat of government was moved in the 1940s. Kingston was at the strategic intersection of the Rideau Canal, Lake Ontario and the entrance to the St. Lawrence River. The fact that Fort Henry was built here reflects the strategic importance that the city had in the 19th century.

Kingston is also a city with a great prospect and a wonderful time. It is the home of Queen's University, one of Canada's premier learning institutions (and presently home to my two boys who go to school there). It is also the home of other great learning institutions such as Royal Military College and St. Lawrence College.

The city of Kingston's tag line is "where history and innovation thrive."

I like to think of our company as being a place "where history and innovation thrive."

I would like to talk a little bit about Electrical Safety Authority's (ESA) heritage and then describe how I see us building upon that heritage to create a great future together. To those of you who are not with ESA, I hope you will enjoy this historical trip—since it mirrors not just ESA but the history of electrical inspection in general. After talking about our heritage I would like to share with you my view of some future directions for our business.

ESA's Heritage: Ontario Hydro Electrical Inspection (OHEI)

Phase 1. In the beginning..."let there be light."

It was only a year or two after the Toronto Incandescent Electric Light Company was established that electrical safety first become an issue in Canada. The initiative came from the Canadian Fire Underwriters Association. Concerned about the massive financial liabilities its members could face from structural fires caused by improper wiring, the association appointed an inspector in 1892 to ensure that all new electric services and equipment were installed in accordance with its own requirements.

Mr. Bruce Smith was the first person charged with enforcement of the new electric code. It was an onerous task. Mr. Smith, if you are up there watching us—we want to assure you that we are continuing the good work that you started.

By 1890, almost all villages with a population over 3,000 had a generator supplying electric street lights—they were using a radical concept we now call distributed generation. The new power source had caught the fancy of consumers and nowhere was this more evident than in the city of Toronto, where scores of itinerant contractors and builders came forward to meet the demand with inferior, often bogus, and clearly dangerous workmanship. When Toronto Hydro was formed, it was often in a dangerous race with Toronto Electric Light Company to see which one could install services first.

"The motive of the Underwriters' Regulations has always been the protection of buildings against fire," wrote H. F. Strickland, chief electric inspector for the Hydro Electric Power Commission in 1918. "...they did not pretend to make regulations for the protection of life." Those regulations would come later.

Regardless of the motive, the decision by the association to introduce Canada's first electrical code has impacted the personal safety of Ontarians for more than a century. It was a business decision that set into motion a system of safety inspection that would continuously improve over time and which prevails today.

Phase 2. "Been there, done that"...the era of Municipal Electrical Inspection

In its infancy, the electrical inspection service was largely confined to the Toronto area and usually only applicable to fire insurance company policy holders. That changed in 1912 and 1914 with significant amendments to The Power Commission Act. By order of the Legislative Assembly of Ontario, rules and regulations were made to cover the design, equipment, and workmanship of electrical installations. Municipal electrical inspectors were appointed, with jurisdiction limited to their own geographical boundaries. When many municipalities failed to appoint inspectors, the commission was granted the power to do so and inspectors were allowed to serve more than one area. As a high number of fires continued to occur, the system was ultimately deemed unacceptable.

Phase 3. Without it there could have never been "deregulation": The Hydro Electric Power Commission of Ontario (HEPC)

The Power Commission Act was amended and, in 1915, Ontario Hydro was granted new powers. Electrical inspection became the responsibility of the Hydro Electric Power Commission of Ontario with the power to make regulations, appoint inspectors, and set fees. The province was divided into inspection districts supported by administration offices in strategic locations. Hydro was given significant authority to enforce its regulations: it was allowed to cut off power to those who were in violation of the regulations; inspectors were granted the right to enter any premises for inspection and were freed of liabilities; and penalties were introduced.

Regulations kept pace with developments in the industry with appropriate amendments put forth by a committee comprised of representatives from manufacturers, contractors, the Toronto Hydro-Electric System and the HEPC. This system worked well until 1927, when due to an increasing lack of uniformity between the various provinces over the regulations and their interpretation, a national Code Committee was established under the auspices of the Canadian Standards Association.

Phase 4. "Speaking in Code," the CEC is established

The committee developed a code for electrical installations, called the Canadian Electrical Code Part I, which

was adopted by the commission as the regulatory foundation for the electrical inspection service in Ontario. Undertaken as a national collaborative effort, the code was, and is to this day, recognized as representing the combined judgment of the best available talent in the field of electrical wiring installations. It was adopted by Ontario, Quebec, British Columbia, Nova Scotia and Saskatchewan.

In 1944 the Canadian Electric Code was adapted to meet the Ontario government's Regulations Act and subsequent revisions have been made as required. Today the code stands as the base for the formal wiring regulation for the province of Ontario.

Phase 5. The phrase that still works... "Hydro Approved"

In 1918, the commission's Approval Laboratory was established to test electrical equipment to determine its adherence to specific and stringent guidelines. Products that met the guidelines were declared "Hydro Approved," an endorsement that brought with it the general acceptance by the electrical industry. This approval process was considered so significant that by 1924 the commission was empowered to prohibit the sale of electrical equipment considered to be unsafe for public use. As a result, the Approvals Section of the Electrical Inspection Department was established.

Soon Ontario Hydro was testing products for all of Canada. When other provinces requested use of the "Hydro Approved" designation, and took steps to include it in their legislation, the need for a national testing body became evident. In 1940, the Canadian Standards Association Testing Laboratories were inaugurated and a decade later became a self-contained, self-supporting unit. Today, virtually all electrical equipment is submitted to accredited certification organizations (e.g., CSA, UL and others) for approval. However, ESA retains its position as the ultimate safety authority in Ontario.

Phase 6. First arrival of management consultants: Decentralization and Restructuring

In 1947, the commission began to decentralize its administration by establishing regional offices. The preparation and interpretation of regulations, matters of policy and the application of rules were established as the responsibility of the inspection group in Head Office, while the actual day-to-day work of supervising these regulations was placed in the Regions. This system had in place work groups throughout Ontario, with responsibility for inspection, supervision and policing the sale of equipment and apparatus, and gathering information for, and advancing prosecutions of, regulatory violations.

Phase 7. Globalization comes to inspection: Free Trade

In recent times Ontario Hydro Electrical Inspection faced a new issue: free trade and its implications on safety regulations for products moving across borders. In 1990, the Standards Council of Canada assumed responsibility for examining and accrediting U.S. laboratories. In addition CSA has received nationally recognized testing laboratory

Hydro Electric Power Commission (HEPC) visitors from the Lakehead at the 1954 Ontario Chapter meeting. *Left to right*: Evert Larson, Kenora; Bill Pirie, Fort William; and Basil Battley, Port Arthur.

(NRTL) accreditation from the U.S. Occupational Safety and Health Administration (OSHA). In 1990, the first harmonization of Canadian/United States standards created a standard for heating and cooling equipment.

Phase 8. Electrical Inspection starts to form its own identity

It was clear that action was required to address these concerns. That opportunity presented itself in 1993 when Ontario Hydro established a new direction. Electrical Inspection was launched as a stand alone, self-sustaining and customer focused business within Ontario Hydro. The organization was divided into five territories, with approximately 25 regional work centers and a staff of 260. Inspection was placed under one provincial manager who exercised full control of the business. In addition the provincial code engineer was clearly made accountable for the final decisions on all electrical and safety code issues. The intent of the new structure was that the inspection business should be self-funding. Initially in 1994, its first full year of operation in the new structure, Inspection lost about $4M even though it was able to rely on infra-structure support for HR and IT from Ontario Hydro. The business steadily improved until 1997 when it reached breakeven.

Phase 9. Restructuring of the electrical industry and the creation of ESA

In the late 1990s many jurisdictions in North America and around the world looked at deregulating their electrical industries. In Ontario this was of particular interest because Ontario Hydro had racked up a staggering debt—heavily based on the Darlington Nuclear project and various other operational problems with Candu systems at Pickering and Bruce. The resulting breakup of Ontario Hydro meant that the Electrical Safety function would need to be carried by a separate entity. Out of this need, ESA was born.

The separation of ESA from Ontario Hydro was not an easy task. Dwayne Eamer, ESA's first CEO and my predecessor, and Dane MacCarthy, ESA's chairman of the board, worked hard to successfully accomplish this task. ESA was set up as a delegated administrative authority reporting to the MCCR—the predecessor ministry to the Ministry of Consumer and Business Services (MCBS) that is ESA's current regulator.

The formation of ESA as a new company involved setup of many new functions: a separate information system, separate HR function, separate pension plan, setup of a Board of Directors, Industry Advisory Committee, Consumer Advisory Committee, etc.

As with any startup there were challenges. The setup of a new computer system and a new call center created transitional challenges from both a customer service and a financial standpoint. In Fiscal Year 2001 and 2002, significant losses were reported in spite of a relatively robust new construction environment in Ontario.

In Fiscal year 2003 ESA embarked on a problem of cost containment and customer service improvement that has stabilized the business financially—but operational challenges that will require the continued co-operation of all staff, remain.

As you can see, ESA has a deep heritage that goes all the way back to 1892. In the 110 years of this heritage there have been ups and downs—that mirror the history of electrical inspection in general. That is why we are proud to be affiliated with the IAEI. We have rich history…but now let's talk about our future.

Phase 10. Future Directions

I see our future directions evolving in the following ways:

1. Brand Awareness. As long as the majority of people who shop for electrical products in a Big Box retailer don't know us we have a problem. On the other hand if every person who purchased a light fixture called us for a permit we would not be financially viable—and our research shows such like-for-like replacements are not safety hazards anyway. Within the next few months we need to aggressively engage the electrical sales channels in Ontario to raise our visibility. In conjunction with this we will attempt to put in place a basic exemption. This basic exemption will allow simple like-for-like work in single dwelling units to be done without a permit. At the same time we will make it clear to the Ontario public as to what work does require a permit. We will also put in place an advertising campaign and a pricing strategy that encourages consumers to use experienced electrical contractors.

2. Increased partnership with electrical contractors. I believe we had this in the past. It is a matter of putting it back in place. One way to accomplish this will be through a new fee program that we offer electrical contractors. Under this option a dedicated inspector is assigned to the contractor. This allows us to gain a better understanding of the contractor's work and allows us to have an open dialog if there are recurring defects. Under this program, the fee to the contractor would not be based on a fee guide. Rather it would be based on hours worked by the contractor using WSIB or other documented evidence.

3. Focus on risk management instead of just inspection. We need to allocate our resources in areas where there are problems which have the highest levels of risk. Where serious safety risks exist in where ESA should be focusing the bulk of its attention. The best vehicle to do this is a performance based inspection concept—where the amount of inspection is proportional to the track record of the contractor and the amount of risk.

4. Increased scope in the deregulated market place. Deregulation in the electrical industry increases the need for ESA's independent assessment of the safety of an installation. As an example, Municipal traffic signals and street lighting monitoring will come into ESA's oversight on January 1, 2003. We have drafted utility regulations that we hope will come into effect early next year. This will cover all LDC's in Ontario. They are currently exempt from the code. I am speaking to the EDA on this topic on Monday of this week. In addition as power generation is sold, there will be need for ESA to be involved in this area. We have already opened up dialog with OPG and other generators on this topic.

In short I think we have a rich history and a bright future—but it will not be without its challenges. I believe that the issues faced by ESA mirror those that IAEI members in all jurisdictions face.

Both the city of Kingston and electrical inspection are areas where "history and innovation thrive."

Excerpted from address by Bob Seltzer to Canadian Section meeting, September 2002.

Building Officials Conference of America

Model Building Codes

This organization, founded in 1915, is a national, non-profit municipal service organization, whose purpose is to promote the improvement of building regulations and the administrative organization, techniques and methods of their enforcement by local governments. It seeks to make possible the use by the public of new materials and construction techniques that have been proven safe and to increase the knowledge and understanding of its members in their proper application.

Active membership in BOCA is limited to governmental units, departments or bureaus which administer, formulate or enforce laws, ordinances, rules or regulations relating to buildings, housing, city planning or zoning. In addition there are various other classes of membership open to associations, companies, etc., having interest in the construction industry.

The organization publishes model codes (building, housing, fire prevention and plumbing) which can be adopted by local communities. In addition, it provides services to its members, including code interpretations, plan reviews, information on approval of new building materials, information on building regulation, administration and construction problems, etc.

Its most important publication is probably the BOCA *Basic Building Code*, which is issued every five years and kept up to date by annual supplements.

The committees that prepare the revision of the code are made up of building officials from widely distributed communities in order to obtain the broadest possible viewpoint. Matters pertaining to the code requirements are open to public review and changes are subjected to a public hearing in which cross-arguments are presented to the committee before final decisions are made.

There are over 400 standards listed in the appendices of the *Basic Building Code*, which recognizes the industry standards as they are produced in preference to modifying them and republishing them in another form. BOCA is a member of virtually all standards producing organizations; its staff and many active members represent BOCA on technical committees of these organizations.

The article of the *Basic Building Code* on electric wiring and equipment provides that all new electrical installations shall conform to accepted engineering practice as defined in the *National Electrical Code*. It indicates a conformity of installations of electrical equipment to the National Electrical Safety Code and other accepted engineering standards listed shall be *prima facie* evidence that such installations are reasonably safe for use. It further provides that materials, appliances, devices and other equipment listed in publications of inspected electrical equipment of Underwriters' Laboratories, Inc., and other accredited authoritative agencies and testing organizations, and installed in accordance with the recommendations of the written approval of these authorities shall be accepted as meeting the requirements of the *Basic Code*.

A pamphlet issued by BOCA contains a statement that has broad significance as to the usefulness of voluntary codes and standards in eventual governmental mandatory application: "The adoption of the BOCA code(s) by any government eliminates the necessity of drafting, typing, duplicating, editing, proofreading and printing, which are both time consuming and expensive. A community could spend as much as five years and hundreds of thousands of dollars in drafting a code similar to the BOCA. Under the BOCA program, less than $150 will usually provide an ample supply of copies of the code for consideration, adoption and initial administration."

Reprinted from *Electrical Safety Study*, NEMA, 1969.

Reprinted from *IAEI News*, November 1957.

American National Standards Institute

Uniting Through Standards

In a position that is both unique and focal in the standardization of activity in the United States, including matters of safety, is the American National Standards Institute, until recently known as the USA Standards Institute.

Originally organized in 1918 as the American Engineering Standard Committee, as a result of cooperative action of several of the engineering societies and others, it was organized ten years later to become the American Standards Association.

The methods and procedures, and even the membership of the institute, have gradually evolved during the fifty-one years of its existence to perfect the methods, means and recognition of voluntary standards in this country.

The membership of the institute is mixed; it comprises some one-hundred sixty technical, professional, trade and labor organizations and also, something on the order of one thousand company members. Membership is also open to federal and other governmental agencies. All of its members may be affiliated with the appropriate one of its three councils, such as the Member Body Council which is comprised of technical, professional, scientific and trade and other membership associations of national scope, as well as representatives from departments or agencies of the federal government or state and regional authorities.

The primary responsibilities of the Member Body Council are to:

1. To approve standards as USA Standards (although approval of USA Standards is delegated to the Member Body Council by the institute's board of directors, the board retains final authority on all matters pertaining to procedures, including approval of USA Standards.)
2. Develop and maintain all procedures relating to the preparation, approval, acceptance and designation of standards.
3. Examine standards developed by competent organizations to determine acceptability for approval as USA Standards.
4. Evaluate the need for new standards and the revision of existing standards.
5. Promote the initiation of new standards' projects.
6. Assure that the U.S. is adequately represented in pertinent international standards development activities concerned with civilian safety, trade and commerce.

A second council, the Company Member Council, has primary responsibility to:

1. Develop programs that represent the interests of commerce and industry in the work of the institute and promote their acceptance as the source of approval for national standards.
2. Promote membership and financial support for the institute.
3. Determine the need for new national and international standards and initiative review or improvement of existing standards.
4. Provide a forum for information exchange leading to the improvement of commercial and industrial practices through proper use of standardizations.
5. Identify areas where certification programs are required for the benefit of society.

Finally, a Consumer Council is designated to assure that the interests of consumers are adequately represented in national standardization. This council is composed of individuals representing institute membership, consumer organizations, government and qualified individuals. The primary responsibilities of this council are to:

1. Determine, through studies and surveys, where standardization can generate improvements in consumer goods and services.
2. Serve as the institute contact between the general public and the industry in matters concerning standards affecting the public.
3. Make the consumer aware of the impact on the U.S. economy of well designed and coordinated voluntary standardization programs and how these programs serve his interest.

The main functions of the institute are:

1. To provide systematic means for the development of American National Standards.
2. To promote the development and use of national standards in the United States.
3. To approve standards as American National Standards, provided they are accepted by a consensus of all national groups substantially concerned with their scope and provisions.
4. To coordinate standardization activities in the United States.
5. To serve as a clearing house for information on American and foreign standards.
6. To represent American interests in international standardization work.

As indicated above, the Standards Institute is a unique organization in that, although standards are its entire business, it does not itself develop standards. It makes use of the combined technical talent and expertise of its member bodies. The standards developed by these organizations may become American National Standards after the institute determines that they have been developed in accordance with its procedures which includes substantial agreement among interested and affected parties. It was organized to provide a single mechanism for the development and approval of voluntary national standards and to assure that all parties with a substantial interest in the scope and provisions of a given standard are afforded the opportunity to participate in its development.

Refinements in the institute's procedures have occurred from time to time, and a substantial new procedure currently being established will institute a circulation of proposed standards for public review and comments prior to their approval with final review concentrated in a judicial board of standards review which will examine all comments received and have mechanisms for further evaluations in cases where a controversy or dissatisfaction is registered.

International work

The world aspect of standardization is becoming increasingly important with increased world trade, international manufacturing organizations and recognition that technical needs and expertise are not limited by national boundaries.

U.S. interest in international standards are represented through ANSI in the two principal world-wide standardization organizations, International Organi-zation for Standardization (ISO) and International Electrotechnical Commission (IEC), as well as in certain other regional international bodies.

ANSI

The institute's long concern with electrical safety is evidenced by the fact that its predecessor's first two electrical standards, C1 and C2, were, respectively, the *National Electrical Code* and the National Electrical Safety Code. The first was already in existence under the auspices of the National Fire Protection Association and that organization has constituted its National Electrical Code Committee to meet all the requirements of and to serve as a standards committee of ANSI. The National Electrical Safety Code, dealing mainly with electrical utilities' installations, previously existed under the auspices of the National Bureau of Standards. That organization also continues to sponsor the NESC and has organized a standards committee under the ANSI set up. While this code does not have actual household implications, it is of importance to the general public, as the safety provisions for utility installations include the safety of the public rights of way. The vast majority of ANSI's electrical safety standards are standards of Underwriters' Laboratories, about thirty in all, which have been developed and adopted by UL and subsequently processed as existing standards through the ANSI procedures. These procedures have involved further review by all organizations having an interest and, while the ANSI activities have not contributed materially to the content of the standards, these further reviews have, in some cases, resulted in additional input leading to improvement.

Many of the other standards committees in the electrical field include safety in their activity. Both C37 on switchgear and C50 on rotating equipment have special sub-projects involving the development of safety standards, although these are not particularly related to household applications. The project designated C101 on leakage current for appliances was organized at a manufacturer's request and its sponsorship was undertaken by Underwriters' Laboratories. It has already issued a draft standard proposed for trail use and criticism. A safety standard of great importance to many residents involving both electrical and other aspects which has been developed under the ANSI rules is the Safety Code for Elevators, Dumbwaiters and Moving Walks.

Reprinted from *Electrical Safety Study*, NEMA, 1969.

Quick Fact

About ANSI

1. In 1916 the American Institute of Electrical Engineers (now IEEE) invited the American Society of Mechanical Engineers (ASME), American Society of Civil Engineers (ASCE), American Institute of Mining and Metallurgical Engineers (AIMME) and the American Society for Testing Materials (ASTM) to join in establishing a national body to coordinate standards development and to serve as a clearinghouse for the work of standards developing agencies. Two years later, ANSI, originally founded as the American Engineering Standards Committee (AESC), was formed on October 19, 1918, to serve as the national coordinator in the standards development process as well as an impartial organization to approve national consensus standards and halt user confusion on acceptability.

2. A year after AESC was founded it approved its first standard on pipe threads. The organization undertook its first major project in 1920 when it began coordination of national safety codes to replace the many laws and recommended practices that were hampering accident prevention. The first American Standard Safety Code was approved in 1921 and covered the protection of heads and eyes of industrial workers. Today there are over 1,200 ANSI-approved safety standards designed to protect the workforce, consumers and the general public. Overall, there are approximately 10,500 ANSI-approved American National Standards. In its first ten years, AESC also approved national standards in the fields of mining, electrical and mechanical engineering, construction and highway traffic.

3. Under the name of the United States of America Standards Institute (USASI), ASA was reorganized in 1966 in response to identified needs for a broader use of the consensus principle in developing and approving standards; making the voluntary standards system more responsive to consumer needs; and strengthening U.S. leadership internationally.

4. ANSI adopted its present name in 1969. Throughout these various reorganizations and name changes, the Institute continued to coordinate national and international standards activities and to approve voluntary national standards, now known as American National Standards. Domestic programs were constantly expanded and modified to meet the changing needs of industry, government and other sectors.

In 1987, the Institute accepted responsibility for the world's largest technical standards effort and the most significant innovation in international standardization — ISO/IEC Joint Technical Committee 1 on Information. Since 1989, ANSI has also advanced its international relationships within the countries of Eastern Europe, the Far East, the Pacific Rim and South and Central America.

5. In late 2000, the first-ever U.S. National Standards Strategy (NSS) was approved. Developed over a two-year period by a diverse group of interested parties, the NSS is a roadmap to developing reliable, market-driven standards in all sectors. It reaffirms that the U.S. is committed to a sector-based approach to voluntary standardization activities, both domestically and globally.

Excerpted from *ANSI—A Historical Overview*, ANSI.org, 2003.

CANADIAN STANDARDS ASSOCIATION

Making Standards Work...

The Canadian Standards Association is a dominion chartered organization which just celebrated its 50th anniversary. Its membership, comprising both organizations and individuals, numbers about 4700, representing manufacturers, consumers, public utilities, universities and all levels of government.

Its standards-writing activities, including all facets of engineering and safety and performance, in a wide range of manufactured products, is carried on through some hundreds of technical committees corresponding roughly to the standards committees of ANSI in the United States and containing balanced representation of all parties at interest.

In addition to standards development and promulgation, the Canadian Standards Association has major activities in the certification and approval of some kinds of equipment, and this is particularly true with respect to safety approval of electric equipment. Approval of electrical equipment is based on tests performed in the association's own laboratories, which were originally founded by the Hydro Electric Power Commission of Ontario, and which became a part of CSA in 1940. This self-contained and self-administered unit of the CSA has a listing approval mark and follow-up inspection service relatively similar to those of Underwriters' Laboratories, Inc.

Throughout Canada the regulations governing the installation of electrical equipment conform very closely to a document known as Part I of the Canadian Electrical Code. This code establishes minimum requirements for safety installation and maintenance of electrical equipment at all potentials in buildings, structures and premises, with the exception of certain utility installations, transportation and mines (which are covered in a separate part of the code). Its scope is, therefore, quite similar to that of the *National Electrical Code.*

Mr. H. L. Freeman of CSA Approvals Division discusses tests on outlet boxes, cable connectors, non-metallic sheathed cable, etc. The guide is Miss Stephanie Starkey, HEPC of Ontario.

Ten editions of the Canadian Electrical Code Part I have been issued at intervals since 1927 under the procedures of the Canadian Standards Association by a committee broadly representative of the electrical industry. Nearly half of the members are provincial and municipal inspectors, but also represented are electrical manufacturers, the publicly owned utilities, the fire and casualty underwriters, the fire marshals, the national research council, the railways and the telephone association, and there is also representation from the CSA Testing Laboratories themselves. Both the British Standards Institution and the American National Standards Institute have associate (non-voting) representatives.

After the Part I committee adopts a revision, the proposal is referred to a provincial chairmen's committee, which consists of the provincial inspectors on the Part I committee and which has final power to accept or reject all submittals. Revisions are processed through a CSA technical council and then published. As so published by the association, the code constitutes a voluntary standard. It obtains legal authority through adoption (in some cases with very minor modifications) by the various provinces or municipalities, which also provide for inspection to determine compliance.

Approvals by the CSA Testing Laboratories are based on compliance with a series of safety standards on a wide range of electrical products which are codified as Part II of the Canadian Electrical Code. Such standards are in charge of the committee on Canadian Electrical Code Part II which is a subsidiary of Part I committee.

Standards for safety on each class of product, of which there are well more than 100, are developed by a subcommittee on that subject. Each subcommittee is chaired by one of the members of the Canadian Electrical Code Committee Part II and is served by a secretary from the CSA Approvals Laboratories, with appropriate representation based upon the particular subject. Drafts of the standards as prepared by the subcommittee, together with a record of the vote and comments by subcommittee members, are considered by the Canadian Electrical Code Committee Part II, and if they are approved, forwarded to the Canadian Electrical Code Committee Part I and to the final processing steps in CSA.

As new developments in technology or products occur, or as new experience is gained in the field, the laboratories require, from time to time, a basis for examination beyond that which may be contained in an existing edition of a Part II standard. To cover this situation, the laboratories, as a staff operation, may issue an "approvals bulletin" with new or modified requirements which will be effective in their approval but having a maximum life of two years. Within that time, it is necessary for the bulletin subject matter to be considered and appropriate changes made in the definitive standard. The Canadian Electrical Code Part II Committee, like the Part I Committee, has arranged for a U.S. associate (non-voting) representative through ANSI.

Final approval of electrical equipment for installation rests with the inspection authorities in the provinces and municipalities. In practice, these authorities depend on recognized independent testing laboratories for approval of repetitively manufactured and consumer types of equipment, and for more household electric equipment CSA approval is required.

CSA maintains liaison representation on a number of American National Standards committees and, in turn, accepts for consideration many comments and suggestions in the interest of safety and uniformity from U.S. organizations.

Reprinted from *Electrical Safety Study*, NEMA, 1969.

Canadian Section News and Notes

Electrical inspection has been carried out in Ontario for more than half a century. In its baby years the Electrical Inspection Department was adopted by one of Canada's largest electrical utilities—The Hydro Electric Power Commission of Ontario. With this so-called adoption the responsibilities of "Hydro" became somewhat unusual.

Hydro is not only a supplier of electric energy, but is empowered to make and enforce rules and regulations governing the safe installation of electrical wiring and equipment in Ontario. Such rules and regulations are enforced by approximately 200 electrical inspectors throughout an area of 412,582 square miles.

In order to keep abreast with numerous technical advancements evident

Mrs. and Mr. F. R. Whatmough, chief engineer at CSA, Mrs. and Mr. R. L. Labelle, Mrs. and Mr. C. T. Ball, and Mrs. and Mr. E. F. Cogan at the 1959 Canadian Section meeting.

Carson Morrison, past chairman of the CSA Certification Policy Board and active in CSA committee work since 1946, began his two-year term as president of the Canadian Standards Association at the 1973 annual meeting of the organization, held June 21, 1973, in Toronto.

Mr. Morrison sees the future for CSA as "significant and bright…In our two prime areas, standards and certification, I see nothing but increasing requirements and CSA growing to meet those requirements," he commented.

Morrison is chairman of the consulting engineering firm of Morrison, Hershfield, Burgess and Huggins, Limited, and editor of *Canadian Consulting Engineer*, a Southam Business publication. From 1954 to 1968 he was head of the Department of Civil Engineering at the University of Toronto.

CSA members elected new members to the board of directors: James A. Burgess, president, Waltec Industries Limited, Wallaceburg, Ontario, and Stuart F. Smith, vice president of manufacturing, Emco Limited, London, Ontario. Joseph L. de Stein, professor of civil engineering, McGill University, Montreal, has returned to the board after an absence of two years.

Re-elected to the board for a further term were: Walter C. Kimball, Alexander M. Matheson, Carson F. Morrison, William J. Pardy, Frederick P. Shand and John P. Watts.

Reprinted *IAEI News*, September 1973.

in the electrical industry, the inspection department has made many changes. Some of the more significant ones which come to mind are the translations of the Canadian Electrical Code—Part I into regulations having such form and intent as to enable them to be used in a court of law as an instrument for prosecution when necessary; the establishment of an Approvals Laboratory and subsequent regulations prohibiting the use, sale or display of unapproved electrical equipment; the implementation of revised inspection procedures designed to further develop the doctrine of electrical safety as a public service.

Recently, Hydro took a rather piercing look at inspection procedure. Very careful scrutiny resulted in changes in inspection activity designed to set an inspection fee schedule on a cost per call basis, segregate clerical duties from those of inspection, increase the standardization of paper work and co-ordinate policy with practice, thereby offering more efficient inspection service.

A brief look into some of the changes may be of interest to other inspectorates. In the revised system "inspection" calls are recorded in relation to various classifications of jobs (installations). The cost to make these calls is then compared with the current fees levied. Appropriate fee adjustments are then considered in an attempt to balance revenue with cost and financially "break even."

The present fee schedule is to be replaced by a new schedule incorporating several items under three main classifications: single family dwellings, apartments or multifamily dwellings and industrial and commercial establishments. A flat-rate fee is anticipated for single family dwellings, irrespective of the equipment and wiring installed. Apartment buildings are calculated on the number of suites and other types of installations (commercial and industrial) on the number of circuits involved.

Other changes include the introduction of a "certificate of inspection." Prior to the new system there was no recognized link between the consumer or people protected by the inspection function and the electrical inspection department. The user of electric energy did not know the inspection department had fulfilled its function until "connection was required."

When an installation now passes inspection, the new system automatically provides a necessary communication between the contractor, consumer and inspector by the issuance of the certificate. This is a definite step in positive identification activity in the eyes of a consumer. It should be realized that certificates are not intended to place a standard upon an installation other than that of the minimum requirements necessary for inspection. It is up to the conscientious contractor to install "adequacy" and further appealing aspects of his work for the ultimate benefit of the consumer.

Chris Bowden, manager, inspection service and Doug Boniface, resident inspector, Far East region for CSA, on the garage roof patio of Doug's residence on Grass Mountain, Taipei, Taiwan. Mr. Boniface was responsible for the factory inspection of CSA Certified products in Taiwan and also audited the inspection work of the various CSA inspection agencies operating in other parts of the far east.

CSA Founded 1919

CANADIAN STANDARDS ASSOCIATION

AFTER 84 YEARS

John E. Leeming, P. Eng., former manager of special projects, Standards Division, has been appointed director of certification, replacing John Kean, who became CSA's new managing director.

Mr. Leeming, a native of Toronto and a graduate of the University of Toronto, joined CSA in 1963 after many years with Canadian General Electric where he was manager of codes and approvals.

In 1970 he became assistant manager of the Certification Division. He was survey director for the Clinical Laboratory and Electro-Medical Equipment Study, which was undertaken by CSA for the Department of National Health and Welfare in the past years.

He is a member of the IAEI board of directors, the IEEE, and the Standards Engineers Society.

Reprinted from *IAEI News*, January 1975.

Within the new procedures, it is understood that the primary responsibility for maintaining a follow-up action as to when a job is "ready" is not part of an inspector's duty. This action is basically the electrical contractor's responsibility. If an inspector retains such a follow-up system, it could increase, unnecessarily, his activity and therefore increase inspection costs which ultimately increase inspection fees.

To eliminate this, contractors are expected to notify the inspector only when jobs are actually ready for inspection. Futuristic dates as to when a job may be ready are not accepted. Further, if a Notice of Deficiency is sent to a contractor informing him that his work is not according to inspection requirement, the inspection work is temporary curtailed until the contractor returns a signed copy of such notice, requesting continuance of inspection.

From this brief explanation, it may be seen that a systematic effort is being made to determine the problems of inspection and analyze them with the object of performing the basic duty of approving electrical wiring and equipment as economically and efficiently as possible.

In this respect, the system brings out more clearly the authority for the approval of installations as well as providing information that will pin-point major problems contributing to the better management of inspection work.

Approval and Certification

It is a well-known fact that the local field inspector and his department are not equipped to assess the suitability of equipment devices or components. This phase of work is in the hands of the Canadian Standards Association Testing Laboratories, a division of the Canadian Standards Association. The CSA Testing Laboratories certify (that the equipment meets the CSA standards) and the CSA Approvals Council (basically the Provincial Electrical Inspection Authorities) approve. This latter situation is accomplished by a 2/3 majority affirmative vote from the members of the council on each approval report.

In order to clear apparent misunderstandings in the terms approval and CSA certification, due no doubt to the semantics regarding such terms, the following may prove helpful.

CSA Certification

The Canadian Standards Association was incorporated by letters patent under the Dominion Companies act in 1919 with powers to co-ordinate the efforts of producers and users for the improvement and standardization of engineering materials, to prepare and promote the general adopt of standards in connection with engineering structures, materials and other matters, and from time to time to revise, alter and amend the same, to register and use its own trade marks, trade names or other distinctive marks applicable to construction or engineering materials, and to enter into any arrangement with any governmental municipal or other authority which may seem conductive to the association's objects, and to obtain from any such authority any rights, privileges and concessions which the association may deem necessary.

The association is a purely voluntary body, and consists of a main committee composed of members and universities in Canada, and sectional or working committees for promoting the association's objects.

Its sustaining members include the Hydro Electric Power Commission of Ontario as well as railway companies, electrical utilities, telephone companies, manufacturers and others interested in the objects of the association across Canada.

With the permission of the Canadian Standards Association, the following excerpt is taken from the *C.S.A. News Bulletin*:

CSA Certification

"CSA Certification is now divided into two categories:

1. CSA General Certification employing the use of Registered CSA Marks 'CSA STANDARD' and 'CSA STD.'

2. CSA Certification based on testing by the Laboratories and using the CSA Monogram.

In order to clearly outline the application of these services, a note will be inserted in the foreword of each of the CSA Standards where it is relevant. Such descriptions will differentiate between the certification which is required by government regulations and certification for which no government regulations exist. The following is an outline of the descriptions of CSA Certification Services for CSA Standards:

Descriptions of CSA Certification Service for CSA Standards

(1) All standards covering products for which no certification is required by government regulations, but which are eligible for general certification under the CSA registered marks 'CSA STANDARD' or 'CSA STD':

CSA Certification

A manufacturer, agent, or distributor wishing to use the registered CSA

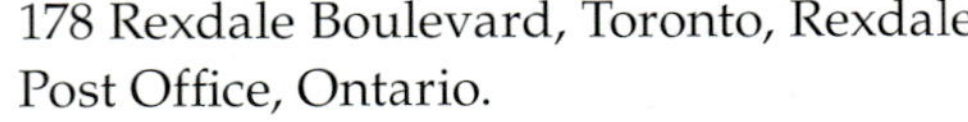

marks 'CSA STANDARD' or 'CSA STD' to certify that a product conforms to this CSA Standard, may do so under license issued by the association. The official marks have been registered and may not be used except by licensees.

For complete details, inquire directly to: The General Manager, Canadian Standards Association, 235 Montreal Road, Ottawa 2, Ontario.

(2) Standards covering products for which certification is required by government regulations and which are eligible for general certification under the registered certification marks 'CSA STANDARD' or 'CSA STD':

CSA Certification

The products covered by the CSA Standard are required by provincial, municipal, or other authority to bear certification that they comply with the requirements of the standard before they may be offered for sale to the public or placed in service.

CSA is prepared to license manufacturers or agents to use the registered certification marks 'CSA STANDARD' or 'CSA STD.' This certification is, in general, accepted by the government authorities having jurisdiction. The official marks have been registered and may not be used except by licensees.

For complete details, inquire directly to: The General Manager, Canadian Standards Association, 235 Montreal Road, Ottawa 2, Ontario.

(2) All standards covering products for which certification is required by government regulations and which are eligible for certification under the registered CSA Monogram.

CSA Certification

The requirements of this CSA Standard have been made mandatory by most provincial or municipal authorities in Canada, and these authorities demand that before products covered by this CSA Standard may be offered for sale or placed in service, representative samples shall have been investigated by a designated laboratory which shall certify that they meet the requirements of the standard.

The registered monogram mark, which is controlled by the CSA Testing Laboratories, is used to indicate this certification. The CSA certification marks 'CSA STANDARD' or 'CSA STD' are not acceptable for this purpose.

For complete details, inquire directly to: The Manager, CSA Testing Laboratories, 178 Rexdale Boulevard, Toronto, Rexdale Post Office, Ontario.

(4) Standards covering products for which no certification is required by government regulations, but which are tested and certified by the CSA Testing Laboratories at the request of interested parties.

CSA Certification

Although not required by government regulations, a laboratory certification of products covered by this CSA Standard is demanded by some interested parties. The CSA is prepared to investigate and certify such products under its registered Monogram service controlled by the CSA Testing Laboratory. The CSA certification marks 'CSA STANDARD' or 'CSA STD' are not acceptable for this purpose.

For complete details, inquire directly to: The Manager, CSA Testing Laboratories, 178 Rexdale Boulevard, Toronto, Rexdale Post Office, Ontario.

Approval

Despite the above explanation, the term approval in such phrases as "CSA Approvals Report" is often confusing. It results from the previous designation of the CSA Testing Laboratories as "CSA Approvals Division." When it was determined a few years ago that this authority should disassociate itself from The Hydro Electric Power Commission of Ontario, inspection authorities across Canada found it necessary to redefine the relative positions of the Canadian Standards Association and themselves.

It should be understood that the authority for approval is in the hands of provincial inspectorates, none of whom have the required testing facilities to perform the investigations concomitant with the powers vested in them.

In view of this the CSA Testing Laboratories has been designated as a recognized testing agency whose "certification" that equipment meets requirements is generally sufficient evidence of acceptability to warrant "approval," without further testing. In a nutshell, the CSA Testing Laboratories "certify" and the provincial inspection authorities "approve."

—Reprinted from *News-Bulletin*, November 1962.

Worldwide certification, testing and inspection services of the CSA play an important part in facilitating international trade to the benefit of both Canada and its trading partners. That was the message CSA Chairman John Brace left with delegates at CSA's week-long tri-annual international workshop September 21–28, 1985. CSA Tri-annual workshop delegates are shown on the front lawn of Rexdale office. Front row *left to right:* Ron Wilson; Jan Lavell, KEMA; Mike Nagata; M. L. Ho, HKSTC; Lo S. Nian, SISIR; John Kean; and Joe Gryn. Second row, *left to right*: Dudley Brown, BSI; Jack Leeming; Hiro Tsunoda, JMI; Alan Walker, SANZ; Serge Bousquet, Atlantic Region; Serge Comtois, Quebec Region and Tom St. John. Third and fourth rows, *mingled left to right*: John Bubany, observer; Merv Burt, SAA; Derek Sawyer, BSI; Pat Paladino; Phil Davies, BSI; Al Godfrey, Taiwan; Theo Stoop, KEMA; Peter Ridout, Pacific Region; Doug Boniface; Mo Polansky; Tom Higgins, Prairie Region; Chris Bowden and Albert Calo, Sil.

ICBO Founded 1922

INTERNATIONAL CONFERENCE OF BUILDING OFFICALS

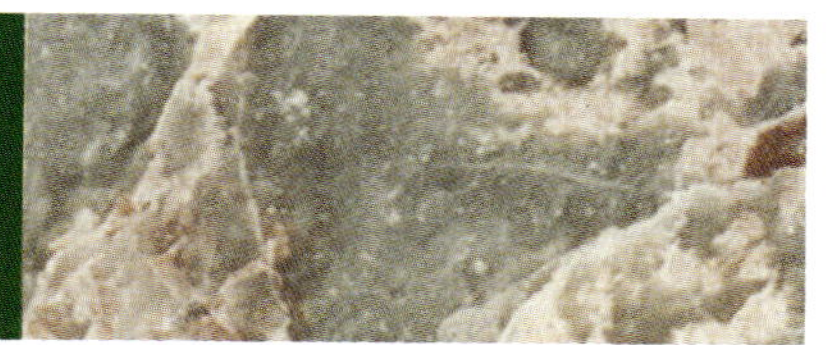

INTERNATIONAL CONFERENCE OF BUILDING OFFICIALS

Uniform Building Code

The ICBO was founded in 1922 on the west coast to discuss building code problems and to compile a uniform building code as minimum requirements for safe construction.

Its active voting membership consists of representatives of cities or counties. Currently it has over 750 members representing governmental agencies in 32 states and in addition to the voting members it has approximately 300 other classes of members from industry and related construction professions.

A principal activity is the development of the *Uniform Building Code* which is a model building code available for adoption by municipalities. This code is revised annually with revisions published in *Building Standards Monthly* and is republished in its entirety every three years. In addition the organization publishes a housing code, a sign code, a dangerous building code, a dwelling house construction pamphlet and a short form of the *Uniform Building Code*.

The conference maintains a technical staff who formulates recommendations on new materials, products and methods of construction; offers a plan-checking service, provides educational courses for building officials in cooperation with various universities and provides a forum through its meetings for discussions of building code and enforcement problems.

While the conference currently does not publish a model code containing electrical requirements its members in many cities are generally responsible for the enforcement of electrical requirements.

The organization plans in the near future to expand a certification program and include approvals for pre-fabricated construction which will encompass the total project in all phases, including electrical.

—Reprinted from *Electrical Safety Study*, NEMA, 1969.

The International Conference of Building Officials Board of Directors takes pleasure in announcing the appointment of **James S. Traw,** P.E., as president; he will assume this position on July 1, 1993. He will be replacing James E. Bihr, P.E., who will be retiring after thirty-three years of service to the conference.

As a member of the ICBO headquarters staff for over sixteen years, Mr. Traw served twelve years in the Codes and Engineering Department with the last five as vice president. When serving as director of ICBO's education and training activities, he was responsible for developing and implementing the conference's seminar and certification programs and training strategies, which still serve as the fundamental guide for conference program activities.

In his career at ICBO, Mr. Traw has been at the forefront of national and international codes and standards development through his involvement as ICBO representative to the Department of Commerce's Trade Barriers Mission to Taiwan and Korea; as United States codes and standards representative to the National Science Foundation Research Project on performance-based codes developments in Australia and the United Kingdom; and as team leader of the Quality Control in Building Construction lecture series for the Ministry of Construction, Peoples Republic of China.

—Reprinted from *IAEI News*, September 1993.

Joint ICBO/IAEI meeting of the Arizona Chapter, circa 1975. ***From left to right:*** **Alan Sleigh, Southwestern Section president; Joe Renesok, by-laws chairman, Arizona Chapter; Chuck Pierce, secretary/treasurer of the Southwestern Section; and Lloyd Nordhelm, third vice chairman of the Arizona Chapter.**

NATIONAL ELECTRICAL MANUFACTURERS ASSOCIATION

Representing the Manufacturers

The National Electrical Manufacturers Association is the principal trade association of the electrical manufacturing industry. It was organized in 1926 by a merger of three existing organizations, the oldest of which dates back to 1908. The membership comprises nearly 500 electrical manufacturing companies in the country. Membership is limited, by its constitution, to firms engaged in the manufacture, for sale in the open market, of products included within the scope of one or more of the nearly seventy product sections. These sections are organized into seven major divisions covering: building equipment, electronics, industrial equipment, insulating materials, lighting equipment, power equipment, wire and cable.

NEMA may, therefore, be considered an aggregate of these various product sections, each representing a group of manufacturers of certain classes of products. These scopes cover most of the kinds of equipment in the power field, such as generation, transmission, distribution and wiring materials, including most of the elements of the fixed wiring system in the home but not appliances, radio, television, home lighting.

Activities of the association include those typical of a trade association such as statistics, public relations, traffic, industrial relations, product promotion, international trade, research and standards and safety regulations. A recent analysis of association activities indicates that approximately two-thirds of NEMA's efforts are related to standards and safety.

NEMA has published over 200 separate standards publications, some of which are multiple standards running to over 300 pages, for electrical apparatus and equipment on the product within its scope.

Although NEMA issues many standards under its own name, a major portion of NEMA standardization activities are in cooperation with other organizations. Standards of interest to NEMA are developed in cooperation with other industries or other branches of the electrical industry through such agencies as the American Society for Testing and Materials, the Edison Electric Institute, the National Fire Protection Association, Underwriters' Laboratories, Inc., the Institute of Electrical and Electronics Engineers and other associations, laboratories or governmental bodies.

Many electrical standards originating within NEMA or initiated by other organizations are of such national significance as to make desirable their adoption as American National Standards under the procedures established by the American National Standards Institute. NEMA supports ANSI through participation in its standardizing activities. It has representation on more than one hundred of the standards committees organized under ANSI, and sponsors more than 20 of them, providing staff assistance for the completion of their work. NEMA, in addition, is represented on several ANSI standards boards and the Member Body Council.

In addition to product standards, NEMA is vitally concerned with and participates in the development of safety standards affecting electrical equipment. There are two principal codes dealing with electrical safety: the *National Electrical Code*, dealing with installations in and around buildings and the National Electrical Safety Code, sponsored by the National Bureau of Standards and dealing with power houses, substations, overhead and underground lines. NEMA, upon invitation, furnishes the military and other governmental standardizing bodies information and recommendations for use in the preparation of their drafts or revisions of various federal and military specifications affecting products within NEMA's scope.

Reprinted from *Electrical Safety Study*, NEMA, 1969.

Geo Pieper, Texas Instruments, and H. P. Mitchener, NEMA, at the Northwestern Section meeting, circa 1960.

Utilization, Distribution, and Supply Installations: NEMA

The National Electrical Manufacturers Association is an association of manufacturers of electrical products going into utilization, distribution and supply installations. It is divided along functional lines into divisions, each handling one group of products. These divisions are divided into sections, each of which is composed of manufacturers of a given type of electrical product. Generally a section comprises the manufacturers of most of the given product. A manufacturer of many types of products is usually a member of each of the sections concerned and sometimes is thus a member of several divisions. It is the aim of each section to support standards for its products which will afford them approval in every inspection jurisdiction, for their proper uses. Besides the original divisions and their sections, there have been added several new sections and some of these have been formed into new divisions, where their problems are similar to require very close coordination of effort. There has also been some rearrangement of divisions and sections, so that NEMA's forty-five sections are now grouped into ten divisions.

With the standardization and development programs of many of NEMA sections, the inspectors, individually and in association, are closely concerned since utilization installations are affected. And many NEMA sections have as one of their main problems the development of their respective products to meet the field needs called to their attention by inspectors and others. Just as the individual inspector finds it necessary to apply a code which governs all alike within his jurisdiction and finds it necessary when the code omits guidance to make a local ruling which governs all alike, so manufacturers find it necessary to follow a code which sets a minimum standard for their products and avoids the dangers and costs which attend products which have not been standardized in the code.

Where national codes are in effect and generally adopted by local inspection authorities, as are the N. E. Code and the various supplementary Underwriters' Laboratories codes under which they examine and list the various electrical products, manufacturers can secure the economy of mass production and be free from a competition from unsafe substandard products. The trend toward

Neither snow nor ice nor...kept circuit riders Bob Pullen, NEMA, and Norm Davis, UL, from their duties at the North Dakota Chapter, November 19, 1981, in Bismarck, North Dakota.

The National Electrical Manufacturers Association (NEMA) named **Dr. Malcolm E. O'Hagan** to succeed Bernard H. Falk as president in 1991. O'Hagan, former president of the Valve Manufacturers Association of America, in Washington, D. C., joined NEMA January 1, 1991, as president-elect and will be appointed president when Falk, who will be 65 in 1991, retires. Born in Ireland, O'Hagan earned B.S. and M. S. degrees in mechanical engineering at the National University of Ireland. He became a naturalized U.S. citizen and earned a Ph.D. in engineering at George Washington University. He was named president of the Valve Manufacturers Association of America in 1981. Prior to that he served as executive director of the U.S. Metric Board, president and chief executive officer of the American National Metric Council, and as a product manager for Bendix Corporation. NEMA Board of Governors Chairman H. John Riley, executive vice president of Operations, Cooper Industries, cited O'Hagan's strong and varied background as the major factor in selecting him for the position.

"He has a unique blend of experiences that really suit him for the post as NEMA president," said Riley. "Not only does he have a strong educational and technical background and the association management skills needed for such a complex organization as ours, but he also has worked in industry. My fellow board members and I are confident that under Dr. O'Hagan's leadership NEMA will continue to play a dominant role as the leading U.S. organization representing electroindustry manufacturers."

Reprinted from *IAEI News*, January 1991.

Joseph A. Ross, NEMA, discussing wiring methods at a Eastern Pennsylvania Chapter seminar, circa 1980.

local adoption of N. E. Code and of Underwriters' Laboratories Standards to govern sales as well as installation of electrical products, is a healthy one. Provisional approvals by local inspectors will still be necessary where products have not yet become thus standardized nationally. Where national codes have omitted necessary guidance and local rulings have been resorted to, mass production of standard safe products becomes difficult and sometimes impossible. NEMA sections are constantly striving to secure better and closer standardization of their products, of the kind which leaves the way open and easy for constant standardized improvements in safety, economy and convenience, but which guards effectively against substandard, low quality, unsafe products and against products which do not fit readily into the wiring installation as a whole. Where other national codes do not exist or are insufficiently developed, NEMA sections as one of their activities develop the necessary complete or supplementary national standards.

NEMA sections welcome and invite suggestions from inspectors for improvements in their products. Naturally it is hoped that through the more effective organization of the International Association of Electrical Inspectors, these suggestions will represent the experience and judgment of a consensus of inspectors so far as possible. Yet no NEMA section would desire to wait its improvements until some seriously unfortunate experience with its products had been repeated in most inspection jurisdictions. Therefore, it is hoped that serious experiences, particularly those which local inspection jurisdictions feel need to be the subject of a supplementary local rules, be called to the attention of the NEMA section concerned. Oftentimes several sections are concerned, as is the case when outlet boxes come under discussions.

Among NEMA sections, which have the closest relation to electrical inspection problems are those whose members manufacture the more highly repetitive and small products entering into wiring installations. For almost every section of N. E. Code, particularly Article 5 dealing with all types of wiring, there is a rather closely corresponding NEMA section. For N. E. Code, Article 7, three NEMA sections are concerned. For Articles 8, 10, and 50 rules on motors there is a NEMA section, and so on. Because several NEMA sections are often concerned with one code rule or local rule, it is desirable that suggestions for improvement and criticisms of performance pass through NEMA headquarters for proper assignment and follow up.

NEMA sections and its headquarters staff are truly at your service in our common effort to afford the public more and better service with the lowest practical over-all cost. Like yourselves, the utilities and others intimately concerned, the manufacturers understand that not only initial safety, but adequacy and durability under expected service conditions, ready and harmonious assembly with other standard products into the wiring installation, freedom from disturbance by mechanical and atmospheric causes—all combine to make for this lowest practicable over-all cost of electrical service. The cost of maintenance versus low first cost are important factors in the design and choice of appliances and wiring systems and unwise decisions when original installations are made may necessitate frequent repair and reinspection service which is always expensive to all concerned.

With the added opportunity of profiting by the field experience of your members and the practical viewpoint of your committees, NEMA feels confident that it can continue to serve you in a constantly better manner.

Reprinted from *News-Bulletin*, May 1929.

Mike Forister is an associate member of IAEI and NEMA field representative. Mike and the other three members of the field team provide a great support to IAEI sections, chapters and divisions in providing valuable information on the code, electrical products and related matters. The field representatives' experience as former inspectors provides a unique line of communications between inspectors and manufacturers.

ESIA Founded 1965 — After 38 Years

Electrical Safety Inspection Association

Electrical Safety Inspection Association

Striving For Safe Electricity in Japan

The Electrical Safety Inspection Association (ESIA) which was inaugurated under the provisions of the Electric Usage Safety Law, and under contract with the power companies concerned, inspects the condition of electric appliances (especially usage of electric power in ordinary households), and conducts safety work in connection with other larger individual utilizers of electric power (mostly industrial companies) while in the process of installing of electric appliances in buildings, maintenance and utilization of electric power and appliances equipment necessary for its use. In addition, ESIA strives, through education and consultations, for the safer, improved usage of electric power by individuals as well as companies. The objective of ESIA is to attain better public interest and attention in the overall safe utilization of electric power, and through the various means described above, attain the said aim and goal.

There are nine such associations throughout Japan. In all cases, each and every one of them has passed the fourth anniversary of its founding, this year. Each of the nine associations is located within the areas of the nine main power distribution companies, namely: Hokkaido, Tohoku, Kanto, Chubu, Hokuriku, Kainsai, Chugoku, Shikoku, and Kyushu ESIA.

Each association is operated individually and independently. The nine associations do consult each other on matters of mutual interest and do exchange information in the same area of interest. For the purposes of improving and enhancing the liaison with the concerned agencies of the Government of Japan, a nationwide liaison committee with necessary subcommittees to supplement its activities has been established. These nine ESIA, within their areas of operation and size, do have their comparative largeness or smallness in size, but, the nature of their administration and their business operations are in all cases identical.

The nature of this association is such that each member does not pay in dues for its operation. Each member of the association hires its own employees, pays salaries to them, and conducts the work of the association itself.

These associations have been created and legalized under the provisions of the Civic Law of Japan, and comes under the purview of the Japanese government insofar as its provisions of the Electric Business Law is concerned, and are duly recognized by the Government of Japan as an official body. The total number of employees of these nine associations, as of 1 April 1970, is approximately 4,000.

Operations pertaining to inspections

In 1965 the new Electric Business Law was promulgated in Japan. But, under the provisions of the old Electric Business Law, the responsibility of the usage of electric appliances within the ordinary utilizer was delegated to the power company providing the electric power. There was no supervision over the usage of such appliances by the ordinary utilizer, and certainly, the power company was not empowered to enter the premises of any of these privately owned properties. These circumstances, of course, were not conductive to the execution of its responsibilities in the proper manner, therefore, under the new law, such responsibilities insofar as pertained to the power company were discarded. The normal, ordinary utilizer of electric power, is, however, not too conversant with the usage of same, not having too much knowledge thereof. Therefore, the inspection at the time of installation of the appliances in the process of construction of building, and the inspection of such appliances in use every other year, was delegated to the power company concerned. Furthermore, it was necessary to ascertain if such appliances were fabricated under the specifications set forth by the Ministry of Industry and International Trade ordinance. And, if after such inspections, it was noted and recognized that technically the appliances or their usage did not meet such specifications, it became necessary for the inspecting party to report such deficiencies, as well as the consequences arising therefrom, if left in the same state of disrepair.

Therefore, as stated above, the responsibility delegated to the electric power company is thus redelegated to this association, which is a duly recognized body by the Government of Japan, under the provisions of its laws. The Electric Business Law specifically states that such work and responsibility will be delegated to ESIA. Therefore, under the provisions of the said law, ESIA is conducting the necessary inspections.

As stated above, the inspections are conducted when the electric appliances are first installed at the time of the construction of the building, and biannually thereafter, on a periodic basis. But, of these two areas of inspections, the first area is done by the power company and what is delegated to ESIA is the latter, or the bi-annual inspection. Throughout Japan there are approximately 35,000,000 households which require these periodic checkups. At the present time, ESIA has accepted the responsibility to inspect 70% of these households, and the remaining 30% is done by the power company. It is scheduled for ESIA to take over the responsibility for the remaining 30% in the near future. Through these periodic inspections, it has been detected that from 2% to 3% of them are reportable in the area of technical deficiencies in fabrication, and these reports have been duly filed.

Although ESIA inspectors may detect deficiencies they do not possess the jurisdiction to make necessary corrections or replacements to correct such deficiencies. This, of course, does not preclude the inspectors from performing such a simple task as replacing a fuse. Such corrective action to be taken is the responsibility of the utilizer of electric

power, and such parties will delegate the corrective action to be taken to a properly designated electric repair or construction company.

The same inspectors can only file a report, as stated above, subjectively. They cannot order the replacement to take place. Such an order for corrective action can only be issued by the Minister of International Trade and Industry.

Administration of preservation of safety in small amount utilizers of electric power

According to the provisions of the Electric Business Law, all parties who use electric power for their own usage (such as factories) will, unless special approval has been received, at all times hire an electrical supervisory engineer who will have in his possession a license issued by the Minister of International Trade and Industry. This engineer will function as the custodian of safety in the use of electric power by such a party. But utilizers of less than 300 kilowatts have an agreement with ESIA to have the inspectors from ESIA inspect their facilities more than once a month. If approved by the Minister of International Trade and Industry such utilizers need not hire such as electrical supervisory engineer.

It is a prerequisite for the inspectors of ESIA to be the possessors of the third class license for electrical supervisory engineers. There are three classes in this license, namely first, second and third class licenses for this type of engineer. According to the power pressure, and how large the utilizers are, it specifies the type of license that is necessary. Third class is of the minimum requirements. There are approximately 70,000 such contracts entered into by ESIA with utilizers throughout Japan. This is the equivalent to about half the number of small scale utilizers of electric power, less than 300 kilowatts. These inspectors, 95 in the case of the others enumerated above, cannot do any repair or replacement work, except such simple tasks as replacing a fuse. Here again, the electric power utilizer will delegate such repair or replacement work to an authorized electric company to do the necessary corrective work.

And, the inspectors cannot order such replacement or repair work to be done. The authority for the issuance of such a directive is vested only with the Minister for International Trade and Industry. At the current time, when there is a scarcity of electrical engineers, the existence of ESIA is a boon for the electric power users. The situation at this present time is that these small scale utilizers of electric power are filing applications with ESIA to contract for their inspection services.

Public information activities

As long as the ESIA is a public organization, it behooves them to conduct such activities as will keep the public informed on the proper usage of electric power. This area of operation is possible while conducting the other activities and operations of ESIA as outlined above. Monthly, ESIA issues pamphlets on the correct use of electricity which are distributed to the utilizers, free of any charge. Monthly, informational services are also given in the orientation of the public as to the proper usage of electric power. Posters are also distributed widely disseminating information on the same subject.

Conclusion

Largely, the ESIA inspectors operate on a single basis when conducting their inspections. Therefore, the ESIA when hiring these inspectors, endeavors to employ only those qualified technically and on a human relationship basis. Daily, ESIA places stress on the education of its staff in relations between human beings, and the technical aspects of their job. Safety, in all areas of daily living, as far as the human is concerned, is of the utmost importance. But, especially in the area of usage of electric power, ESIA is striving its best at all times to improve its usage in a safe manner. To attain this aim and goal, we, of the association, are endeavoring our utmost to conduct further studies in the technical aspects of equipment, and usage of electric power itself. We hope to receive the continued support and guidance from all quarters concerned.

Waichi Nakajima, director, Executive Office, All Japan Liaison Committee of the Electrical Safety Inspection Association. Excerpted from speech given at the annual meeting of the Japan Chapter, IAEI, in May 1970. Reprinted from *IAEI News*, March 1971.

Original Class "C" and "D" Cooperating Members

In 1930, cooperating members consisted of organizations or firms interested in promoting the objectives of the association. These firms could have a representive in each section, or be confined to a local territory.

Alabama Power Company,
Birmingham, Alabama.
American Circular Loom Company,
90 West St., New York, New York
American District Telegraph Company,
155 Sixth Avenue, New York, New York
Anaconda Wire & Cable Company,
Pawtucket, Rhode Island
Appleton Electric Company,
1713 Wellington Avenue, Chicago, Illinois
Arrow-Hart & Hegeman Electric Co.
103 Hawthorne Street, Hartford, Connecticut
Association of Electragists Int'l.
420 Lexington Avenue, New York, New York
Autocall Company,
Shelby, Ohio
Banash, J. I.,
176 W. Adams Street, Chicago, Illinois
Birmingham Electric Company,
2100 First Avenue, Birmingham, Alabama
Board of Fire Underwriters of Allegheny
County, Commonwealth Building, Pittsburgh, Pennsylvania
Board of Fire Underwriters of the Pacific, Merchants Exchange Building, San Francisco, California
Bryant Electric Company,
Bridgeport, Connecticut
Bulldog Electric Products Company,
7610 Jos. Campau Avenue, Detroit, Michigan
Bureau of Power and Light,
Department of Water and Power, Los Angeles, California
Caldwell & Company, Incorporated,
Edw. F., 38 West 15th Street, New York, New York
Central Illinois Public Service Co.
217 N. Ninth Street, Springfield, Illinois
Century Electric Company,
1806 Pine Street, St. Louis, Missouri
Cleveland Electric Illuminating Co.

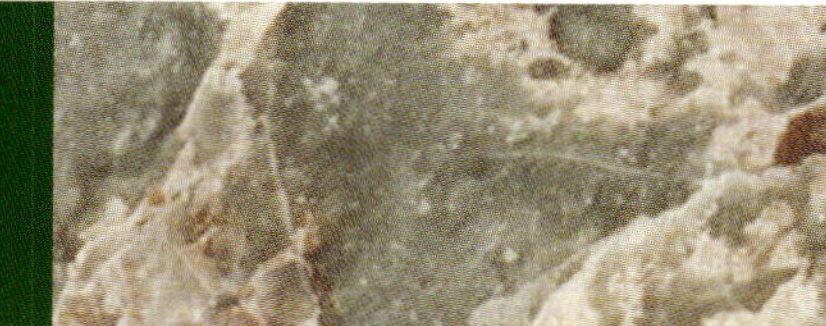

Illuminating Building, Cleveland, Ohio
Colt's Patent Fire Arms Manufacturing Company, Hartford, Connecticut
Columbia Cable & Electric Co. Thompson Avenue, Long Island city, New York
Columbia Metal Box Company, 226 E. 144th Street, New York, New York
Copperweld Steel Company, Glassport, Pennsylvania
Crescent Armored Wire Company, Trenton, New Jersey
Crouse-Hinds Company, Syracuse, New York
Cutler-Hammer, Incorporated, 12th & St. Paul Avenue, Milwaukee, Wisconsin
Eastern Tube & Tool Company, 594 Johnson Avenue, Brooklyn, New York
Economy Fuse & Manufacturing Co. 2717 Greenview Avenue, Chicago, Illinois
Edison Electric Illuminating Co. 39 Boylston Street, Boston, Massachusetts
Erie Malleable Iron Company, 20 N. Wacker Drive, Chicago, Illinois
Erikson Electric Company, 6 Power House Street, Boston, Massachusetts
Frank Adam Electric Company, 3650 Windsor Place, St. Louis, Missouri
General Electric Company, 1 River Road, Schenectady, New York
General Electric Vapor Lamp Co., 410–8th Street, Hoboken, New Jersey
General Inspection Bureau, 1229 Plymouth Building, Minneapolis, Minnesota
Georgia Power Company, Electric & Gas Building, Atlanta, Georgia
Graybar Electric Company, 420 Lexington Avenue, New York, New York
Harvey Hubbell, Incorporated, Bridgeport, Connecticut
Howell Electric Motors Company, Howell, Michigan
Illinois Inspection Bureau, 108 E. Ohio Street, Chicago, Illinois
Illinois Power & Light Corporation, 231 S. LaSalle Street, Chicago, Illinois
Indiana Inspection Bureau, 320 N. Meridian Street, Indianapolis, Indiana
Indiana Rubber & Insulated Wire Co., Jonesboro, Indiana
Indiana Service Corporation, 122 E. Wayne Street, Fort Wayne, Indiana
Iowa Insurance Service Bureau, 431 Insurance Exchange, Des Moines, Iowa
I-T-E Circuit Breaker Company, 19th & Hamilton Streets, Philadelphia, Pennsylvania
Jefferson Electric Company, 1500 S. Laflin Street, Chicago, Illinois
Kansas City Power & Light Company, Kansas City, Missouri
Kansas Inspection Bureau, 701 Jackson Street, Topeka, Kansas
Kentucky Actuarial Bureau, 940 Starks Building, Louisville, Kentucky
Kentucky Utilities Company, 455 S. Fourth Street, Louisville, Kentucky
Kerite Insulated Wire & Cable Company, 30 Church Street, New York, New York
Louisiana Rating & Fire Prevention Bureau, 606 Canal Bank Building, New Orleans, Louisiana
Metal Ware Corporation, 1710 Monroe Street, Two Rivers, Wisconsin
Michigan Inspection Bureau, 1200 Cadillac Square Building, Detroit, Michigan
Milwaukee Electric Railway & Light Company, Public Service Building, Milwaukee, Wisconsin
Missouri Inspection Bureau, 1330 Pierce Building, St. Louis, Missouri
Monitor Controller Company, 500 E. Lombard Street, Baltimore, Maryland
Mountain States Inspection Bureau, 801 Gas & Electric Building, Denver, Colorado
National Board of Fire Underwriters, 85 John Street, New York, New York
National Electric Light Association, 420 Lexington Avenue, New York, New York
National Electric Products Company, 1110 Fulton Building, Pittsburgh, Pennsylvania
New Era Electric Manufacturing Co., 6725 Machinery Avenue, N.E. Cleveland, Ohio
Northern States Power Company, Minneapolis, Minnesota
Oklahoma Gas & Electric Company, Oklahoma City, Oklahoma
Otis Elevator Company, 260 Eleventh Avenue, New York, New York
Pass & Seymour, Incorporated, Solvay Station, Syracuse, New York
Plainville Electrical Products Company, Box M, Plainville, Connecticut
Public Service Company of Colorado, Denver, Colorado
Public Service Company of No. Ill. 72 W. Adams Street, Chicago, Illinois
RCA Victor Company, Incorporated, 233 Broadway, New York
Ralco Manufacturing Company, 125 N. Albany Avenue, Chicago, Illinois
Rockbestos Products Corporation, New Haven, Connecticut
Rome Wire Company, Rome, New York
Russell & Stoll Company, 53 Rose Street, New York, New York
San Joaquin Light & Power Corporation, Fresno, California
Southeastern Underwriters Assn. P. O. Box 1743, Atlanta, Georgia
Square D Company, 6060 Rivard Avenue, Detroit, Michigan
Steel & Tubes, Incorporated, 224 East 131st Street, Cleveland, Ohio
Tennessee Inspection Bureau, 1032 Stahlman Building, Nashville, Tennessee
Toledo Edison Company, Jefferson Avenue and Superior Street, Toledo, Ohio
Triangle Conduit Company, Inc., Dry Harbor Road and Cooper Avenue, Brooklyn, New York
Trumbull Electric Manufacturing Co. Plainville, Connecticut
Underwriters' Laboratories, Inc. 207 E. Ohio Street, Chicago, Illinois
Union, The, (Western Insurance), 175 W. Jackson Boulevard, Chicago, Illinois
Wadsworth Electric Manufacturing Co. Covington, Kentucky
Wagner Electric Corporation, 6400 Plymouth Avenue, St. Louis, Missouri
Washington Surveying & Rating Bureau, 1100 Alaska Building, Seattle, Washington
Westinghouse Electric Manufacturing Co. 150 Broadway, New York, New York
Wiremold Company, The, 83 Woodbine Street, Hartford, Connecticut
Wisconsin Inspection Bureau, 490 Broadway, Milwaukee, Wisconsin

—Reprinted from *Year Book Directory*, IAEI, 1930.

Business Evolution

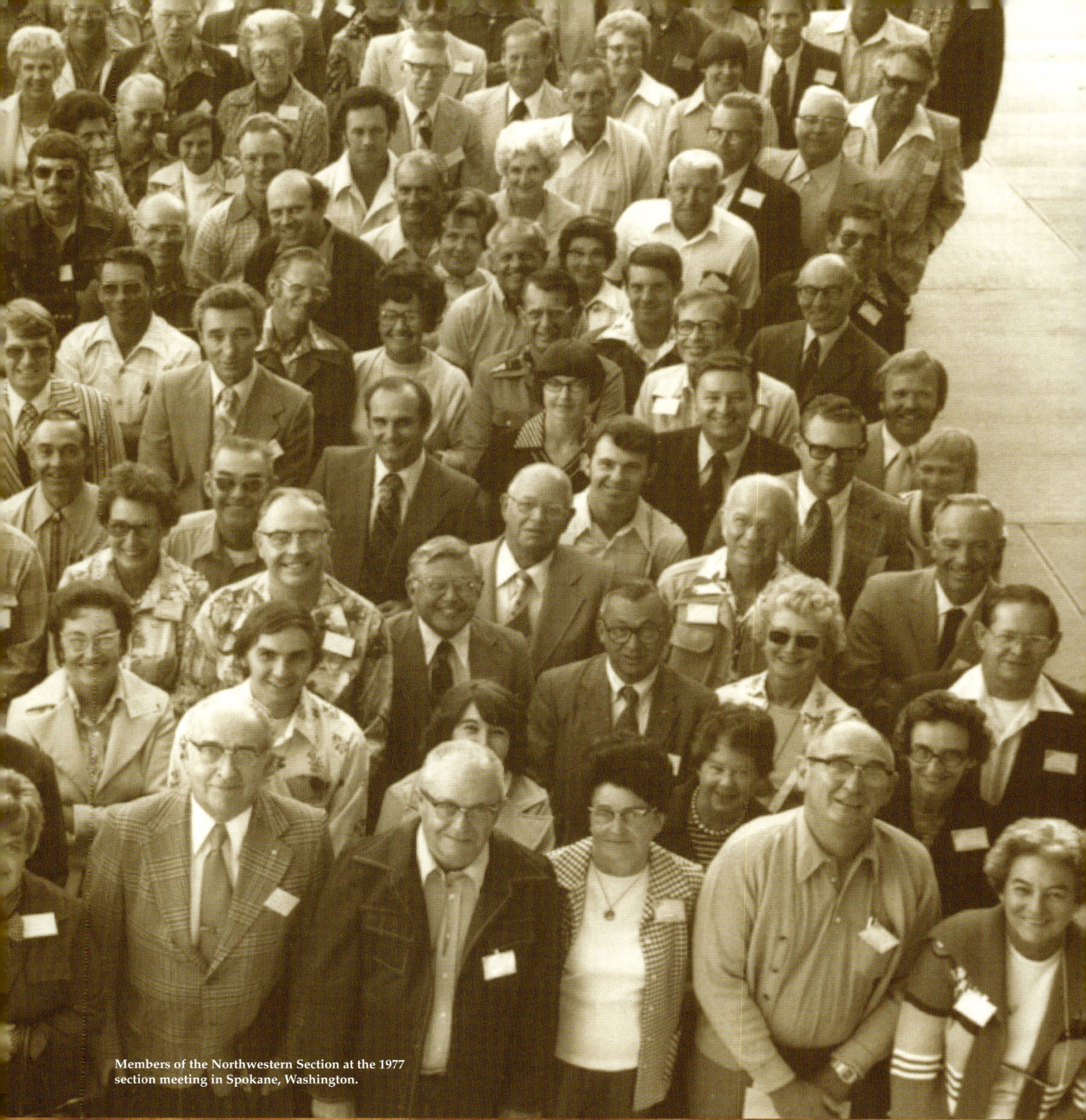

Members of the Northwestern Section at the 1977 section meeting in Spokane, Washington.

That mission has always been about safety. As the mission has expanded, the character of the association has grown from that of a brotherhood to one of a serious business environment. Through that growth has emerged three streams: service, publishing, and education. Each stream is focused on helping the inspectors and associates fulfill the mission in the quickest, most effective way possible.

1964-1969

Flower Power

As the 70 million children from the post-war baby boom became teenagers and young adults, the movement away from the conservative 1950s continued and eventually resulted in revolutionary ways of thinking and real change in the cultural fabric of American life. Rebellion became the key word of the decade, against everything: authority and the revolt against authority, sexual liberty and its threat to the order of things, assertions of rights by members of despised groups, followed by counters from everyone else—these are old themes in American life, as moral upheavals during this decade found fervent reverberations around the globe, thanks in part to the media spotlight. Individual choice was enshrined, and who knew what might start the world over again? In the slogan of the women's movement, the personal was felt to be political.

The Electrical Inspector

The word "image" has many shades of meaning, ranging from a low of "effigy" to a high of "idol"; we hope that all concerned will realize that in this article an impression in the better sense is intended to be conveyed to the reader.

In the past, the public's "inspector-image" has left something to be desired. This attitude on the part of contractors, supply and other authorities, and the public, is quite understandable, when one recalls some of the "salty" old inspectors, most of whom are now, (fortunately), no longer with us.

The inspector-image created by some of these old-timers was that of a policeman with a big stick; and how some of them swung that stick! In many cases there was no velvet glove encasing the iron hand. The inspector of those days had plenty of detractors and very few supporters, because he usually failed to inform the public that he was operating for their benefit and protection.

All they could see was an "ogre," whose defect notices flew in all directions like the autumn leaves, and who always required the impossible, even if he had to "split hairs" in an attempt to justify his demands.

This condition, however, was not altogether the inspector's fault, because the public attitude towards inspectors of all kinds and types was that the inspector's only purpose in life was to make trouble for them, and to cause them unnecessary expense. The old concept of the police officer as a "big bad wolf" is a good example of the public image of all law and regulation officials in the past.

A much happier state of affairs exists nowadays, however, as the direct result of efforts on the part of our electrical inspectors. Our modern electrical inspector can be truly represented to the public as a friend, a counselor and adviser who is trying to keep people *out of trouble.*

He helps them to avoid needless expense in their actual wiring installations, by aiding in fire prevention, to obtain better value for the money which

The summer meeting of the Western New York Chapter was held at the Hotel Jamestown in Jamestown, New York. A talk by Norman Johnson, district manager of Bryant Electric Company, on service equipment, highlighted the opening of the meeting. The mayor of Jamestown, Frederick Dunn (*far left*), extended greetings and the hospitality of the city. With him are Robert E. Rindell, chief inspector, Buffalo and Western New York; John W. Schlehr, secretary-treasurer; Walter Cole and Inspector William Pihl (*at blackboard*) who handled the arrangements.

1964 International President

R. E. Ward did electrical work prior to finishing high school—doing house wiring for an uncle who was a building contractor. He worked as farmer, electrician and plumber, owning and operating the business, for some few years prior to being appointed electrical inspector for the Tennessee State Department of Insurance and Banking in 1938. His first assignment as a deputy electrical inspector was under the supervision of the deputy fire marshall. In 1940 he was appointed the first chief electrical inspector for the department, and continues to hold that position. Tennessee has statewide inspection service, with 48 deputy inspectors under Mr. Ward's supervision. In 1949 Mr. Ward took a leading part in organizing Tennessee Chapter of the IAEI, served as its first chairman, and for the past several years has served as secretary-treasurer.

He is a past president of the Southern Section; in 1953 was elected to the executive committee of the section as chairman, and continues to serve as chairman, having been re-elected in 1963; member of code-making panel 5; chairman of the electrical subcommittee NFPA 501A and 501B, and has represented the IAEI on various other NFPA and ASA committees, as well as serving on many IAEI committees.

Mr. Ward is also a member of Underwriters' Laboratories Electrical Council; consulting editor *for Electrical Construction and Maintenance*, a McGraw-Hill publication; and has been a contributing editor to the *News-Bulletin*, and *The Tennessee Magazine.*

Reprinted from *News-Bulletin*, January 1964.

they do spend for electrical service, by assisting in planning their wiring layouts, and to obtain proper equipment. Thus, both efficiency and convenience are more readily obtained.

While the inspector's primary reason for existence is still the enforcement of regulations, a new attitude obtains today, in that the iron hand is encased in the proverbial velvet glove. This does not imply or necessitate any relaxation of enforcement, but does facilitate much better understanding while still maintaining the desired standards of materials, wiring methods, and workmanship.

An explanation of the "whys and wherefores" of the regulations does much to prevent friction which might otherwise arise in enforcing the "law." People who understand the reasoning behind inspection requirements are more likely to be cooperative, and will be in a more receptive mood than if they felt that a certain procedure was only an inspector's or a code committee's "notion," unsupported by reason.

The contractor and customer should be informed, firmly and clearly, but diplomatically, that, after all, the entire inspection procedure is for their benefit and protection. The need today, and it is, we are happy to say, being partially satisfied, is for better understanding between electrical inspection staffs and the people with whom they deal.

It should be possible to speak of your "friendly" electrical inspector. A good friend can still submit constructive criticisms and suggestions. Fortunately, recalcitrant contractors and customers are in the minority, and these "culprits" can be dealt with as required by the current circumstances.

An intensification and extension of the present "good-will" policy can eradicate remaining objectionable attitudes on the part of the public and will result in more consultation with inspection authorities prior to the installation of jobs which otherwise might have to be rejected. This, in turn, removes the annoyance of defect issuance procedure.

A service to the customer which is often omitted due to pressure of work is a general inspection of the customer's wiring and equipment. This need not be a lengthy, or arduous procedure, because even when inspecting a small job such as a stove or dryer installation, it is necessary to check at the source of supply, i.e., the service entrance and distribution panel.

While at this point, why not give a quick check of the service entrance switch, main ground wire, and branch circuit fuses. If oversize fuses are found, or any other simple fault, two or three minutes spent in explaining the situation to the customer would be well spent.

It may not only clear up a fire and personnel hazard, but will show the customer that the inspector is interested in his welfare. At the same time, a glance at the basement wiring may reveal unsafe conditions, such things as cords run out through basement windows in lieu of proper outdoor weather outlets.

Even an adequate inspection of a minor new installation takes only a short time, and some customers may feel that they aren't getting much for their money, if the inspector rushes through the job and doesn't give the customer "that little extra."

It has been said "I don't know why we pay inspection fees – that inspector didn't do much for the money." A little more time, a little more trouble, a little more explanation of inspection benefits to the customer, can remove most, if not all, of the objections which the customer may have to inspection staff and procedures.

Now that we, as inspectors, have embarked upon a program of understanding and co-operation, let's all expend that extra little bit of effort which will convince the contractors, supply authorities, and the general public, that their electrical inspector is prepared and happy to act as guide, counselor and adviser and will if they will only permit him, be their best friend in all matters electrical.

By A. S. Prior, Matheson, Ontario. Reprinted from *News-Bulletin*, March 1964.

Eustace C. Soares

Eustace C. Soares, P.E., author, teacher and technical advisor of electrical engineering, and an international honorary member of IAEI, died March 4, 1976. He had been a long-time member of the Eastern Section of IAEI.

Mr. Soares was awarded many honors in his field. In 1963 he was presented a certificate of appreciation from the National Electrical Contractors Association as a *National Electrical Code* conference leader. In 1968 the Brooklyn Engineers Club awarded him the citation of "Engineer of the Year" for meritorious services to the engineering profession and to the club. His U. S. Letters patent, covering a protective circuit used for clearing ground faults, licenses many electrical manufacturers to apply the patented circuit to their equipment.

In 1969 Mr. Soares served as a technical advisor on an *ad hoc* committee of President Nixon's Commission on Product Safety.

Over the years he contributed many technical articles, mainly on grounding, to magazines including the *IAEI News*, *Electrical Construction & Maintenance*, *Specifying Engineer, Consulting Engineer* and *Electrical Construction Design*. He is the author of the book, *Grounding Electrical Distributions Systems for Safety*, published in 1966. The book can be purchased through IAEI.

Born in England, Mr. Soares attended Cambridge University Junior, then came to the United States and completed his electrical engineering education at Cooper Union, New York, and the American School of Correspondence.

He is survived by his wife, Marie.

—Reprinted from *IAEI News*, May 1976.

Western Section Timeline

1964 A secretary is finally named for the newly-created **Oklahoma-Arkansas Chapter**.

1970 International executive board members approve the creation of the Missouri-Kansas Chapter, **Kansas City Division**.

1971 Illinois Chapter creates the **Chicago Division**.

After the dissolution of the Oklahoma-Arkansas Chapter, the **Arkansas Chapter** charter is approved by International board members in November 1971.

Oklahoma Chapter, **Greater Tulsa Division**, is approved by the International board.

International board approves the formation of the Ohio Chapter, **Western Reserve Division**.

1976 Bylaws of the Ohio Chapter, **Southwest Division**, are approved by the board.

1979 **Western Section holds its 75th Diamond Jubilee** on September 24–26, 1979 in Oklahoma City, Oklahoma.

1981 Board approves the creation of the Ohio Chapter, **Central Ohio Division**.

Rocky Mountain Chapter, created in 1931, celebrates its 50th anniversary with the creation of the **Wyoming Division**.

1983 Chicago Division of the Illinois Chapter (formed 1971) changes its name to the **William P. Hogan-Chicago Division**.

1985 **Oklahoma Chapter** becomes part of the Southern Section.

Ben L. Auger, of Huntington Woods, MI, is elected Western Section secretary.

International board approves the creation of the short-lived Illinois Chapter, **Blackhawk Division.**

1986 **Northwest Division** of the Ohio Chapter is formed.

International board of directors approves the official creation of the **Northwest Indiana Division** of the Indiana Chapter.

1989 **Edward C. Lawry**, from Madison, Wisconsin, becomes the Western Section secretary.

1990 Illinois Chapter welcomes its latest division, the **South Suburban Division**.

The charter of the newly-created **Kansas-Sunflower Chapter** is approved.

1993 Illinois Chapter, **Blackhawk Division** is officially disbanded.

1994 **Northwest Division** of the Illinois Chapter is created.

Coletta Hogan and family shown at the Illinois Chapter meeting receiving a wall certificate in honor of her departed husband, William P. Hogan. At this meeting in 1984, it was announced that the Chicago Division has been renamed the William P. Hogan-Chicago Division.

1965 International President

F. R. Whatmough joined the Western Section in 1947, and became chairman of the Ontario Chapter in 1950. After the forming of the Canadian Section, he served as president in 1959. Always active in IAEI affairs, he served on various committees and was author of technical papers at intervals.

Born in Stratford, Ontario, where he received his primary and secondary education, he graduated in electrical engineering from the University of Toronto in 1925 with the degree of B.A.Sc. He spent the following two years on test and design courses of the Canadian General Electric Company in Toronto and Peterborough, with particular reference to transformers and industrial controls. For one year he acted as instructor in electrical engineering at the University of Toronto.

In 1928 he joined the research laboratories of the Hydro-Electric Power Commission of Ontario where he was engaged in testing, examining and compiling technical reports relating to the safe operation of domestic and industrial electric equipment. With the transfer of this type of engineering from Ontario Hydro to the Canadian Standards Association in 1950, Russ became chief engineer with responsibility for engineering and standards.

Since 1938 he has been active on numerous CSA committees, compiling the Canadian Electrical Codes, Parts I, II, IV, V and VI. Since 1950 he has served as chairman of the CSA committees on codes, Parts II and VI.

He is secretary of the IEEE committee dealing with safety of electric equipment; member of the Standards Engineering Society of America, Toronto-Hamilton Chapter; member of the Ontario Professional Engineers Association; member NFPA and the American Society for Testing Materials; liaison member of ASA Sectional Committees C73 and C97; as well as a member of the Engineer's Club and the Electrical Club both of Toronto; a graduate life member of Hart House of the University of Toronto.

Reprinted from *News-Bulletin*, January 1965.

TEN THOUSAND PLUS!

IAEI membership passed the 10,000 mark in July 1965. Like a milestone, this goal has been in sight for sometime. Last January, our growth chart indicated that the 10,000 mark would be reached between May and August.

Climbing over the 10,000 figure didn't happen as a matter of course and time. This point was reached through the efforts of every member who brought in a new member this year – and in prior years.

Special credits go to Mr. L. E. Peterson, general membership chairman. Also, to his committee and all the membership committees in the sections and chapters.

The New York Chapter played the biggest part in this effort. Their record of 228 new members this year represented more than 50 percent of the total needed to pass the 10,000 mark. A special "Thank You" goes to such hard working people.

With but few exceptions, all chapters contributed new members to help reach the new mark. They, too, are commended for their effort.

The New Mexico Chapter contributed in an unusual way. They did this by having no delinquents or cancellations for 1965. "Let's keep what we have and see what we can get" is perhaps their motto. Whatever their motto is — their example paid off and could be copied by others as a benefit to the association.

Attrition (drop-outs) has been a depressing factor in our growth rate for many years. Overcoming this problem isn't easy since it takes a personal follow-up by an endorser, the membership committee or a secretary when a delinquent notice appears on a member. Apparently, the New Mexico Chapter has a method of accomplishing this.

The International office, in 1964, established an "endorser identification" system for new members. This means that in following years the International office can provide chapters and sections with the name of the member who endorsed a new member listed as delinquent. So Bill Smith (endorser) can be informed that John Jones (his new member in a prior year) hasn't paid his dues. This is where Bill Smith applies his personal touch and thus keeps John Jones as a member. This system should help all chapters to reduce their delinquent list.

Reaching the 10,000 mark doesn't mean membership recruitment should be relaxed. Now let's go for 11,000.

IAEI has always offered much and asked for little from its members. Our services to members, to the industry and to the public are much too extensive to enumerate here. Our services and accomplishments are selling points in approaching a prospective member. Now, we have added a new and important feature, "anniversary membership."

A new member coming into membership in July isn't cut off in January (billed for another year's dues) as was done heretofore. Every new member now receives a full year of membership for his dues. July to July of next year, May to May, etc.

This system is eminently fair to the new member even though the mechanics involved (in the next few years) create operational problems in the International office.

The mechanical operations needed to keep old and solicit new members have been established.

The job left for you is to get that new member.

Reprinted from *News-Bulletin*, September 1965.

1966 International President

John W. Hager, borough superintendent, Department of Water Supply, Gas and Electricity, city of New York, pursued individual courses in advanced mathematics, physics, electricity, electronics, and electrical engineering, while attending Mechanics Institute, RCA Institute, and New York University.

After having served with the United Electric Light and Power Company, the Western Electric Company, the New York Central Railroad, and the electrical industry, he was appointed in 1923, after competitive examination, to the position of electrical inspector, city of New York. He served on the code interpretation and revision committee of his department since its inception in the early 30s and until 1958.

In 1945 he was designated assistant chief inspector, borough of Manhattan, and in 1954 advanced to the position of assistant supervising chief inspector of code inspection citywide. At that time he was made secretary of the advisory board which examines and recommends for approval electrical materials and devices for use in the city of New York. In 1958 he succeeded to his present position as borough superintendent.

In 1928, he became a member of the New York Chapter, and did much to promote and build its membership. He has held various chapter offices including secretary-treasurer, and served as chairman in 1934, 1936 and 1945. He is past president, a past secretary-treasurer of the Eastern Section and served on the IAEI executive council (now board of directors), since 1944.

Mr. Hager is a veteran of World War I, having served with the 12th N.Y. Infantry and the 107th U.S. Infantry, and is past commander of American Legion Post 1008, Department of Water Supply, Gas and Electricity, city of New York.

—Excerpted from *News-Bulletin*, January 1966.

C. B. Wolfe

C. B. Wolfe (Mrs.) by unanimous vote of the board of directors was elected international secretary-treasurer of IAEI at the opening session of the board meeting on November 9, 1966.

Mrs. Wolfe, "Ceil" to IAEI and the electrical family, becomes IAEI's 5th international secretary-treasurer and the first woman to hold this office. Ceil is an associate member of IAEI and has been a staff employee in the International office for over fifteen years. She has worked in the international office under three administrations: Charles L. Smith, Everett F. Cogan, and L. E. LaFehr. From 1958 through mid-1962 she was secretary to Frank Stetka, NFPA's electrical field engineer who occupied space in IAEI's offices and was furnished secretarial services.

Ceil has advanced from office secretary to administrative assistant in IAEI employment. Under IAEI's managing director she is in charge of the internal affairs of the International office.

As secretary-treasurer, she receives no pay. Her paid job is as administrative assistant. Major changes in the articles of association and the addition of bylaws in 1964 changed IAEI's international secretary-treasurer office from an administrative to a functional responsibility.

Among those who know, Ceil is recognized as one of the very few women in the USA with a complete structural knowledge of the *National Electrical Code*. From the beginning of her employment by IAEI she has been dedicated to the objectives of the association, devoted to its members and serves with a degree of efficiency and integrity far beyond the ordinary. IAEI owes much of what it is today to Ceil. Behind the scenes, so to speak, she has virtually been our secretary-treasurer, without portfolio, for many years.

Ceil's election and recognition as secretary-treasurer is a classic example of calling a "spade a spade."

Note: In IAEI's structure the office of international secretary-treasurer is not a chain-of-command or a line office. The international secretary-treasurer is not a member of the board of directors and has no vote in that body.

Reprinted from *IAEI News*, January 1967.

Quick Fact

After due consideration, your officers and directors are pleased to announce a special low cost group insurance program for eligible members.

There is available a program designed to pay you an income up to $500 per month when you are unable to work because of sickness or an accident. Benefits can begin immediately or be "tailor-made" to increase and extend "sick leave," or any other type of group coverage you may have. In addition, a convertible term life insurance policy is available to supplement and strengthen your life insurance estate at very low cost.

You will be hearing more about the program by mail and in the *IAEI News*. A letter is being sent to you with a self-addressed, stamped card to provide immediate local insurance service at your option.

The success of this program depends upon membership participation, and we urge you to look into this coverage, as there are many benefits for you and your dependents.

—Reprinted from *IAEI News*, March 1967.

Central California Chapter booth has content for wiring violations thus evoking electrical safety interest among contractors, designers and manufacturers. The booth displays 50 years of *NEC* progress. Code books dating back 50 years are shown.

Southwestern Section Timeline

1966 Southern California Chapter, **Los Angeles Metropolitan Division** (later changed to Greater Los Angeles Division in 1973) is formed.

1967 **Southern Nevada Division** of the Nevada Chapter is created.

1972 **Los Angeles County Division** becomes the Los Angeles Division.

1976 Executive board of directors grants the charter of the **Border County Division** of the Southern California Chapter.

1977 **Pima Division** of the Arizona Chapter receives its charter from the executive board.

1985 **Orange Empire Division** of the Southern California Chapter is formed.

1986 **Northern Nevada Chapter** and **Southern Nevada Chapters** are formed.

Robert Milatovich, from Clovis, California, is elected Southwestern Section secretary.

1987 Executive board of directors approves the split of the Arizona Chapter into two chapters—the **Central Arizona Chapter** and the **Southern Arizona Chapter.**

1989 **Northern Arizona Chapter** is formed.

Northwestern Section Timeline

1964 **L. F. Lynch**, of Portland, Oregon, is elected Northwestern Section secretary.

1967 First annual meeting of the **Alaska Chapter** is held on February 26-28, 1967.

1973 **L. D. Sisson**, of Beaverton, Oregon, is elected Northwestern Section secretary.

1978 **C. Landin**, of Seattle, Washington, is elected Northwestern Section secretary.

1981 **Arel R. Sessions**, of Rexburg, Iowa, is elected Northwestern Section secretary.

1982 Executive board of directors approves the charter for the **Eastern Division** of the Idaho Chapter. The charter was rescinded in November 1988.

1985 **Columbia Basin Division** of the Eastern Washington Chapter is formed. The board of directors dissolved this chapter in 2000.

Gaylen D. Rogers, of Highland, Utah, is elected Northwestern Section secretary.

1988 **J. Philip Simmons**, of Olympia, Washington, is elected Northwestern Section secretary.

1990 **Billy C. Barclay**, of Kennewick, Washington, is elected Northwestern Section secretary.

1993 **Victor O. Jivetin**, first Russian member, joins IAEI Alaska Chapter

Alaska Chapter expanded to include all of Russia East of the Ural Mountains - Passed by resolution at the 1993 Northwestern Section meeting.

1994 **Fairbanks Division** of the Alaska Chapter is created.

Jack Watterson, of Amboy, Washington, is elected Northwestern Section secretary.

Thirty-ninth annual Northwestern Section meeting in Portland, Oregon, on September 27, 1965.

IAEI Welcomes Alaska Chapter

Alaska—a vast and rugged land of magnificent grandeur, minerals, timber, fishing, oil, air transportation—crossroads of the North. There is a lot more than just land in the 49th state. It has people. Like the other states. Not very many in comparison with most other states, but people just the same, Alaskans.

Adopts *National Electrical Code*

Alaska adopted the *National Electrical Code* several years ago and at the same time established provisions for enforcement of the *Code* as state law. This is typical of the progressive, forward looking people who live in Alaska. Many of our older states have yet to establish electrical rules and regulations. Alaska is to be congratulated for recognizing and using the *National Electrical Code.*

Use of the Code Brings Chapter Recognition

Adoption and use of the *Code* by Alaska brought a need for a *Code* discussion forum in the Alaskan electrical industry. IAEI was ready to fill this need. Our Northwestern Section, of which Alaska is now a chapter, has been working toward this goal for many years. The officers and other leaders in the Northwestern Section established a liaison with NECA's Alaska Chapter and together they laid the ground work which brought IAEI chapter status to Alaska.

Major credit for this successful venture goes to NECA's Alaska Chapter Manager, John A. Scheffer and IAEI's Northwestern Section secretary, Les Lynch. To match the work of these men and others, the electrical industry gave wholehearted support to the project. They sent their *Code* experts and technical leaders to the key meetings which were held with a view towards embracing Alaska as a new chapter in IAEI.

Centennial Celebration

Our cover for September 1967 salutes Alaska's centennial year and the formation of our Alaska Chapter. IAEI's International President, Mr. William P. Hogan, presented the chapter charter to the first chairman of the chapter, Mr. R. L. Hufman. For more detail on this event, the first report and pictures of the Alaska Chapter Meeting appear in "General News" as an introduction of the Alaska Chapter to the IAEI family.

Alaska Chapter Report

The First Annual Meeting of the Alaska Chapter of the International Association of Electrical Inspectors was held on February 25, 27 and 28, 1967, at the Anchorage-Westward Hotel, Anchorage, Alaska.

February 26, 1967

The activities of registration, world champion dog sled racing, the annual fur rendezvous events were well-rounded out with a "get acquainted" social hour sponsored by Mr. Bob Stark of Coast Electric & Manufacturing Company, Portland, Oregon.

February 27, 1967

The meeting, with ninety-seven in attendance, was called to order by Chairman Hufman. The following guests were included: William P. Hogan, international president; Lou LaFehr, managing director, Daniel Boone, Federal Pacific Electric Company; Norman Davis, Underwriters' Laboratories, Santa Clara, California;

1967 International President William P. Hogan welcomes Alaska Chapter members to the IAEI at the inaugural chapter meeting on February 26–28, 1967. The first meeting was held at the Anchorage-Westward Hotel in Anchorage, Alaska. Major credit for this successful venture goes to NECA's Alaska Chapter Manager John A. Scheffer and IAEI's Northwestern Section Secretary Les Lynch. They sent their code experts and technical leaders to the key meetings which were held with a view towards embracing Alaska as a new chapter in IAEI.

Bob Start, Coast Electric & Manufacturing Co., Portland, Oregon; Richard Lloyd, Underwriters' Laboratories, Melville, Long Island, N.Y.; Creighton Schwan, National Electrical Manufacturer's Assn.; and Les Lynch, secretary-treasurer, Northwestern Section IAEI.

Mr. Hufman introduced John A. Scheffer, manager, Alaska Chapter National Electrical Contractors Association, Inc., who gave the welcoming address.

Mr. Lou LaFehr gave a very informative talk on the functions of the International Association of Electrical Inspectors and its important role in the electrical industry.

Manufacturers – Inspectors Relations was explained by Mr. Daniel Boone.

Mr. Norman Davis gave a talk on listings by Underwriters' Laboratories and how it is accomplished.

Mr. Jack Schratz, Montgomery Brothers, covered electric heating concept.

A talk was given by Mr. William Elam, Minneapolis-Honeywell, on proper controls under given circumstances.

After lunch, the first speaker was Bob Stark, Coast Electric & Manufacturing Company, who explained the meaning of the new C.T.L. Panels.

The balance of the day was spent on *Code* discussion with panel members: William P. Hogan, Lou LaFehr, Norman Davis, Daniel Boone, Richard Lloyd, Creighton Schwan, with Les Lynch as moderator.

Monday evening, the banquet was highlighted by a speech by Mr. William P. Hogan, international president IAEI, and the charter presentation. Robert "Bob" L. Hufman accepted the charter for the Alaska Chapter.

Les Lynch, on behalf of the Oregon Chapter IAEI, presented the Alaska Chapter with an engraved gavel, chrome plated pliers and a congratulatory message on white ribbon signed by all the members of the Oregon Chapter IAEI.

February 28, 1967

The morning session started with Creighton Schwan's talk on National Electrical Manufacturers Association and the *National Electrical Code*.

This was followed by Gene Morgan's, Robert W. Retherford & Associates, presentation "Underground Residential Distribution in Alaska." Open discussion on URD continued until noon.

After lunch, Moderator Les Lynch and his panel provided an enlightening *Code* discussion.

After a short coffee break, the meeting was called to order by Robert L. Hufman.

The bylaws committee recommended the model chapter bylaws be accepted together with several modifying insertions.

A motion made by William Whitcher and seconded by James Dawson that the bylaws be accepted. motion carried.

The nominating committee submitted nominations of officers, as follows: Chairman, Robert L. Hufman; Vice Chairman, Roy Banta; Secretary-Treasurer, Donald O. Thompson.

Motion made by Frank Stowman, seconded by Jorge Hix, that the secretary be instructed to cast a unanimous ballot for the officers nominated. Motion carried.

The new officers were installed by International President William P. Hogan.

Alaska Chapter Chairman Hufman thanked John Scheffer for his outstanding work in arranging the details of the meeting and the banquet.

John Scheffer presented certificates and pins to William P. Hogan, Norman Davis, Creighton Schwan and Daniel Boone signifying their "membership" in the "Order of the Walrus."

Motion made and carried to purchase stationery with appropriate International Association of Electrical Inspectors emblem and showing the names of the newly elected officers.

With no further business, the meeting adjourned at 5:30 p.m.

Reprinted from *IAEI News*, September 1967.

1967 International President

William P. Hogan, chief electrical inspector of the city of Chicago, became an apprentice electrician in 1939, and at the same time attended night school at the Armour Institute. In 1941, he became a journeyman electrician.

January 1942, found Mr. Hogan in the Navy where he served as electrician's mate 3/c. Having served aboard several ships on convoy duty in the North Atlantic from 1942 to 1944, he returned to Washington, D. C., where he attended the Electrical Interior Communication School. In 1945 he was made chief electrician's mate and was discharged from the Navy later that year.

Mr. Hogan became a civil service electrical mechanic for the city of Chicago in December 1948. He worked as an electrical mechanic, foreman of electrical mechanics and general foreman until September 1954. At this time, he became a civil service electrical inspector, trading this title in April 1955, for that of chief electrical inspector. Mr. Hogan placed first in statewide examinations for this position.

In November 1956, he became an associate member of the Underwriter's Laboratories and a member of the Electrical Council of UL. Mr. Hogan is a past chairman of the Illinois Chapter and past president of the Western Section. He is chairman of code-making panel 9 and represents IAEI on CMP-6. He is also a member of several NFPA committees as an IAEI representative. In January 1965, he was promoted to the position of deputy building commissioner (chief electrical inspector).

Excerpted from *News-Bulletin*, January 1967.

IAEI starts a new project. A new special committee on electrical fires and accidents was established in 1970. The new committee is shown above during their initial meeting at UL in Chicago. Seated *left to right:* Peter J. Meyer, J. Gordon Maltby, and Ivey Johnson. Standing *left to right* are Paul L. Miller, P. L. White, and D. S. Martin. The committee is revising and updating IAEI systems and brochures on the subject of reporting electrical fires and accidents. They welcome suggestions that will be helpful in their work.

Arthur W. Welklin

Arthur H. Welklin, 86, honorary member and former president of the Western Section IAEI, and author of *The Electrical Inspector,* died recently. He had been a member of the Indiana Chapter, IAEI, for many years when he was the chief electrical inspector for the city of Fort Wayne, Indiana. He had resided in Bradenton, Florida for the past 10 years.

His book, *The Electrical Inspector,* published in 1969, has been popular with readers of the *IAEI News* as a history and guide for the electrical inspector in the development of electricity and safe standards for its use.

Welklin had authored a weekly astronomy column, "Our Amazing Universe," in the *News-Sentinel* since 1967. He was a graduate of the International Business College in Fort Wayne and was an electrical contractor before serving many years as chief electrical inspector. He had also taught night classes in electricity.

A veteran of World War I, he was associated with the Fort Wayne Astronomical Society and was active in affairs of its small observatory in Allen County called Mount Willig Observatory.

A member of IAEI since 1921 (Western Association of Electrical Inspectors), Welklin has served on numerous committees for the association. For many years, he served as chairman of the IAEI Public Relations Committee. In addition, he has also served as chairman of the Indiana Chapter, IAEI, and as president of the Western Section, IAEI.

Surviving are his wife, Carolyn, a daughter and three sons and a brother.

Reprinted from *IAEI News,* May 1981; and *The Electrical Inspector,* A. H. Welklin, 1969.

1968 International President

Walter (Wally) F. Reed first went to work in the electrical industry in 1926. The year 1935 found him employed at L. B. Marsh Wholesale Electric Company. After working several years in Long Beach, he was transferred to the Santa Ana office in the sales division. This is where he met Mr. Charles Donohue, who at that time was chief electrical inspector of Orange County, California, and has since become superintendent of building and safety.

At the start of World War II, Wally was employed as an electrician for Bethlehem Ship Building Corporation in Long Beach, California. From there he enlisted in the U. S. Coast Guard. Upon receiving his honorable discharge, he went to the Naval Operating Base and then back to Marsh Electric Company in Santa Ana as assistant manager.

In 1951, Mr. Reed went to work as electrical inspector for the county of Orange, California. In 1956 he was promoted to senior electrical inspector and upon the retirement of Mr. Jimmie Hutchins, passed the necessary examinations, and in 1957 became supervising electrical inspector. He has been with the county of Orange for 14 years.

The purpose and goal in Wally's career is to strive for uniformity, and if it is not accomplished in the near future he feels the industry will be under state and government control. It is his opinion that we are contributing much more to the writing of the *National Electrical Code* than ever in the past. Therefore, he feels there is no reason why we should not take it as our *Code*, that is, the latest edition.

Excerpted from *News-Bulletin,* January 1964.

1969 International President

John C. Hewitt first entered the electrical industry in 1936. In 1943 he started the Broadway Electrical Company in Seattle. During the latter part of World War II, he was with the Merchant Marines. When he returned, he went to work for electrical contractors in the northwest.

In 1949, Mr. Hewitt was appointed chief electrical inspector for the state of Washington. In the early part of 1954, he left the state for a position as superintendent for electrical construction with the Seattle School District. In the fall of 1961, he resumed the position of chief electrical inspector for the state of Washington, which he retains today.

He served on numerous apprenticeship boards and code advisory committees in and around Seattle for quite a number of years. During the years 1955-1959, he was on the mayor's advisory board for the city of Seattle. He served on NFPA code-making panel No. 9. He is presently secretary of the Washington State Governor's Electrical Advisory Board.

Mr. Hewitt was presented the Man of the Year Award by the Puget Sound Electrical League for his contribution in bringing about uniform inspection programs and his contribution regarding state legislation. In 1963 he received the Man of the Year Award from the National Electrical Contractor's Association for creating 100 percent inspections for the state of Washington.

Reprinted from *IAEI News*, January 1969.

Southern Section Timeline

1969 **Mel L. Young**, from Springfield, Virginia, is elected Southern Section secretary.

1977 International board of directors approves the charter for the **Rio Grande Valley Chapter**. Its charter was revoked in November 1986.

Palm Beach County Division of the Florida Chapter is created.

1978 Sabine Division of the Texas Gulf Coast Chapter becomes the **Sabine Chapter**.

1980 International board of directors approves charter for newly developed **South Texas Chapter** at a meeting on October 30, 1981.

1984 International executive board approves the creation of the **Central Florida Division** of the Florida Chapter.

1985 Tennessee Chapter welcomes its new division, the **Chattanooga Division**.

Oklahoma-Arkansas Chapter officially splits apart in 1971 to form two different chapters: the **Oklahoma Chapter** and the **Arkansas Chapter**. The **Oklahoma Chapter** formed in 1971 part of Western Chapter, but became part of the Southern Section in 1985.

1986 **Suncoast Division** of the Florida Chapter is created.

Broward Division of the Florida Chapter is granted its charter. The division changed its name to **Maynard Hamilton/Ft Lauderdale Division** in 1998

1987 **East Texas Division** of the Texas Chapter is created.

1989 **Treasure Coast Division** was formed for the Florida Chapter, but the division was later dissolved in 2001.

Miami/Dade Division of the Florida Chapter is formed.

1990 International board of directors approves the charter for the **Kansas Sunflower Chapter**.

Central Alabama Division of the Alabama Chapter is formed.

1992 Georgia Chapter welcomes its new division, the **North Georgia Division**.

Florida Gulf Coast Division of the Florida Chapter is born.

North Florida Division of the Florida Chapter is created.

1994 **James W. Carpenter**, from Durham, North Carolina, is elected Southern Section secretary.

Valley of the Dolls...or not.

A cordial welcome was in store for the Eastern Section members at the 1972 annual meeting at the fabulous Playboy Club-Hotel.

"This new hotel is a year-round resort featuring a sidewalk café, discotheque, deli, 27 holes of golf, miles of ski runs, stables and bridle paths, skeet and trap shooting, indoor-outdoor swimming and tennis, game room, health club, and shops.

"Our Ladies Committees, as usual, has lined up a lot of new ideas to keep our ladies entertained. There are many indoor recreational facilities as well as the outdoor ones.

"The people at Playboy who are responsible for our stay here have been most cooperative and indeed we should have a most enjoyable meeting.

"The Eastern Section officers are looking forward to seeing all of you at the meeting. Be sure to have your 1971 National Electrical Code books with you at all sessions and above all—be interested and attend."

— *IAEI News*, July 1972

The Electrical Inspector

A strange breed is the electrical inspector. Try to think of any one place where you might find a definition to fit same. What is said here could in part apply to other inspectors, but the electrical inspector must be a specialist with a highly technical knowledge that is well-rounded. The order in which I place the qualifications of the electrical inspector are not necessarily as you might place them. I do not feel that any one qualification is more important than another — they must all dovetail together.

The electrical inspector's job is fundamentally one of safety to both life and property, and to see that adequacy is incorporated into the wiring job for the demands which will be imposed upon the wiring system. The key theme of our job is safety, and this fact shall never be overlooked. All other qualifications and duties of our job will be secondary to safety.

The importance of codes and inspections is brought out forcefully by the fact that the federal government is definitely becoming interested in inspection programs and licensing of inspectors. In order for us to maintain local control of this, our state and local governments must take steps to demonstrate they are capable of doing the job in a satisfactory manner. Many state and local governments are doing a splendid job, some are not.

We have the *National Electrical Code* (NFPA 70) and this is well accepted. One will not find a more democratic code. Should anyone question this statement, they should submit a proposal for change with the proper supporting comments, etc., for any changes they feel are needed in the *Code*. The proposal will go to the proper code-making panel for consideration, if it is submitted as outlined in the *NEC*.

These proposals will be published by the NFPA in what is called the "Preprint," which will be available about July of this year. Everyone should secure a copy, and we have until December 1st to make our comments to the code makers. So if you do not like what comes out in the *Code* and have done nothing to assist in making proper changes, just accept them, profit by your experience, and participate in the next issue of the *Code*.

We have the organization — the International Association of Electrical Inspectors, with Mr. L. E. LaFehr as managing director, and a very efficient staff to back him up. These items in themselves are not enough. We inspectors must qualify in keeping abreast with our ever growing industry and its new developments. The IAEI has engaged the University of Nebraska to supply, under our supervision, a correspondence course for electrical inspectors. We also have a certification as certified electrical safety engineers for those who may qualify.

I would place public relations as the head item on my list of qualifications. These public relations are between the inspector, contractor, wireman, manufacturer, design engineer, building owners, and the public in general. We must be continually alert in selling our safety job, our department and ourselves, and the benefits the public receives from inspections.

Many articles have been written on public relations, and many of them are good. It could be suggested the book by Dale Carnegie, *How to Win Friends and Influence People*, should be in every inspector's library, and it should be reread often.

Everyone has a right to his own opinion and this opinion must be respected. Should we feel he is wrong, give him the benefit of his opinion and then subtlety put your ideas forth, even in such a manner that he might feel that they were his own ideas. It doesn't matter whose ideas they were, as long as the job gets done. Be a good listener, then weigh what you think very carefully before saying it.

Knowledge of the subject is highly important. In our work we are in a technical field. Gaining a good knowledge of electrical inspections is far from being the easiest task in the world. The inspector may often be told that he is wrong, but who do people go to for information? The inspector. How many hours and minutes do you throw away each day? The answer cannot be anything but "many." It is easy to create habits, since we are creatures of habit. One of the best habits that I know of is to find half an hour or more a day for study. If you are not doing this, you will find you have to force yourself to start it. Once started, it will be as easy as eating. You will never really realize you are doing this, and it will not take time from your family life either. Anything that is good is not free and if we progress on our inspection job, we must prepare ourselves, especially with the changes that are constantly being made in our industry.

The number one item in our libraries must be the *National Electrical Code*. Other books are: The *NFPA Handbook of the National Electrical Code*, by Frank Stetka; *Electrical Code Diagrams*, by B. Z. Segall; *Questions and Answers for Electricians' Exams*, by Roland Palmquist; The *1968 Guide to the NEC*, by Roland Palmquist; *The Electrical Inspector* by A. H. Welklin; and *The Grounding Book*, by Eustace Soares. These are all available through your IAEI.

In addition, there are many handbooks and books on special subjects that you may want in your library.

A membership in the International Association of Electrical Inspectors is probably one of the most valuable investments that one might make. The membership fee is nominal. There are six copies of the *IAEI News* mailed out each year. These are full of *Code* information and related subjects, plus many other pieces of literature given to the IAEI to be mailed to its members. Also, when a new *Code* appears you automatically receive a copy.

When you join, or if you are a member, take active part in your chapter. The members that set up the meeting of the chapter spend many hours attempting to see that information of interest is available to you at these meetings. I will speak of my chapter, the Rocky Mountain Chapter of the Western Section, as I am acquainted with its activities. A two-day annual meeting is held every March and many *Code* authorities are in attendance to pass on to you what information they have. Much of the time at our meetings is spent in code panel discussions, at which questions are presented from those in attendance and answered by a code panel. This also takes into consideration problems in locals areas. Four additional meetings are held throughout Wyoming and Colorado during each year to further cover our industry. One need not be a member to attend, but let us not be selfish. Carry membership applications and share with others the good that we get out of IAEI.

One way to improve yourself as an inspector is to teach *Code* classes. You will gain much more than the students do, this I will assure of. You will usually receive pay for your teaching time.

Those of us who have been inspectors realize that at the moment, the pay scale leaves much to be desired in many cases, but it is gradually rising. Many of us have received very good positions fundamentally due to our success as inspectors.

Dedication is a must. Any job worth doing is worth doing well. Should you be an inspector, or choose to be one, be dedicated and feel that you are doing one of the most important jobs in the world. Actually, you are.

Be positive. When inspections are being made, or you are asked questions, be sure that you are right before you answer or give your decision. If necessary, call on someone else for an opinion. It is never a disgrace to ask others for their opinion, the disgrace is in not asking for advice. Do not "bull" something through, be sure you are right and then be positive in your statements. The highest respect can be gained by having a thorough knowledge of electrical inspections and installations, and then staying with your convictions. Do not be swayed by pressures or threats.

Be fair in all of your decisions. Sometimes you might have to digress a little, but never where safety is involved. By all means, treat everyone whose job you might be inspecting the same. Any favoritism to one contractor will break you as an inspector. Never ask for the impossible, and never put yourself on a pedestal as a "tough watchdog." Be kind.

The rights of others must always be considered — politeness pays well. Being clean about your work pays big dividends, so do not track in dirt. Little things? No, big things which leave a good impression with the owner of the property that you are inspecting.

Be familiar with the laws provided for inspections and, if in doubt, consult your supervisor. I am sure that at times, we have all had to be ruggedly firm, however, it is prudent to wait until routine methods have been exhausted. One can always be firm without the use of foul language or abuse. Use finesse.

Keep records of your activities each day. If there is a case that may backfire on you, make a complete record of all that transpired in the matter. Do not wait until tomorrow to do so—write it up at the earliest opportunity. Date it, sign it, and file it away just in case. Most of this you will never use, but memory is deceptive, and is not to be relied upon. Time, date, names, conversations, and all—get it down in writing.

An electrical inspector will never know just how many lives or how much property he has helped protect, but records show that thorough inspections do just that. Always treat those involved as you yourself would like to be treated.

I have had a few cases where it was necessary to take extreme means in order to get installations corrected. I think one of my most embarrassing moments involved a case I had to take to court. Afterwards, the man thanked me, stating he did not realize what he was doing in possibly creating a condition where people or property could be injured.

There have also been times when steps for revocation of a license were necessary. One case came very close to revocation and sometime later I was thanked and told that I had done more for him in the electrical industry than anyone he knew. I value such a statement highly because it took a big man to come to me and say such a thing.

Last of all, remember that our job is one of the most interesting there is, so let us strive to do the best job possible.

By Roland E. Palmquist, electrical inspector. Reprinted from *IAEI News*, July 1970.

1970-1979

The Silent Majority

The chaotic events of the 60s, including war and social change, seemed destined to continue in the 70s. The "Silent Majority," which Richard Nixon called the voice of middle Americans, were characterized by scorn for both the establishment and antiestablishment, anger towards attacks on the American Way, and felt threatened by the fact that hard work and hard knocks earned less money—and this majority became a powerful force during the 1970s. Trends among this majority included a growing disillusionment of government, advances in civil rights, increased influence of the women's movement, a heightened concern for the environment, and increased space exploration. Many of the radical ideas of the 60s gained wider acceptance in the new decade, and were mainstreamed into American life and culture. Amid war, social realignment and presidential impeachment proceedings, American culture flourished.

1970 International President

Richard B. Boyd, Jr. was employed by the North Carolina Insurance Department shortly after graduation and presently is head of the electrical section of the Engineering Division. The section cooperates with and assists local inspection departments throughout the state in the enforcement of state and local regulations governing electrical installations, and is also responsible for the electrical inspections of state-owned buildings.

Mr. Boyd joined IAEI more than twenty years ago and has served on numerous committees at the chapter and section level. He has served as chairman of the Ellis Cannady Chapter; president of the Southern Section; and presently is chairman of the Southern Section executive committee.

In February of 1960 he became an associate member of Underwriters' Laboratories and a member of the Electrical Council of UL. He has served as IAEI's representative on code-making panel 16 and presently represents this organization on code-making panel 13. Mr. Boyd is also a member of the electrical section of NFPA.

He is a registered professional engineer and is presently serving as chairman of the State Board of Examiners of Electrical Contractors. He is active in teaching short courses for electrical inspectors and serves as moderator on *Code* discussions at many of the *NEC* sessions at the Ellis Cannady meetings.

Reprinted from *IAEI News*, January 1970.

1971 International President

Keith L. Bellamy graduated from Queen's University with a bachelor of science degree in electrical engineering. He conducted an electrical contracting business for several years prior to joining Ontario Hydro as an electrical inspector at St. Catherine's. Moving to Toronto shortly thereafter, he became chief electrical inspector in 1958.

He has been a member of IAEI since about 1946 (initially as a member of the Western Section), becoming the first secretary of the Canadian Section; he served as president of the section in 1960, and again acted as secretary until elected as candidate for office to the board of directors. He is also a member of the Association of Professional Engineers of Ontario Engineering Institute of Canada, Standards Engineers Society, and the electrical section, NFPA.

Keith was a member of several code committees, including the main committees of the Canadian Electrical Code, Part I, Part II, and Part III; also active in many of the Part II subcommittees, chairing those dealing with hairdressing equipment, PVC conduit, decorative lighting, and grounding of electrical equipment, as well as chairing a task group on derating factors under the general subject of compatibility. He is a member of the CSA Approvals Council, chairman of the Chief Inspectors for Canada, and was recently appointed vice chairman of the CSA Committee on Emergency Systems.

Reprinted from *IAEI News*, January 1971.

James H. McGraw Awards

Robert E. Ward, *right*, was the first IAEI winner of the James H. McGraw award in 1970.

The **James H. McGraw Award** was established in 1925 by the McGraw Committee of Awards. This award is presented to a person from the electrical contracting industry for some new and useful idea or for having performed an industry service over and above his normal responsibilities to his own or his company's progress. The awards consist of a bronze medal and purse. The awards endowment is administered by a committee of awards made up of leading industry executives.

Candidates for awards may be designated from any one of six segments of the electrical industry: manufacturing, utility, engineering design, contracting, distribution, and inspection. Selection of a candidates is made by the industry association serving that phase of electrical work. Final approval of candidates is made by the committee of awards. 1970 was the first year that IAEI was allowed to be included in this award. In 1990, the award was replaced by the IAEI Medal of Honor.

1970	Ward, Robert E.
1973	Hogan, W.P.
1974	Carlton, E.E.
1976	Barker, A.O.
1976	Boyd Jr., Richard B.
1977	Bellamy, K.L.
1978	Riley, G.E.
1979	Love, H.B.
1980	Wintz, G.A.
1981	Niedermeyer, R.A.
1982	Flach, G.W.
1983	Leeming, J.E.
1984	Reed, A.J.
1985	Nagel, Leo
1986	Fujihara, E.Y.
1987	Simmons, J.P.
1988	Young, M.L.
1989	Waller, J.D.
1990	Lounsbury, M.H.

1972 International President

C. E. Schaad was employed from 1929 to 1942 as electrician and substation operator in the chemical, grain milling and gypsum industries in the Niagara frontier area. He joined the New York Board of Fire Underwriters in 1947, and was assigned as an electrical inspector to the Buffalo district. He was appointed general manager of the electrical department in 1956; and elected secretary to the board in 1965.

Mr. Schaad became a member of the original Empire Chapter of the International Association of Electrical Inspectors in 1950, serving as secretary to the chapter. He transferred his membership to the New York Chapter in 1952, and later was elected to the executive committee as well as serving on various chapter committees. He was elected to the Eastern Section executive committee, serving as a member to date. He was also elected Eastern Section president for the year 1966, and presently represents the Eastern Section on the IAEI board of directors, and various standing committees.

Mr. Schaad is a consulting editor for *Electrical Construction and Maintenance*, a magazine published by McGraw-Hill, Inc. He is also a member of the following organizations: Association of Electrical Construction Engineers; Underwriters' Laboratories, Inc.; National Fire Protection Association's educational committee for electrical safety; National Fire Protection Association's committee on electrical equipment maintenance; International Association of Electrical Inspectors' educational committee; insurance group representative on code-making panels 2 and 14; New York State Electrical Contractors and Dealers Association; and the Nassau Electric League.

Excerpted from *IAEI News*, January 1972.

1973 International President

Heilbron B. (Bill) Love, chief electrical inspector, Detroit Buildings & Safety Engineering Department, and 1973 president of IAEI, became interested in things electrical in his early teens when he worked simultaneously as a carpenter's helper and electrician's helper while attending the famed Cass Technical High School in Detroit taking electrical courses. While earning his bachelor's degree in electrical engineering from the University of Michigan, his part time work continued until he graduated with a BSEE in 1931.

For ten years Love worked with various electrical contractors until joining the city of Detroit staff in 1941 as an electrical inspector for the Department of Building & Safety Engineering. During World War II, he served in a number of city electrical and engineering posts in the Public Lighting Commission and the city engineer's office of the Department of Public Works; returning to the Building and Safety Engineering Department in 1946.

Love's emphasis on education and training was evident throughout his career. He was instrumental in the planning and initiation of *National Electrical Code* classes at Wayne State University, Applied Management and Technology Center. He has been an instructor there for the past eight years. He also sparked an annual series of code classes for engineers, journeymen, masters, contractors and inspectors through the Reciprocal Electrical Council, a southeastern Michigan regional association of more that 130 communities which set uniform standards in licensing and registration of electricians.

Professional and technical organizations in which Love presently holds membership and affiliations include: Industrial Electrical Engineering Society; Institute of Electrical & Electronics Engineers; Michigan Society of Professional Engineers, Detroit Chapter; Associated Electricians, Inc.; National Electrical Code, code-making panel 11; Underwriters' Laboratories, Inc., Electrical Council; NFPA, metalworking and machine tool committee #79; IBEW, Local 58; Society of Municipal Engineers; state of Michigan Electrical Administrative Board (gubernatorial appointment); Reciprocal Electrical Council, past chairman; Fifth Wheel Club, and the city of Detroit Management Group.

Excerpted from *IAEI News*, January 1973.

First Female Electrical Inspector

Rovena S. Bazzrea is the electrical, building and plumbing inspector for the Department of Buildings in the jurisdiction of Alleghany County, state of Virginia.

Ms. Bazzrea became an IAEI member during the June 9–10, 1975 meeting of the Virginia Chapter which was held in Danville, Virginia.

Although IAEI has female associate members, Ms. Bazzrea is the first active governmental electrical inspector according to our records.

—Reprinted from *IAEI News*, September 1975.

1974 International President

Colin J. Watt, president of the IAEI, is from Fresno, California. Mr. Watt has been a member of the association for over 15 years. He had his formal education in Indiana and in 1935 entered the Navy and was assigned to the U.S.S. *Tennessee* in the electrical division. After his discharge, he went to work for the Pacific Gas and Electric Company as an electrical operator. When World War II broke out, he was back in the Navy and working in the Pacific as a warrant electrician. After the war ended, he went to Los Angeles where he held the position of electrical inspector. Interest in education brought Mr. Watt to the Los Angeles Evening Technical College first as a student taking math and electrical courses, and then as a teacher for eleven years.

In 1957 he became a state of California employee holding the position of electrical safety engineer. He holds this position today. Mr. Watt has a great interest in education and still attends class at night. His present responsibilities do not permit him to teach; nevertheless, teaching is a source of great enjoyment to him.

Excerpted from *IAEI News*, January 1974.

IAEI Quad Chapter meeting in Fresno, on May 5–6, 1972. *From left to right*: Max Van Dyke, chairman Central City Chapter; Arthur K. C. Chong, Honolulu, president of Southwestern Section, and George Harvis, chairman of the Northern California Chapter.

1975 International President

Artie O. Barker, president of the IAEI, has been an associate and active member of the IAEI for over 25 years, and is currently the secretary-manager of the Idaho Electrical Board and chief of the Electrical Safety Bureau for the state of Idaho. Mr. Barker began his work with the state of Idaho in 1963 as an electrical inspector. In 1965 he was promoted to assistant chief, and in 1966 he was made chief inspector and director of the Idaho State Electrical Board.

Mr. Barker was an electrical contractor for over twenty years and was serving on the board of directors for Idaho Electrical Contractors when the licensing and inspection law was enacted in 1947.

He is a member of the Snake River Valley Electrical Association and president of the Chief Electrical Inspectors Association, which is a section of the NFPA. He is also the chairman of the *NEC* panel 19 and member of panel 9 and chairman of the Intersectional Committee Electrical Task Force for mobile homes, parks, and recreational vehicles and parks. He is also a member of the following: Correlating Committee for Mobile Homes and Recreational Vehicles; NFPA 501A Sectional Committee on Mobile Home Parks, 501B on Mobile Homes, 501C on Recreational Vehicles, 501D on Recreational Vehicle Parks; Underwriters' Laboratories, Electrical Council and corporate member of Underwriters' Laboratories, Inc. He also served on the technical committee for irrigation sprinklers.

Excerpted from *IAEI News*, January 1975.

Y. Ikeda, chairman, holds a certificate of achievement at the May 1970 Japan Chapter meeting. Vice Chairman A. P. Sapiro (*second from right, first row*), Secretary Y. Shimura (*far right, first row*), and Waichi Nakajima (*second from the left, back row*) also attended the meeting. The other gentlemen are unidentified.

The Electrical Hall of Fame awards for 1974, presented at the Northwestern Section Meeting in Boise, Idaho, went to (*left to right*): Park Forte, Joe Triplett, Claude C. Haggard, and Richard Lloyd. The annual presentations, first awarded in 1970, are given to recognize and honor persons of long tenure and outstanding efforts in the electrical industry and related areas, participation in civic electrical organization activities, and good standing in the community. The awards are sponsored by the Magic Valley Chapter, Snake River Valley Electrical Association. — Reprinted from *IAEI News*, March 1975.

International Timeline

1969 **Japan Chapter** is created.

1980 Board of directors approves charter for newly developed **Saudi Arabia Chapter** at meeting on October 30, 1981

Members of the Northwestern Section at the 1974 Northwestern Section meeting.

Benefits of IAEI Membership

For electrical contractors and others engaged in electrical construction and maintenance, membership in IAEI is as essential as the tools required to make an electrical installation. It has long been known that electrical contractors succeed best in an environment where competent qualified electrical inspections holds forth. It is basic understanding in the industry that when electrical installation rules are enforced with equality, a bidding contractor who may not obtain the bid knows that the installation will perforce be installed according to the standards set by the rules.

To understand electrical inspectors and the rules they enforce, it seems that nearly everyone in the electrical industry would recognize the benefit of becoming a member of IAEI. This is the avenue which associate members in IAEI use to discuss installation situations and problems with electrical inspectors, and to hear electrical inspectors themselves discuss the *Code* rules. Furthermore, the association makes available to all members the most profound *Code* discussions available in the industry.

Associate membership in IAEI is open to individuals who are interested in the *National Electric Code* and interested in promoting the objectives of the association, which basically is "an understanding of the *National Electrical Code*."

Dues for associate membership are only $20.00 per year, and this is a bargain considering the information available to members through the meetings and publications of the association.

The electrical inspectors themselves govern the IAEI, through a board of directors, which is elected in the sections by the active membership. The association maintains an executive office where the administrative work of the association is handled. In addition to electrical contractors, journeymen and apprentice electricians, the association has members from throughout the electrical industry. Represented in the membership of IAEI are utilities, electrical dealers, insurance groups, electrical manufacturers, testing laboratories, and electrical safety experts.

The association is structured so that an individual member may associate with a small local group (chapter), which considers and handles local situations. Larger meetings are held annually in the regional areas of the United States and Canada, and these are known as section meetings, where members may hear *Code* discussions as given by *Code* authorities representing nearly all of the National Electrical Code-making panels.

There are more than 14,000 members in IAEI, and this membership helps maintain the position of the electrical inspector in the industry. Members find that they can develop a reciprocal interest with the inspector. Support of the association through membership assists the electrical inspector in advancing the techniques of his work through education and certification in which the association is involved.

Everyone in the electrical industry is in favor of safe electrical wiring, and the safe use of electricity. This is effectively promoted through membership in the association.

Membership in IAEI helps protect the electrical inspector from political interference. Political interference with the duties of the electrical inspector can be most damaging to a qualified electrical contractor whenever the competition can influence political interference with the electrical inspector. Think about that; membership can help insulate the electrical inspector from political interference. As an organization, IAEI provides a shield protecting the inspector from politics.

Association membership in IAEI helps to provide a means for IAEI electrical inspectors to inform the public in the safe use of electricity and can be a big influence toward better public understanding of the benefits of electricity.

IAEI is a partner in the formulation of standards for the safe installation and use of electrical materials, devices and appliances.

The association is continually promoting a uniform understanding and application of the *National Electrical Code* and the Canadian Electrical Code.

The association provides representation by electrical inspectors in the electrical industry, both nationally and internationally.

IAEI cooperates with national and international organizations towards the further development of the electrical industry. Membership in IAEI helps

1976 International President

Native Texan, **Marvis S. "Dude" Parmley,** is the new president of IAEI. An active member of IAEI for many years, he is currently the chief electrical inspector, environmental safety and maintenance, city of Houston. Mr. Parmley began his work for the city of Houston as an electrical inspector in 1952. He was made chief electrical inspector for the city in 1954, and in 1964 was promoted to deputy building official, serving that capacity until 1974, at which time he was transferred to take over his present position.

Born in Houston in 1925, he joined the U.S. Navy as an apprentice seaman in 1942 and served three years in the South Pacific with the 135th Construction Battalion (Sea Bee's) as an electrician's mate.

Mr. Parmley joined the International Brotherhood of Electrical Workers (IBEW) Local Union 716 in 1946 as an apprentice electrician and graduated as the outstanding apprentice of 1950. He was elected president of that Local in 1952. He taught in Local Union 716 for eight consecutive years.

Mr. Parmley serves on *NEC* panel 18; holds a master electrician's license in the city of Houston; and is a certified electrical safety engineer.

Excerpted from *IAEI News,* January 1976.

J. N. Johnson, *left*, past chairman of the Ohio Chapter, presents the gavel to the new chairman, M. R. Wilson, at the annual meeting of the Ohio Chapter in Cleveland, Ohio, on May 2–3, 1974.

develop cooperation and uniform *Code* interpretation among inspectors and inspection departments at all levels of government: city, county, state and national. Associate with your electrical inspector through associate membership in IAEI, it will pay dividends.

Membership will entitle you to a number of benefits provided by the association. There are insurance programs — life insurance, hospitalization insurance, income protection insurance and for the electrical inspector, electrical inspector liability insurance. The association usually provides a complimentary copy of the *NEC* in its year of issue. The next issue is expected to be the 1978 *NEC*, which should be available in the fall of 1977.

The association is approaching its 50th Anniversary. It will celebrate its Golden Jubilee and the 1978 *NEC* in the city of New Orleans during the week of September 10 – 15, 1978. This meeting is expected to attract electrical industry people from around the world. It is expected that there may be more than 750 electrical exhibits, some of which will bring together, in one location for everyone to see and hear, the most renown *Code* authorities, not only from the United States and Canada but from other countries as well. The Golden Jubilee 50th Anniversary meeting of IAEI is the affair that should not be missed by anyone in the electrical industry. It is expected to be the biggest show and educational forum to take place in the last quarter of this century. As a member of the IAEI you can be a part of this celebration.

By Lou LaFehr, editor. Reprinted from *IAEI News*, September 1976.

Mary Fetzer Lopez

Mary Fetzer Lopez has a class B electrical license from the city of Cleveland, Ohio, and is one of a crew of four electricians working for Bardons and Oliver Company. She is qualified to put in installations and do wiring in any of the buildings owned and operated by her employer. Ms. Lopez is a member of the Western Reserve Division, Ohio Chapter IAEI.

After jobs as a nurse's aide, dancer and clerk, Mrs. Lopez got started in the electrical field as an assembly line worker for a company manufacturing printed circuit boards for numerical control machinery. She joined Bardons and Oliver and began wiring panels with starters and relays that operated turret lathes and cut-off machines. She has completed courses in AC and DC theory, air conditioning, blueprint reading, motor control, and, of course, the *National Electrical Code.*

Reprinted from *IAEI News*, July 1976.

The *Electrical Construction and Maintenance* staff receiving their membership cards from Sol Leiman, New York Chapter membership chairman. *From left to right*: Sol Leiman, membership chairman, Joseph F. McPartland, William J. Novak, Gerry C. Quinn, Jill P. Wentz, Joseph R. Kinsley, Robert J. Lawrie, and Jerry S. Ryan.

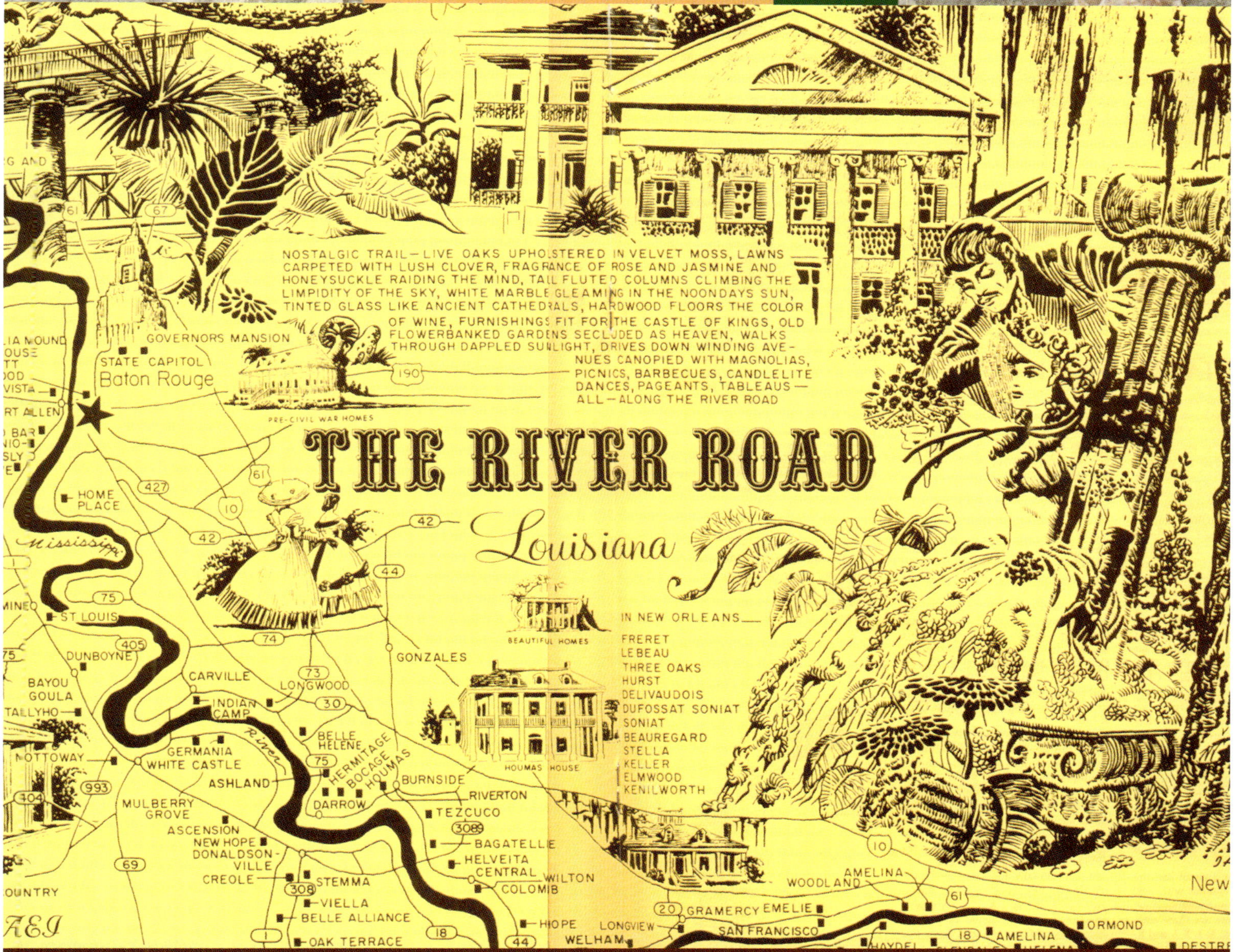

NOSTALGIC TRAIL—LIVE OAKS UPHOLSTERED IN VELVET MOSS, LAWNS CARPETED WITH LUSH CLOVER, FRAGRANCE OF ROSE AND JASMINE AND HONEYSUCKLE RAIDING THE MIND, TALL FLUTED COLUMNS CLIMBING THE LIMPIDITY OF THE SKY, WHITE MARBLE GLEAMING IN THE NOONDAYS SUN, TINTED GLASS LIKE ANCIENT CATHEDRALS, HARDWOOD FLOORS THE COLOR OF WINE, FURNISHINGS FIT FOR THE CASTLE OF KINGS, OLD FLOWERBANKED GARDENS SECLUDED AS HEAVEN, WALKS THROUGH DAPPLED SUNLIGHT, DRIVES DOWN WINDING AVENUES CANOPIED WITH MAGNOLIAS, PICNICS, BARBECUES, CANDLELITE DANCES, PAGEANTS, TABLEAUS—ALL—ALONG THE RIVER ROAD
THE RIVER ROAD
Louisiana
GOVERNORS MANSION
STATE CAPITOL
Baton Rouge
PRE-CIVIL WAR HOMES
HOME PLACE
Mississippi
River
ST LOUIS
DUNBOYNE
BAYOU GOULA
TALLYHO
NOTTOWAY
CARVILLE
INDIAN CAMP
LONGWOOD
GONZALES
BEAUTIFUL HOMES
IN NEW ORLEANS
FRERET
LEBEAU
THREE OAKS
HURST
DELIVAUDOIS
DUFOSSAT SONIAT
SONIAT
BEAUREGARD
STELLA
KELLER
ELMWOOD
KENILWORTH
GERMANIA
WHITE CASTLE
ASHLAND
BELLE HELENE
HERMITAGE
BOCAGE
HOUMAS
HOUMAS HOUSE
BURNSIDE
DARROW
MULBERRY GROVE
ASCENSION
NEW HOPE
DONALDSONVILLE
CREOLE
STEMMA
VIELLA
BELLE ALLIANCE
OAK TERRACE
RIVERTON
TEZCUCO
BAGATELLE
HELVEITA
CENTRAL
WILTON
COLOMIB
HOPE
LONGVIEW
WELHAM
GRAMERCY
EMELIE
SAN FRANCISCO
WOODLAND
AMELINA
ORMOND
COUNTRY
AEI

"Hey Mister—Throw Me a Doubloon"

Golden Jubilee

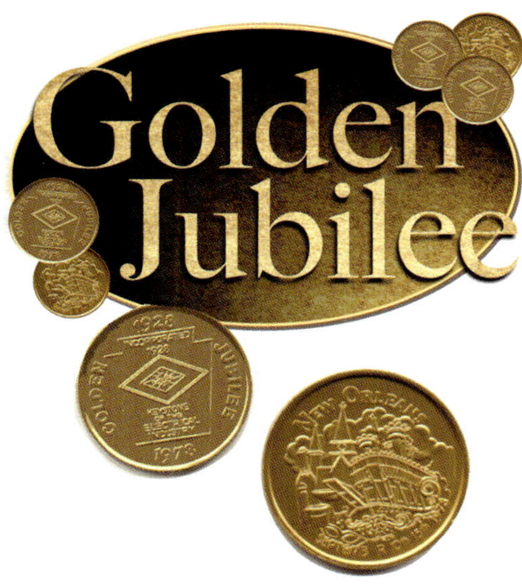

The year 1960 was a momentous one for the whole New Orleans Carnival scene. That was the year that the Rex Doubloons made their appearance. (The parade of Rex held on Mardi Gras Day is the singular highlight of the entire Carnival parade season that lasts for eleven days.) Years before, Rex had produced medallions, 1884 and 1893 to be precise, but the idea of a Rex doubloon to be tossed to parade watchers was spawned in 1960.

The Rex doubloon won instant favor of the parade crowd and immediately the traditional cry, "Hey, Mister, throw me something," became "Hey, Mister, throw me a doubloon."

Other Carnival organizations soon followed suit in the issuance of these medallions. It is estimated that literally millions of these tokens are tossed from parade floats each year.

So in the true New Orleans Mardi Gras tradition this doubloon will be minted to commemorate the 1978 Golden Jubilee of IAEI to be held September 10-15, 1978 in New Orleans. The nominal price of 50 cents each will cover the cost of producing and handling.

Reprinted from *IAEI News*, May 1977.

Reprinted from *IAEI News*, May 1976.

Advanced Program
Golden Jubilee Meeting
September 9–15, 1978

Saturday, September 9

12:00 noon to 5:00 p.m.	Registration and advance registration credentials	Rivergate

Sunday, September 10

12:00 noon to 5:00 p.m	Registration and advance registration credentials	Rivergate
12:00 noon to 3:30 p.m	Meeting Executive Committee members of all sections, Luncheon included.	Marriott Hotel
6:00 p.m. to 9:00 p.m	Exhibits open with reception in the Exhibit Hall	Rivergate

Monday, September 11

8:00 a..m. to 5:00 p.m	Registration and advance registration credentials	Rivergate
9:00 a.m	Meeting convenes. Opening ceremonies. Official welcome. Introductions. Theme	Louisiana Superdome
12:00 noon to 2:00 p.m	Luncheon. All members and guests. Nationally known speaker (Ladies have a separate function)	Louisiana Superdome
2:00 p.m	Meeting transfers to exhibits at Rivergate (until 6:00 p.m.)	

NOTE: This evening is open. Some sections plan a social event in the section hotel. Look for section announcements.

Tuesday, September 12

8:00 a.m. to 5:00 p.m	Registration	Rivergate
8:45 a.m	Announcements	Hilton Hotel Ballroom
9:00 a.m. to 10:00 a.m	CSA and UL presentations	Hilton Hotel Ballroom
10:15 a.m. to 12:00 noon	National Electrical Code Seminar	Hilton Hotel Ballroom
12:00 noon to 2:00 p.m	Secretaries (Divisions, Chapters, Sections) Luncheon	Hilton Hotel
12:30 p.m. to 5:30 p.m.	Exhibits open	Rivergate

Evening-Open

Wednesday, September 13

9:00 a.m. to 1:00 p.m	Exibits-closing session Registration	Rivergate Rivergate
1:15 p.m.	Announcements	Hilton Hotel Ballroom
1:30 p.m. to 3:30 p.m.	Health Care/Medical Symposium, Article 517 *NEC*	Hilton Hotel Ballroom
4:00 p.m. to 5:30 p.m.	Section meetings. Each section conducts own business and elections separately	Section Headquarters Hotel

Evening-Open

Part of the New Orleans Jazz scene is the Dejans Olympia Brass Band. The band participates in most city-sponsored jazz events and can be seen struttin' through the French Quarter on their way to a concert. Wherever they go, crowds are sure to gather to enjoy the Dixie beat.

Longue Vue Gardens, a privately owned estate in New Orleans, located within miles of Canal Street, is one of the nation's great showplaces. Here you walk through a series of five gardens, each with its own plan, color scheme, and personality. Fourteen fountains, statues, patios, pebbled walkways and 100 varieties of flowers add to the enchantment of this exquisite estate garden.

The unique Rivergate in New Orleans covers six city blocks and rests at the foot of Canal Street. The main hall will accommodate crowds up to 17,000. It is readily accessible to 32 major hotels in the central business district and French Quarter and is ideal for conventions, exhibits, banquets, parties, and trade shows.

Ladies' Program – Golden Jubilee

Following are the planned activities for the Ladies' Program during our Golden Jubilee. The program, planned by Mrs. Lou Flach, has been arranged so that all ladies in attendance may participate in each activity, if they so desire.

Each group will be comprised of 375 ladies. Buses will alternate at locations as well as luncheons.

This program will be repeated for four days. Monday through Thursday, thereby allowing 3,000 ladies to participate.

Because of the complexities of arranging a four-day rotating program for an estimated 3,000 ladies, registration must be received by June 30, 1978. Ample registration is a vital factor for this program to be successful: insufficient registration may necessitate program changes. We are sure you will find the program very enjoyable so register now.

1. Garden District Personalized Tours & Luncheon
10:00 a.m.-3:00 p.m.
"Original American Section of the City"

Leave hotels by chartered bus with professional guides. Interesting sights will be pointed out as we travel the Garden District, New Orleans' loveliest residential area, the Coliseum Square Area, the University Section, as well as the Old Riverbend Township of Carrollton.

Two private homes in the Garden District will be visited. After this lovely tour, we will enjoy a savory Creole luncheon and live entertainment at the beautifully appointed "Gallier Hall."

The buses will return to the hotels at approximately 3:00 p.m.

2. Mississippi River Cruise & Buffet Luncheon
11:30 a.m.-1:30 p.m.
"The Way Life Was"

From Toulouse Street Wharf, across from Jackson Square, in the heart of the French Quarter, you will board the Steamboat *Natchez IX*. This guided cruise takes you "On the River," along the banks of commerce that date back 250 years. During this relaxing cruise, and buffet luncheon, you can turn back the clock and relive life the way it was.

Social Events
Sunday: 6:00 p.m.-8:00 p.m.
Cocktail Party–Rivergate
Monday: 7:00 p.m.-till
All Section Banquets
Tuesday: Free Evening
Wednesday: Free Evening
Thursday: 7:00 p.m.-1:00 a.m. Mardi Gras Extravaganza. Superdome. Midnight breakfast.

For the Avid Shopper
We plan to furnish transportation on Friday after our pause to take all interested shoppers to the Lake Forest Shopping Mall, the largest mall of its kind in the south.

What to Wear and Weather
New Orleans has a balmy, subtropical climate with an average September temperature of about 80 degrees. In the summer and fall, lightweight clothing is most comfortable. Raincoat and umbrella are necessary at times.

3. River Road Plantation Tour
10:00 a.m.-3:00 p.m.
"Our Past"

Leave hotels by chartered bus for a journey into the magnificent past of Louisiana. Many fascinating points of interest will be explained along the route as we journey to the "San Francisco Plantation" which is noted for its outstanding Steamboat Gothic architecture. Then, on to an internationally renowned French restaurant where we will enjoy an especially prepared seafood luncheon and live entertainment.

4. French Quarter Personalized Strolling Tour
10:00 a.m.-3:00 p.m.
"European Corner Of America"

Tour guides will meet the ladies at their headquarter hotels where they will proceed to our famous "French Quarter" for an informal stroll through the quaint streets of the Vieux Carre where they will observe a factual and informative look at the "Paris of the Americas." Two historic homes, including romantic patios rich in history, will give you an insider's view of the oldest section of New Orleans. A pause for petite refreshments along the tour will be included. Comfortable walking shoes are highly recommended.

5. "Farewell"
10:00 a.m.-11:30 p.m.
Friday, September 15, 1878
(A coffee break to say goodbye)

Café D'Adieu to be hosted at the Marriott, the Southern Section Hotel. This event will bring all Mesdames together for a final gathering and tearful goodbye.

All local hostesses will be available for last minute requests.

Most New Orleans restaurants hold fast to the rule that ladies are not allowed in slacks; however, matching slacks suits are usually acceptable. Gentlemen must wear a coat and tie. Comfortable walking shoes are a "must" for the ladies' walking tour.

"After Five" wearing apparel for ladies is acceptable dress for cocktail parties or dinner. A long dress or costume for the lady and an evening jacket, tuxedo, dark suit or costume for the man will be the dress for the September 14th Mardi Gras Extravaganza.

Reprinted from *IAEI News*, March 1978.

Thursday, September 14

9:00 a.m.	Announcements	Hilton Hotel Ballroom
9:10 a.m. 12:00 noon.	*National Electrical Code* Luncheon Recess—on your own	Hilton Hotel Ballroom
2:00 p.m to 4:30 p.m.	*National Electrical Code*	Hilton Hotel Ballroom
7:00 p.m. until? Breakfast.	Golden Jubilee Extravaganza. Mardi Gras and Midnight IAEI's 50th Birthday	Louisiana Superdome

Friday, September 15

10:00 a.m. to noon.	*National Electrical Code*	Hilton Hotel Ballroom
12:00 noon	Luncheon Recess—on your own	
1:30 p.m. to 4:30 p.m.	*National Electrical Code*	Hilton Hotel Ballroom
4:30 p.m.	Adjourn the 50th Anniversary Meeting	

Notes:
1. A souvenir program is to be printed. It needs your support in advertising. Get an ad—even a one liner will help.
2. *National Electrical Code* segments of the program will be detailed later. There will be time for discussion and proposals under controlled conditions.
3. The program events will be recorded and cassettes will be available for purchase.

Reprinted from *IAEI News*, March 1978

Memories of Golden Jubilee

The IAEI Golden Jubilee in 1978. It's history now. Were you there to participate in celebrating the 50 years of IAEI's existence?

It was held the week of September 10-15 in New Orleans, Louisiana. There were approximately 2500 members and guests registered and some had come great distances to make this a truly international affair: over 20 Japan Chapter members attended; many came from the various provinces of Canada; and representatives from all sections of the United States fanning out from the Mason-Dixon line traveled South to discuss a common interest: the safe use of electricity.

Over 100 outstanding exhibits of manufacturers, associations and testing laboratories of the electrical industry were displayed at Rivergate, a modern, sweeping structure adjacent to the famous French Quarter. Exhibitors were able to introduce their new products and methods, inspectors could ask questions and get answers and everyone was enthusiastic about the response.

The hotels where most members stayed such as the Marriott, Monteleone, Hilton, Fairmont and International were all conveniently located to get to the many activities planned at the Rivergate and the Hilton.

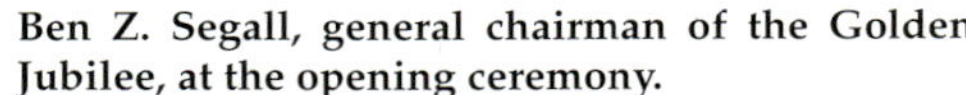

Ben Z. Segall, general chairman of the Golden Jubilee, at the opening ceremony.

The balconies of New Orleans.

There were superb speakers who informed us on developments in the industry, the problems of the electrical inspector and some of the ways in which they can be solved.

The *Code* discussions and seminars were well attended and resulted in interesting discussions. The *Code* proposals and questions sessions and panel meetings were productive.

Each section conducted its own business meeting and election as it would have had there been the separate section meetings held every year.

For those of us as first time tourists to New Orleans, we found this southern city a unique one. Southern hospitality lives!

The city is a mecca for history buffs. Exploring the French Quarter with its Royal Street and Basin Street, Pirate's Alley, its charming courtyards, marvelous cafes and restaurants and delightful antique and curio shops was exciting. We viewed with awe and respect the splendor of St. Louis Cathedral. We strolled through Jackson Square with its artists, magnolias and ferns and other lush tropical plants that grew so casually everywhere, the same ones we nursed so carefully back home in our living rooms with only half the results. Is it the humidity?

We walked slowly through the Cabildo where the transfer of the Louisiana purchase took place and thought we could hear voices from the past as we stood silently looking over the artifacts of history in the now quiet museum. We went aboard the Steamboat *Natchez* up the muddy Mississippi along the banks of commerce dating back to the 1700's and even imagined Huck Finn on his raft right around the bend.

We stood in one of the unique burying grounds of New Orleans where the swampy terrain necessitates above ground family crypts.

We'll never forget the 30¢ ride on the streetcar down St. Charles Avenue that traveled through the Garden District where so many large stately homes of an era forever gone still stand. We visited a grand restored plantation with the lofty ceilings, intricate woodwork and superb antiques. How did they ever paint to the top of those high walls and ceilings? And the sweeping verandah, live oaks and Spanish moss, the fireplaces and chandeliers, rich heavy draperies and huge portrait paintings hung from silk interwoven cords to the top of the wide

Getting a tour of New Orleans.

The Japan Chapter of IAEI was well represented at IAEI's 50th Anniversary convention in New Orleans, Louisiana, in September. We were delighted that over 20 members had come such a great distance to participate in the programs and activities.

Members of the Japan Electrical Construction Association, Incorporated, and the Kanto Electrical Safety Inspection Association, both of Tokyo, offered their congratulations to IAEI on their 50th Anniversary in letters presented to our editor, L. E. LaFehr, while in New Orleans. The original letters were beautifully hand written in black and red ink on 18 ½-inch by 12 ½-inch rice paper

Excerpted from *IAEI News*, November 1978.

moldings; ladies' sitting rooms, separate gentlemen's drawing rooms. Great balls of fire! It was *Gone With The Wind* come alive.

New Orleans cuisine certainly isn't the type of fare found in health food stores. The calories are only outnumbered by cholesterol content. But who can refuse the kaleidoscope of flavorful preparations of New Orleans chefs and rich, brown chicory coffee?

But what is the French Quarter without Dixieland jazz? Our fingers and toes could not resist a synchronous tapping to Al Hirt's inspired rendition of "When the Saints Go Marching In."

Top it off with IAEI's Mardi Gras extravaganza with its floats, costumes, food and prizes and the end result was an unquestionable success. Congratulations to the grand prize winner…it must have been great driving home in a brand new Chevy Malibu Classic.

New Orleans, thanks for the memories. See you in 2003?

Reprinted from *IAEI News*, November 1978.

Al Hirt and his band—Superb Dixieland.

Bourbon Street in New Orleans

The Oklahoma Chapter at the 1978 Golden Jubilee in New Orleans, Louisiana.

At the ribbon cutting ceremonies (*left to right*): James Fitzmorris, Louisiana lieutenant governor, George Riley, Joseph Roohan, Gilbert Hazzard and Ben Segal.

1977 International President

John E. Leeming, P. Eng., native of Toronto, Canada, has been a member of IAEI since 1956. Currently director of the Certification Division of Canadian Standards Association, Mr. Leeming joined CSA in 1963 after many years with Canadian General Electric, where he was manager of Codes and Approvals.

Mr. Leeming has served in various managerial positions at CSA, including manager of the Electrical Department, manager of the Engineering Services Department and assistant manager, Certification Division. Prior to becoming director of the Certification Division in 1974, he was manager of Special Projects, CSA Standards Division.

Mr. Leeming has been involved with every aspect of standardization and certification, including testing and inspection of electrical and non-electrical products. He was survey director for the "Clinical Laboratory and Electro-Medical Equipment Study," which was undertaken by CSA for the Canadian Department of National Health and Welfare in the early '70s and resulted in CSA's current program of standardization of hospital equipment.

As director of certification he is responsible for administering CSA's total program of certification. This includes the operations of CSA's laboratories in Toronto, Ontario, and the four Canadian regional branch offices, plus the certification and inspection activities at CSA agencies in the United Kingdom, continental Europe, Japan and other inspection offices throughout the world. Currently, electrical inspections involved with CSA certification activities are conducted in 33 countries by 80 inspectors.

Mr. Leeming is a member of several other organizations including the Institute of Electrical and Electronic Engineers, the Standards Engineers Society and the Electric Club of Toronto.

—Excerpted from *IAEI News*, January 1977.

1978 International President

IAEI's new president for 1978 is native New Yorker, **George E. Riley**. He has been an active member of the New York Chapter since 1949 and is currently principal electrical inspector in the city of New York.

He served with the U.S. Coast Guard from 1942 to 1945 and was discharged as an electrician's mate. He immediately entered the electrical industry and worked for an electrical contractor. He entered civil service in 1947 and was appointed an electrical inspector, then became supervising electrical inspector, and then advanced to his present position.

Mr. Riley's participation in the IAEI has been extensive. In 1968 he was the Eastern Section president. He has served on the IAEI executive board for 25 years, the Eastern Section executive board for 20 years and has been a member of the board of directors since 1966, was New York Chapter chairman for two years and represents IAEI on code panel 23. He is now chairman of IAEI's educational committee studying inspector certification. Since 1960 he has been annually appointed to serve as chairman of New York's Electrical Licensing Board.

Other membership affiliations include Underwriters' Laboratories Electrical Council, past secretary of the Electrical Inspector's Division, Local #3, IBEW for eight years and former member of New York's Electrical League's board of directors.

He also holds honorary membership in the Association of Electrical Construction Engineers and the Nassau Electrical League of Long Island.

Excerpted from *IAEI News*, January 1978.

Gersil Kay

Gersil Kay, a licensed electrical contractor with Morris Newmark Brothers in Philadelphia, became the first woman member of the Eastern Pennsylvania Chapter executive committee.

All committee members are presented with a blazer with the IAEI emblem. Ms. Kay shown at a 1979 chapter meeting, designed her own jacket and had it tailored.

Reprinted from *IAEI News*, July 1979.

Northern California Chapter officers for 1974 at the January 12, 1974, installation meeting. *From left to right*: **E. E. Carlton, Division of Industrial Safety, past IAEI president who installed the officers; Al Cooper, Contra Costa County, chairman; John Thompson, Berkley, past chairman; Charles Waldron, San Leandro, secretary/treasurer; and Dave Forsythe, Hayward, vice chairman;**

Wilford "Bill" Summers

Wilford I. Summers, chief electrical field specialist of the National Fire Protection Association since 1973 and secretary of the National Electric Code Committee became the new executive director of the International Association of Electrical Inspectors on November 1. He has been an active member of IAEI, has served as a panelist and moderator on numerous IAEI code conferences and is a past chairman of the Rocky Mountain Chapter IAEI.

Summers is also secretary of the NFPA electrical section and executive secretary of the National Association of Chief Electrical Inspectors. Well-known for lectures on electricity before many trade groups, he has 27 years' experience in the electrical construction industry, including 10 years as chief electrical inspector for the city of Colorado Springs and the county of El Paso, and 11 years as a licensed journeyman electrician.

He is a corporate member of Underwriters' Laboratories as a safety expert, a member of the UL Electrical Council and a member of the American National Standards Institute Electrical and Electronics Standards Management Board and the International Brotherhood of Electrical Workers.

He is the editor of the 4th edition of the *Handbook of the National Electrical Code* and the 10th Edition of *American Electrician's Handbook*, both McGraw-Hill publications, and editor of NFPA's *1978 National Electrical Code Handbook*.

Summers is a Purple Heart veteran of the Korean War.

His Legacy

The 1980s were busy times for the association with unprecedented growth of both members and assets. In December of 1979 the association had 13,522 members. At the end of February 1990 membership had expanded to 20,591 members, and increase of over 52 percent. At the end of December 1979 the association's assets were $276,500. At the end of December 1989 the assets were $1,349,529, an increase of 358 percent.

The September/October 1980 *IAEI News* contained an *Analysis of the 1981 NEC* by Bill Summers. This was later published in an illustrated version and has become an integral part of chapter and section meetings as well as study material for IAEI seminars.

On September 19-20, 1980, the first of four IAEI-sponsored *Code* seminars was held in Houston, Texas, with an attendance of over 250. Later in October a Denver seminar had an attendance of over 400! The Los Angeles and Rochester, New York, seminars were also huge successes and the association has continued this successful and rewarding program to this day.

On March 28, 1981, the first certification examinations for construction code inspectors was given in over 100 cities. IAEI had become a partner in the National Board of Governors for the Certification of Construction Code Inspectors along with the building officials associations and several states utilizing certification requirements for electrical inspector. International Conference of Building Officials and Southern Building Code Congress International eventually went their way, but our program has continued to grow until there are now more electrical inspectors certified in our program than all other programs combined. At last count over 8,000 electrical examinations have been given.

Reprinted from *IAEI News*, November 1979 and May 1990.

1979 International President

A native of North Dakota and a member of the International Association of Electrical Inspectors for 28 years, **Leo Nagel** is executive director of the North Dakota State Electrical Board. Nagel was instrumental in organizing the North Dakota Chapter of IAEI in 1961 and served as its first chairman.

He got his electrical training in the U.S. Army during World War II and served as a technician in an army searchlight unit. After the war, he worked as an apprentice electrician on electrical construction and became a state journeyman wireman. After receiving his North Dakota master electrician's license in 1949, he became interested in electrical inspection and became a state inspector for the North Dakota State Electrical Board. In 1958 he was named chief electrical inspector for the state. The title was changed to executive secretary in 1962, and to executive director in 1973, and in that capacity he is responsible for enforcement of the *National Electrical Code* and State Wiring Standards, the supervision of state electrical inspectors, formulation and administration of electrician's examinations, issuance of licenses, maintaining a complete record of all persons holding North Dakota licenses and the updating of State Wiring Standards to avoid conflict with the *NEC*. He implemented a bimonthly meeting for state inspectors to provide information and training towards a uniform statewide inspection program.

In 1968 he served as president of the IAEI Western Section and was elected to the IAEI board of directors. He is past president of the National Association of Chief Electrical Inspectors and is certified electrical safety inspector.

He is a member of code-making panel 5, and the Electrical Council Underwriters' Laboratories Inc., Chicago, Illinois.

Excerpted from *IAEI News*, January 1979.

The 1980s became the Me! Me! Me!–generation of status seekers. Binge buying and credit became a way of life and "Shop 'til you drop" was the watchword. Labels were everything. Tom Wolfe dubbed the baby-boomers as the "splurge generation." Video games, aerobics, minivans, camcorders, and talk shows became part of our lives. The decade began with double-digit inflation, Reagan declared a war on drugs, hospital costs rose, the AIDS epidemic was discovered, and unemployment rose. At the very end of the decade the Berlin Wall was removed—this ending of the Cold War was so pivotal that British historian Eric Hobsbawn called 1989 the end of the 20th century.

1980-1989

A Material World

Ten Guidelines for Electrical Inspectors

It takes some of us many years — some a lifetime — to learn that most useful rules on doing a better job are so deceptively simple as to escape recognition. We often tend to wave aside the simplest things as lacking in deep and profound significance. Anyone who takes the time to heed the following simple suggestions, however, should have ten fewer obstacles before him in pursuit of success on the job. These tips may be hard to follow, but they are easy to understand.

1. Do One Thing At a Time.
Remember, no man can do more. Two things at a time or three things at a time are less than one thing at a time. Here, mathematics stands confounded, for here always — more is less.

2. Know The Problem.
Much time is skillfully wasted by people tying to find the answer when they really don't understand the problem. Be sure you have a clear (and agreed upon) description of the problem first.

3. Learn To Listen.
No one has a monopoly on good ideas, so listen. Open your ears before you open your mouth — it may open your eyes.

4. Learn to Ask Questions.
Make a point to ask questions if only to double check your position. Do not approach a problem with a preconceived notion of the answer. This may be quite satisfying to the ego, but seldom to the solution of the problem at hand.

5. Distinguish Sense From Nonsense.
If it takes a five page memo to explain or justify 25 words of text, stop and take a second look.

6. Accept Change As Inevitable.
Every job is subject to change. Beware of the pat solution. A rule good enough ten years ago — or even one year ago — may not be good enough for today.

7. Admit Your Mistakes.
It is a great temptation to rationalize our mistakes into a towering edifice built on a foundation of words. No matter how glittering the fabrication, there is the inevitable risk that someone else will see through it. Build on a foundation of reality — or you will not be building at all.

8. Be Simple.
Five or six syllable words depress readers and may not communicate, but serve only to inflate the writer's ego. Use words as if you were charged five cents for every one.

9. Be Calm.
Sensible and sound opinions are seldom reached in a frenzy. Judgment and maturity are more likely to thrive in a contemplative atmosphere than a hurricane. Once you depart from calmness, you risk confusion and chaos.

10. Smile.
Effective workers are usually serious, but the best try not to show it too much. One of the most common failures of many persons is loss of perspective. After arduously scaling the molehill, we plant our success flag triumphantly at its crest, proclaiming it to be greater than Mount Everest. We take ourselves too seriously.

Joseph A. Tedesco, assistant electrical inspector, city of New Haven, Connecticut. Reprinted from *IAEI News*, November 1971.

History of the Electrical Field Service Project

The history of the Electrical Field Service Project of the *National Electrical Code* is one of cooperation between the National Fire Protection Association and the International Association of Electrical Inspectors.

The Electrical Field Service had its beginnings in 1925 when several of the leading organizations interested in the *National Electrical Code*, representing electrical manufacturers, contractors, inspectors, utilities and fire insurance, agreed to subscribe funds to the NFPA to enable it to employ a competent specialist who would devote his full time to advancing the adoption and application of the *NEC*. Up to the present time six men have served as head of the Electrical Field Service project. The first was W. J. Canada who held the post briefly, and was replaced by Victor H. Tousley in 1928. Tousley had been chief electrical inspector of Chicago prior to his appointment. He was succeeded by Charles L. Smith, former chief electrical inspector of the city of Detroit. Smith served from 1948 until his death in 1957. Frank Stetka, former chief electrical inspector for the District of Columbia, was then appointed and he continued in the post until his retirement at the end of 1968. On January 1, 1969, John H. Watt, former chief electrical inspector for the city of Seattle, assumed the post until his untimely death December 26, 1973. The post was then filled by Wilford "Bill" Summers, former chief electrical inspector of Colorado Springs, who held the position until November 1, 1979.

Prior to the appointment of Frank Stetka, the NFPA electrical field engineer served a dual role, acting also as secretary-treasurer of IAEI. After Smith's death in 1957, Everett F. Cogan was appointed secretary-treasurer of IAEI continuing in this capacity until 1962. L. E. LaFehr was appointed managing director in 1962 and continued as head of the organization until his retirement. The two parallel jobs have now come full cycle as Summers has resigned as chief electrical field specialist with NFPA and assumed the reins as executive director of IAEI.

With the end of an old administration and the coming of the new it becomes incumbent upon us all to take a fresh look at our organization. The IAEI logo incorporates the keystone with the motto that we are "The Keystone of the Electri-

James D. Kennedy, *left*, Winston-Salem/Forsyth County inspector shown receiving the plaque for the North Carolina Electrical Inspector of the Year Award presented by Curtis R. Kennedy, *right*, chairman of the nominating committee of the Ellis Cannady chapter in 1980.

1980 International President

Beginning the new decade for IAEI, native Californian, **Robert D. Sappington**, is the association's president of 1980. He has been a member of the Northern California Chapter since 1952 and the chief electrical inspector of San Jose, California, since 1961. He worked as an apprentice, journeyman electrician, and superintendent in the electrical industry, prior to commencing his electrical inspection career with the city of San Jose in 1953.

He has served in various IAEI chapter and section offices, including two consecutive years in 1968 and 1969 as president of the Southwestern Section, and the Northern California Chapter chairman in 1964 and secretary-treasurer 1964 to 1966. He is a member of the IAEI board of directors. He is also past president of the National Association of Chief Electrical Inspectors, National Fire Protection Association, and was elected as a corporate member of Underwriters' Laboratories, Inc., presently serving on UL's Electrical Council. He is chairman of code-making panel 7 of the National Electrical Code Committee and has served on the National Fire Protection Association's technical committee on grounding portable equipment. He is a registered electrical safety engineer.

Excerpted from *IAEI News*, January 1980.

Duane Lauf at the North Dakota Chapter meeting held November 19–20, 1981, at the Kirkwood Motor Inn, Bismarck, North Dakota. Ten-gallon Stetsons serve just as well for keeping snow off the head as an overhang on the porch! Besides an electrical inspector needs a mark of distinction to inspect oil wells and travel the Badlands of North Dakota.

cal Industry." Our primary function is the safe installation and use of electrical materials, devices and appliances, and to that end we cooperate with all groups having a similar goal. We pride ourselves on this close cooperation and intend to continue this relationship. On the other hand, times are changing and we must also open up other avenues of communications with federal agencies, model code groups, Institute of Electrical and Electronics Engineers, Incorporated, and other groups who are vitally concerned with safe electrical installations. We have been fortunate to have the assistant of the "circuit riders," who represent many associations, to assist us in the education of our membership. Certainly we wish to continue this close relationship in years to come. The keystone is indicative that IAEI serves as the catalyst to bring all the groups together with the common purpose of promoting the welfare of the public by providing safe electrical installations. IAEI is the contact group between the public and the electrical industry on all items relating to public safety; no other group can claim that distinction.

As with every association we have a goal to grow and to prosper. To attain these goals your board of directors has made a bold decision to move ahead in the education field in the area of field seminars. Many organizations and individuals are in the business of seminars, for the most part as a profit venture. We foresee seminars on the *National Electrical Code* not as a profit-making venture, but as a way of putting our association before the public, and hopefully, to attract some of these people to our association, because we do have so much to offer. Education is our beacon light to the future and we hope to improve our association through seminars, suggestions to our chapters and sections on ways to improve their meetings, and also, by changing the editorial policies of the *IAEI News.*

In the future we will have only one *Code* column and it will be called "Focus on the Code." The contributors will be the IAEI representatives on the various code-making panels plus other selected experts. This new policy is being undertaken as it is essential that every answer given in our columns should be as definitive as can reasonably be expected. Our representatives on the code-making panels have a unique advantage of having participated in *Code* discussions at the highest level and thereby can impart words of wisdom to our readers that can be obtained in no other way. Our association embraces the entire electrical industry and our magazine should have a broad appeal to all of our readers. Articles on the *Code* and responses to field problems should be such that electricians, electrical contractors, or electrical inspectors can apply the principles they learn in the *News,* on the job, with reasonable assurance that the installation will meet the *Code*. We intend that the *News* become an educational medium to eliminate some of the needless conflicts that arise in the field due to a lack of knowledge. By increasing our credibility through "professionalism" our membership will become more confident in applying the interpretations found in the *News.*

Our entire association owes a special word of appreciation to our *Code* consultants who have maintained regular code columns in the *News.* They have built up their own special following and in coming years will always be looked up to for their major contributions to the welfare of our association. To you all a rousing "well done."

As we go forward we must do so with enthusiasm and hope, not with fear and trepidation. It has been said very

1981 International President

Roger Niedermeyer, a native of Portland, Oregon, is the new 1981 president of IAEI. In his 35th year as electrical inspector for the city of Portland, he has been the chief inspector for the city for the past 20 years. He is a member and past chairman of IAEI's Oregon Chapter and a member of IAEI Northwestern Section executive board and board of directors.

After the war, Niedermeyer became a licensed supervising electrician in the state of Oregon and was a member of the International Brotherhood of Electrical Workers' local examining board for eleven years. He has taught apprentice, journeyman and advanced *Code* for thirteen years and revised and edited two different city electrical codes.

He is a prior member of the National Steering Committee on Use and Application. He is also a member of code-making panel 4 of the National Electrical Code Committee, Underwriters' Laboratories Electrical Council and a UL corporate member, American National Standards Institute C-73 Committee–attachment caps and plug receptacles. He was sent by the city of Portland to Germany to inspect $40 million worth of electrical equipment coming to industrial plants in Portland.

During World War II Niedermeyer served as a fire control man, 1st class, in charge of the main battery plotting room and 14-inch turrets on the USS *California* and attended fire control and radar and sonar school in the Navy.

Excerpted from *IAEI News*, January 1981.

well that people react to change in three ways: to the timid, change is threatening, as things might get worse; to the confident, change is encouraging, as things may get better; and to the enthusiastic, change is inspiring, as it is a challenge to make things get better. With these thoughts foremost in our mind let us go forward with confidence and enthusiasm for there is much to do, and with hard work we can do it…together.

—By W.I. Summers, editor. Reprinted from *IAEI News*, January 1980.

Eastern Section Timeline

1964 **M. F. Hoffmann**, of Queens, NY, is elected Eastern Section secretary.

1966 **Delmar Division** of the Chesapeake Chapter is granted.

1969 **Arthur J. Jacobsen**, of Brooklyn, NY, is elected Eastern Section secretary.

1973 **Peconic Division** of the Long Island Chapter is granted its charter.

1975 **Southern Division** of the New Jersey Chapter is created. Reorganized in 1996 to form the **South Jersey Chapter**

Board of directors approves the creation of the **Putnam Division** of the Westchester Chapter.

1978 **Ray Millet, Jr.,** of Brooklyn, NY, is elected Eastern Section secretary.

1983 **Central Pennsylvania Chapter** is formed on February 24, 1983.

Northeast Division of the Eastern Pennsylvania Chapter is created.

1986 **Northeastern Pennsylvania Chapter** is born.

1989 Board of directors approves the creation of the **Green Mountain Chapter**.

Putnam Chapter is formed.

1992 Charter for the **Cape and Islands Chapter** is granted.

Western Massachusetts Chapter charter is granted.

Granite State Chapter is formed.

Eastern Section 1974 officers and executive committee. Front row (*left to right*): George Riley, fourth vice president international; Carl Schaad; James Sheppard, third vice president; Artie Jacobsen, secretary-treasurer; Bill Love, Jr., international past president; Milton Lounsbury, 1974 section president; Mel Borleis, Jr., Eastern Section past president; Robert Rindell, first vice president; Sol Leiman, fourth vice president. Middle row (*left to right*): Bill Fleischauer; Olive Dore; George Sullivan; Robert Kimball; John Fetty; Ernie McNeill; Harry Buss; Edward O'Connell Jr.; Raul Schweinberg. Back row (*left to right*): James Dillon; Albert Reed; Russell Hendrick; William Hauze Jr.; Andre Cartal; Jack Webster; Edward Sargent; Edward Williams; William O'Connell; and Len Turner.

New Saudi Arabia Chapter Chairman Visits IO

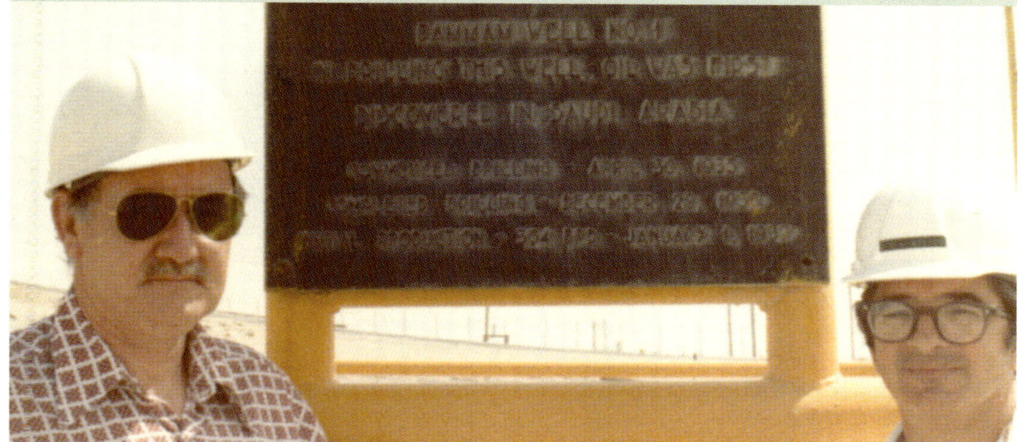

Taken at the site of the first oil producing well in Saudi Arabia are *left to right:* **Carlon Will, secretary of the Saudi Arabia Chapter IAEI, and James C. Librande, chairman. The first drilling by the Arabian American Oil Company at this Saudi Arabian well was in 1935.**

James C. Librande, supervisor and electrical inspector, at ARAMCO's Saudi Arabia's oil operations in Dhahran, Saudi Arabia, visited the International office of IAEI in Park Ridge, Illinois, in October 1980. Librande is an active member of IAEI's new Saudi Arabia Chapter.

He states the situation in Saudi Arabia is stable at this time and he does not see any changes in the immediate future. He has worked in that country for many years and; although he misses many American ways of life and conveniences, he states that ARAMCO has provided its employees a good quality of life within the perimeters of its operations, including good housing, schools and stores. Families of the company are not allowed to go outside of the village, however, in automobiles. An average daytime temperature may be 110°.

2003 officers: *seated left to right*, **Robert Bushman, vice president and Mark Regan, president;** *back row left to right*, **Daniel Billones, third vice president and Manuel Reyes Mon, director of membership.**

Electrical wiring in housing units and cities are mostly underground. The need for safe electrical practices is of paramount importance at the ARAMCO oil sites.

Excerpted from *IAEI News*, January 1981.

1982 International President

George W. Flach, chief electrical inspector of the city of New Orleans, started his career when he enrolled in the electrical course at Delgrado Trade School in 1936. As a 1949 graduate of Tulane University of Louisiana with a bachelor of science in electrical engineering he worked as an electrical field engineer during the construction of a large industrial complex until his appointment in 1953 as chief electrical inspector and secretary to the Board of Electrical Examiners of New Orleans.

He has devoted many hours to the promotion of electrical safety by speaking before civic groups, teaching the *National Electrical Code*, conducting seminars on *NEC* changes, grounding, etc., and serving on various committees.

Flach is a member of the board of directors, IAEI, and the executive committee of the Southern Section IAEI. At the Southern Section annual meetings, he usually acts as moderator during the *Code* discussions. He is a senior member of the Institute of Electronic & Electrical Engineers. He is past chairman of the George Welman Chapter of IAEI, past president of the Southern Section IAEI, and past president of the Chief Electrical Inspector Section of National Fire Protection Association. He is a registered professional engineer in the state of Louisiana and a certified electrical safety engineer in IAEI.

Much of his spare time is devoted to writing articles dealing with electrical safety and the *National Electrical Code.* His answers to questions appear in the "Focus On The Code" column in the *IAEI News*, and he has a monthly column, "Code Q&A" in *Electrical Contractor* magazine. His articles on electrical safety and electric heating have appeared in many magazines.

Excerpted from *IAEI News*, January 1982.

The National Electrical Code Circuit Riders and The Roadrunner Club

The *National Electrical Code* circuit riders were a group of individuals that contributed immensely to the discussion of the *Code* at the various IAEI section and chapter meetings. This group of men because of their broad electrical backgrounds and a willingness to share their knowledge have done more to promote the welfare of the IAEI membership than any other single factor.

During the late 1960s at some of the IAEI section meetings, a group that had been regularly attending all of these meetings for the past ten years, discussed the desirability of forming a club of circuit riders. The Canadian Section was not included because they have their own electrical code. This group consisted of Dan Boone, Frank Stetka, Kent Stiner, Lou LaFehr and Dick Lloyd. In addition to attending section meetings, we also had been attending many chapter meetings throughout the United States including Alaska and Hawaii as well as the six-chapter meetings in Texas and Louisiana and the tri-chapter meetings in California.

In the early years, Bill Gaffney, and later, Les Lynch, servicing as secretary of the Northwestern Section would arrange some of the chapter meetings to be in sequence so that the circuit riders could attend them in a single trip. They would invite them well in advance so that the circuit riders could include their meetings in their travel schedules. Many of the chapters had spring meetings or other regular times for their meetings and the circuit riders would try to attend unless a conflict occurred. These circuit riders either served on code panels or had sufficient contact with code panel members so that a uniform interpretation of the latest *Code* requirements were made available to those attending the meetings. Most of these meetings were well attended and had good *Code* discussions, such as those in Raleigh, Denver, Minneapolis, Nashville, Buffalo, Portland, Michigan, Idaho, Florida, Ohio, Indiana, and many others.

Although we never formed a formal club, the executive committee of the Southern Section decided to honor the circuit riders by awarding them solid gold roadrunner tie tacs/lapel pins that had ruby eyes. They were presented by Dude Parmley to Dan Boone, Ed Brand, Money Brandon, Lou LaFehr, Dick Lloyd, Len Sessler, Frank Stetka, Kent Stiner, Hank Watson and John Watt at the Southern Section meeting in Dallas, Texas, on October 20, 1970. Later, awards of the gold roadrunner pins were made to Clem Baxter, Alan Reed, Ben Segall, Dick Shaul, Bill Summers, Jack Wells, and Baron Whitaker by Dude at the Southwestern Section meeting in Fresno, California, on September 15, 1976. Dude also presented a gold roadrunner to Gene Carlton at the six-chapter meeting in San Antonio, Texas, on April 23, 1977, and to Earl Roberts at the electrical section meeting of the annual National Fire Protection Association in Boston, Massachusetts on May 19, 1980.

Mention should be made of some of the others that did not receive pins but did make significant contributions to

Road Runners and Circuit Riders who attended all five section meetings at the 1996 Southern Section meeting are, from *left to right*: Richard Lloyd, Phil Cox, Andy Cartal, Doug Geralde, Charles Forsberg, Jim Pauley, John Erickson, Hal Lichenstein, Earl Roberts, Harvey Johnson, Herb Moulton and John Troglia.

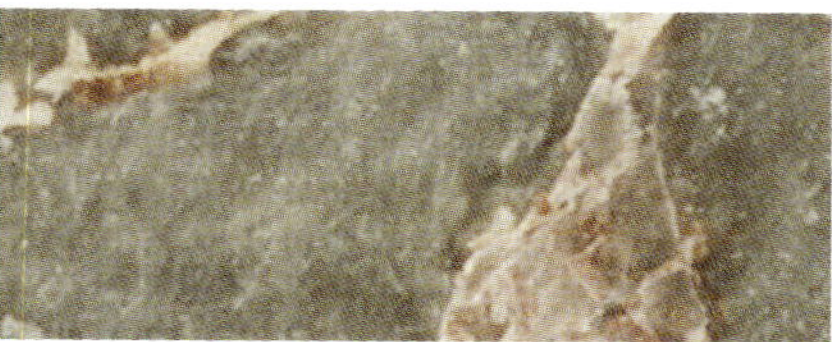

discussions of the requirements in the *National Electric Code* at IAEI meetings. These include Bill Hildebrand, George Flach, Orville Cavanagh, Norm Davis and NEMA regional representatives; Creighton Schwan, Bob Pullen, D. J. Clements, Bill Worthing and Joe Ross.

Note: Roadrunner Club members Clem Baxter and Dick Shaul not shown. By Richard Lloyd. Excerpted from *IAEI News*, May 1981.

Daniel Boone

Money Brandon

Gene Carlton

Lou LaFehr

Dick Lloyd

Alan Reed

Earl Roberts

Len Sessler

Frank Stetka

Kent Stiner

Bill Summers

Hank Watson

John Watt

Jack Wells

Baron Whitaker

1983 International President

George Wilf Lawson, executive director of the Safety Engineering Services Division, Ministry of Labour, British Columbia, Canada, is an active member of the British Columbia Chapter IAEI.

Lawson was employed in the electrical industry prior to serving with the Royal Canadian Air Force in World War II. His technical, professional and management education background includes graduation from the Institute of Technology and Art in Calgary, and in course studies at the University of Alberta and the Banff School of Fine Arts.

Following graduation and completion of an apprenticeship in the electrical field where he obtained the status of a first class and master electrician, he was employed in private industry. In 1949 he assumed the position of assistant to the electrical superintendent for a municipal utility and was responsible for establishing an electrical inspection department. Through a competition, he received an appointment as an electrical inspector with the Alberta provincial government electrical inspection branch in 1951. After serving in various capacities he was appointed assistant chief inspector and subsequently chief electrical inspector for the province in 1959.

His involvements have included membership on the Canadian Electrical Code Part I Committee, the Canadian Standards Association Council (Electrical), chairman of the Alberta Provincial Code Committee, as well as chairman for the Board of Examiners for a master electrician certificate program, chairmanships for the Canadian Electrical Code Committee on grounding, mobile home courts, mobile housing, pre-fab buildings, as well as chairman and member of various committees developing electrical safety programming. He was a member of the advisory committee for the Alberta Institute of Electrical Technology courses, and conducted lectures on the Canadian Electrical Code for several years for adult evening classes. He has served on various other national and international committees extending beyond the electrical field including the *ad hoc* group which established the criteria for accreditation of Canadian certification organizations and testing laboratories, training programs for inspectors from the Bahamas, and represented Canada in Geneva on safety in the petroleum industry.

—Excerpted from *IAEI News*, January 1983.

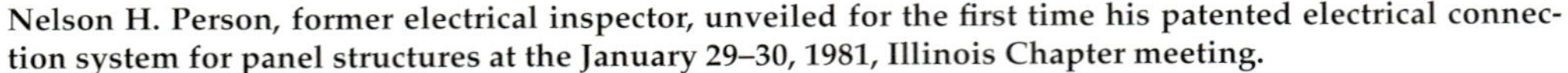

Nelson H. Person, former electrical inspector, unveiled for the first time his patented electrical connection system for panel structures at the January 29–30, 1981, Illinois Chapter meeting.

1984 International President

Albert J. Reed, vice president of the New York Board of Fire Underwriters, New York City, and general manager of the Electrical Department, has been a member of the Long Island Chapter since 1956. He has been a member of the Eastern Section executive committee since 1961 and a member of the board of directors since 1979. He served as a member of IAEI's education certification committee, assisting in assembling the material for the first edition of the *Electrical Inspectors Guide*. He is certified in electrical inspector one and two-family, electrical inspector general and electrical plan review.

He joined the electrical department of the New York Board of Fire Underwriters in 1956 as an electrical inspector, advanced to chief inspector of the Long Island Division in 1960, regional metropolitan manager in 1969, and general manager in 1975.

In 1963 he satisfied the requirements of the state of New York Department of Education and was certified to teach the subject of "Interpretation and Application of the *National Electrical Code*." He taught the subject for Nassau County's Board of Cooperative Educational Service for twelve years, and fire science courses at Suffolk County Community College for three years.

He is past president of the National Association of Chief Electrical Inspectors of NFPA, a member of the NFPA subtechnical committee on electrical equipment maintenance, code-making panel 4, Underwriters' Laboratories Electrical Council, New York State Association of Electrical Contractors, Nassau Electric League, Suffolk County Electrical Contractors Association, and Building Inspectors Association of Nassau County, Long Island.

He participated as a member of the Electrical License Boards of the city of Long Beach, the village of Floral Park and the township of Huntington for thirteen years.

Reprinted from *IAEI News*, January 1984.

After watching the horse Winagaingin at the races attended by the Northwestern Section members September 18, 1985, during the annual section meeting held in Spokane, Washington, members help hold up the horse blanket with "N. W. Section – IAEI," clearly noted. Identified in center holding blanket are: Ed Lawry, 1985 international president (*dark trousers and white shirt*); and to his right, Bill Summers, executive director, IAEI; Laura Summers; and Jan Lawry.

Chief Eiichi Ikeda at his opening address during the IAEI Japan Chapter meeting on June 17, 1982. He told about the relations between the Japan Chapter and the many recent topics and subjects in the field of electrical safety.

1985 International President

Edward C. Lawry, supervising electrical engineer of the Division of Safety and Buildings, Department of Industry, Labor and Human Relations, state of Wisconsin, is the new 1985 president of IAEI. He has been a member of IAEI since 1961, serving as Western Section IAEI president in 1973 and Wisconsin Chapter secretary-treasurer from 1963 to 1968 and 1977 to the present.

Following graduation from the University of Wisconsin in 1957 he was employed in private industry as an application engineer for an electrical equipment manufacturer. In 1961 he was employed by the state of Wisconsin and served in various electrical inspections and enforcement positions until assuming his current position on July 1, 1984. He is responsible for developing and implementing a new statewide program of electrical inspection, certification of commercial electrical inspectors, and examination and certification of master electricians.

He is currently chairman of *NEC* code-making panel 3, and is a past chairman of CMP-12 and member of CMP-11. Lawry has previously served on National Fire Protection Association (NFPA) *National Electrical Code* technical subcommittees on control circuit protection, disconnecting means for appliances and wiring in ducts and plenums. He is currently serving on the *NEC* technical subcommittee on solar photovoltaic and NFPA task force on marking and illumination of means of egress.

He is a member of the NFPA, National Electrical Safety Code Committee—ANSI C2, and corporate member of Underwriters' Laboratories and has served on UL's Electrical Council since 1965. In addition, he has served on a UL advisory committee on combustion products for PVC in building construction and *ad hoc* committee on cables in air handling plenums.

—Excerpted from *IAEI News*, January 1985.

THE SECOND CENTURY OF ELECTRICITY

Continued dependence on reliable sources of power has created a demand for electrical generation since 1982. And things are not likely to change in the next 100 years…

Electricity. It's as simple as turning on a switch. Always there when you need it and very versatile. Electricity can meet most energy demands, from residential heating and cooling to lighting up America's stores and office buildings to running heavy machinery in industrial facilities.

Almost everyone in this country uses electricity daily. In many ways, our life-styles are based on the premise that electricity will always be available in abundance.

Yet, it was only 100 years ago that Thomas Alva Edison first introduced the commercial sale of electricity. It was in September 1882, in fact, that Edison introduced direct-current electricity to some 50 customers. Edison's utility company served a variety of commercial customers in lower Manhattan's Pearl Street area. One of these initial customers, *The New York Times*, wrote about the event in glowing terms, discussing how clear and easy electric lighting was on the eyes. *The Times* noted that, "To turn on the light nothing is required but to turn the thumbscrew; no matches needed, no patent appliances….you turn the thumbscrew and the light is there with no nauseous smell, no flicker, no glare…"

By the end of 1882, there were some 225 houses wired for about 5,000 lamps, lit by electricity generated from that one Pearl Street station. By 1888, 185 Edison central electric illuminating companies were operating around the country.

With the advent of this new, efficient, and clean source of power, society began to take on an entirely new look. Electrically powered elevators gave man the opportunity to build the first skyscrapers, and cities began to rise upward, higher and higher. Electric trolleys provided a new means of transporting people. Electricity also offered new methods of working at the factory and in the home. It became available to just about everyone, everywhere in the country, and even provided new means for recreation—such as the electric carousel and night baseball.

With time, electricity offered Americans more freedom than our forefathers ever dreamt was possible. And today, that desire for freedom is more prevalent than ever, as evidenced by our quest for laborsaving devices, both in the workplace and home. Electric word-processing units, small computers for billing systems and computer-operated assembly lines became the logical step after the electric typewriter. Computers and telecommunications devices are playing an ever-increasing role in our work-reducing effort increasing productivity.

Microwave ovens, electric clothes dryers, and washing machines, dishwashers and vacuum cleaners have all

Enjoying the evening banquet at the 36th annual Nevada Chapter meeting on April 27, 1985, at the Frontier Hotel were: (front row, *left to right*): Chairman Larry Crouch, Londa Crouch, Pat and Bill Worthing, Gwen Holmes; (back row, *left to right*): Bill Morris, Gene Carlton, Bob Newton, and Dick Holmes

Peggy Reese of the Tennessee Chapter, Chattanooga Division IAEI, is shown accepting the silver goblet from Bill Summers, executive director of IAEI, on behalf of John Mulligan for having signed up the most new members during the IAEI 1987–88 membership contest.

helped reduce the workload in the home. And it is expected that within the next several years computers and telecommunications devices will increasingly enter the home, helping us to do everything from balancing our checkbooks, monitoring room temperatures, turning on the lights, ordering the groceries and planning menus, to providing warning systems against intruders or fire, watching our children and even entertaining us.

All of these devices have enhanced our lives by providing increasing numbers of Americans with more freedom for leisure activities.

But they're also based on one important premise. They are all dependent on constantly reliable sources of electricity at reasonable prices.

As we enter the "second century" of electric utilities, this nation will be facing some important decisions as to how to plan its economic future. America will gear up again when the economy begins its recovery. The question here, however, is which future should we invest in. Should we, as some have suggested, retool our basis industries—steel, aluminum, automotive, chemical and rubber—or should we move more heavily into the high technology and telecommunications industries? One thing is for certain: either way there will be a continued dependence on reliable sources of power. Future electricity users will be more efficient consumers than in the past, but they may also be more dependent.

So, what's the problem? The electric utilities have been providing good service for 100 years and are already in the position to meet future energy demands. Right?

Well, not necessarily. More and more of the nation's investor-owned electric companies, which fulfill some 80 percent of America's electric needs, are finding their finances are preventing them from making economic decisions which will allow them to plan intelligently for the future. Some of the utilities are being forced to put "band aids" on old, inefficient generating facilities. Others are continuing to burn expensive OPEC oil and natural gas because they are not able to raise the necessary capital to make investments to replace those plants.

Critics of the utility companies claim electric rates are already way too high, and that the electric companies have greater earnings than they could possibly know what to do with. They say the

In lieu of the regular monthly meeting, the Texas Gulf Coast Chapter conducted its 3rd annual bar-b-que cook-off on April 27, 1985, at the Charity Oaks in Houston, Texas. Brisket, ribs, and chicken were prepared and cooked by teams in the contest with only the brisket being judged. Pictured above are (*left to right*): Ernest Banks, Rus Wilkins, Paul Pierson, Larry Cobble, Bill Bean, and Max Langham. Chairman Harold Saunders was asked to lead in prayer for the food serving over 800 people. The evening concluded with the people dancing to the country music western band, *The Good, the Bad, and the Ugly*.

1986 International President

Eugene Y. Fujihara, chief electrical inspector of the city and county of Honolulu, Hawaii, is the new 1986 president. He has been a member of IAEI since 1965, was the Hawaii Chapter president in 1974, and served as Southwestern Section president in 1979.

Hawaii has always been his home. He began his electrical career as an electrician's helper working for the Byrnes Organization at Pearl Harbor. From 1945 to 1947 he served in the U. S. Army Engineers Corps as a material expeditor. The following year he began work as an electrician, completed an electrical apprenticeship program in 1949 and in 1953 completed and received a certificate for industrial electrical engineering from the International Correspondence School of Scranton, Pennsylvania. In 1956 after receiving his license for supervising electrician in the city and county of Honolulu, he joined the Public Works Department as electrical and mechanical maintenance supervisor. In 1965 he was transferred from the Public Works Department to the Building Department and became an electrical inspector. He was promoted to senior electrical inspector in 1971, and in 1980 was promoted to chief electrical inspector of the city and county of Honolulu.

Fujihara served on the 1974 IAEI membership committee, and in 1979 was on the executive committee in the Southwestern Section.

He was elected as a member of the Underwriters' Laboratories, Inc., Electrical Council, in 1982 and in 1983 he served on the special subcommittee of the examination for electricians in the state of Hawaii.

He is a member of IBEW Local 1186 and served as shop steward for the Hawaiian Government Employee Association from 1956 to 1979. He was a member of the Hawaii Association of County Building Officials from 1980 to 1985.

From 1965 to 1979 he attended twenty different night school classes ranging in subjects from grammar and public speaking to report writing. He has given presentations on electrical safety for Hawaiian Electric Company, Electrical Union, Pacific Coast Electrical Contractors, Illuminating Electrical Engineer Society, nursing home owners, and the fire department.

Excerpted from *IAEI News*, January 1986.

All members of the Arizona Chapter for 29 years and retiring after 30 years each with the city of Phoenix, Arizona, are (*left to right*): Rudy Kruse, Elmer Williams, and Dave Houseman in 1988.

electric companies could save consumers money if only they chose to. Unfortunately, that is not true. The collection of information from a wide variety of sources actually indicates that the nation's utility industry is in a weakened financial situation.

While it is true that electric rates have greatly increased, the cost of fuel, interest payments, equipment, taxes, labor, and inflation have also gone up dramatically. When everything is paid out for the cost of operations, electric utilities must have adequate earnings to reinvest in their operations so they can meet the future needs of their customers.

What seems like a lifetime ago, before the Arab oil embargo and sky-high interest rates, electric rates seemed reasonable and the utilities were in a strong financial situation. Americans were told that the more electricity they used, the cheaper per-unit costs would be. And many followed that advice.

Consumption patterns indicated that Americans were enamored of available, cheap electricity. All-electric homes and energy-thirsty industrial facilities became commonplace. All that changed, however, with the energy crisis.

"Conservation" has since become a common word in this nation's vocabulary. Insulation, weather-stripping and new awareness of energy consumption have entered our homes. In the workplace, energy efficiency, is now a key word and many industrial electric users have just about halved their electricity usage from pre-Arab oil-embargo days.

Some critics of the industry claim that conservation will be the solution to the nation's energy problems, if only the utilities will make the necessary investments; if only the utilities will support the concept of conservation. The nation's electric utilities have had active conservation programs for a number of years, now. Some electric companies offer energy audits; others, weatherproofing assistance; low-interest conservation loans; and still others offer special off-peak electric rates to help moderate the highs and lows of electric consumption. Just about every utility takes some kind of active role in helping their customers conserve energy. Conservation helps the utilities because it reduces the need for the generating capacity; it helps consumers to achieve lower electric bills. The utilities rightfully view conservation as another means of helping the nation out of its energy fix. It does not, however, represent the total solution

In fact, if one takes the complex view of the nation's energy problems and recognizes that there is no one "total solution," it becomes apparent that there are many things the utilities can and should be doing. Perhaps the greatest single action that can be taken now is to reduce the use of oil and natural gas for electric generation. It makes far more economic sense for utilities to burn coal or use nuclear energy to generate electricity. And in the future, solar, municipal waste, biomass, and other supplemental fuels will also be sensible alternatives, as they become cost-effective.

So why the continued dependence on foreign oil and natural gas? Again, the answer is complicated. Despite the

1987 International President

J. Philip Simmons, chief electrical inspector and acting assistant director for the state of Washington, Department of Labor and Industries, is the new international president of IAEI. A member of the Puget Sound Chapter IAEI, since 1976, he was chairman in 1982 and has been secretary-treasurer of the chapter since 1983.

Simmons has worked in several areas of electrical, plumbing, welding and mechanical employment. In 1969 he became an electrical contractor and as owner and manager of Simmons Electric Inc., he designed and installed electrical equipment and systems in many types of commercial, industrial and residential occupancies. In 1975 he became a state electrical inspector in the state of Washington, Department of Labor and Industries. In 1979 he became state electrical plans examiner in health care and educational facilities and developed and administered examinations for electricians and electrical contractors. He became an electrical inspector for the state of Washington in 1983, and in 1984 served as administrator in the electrical inspection, contractor registration and plumber certification sections. He also served as a member of the Electrical Advisory Board and as secretary to the Board of Electrical Examiners and Plumbers Advisory Board. In 1985 he became the chief electrical inspector and since 1986 he has also been the acting assistant director, state of Washington, of the Building and Construction and Safety Inspection Services Division.

He was a member of code-making panel 17 and is chairman of code-making panel 19 and serves on the Underwriters' Laboratories electrical advisory council. He was elected vice president of the NFPA electrical section in 1985 and serves on the IAEI board of directors.

He is an instructor for electrical code-related courses for IBEW and since 1977 for the Puget Sound Chapter of IAEI. He is a seminar speaker for the IAEI seminars on the changes in the 1987 *National Electrical Code.*

Simmons is a journeyman electrician and certified as a general electrician administrator. He is a member of IBEW Local 46, Seattle, and The Electric League of the Pacific Northwest. He has a certificate in public administration from Olympia Technical Community College.

Excerpted from *IAEI News*, January 1987.

1988 International President

Melvin L. Young, chief electrical inspector for the city of Manassas, Virginia, and a member of IAEI since 1951, is the new International president. He has served as the IAEI Southern Section secretary since 1969. He has been assistant secretary-treasurer of the Southern Section from 1966 to 1969, and also was secretary of the Virginia Chapter from 1966 through 1986, and chairman of the chapter in 1959.

After completing high school in 1940, he worked as an apprentice machinist for the U. S. government at the torpedo station, Alexandria, Virginia. In 1942 he began work in building maintenance for Cafritz Corporation, Washington D. C. Interested in the electrical trade, Young became an electrical apprentice and after completing his training with electrical contractors in the Northern Virginia area, he became a journeyman electrician. He continued in the electrical trade as an electrician and foreman and qualified as an electrical contractor and master electrician.

In 1950 he became an electrical inspector in Arlington County, Virginia. From 1955 to 1979 he was employed by Fairfax County, Virginia, as chief electrical inspector. He became the building official for the city of Manassas, Virginia, in 1979, and in September 1981 became the chief electrical inspector of that city.

He has attended training classes in the electrical, building, plumbing and mechanical trades and in personnel administration and became certified in the state of Virginia in 1978 as building official. In 1962 he was certified as an instructor by the Virginia State Board of Education to instruct electrical courses in the JATC program and adult education classes; he was active in the JATC program from 1960 through 1975 and has continued to instruct code classes for the adult education program in Fairfax County Schools.

Young has represented IAEI on code-making panel 8 since 1970. Previously he had served on panel 17 from 1964-1970.

He has been a member of NFPA since 1964, served on several NFPA committees, has been a member of the UL Electrical Council since 1969 and a corporate member of UL in the public safety category. He has been a recipient of achievement awards from the Virginia Chapter and the county of Fairfax as a county employee.

—Excerpted from *IAEI News*, January 1988.

A unique and notable occurrence was the gathering of eight past IAEI international presidents, from various sections, attending the 1988 Northwestern Section held September 19–22, 1988, at the Red Lion Inn, in Bellevue, Washington, making this photo possible. Shown are (*left to right*): Mel L. Young, Southern Section, 1988 IAEI president; Eugene E. Carlton, Southwestern Section, 1962 IAEI president; J. Philip Simmons, Northwestern Section, 1987 president; Artie O. Barker, Northwestern Section, 1975 president; Leo Nagel, Western Section, 1979 president; George W. Lawson, Canadian Section, 1983 president; George W. Flach, Southern Section, 1982 president; and Roger A. Niedermeyer, Northwestern Section, 1981 president.

perception that utilities are charging sky-high rates, most utilities are not in the financial position to replace old, inefficient or oil-fired generators. Too many state regulators have attempted to shield consumers from rising electric costs by holding down the utilities' returns on equity. That step has made many in the financial community uneasy, and makes the utilities appear to be riskier ventures than many other investments. This has, in turn, diminished the utilities' ability to borrow capital at reasonable rates. Considering that the utilities are second only to government in their need for capital, this situation is very significant.

When faced with the prospect of borrowing, at sky-high interest rates, the $340 billion the utility industry is predicted to need during the remainder of 1982 to maintain existing facilities for new construction, many of those in the industry are shying away from commitments to build any new generating capacity. Some utilities have indicated that they will wait to see how demand shapes up in future years. Others acknowledge that the financial pressures they face preclude them from embarking on any construction projects.

Yet, to fully understand the implications of such actions, it is necessary to consider that the construction of new generating facilities now takes an average of ten years. So, what will happen if additional generating capacity is needed and not planned for now? What will happen when the economy recovers and industrial demand, although different from before, still requires electricity to be reliable and available at reasonable costs?

Those are questions that are starting to receive some attention from people outside the industry. Two recent studies by the Department of Energy, for example, claim that electric generating capacity will be inadequate by the mid 1990s, if something is not done now. They analyze the impact on the economy if such a scenario develops.

In addition, knowledgeable people from the financial community, from academia, from state government and even labor unions are thinking about this potential problem. Some of these people have concluded that, faced with

Australia's first IAEI member, John Blandy, shown with Bill Summers and his Royal Artillery slouch hat that was given to him by the Victoria Division of the Institute of Electrical Inspectors as a memento in 1987.

inadequate electric service, many U.S. industries will decide to relocate.

With such relocation, communities will lose jobs, and will face a reduced tax base and a decrease in total revenues. Some of these people are concerned that relocation will be to foreign countries and, at a time when the nation is working for economic recovery, this could be tragic.

One group that could be severely affected by this situation is minority workers. In fact, the National Conference of Black Mayors took this view recently when it voted to endorse the revitalization of the electric industry.

So, what's the solution? Electric utilities must receive a fair rate of return on equity to attract investors. This means utility commissioners must be willing to increase a small part of our electric rates by a few pennies now. Taking such action will give the utilities the incentive and the economic freedom to plan effectively for the future. Unfortunately, this is not an easy solution, but still it's absolutely vital if this nation is to continue to grow and be great.

It also means that consumers will have to accept the hard truth that electric rates will have to go up somewhat now to keep them moderate in the future and to assure reliability of service. Utility commissioners are constantly faced with economic pressures to keep rates low. If the public provides them with the opportunity to act responsibly by planning for the future, the great majority of commissioners will choose to do so.

It's a hard solution to a difficult problem. But, this country has had a history of acting on difficult problems and planning for the future. Only 100 years ago Edison took some difficult steps and changed the course of history for the better. Although our actions seem less dramatic in comparison, they too will have a great effect on America's future. It's something to consider.

Don D. Jordan, chairman, Edison Electric Institute. Reprinted by permission from *SKY*, September 1982. Reprinted from *IAEI News*, May 1983.

1989 International President

John D. Waller, a supervising electrical inspector for Ontario Hydro, is the 1989 International president of the IAEI. John is responsible for an inspection district, which is centered by the twin cities of Kitchener and Waterloo, Ontario. In 1987 Ontario Hydro served 3.3 million customers and had assets of over $32 billion, making it one of the largest public utilities in North America.

Before he joined Ontario Hydro in 1971, John was employed by the Canadian Standards Association in Rexdale, Ontario. He worked on various product lines in CSA's testing laboratories, spent ten years as a laboratory supervisor in the electronic medical and transformer operated equipment, and also worked in the audits and investigation group. Prior to his appointment as supervising electrical inspector, John's background at Ontario Hydro included positions as inspection supervisor, in the regional office, field electrical approvals inspector in the Willowdale office, and approvals control inspector in head office.

John has been an IAEI member for many years, serving as Ontario Chapter chairman in 1978 and Canadian Section president in 1981. In his executive role with the Canadian Section, some of the activities he has spearheaded included gaining IAEI representation on a number of sections of the CEC, promoting the concept that the IAEI section leadership come from field inspectors and the creation of officer duty rosters. John was also a member of a team of four, which wrote the first Provincial Special Inspection requirements that have recently been accepted by every Canadian province.

John works closely with local electrical contractor associations, representing inspection at their monthly meetings and hosting annual "Inspector nights." He also works with a local community college's electrical apprenticeship program. He is a long-time member of Ontario Association of Certified Engineering Technicians and Technologists (OACETT).

Excerpted from *IAEI News*, January 1989.

Technology empowers. It floods our lives with options and overwhelms us with choice, and it places us squarely in the middle of the revolutions it generates. The 1990s were evolving and truly becoming the electronic age. The World Wide Web was born in 1992, changing the way we communicate (email), spend our money (online gambling, stores), and do business (e-commerce). Internet lingo like plug-ins, BTW (by the way), GOK (God only knows), IMHO (in my humble opinion), FAQS, SPAM, FTP, ISP, and phrases like "See you online" or "The server's down" or "Bill Gates" became part of our everyday vocabulary. By 1994, over three million people were *online.* With the rush of technology came information overload, and we were deluged with information on big issues such as health care, social security reform and gun control—hidden dangers lurked around every corner. As Socrates observed, "Nothing vast enters life without a hidden curse." So it could be said that technology not only empowers us, but conversely, it can be a debilitating dependence as well.

Taking part in the ceremony in Halifax November 8, 1976, where the newly formed Nova Scotia Chapter of IAEI received its provincial charter are (*left to right*): John Henselwood, secretary Canadian Section; Floyd Coolen, chairman of the Nova Scotia Chapter; Harvey Putnam, president Canadian Section; and John Leeming, international president of IAEI.

Canadian Section Timeline

1965 **J. E. Henselwood**, of Downsview, Ontario, is elected Canadian Section secretary.

1976 **British Columbia Chapter** is christened.

Canadian Section welcomes the **Nova Scotia Chapter.**

1982 **Gordon R. Orr,** of Bramalea, Ontario, is elected Canadian Section secretary.

Entering the Technological Era

Toll-Free Telephone Number.
A toll-free telephone number to our office is now available. The number is effective from all 50 states of the U.S. and from Canada. This number is for membership services such as changing your address, employer or similar changes to our records. You can also order books, other products or register for seminars this way. The toll-free number is 800-786-IAEI.

Charge Cards
We are now accepting charge cards for membership services (both new and renewal), books and other products and seminar registrations. We accept Visa and MasterCharge cards. The combination of toll-free phone number and charge cards give us a great deal of additional flexibility in serving our members and customers.

Long Distance Telephone Savings
Want to save a lot of money on your long distance telephone bill without comprising quality of service? IAEI members can now do exactly that. We have joined forces with US Sprint, an excellent provider of long distance services, to give our members a ten percent reduction below Sprint's already very competitive rates.

Just think. If you presently spend no more than $25.00 per month ($300.00 per year) on long distance, your IAEI membership is, in essence, free! In addition, the IAEI receives a royalty for sponsoring the program.

This long distance service is also available for your business where you can really save big. All members who sign up for this program receive a free US Sprint "Fon Card" for making long distance calls while away from your home or business. The card will have both the cardholder's and IAEI name on it.

Why not call the US Sprint toll free number shown on the ad in this issue and sign up today so you can enjoy the savings right away. Saving our members money on their long distance telephone bill is not the purpose for our existence, but we hope you will agree that it is a pleasant bonus.

Reprinted from *IAEI News,* May 1991.

THE PRESIDENTIAL MEDAL OF HONOR

The IAEI Presidential Medal of Honor was first established in 1990, after the James H. McGraw Award for Electrical People was discontinued. This coveted medal of honor is presented on an irregular basis to those who are dedicated to helping the IAEI fulfill its mission of promoting electrical safety and education.

Presidential Medal of Honor honorees include:

1992, Edward C. Lawry

1993, Russell Helmick

1998, Andre Cartal

2000, Thomas E. Trainor

2002, Philip H. Cox

1990 International President

Milton H. Lounsbury, branch manager of the Albany Division of the New York Board of Fire Underwriters, is the 1990 International president of IAEI. Lounsbury has been a member of IAEI since 1955. He served as president of the Adirondack Hudson Chapter in 1961 and Eastern Section president in 1974. He has been a member of the Eastern executive committee since 1963 and a member of the International board of directors since 1985. He has been a member of code-making panel 8 for 23 years.

He joined the electrical department in 1956 as a field electrical inspector and was appointed assistant chief electrical inspector in 1960 and advanced to chief inspector in 1962. In 1969 he was named Albany Division branch manager.

Prior to joining the New York Board of Fire Underwriters, he was a licensed electrical contractor in Albany and Greene County. He has served as an IAEI representative on the *ad hoc* committee on electrical grounding of agricultural buildings.

He is an instructor at the Hudson Valley Community College teaching the *National Electrical Code* and a member of the advisory board of the college. He is chairman of the Board of Electrical Examiners for the city of Albany.

—Excerpted from *IAEI News*, January 1990.

1991 International President

William L. (Bill) Raines, supervisor of electrical inspection for St. Louis county since 1973, is IAEI's new International president for 1991. Prior to his appointment as supervisor he was with the city of St. Louis Electrical Inspection Department for seventeen years, serving as assistant chief electrical inspector.

He has been a member of IAEI's St. Louis Chapter since 1956, and has served as chapter secretary-treasurer and chapter chairman. He has served on the Western Section executive committee for the past eighteen years, and was Western Section president in 1982.

Raines served his electrical apprenticeship and spent seven years as a journeyman electrician as a member of IBEW, Local 633. He has been a member of Local No. 1 since the beginning of his electrical inspection career.

He has been an instructor of the *National Electrical Code* for the IBEW apprenticeship training school and for the local electrical contractor's associations. He represents the IAEI on code panel 14.

Excerpted from *IAEI News*, January 1991.

J. Philip Simmons

The 1990s began with a new director and a new home. **J. Philip Simmons**, IAEI Northwestern Section secretary and 1987 international president, became the new executive director of IAEI on April 1, 1990. He had been a member of the board of directors from 1984.

Under the direction of Simmons, the IAEI relocated the International office to Richardson, Texas, and sold the property in Park Ridge, Illinois. This change included not only locating and purchasing of the new facility, but also working with the architect and contractors to finish the building interior while hiring and training a new expanded staff to produce the *IAEI News*, books and other publications by desktop publishing software rather than outsourcing the publications. This new software was made available by a new local area network (LAN) that was installed for the first time.

This new software and expanded staff allowed the IAEI to take on greater responsibilities in promoting electrical safety through publications. During this period, Simmons reorganized, expanded and re-illustrated the *Soares' Book on Grounding* from a small pocket book to develop it into the most respected authority on the subject of grounding of electrical systems and equipment. He acquired the rights to the *Ferm's Fast Finder* book and improved and expanded the illustrations and updated it to the current edition of *National Electrical Code*. He acquired the rights to, developed and published the *Neon Installation Manual*. Simmons and Joe Tedesco, codes, standards and seminar specialist, were co-contributors to the first edition of IAEI *One- and Two-Family Dwelling Electrical Systems*; Simmons illustrated the book. He updated the book to the current *NEC* through its fourth edition.

During this time, IAEI membership and assets were at an all-time high. In 1993, IAEI developed and implemented a Bonus-point Plan for member retention and rewards. The organization also developed and implemented the marketing of membership logo products.

The education department developed partnership on joint seminars with sections, chapters and divisions in the early nineties.

Simmons also represented IAEI as a charter member of the board of directors of the original National Electrical Safety Foundation (now the Electrical Safety Foundation International).

Previously, Simmons had been chief electrical inspector for the state of Washington, Department of Labor and Industries from 1985. He has been a member of the IAEI Puget Sound Chapter since 1976 and was chairman in 1982 and secretary-treasurer of the chapter from 1983–1987. In 1987 he received the inspector/medal of the year and purse of James H. McGraw Award for Electrical People.

He has worked in several areas of electrical, plumbing, welding, and mechanical employment. In 1969 he became an electrical contractor and as owner and manager of Simmons Electric Inc., he designed and installed electrical equipment and systems in many types of commercial, industrial and residential occupancies. In 1975 he became a state electrical inspector for the state of Washington, Department of Labor and Industries. In 1979 he became state electrical plans examiner for health care and educational facilities and developed and administered examinations for electricians and electrical contractors. He became an electrical inspector supervisor for the state of Washington in 1983, and in 1984 became administrator of the electrical inspection, contractor registration and plumber certification sections. He served as secretary to the state Electrical Board.

In 1985 he became the chief electrical inspector for the state of Washington, and in 1986 he served as acting assistant director of the state of Washington Department of Labor and Industries, Building and Construction Safety Inspection Services Division.

He was a member of code-making panel 1 from 1990–1996. Previously he was chairman of code-making panel 19 from 1984–1990, and a member of code-making panel 17 from 1981–1984. He is a past vice president and president of the National Fire Protection Association Electrical Section and has served on the NFPA Standards Council since 1987. He serves on the Underwriters Laboratories Electrical Advisory Council.

Simmons has been a moderator at the IAEI seminars on changes in the 1987 and the 1990 *National Electrical Codes*, and has been an instructor for the Washington State Electrical Inspection Section in the Department of Labor and Industries, developing and presenting electrical *Code* and electrical industry-related courses, for the training of electrical inspectors, engineers, contractors and electricians.

Simmons is a journeyman electrician and is certified as a general electrical administrator. He is a member of IBEW Local 46, Seattle, and the Electric League of the Pacific Northwest. He has inspector certification for electrical inspector general, electrical plan review and electrical one- and two-family. He has a certificate in public administration from Olympia Technical Community College.

Excerpted from *IAEI News*, May 1990 and from a personal email from Simmons, June 2003.

YOUR NEW INTERNATIONAL OFFICE IN RICHARDSON, TEXAS

Your new International office is located at 901 Waterfall Way, in a small office park, in Richardson, Texas. Richardson is a suburb situated just northeast of the city of Dallas and is easily accessed off the LBJ Freeway I-635, and the US 75 freeway from Coit or Spring Valley roads.

The office is a 12, 000 square foot, two story, brick building built in 1985 for speculation and was unfinished inside when we bought it. The property was purchased for $150,000 or about $12.50 per square foot, an unheard of value. At this time, we are finishing the corridors on both floors and one half of the office space. We have placed the Park Ridge office (which we own free and clear) on the market and expect to finance the new office purchase and finish-out of the space we will occupy from the proceeds of that sale.

Other questions that have been asked about the transaction include:

1. What's wrong with our present office? Why did we need to move?
Faced with the need to remodel the existing building to add a freight elevator as well as more office space, the board chose to look for more suitable quarters.

2. Did the board consider other properties in the Chicago area as well as other cities in the country? Yes. A relocation task force of the board considered properties in the Chicago suburbs as well as in a number of other cities having airline hubs.

3. Why Richardson, Texas? This property seemed to be the best value by far in a suitable location.

4. What will be done with the extra space? That has yet to be determined. The extra space gives us adequate room for growth and flexibility for years to come. The new facilities will allow us to offer on-site seminar instructor training classes and to enhance our production of educational materials and seminars.

We hope that whenever your travel plans take you near the Dallas area, you will stop and see us at your new office.

Reprinted from *IAEI News*, November 1991.

Quick Fact

The IAEI board of directors, at the November 1991 meeting, approved revisions in the articles of association and Bylaws for present classes of cooperating class C, D, E and F memberships to become section, national, international, sustaining and inspection agency classifications.

Excerpted from *IAEI News*, January 1992.

1992 International President

Russell J. Helmick, Jr., supervising inspector and chief electrical inspector for the city of Irvine, California, is the new international president of the IAEI. A member of the Southern California Chapter since 1976, he was chairman of that chapter and also chairman of the Orange Empire Division. Russ, aside from serving on many committees, has served on the Southwestern Section's executive board, and the Southern California Chapter's executive board since the early 1980s. He has also served as membership chairman for his section, chapter, and division since 1983.

Russ, after serving four years in the U.S. Navy, started his electrical career in 1962, beginning as a helper, and served his apprenticeship in Local 441. He then became an electrical contractor and performed various types of electrical work until he started with the city of Irvine in 1976. He continued his electrical work on a part time basis, and still continues to do so.

In 1978, Russ received lifetime teaching credentials from the state of California after finishing some of his education at UCLA, and has been teaching two classes every semester since 1978. The subjects he has been teaching are electrical inspection and codes, building code and law, and contractor's license law.

Russ is certified by ICBO/IAEI as an electrical inspector. He is also certified by the American Public Works Association for all public works construction, and was a registered electrical inspector for the state of California. Recently Russ also received his certification from the Council of American Building Officials (CABO) as a certified building official.

Russ has served on code-making panel 18 as the principal member, and is now chairman of code panel 20. He is also a member of the Underwriters' Laboratories Electrical Council and a member of the National Fire Protection Association.

Excerpted from *IAEI News*, January 1992.

IAEI Membership Categories Revised

The articles of association were revised last year by the board of directors and by the membership. These changes were made to clarify membership classifications and to make the titles descriptive of the classification and thus more user friendly.

The old membership classification titles that were changed are class C, class D, class E and class F. In addition, two new membership classifications were established. One new classification is the senior associate member category that associate members who have been an active, contributing member for at least five years can be nominated for. The second new classification is the sustaining membership category which recognizes the significant support and contribution to the IAEI by those members.

The details of the new or revised membership categories are:

Senior Associate Member. This new membership classification is defined as "An individual not qualified for membership in the inspector classification who has been an associate member in good standing of a chapter or division for not less than five years and who is interested in promoting the objectives of the IAEI. This member shall be nominated for this classification by the chapter or division executive committee."

This new classification can be adopted by chapters or divisions. Senior associate members are permitted to serve as an officer of the local organization, including the position of chairman, in the model chapter and division bylaws.

Section Member. The section member is defined as "An organization or firm interested in promoting the objectives of the IAEI, which operates within the territory of a single section. Such section member may have one (1) representative in the section where their operations are conducted." This membership classification replaces the old class C membership.

National Member. The national member category replaces the old class D membership. It is defined as "An organization or firm interested in promoting the objectives of IAEI, which confines its operation to a single country. Such national member may have one (1) representative in each section within the boundaries of the country where operations are conducted."

International Member. This new membership classification is intended to give proper recognition to the several organizations that support the purposes of the IAEI in a substantial manner. It is defined as "An organization, firm, association or group which is particularly interested in supporting the objectives of IAEI by paying dues not less than that shown in this section. Such sustaining member is entitled to one (1) representative for each section." "Sustaining memberships are further established as bronze, silver, gold and platinum types." The membership dues vary from $500 for the bronze category to $5,000 or more for the platinum category.

Inspection Agency Member. This membership classification replaces the previous class F member.

It is hoped that these new and revised membership classifications will enhance the membership of the IAEI and make the classifications easier to understand. In addition, the new senior associate classification will permit chapters and divisions to recognize associate members who have supported the local group. The sustaining membership classification will give recognition to the many friends and supporters of the IAEI who have chosen to express their support in this manner.

Reprinted from *IAEI News*, July 1993.

Trial Membership

We will soon be introducing a test program in recruiting members for the IAEI. While the concept is not new, this is the first time it has been offered by our association. Each inspector member will receive a membership nomination form for sponsoring another inspector. The new inspector will receive a complimentary six-month membership in the IAEI.

This will give another approximately 7,000 inspectors the opportunity to become familiar with the many benefits of belonging to your association. At the end of the trial period, the inspector will be given the opportunity of renewing his or her membership under the standard terms.

Why are only inspector members being given this opportunity at this time? Since this is a "first" for us, we want to test the program in this way before implementing it on a broader scale. By the board of director's meeting in November, we should have sufficient data for evaluation of the project.

Excerpted from *IAEI News*, March 1993.

Visiting members of the Quebec Chapter with their tour guide on July 9, 1992, at the La Grande-2A site *(from left to right)*: Daniel Dubé, Ronald Quimper, Nancy Vermette (tour guide, James Bay Power Corporation), Nora Manoli, and Rolland Dagenais.

1993 International President

John H. Stricklin, electrical inspector for the state of Idaho, is the new international president. A member of IAEI since 1971, he is currently secretary of the Idaho Chapter and public relations chairman of the Northwest Section.

Stricklin attended schools in Teague, Texas, and technical classes at Idaho State University in Pocatello, Idaho, and Boise State University in Boise, Idaho. He served four years in the United States Air Force where he was a multi-jet engine specialist.

Stricklin began his electrical career serving as an apprentice electrician for two years. He has been a journeyman electrician for thirty-three years, passing the Idaho state journeyman electrician's test in 1959.

In 1963, John became an electrical contractor, opening Intermountain Electric of Mountain Home, Idaho, and operated the business until 1979. During his sixteen years as an electrical contractor, and his years as a journeyman electrician, Stricklin worked on residential, commercial, industrial and high voltage installations. He is, or has been, licensed as a journeyman or contractor in Idaho, Nevada, Oregon and Washington.

Stricklin has instructed electrical or *National Electrical Code* classes for the state of Idaho, United States Air Force, Boise State University and IAEI.

John is presently chairman of code-making panel 19, representing the IAEI. He is past principal and alternate to code panel 4.

As an electrical inspector for the state of Idaho, Stricklin has inspection experience in residential, commercial, industrial, high voltage and cogeneration.

Excerpted from *IAEI News*, January 1993.

Bonus Point Program Established

How about a free car? Or something like that!

The IAEI board of directors has continued, for many years, the practice of awarding the new IAEI member with a free *National Electrical Code.* I can't tell you when the practice first started but it has been in place for as long as I have been involved with IAEI. Many members have used this new-member benefit as a selling point in convincing a friend or associate to join the IAEI. Instructors at several electrical trade schools have encouraged or required new students to their programs to join IAEI to get a free *Code* book for use in their class.

The value of this new-member benefit is obvious. A new IAEI member gets a 1993 *National Electrical Code* book with a list price of $37.50 for the $36 membership dues. Along with that comes a one year subscription to the *IAEI News.* We work hard to keep the *News* a great source of worthwhile information. Other member benefits only increase the value of IAEI membership. These include reduced prices for attending IAEI seminars, savings on many books and products along with reduced price access to really neat programs like the recently announced Quest International Travel Club where you can save many times the cost of your IAEI membership. Add to this the incalculable value of attending local section, chapter or division meetings with their educational programs and opportunity for dialog with associates and one can soon see what a great value IAEI membership is.

You probably agree that all this is a great value for $36. Try $26 membership dues for student members and you can readily see why instructors of these classes recommend that their students join IAEI.

Simple mathematics will demonstrate where the problems begin. Nine dollars of the $36 goes back to and is divided among sections, chapters and divisions. Subtract from the remainder the cost of the *Code* book, shipping costs, producing and mailing the *IAEI News* along with producing and mailing membership cards and renewal notices and you can

Chattanooga Division's January 1994 program was presented by Chris Crimmins of the River City Company who discussed past, present, and future plans and accomplishments in the Revitalization Plan for downtown Chattanooga and along the Tennessee River. Pictured (*left to right*): Chattanooga Division Chairman Don Fowlkes; Mr. Crimmins; and David Perry, chief electrical inspector for the city of Chattanooga.

see that we lose money the first year on every new member who joins IAEI. (The results get worse for foreign members who pay in non-U.S. funds by the ratio of foreign to United States funds along with increased mailing and shipping costs to service these members.)

Membership dues have to be adjusted upward from time to time to take these and many production and operational costs into account. Membership dues made up only 33 percent of our revenue last year. Other sources of revenue include such things as sale of books, conducting seminars and advertising.

The board of directors has also continued, for many years, the practice of awarding the IAEI member whose dues are paid by some certain date with a free *National Electrical Code* book when a new edition is published.

The policies regarding the free *Code* books when joining and on publication of a new *NEC* were clarified at the last board of directors meeting. In addition, steps have been taken to make it more difficult for persons to join every three years to get a free *Code* book and then not renew for the next two years. Now, these former members are reinstated in their former or revised membership classification but are not treated as a new member.

Under the present board policy, new, first-time members will get a letter in their new-member kit giving them a choice of a free *National Electrical Code* book or an IAEI publication like *Ferm's Fast Finder Index* or *Soares Book on Grounding*. New members who join late in the *Code* cycle will have the choice of getting an existing *Code* book or IAEI publication or waiting for the new one.

Members who renew their membership will earn 100 bonus points for each year they renew. We will keep track of these "bonus points" in our membership database. A maximum of 300 points can be accumulated. When a member has 300 points, he can choose to obtain a current edition of the *National Electrical Code* without cost. As can be seen, a member will be eligible for another free *Code* book only when the member has renewed his membership three times. This will allow us to spread the cost of providing free *Code* books over three years. As you might expect, providing free *Code* books to our members gets more difficult with every price increase. We don't know of anyone who expects the price of *Code* books to go down anytime soon!

A member will also have the option of applying 100 bonus points toward the purchase of an IAEI publication. The value of the bonus points will be set each year and will be based on a cost formula. When our member receives his membership renewal card, the number of available bonus points will appear. Order forms will include the provision for cashing in bonus points.

While this bonus point program may appear a little complicated, every effort has been made to be fair and allow members additional flexibility in the use of bonus points. Some members have asked us if they can get an IAEI book rather than an *NEC* book when joining as they get one or more *Code* books from their employer or from previous activities like attending seminars.

These policies are reviewed from time to time by the board of directors and, of course, are subject to change. In this, as in other policies, the board and management strives to be prudent with association resources. Please feel free to share your ideas for improving the operation of your association with us.

Oh, about the free car. Simple mathematics will yield the annual dues needed to allow us to give members a free new car every three years. The dues might be a little steep!

Reprinted from *IAEI News*, July 1994.

Quick Fact

At the 1994 IAEI board of directors meeting, the board decided to look into expanding the IAEI trademark registration on an international basis. The International office will proceed with registering IAEI's trademark in Canada and Mexico. The board also provided for the bonding of IAEI staff and section secretaries. IAEI is protected by an employee theft policy. Section secretaries have arranged for individual bonds.

Reprinted from *IAEI News*, January 1995.

John Minick

John Minick celebrated a "Half Century of Greatness" on October 31, 1993. John was surprised with a birthday cake at the Tennessee Chapter meeting on November 1, 1993.

Minick, 1987 Southern Section president, was the chief electrical inspector for the city of Grand Prairie, Texas, from 1982 and also from 1974 to 1981. He had previously been rehabilitation officer in Grand Prairie from 1969 to 1974.

Minick received his B.A.A. from the University of Texas at Arlington in 1974. He holds a journeyman electrician's license, a master electrician's license and adult apprentice electrician's instructor certification. He received his electrical inspector general certification from IAEI in 1985.

A member since 1974, he served as the Texas Chapter chairman in 1983 and is currently on the chapter executive committee and Southern Section executive committee. He is past secretary of the Dallas County Examining Board and now serves on that board developing testing materials for examinations.

He has been an electrical and *Code* instructor for several colleges including Texas A & M University, North Lake College, Mountain View College, Dallas Independent School District and the Independent Electrical Contractors Association.

Excerpted from *IAEI News*, March 1987 and May 1994.

Canadian Section officers at the 1994 Canadian Section meeting. Front row, *left to right*: Dave Rae, Gordon Orr, Ross Wilson, Dave Conrad, and International President Don Germain. Back row, *left to right*: John Butts, Dave Clements, Doug Geralde, Tom Scott, Norm Scott, and Tom Arbanas.

Southern Section chapter and division secretaries at the 1994 Southern Section meeting in Nashville, Tennessee. First row (*left to right*): Earl Massey, Harold Sanders, Charles Gilliand, Ed Gregory. Second row (*left to right*): Sonny Lamb, unidentified representative from Florida, Darrell Linthicum, and Mel Young. Third row (*left to right*): Ron Purvis, James Carpenter, Peggy Reese, and Don Smedley. Back row (*left to right*): John Minnick and Lewis Ryan.

1994 International President Don Germain installing the new Northwestern Section President Brad Zempel at the 1994 Northwestern Section meeting in Portland, Oregon.

The weight of power shifts as outgoing Southern California Chapter President Herb Graham passes the gravel to Jerry Williams, with Russ Helmick looking on at the November 1994 meeting of the chapter in Pasadena, California.

Northwestern Section presents IAEI jacket to Alaska Chapter member Victor Tivetin from Magadan, Russia, at the 1993 Northwestern Section meeting.

1994 International President

Donald G. Germain, field inspector for ETL Testing Laboratories, Inc. and past member of their technical advisory council, is the new international president of the International Association of Electrical Inspectors.

A member of IAEI since 1972, he is currently a member of the Southern Section executive board, a position he has held since 1984. Don has also served as chairman of the Florida Chapter and as chairman of the Southern Section executive committee for five years.

Germain was born, raised and attended school in St. Augustine, Florida. He began his career in the electrical industry in 1950 with Marineland of Florida where he was responsible for their entire operational system including electrical, water, sewer and new construction. Don became chief electrical inspector of St. John County, Florida, in 1971 and served as director of code enforcement from 1984 to 1992. He held a Florida Department of Education teacher's certificate for *National Electrical Code* code instruction from 1972 to 1982 at the St. Augustine Technical Center.

Germain is a state-certified building official and a state-certified municipal fire safety inspector. He is licensed as a general contractor with the Florida Department of Professional Regulations and holds a certificate in electronics – basic concepts and dc circuits plus electronics fundamentals of ac and ac circuit analysis.

Excerpted from *IAEI News*, January 1994.

Quick Fact

The board of directors at the November 1993 meeting decided to support the concept of including all of Russia east of the Ural Mountains, as part of the Alaska Chapter.

Reprinted from *IAEI News*, January 1994.

Alton R. Thompson

Alton R. Thompson, a native of Durham, North Carolina, has been a member of IAEI since 1963 and of the North Carolina Ellis Cannady Chapter since 1966. After 27 years of service to the city of Durham, he retired as its chief electrical inspector in September 1989; he is now a *National Electrical Code* consultant, working part-time with a national firm teaching the *National Electrical Code* during public and in-house seminars, and an electrical contractor.

He began his work in the electrical field in 1944 as an electrician's helper with Modern Electric Company, Durham, after graduating from Bethesda High School. He attended Durham Technical Community College for three years of *National Electrical Code* classes.

He worked for Western Electric Company, in Burlington, North Carolina, and in 1947 he became a journeyman electrician at Whitley Electric Company in Durham until 1954, when he became an electrical inspector. In 1962 he became the assistant chief electrical inspector for the city of Durham, and in 1976 he became the city's chief electrical inspector.

He was a member of code-making panel 13 since 1981 and wrote for the "Focus on the Code" column in the *IAEI News*. He is a past chairman of the North Carolina Ellis Cannady Chapter. In 1981 he received the North Carolina Electrical Inspector of the Year Award.

Thompson has taught at the Durham Technical Community College for 21 years; his classes include electric apprentice 1, 2, 3, and 4; basic electricity A/C and D/C; basic electronics A/C and D/C; and A/C and D/C solid state. As a member of Durham Electrical Contractors Association from 1968 through 1990, he has reviewed the *National Electrical Codes* from 1968 through 1999. He served on the North Carolina Code Qualification Board from 1978 to 1990 and taught electrical inspector levels I, II, III courses and participated in seminars at the Marshall Institute since 1984. He has attended the North Carolina Institute meeting since 1953.

He has held a North Carolina electrical contracting license (unlimited) since 1954, a standard certificate electrical inspector level III from North Carolina Code Officials Qualification Board since certificates were first issued in 1981. He is a certified instructor for electrical standard inspection course levels I, II, III issued from the North Carolina Code Officials Qualification Board and has held a Durham city journeyman electrical license since 1947.

Thompson states: "My plans are to maintain my membership and to keep active in IAEI. I shall ever be indebted to the IAEI for services that they have rendered to me over the years. If IAEI should ever need my services in any way, feel free to let me know."

For the many years of service and expertise Thompson has given IAEI, the association takes this opportunity to express its gratitude and appreciation and many thanks. IAEI salutes Alton R. Thompson!

Reprinted from *IAEI News*, September 1990.

Southwestern Section executive committee members at the 1994 Southwestern Section meeting in Honolulu, Hawaii.

The Cape and Islands Chapter, Western Massachusetts, and Granite State Chapter share the congratulations after receiving their charters at a meeting held August 12–14, 1993. (*From left to right*): Andre Cartal (*far left*), code panel expert; Doug Sartwell, president of Granite State Chapter; Jeff Sargent, secretary of the Granite State Chapter; John Glennowicz, chairman of the Western Massachusetts Chapter; Fred Hartwell, secretary of the Western Massachusetts Chapter; James Rogers, secretary of the Cape and Islands Chapter; George LeBlanc of the Cape and Islands Chapter, and Ray Lease (*far right*), president of Eastern Section.

Their Future

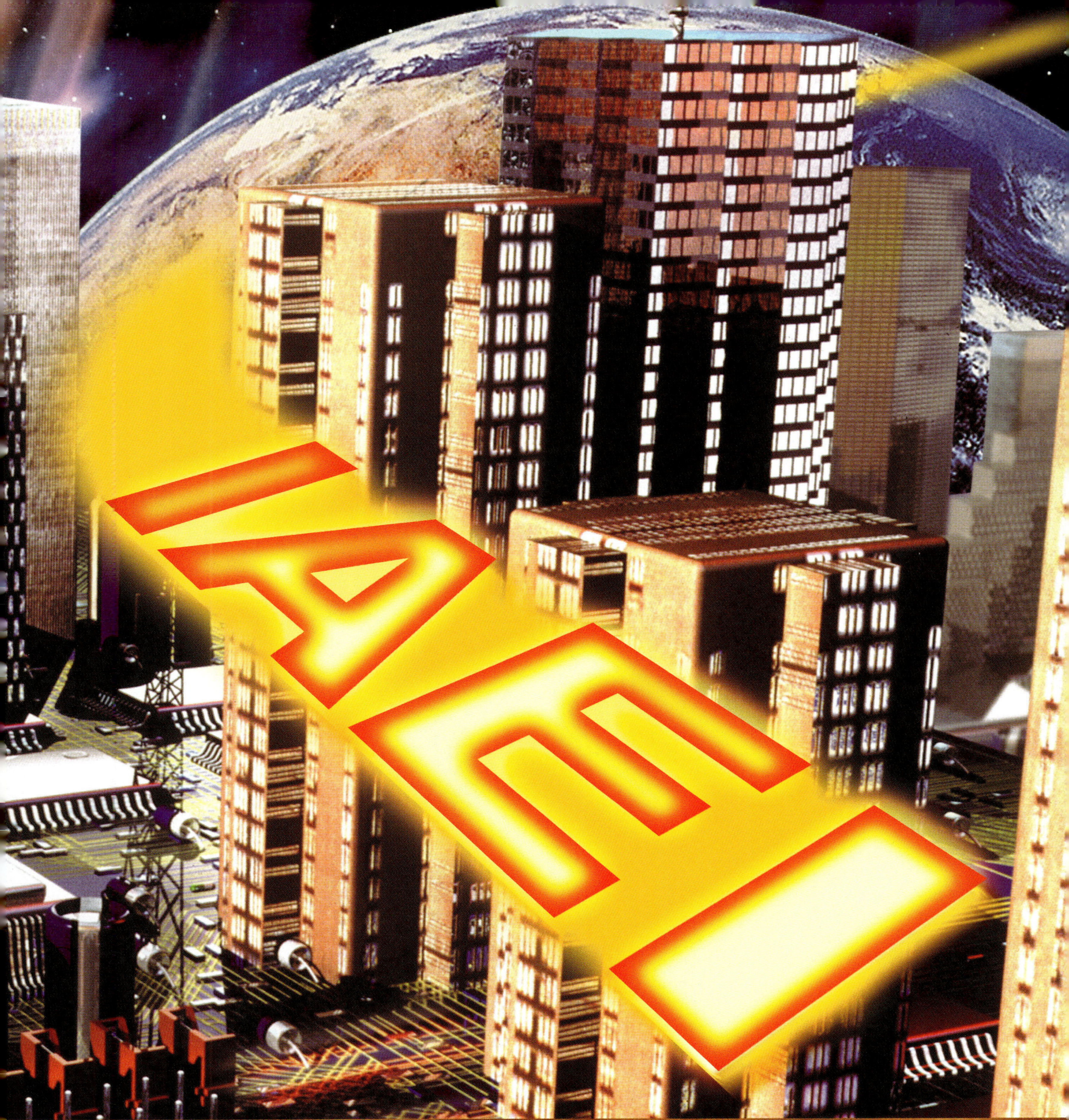

Therein lies our future. What impact will we have on our industry and the safety of our friends and families? How can we maintain the stance of unbiased focus on safe installations? Will we expand the business opportunities that enable a wider dissemination of information and education? Will we become a political action committee that persuades governments to give more careful consideration to electrical safety? What price are we willing to pay to fulfill this mission?

1995-2003 *Back to the Basics*

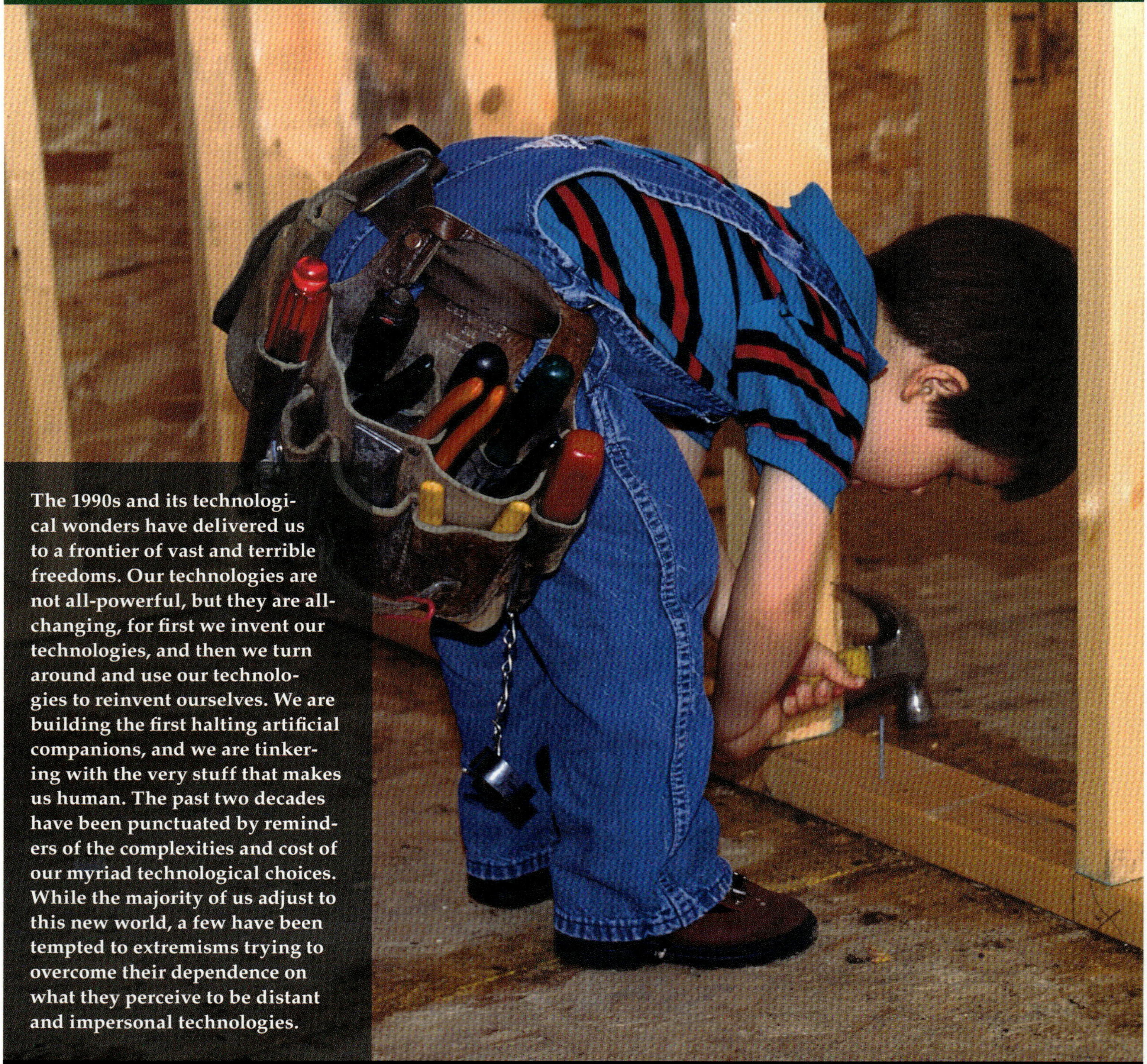

The 1990s and its technological wonders have delivered us to a frontier of vast and terrible freedoms. Our technologies are not all-powerful, but they are all-changing, for first we invent our technologies, and then we turn around and use our technologies to reinvent ourselves. We are building the first halting artificial companions, and we are tinkering with the very stuff that makes us human. The past two decades have been punctuated by reminders of the complexities and cost of our myriad technological choices. While the majority of us adjust to this new world, a few have been tempted to extremisms trying to overcome their dependence on what they perceive to be distant and impersonal technologies.

Western Section Timeline

1995 International board of directors approves the charter of the **Northern Illinois Division** of the Illinois Chapter.

Robert R. Sallaz, of Cuyahoga Falls, Ohio, is elected Western Section secretary.

1996 International board of directors approves the creation of three new divisions of the Illinois Chapter: the **Northeast Suburban Illinois Divisio Central Illinois Division,** and the **Southern Illinois Division.**

1998 **Edward C. Lawry**, from Madison, Wisconsin, is re-elected Western Section secretary.

Tim Arendt, Philip Cox, Mike Forister, and Jim Conway discuss a serious point of the *Code* at the 1999 Western Section meeting.

IAEI Becoming More International

An agreement of cooperation was recently signed between IAEI and the Asociación de Ingenieros Universitarios Mecánicos Electricistos (AIUME). Phil Simmons represented IAEI at this ceremony. Signing the agreement for AIUME was their presdent, Ing. Enrique Jiménez Espriú.

Asociación de Ingenieros Univer-sitarios Mecánicos Electricistos (AIUME) is a professional association of electrical and mechanical engineers having several thousand members. This group is actively promoting education and training on the Mexican Electrical Code commonly referred to as the "NOM." As can be readily seen, IAEI and AIUME are closely aligned in our mission of providing electrical education for our members and the electrical industry.

The agreement was signed at the Trinational Meeting of Electrical Engineers in early February 1995. This meeting was attended by high-level officials in government and industry including: Dr. Héctor Olea, president, Mexico National Commissioner of Energy; Dr. Carlos A. Puig H., secretary of Urban Development and Public Works for the state of Morelos; Dr. Josés Louis Fernandez Zayos, director of the Institute of Engineering, National University of Mexico; and Julián Adame Miranda, director of Lapem Testing Laboratories for the Feral Commission of Electricity.

Reprinted from *IAEI News*, March 1995.

Pedro Sanhua, Phil Simmons, Enrique Jiménez Espirú and Francisco Lira at signing ceremony in February 1995.

1995 International President

Norman T. Scott is the 1995 international president of the International Association of Electrical Inspectors. Norm was born in Dunnville, Ontario, raised and educated in Hamilton, Ontario, and Victoria, British Columbia. He began his electrical career installing and repairing automobile radios at a radio shop while attending high school. He apprenticed as an electrician prior to obtaining a Certificate of Qualification in electrical construction and maintenance from the Ontario Ministry of Colleges and Universities. Norm has attained master electrician status by passing the electrical contractors exam in Hamilton, Ontario. He is also certified as an electrical inspector for installations, investigations and equipment approvals by the Canadian Section of IAEI.

His work experience includes electrical construction as an apprentice, electrician and project supervisor, as well as a number of years in the electrical contracting field prior to joining the electrical inspection department in Ontario where he held positions as inspector and supervising inspector at the Barrie Ontario Inspection Office. Norm presently operates Electrical Safety Services which provides electrical inspection and safety services to a number of clients which include municipal and provincial authorities in Ontario, as well as safety and risk management inspections for insurance companies.

Norm has been very involved with the IAEI since 1977 and has held positions on the IAEI Ontario Chapter and Canadian Section conventions including technical programs, moderator, speaker, trade show publicity, and convention chairman. He was the Ontario Chapter chairman in 1984 and the Canadian Section president in 1986. In 1988 Norm was elected as a Canadian representative to the International board of directors and has also served as vice president since 1989, He serves IAEI as a member of the Section 14 (Protections and Control) subcommittee for the Canadian Electrical Code. He chairs the certification of inspectors committee for the Canadian Section.

Norm is a member of the Ontario Electrical League and has served on the city of Barrie Master and Electrical Contractors Licensing Board as well as teaching classes in the electrical code and electrical installations for school boards and colleges.

Reprinted from *IAEI News*, January 1995.

Philip H. Cox

Philip H. Cox has announced that he is stepping down from the position of CEO/Executive Director of the International Association of Electrical Inspectors. His plans include leaving the position in June 2002 after his successor has been employed.

In the seven years Mr. Cox has been employed by IAEI he has focused on publishing, education, certification, and relationships. Among his accomplishments are enhanced relationships with other organizations and with association members; developing, together with NFPA, a certification program; establishing an education department; revamping the *Analysis* book and *IAEI News*, along with other publications; and the development of a new web site, which will be launched in January 2002.

Mr. Cox indicated that it has been both a privilege and a pleasure to have met and worked with many of the great leaders of the association during his thirty-five years as a member. He expressed appreciation for being granted the opportunity to serve the IAEI as CEO/Executive Director since 1995 but emphasizes, "It is time to slow the pace in order to spend more time with my family and to devote time to some things that the schedule previously has not permitted. I plan to remain active in my home chapter and section and want to be able to help other members as I was helped during my growth in the organization."

During his tenure, Mr. Cox developed a reputation of being a tireless leader and charismatic diplomat. Doug Geralde, junior past president and vice president of international affairs says, "Whether it has been preparing for the IAEI section conventions, working with the staff in the office, expanding the IAEI's presence by meeting with other organizations, working on committees, editing articles for education material or the magazine, or just chatting with the members, Phil has always been there. He has a gift that allows him to listen to all the diverse views of the members, board of directors and other constituents, then to formulate the best position for the IAEI organization as a whole.

"Phil is a tireless worker, who always maintains the highest integrity for both himself and the organization and is an inspiration to those who know him. In the end, for the IAEI, Phil Cox is a man for all seasons."

A man's character and sense of commitment establish his legacy. So believes Ray Weber, international 1st vice president representing the Western Section. As a leader in Cox's home section, Weber has observed him through many years of membership.

"The IAEI has been truly blessed," Weber says, "with dedicated and caring individuals that ask not what can be done or given to them; but simply ask, *What can I do to help? What talents do I possess that can be of use to this great organization?* Phil Cox exemplifies those character traits and personifies the terms of honesty, integrity, sense of duty and willingness to listen to all great and small as an equal, while putting them at ease. A review of our association's history shows that through his steady hand at the helm, what Phil has done and managed as well as what he has produced has been built on the foundation of earlier leaders and has brought our association a quantum leap forward in the electrical safety industry and electrical code knowledge arena. His ability to see the invisible has allowed us to do what to some might seem to be the impossible. Yet through it all, his Arkansas kindness and humor has made him a friend to us all.

"It is with great sadness that we accept his decision to retire and enjoy the quieter times back home with family, friends, and his beloved wife Jama, where his heart truly lies. Just as he has given in the past, he will be there to assist and advise in the future for the good of our association. One of Phil's axioms for living is, 'Life is not to be measured in length of time on earth but in a person's regard for doing the right thing and the quality of his friends.'"

International President Anthony Montuori comments, "Phil Cox will be sorely missed when he retires in June 2002. I am sorry that I will be unable to complete my term as president without his guidance and wisdom. Phil has been an asset to this organization; his administrative and technical abilities have benefited the entire membership. I would like to take this opportunity to wish Phil and his wife many years of a happy retirement."

Reprinted from *IAEI News*, January 2002.

1996 International President

Andre (Andy) R. Cartal was named the 1996 international president of the International Association of Electrical Inspectors at the Board of Directors' Meeting on November 3-4, 1995.

Andy began his career in 1948 as an electrical inspector trainee for the Middle Department Association of Fire Underwriters. Through the years, he held various supervisory positions, and in 1969 was appointed regional manager for the Eastern Region consisting of New Jersey and northeastern Pennsylvania.

With the privatization of the Fire Underwriters in 1972, he continued to represent the successor organization, Middle Department Inspection Agency Inc., in government and industry relations. In addition, Andy presently chairs the Code and Standards Division as well as manages Middle Department's Philadelphia Office.

In 1959, Andy conducted his first code seminar and has since done seminars for NECA, IBEW, New Jersey State Council of Electrical Contractors as well as various colleges throughout the area.

Due to his belief in inspector education and the IAEI certification program, Andy is the chairman of the International education committee.

He is also a member of CMP-12, Underwriters Laboratories Electrical Council and a life member of NFPA. He is past chairman of the Eastern Section and the New Jersey Chapter, and currently, he serves as secretary of the South Jersey Division. — Reprinted from *IAEI News*, January 1996.

What Do I Get for My Money?

At the annual section meetings this year, you will be asked to support an increase in membership dues. As a long-term member of IAEI, I know that the first response of some will be: "What do I get for my money?" That's a fair question and I'd like to answer it. IAEI is an organization with very specific purposes. These objectives were originally developed by the members and are intended to support the work of electrical inspectors. Your dues support these activities. Whenever the organization asks for a dues increase, it is time to review just how well these objectives are being met. Let's take a minute and look at each of them in terms of what the organization has done, what it is doing that's new, and what is being proposed.

Objective: To cooperate in the formulation of standards for the safe installation and use of electrical materials, devices and appliances.

IAEI funds two members on each of the twenty code-making panels for the *National Electrical Code* and on the *NEC* technical correlating committee. The work of these members assures that the inspection point of view is considered and that safety continues to be the main focus of the *Code*. We previously sent both members to the proposal meetings and only the principal member to the comment meeting.

New: Starting with the 1999 *NEC* meetings, we are sending both members to both meetings. This provides better representation at the comment meeting and assures that the alternate members are better prepared if and when they are called on to be principal members.

We have always had a procedure for *Code* change proposals to be approved as official IAEI proposals. IAEI CMP members support and vote for these proposals at the Proposal Meeting. However, we have never been able to follow through on these proposals in the Comment stage.

New: For the 1999 *NEC* cycle, we instituted a new codes and standards committee. This committee worked with our CMP members to develop responses regarding IAEI proposals so that their comments could be identified as the of-

Installation of 1995 Central Alabama Division officers. *From left to right*: Arthur Adams, past Alabama Chapter chairman installed officers, Past Chairman Reggie LeCren, Chairman Ernie Wilson, Secretary/Treasurer Donny Cook, and executive committee members Steve Owen, LeRoy Meacham, and Vice Chairman Dak Sims.

Virginia Chapter Secretary H. J. "Sonny" Lamb consults with Virginia Chapter President Terry Moore at the 2002 annual Virginia Chapter meeting.

Southern Section Timeline

1995 Panhandle Division of the **Florida Chapter** has its charter approved.

1996 Alabama Chapter welcomes its newest division, the **Southwest Alabama Division**.

South Georgia Division of the Georgia Chapter is created.

1998 South Texas Chapter welcomes two new divisions: the **Corpus Christi Division** and the **Alamo Division**.

2002 Virginia Chapter welcomes its first division, the **Eastern Virginia Division**.

Donald R. Cook, from Pelham, Alabama, is elected Southern Section secretary.

ficial IAEI position. More importantly, CMP members identified other proposals that directly impacted inspectors and worked with the IAEI codes and standards committee to develop official IAEI positions where necessary. The activity of this committee has significantly increased the inspector's influence in the code-making process.

In addition, IAEI funds members on the following industry-related committees associated with the formulation and adoption of electrical safety codes and standards:

- NFPA Standards Council
- NFPA 70B, Committee on Electrical Equipment Maintenance
- NFPA 73, Committee on Electrical Reinspection Code for Existing Dwellings
- ANSI-C73, Committee on Receptacles and Attachment Plugs
- ANSI-C80, Committee on Raceways for Electrical Wiring Systems
- NFPA 79, Committee for Electrical Equipment for Industrial Machinery
- NFPA Advisory Committee on the Adoption and Use of the *National Electrical Code*
- UL Committee on Intrinsically Safe Electrical Equipment
- Correlating Committee on Electrical Installation Codes of America

New: UL Technical Advisory Panel. This panel was established in 1997 and includes three IAEI members and the executive director. Its function is to take inspection issues directly to UL and to work with them on an effective resolution. The issues raised at the first meeting included lighting fixtures that rely on marking for safe operation, armored cable and metal raceways used as equipment grounding conductors and polymeric material used in neon sign electrodes. We anticipate that similar committees will be formed with other testing laboratories, as needed to address

1997 International President

Paul M. Bowers was named the 1997 international president of the International Association of Electrical Inspectors at the board of directors meeting November 8 – 9, 1996.

Bowers started in electrical inspection in 1972 for the city of Iowa City. He began working for the city of Iowa City in 1969 as housing inspector. After being appointed electrical inspector, he attended a number of short courses at Southern Illinois University, University of Wisconsin, University of Iowa and various other *Code* classes and reviews. He has organized *Code* classes locally and occasionally taught classes, including one- and two–family dwelling electrical systems for Iowa's housing inspectors. He continues to work at setting up classes in the local community college for *Code* updates and preparing candidates for the electrical exam.

Bowers has been on the executive board of the Iowa Chapter of IAEI for almost all of his career as an electrical inspector, serving as chapter president. He has been the Iowa representative to the Western Section executive board since 1982 and on the International board of directors since 1987. Currently, Bowers is serving as alternate to the NFPA *NEC* code-making panel 5.

Reprinted from *IAEI News*, January 1997.

the concerns of inspector members.

The board of directors has recommended IAEI representation on the following committees, subject to available funding, for the reasons noted.

Proposed: NFPA 72, Committee on Fire Alarm Codes. We believe that IAEI should have representation on this committee because it is becoming more and more common for electrical inspectors to be required to inspect fire alarm systems.

Proposed: National Electrical Safety Code. We believe that IAEI needs representation on this committee since more and more primary and medium voltage service installations are being installed and maintained by owners instead of public utilities. The standards for overhead and underground installations of these types are developed by this committee.

Proposed: International Electrotechnical Commission. We believe that IAEI representation on this committee is vitally important. International codes are being proposed for adoption in this country which do not even include an inspection process, relying instead on self-certification of manufacturers and installers. We need to be sure that global free trade doesn't result in unsafe electrical products and installations.

OBJECTIVE: To promote the uniform understanding and application of the *National Electrical Code* and other electrical codes. Your organization develops educational material aimed directly at improving the understanding and proper application of the *National Electrical Code*. These materials, listed below, are considered to be some of the best in the industry.

- *Analysis of the National Electrical Code*
- *One- and Two-Family Dwelling Electrical Systems*
- *Soares Book on Grounding*
- *Ferm's Fast Finder*
- *Neon Installation Manual*
- Certification Study Guides for Electrical Inspectors and Plan Reviewers
- *Analysis of the National Electrical Code*, in Spanish (new)

IAEI members receive a discount on the retail price of all of these materials, as well as on many other products available through IAEI.

Your organization presents electrical seminars which promote better understanding of code requirements. These seminars draw attendees from all segments of the electrical industry and receive excellent evaluations. Members attend at a discounted fee. All seminar material is available to chapters and divisions without charge for educational programs for members only.

Current seminar topics include grounding, one- and two-family electrical systems, and the analysis of the *National Electrical Code*.

Under Development: Additional educational material in the areas of generators, motors, transformers, hazardous locations and medical facilities is being developed. Seminars for these topics and for neon signs are planned to follow.

New: IAEI has a formal MOU with ICBO under which it provides seminar material and instructors for all of the ICBO electrical seminars. These seminars are good refreshers for electrical inspectors and an excellent training experience for combination inspectors.

Proposed: IAEI is working with BOCA and SBCCI regarding the possibility of cooperative efforts in education where IAEI can provide educational material and qualified instructors.

IAEI provides technical articles in the *IAEI News*, which are aimed at improving the understanding of *Code* requirements and the proper use of products and materials in electrical installations.

New: IAEI funded two members on the NFPA task group on usability of the *NEC*. This effort was directly aimed at making the *NEC* easier to read, understand and apply. The very positive work of this group is reflected in the major editorial changes accepted for the 1999 *NEC*.

OBJECTIVE: To promote cooperation between inspectors, the electrical industry and the public.
IAEI promotes cooperation between inspectors and the industry through its work on NFPA committees and by ongoing work with testing laboratories, manufacturers, contractors and electricians. This cooperation is apparent at section meetings where these industry members display their products and

William "Bill" Clark, of the city of Sacramento, discussing changing jobs in service and technology at the 1996 Southwestern Section meeting. Bill Clark is also an IAEI instructor.

Jim Pauley presents Executive Director Phil Cox with a plaque of appreciation from the Western Section at the 1995 Western Section meeting.

Eastern Section held its 72nd annual code workshop on the shores of New Jersey, at Harrah's Casino and Hotel in Atlantic City in 1996.

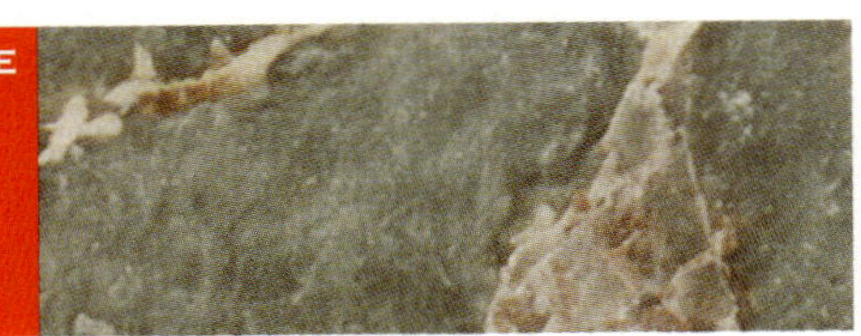

1998 International President

Thomas E. Trainor, newly elected international president, is the manager of Inspection Services for the city of San Diego and has 35 years of service with the city. Tom started as an apprentice electrician with the city in 1963 and worked as a journeyman electrician, electrical inspector, and senior electrical inspector prior to his appointment as chief electrical inspector in 1979. He still holds that technical position and, since his promotion to inspection services manager in 1991, is also responsible for the administration of all construction inspection services in the city of San Diego.

Mr. Trainor has served as secretary and chairman of the Border Counties Division, chairman of the Southern California Chapter, and is an ongoing member of the chapter executive committee. He was Southwestern Section president in 1989 and serves on the past president's council which provides fiscal review and historical continuity for Section operations. He has been chairman of the Southwestern Section educational committee since 1981, organizing and presenting the educational programs for seventeen annual meetings and nearly as many Quint Chapter meetings. Tom represents IAEI as a principal member on CMP-18 and is a member of NFPA and the UL Electrical Council.

Tom developed the electrical newsletter concept in the San Diego area. Local jurisdictions adopt the *National Electrical Code* without amendment and then work together to develop and publish newsletters which identify code interpretations and electrical installations that are acceptable throughout the county area. This concept is well received by the local electrical industry and makes everyone's job a little easier. Tom has also created a combination permit for residential construction; designed phone systems and work flow procedures for the department, and implemented an automated inspection request line to improve customer service.

Mr. Trainor was instrumental in the development of electrical seminars, which are jointly sponsored by IAEI and ICBO. This program, which originated in the Southwestern Section, has expanded into a formal agreement between IAEI and ICBO and is the keystone of our effort to partner effectively with the model building code groups. Tom has instructed in these seminars since 1987, is an IAEI instructor and has also served as an IAEI instructor in seminars for the International Sign Association.

As a board member, Tom has worked to improve cooperation between IAEI and NFPA, which is most noticeable in their support of our code analysis seminars. He has worked to develop our relationship with the three model building code groups and with the new ICC with the ongoing aim that IAEI provide electrical education for the members of all of these organizations. Most recently, Tom was involved in the creation of the IAEI/UL technical advisory panel (TAP) which gives IAEI more direct involvement in the review of UL standards. The TAP is currently reviewing UL's Standards related to light fixtures, armored cable, grounding of metal raceway systems, and polymeric neon sign materials. Tom was instrumental in forming the IAEI codes and standards committee to assist code-making panel members in the review of proposals and to identify code issues where IAEI should take an official position. Tom was also a member of the NFPA usability task group and strongly supports the effort to make the *NEC* more user friendly. He feels that the rewrite of Article 250 may be the single most important issue he has been involved with in the area of electrical safety.

— Reprinted from *IAEI News*, January 1998.

services, participate in the education programs, and support effective *Code* enforcement.

New: IAEI is working with the three major building code groups to demonstrate the importance of electrical inspection and the significant role professional electrical inspectors have in safe electrical installations.

New: IAEI proactively supports the Inspectors Initiative developed through the efforts of industry organizations.

New: IAEI has embarked on a partnership with the National Electrical Safety Foundation to provide information to the public on the importance of electrical safety.

OBJECTIVE: To collect and disseminate information relative to the safe use of electricity.

The goal of the *IAEI News* is to provide the very best information on code requirements, electrical products and installations all of which promote the safe use of electricity. IAEI has provided field reports and other information to the Consumer Products Safety Commission, the National Electrical Safety Foundation and various test labs in support of safe electrical products and installations.

IAEI publishes accident reports which help others to avoid repeating dangerous practices.

OBJECTIVE: To represent the electrical inspectors in all matters which are dealt with nationally and internationally by the electrical industry.

Most of the activities previously mentioned result in the effective representation of electrical inspectors and what they do today. In these changing times, there is a real need to demonstrate the continuing importance of professional electrical inspection in the construction process.

New: IAEI is working with the International Code Conference on the development of professional standards for inspectors and with the three member building code groups on training and certification programs for electrical inspectors.

New: IAEI simply has to participate on committees of the International Electrotechnical Commission which are developing worldwide electrical safety standards.

New: In addition to the United States, Canada, Saudi Arabia and Japan, IAEI now has an active chapter in Mexico. Expansion into Russia, Puerto Rico and Chile is being considered. The new focus on an international electrical safety system aimed at supporting international trade requires that we take a global approach to electrical safety.

OBJECTIVE: To cooperate with other national and international organizations in furthering the development of the electrical industry.

IAEI works with NFPA, CSA and AUME in the development, adoption and use of electrical codes. IAEI works with UL and CSA in the development of standards for electrical products and materials. IAEI works with building code groups in the training and certification of inspectors. IAEI works with electric utilities to assure an effective interface between distribution and premises electrical systems. IAEI works with manufacturers in the field review of their products and with contractors in the inspection of their installations. IAEI works with both union and non-union electricians to support safe electrical installations. IAEI is, as our logo proclaims, the keystone of the electrical industry.

This is what your organization does to represent you and to support and defend the importance of your work. These activities benefit you every day in ways you may not always recognize. Building officials are more aware of the importance of what you do and your role in maintaining electrical safety in your community. Test Labs are more responsive to your complaints or concerns about the products they list. Manufacturers are more diligent in responding to your issues with their products. Contractors and customers have a better understanding of your role in the industry and the value of knowledgeable and professional electrical inspectors. Most importantly, you are better prepared in every way to do your job on a daily basis.

But, clearly, these efforts on your behalf cost money. IAEI has functioned for years on the proverbial "shoestring." Our dues are undoubtedly the lowest of any comparable organization. (They cover only about a third of the organization's expenses.) We continue to be cost conscious and frugal in our efforts to provide good member services at a minimum cost, but we are at our limit at this point.

These are new and dynamically changing times. The electrical industry continues to grow and expand into a global economy. Electrical safety standards are in danger of being negotiated away in the interests of free trade. Objective third-party inspections of products could be replaced by manufacturer's self-certification programs. Self-certification by contractors is the next logical step. Changes are occurring on an almost daily basis that could seriously impact you and your work. IAEI must be able to represent you effectively and protect your interests. This is its mission. So when you consider the proposed dues increase, I encourage you to review the benefits you derive from your membership in IAEI, the value you receive from your organization and vote to support IAEI so that it can continue to support you. Thank you.

Thomas E. Trainor, IAEI international president, is the manager of Inspection Services for the city of San Diego and has 35 years of service with the city. Tom represents IAEI as a principal member of CMP-18 and is a member of NFPA and the UL Electrical Council. Reprinted from *IAEI News*, September 1998.

Northwestern Section Timeline

1995 Southern Utah Division of the Utah Chapter is granted its charter.

1998 Herb Stabenow, of Hillsboro, Oregon, is elected secretary of the Northwestern Section.

CHALLENGES FOR 1998: SUPPORTING IAEI

Global Influences: The coming year brings a number of significant challenges to the International Association of Electrical Inspectors. Those attending the 1997 annual section meetings were given a brief description of what is taking place in the global market. Information was also provided as to how this will affect IAEI members in general and electrical inspectors in particular. Code enforcement jurisdictions will be affected by international agreements established between their own country and foreign governments. This will involve electrical equipment made in one country and used in another. Electrical inspectors may be required to accept the installation of foreign made electrical equipment within their jurisdiction even though the equipment was neither manufactured nor tested according to product standards and testing procedures they have been familiar with in the past. It is hoped that inspector members will take this issue seriously and prepare for what is likely to happen in the future. The IAEI must become more involved in global affairs affecting electrical inspectors and the electrical industry if it is to operate effectively in the future. This will involve active participation and financial commitment from IAEI members to make it work. How the IAEI grows and how it functions in international affairs will be determined

Code discussion at the 2001 Northwestern Section meeting.

Central Mexico Chapter received its charter in February 1998. ***From left to right*:** **John Calloggero, NFPA; Antonio Macias, secretary/treasurer; Javier Velez, vice president; Manuel Villa, president; Doug Geralde, CSA; Mark Earley, NFPA; Phil Cox, IAEI; Victor Espinola, manager of Americ.**

by the members. The board of directors recognizes the importance of becoming more involved and has authorized the establishment of an IAEI global affairs committee to provide guidance for the organization.

International Growth: The IAEI board of directors, in its November 1997 meeting, approved the formation of a new chapter in the country of Mexico. It is known as the Central Mexico Chapter and is made up of Mexico City and states surrounding it. It is good to see IAEI members in the country of Mexico actively expressing their interest in promoting electrical safety through education, inspection, and the enforcement of electrical safety rules. Those individuals who worked hard to get the Central Mexico Chapter started are to be commended. Their extensive effort has resulted in forming a small but strong group of individuals upon which this new chapter can grow. The IAEI must provide the necessary support to ensure the progressive development of the new chapter.

The IAEI is fortunate to have a strong organizational structure in both Canada and the United States. With the interest shown by members in Mexico, it is anticipated that the organization will soon be strong there also. The IAEI must be ready and willing to act when the opportunity to promote interest in electrical safety in other countries presents itself.

Support for Qualified Electrical Inspectors: Friends of the IAEI have openly supported a quality electrical inspection program. The Inspection Initiative includes representative organizations from different areas of the electrical industry. Those organizations have joined together in an effort to make known the importance of having good electrical programs with qualified electrical inspectors. Inspectors know the value of making thorough electrical inspections in enforcing electrical safety rules and of the benefit it brings to the consumer. Electrical inspections made by dedicated qualified electrical inspectors are a proven value.

IAEI Membership: A major challenge for 1998 is for IAEI members to bring in additional members. The cost of membership in the IAEI is one of the best values to be found. There are too many electrical inspectors who are not members. In addition, there are too many others in other electrical trades or professions who are not part of this organization. They are missing an opportunity to learn from the collective knowledge and experience of IAEI members. The ability to meet in IAEI meetings to discuss code related problems, to gain from nationally recognized experts, and to keep abreast of the many industry changes is too great an opportunity to ignore. Continuing education of electrical inspectors and other members through participation in educational conferences and seminars provides the basis for more uniform interpretation and enforcement of electrical rules. Past International President Paul Bowers offered a challenge for each IAEI member to recruit one member during 1998. If we all accomplish that, the stated goal of 30,000 members by the year 2000 will be reached far ahead of schedule. It can be done.

The IAEI staff wishes you a happy and prosperous New Year.

Reprinted from *IAEI News*, January 1998.

Edward C. Lawry Award

John Schwab presents to Ron Massen the first Edward C. Lawry Award on May 14, 1998. This award was created by the Wisconsin Chapter for members who distinguish themselves as to merit an award of this magnitude. The attributes include more than three decades of service, participation on committees, commitment to the organization and the standards-making process, honesty, integrity, wisdom and more. Jerome C. Kortendick was awarded the honor on May 24, 2001.

There have always been those members of IAEI who attend each and every section meeting each year. Some of those members, at the 1998 Eastern Section meeting, are (*left to right*): Maggie and Harvey Johnson, Patty and Charlie Forsberg, Liz and John Erickson, Nancy and Richard Loyd, Doris and Tom Trainor, and Phil Cox.

Dick Widera, the Florida Chapter secretary/treasurer, (*second from left*) presented Jim Yost, 1997 division chairman, with a certificate for 25 years of membership. Nelson Montgomery, chief electrical inspector for the city of Tampa, (*second from right*) also presented a certificate for 35 years of membership with Julian Burnside, retired chief electrical inspector for the city of Tampa.

Doris and Tom Trainor visit with Antonio Macias, secretary/treasurer of the Central Mexico Chapter.

Chattanooga Division's July 1998 meeting was presented by the Electric Power Board of Chattanooga. Pictured from *(left to right)* are: Speaker Randy Snorek, EPB safety director; Chattanooga Division Vice Chairman Steve Clark; Sam Stephens, EPB; Speaker Alan Roderick, manager; Meter Department, and David Perry, city of Chattanooga chief electrical inspector.

1999 International President

It is said that one can read a man by knowing where he is from and what he does with the time that is his own. That being the case one would expect that the new president of IAEI would be a rugged individualist, who is persistent, unafraid of obstacles, a careful and patient observer who achieves his goals, quietly and steadily, without fanfare.

IAEI was only 19 years old when **Elver Madsen** began his fifty-two year career in the industry by installing electrical substations in Savage Circle, Wolfpoint and Fort Peck, Montana. Young Madsen had a goal and he moved steadily toward it, moving through such business positions as office manager and bookkeeper and marketing, as he gathered more training from ICS Electrical School, General Motors Institute, and from specialized classes through IAEI in one and two-family and electrical general and electrical plan review. Even when he was drafted into the U.S. Army Signal Corps, he continued his studies. He was graduated from the Southeastern Signal School, Ft Gordon, Georgia, and was chosen to teach the operation and installation of electrical generators to supply power for C.P.O. Command Post.

After leaving the Army, he continued his education and obtained a journeyman license in the states of Washington and Idaho and the master electrician's license in 1967. In 1964, he established and operated Madsen Hardware and Electric Company, along with a radio and TV shop. During the next thirty years, his involvement in the electrical industry escalated, from serving as a part-time electrical inspector for the city of Boise, Idaho, to electrical inspector for the city of East Helena, Montana, to state electrical inspector where he was responsible for both inspections and the checking of electrical licenses. In 1983, he was promoted to chief electrical inspector for the state of Montana, with the responsibility of interpreting the *Code* and supervising twelve inspectors.

Following his love of teaching, he taught low voltage systems to U.S. West employees in Portland, Medford, and Klamath Falls, Oregon; the 1996 *Code* for Shell and Texaco Oil Refineries in Anacortes, Washington, and for Conoco Oil Company in Billings, Montana. He has taught *NEC* classes at Clackamas Community College in Oregon. In 1990, he started ELM Code Seminars, which has provided other teaching opportunities across the northwest.

Along the way, Madsen has steadily racked up a string of credits. He is past president of Northwestern Section of IAEI, past member of code-making panel 17, member of NFPA, member UL electrical advisory council, board member of the NBEE, and IAEI board member.

Throughout his career, Madsen has been the rugged individualist, thinking private thoughts, silently watching and learning, overcoming whatever obstacles blocked his path, and most usually reaching his goals. It is expected that this president from Montana will bring a touch of the explorer, the hunter, the fisherman to the international offices of IAEI — persistence without fanfare, willingness to press forward despite hardships, a sense of direction and growth.

Excerpted from *IAEI News*, January 1999.

IAEI Focuses on Education

Meet Michael Johnston

Amid the ring of hammers, muffled conversations of electricians busy pulling wires bleed over into the offices at the IAEI headquarters office. Dust, clutter and stacks of materials have shifted from point to point through the weeks as work has progressed. Excitement rises as the educational training area is nearing completion.

Officially, as of June 1, the Education Department, of IAEI has been formed. Michael J. Johnston, formerly electrical field inspections supervisor of the city of Phoenix, Arizona, will serve as acting manager. Thoughtful, perceptive and highly organized, Johnston is in the process of launching the various functions of the department.

His first task is to ensure that the role of the department conforms to the mission of IAEI to focus on education, to be innovative, accessible, educational, and informed.

He wants to encourage all IAEI members to stay at the top of the game when it comes to the *NEC*, to stay on the learning edge. With this mission in mind, he will ensure that the department communicates knowledge and keeps the members informed.

Not only does he want to keep members informed but he wants also to extend education, formal instruction and supervised practice into the profession. He believes that when apprentices grow to journeymen and journeymen achieve the level of master craftsmen, the industry grows.

But growth cannot happen without accessibility – to materials that are easy to understand and easy to use and to mentors who share knowledge and insight. These mentors will consist of competent inspectors, code panel members and leaders in the industry who will present seminars and answer questions that come in through the magazine, the web site and through fax or e-mail. Johnston wants to use every communications avenue available to promote both accessibility and innovation.

For innovation to happen, however, we have to be willing to do some things in a new way. Although IAEI has been active for more than seventy years, there is an ongoing upgrading in materials and methods. One of Johnston's goals is to see every publication have multimedia counterparts, such as powerpoint, electronic books, videos, slides, and transparencies.

Michael Johnston

Another innovation is the addition of new publications on such subjects as hazardous locations, electric motors & motor control, swimming pools, and health care facilities. Johnston would like to hear from members and other supporters of good education to get recommendations on subjects that need educational material developed and made available. He stresses that the Education Department exists to serve the membership and to provide the instruction materials that are needed.

In addition to developing new materials with multimedia counterparts, a schedule will be developed for the International office training facility. These sessions will be conducted with state-of-the-art multimedia presentations that focus on the real need of electricians and seek to clearly show exactly what he or she needs to know.

So will the three types of seminars that will be held away from the International office—International Seminars, Joint Seminars and On-Site Seminars. Johnston strongly emphasizes that he believes communication, education, and teamwork are the keys to growth and the future of IAEI. He hopes to quickly work out a schedule for each of the three types of seminars that will offer the greatest benefit to members.

Mike's greatest interest seems to be helping members achieve more out of their profession. Perhaps that is because he himself came up through the ranks and has come to value education. He spent more than ten years in electrical code enforcement both as a senior electrical inspector and field supervisor. His career spanned many years in the electrical industry and includes work as

a journeyman electrician on residential, commercial, and industrial projects. He also worked as project superintendent for several major electrical construction projects.

Johnston is fully certified in many areas. He is a member in good standing of the International Brotherhood of Electrical Workers. He served a full apprenticeship and achieved both journeyman E-2 and master electrician E-1 licenses in the state of Connecticut. Additionally, he holds all IAEI certifications: one- and two-family dwelling electrical systems, electrical general, and electrical plans review. He also holds ICBO electrical inspections certifications.

His involvement with IAEI began in 1989. He has served at the section level as 3rd vice president of the Southwestern Section and also served the Central Arizona Chapter as chairman of the chapter in 1996 and chairman of the education committee in 1996 and 1997.

Teaching has come naturally to Mike. He has been an active electrical code and educational instructor for the Central Arizona Chapter since 1990. Certified by the state of Arizona to instruct at the community colleges in electrical code and theory, Mike has taught at Phoenix College and at Gateway Community and also was an active instructor for the Electric League of Arizona.

Keenly interested and experienced in computers and multimedia, Johnston brings with him many innovative and exciting ideas to enhance the new Education Department.

Reprinted from *IAEI News*, March 1999.

Quick Fact

At the IAEI board of directors meeting in 1996, the board approved proposed changes in the Articles of Association to permit the secretary to be elected each year from the board membership. The treasurer's position would be filled each year by the chairman of the fiscal affairs committee (first vice president) for that year. This was to be submitted to the membership for vote.

Northwestern Secretary Herb Stabenow recognizes the ladies that handled the companion program as Executive Director Phil Cox looks on at the 1999 Northwestern Section meeting. *From left to right*: Beth Burns, Carrie Dove, and Susan Hughes.

Ronald L. Hughes and his wife, Marilyn, celebrated their 50th wedding anniversary at the 1999 Southwestern Section convention.

Robert J. Falconi, CSA International; Dave Clements, Canadian Section; Ray Millet, Eastern Section; Rick Gilmour, Canadian Section, visit at the 1999 board meeting.

Anytime is a good time for inspectors to talk code. Western Section members discuss their opinions at the 1999 Western Section meeting.

Members of the Eastern Section at the 1999 Eastern Section meeting felt that Andy Cartal needed a friend. He is shown here with his new best friend at the 1999 annual section meeting.

Chairman Marvin Bouchardt talks with students and members at the April 15, 1998, South Texas Chapter meeting.

2000 International President

A son of the land, **Jimmy Bonds** embraces earthy values often not seen in the cities, values like practicality, vigor, openness and straightforwardness. His occupation is that of an electrical inspector, a responsible and respectable business, in which his physical strength, practical knowledge, and sagacity made him a leader among inspectors. The new international president of IAE carries with him a deep pride and love of the electrical industry not found in many, and approaches industry issues with the highest level of professionalism.

Jimmy Bonds started gaining the practical knowledge of electricity as an apprentice and worked his way, over a period of eighteen years, through the stages of journeyman and contractor to become, in 1983, the first electrical inspector for the state of Oklahoma.

He joined the International Brotherhood of Electrical Workers (IBEW), NJATC Program, in Ft. Smith, Arkansas, in 1965, and the IAEI in 1983.

Carl Albert State College in Poteau, Oklahoma, awarded him the associate degree in trades and industry education. He has obtained further certificates through IAEI in one and two-family electrical systems, electrical general, and electrical plan review.

During the 1999 *Code* cycle, he served as alternate member of the *National Electrical Code* code-making panel 14, representing IAEI, and will serve as alternate on CMP-8 during the 2002 *Code* cycle.

He is a member of the IAEI/UL technical advisory panel and of the NCPCCI electrical test development committee for Experior Assessments.

Bringing with him a wealth of knowledge and wisdom to the office of international president, Bonds has expressed his goals as centering on education, membership issues, and global expansion. A strong advocate of education, he feels that it is important for electrical inspectors and other members of the electrical industry to continually increase their knowledge of the electrical field in order to stay abreast of rapidly changing technology.

Consequently, he wants to continue the progress that has been made in the certification program, to complete the training facilities and continue the training of instructors, to expand the production and upgrading of the magazine and books, and to increase the sales of the books and other learning materials.

The membership friendly approach of the association should be continually enhanced. Additional members should be sought from among inspectors, apprentices, journeymen, contractors and associates, as well as other from all segments of the industry.

Global expansion is the wave of the future, he believes, and IAEI should be in the forefront of this growth and aggressively continue with the progress that has been made in this area.

Reprinted from *IAEI News*, January 2000.

Quick Fact

The board of directors, at their November 10–11, 2000, board meeting eliminated the senior member retired classification effective July 1, 2001. Those who are presently classified as senior member retired members are permitted to maintain that classification as long as they hold the qualifications. This action is to be included in the summary of the 2000 board of directors meeting scheduled for the March/April Issue of the *IAEI News*. Senior member retired members will be contacted for verification of their status and their desire to be retained in this status.

— Reprinted from *IAEI News*, March 2001.

These members of the Central Illinois Division won the coveted Charlie Trout plaque in fierce competition at the Illinois Chapter annual meeting in 2000. Front row, *left to right*: Art Cummins, Mike Leahy (holding plaque), and Mike Alwes. Back row *left to right*: Rex Snider, William Miller, and Phil Yehl. It is the second time the Central Illinois Division has won the traveling plaque in as many years. The Trout plaque is given in "Code Competition" at the annual Illinois Chapter meeting each year.

A Time To Say Thanks!

When the IAEI needed help to do a job, many of its members rallied to provide that help and support its effort. Thanks to that support, the project to finish a portion of the second floor of the IAEI headquarters office building is almost complete. Converting this portion of the building into a training room with adjacent office space for the IAEI education department and the installation of an elevator has been made possible by the generous contribution of funds from several IAEI sections, chapters, divisions, outside organizations, and individuals. Those contributors have made it possible for the IAEI to have a very functional area that will enhance its ability to promote good electrical education. By using this training room for seminars and for board meetings, the IAEI has already saved money by not having to rent outside meeting room space.

The contributors who made this construction project possible are shown (below), ranging from those who made both large and multiple donations to those dedicated individuals who rose to the occasion and gave their share. Each of these organizations and individuals are to be commended for their willingness to participate. All contributors will be contacted to give individual recognition for their support and a plaque with their names will be displayed in the training room. This plaque will be a constant reminder of the unselfish commitment of members who willingly accepted the challenge and made a sacrifice to promote the IAEI and its work.

The following photographs of the unfinished area, of varying stages of construction, and of the finished area will give an idea of what has been accomplished. If you have an opportunity to visit the IAEI international office, it will be our pleasure to give you a tour of the building.

Thanks for your generous support.

Reprinted from *IAEI News*, July 2000.

Before: Elevator

After: Elevator

Training Center Champions

Wisconsin Chapter
Western Section
Southwestern Section
Southern Section
Kentucky Chapter
Puget Sound Chapter
Rocky Mountain Chapter
Canadian Section
Nebraska Chapter
Central Arizona Chapter
Northwestern Section
South Dakota Chapter
Ellis Cannaday Chapter
North Carolina Electrical Institute
Southern California Chapter
St. Louis Chapter
South Dakota Chapter
North Dakota Chapter
Iowa Chapter
Ontario Chapter
Minnesota Chapter
Arkansas Chapter
Oregon Chapter
Nova Scotia Chapter
EUSERC
Akron Division
South Jersey Chapter
Western Section
Alabama Chapter
Philip and Jama Cox
Raymond Millet
Ed Lawry
Fred W. Brown
Pavlick Electric Company
Ray and Donna Weber
Doug Geralde
Lanny McMahill

Total Contribution $117,253

Before: Training Area

After: Training Room

Wisconsin Chapter

Model of Performance

IAEI members and associated organizations rose to the occasion to make possible the completion of a construction project at the IAEI headquarters building in Richardson, Texas. Finishing the second floor area to create an educational facility has provided a more suitable environment in which to conduct meetings and perform training. In a previous editorial, those individuals and organizations who contributed to make this work possible were identified. I believe it is appropriate to give special recognition to one contributor who has not only risen to the challenge, but has achieved a level of support that could not have been anticipated.

Wisconsin Chapter officers and members have supported the International office in the IAEI education program by joining with it to conduct seminars within the state of Wisconsin that benefited both the chapter and the IO. Recognizing that developing and producing quality educational material is very expensive for the IAEI International office, the chapter board of directors chose to work directly with the IO in conducting seminars and to share the proceeds. The chapter had an option of purchasing the material from the IO and conducting those seminars on its own in order to realize a greater return, but chose not to do so. For several years the Wisconsin Chapter has conducted jointly sponsored seminars within the state, and that effort has not only been good for the chapter, but has also significantly helped the International office. Another result of the seminar activity is the increase in chapter membership to the point that it now has the greatest number of members of any chapter in the IAEI. This model of performance is an example of what can be done when there is the determination to do so.

The Wisconsin Chapter was one of the top two contributors to the IAEI building fund for the education facility at the International office. However, the chapter did not stop there. After learning that there were not enough funds to install audio-visual equipment in the new education facility, the chapter board of directors authorized funding for the purchase and installation of an LCD projector, screen, and supporting AV equipment. As a result of this action, quality equipment has been installed in the training room that makes it possible to present information through audio and video mediums from different sources. The system has versatility and can be used as part of the needed equipment when the IAEI is able to develop and implement a remote learning program. Those who have seen the equipment in operation can attest to the value it adds to the education facility.

The IAEI is made stronger by the dedication and support of a multitude of people who never ask, *What's in it for me?* but rather, *What can I do to make the IAEI better?* Every successful organization has this caliber of people who do their job well, and frequently, the extent of that work is unknown by most members.

The Wisconsin Chapter board of directors deserves recognition for its decision to support the IAEI education program and the leadership standards it has set. A special thanks goes to Joe Hertel, chapter secretary/treasurer, for his hard work and dedication in making sure all things came together to make the joint seminar program a success. Instructors for the latest series of seminars were Ed Lawry, Tom Garvey, and Joe Hertel. Thank you, officers and members of the Wisconsin chapter.

Reprinted from *IAEI News*, September 2000.

High lumen output LCD projector

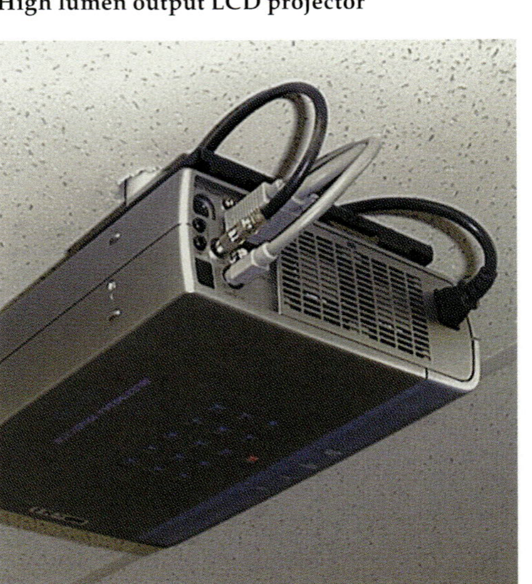

Ceiling recessed motorized screen

Supporting current technology rack mounted audio equipment

2001 International President

In November, **Doug Geralde** was elected the 73rd president of the International Association of Electrical Inspectors. In this role, he hopes to encourage a more global outlook and greater connectivity through computerization.

"Doug Geralde is a natural fit as president for this time of our development," Phil Cox, executive director of IAEI, said. "His input on globalization and greater computerization will greatly facilitate our forward progress. Through his years of involvement with IAEI, we have found Doug to be informative, cooperative, and a global ambassador for the IAEI. His dedication to the IAEI and to promoting electrical safety has been demonstrated through the work he has done and the time he has devoted to this task. As with other dedicated leaders of organizations, Doug gives much more of his time and energy than is expected and the IAEI is better because of it.

"Doug has traveled extensively throughout much of the world. During his trips abroad, he made contact with many potential IAEI members and promoted the organization and its objectives. His work in international affairs has benefited the IAEI in the past and is expected to continue in the future. The IAEI board of directors expressed its confidence in Doug's ability to help the organization in the international arena by appointing him as vice president for international affairs."

IAEI focuses on expanding electrical education and safety. The association is actively involved in making recommendations to the standards committees and testing laboratories, promoting the uniform application of standards and inspection methods, publishing instructive and interpretive information, and fostering global cooperation in developing the electrical industry.

In April, Mr. Geralde was appointed director of Corporate Audits and Investigations (CAI), part of the legal department of Canadian Standards Association. In this role, he focuses on liaisons with regulators throughout North America and on a global basis.

The CAI group investigates incidents reported by regulatory authorities, police, coroners and fire marshals involving CSA-certified equipment. Through their work, the team — who work across all CSA divisions — recommend changes to CSA standards committees; conduct audits on internal processes; and initiate, with manufacturers, voluntary recalls and all-points bulletin (APBs). CAI also exchanges information with regulators; sits on many of their boards; and provides them with new information on the marketplace with respect to investigations involving CSA-certified products.

"Over the past 20 years, Doug has established a very good working relationship with regulators across North America," said R.J. Falconi, vice president, general counsel and corporate secretary at CSA International. "This appointment reflects the higher profile that Doug now has, and it recognizes the importance of his work and his team to the organization. It will greatly serve to fulfill our ability to protect the integrity of the family of CSA certification marks."

Mr. Geralde started his career with CSA International in July 1977 as an engineering technologist. He then joined the CAI team in 1980 as a special service investigator. In 1986, he was appointed to the position of supervisor, Audits and Investigations and later to his just-concluded role of manager, Audits and Investigations.

Doug Geralde is avid about education, has served as chairman of the IAEI education committee, and presently works as the Canadian Section representative on that committee. He advocates the greater use of computer technology in the IAEI training program as well as in the general business of the organization.

A man of vast knowledge and wisdom, he has the vision needed to help IAEI along its path to success. His contributions and dedication to the IAEI over the years are immeasurable.

Mr. Geralde is also secretary of the National Laboratory Accreditation Cooperation (NACLA); and active on several committees of the Canadian Council of Fire Marshals and Fire Commissioners (CCFM&FC). Reprinted from *IAEI News*, January 2001.

2001 International President Doug Geralde sports new hockey jersey presented to him at the 2001 Canadian Section meeting.

IAEI members at one of several technical presentations that highlighted the 1999 Southwestern Section meeting held at the Cathedral Hotel in San Francisco. Topics ranged from grounding and bonding to hazardous location wiring.

Southwestern Section Timeline

1997 International board of directors approves the formation of the **Central Mexico Chapter**.

California Section District is approved and created.

1998 The **Mexico Chapter** is renamed the **Sinaloa Chapter**.

2002 Board of directors approves the creation of the **Korea Chapter**.

Quick Fact

The board of directors, at their November 10–11, 2000, board meeting:

1. Received and accepted the report of the restructuring of the United States National Committee into a council and a technical committee and the change to IAEI participation. James Carpenter was accepted by the USNC as a member of the technical committee. The IAEI was not elected as a member of the newly instituted United States National Council.

2. Established a position of vice president for international affairs, and appointed Doug Geralde, Canadian Section, to the position.

Reprinted from *IAEI News*, March 2001.

William Wusinich

William Wusinich, a 28-year member of IAEI and a 40-year member of the International Brotherhood of Electrical Workers, passed away on May 5, 2001.

Bill was a member of the IBEW Local Union 98, located in Philadelphia, Pennsylvania.

Bill served in the Navy and as a volunteer fireman in Narberth. After working for several years at the trade, Bill began a job he would hold for over 30 years as an instructor for young apprentices learning the electrical trade. He soon began a lifelong battle to improve the codes and standards that regulated all aspects of the electrical industry.

He is credited with single-handedly awakening the IBEW to the importance of and the need for effective participation in the development of codes and standards. Several years ago, Bill accepted a position with OSHA that allowed him to focus more on fulfilling the need of working men and women.

Word spread quickly of his electrical safety program and he preached his message from coast to coast. His greatest gift was his ability to communicate ideas and motivate the audience to join the fight. He firmly believed that God had given him a special talent and he remained dedicated to his gift throughout his entire life.

William is survived by his wife, Carol, and three sons: Mark Wusinich; Scott Wusinich; and Matthew Wusinich: brother, John Wusinich; and sister, Margaret Scott.

Excerpted from *IAEI News*, July 2001.

Some members of the Canadian Section gather together at the 2001 Canadian Section meeting in Sudbury, Ontario.

Importance of IAEI Membership to Manufacturers

Electrical inspectors demonstrate support of electrical manufacturers and feel they are an integral part of the team dedicated to providing an environment in which consumers can safely use electrical energy. In keeping with that objective, many of these manufacturers have traditionally been and continue to be an important part of the International Association of Electrical Inspectors membership. Many actively participate in section and chapter meetings. Some of those individuals are often involved in code discussion panels and technical presentations and contribute in many other ways to the betterment of the organization and industry. Their involvement is an asset to the IAEI and in its effort to promote electrical safety.

Unfortunately, the level of participation of electrical manufacturers as members of the IAEI has decreased over the past few years and that adversely affects both the IAEI and manufacturers. It is readily understood that factors such as the necessity of being involved in both national and international activities and the impact of prevailing economic conditions have significantly affected planning and operations of industry organizations and have placed a heavy demand on resources. In view of these and other conditions, some may conclude that being part of the IAEI is not economically practical because electrical inspectors are not primary purchasers of electrical products and don't contribute to the bottom line. While electrical inspectors are not customers in the general sense, the normal performance of their code enforcing responsibilities can have a significant effect on the use of products within their jurisdiction.

John Minick, National Electrical Manufacturers Association field representative and former IAEI Southern Section president, stresses the importance of NEMA's association with inspectors in his contribution to an article in the November 15, 2001, issue of the NEMA publication *electroindustry*. That recognition is appreciated and manufacturers not already involved are encouraged to become active participants in the IAEI as membership in the association is one of the best investments they can make. Qualified electrical inspectors are one of the best friends manufacturers have.

The electrical inspector's primary obligation is to the consumer or user of electricity within his or her jurisdiction. It is in the best interest of the consumer as well as the inspector that quality electrical products be used and that they be installed and maintained by qualified people so that a high degree of consumer safety can be achieved. It is also in the best interest of manufacturers that their products comply with safety standards and be installed and used correctly. A representative of a well-known manufacturer actively involved with the IAEI made a comment something to the effect that "It would be foolish and contrary to our company's goals for it to produce an unsafe product." It actually goes beyond that. Even a product designed to operate safely can easily be installed or used in a way to render its operation unsafe. Inspectors are instrumental in locating and identifying many of those abuses and enforcing corrective measures.

The IAEI is considered as a keystone of the electrical industry because of its unique position and composition. It provides a focal point of interest because the work of electrical inspectors affects most segments of the electrical industry. Being a part of the IAEI provides a variety of benefits regardless of which part of the electrical industry the member represents. Some of those that apply to manufacturers are:

Establishing contacts and developing effective communications: Experience as a governmental electrical inspector and as a field representative for the National Electrical Manufacturers Association has provided some valuable insights for me as to the different needs and constraints of inspectors and manufacturers. Shortly after being employed by NEMA, I became aware that a real problem existed as to how each profession perceived the other. The expectation of each as to what the other could do was often miles apart in concept. This observation caused me to set an objective to encourage both groups to become better acquainted and to communicate with one another more effectively. Each needs to develop a better understanding of the capabilities, obligations, and constraints of the other. This objective has been successful on a limited basis but there is a great amount of work that needs to be done. Where good communications are established between inspection authorities and manufacturers, it significantly reduces problems and misunderstandings. This can translate into a significant saving of time and money for both sides.

IAEI meetings are places where inspectors and other members of the industry can meet and become acquainted in an environment where people of similar interests assemble to learn, exchange new ideas, and address other important industry issues. These settings not only result in educational achievements, they also result in an opportunity to develop better communications between and within groups. It is well understood that knowing someone to contact when information is needed or problems need to be resolved is far better than having to start cold in the search for solutions.

Being a source of product information: Electrical manufacturers are the ideal source of technical expertise regarding the design and use of their products. Individuals from those companies who have the technical knowledge of product standards, products, and how they relate to *Code* rules can serve as an important source of reliable information for designers, installers, and enforcers. Many electrical products are becoming much more complex and create a challenge for enforcing authorities to keep up with those advancements. Designers and installers often use a limited variety of materials and equipment because they generally select specific lines of known products that they use as standard operating procedures. Enforcing authorities must be prepared to inspect the installation of any type of foreign or domestic electrical equipment and be knowledgeable enough to determine if the installation complies with *Code* rules. Electrical inspectors need considerable information regarding specific electrical equipment and materials to effectively do their jobs. The best source for reliable information is from the product manufacturer. This is a significant reason why manufacturers need representatives known to and involved within the inspection community. Other sources of information are also necessary, but they are no substitute for the data available from makers of products.

Addressing the problem of counterfeit products: Counterfeit electrical products are a serious problem for both inspectors and manufacturers. From the inspector's side it presents several problems, but the most significant one is that of safety. For manufacturers, this is a severe problem from several aspects and can have a serious impact on them. Inspectors need to be able to recognize counterfeit products and this information should come from manufacturers. This has already been demonstrated by a few product manufacturers where representatives made presentations at IAEI meetings showing examples and specific details of counterfeit products and the differences between them and the authentic ones. Viewing samples of counterfeit products made it clear that unless one knows exactly how to distinguish between them and legitimate products, the imitation will likely be undetected. The best source for that information is the product manufacturer and the best location for dispensing it is at IAEI meetings.

Providing information during the *Code* development process: The IAEI has an established procedure to allow *Code* proposals to be processed for organizational endorsement. Where proposals involve electrical products, information from manufacturers is frequently needed to give inspectors adequate data to consider before taking a position on those proposals. Those hearings often involve extensive discussion of the merits of the issue and where an electrical product is concerned, it is best that a

Art Buxbaum

Art Buxbaum was a unique and independent individual. He left home at 14 and worked in upstate New York at such varied jobs as farm hand, dairy cattleman and resort lifeguard. Art served in the navy in World War II and picked up his basic electrical training there. He served in both ships and submarines as an electrician and also served on a base security force. Following his military service, he returned to New York City and worked as a subway maintenance electrician before opening his own electrical contracting business. In addition to contracting, he owned and operated a marine boat and engine business. He said it was the only way he could afford his own boat. He picked up his interrupted education, obtaining a high school diploma, and going on to gain a doctorate in education. He rarely used the title, Doctor, but would bring it up on occasions when he ran into professional snobbery.

Art moved his family to California in the late 50s. After working some time as an electrician, he joined the city of Los Angeles, Department of Building Safety as an electrical inspector. Art worked 27 years for the city of Los Angeles as electrical inspector, fire and life safety inspector and senior electrical inspector. Following the 1971 Slymar earthquake, Art participated in the investigation of quake damaged buildings and the development of new building regulations for high rise construction. As the first fire and life safety inspector, he established procedures for effective cooperation between the Fire and Building Safety Departments which remain in place today. He was awarded an honorary fireman's badge of which he was especially proud.

During this period, he also obtained his private pilot's license. Flying was one of the loves of his life and his stories about flying adventures are second only to those about his "Uncle Guido" in New York (a purely fictitious character).

Following his retirement from L.A., Art and Marilyn had planned to tour the country in their motor home and, indeed, did make a few trips which were also the source of some of Art's better stories. However, Art was not cut out for retirement and, in 1989, he joined the city of San Diego as chief combination inspector. He took over a newly formed division and provided organization and training to support a single inspector reviewing the work of all trades in one- and two-family construction. This is now a very successful program that has been studied and copied by other building departments across the country. Art also brought a business attitude to the department and helped to develop the concept of a bureaucracy that works like a business.

Art was a strong and active participant in the International Association of Electrical Inspectors. He held every office at the division, chapter, and section level. He helped to form and was a charter member of the Los Angeles Division. He represented IAEI on *NEC* code-making panel 7 and on NFPA 73 and served on the International education committee. He was a member of the International board since 1992. At the time of his death, he was an international vice president and on track to be international president in 2004.

Reprinted from *IAEI News*, September 2001.

Puget Sound Chapter 2001 officers sworn in at the January 13, 2001, meeting. *Front row, from left to right*: Joe Andre, code panel and education; Joe Guinasso, associate member, membership; Russ Bath, code panel; and Dobbe Spasojevich, junior past president, by-laws. *Center row*: Bob Thomas, president; Jack Waterson, first vice president, inspector member, membership; Mike Buettner, by-laws, inspector member; Chris Porter, section representative, education; and Jim Hinrichs, section representative, second vice president. *Top Row*: Don Millar, secretary/treasurer, by-laws, code panel; Jim Simmons (Roland LaVasseuer standing in), associate member, membership.

manufacturer is present to both present information and respond to inquiries.

Identification of field problems: Electrical inspectors are a good informational source for manufacturers regarding how their products are installed and used in the field. Regardless of how good a product is designed and made, if it is not applied in the field as it was designed, it can become a problem. Identifying field problems provides manufacturers information that can lead to the development of new products, the modification of existing ones, or changes in instructions included with products. Getting this type of information either at inspector meetings or through contacts established within the IAEI can be helpful to manufacturers. It is especially advantageous to a manufacturer if its representatives are able to deal directly with the source of such information where it is product specific.

Correcting misinformation: Inspectors need accurate product information to aid them in making many of their enforcement decisions. It is in the best interest of manufacturers to make that type of information accessible to inspectors and to address misinformation whenever it occurs. During inspector meetings where code discussion or other educational programs are conducted, it is not uncommon for material to be presented or questions to arise regarding the installation and use of specific products. It is highly desirable that someone knowledgeable of the product, its application and performance, related standards, and *Code* rules either be the presenter or be present to provide correct information should questions arise.

Scranton/Wilkes-Barre Division Chairman Bill Hopple accepts division charter from Eastern Section representative John E. Brezan and Northeast Pennsylvania Chapter chairman John K. Brezan.

Eastern Section Timeline

1996 **South Jersey Chapter** replaces the old Southern Division of the New Jersey Chapter.

1999 Board of directors approves the creation of the **Scranton/Wilkes-Barre Division** of the Northeastern Pennsylvania Chapter.

2000 **Keystone Chapter** is first mentioned in the Secretary's List.

Product exhibitions as classroom: Most IAEI meetings make provisions for electrical manufacturers to display their products. Exhibits staffed with people who have extensive knowledge of the products they display can be extremely effective educational settings for inspectors for product recognition and application. While inspectors don't purchase those products as part of their job, the more they know about them, the more effective they can be as inspectors. There is no substitute for seeing the actual product and getting detailed information on it. Product displays at meetings generally result in inspectors plying exhibitors with questions about products in order to learn as much as they can.

It is difficult to identify all the positive aspects of IAEI membership beneficial to manufacturers. The small fee for membership and the cost of attending meetings pales in relation to the direct benefits realized. IAEI gains from that association also, but the greatest value is not from membership dues or exhibit fees, but rather from the sharing of information, the open lines of communications, and in the cooperative effort to promote safety.

IAEI CEO and Executive Director Philip Cox is a member of NFPA NEC Technical Correlating Committee and CMP-1. He has served on CMP-1 since 1996—representing NEMA as chairman in the 1996 cycle and IAEI as acting chairman in the 1999 cycle. He also served on CMP-6, representing IAEI during the 1984 and 1987 cycles. He is a member of NFPA Electrical Section. — Reprinted from *IAEI News*, January 2002.

"Grampa" Don Nissen of UL consults the oracle (a jack-a-lope), having failed to get a proper answer from the Nebraska Chapter meeting code panel at the 2001 annual Nebraska Chapter meeting.

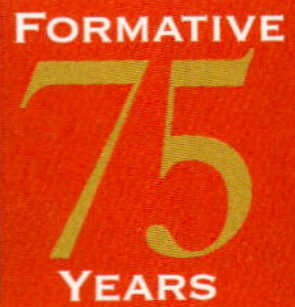

2002 International President

He is the seventy-fourth person to be honored as such. Through his efforts and contributions, IAEI has grown in stature and has become a viable force in developing and enhancing codes that help to assure greater electrical safety in homes and businesses throughout the nation and beyond.

Anthony Montuori has manifested interest in, and concern for, improved electrical services for virtually his entire adult life. He has worked diligently for decades in an effort to direct the focus of the organization and to enable it to function with efficacy. He has earned the respect and admiration of his colleagues, all of who heartily endorse his dedication to the position of president.

He has served in every capacity of the electrical industry, beginning as an inspector for the New York Board of Fire Underwriters in August 1963. He was promoted to senior inspector in 1982, and to chief electrical inspector in 1984. He obviously has worked his way "up the line."

Anthony displayed an affinity for his future field of endeavor at an early age, graduating from Alexander Hamilton Vocational High School in Brooklyn, New York, in 1950 with a major in electrical theory. He worked as an apprentice for two years before his employment was interrupted between 1953 and 1954, during which time he served with distinction in the Korean War with the U.S. Army.

Following the two-year hiatus for military service, Anthony immediately resumed pursuit of his career. He began employment with Gal Electro Mechanical Service in New York City where he honed his skills wiring and servicing controllers for self-service elevators and testing control panels. While at Gal, his interest in electricity burgeoned, motivating him to enroll at the Pratt Institute evening school in Brooklyn in 1957. He studied at Pratt until 1961, majoring in physics and electrical engineering, complementing his practical experience with advanced theory. The combination of the two provided the foundation for his future achievements as an inspector and exceptional leader in the field of electrical safety.

Through the years, Anthony's accomplishments have been numerous, and his expertise has been recognized through his appointments to many prestigious committees, both locally and nationally.

In 1984, he was appointed to the Master Electricians Licensing Board and the Advisory Board, Department of Buildings, city of New York. He remains with both groups to this day, where he is instrumental in reviewing qualifications of prospective licensed electricians and conducting hearings predicated on charges against license holders. Additionally, he reviews and recommends to the department the issuance and approval of 1000 kVA electrical installations. The granting of special permission for the use of wiring or appliances for those cases not covered by the New York City Electrical Code are within his purview. In New York City, he also serves as a member of Electrical Code Revision, Panel #5, and the Steering Committee for Code Revision.

On the national level, Anthony was appointed as a principal member of NFPA 73, representing New York Board of Fire Underwriters in 1991. In 1996, he was appointed as a principal member of CMP-9, and has served through three code cycles in that capacity representing IAEI.

Anthony is one of those rare individuals who, despite the enormity of his professional involvement, finds time to serve the community as a caring and concerned citizen. He is past president of Kiwanis International, which, under his leadership, contributed many thousands of dollars to worthy and charitable organizations.

Anthony Montuori is a visionary and catalyst whose vast knowledge, background and experience will enable him to provide the necessary leadership for IAEI in his quest for continued excellence in electrical safety throughout the world. He is worthy and admirable successor to the presidency.

Excerpted from *IAEI News*, January 2002.

1999 Eastern Section and International officers. *Back row left to right:* Bob McCullough, International delegate; Les Jones, president-elect of Eastern Section; Phil Cox, executive director; Ray Millet, Eastern Section secretary/treasurer. *Front row, left to right*: Anthony Montuori, candidate for office; Dennis Rowe, Jr., past president; and Elver Madsen, 1999 international president.

Another Step Forward

The electronic age has opened the way to an exciting world involving advanced methods of communications. What was once thought to be science fiction or unrealistic dreams is now reality. The feverish pace being experienced in the electronic or informational technology industry is difficult for many to understand well, much less to become skilled in its use. Improvements in computer hardware and software are constantly being made and users are at the mercy of those changes. By the time a new computer is purchased and put into use, it is likely that a newer and more advanced model is already being produced. Those newer computers often come with new types of pre-loaded software or a later version of programs than the purchaser has been using. With those changes, the user is required to learn the new systems if they are to be adequately utilized. Keeping up with the evolution of the information technology industry is both expensive, time consuming, and takes a serious commitment to study and grow. It is the way of the future, or should we really say, the present. The reality is that we are forced to continue learning or be left behind.

Rather than dwelling on the negative side, it is better to focus on the positive side and grow with the industry as fast and as much as resources permit. That struggle is difficult and takes a strong dedication of some very talented people. Successful organizations have to not only incorporate new technology into their operations, they also must continually look for better ways to utilize available features and make choices that are to their advantage.

While many don't truly understand the Internet and how it operates, the number of users of that service is increasing rapidly. The Internet is a valuable means by which people can communicate with one another, obtain a broad variety of information, and do a variety of other things. Web sites or home pages have been developed by organizations and individuals and are accessible to those who use the Internet. These web sites provide information on the host organization, and often have the capability to conduct business through it.

The IAEI in its effort to continually improve services provided to its members, has maintained a web site for the last few years and recently has added another one that will allow members and other users to have more effective contact with the international office and other parts of the organization. The IAEI plans to be part of advancing technology and to grow with the industry in this area even though it places a heavy demand on resources. This participation is viewed as an exciting challenge because of the multitude of possible uses of the technology that will help the IAEI in achieving its stated objectives.

IAEI staff takes pride in announcing the launching of its new web site, iaei.org, as another step toward a productive future. This is a significant step forward in the on-going effort to continually improve products and services to IAEI members, customers, and others associated with the organization. The initial site has a limited number of interactive features but new ones are being added as they are developed. The IAEI web site will grow into a leading source of industry related information with links to other key sites.

An e-commerce feature will be part of iaei.org in the near future. It will become an important part of the web site and will significantly improve the accessibility of members and customers to services and products offered by the IAEI. Providing adequate security for e-commerce activities is a very high priority and the program will not be activated until that protection is in place. The e-commerce program will allow people to apply for new membership, renew membership, order products, register for seminars, and perform other transactions that presently have to be done by mail or by phone.

You are encouraged to visit the site on a regular basis to learn when and where chapters, sections, and divisions are meeting, to get information on the IAEI, to review educational opportunities, to learn of new publications and products and just to see the progressive changes that are made. Your comments and suggestions are also welcome and are considered to be an important contribution. IAEI staff will monitor and update the site on a regular basis and will make every effort to ensure that it is a pleasant experience for those logging on to it and something of which members can be proud.

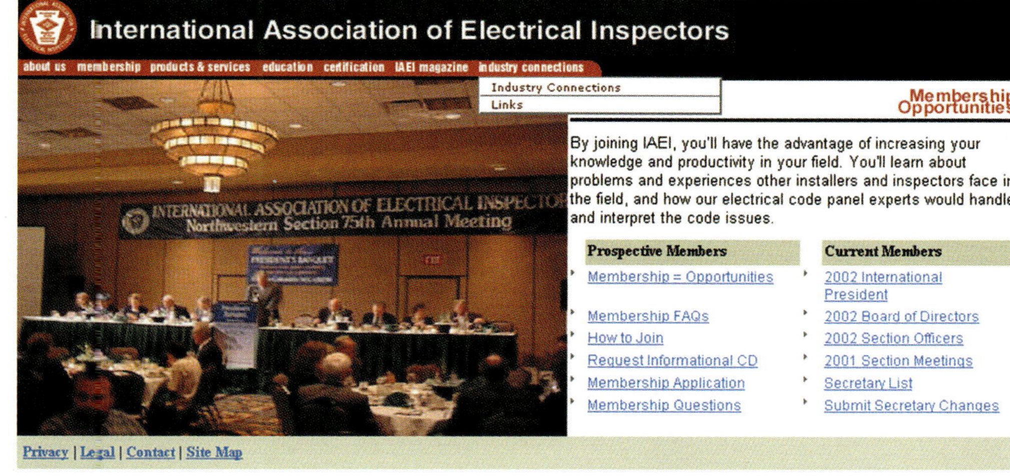

A sample IAEI.org web page.

Reprinted from *IAEI News*, March 2002.

James W. Carpenter

It is a pleasure to introduce **James Carpenter** as the new chief executive officer and executive director of the International Association of Electrical Inspectors. In many cases, the outgoing person has reservations regarding the one who assumes his or her position. There are no such reservations in this transition and it is felt that the search committee made an excellent choice in the selection of Jim Carpenter and the entire board of IAEI board of directors strongly supports his appointment. Many within the electrical industry already know Jim and his proven record of achievements and those who do not know him or of his work will soon understand his value to the IAEI.

Jim brings a valuable set of credentials to the office that will enable him to provide strong and stable leadership for the IAEI. The primary responsibilities associated with the position of CEO/executive director have shifted more toward the administrative and business side of the operation with less emphasis on the technical side associated with codes and standards. However, Jim's sound electrical training and experience will be an asset in his role as editor-in-chief as he is responsible for the review and approval of articles and material included in the *IAEI News*, the IAEI web site, and the other published materials produced by the IAEI.

Years of experience in code enforcement and his advancement to the administrative level of code enforcement has provided Jim with sound leadership and decision-making skills. As chief electrical engineer/state electrical inspector, with the North Carolina Department of Insurance, he was responsible for managing the inspection program and the third party certification program. In that position, he also provided consultations services for the state electrical code.

The quiet and reserved manner Jim demonstrates belies the inner strength and organizational ability he possesses, and those of us who have watched him work over the years are impressed with his ability to analyze and address complex situations. These characteristics will be important as he moves forward and provides leadership that will enable the organization to realize its great potential. Understanding the inspector's needs and those of other partners within the electrical industry are vital elements in the quest for industry support for electrical safety, and Jim is very familiar with what electrical inspectors face.

The assumption of the position of CEO/executive director carries with it a heavy workload and a heavy burden of responsibilities. It is my firm conviction that Jim is the right person for the time and is capable of handling whatever he must face. The IAEI will be better because of his commitment to serving the organization and his willingness to make the necessary sacrifices to properly do the job. Each member is encouraged to welcome Jim and to give him the support necessary to do his job.

By Philip H. Cox. retiring CEO/executive director. Reprinted from *IAEI News*, July 2002.

SUPPORTERS OF THE IAEI

Contributors to the Education Technology Fund

The IAEI is fortunate to have many supporters who willing give of themselves to help the organization do its work better. With ever increasing cost to operate and to provide services to both members and customers, it is difficult to find the resources to do everything that should be done.

When a need arose to add an elevator to the IAEI office in Richardson, Texas, to provide better access to the building and to convert unused space into much needed and functional meeting and office space, the response was quick and sufficient. Sections, chapter, divisions, outside organizations, and individual members contributed to the effort and made it successful.

The IAEI provides important training for many within the electrical industry. Electrical inspectors, designers, installers, and many others benefit from the types of programs developed and made available by the IAEI. Technology involved in the type of educational material developed and the method of presenting that information in training settings has improved dramatically within the last few years.

The IAEI is focusing on a versatile and effective form of training as part of its current seminar program. Electronic forms of presentations have been well received by participants and is much more flexible than earlier technology. Computer generated slides incorporating both actual photographs and created graphics bring much more realistic images with which to work. The more training images look like the real world, the more effectively they can be used to help students identify with situations encountered in the field.

Developing this type of training material and presenting it in the seminar or classroom setting requires a serious commitment of both time and other resources. In an effort to keep the IAEI abreast of this advanced technology and to keep up with future changes, an education technology fund has been established to provide a means whereby IAEI supporters can become involved in that work. Contributions made to the fund go to the purchase of laptop computers, LCD projectors, and related equipment necessary to develop and use this form of technology. This equipment is used by IAEI staff and other instructors who are part of IAEI International office education program.

Technical staff members and other program instructors are using this new technology where possible and the support by several sections, chapters, and individuals has made that possible in several cases. As funds become available, equipment is purchased to enable specific instructors in the IAEI sponsored program to convert to this newer technology.

The following individuals and groups have provided support for the education technology fund:

IAEI Sections:

Canadian Section; Eastern Section; Southern Section; Southwestern Section; Western Section.

IAEI Chapter:

Arkansas Chapter; Nebraska Chapter; New York Chapter; North Dakota Chapter; North Carolina Ellis Cannady Chapter; Ohio Chapter; Ontario Chapter; South Jersey Chapter; Southern California Chapter; Texas Chapter; Utah Chapter; Nova Scotia Chapter.

Individuals:

Andy and Christa Cartal; Philip and Jama Cox.

By Philip Cox, IAEI CEO and Executive Director and member of NFPA, NEC Technical Correlating Committee and CMP-1. He has served on CMP-1 since 1996, representing NEMA as chairman in the 1996 cycle and IAEI as acting chairman in the 1999 cycle. He also served on CMP-6, representing IAEI during the 1984 and 1987 cycles. He is a member of NFPA Electrical Section.

Reprinted from *IAEI News*, July 2002.

Canadian Section Timeline

1998 **N.B. P.E.I. Chapter**, covering New Brunswick and Prince Edwards Island, is initiated.

1999 **Rick Gilmour**, of Etobicoke, Ontario, is elected Canadian Section secretary.

2000 IAEI board of directors approves the charter for the newly developed **Prairie Chapter**.

Prairie Chapter held its inaugural meeting in Regina, Saskatchewan, on May 5, 2001. The meeting was held in conjunction with a training seminar.

First Female Section President

Leslie Sabin-Mercado was the first woman to achieve a section presidency at the 2002 Southwestern Section meeting in Honolulu, Hawaii.

YESTERDAY THINGS WERE DIFFERENT... TODAY, THEY ARE DIFFERENT AGAIN"

The opening line from a southern gospel music song by the Cathedrals has special meaning for me at this point of my life. Yesterday, I was very comfortable in my position as the chief electrical engineer, state electrical inspector with the North Carolina Department of Insurance. Today, I find myself moved to another state and with a new position—CEO & Executive Director of the International Association of Electrical Inspectors. Now you may surmise from the opening of this editorial that big changes are coming as I begin this experience as your CEO, but I am not one to rush in and make a lot of changes.

I have served with and worked for many good people in my career, starting as an electrician with Modern Electric Company in Durham, North Carolina, some forty years ago, then as an electrical inspector for Durham County, and ending with the North Carolina Department of Insurance, Office of the State Fire Marshal for the last twenty years. Since 1972, I have been a member of the IAEI and, through the years, have been involved in chapter and section meetings and even on the International board of directors. Over these many years I have witnessed many changes in our association under the four previous executive directors: Lou LaFehr, Bill Summers, Phil Simmons, and Phil Cox. Each leader brought changes that furthered the goals of the IAEI. Just compare the *IAEI News* today with the *News* of thirty years ago. Look at the educational opportunities, books, CDs, and PowerPoint educational programs available today, and look at the growth in membership over the last thirty years. The International office has moved from Chicago, Illinois, to Richardson, Texas, and the number of people that staff the office has increased.

So! What needs changing?

Not so much needs changing as needs continuing. We need to continue to produce the best educational materials at a cost that will allow us to offer them at a price that our members can afford. We need to continue to produce the *IAEI News* at the quality that we have learned to appreciate. We need to continue to offer our members opportunities and products that they need and want. Oh yes!

There are also things that need changing, or maybe that should be termed improved. We have to improve on the customer service segment of our operation. We have to improve on the membership handling—and we will. You members are the backbone of the IAEI, and we have to do things that make you want to remain a member. We also have to do things that make nonmembers want to be members of the IAEI. Being a member of this association, it seems to me, is all the more important in this day and time. Training, educational opportunities, timely publications, and member support are benefits that this association can and does provide.

There have already been some changes. Annette Thomas has been named as director of customer service, with the primary responsibility of general supervision of the customer service staff. Their task is to maintain members' records, order processing, and shipping. In the past, this function was just a part of Natalie Coleman's responsibilities. Natalie's new title is director of administrative services. She will now be able to devote more time to the general administration and financial part of the International office operations. We expect this change to enhance our ability to serve our members and customers. Other staffing changes are in the works. We are working toward a full-time person to be in charge of maintaining the financial records. This will enable us to have a better handle on where our money is coming from and, better yet, where it goes. We will be expecting each section director to help in creating a budget and to be aware of how the available money is spent.

What other changes are coming?

If you have ideas, please let us know. I am looking forward to working with you to make the changes that improve our International Association of Electrical Inspectors.

George Washington Chapter members brandish various samples provided by the evening's speaker, Ben Bird, of Certified Insulated Products—including insulated screwdrivers and ratchet drives— at the January 15, 2002, business meeting.

By the way....

It is not too early, in fact it is getting very close to the time, to start planning for the Diamond Jubilee coming up September 7 – 12, 2003. The Jubilee committee is hard at work making plans for this 75th Anniversary, which is being held at Disney's Coronado Springs Resort, right on the property of Disney World in Florida. Room costs and hotel registration information should be available by the time you read this. The program committee will be making final decisions about the program format and educational opportunities this August. Solicitation for advertisement for the program book and for display space has been disseminated. Registration information for the meeting can be found elsewhere in this issue of the *IAEI News*. So get to it—start planning.

As usual, there are many informative articles in this issue. Grandma's string from the bedpost to the light fixture (Grandma did not have luminaries back then) in the ceiling is long gone. Many interesting things are happening. Happy reading.

Late Breaking News

IAEI News recently placed silver in the scientific and technical journals (web) category of the prestigious *Gold Ink Awards Competition.* The March/April 2002 issue was submitted by IPC Communication Services, who print the magazine. This rigorous competition about quality was judged by accomplished professionals in the printing industry. Criteria for award-winning pieces included quality of printing, technical difficulty and overall visual effectiveness. Nearly 1800 entries competed in 40 categories; each category awarded only one gold, one silver, and one bronze. Winning entries will receive recognition in the special Gold Ink issue of *PrintMedia* magazine to be published in October. The Annual Gold Ink Awards Reception and Banquet will be held at McCormick Place in Chicago on the evening of October 7, 2002.

Reprinted from *IAEI News*, September 2002.

One of the highlights of the 2002 Eastern Section meeting was the costume party, complete with dancing, games, and multiple laughs.

Southern Section members at the Tuesday evening banquet at the 2002 Southern Section meeting, that was provided by a local Shriners group that included Metro Nashville inspectors.

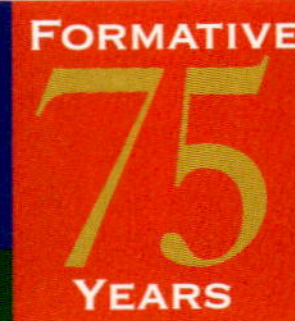

2003 International President

Ray Weber is both a man of vision and practicality. While he is not daunted by challenges, he examines each carefully for its service to others, application to electrical safety, and affordability. These instincts make him a strong and outspoken leader for the IAEI.

His most recent position of leadership is that of international president, which he assumed in November 2002. Weber has been involved with leadership at the national, section and local levels for more than 35 years as he specialized in the electrical inspection field and in the codes and standards making process. Additionally, he has actively provided presentations, taught code classes, and conducted electrical safety training for inspectors, designers, contractors and electricians.

Weber's background and training eminently qualify him for his involvement in the electrical field and in leadership. He has an associates degree in electrical and electronics technology from the Wausau Technical Institute and is acknowledged by the state of Wisconsin as a licensed designer of engineering systems, certified master electrician, certified commercial electrical inspector, and certified uniform dwelling code inspector. He is the north district state electrical inspector for the state of Wisconsin, Department of Commerce, Safety and Building Electric, that has consistently supported IAEI.

On a national level, he is chairman of the *National Electrical Code* CMP-2 and a member of National Fire Protection Association of Quincy, Massachusetts; he is past chairman of *National Electrical Code* CMP-3, and past member of the technical appeals board of Underwriter's Laboratories, Northbrook, Illinois. In Wisconsin, he is a member of the State Committee for the Adoption of Electrician Certification rules and renewal program and is a past member and chair of the Wisconsin State Electrical Code for the amendments and adoptions of the *NEC*.

"The learning process is a never-ending quest," believes Weber, "and so is the need to be of service to others through sharing the knowledge of the electrical code and application for the enhancement of electrical safety." Consequently, he has added writing technical articles on the electrical code for trade magazines and journals to his other skills.

"The IAEI has given me so many opportunities for personal growth and development that I feel my remaining life-long service to the association will never fully repay the membership for the honor they have bestowed upon me. The professionalism of the International staff and board and of the section officers and dedicated membership bring out the best in us all. 'As constant as the flight of time occurs,' it has been said, 'so should we make a contribution to the well-being of others and share what talents life has bestowed on us,'" he concludes.

Ray and his wife Donna, a recently retired elementary school principal, reside on a 125-acre tree farm in Central Wisconsin. They own a sawmill and have utilized timber from their land to build rental dwellings and have sawed timber for others. Ray gets involved as sawyer. "One of life's rewards is to smell freshly sawed pines coming off the mill; it is a great stress remover," he comments.

Another of life's rewards, in Ray's eyes, are the days he and Donna spend with their three daughters—Donna Rae, Kristina and Joanna—and extended family at their lake-front cottage in the Minocqua, Wisconsin area. "The quality time spent with each other and friends either hunting, fishing, listening to the loons call out or watching the eagles soar above Little Bearskin Lake make us all appreciate what freedom and America, as the land of opportunity, have given us."

Even when he is not doing electrical work, Weber is serving others with his talents. He and Donna attend Saint John's Lutheran Church of Kellner, Wisconsin, where he is past president and Donna is one of the organists. He is treasurer of the Rapids Municipal Credit Union; chairman of the township of Grand Rapids Planning Commission; former 1st vice chairman of the Wood County Board of Supervisors; and a graduate of the state of Wisconsin ARNG Military Academy. He retired with twenty-one years of service with the Wisconsin National Guard as a field grade officer with the rank of major, field artillery and as the 32nd Brigade fire support officer, where he coordinated all weapons systems assets for the unit's mission.

When asked about his goals for the IAEI, Weber responded, "As international president, I know full well that I am working for and representing each and every member of the IAEI for the betterment of electrical safety and education, as well as supporting our association's vision and goals for the future. Our first priority is to attract new members and sustain our current membership by providing useful as well as the most current, state-of-the-art magazine, publications and training to assist them in being the best they can be. We are the keystone of the electrical field, and I will continue to lead our organization to the pinnacle position amongst our peers, and continue the proud tradition those who have gone on before have achieved."

Reprinted from *IAEI News*, January 2003.

IAEI Announces Establishment of the Anthony J. Montuori Memorial Fund

IAEI has announced the creation of the Anthony J. Montuori Memorial Fund in honor of its 2002 international president who died in office. Montuori is survived by his wife Madeleine.

"The Memorial Fund has been established to honor Tony's vision and quest for continued excellence in electrical safety throughout the world, and to provide a living legacy and message of leadership in tribute to him. This memorial fund is a way for Tony's friends and colleagues to honor his life and contributions to the industry," said James Carpenter, chief executive officer and executive director. "IAEI is proud to establish this fund, together with Tony's family, with the first contribution."

"Tony's death has been a great professional and personal loss for all of us at IAEI. He was a caring and concerned individual who put the needs of the association above his personal interests. He made many significant contributions to our association and was a friend for many of us. His main focus was to improve electrical services and safety through his involvement with IAEI. The electrical industry has lost a champion and IAEI has lost a good friend, " Carpenter continued.

A spontaneous effort for this memorial was started by individuals who have a strong desire to see this living legacy become a reality. The memorial fund will be administered by IAEI. A portion of the proceeds will be used for educational technology. Other portions will be used for the maintenance and upkeep of the international office and conference center. An immediate goal of $200,000 has been established. Corporate and individual contributions are greatly valued and appreciated. All gifts are tax deductible.

Donations can be made payable to:
IAEI
Mark for the Anthony J. Montuori Memorial Fund
P. O. Box 830848
Richardson, TX 75083-0848

Benefactors contributing over $250 will be given special acknowledgement in the conference center.

For more information on the memorial fund, please call James Carpenter at (972) 235-1455.

International Association of Electrical Inspectors (IAEI) is engaged in training electricians and inspectors in the safe use and installation of electricity and in publishing pertinent materials, including a bi-monthly magazine and textbooks. Headquartered in Richardson, Texas, the company is a not-for-profit [501(c)(6)] corporation. Membership is divided into six regions — Western, Southwestern, Northwestern, Southern, Canadian, and Eastern — and several international chapters. For more information, visit the company's web site at www.iaei.org.

Reprinted from *IAEI News*, March 2003.

Director of Customer Service Annette Thomas and Director of Administrative Services Natalie Coleman work the display booth at the NFPA trade show held on May 20, 2003.

LEADERS FOR THE FUTURE

IAEI Board of Directors for 2003. *First Row (from left to right)*: Gaylen Rogers, Lanny McMahill, Ray Weber, Robert McCullough, and David Clements. *Second Row (from left to right)*: Chuck Mello, Robert F. Smith, Robert Milatovich, Wayne Lilly, Steve Douglas, Doug Geralde, and James Carpenter. *Third Row (from left to right)*: Ray Millet, Herb Stabenow, Gerald Williams, Dick Owen, Phil Cox, Donald Cook, Stan Benton, and Rick Gilmour.

Officers of the 2003 Board of Directors. *Front row, left to right:* Gaylen Rogers, Lanny McMahill, Ray Weber, and Dave Clements. *Back row, left to right:* James Carpenter, Robert McCullough, Doug Geralde, and Wayne Lilly.

International representatives for 2003 from the Eastern Section include, *left to right*. Robert F. Smith, Robert A. McCullough, and Ray Millet.

2003 Canadian international representatives, *left to right:* Rick Gilmour, Doug Geralde, Steve Douglas, and David Clements.

2003 Northwestern Section representatives to the IAEI board, *left to right:* Herb Stabenow, Gaylen Rogers, and Chuck Mello.

Southern Section 2003 representatives include, *left to right:* Wayne Lilly, Donald Cook, and Stan Benton.

2003 Southwestern representatives to the board, *right to left:* Robert M. Milatovich, Lanny McMahill, and Gerald Williams.

2003 Western Section representatives to the board, *left to right:* Dick Owen, Ray Weber, and Philip Cox.

THEIR FUTURE 1995-2003
GROWING INTO IAEI LEADERS
FORMATIVE 75 YEARS
Diamond Jubilee Celebration
INTERNATIONAL ASSOCIATION
75 Anniversary
ELECTRICAL INSPECTORS

Diamond Jubilee Celebration

Saturday, September 6

12:00 Noon to 5:00 p.m.
Registration and Advanced Registration Credentials

Sunday, September 7

9:00 a.m. to 12:30 p.m.
Western Section Board Meeting

9:00 a.m. to 1:30 p.m.
Southwestern Section Board Meeting

9:00 a.m. to 12:30 p.m.
Eastern Section Board Meeting

12:00 Noon to 5:00 p.m.
Registration and Advanced Registration Credentials

1:00 p.m. to 6:00 p.m. Display Setup

1:00 p.m. to 5:00 p.m.
Southern Section Board Meeting

1:00 p.m. to 5:00 p.m.
Canadian Section Board Meeting

1:00 p.m. to 5:00 p.m.
Northwestern Section Board Meeting

6:00 pm to 8:30 p.m.
Welcome and Get Acquainted Reception
Displays Open

Monday, September 8

7:00 a.m. to 5:00 p.m.
Registration and Advanced Registration Credentials

8:00 a.m. to 5:00 p.m.
Displays Open
All attendees attend Opening Session at 9 a.m.

9:00 a.m.
Diamond Jubilee Meeting

10:30 a.m. to 11:00 a.m. Break

11:00 a.m. to 12:00 Noon
Presentation of Code Development Organizations

12:00 Noon to 2:00 p.m.
Lunch on your own and Visit Displays
International Membership Committee Meeting
International Education Committee Meeting

2:00 p.m. to 3:20 p.m.
Presentation from Testing Laboratories

3:20 p.m. to 3:45 p.m. Break

3:45 p.m. to 5:00 p.m.
Introduction of Displayers

5:00 p.m. 6:30 p.m.
Governmental Inspectors Meeting

Tuesday, September 9

8:00 a.m. to 5:00 p.m.
Registration
Displays Open

8:30 a.m. to 10:20 a.m.
General Announcements
Special Presentation by NECA
Introduction of International Attendees
IAEI Global Affairs Committee
Presentation by
Jack Wells and Jim Pauley
Managing Change by Tom Moses

10:20 a.m. to 10:45 a.m. Break

10:45 a.m. to 12:00 Noon
Electrical Safety and the Electrical Inspector, by Mike Callanan

12:00 Noon to 2:00 p.m. Members Luncheon

2:00 p.m. to 3:30 p.m.
Neon Lighting by Mike Johnston, IAEI

3:30 p.m. to 3:45 a.m. Break

3:45 p.m. to 5:00 p.m.
Section Business Sessions

5:00 p.m. to 6:30 p.m.
Utility Caucus

Diamond Jubilee Celebration

Jim Carpenter

Bob Duncan

Ray Weber

Wednesday, September 10

8:00 a.m. to 5:00 p.m.
Registration/Displays Open

8:00 a.m. to 8:30 a.m.
Announcements/Installation of all Section Officers

8:30 a.m. to 10:00 a.m.
CMP Reports on Significant Proposals
for the 2005 ***NEC***

10:00 a.m. to 10:30 a.m.
Consideration of comments for CMP-1 through 6

10:30 a.m. to 11:00 a.m. Break

11:00 a.m. to 12:00 Noon
Continuation of CMP Reports

12:00 Noon to 12:20 p.m.
Consideration of Comments for CMP 7 through 10

9:00 a.m. to 10:30 a.m.
Canadian Workshop/Anti-Counterfeiting

10:30 a.m. to 11:00 a.m. Break

11:00 a.m. to 12:00 Noon
Canadian Workshop
Canadian Electrical Inspection Program

12:00 Noon to 2:00 p.m. Lunch on your own

2:00 p.m. to 5:00 p.m.
Caucuses for Sections/Chapters/Divisions
Florida Training
Florida Chapter Code Seminar
2:00 p.m. to 4:00 p.m. IBEW Caucus

Thursday, September 11

8:00 a.m. to 5:00 p.m.
Registration/Displays Open

8:00 a.m. to 10:15 a.m.
Announcements
Code Question Panel

10:15 a.m. to 10:30 a.m. Break

10:30 a.m. to 11:45 Noon
Continuation of CMP Reports

11:45 a.m. to 12:00 Noon
Consideration of comments for CMP-11
through 15

10:45 a.m. to 12:00 Noon
Canadian Workshop
CEC Changes

12:00 Noon to 2:00 p.m.
Members Luncheon

2:00 p.m. to 3:20 p.m.
Code Question Panel

3:20 p.m. to 3:45 p.m.
Break

3:45 p.m. to 5:00 p.m.
Code Question Panel

6:30 p.m. to 7:00 p.m.
Social

7:00 p.m. to 11:00 p.m.
Diamond Jubilee Gala Dinner

Friday, September 12

8:00 a.m. to 10:00 a.m.
Announcements
Past, Present, & Future

10:00 a.m. to 10:25 a.m.
Break

10:25 a.m. to 11:25 Noon
Continuation of CMP Reports

11:25 a.m. to 12:00 Noon
Consideration of comments for
CMP-16 through 19

10:45 a.m. to 12:00 Noon
Canadian Workshop
Electrical Fire Investigations

12:00 Noon to 2:00 p.m.
Lunch on your own
Sections/Chapters/Divisions Secretaries Lunch

2:00 p.m. to 4:00 p.m.
Training Sessions
1 & 2 Family Dwellings
Soares Grounding and Bonding
Health Care Facilities
Swimming Pools & Similar Locations
Motors and Air Conditioning Equipment
Hazardous Locations
IAEI Study Guides Overview

4:00 pm. to 5:00 p.m.
Closing Session

Saturday, September 13

8:00 a.m. to 12:00 Noon

Section Secretaries and IAEI Staff
Final Paperwork Session

Section/Chapter/Divisions
Closing Meetings

Diamond Jubilee Celebration

We would like to take a moment to salute the following members, who have been a part of the IAEI family for over fifty years!

Adams, James L.
Adams, Nicholas
Arnold, Everett B.
Bellamy, Keith L.
Botto, John V.
Boyd, Richard B.
Bray, Norman F.
Budil, Ben J.
Carey, Richard
Cavanagh, O. A.
Curtiss, L. M.
Davis, Ben
DeFelippo, Charles
Ferroni, Frank A.
Flach, George
Gehm, Herman V.
Gibaratz, Jos F.
Girard, J. Megler
Glover, William A.
Gustafson, Robert L.
Herlache, Lloyd A.
Houck, Eugene B.
Kennedy, Curtis R.
Kubacki, Joseph W.
Labourr, Donald C.
Lawson, George W.
Leiman, Sol
Lind, Maynard M.
Lowe, Robert J.
Lower, J. Joseph
Mason, Gerald H.
McFeely, John A.
Mellen, Schuyler V.
Metz, Richard F.
Miller, Paul L.
Mugavero, Salvatore C.
Mullooly, Patrick J.
Naquin, Clyde J.
Nelson, Morris T.
Otero, George G.
Parmley, M. S. "Dude"
Parmley, Mark S.
Peterson, Harry A.
Pyette, Arthur G.
Rearic, Michael T.
Robinson, Markle C.
Rose, Morris J.
Schmitz, Nick A.
Schneeberger, Joe
Silvestri, Anthony
Slavin, William H.
Smith, Ray T.
Taggart, Ranson
Taylor, Ralph A.
Turner, Garland L.
Watts, Charles W.
Wilkins, Solomon A.
Williams, Harold
Young, Melvin L.

Researchers/Contributors:

American Cultural History, Kingwood College Online, 1999.
Andy Cartal
Bob Seltzer
Book of Historical Records, by Norris McWhirter, Virgin Publishing Ltd, 2000.
Canadian Standards Association
David Conrad
David Shapiro
Doug Geralde
Edward Lawry
Gerald W. "Jerry " Williams
IAEI Archives
Infoplease.com, Family Education Network Inc., Pearson Education Publishing, 2003.
James W. Carpenter
Joe Tedesco
Laura Hildreth
Life: Our Century in Pictures, Time Incorporated, 1999.
Michael Johnston
National Electrical Manufacturers Association
National Fire Protection Association
Philip Cox
Philip Simmons
Ray Millet
Rick Gilmour
Smithsonian Institution
Timelines of World History, Dorling Kindersley Limited, 2002.
Underwriters Laboratories'

Photo Credits:

Ansgar Johnson Photography
Bettmann/Corbis
Bob Miller Photography
Bulldog Electric Products Company
Business & Industrial Photographers, Ltd.
C. "Pop" Laval Commercial Photography
Canadian Standards Association
Chicago Daily News negatives collection, DN-0003451, DN-0062405, DN-0071983, DN-0008925. Courtesy of the Chicago Historical Society.
Civil War Treasures from the New-York Historical Society, [PR-065-812-38].
Corbis Images
Culberson—Ashville, N.C.
Denver Public Library, Colorado Historical Society, and Denver Art Museum
Edward A. Bourdon
Electrical Contracting & Maintenance
Electrical West
Elibrary.com. *Early Washing Machine,* Archive Photos, 01-01-1995.
Elibrary.com. *The Jazz Singer,* Archive Photos, 1927.
Federal Photos
Franklin D. Roosevelt Library & Museum
Hassen Enterprises, Inc.
Hulton-Deutsch Collection
Hydro Electric Power Commission of Canada
IAEI Archives
Jeffrey Sellon Collection
Jimmy Roberts
Jon Sullivan
Julius R. Young
Kaufmann & Fabry Company
Larry Griffith
Leedom Photo Shop
Library of Congress American Memory Collection.
Library of Congress, Prints & Photographs Division, FSA-OWI Collection, [LC-USF33-003217-M1 DLC]
Library of Congress, Prints & Photographs Division, FSA-OWI Collection: LC-USW3-001523-D DLC;
Library of Congress, Prints and Photographs Division, Detroit Publishing Company Collection.
Library of Congress, Prints and Photographs Division, Theodor Horydczak Collection [LC-H814-T-2241-071 DLC; LC-H824-T-1806-002 DLC; LC-H813-1999-001-x DLC; LC-H814-T-1979-101 DLC].
Mensa International, Ltd.
Moffett Studio
National Fire Protection Association
National Photo Company Collection.
Nebraska State Historical Society, [nbhips 13065; nbhips 10135]
Nova Development Corporation.
Omaha Photographic Laboratories
Oscar & Associates, Inc.
PBS.org. MacNeil-Lehrer Productions.
Philip Cox
R. G. B. Studios
R. G. Electric Company
Scamahorn Studio
Schenectady Museum; Hall of Electrical History
Stock.XCHNG.com
The Shamrock
The Truman Library Online
U.S. National Archives & Records Administration
Underwriters' Laboratories
US National Oceanic and Atmospheric Administration
W. L. Gaffney
Western History/Genealogy Department, Denver Public Library.
William James Topley / National Archives of Canada / C-005647.

Chief Researcher/Production Coordinator:
Laura Hildreth

Art Direction/Design:
John Watson

Managing Editor:
Kathryn P. Ingley

Editor-in-Chief:
James W. Carpenter

Composed at:
International Association of Electrical Inspectors
Type set in Compact, Palatino, Arial, Folio, Copperplate and Garamond

Printed by The Odee Company on Avalon Gloss Book
Binding: Hard Case, Smythe sewn, Kennett

IAEI wishes to thank its entire staff and all other individuals who, in some form or other, had a hand in the development of this book.